# Handbook of Research on Implications of Sustainable Development in Higher Education

Eleni Meletiadou
*London Metropolitan University, UK*

A volume in the Advances in Higher Education and Professional Development (AHEPD) Book Series

Published in the United States of America by
IGI Global
Information Science Reference (an imprint of IGI Global)
701 E. Chocolate Avenue
Hershey PA, USA 17033
Tel: 717-533-8845
Fax: 717-533-8661
E-mail: cust@igi-global.com
Web site: http://www.igi-global.com

Copyright © 2023 by IGI Global. All rights reserved. No part of this publication may be reproduced, stored or distributed in any form or by any means, electronic or mechanical, including photocopying, without written permission from the publisher. Product or company names used in this set are for identification purposes only. Inclusion of the names of the products or companies does not indicate a claim of ownership by IGI Global of the trademark or registered trademark.

Library of Congress Cataloging-in-Publication Data

Names: Meletiadou, Eleni, 1971- editor.
Title: Handbook of research on implications of sustainable development in
   higher education / Eleni Meletiadou, Editor.
Description: Hershey, PA : Information Science Reference, [2023] | Includes
   bibliographical references and index. | Summary: "Implications of
   Sustainable Development in Higher Education: Teaching, Learning, and
   Assessment provides insight regarding the implications of ESD for
   teaching, learning, and assessment in higher education and demonstrates
   the value of adopting an ESD lens by broadening and strengthening the
   evidence base of the impact that this can make for students, educators,
   and society as a whole. Covering key topics such as assessment,
   globalization, and inclusion, this reference work is ideal for
   university leaders, administrators, policymakers, researchers, scholars,
   practitioners, academicians, instructors, and students"-- Provided by
   publisher.
Identifiers: LCCN 2022043123 (print) | LCCN 2022043124 (ebook) | ISBN
   9781668461723 (hardcover) | ISBN 9781668461730 (ebook)
Subjects: LCSH: Education, Higher--Social aspects. | Sustainability. |
   Social accounting. | Sustainable Development Goals.
Classification: LCC LC191.9 .I47 2023  (print) | LCC LC191.9  (ebook) | DDC
   378--dc23/eng/20220921
LC record available at https://lccn.loc.gov/2022043123
LC ebook record available at https://lccn.loc.gov/2022043124

This book is published in the IGI Global book series Advances in Higher Education and Professional Development (AHEPD) (ISSN: 2327-6983; eISSN: 2327-6991)

British Cataloguing in Publication Data
A Cataloguing in Publication record for this book is available from the British Library.

All work contributed to this book is new, previously-unpublished material. The views expressed in this book are those of the authors, but not necessarily of the publisher.

For electronic access to this publication, please contact: eresources@igi-global.com.

# Advances in Higher Education and Professional Development (AHEPD) Book Series

Jared Keengwe
University of North Dakota, USA

ISSN:2327-6983
EISSN:2327-6991

MISSION

As world economies continue to shift and change in response to global financial situations, job markets have begun to demand a more highly-skilled workforce. In many industries a college degree is the minimum requirement and further educational development is expected to advance. With these current trends in mind, the **Advances in Higher Education & Professional Development (AHEPD) Book Series** provides an outlet for researchers and academics to publish their research in these areas and to distribute these works to practitioners and other researchers.

**AHEPD** encompasses all research dealing with higher education pedagogy, development, and curriculum design, as well as all areas of professional development, regardless of focus.

COVERAGE
- Adult Education
- Assessment in Higher Education
- Career Training
- Coaching and Mentoring
- Continuing Professional Development
- Governance in Higher Education
- Higher Education Policy
- Pedagogy of Teaching Higher Education
- Vocational Education

IGI Global is currently accepting manuscripts for publication within this series. To submit a proposal for a volume in this series, please contact our Acquisition Editors at Acquisitions@igi-global.com or visit: http://www.igi-global.com/publish/.

The Advances in Higher Education and Professional Development (AHEPD) Book Series (ISSN 2327-6983) is published by IGI Global, 701 E. Chocolate Avenue, Hershey, PA 17033-1240, USA, www.igi-global.com. This series is composed of titles available for purchase individually; each title is edited to be contextually exclusive from any other title within the series. For pricing and ordering information please visit http://www.igi-global.com/book-series/advances-higher-education-professional-development/73681. Postmaster: Send all address changes to above address. Copyright © 2023 IGI Global. All rights, including translation in other languages reserved by the publisher. No part of this series may be reproduced or used in any form or by any means – graphics, electronic, or mechanical, including photocopying, recording, taping, or information and retrieval systems – without written permission from the publisher, except for non commercial, educational use, including classroom teaching purposes. The views expressed in this series are those of the authors, but not necessarily of IGI Global.

## Titles in this Series

*For a list of additional titles in this series, please visit: http://www.igi-global.com/book-series/advances-higher-education-professional-development/73681*

*Collaborative Models and Frameworks for Inclusive Educator Preparation Programs*
Beverly Sande (Prairie View A&M University, USA) and Charles William Kemp (Shawnee State University, USA)
Information Science Reference • © 2022 • 244pp • H/C (ISBN: 9781668434437) • US $215.00

*Instilling Diversity and Social Inclusion Practices in Teacher Education and Curriculum Development*
Olga María Alegre de la Rosa (University of La Laguna, Spain) and Luis Miguel Villar Angulo (University of Seville, Spain)
Information Science Reference • © 2022 • 252pp • H/C (ISBN: 9781668448120) • US $215.00

*Rethinking Perception and Centering the Voices of Unique Individuals Reframing Autism Inclusion in Praxis*
Jessica Block Nerren (California State University, San Bernardino, USA)
Information Science Reference • © 2022 • 289pp • H/C (ISBN: 9781668451038) • US $215.00

*Handbook of Research on Practices for Advancing Diversity and Inclusion in Higher Education*
Eleni Meletiadou (London Metropolitan University, UK)
Information Science Reference • © 2022 • 451pp • H/C (ISBN: 9781799896289) • US $270.00

*Self-Care and Stress Management for Academic Well-Being*
Karis L. Clarke (Clark Atlanta University, USA)
Information Science Reference • © 2022 • 302pp • H/C (ISBN: 9781668423349) • US $215.00

*Preparing Agriculture and Agriscience Educators for the Classroom*
Andrew C. Thoron (Abraham Baldwin Agricultural College, USA) and R. Kirby Barrick (University of Florida, USA (retired))
Information Science Reference • © 2022 • 381pp • H/C (ISBN: 9781668434208) • US $215.00

*New Models of Higher Education: Unbundled, Rebundled, Customized, and DIY*
Aaron M. Brower (University of Wisconsin Extended Campus, USA & University of Wisconsin-Madison, USA) and Ryan J. Specht-Boardman (University of Wisconsin Extended Campus, USA)
Information Science Reference • © 2022 • 425pp • H/C (ISBN: 9781668438091) • US $165.00

*Contributions of Historically Black Colleges and Universities in the 21st Century*
Anisah Bagasra (Kennesaw State University, USA) Alison Mc Letchie (South Carolina State University, USA) and Jonathan Wesley (Independent Researcher, USA)
Information Science Reference • © 2022 • 359pp • H/C (ISBN: 9781668438145) • US $215.00

701 East Chocolate Avenue, Hershey, PA 17033, USA
Tel: 717-533-8845 x100 • Fax: 717-533-8661
E-Mail: cust@igi-global.com • www.igi-global.com

# List of Contributors

**Albuquerque, Fábio** / *Lisbon Accounting and Business School, Portugal & Instituto Politécnico de Lisboa, Portugal* .................................................................................................................. 71
**Alfalagg, Abdullah Rajab** / *Hadhramout University, Yemen* ............................................................. 251
**Ba-Udhan, Hassan Saeed Awadh** / *Seiyun University, Yemen* ........................................................ 251
**Blignaut, Jean Henry** / *Research Unit Self-Directed Learning, Faculty of Education, North-West University, South Africa* ................................................................................................................ 293
**C., Therasa** / *SASTRA University (Deemed), India* ............................................................................ 183
**Cabral, Ana** / *Queen Mary University of London, UK* ......................................................................... 43
**Chen, Yue** / *Queen Mary University of London, UK* ............................................................................ 43
**Chowdhury, Jahid Siraz** / *Department of Social Administration and Justice, Universiti Malaya, Malaysia* ...................................................................................................................................... 314
**Dias, Ana Isabel** / *Lisbon Accounting and Business School, Portugal & Instituto Politécnico de Lisboa, Portugal* .................................................................................................................... 71
**Domingos, Alexandra** / *Lisbon Accounting and Business School, Portugal & Instituto Politécnico de Lisboa, Portugal* ............................................................................................................... 71
**du Toit-Brits, Charlene** / *North-West University, South Africa* ......................................................... 293
**Fuller, Stephanie** / *Queen Mary University of London, UK* ................................................................. 43
**Gill, Sukhpal Singh** / *Queen Mary University of London, UK* ............................................................. 43
**Goosen, Leila** / *University of South Africa, South Africa* ................................................................... 167
**Gruber, Sibylle** / *Northern Arizona University, USA* .......................................................................... 272
**Gurbuz, Akin** / *Mugla Sitki Kocman University, Turkey* ..................................................................... 230
**Hamidi, Mashitah** / *Universiti Malaya, Malaysia* ............................................................................... 97
**Hart, Clare** / *Manchester Metropolitan University, UK* ...................................................................... 202
**Hashmi, Anita** / *Manchester Metropolitan University, UK* ................................................................. 202
**Hays, Jay** / *Melbourne Institute of Technology, Australia* .................................................................. 115
**Hosen, Shamim** / *Bangladesh Public Administration Training Centre (BPATC), Bangladesh* ........ 337
**Islam, Md. Shafiul** / *University of Rajshahi, Bangladesh* ................................................................... 337
**Kettleborough, Helena Mary** / *Manchester Metropolitan University, UK* ......................................... 202
**Kwai Nam, Chan** / *Icetech Education, China* ..................................................................................... 144
**Lau, Yui-Yip** / *College of Professional and Continuing Education, The Hong Kong Polytechnic University, China* ....................................................................................................................... 144
**Marron, Roz** / *Manchester Metropolitan University, UK* ..................................................................... 202
**Meletiadou, Eleni** / *London Metropolitan University, UK* ............................................................... 1, 24
**Nghuulondo, Patrick** / *University of South Africa, South Africa* ....................................................... 167
**Randles, Sally** / *Manchester Metropolitan University, UK* ................................................................. 202

**Reinders, Hayo** / *King Mongkut's University of Technology, Thonburi, Thailand* ......... 115
**Roy, Parimal** / *Universiti Malaya, Malaysia* ......... 97
**Shih-Kuei, Hsiao Arthur** / *Top-BOSS International Corporation, Taiwan* ......... 144
**Skritsovali, Konstantina** / *Liverpool John Moores University, UK* ......... 202
**Tucker, Megan** / *Manchester Metropolitan University, UK* ......... 202
**Uhlig, Steve** / *Queen Mary University of London, UK* ......... 43
**Wadham, Helen** / *Manchester Metropolitan University, UK* ......... 202
**Wahab, Haris Abd** / *Universiti Malaya, Malaysia* ......... 97
**Wong, Macy** / *College of Professional and Continuing Education, The Hong Kong Polytechnic University, China* ......... 144
**Yang, Zhuang** / *The Hong Kong Polytechnic University, China* ......... 144
**Yildirim, Rana** / *Çukurova University, Turkey* ......... 230

# Table of Contents

**Preface** .................................................................................................................................. xvii

**Chapter 1**
Leadership for Sustainability in Higher Education Amidst the COVID-19 Crisis: Exploring
Female Educational Leaders' Strategies for Transformation .................................................. 1
    *Eleni Meletiadou, London Metropolitan University, UK*

**Chapter 2**
Using Virtual Professional Learning Communities to Foster Sustainable Learning and Close the
Awarding Gap in Higher Education Amidst the COVID-19 Pandemic .................................. 24
    *Eleni Meletiadou, London Metropolitan University, UK*

**Chapter 3**
Facilitating an Online and Sustainable Learning Environment for Cloud Computing Using an
Action Research Methodology ................................................................................................ 43
    *Sukhpal Singh Gill, Queen Mary University of London, UK*
    *Ana Cabral, Queen Mary University of London, UK*
    *Stephanie Fuller, Queen Mary University of London, UK*
    *Yue Chen, Queen Mary University of London, UK*
    *Steve Uhlig, Queen Mary University of London, UK*

**Chapter 4**
Exploring Drivers and Barriers of Accounting Students' Motivation for Non-Financial Information 71
    *Alexandra Domingos, Lisbon Accounting and Business School, Portugal & Instituto*
        *Politécnico de Lisboa, Portugal*
    *Fábio Albuquerque, Lisbon Accounting and Business School, Portugal & Instituto*
        *Politécnico de Lisboa, Portugal*
    *Ana Isabel Dias, Lisbon Accounting and Business School, Portugal & Instituto Politécnico*
        *de Lisboa, Portugal*

**Chapter 5**
A Philosophical Discussion of Sustainable Development: A Case From the Bangladeshi Santal
Community ............................................................................................................................. 97
    *Parimal Roy, Universiti Malaya, Malaysia*
    *Haris Abd Wahab, Universiti Malaya, Malaysia*
    *Mashitah Hamidi, Universiti Malaya, Malaysia*

**Chapter 6**
Discontinuity, Sustainability, and Critical Learnership: Development, Dynamics, and Demand ...... 115
    *Jay Hays, Melbourne Institute of Technology, Australia*
    *Hayo Reinders, King Mongkut's University of Technology, Thonburi, Thailand*

**Chapter 7**
Enhancing Student Professionalization Through Business Simulation Games ................................. 144
    *Yui-Yip Lau, College of Professional and Continuing Education, The Hong Kong Polytechnic University, China*
    *Macy Wong, College of Professional and Continuing Education, The Hong Kong Polytechnic University, China*
    *Zhuang Yang, The Hong Kong Polytechnic University, China*
    *Chan Kwai Nam, Icetech Education, China*
    *Hsiao Arthur Shih-Kuei, Top-BOSS International Corporation, Taiwan*

**Chapter 8**
Implications of Using Mobile Technologies in Higher Education Amidst the COVID-19 Pandemic: Accessing Teaching, Online Learning, and Assessment ..................................................... 167
    *Patrick Nghuulondo, University of South Africa, South Africa*
    *Leila Goosen, University of South Africa, South Africa*

**Chapter 9**
Learning Styles and Enhancing Learner Engagement in Online Platform Strategies for Sustainable Development in Higher Education ....................................................................................................... 183
    *Therasa C., SASTRA University (Deemed), India*

**Chapter 10**
Sustainability Education Beyond the Classroom: How the "Exploding University" Nurtures Collective Intelligence Across Local and Global Communities ...................................................... 202
    *Helen Wadham, Manchester Metropolitan University, UK*
    *Clare Hart, Manchester Metropolitan University, UK*
    *Anita Hashmi, Manchester Metropolitan University, UK*
    *Helena Mary Kettleborough, Manchester Metropolitan University, UK*
    *Roz Marron, Manchester Metropolitan University, UK*
    *Sally Randles, Manchester Metropolitan University, UK*
    *Konstantina Skritsovali, Liverpool John Moores University, UK*
    *Megan Tucker, Manchester Metropolitan University, UK*

**Chapter 11**
Tackling the Challenges Posed by Linguistic and Cultural Diversity in EFL Classrooms ................ 230
    *Akin Gurbuz, Mugla Sitki Kocman University, Turkey*
    *Rana Yildirim, Çukurova University, Turkey*

### Chapter 12
Teachers' Perceptions on Using Arabic L1 to Teach English in Higher Education in Yemen ........... 251
    *Abdullah Rajab Alfalagg, Hadhramout University, Yemen*
    *Hassan Saeed Awadh Ba-Udhan, Seiyun University, Yemen*

### Chapter 13
Teaching and Learning in the Age of Climate Change: Postcolonial Ecofeminism and the Rhetorics of Sustainability ........................................................................................................... 272
    *Sibylle Gruber, Northern Arizona University, USA*

### Chapter 14
The Significance of Collective Self-Directed Learning Competencies for the Sustainability of Higher Education ......................................................................................................................... 293
    *Jean Henry Blignaut, Research Unit Self-Directed Learning, Faculty of Education, North-West University, South Africa*
    *Charlene du Toit-Brits, North-West University, South Africa*

### Chapter 15
Voice and Photovoice of the Bangladeshi Migrant Workers in Malaysia: An Ethnography of the 3rd Space With Reciprocity ......................................................................................................... 314
    *Jahid Siraz Chowdhury, Department of Social Administration and Justice, Universiti Malaya, Malaysia*

### Chapter 16
Ensuring Quality Education to Achieve the Sustainable Development Goals (SDGs) in Bangladesh .................................................................................................................................. 337
    *Shamim Hosen, Bangladesh Public Administration Training Centre (BPATC), Bangladesh*
    *Md. Shafiul Islam, University of Rajshahi, Bangladesh*

**Compilation of References** ..................................................................................................... 361

**About the Contributors** ........................................................................................................... 420

**Index** ............................................................................................................................................ 428

# Detailed Table of Contents

**Preface** ........................................................................................................................................... xvii

**Chapter 1**
Leadership for Sustainability in Higher Education Amidst the COVID-19 Crisis: Exploring
Female Educational Leaders' Strategies for Transformation ................................................................ 1
    *Eleni Meletiadou, London Metropolitan University, UK*

Through assisted thematic content analyses of 40 female educational leaders' interviews, the chapter investigates the crisis management and leadership practices which foster sustainable development in higher education from their perspective. Drawing on diversity, gender, and upper echelon theories, the authors propose that the addition of unique female perspectives and leadership styles will afford gender-diverse senior leadership teams (SLTs) a leadership capability advantage over equally talented yet homogeneous male teams. This link between gender diversity and leadership capability is more pronounced in times of crisis such as the current pandemic. The study suggests that increasing female representation in SLTs may have a substantial and direct impact on overall leadership capabilities and elicit positive performance effects in times of crisis. Notably, and unique to this study, they show that feminine traits and inclusive leadership styles may be more efficacious in contemporary leadership contexts than generally believed.

**Chapter 2**
Using Virtual Professional Learning Communities to Foster Sustainable Learning and Close the
Awarding Gap in Higher Education Amidst the COVID-19 Pandemic .............................................. 24
    *Eleni Meletiadou, London Metropolitan University, UK*

In the current study, a combination of synchronous and asynchronous online strategies has been used to support undergraduate students at a University in the UK, as VPLC embraces individual students' needs for learning development and professional growth through peer support building community among the student population. The intent of this research study was to unravel students' perceptions of the benefits and the challenges that VPLC may have amid the pandemic. An exploratory anonymous survey design was employed to explore their impact. Students were also asked to provide anonymous feedback at regular intervals during the implementation using Mentimeter. Descriptive statistics and thematic analysis were used to examine the data. Findings suggest that VPLCs can be used as a means to support students through collaboration, peer mentoring/coaching, networking, and sharing of resources.

## Chapter 3
Facilitating an Online and Sustainable Learning Environment for Cloud Computing Using an Action Research Methodology.................................................................................................................43
    *Sukhpal Singh Gill, Queen Mary University of London, UK*
    *Ana Cabral, Queen Mary University of London, UK*
    *Stephanie Fuller, Queen Mary University of London, UK*
    *Yue Chen, Queen Mary University of London, UK*
    *Steve Uhlig, Queen Mary University of London, UK*

In this chapter, a research plan is presented to investigate online teaching and evaluation analysis for cloud computing using an action research methodology to enable sustainable learning environment. Using online teaching, the authors planned to conduct a thorough evaluation of student learning implementation in order to identify both merits and challenges. An investigation of the authors' own teaching and learners' understanding while working together as a team on a cloud computing project has assisted in finding the perfect methods for improving both. Further, the authors used action research methodology to analyze the literature and scholarship critically and designed best practices for action plan to facilitate an online and sustainable learning environment for cloud computing. Moreover, possible ethical concerns have been considered as students worked in a team for a group project. Finally, they have discussed the plans for monitoring and evaluation of the action and impact assessment.

## Chapter 4
Exploring Drivers and Barriers of Accounting Students' Motivation for Non-Financial Information 71
    *Alexandra Domingos, Lisbon Accounting and Business School, Portugal & Instituto*
        *Politécnico de Lisboa, Portugal*
    *Fábio Albuquerque, Lisbon Accounting and Business School, Portugal & Instituto*
        *Politécnico de Lisboa, Portugal*
    *Ana Isabel Dias, Lisbon Accounting and Business School, Portugal & Instituto Politécnico*
        *de Lisboa, Portugal*

Recent developments related to non-financial information (NFI) reporting encourage the adoption of a long-term vision approach to sustainable development. In turn, the self-determination theory (SDT) describes which elements explain the students' motivation and how their skills can be better developed from their choices. Using NFI as the subject and the SDT as the theoretical framework, this chapter links both topics aiming to identify the types of students' motivation and for what specific interests are accounting students motivated to learn topics related to NFI. Data were gathered from a questionnaire. The results, using frequency and textual analyses, indicate a higher level of intrinsic motivation. Environmental and social matters are the topics of concern, while governance issues are absent. As an exploratory analysis, this chapter provides insights into how students of an accounting course are motivated to acquire skills in NFI reporting, which is particularly relevant to higher education institutions, professors, students, and organizations related to accountancy education.

## Chapter 5
A Philosophical Discussion of Sustainable Development: A Case From the Bangladeshi Santal Community ....................................................................................................................................97
    *Parimal Roy, Universiti Malaya, Malaysia*
    *Haris Abd Wahab, Universiti Malaya, Malaysia*
    *Mashitah Hamidi, Universiti Malaya, Malaysia*

This chapter aims to present a logical discussion on the Sustainable Development Goals (SDGs) and how they are being treated as incorrect concepts in the academic world and the ethnic community. The Santal is one of the examples from Bangladesh. Methodologically, this chapter follows the 'capability approach' by Amartya Sen to understand the changing trend in the Santal community of Bangladesh. The discussion shows that despite being a global phenomenon, sustainable development is not an ideal coupling phrase to combat global issues because it falls into the global trap within. Based on secondary data from the literature and the first author's reflections, the study of versatile literature has been noted in this chapter.

**Chapter 6**
Discontinuity, Sustainability, and Critical Learnership: Development, Dynamics, and Demand ...... 115
    *Jay Hays, Melbourne Institute of Technology, Australia*
    *Hayo Reinders, King Mongkut's University of Technology, Thonburi, Thailand*

It is generally understood that we are in an age of upheaval, accelerating change, and global fragility. The increasing complexity of problems we are facing and the discontinuity we have been experiencing are only likely to escalate as we proceed into the new millennium. These challenges are more daunting when one considers dwindling resources, potential conflict, and environmental vulnerability. Less clear is what we can better do to prepare the next generation of leaders to guide and support engaged employees and citizenry to work together to solve immense problems. The chapter's subtext is that conventional education and professional development are insufficient—if not counterproductive—to equipping current and future generations with the skills and dispositions to contend with the chaos and complexity of the emerging millennium. To the degree this is true, approaches to learning and professional development need to change. To this end, readers might benefit most from the practical and realistic recommendations outlined herein for schools, organisations, and communities.

**Chapter 7**
Enhancing Student Professionalization Through Business Simulation Games ................................. 144
    *Yui-Yip Lau, College of Professional and Continuing Education, The Hong Kong Polytechnic*
        *University, China*
    *Macy Wong, College of Professional and Continuing Education, The Hong Kong Polytechnic*
        *University, China*
    *Zhuang Yang, The Hong Kong Polytechnic University, China*
    *Chan Kwai Nam, Icetech Education, China*
    *Hsiao Arthur Shih-Kuei, Top-BOSS International Corporation, Taiwan*

A traditional classroom approach focuses on teacher-centric learning, and theoretical knowledge transition is often reinforcing spoon-feeding education. To this end, it leads to demotivating students' learning and failing to fulfill the employers' expectations. The business simulation game is a new, innovative educational tool for students to enjoy in an interactive learning classroom. The use of support tools can help students to improve their professionalization. This study mainly uses an illustrative real-life case study, Macro Business Simulation, as the target study area. In response, the study invited 64 university students to complete both pre-activity and post-activity surveys, along with 10 semi-structured, in-depth interviews with relevant parties including teachers, students, Macro Business Simulation operators, and business enterprises. Implications of the findings are also discussed.

**Chapter 8**
Implications of Using Mobile Technologies in Higher Education Amidst the COVID-19
Pandemic: Accessing Teaching, Online Learning, and Assessment................................................ 167
    *Patrick Nghuulondo, University of South Africa, South Africa*
    *Leila Goosen, University of South Africa, South Africa*

The purpose and objectives of this case study are to explore the effective use of mobile technologies by first year students amid the COVID-19 coronavirus pandemic, using a situational analysis and active theory. Moreover, this study will unveil intersectional problems and educational inequality among 'digital natives' and 'digital immigrants' at the Rundu campus of the University of Namibia (UNAM). The study aims at examining how the interventions of distance and/or online learning are exclusive, exposing many, especially first year, students to educational inequality. Finally, the implications of sustainable development in higher education in terms of teaching, learning, and assessment will be considered.

**Chapter 9**
Learning Styles and Enhancing Learner Engagement in Online Platform Strategies for Sustainable
Development in Higher Education................................................................................................... 183
    *Therasa C., SASTRA University (Deemed), India*

Online learning replacing face-to-face interactions is a preferred medium now and gained popularity especially after pandemic. The success in online learning would depend upon different learning styles, and it is highly necessary to understand the strategies to handle Gen Z for developing learner engagement. The purpose of this paper is to throw light on the inter-relationships between different learning styles and learner engagement and also to understand the characteristics of Gen Z and the strategies used to create engagement with Gen Z. The suggestions from this chapter insist that the different learning style require different pedagogies to create engagement among learners. The sociability skills and care about sustainability are incredibly more for Gen Z than previous generations, and hence, the learning environment can be carefully structured using these strategies, which brings in sustainable development.

**Chapter 10**
Sustainability Education Beyond the Classroom: How the "Exploding University" Nurtures
Collective Intelligence Across Local and Global Communities ....................................................... 202
    *Helen Wadham, Manchester Metropolitan University, UK*
    *Clare Hart, Manchester Metropolitan University, UK*
    *Anita Hashmi, Manchester Metropolitan University, UK*
    *Helena Mary Kettleborough, Manchester Metropolitan University, UK*
    *Roz Marron, Manchester Metropolitan University, UK*
    *Sally Randles, Manchester Metropolitan University, UK*
    *Konstantina Skritsovali, Liverpool John Moores University, UK*
    *Megan Tucker, Manchester Metropolitan University, UK*

This chapter explores how the authors expanded their teaching and learning beyond the classroom at Manchester Metropolitan University in the UK. It puts forward the theoretical concept of the "exploding university" as a way to help develop a critical yet hopeful understanding of collective problems at local and global scales. This helps them explore three interrelated initiatives that brought teachers, students, and communities together, namely a sustainability festival, research project on animal rehoming, and community tree-planting drive. The chapter illuminates how exploding the work beyond the classroom enabled everyone involved to take action on the challenges that matter to them, while also developing a "collective intelligence" about their underlying causes. The exploding university thus emerges as a theoretical and practical model, which we can use to inspire students to actively critique, reimagine, and reconstruct the world around them. The authors conclude by encouraging and supporting others who might wish to embark on similar journeys themselves.

**Chapter 11**
Tackling the Challenges Posed by Linguistic and Cultural Diversity in EFL Classrooms ................. 230
    *Akin Gurbuz, Mugla Sitki Kocman University, Turkey*
    *Rana Yildirim, Çukurova University, Turkey*

One of the main purposes of multicultural education is to approach all individuals at an equal distance in educational environments, provide a sense of belonging by ensuring unity and integrity, and eliminate the gap in academic achievement among diverse groups by ensuring equal opportunities for all. In this regard, the present study intends to contribute to the existing research by providing a rich amount of evidence as to the challenges posed by linguistic and cultural diversity, and the strategies employed by the instructors to effectively overcome those challenges. The data of the study were collected through video-stimulated interviews with four instructors and semi-structured interviews with 20 lecturers. The study revealed that the EFL instructors most frequently experienced challenges in regards to language and communication, and they developed numerous strategies to overcome these challenges. Considering the research process and its results, the current research study provided various pedagogical implications and suggestions for the main stakeholders of education.

**Chapter 12**
Teachers' Perceptions on Using Arabic L1 to Teach English in Higher Education in Yemen ........... 251
    *Abdullah Rajab Alfalagg, Hadhramout University, Yemen*
    *Hassan Saeed Awadh Ba-Udhan, Seiyun University, Yemen*

This chapter aims at exploring teachers' perceptions of using Arabic (L1) as a pedagogical tool to mediate teaching English in higher education. It further investigates the reasons for abstaining from using Arabic and its functions and attempts to determine the factors that affect teachers' decisions on whether or not to use L1. Forty teachers from different universities responded to an online questionnaire. The results revealed that the teachers had positive perspectives toward the selective use of students' L1 (M= 2.89; SD= 0.39). The results showed a moderate positive correlation between the respondents' perceptions of using L1 and their classroom practices (r=0. 498; p=0.001). The results suggested that the teachers were hesitant about using students' L1 because of the misconception about its role in learning the target language. The chapter concludes with implications on functions for utilizing L1, its determining factors, and the reasons for abstaining from it.

**Chapter 13**
Teaching and Learning in the Age of Climate Change: Postcolonial Ecofeminism and the
Rhetorics of Sustainability ................................................................................................................. 272
    *Sibylle Gruber, Northern Arizona University, USA*

The chapter foregrounds the important role of teaching and learning in the age of climate change. The author shows that education for sustainable development needs to promote communication practices that not only emphasize transition and betweenness, but that transcend current definitions of disciplines to create sustainable solutions to existing problems. Such writing and communication practices are necessary to contribute to 21st century solutions to such monumental issues as increased migration due to conflict, persecution, and natural disasters; food insecurity across the globe; the erasure of economic, social, cultural, gender, civil, and political rights; and pandemics that know no borders. The chapter concludes by emphasizing the importance of encouraging students to practice transdisciplinary writing and communication skills to ensure that they can participate successfully in a world where disciplinary boundaries often hinder new and innovative approaches to finding solutions to the pressing issues raised by the current climate emergency.

**Chapter 14**
The Significance of Collective Self-Directed Learning Competencies for the Sustainability of Higher Education ................................................................................................................. 293
    *Jean Henry Blignaut, Research Unit Self-Directed Learning, Faculty of Education, North-West University, South Africa*
    *Charlene du Toit-Brits, North-West University, South Africa*

Few scholarly studies have addressed SDL in HE. Competency improvement and curriculum change are important HE learning opportunities. Curricula should emphasize knowledge acquisition, future-oriented evaluation, and global accountability to meet HE's SDGs. Sustainable learning, living, and working must be explored alongside HE for sustainable development. New learning strategies and cultures are needed. It should be sustainable, open-minded, self-directed, and participatory. CSDL is essential for sustained capabilities and HE's growth. HE must promote SDL to engage pupils. This chapter claims that SDL skills are vital for HE's progress. Participatory learning builds these skills, which needs a university-wide approach. Using explicit, null, and hidden curricula creates meaningful learning experiences, linking theory and practice. Self-directed, sustained learning ought to be HE's focus. SDL should replace directed learning in HESD. Lastly, participatory learning might generate independently responsible and accountable thinkers who respect sustainable development.

**Chapter 15**
Voice and Photovoice of the Bangladeshi Migrant Workers in Malaysia: An Ethnography of the 3rd Space With Reciprocity .......................................................................................................... 314
    *Jahid Siraz Chowdhury, Department of Social Administration and Justice, Universiti Malaya, Malaysia*

This chapter has an inspirational event. During this pandemic, the authors have been volunteering among the Bangladeshi migrant workers in Malaysia, concomitantly finding that marginal people are unsecured for the severe food crisis. In doing this volunteering, a few questions were raised: What is the state's responsibility for the marginal people's food supply? Why does the state ignore its presence? Is there any philosophical reason? And how can these activities be theorized? Finally, how can these people survive? How can it be theorized? The authors endeavoured to answer these questions from the critical paradigm by adopting the philanthropic accountability model. In this empirical study, they argue by applying or testing the Ubuntu for politics and policy about a practical way forward in this new normal for a happier, sustainable, and healthier community.

**Chapter 16**
Ensuring Quality Education to Achieve the Sustainable Development Goals (SDGs) in
Bangladesh ................................................................................................................................. 337
    *Shamim Hosen, Bangladesh Public Administration Training Centre (BPATC), Bangladesh*
    *Md. Shafiul Islam, University of Rajshahi, Bangladesh*

Bangladesh's development paradigm would change visibly once the Sustainable Development Goals (SDGs) are implemented by 2030. Quality tertiary education can act as a catalyst for the country's economic and social development, enabling it to realize its full potential. By 2030, the entire national system will have undergone gradual modification to accommodate the "Development Junction." Therefore, the main goal of this research is to identify the institutional and procedural barriers to ensuring quality tertiary education to fulfil the Sustainable Development Goals. Multiple primary data gathering techniques have been used in this study's mixed (qualitative and quantitative) approach. Again, in this study, both thematic and descriptive analyses were used. Finally, based on the findings, several recommendations have been put together for policy formation to ensure quality tertiary education in order to meet the Sustainable Development Goals.

**Compilation of References** ................................................................................................. 361

**About the Contributors** ...................................................................................................... 420

**Index** ..................................................................................................................................... 428

# Preface

One of the major challenges that we are facing nowadays is sustainability - that is exploring ways in which we can protect the planet's natural environment and resources while fostering prosperity and well-being for a growing population (United-Nations, 2014; Holden et al., 2017). Therefore, sustainable development (SD) remains a significant global endeavor. In the past few decades, the United Nations (UN) has led the international governments as they tried to collectively resolve SD issues in their countries and promote collaboration and willingness to learn from the mistakes of the past.

Education for Sustainable Development (EDS) has become a buzzword and is now viewed as one of the common points of reference for Educational Institutions worldwide as they strive to ensure Sustainable Learning and Development for their students and staff. In terms of the ESD Framework students are equipped with sustainable expertise through an integrated multidisciplinary viewpoint on democratic teaching, learning and assessment strategies based on content and pluralistic learning. As part of the DESD (UNESCO, 2005), member states are asked to implement ESD according to their priorities, methods and approaches. In response, the participation of global higher education institutions (HEIs) in SD has increased considerably by simultaneously changing the scope of their education, research, operations and community outreach tasks (Wals, 2014). Nevertheless, education and research on sustainable development and inclusive learning, teaching and assessment in universities and institutions are still in its infancy (Farinha et al., 2018). It is vital, therefore, to create links between the various dimensions of SD and possibly Social Justice (SJ) in Education while working on and piloting ESD globally, so that people may apply SD concepts in their everyday lives (Rieckmann, 2018).

HEIs can assist in overcoming the barriers of achieving SD by creating and implementing new processes of change, adaptation and development for individuals (students and members of staff) and stakeholders (academic and non-academic) (Sinakou et al., 2018; Vargas et al., 2019). Nevertheless, the students and their families are also key stakeholders of HEIs as Aleixo et al. (2018) identify the key stakeholders of HEIs as leaders/managers, faculty, administrative staff, research staff and students. In the current handbook of research, we tried to focus on students and members of staff consciousness and understanding of SD. The concept of SD consciousness is a comprehensive term that is closely related to UNESCO's themes and sub-themes. It offers personal psychological and emotional construction based on the knowledge, attitudes, and behaviors of students and members of staff in all three dimensions of SD. To ensure we achieve the long-term Sustainable Development Goals (SDGs), it is crucial to develop positive attitudes and behaviors both at an individual level and at an institutional level and to deepen members of staff and students' understanding of what SD mean and how we can achieve it. Educational projects should try to develop leadership skills and respond to the significant features of the transition to a sustainable era in which ESD will play a vital role.

*Preface*

ESD is one of the main ways to respond the calls for SD. This concept quickly became a global movement. Today, ESD is receiving more and more attention as an effective tool to ensure SD, especially in HEIs (Leal Filho, 2018). ESD focuses on developing skills among students and individuals to encourage and motivate them to engage in sustainable behavior by considering current and future economic, political, cultural, and environmental impacts, both locally and globally (Hopkins and McKeown, 2002; Rieckmann, 2018). As stated by Leal Filho (2015), ESD is the "Educational process characterized by approaches and methods aimed at fostering awareness about the issues pertaining sustainable development".

According to the definition of UNESCO, the concept of ESD has two basic characteristics: holism and pluralism (Hopkins, 2012). The former relates to the content and the latter relates to pedagogy. In terms of content, ESD covers all disciplines that are important in discussing the complex concepts of SD (Vare and Scott, 2007; Venkataraman, 2009). ESD emphasizes the need to include three dimensions (social, economic, and environmental) and emphasizes interrelationships and time–space interactions (Summers and Childs, 2007). The overall approach of SD recognizes that cultural and social impacts are often the root cause of environment-related issues and that there are conflicts of interest between individuals and societies on economic, social, and environmental priorities (Borg et al., 2014). In one study, Öhman (2008) pointed out three key aspects of holism in his outline of ESD as a teaching tradition: linking the environmental, social, and economic aspects of SD issues; integrating their past, present, and future impacts; and paying attention to their local, regional, and global nature.

The process of learning and teaching (pedagogy) is another essential feature of ESD. For sustainability, ESD emphasizes the development of individual skills and their ability to act through learning and teaching, which is called diversity (Rudsberg & Öhman, 2010). In addressing sustainability issues, pluralism is described as an attempt to consider and involve different perspectives and beliefs. The basic idea is that the nature of such problems and conflicts of interest makes pre-defined answers difficult to teach (Englund, 2006). An innovative and revolutionary approach to teaching promotes critical assessment of alternative perspectives and includes learner-centered teaching strategies such as critical thinking, participatory decision-making, value-based learning, and social learning (Wals, 2012). Basically, ESD seeks to promote education in a way that allows students to understand the world based on their own experience and develop sustainable practical skills.

The current handbook of research presents an array of chapters which describe learning, teaching and assessment practices that can Sustainable Development in education although the holistic and pluralistic approach which is promoted in terms of the Education for Sustainable Development Framework is often considered a complex issue. Research indicates that education is obtained through the pluralistic understanding of cultural, economic, and environmental perspectives (Sterling, 2010). However, the challenges in implementing holism and pluralism in ESD are considered to be obstacles for lecturers and Higher Education Institutions seeking to adopt ESD (Borg et al., 2014). Consequently, focusing on holism and pluralism in education are considered to be important for promoting Sustainable Development. There is no 'correct' pedagogy for sustainability education. However, there is a broad consensus that it necessitates a shift towards active, collaborative, and experiential learning methods that engage students, promote interaction, and make a real difference to their understanding, thinking and ability to act. As indicated in this handbook of research, critical reflection, participatory collaborative learning and creative thinking are guiding pedagogical approaches that educators in HIE should promote while teaching students.

*Preface*

## ORGANIZATION OF THE BOOK

The book is organized into 16 chapters. A brief description of each of the chapters follows:

Chapter 1 discusses investigates 40 female educational leaders' crisis management and leadership practices which foster sustainable development in Higher Education from their perspective. Drawing on diversity, gender, and upper echelon theories, we propose that the addition of unique female perspectives and leadership styles will afford gender-diverse senior leadership teams (SLTs) a leadership capability advantage over equally talented yet homogeneous male teams. This link between gender diversity and leadership capability is more pronounced in times of crisis such as the current pandemic. Our study suggests that increasing female representation in SLTs may have a substantial and direct impact on overall leadership capabilities and elicit positive performance effects in times of crisis. Notably, and unique to this study, we show that feminine traits and inclusive leadership styles may be more efficacious in contemporary leadership contexts than generally believed. Based on these insights we consider our limitations and offer suggestions for theory, research, and practice.

Chapter 2 explores why Virtual Professional Learning Communities (VPLC) have become an increasingly popular means to meet the learning and professional development needs of students in the online learning environment amid the Covid-19 pandemic. In the current study, a combination of synchronous and asynchronous online strategies have been used to support undergraduate students at a University in the UK, as VPLC embrace individual students' needs for learning development and professional growth through peer support building community among the student population. It also provides networking and mentoring opportunities for students as they can interact with experts and professionals in their chosen field of study and work. However, previous research into VPLC has explored either exclusively synchronous or asynchronous settings and has primarily focused on the processes of the community rather than revealing students' response to this innovative learning approach or how VPLCs can help students through the provision of peer coaching/mentoring. In this study, peer coaching/mentoring consisted of four factors: academic support, technical (IT) support, emotional support, and reflective support. The intent of this research study was to unravel students' perceptions of the benefits and the challenges that VPLC may have amid the pandemic. An exploratory anonymous survey design was employed to explore their impact. The survey was administered to volunteers from the population of students who participated in the study within a one-year time frame. Students were also asked to provide anonymous feedback at regular intervals during the implementation using Mentimeter. Descriptive statistics and thematic analysis were used to examine the data. Findings suggest that VPLCs can be used as a means to support students through collaboration, peer mentoring/coaching, networking, and sharing of resources. They were significantly beneficial for BAME students supporting them in closing the awarding gap. Finally, they may include suitable learning and professional development activities to allow for knowledge transfer, student peer support, development of valuable professional skills and sustainable learning.

Chapter 3 discusses a research plan which is presented to investigate online teaching and evaluation analysis for cloud computing using an action research methodology to enable sustainable learning environment. Using online teaching, we planned to conduct a thorough evaluation of the student's learning implementation in order to identify both merits and challenges. An investigation of our own teaching and learners' understanding while working together as a team on a cloud computing project has assisted us find the perfect methods for improving both. Further, we used action research methodology to analyze the literature and scholarship critically and designed best practices for action plan to facilitate an online and sustainable learning environment for cloud computing. Moreover, possible ethical concerns have been considered as students worked in a team for group project. Finally, we have discussed the plans for monitoring and evaluation of the action and impact assessment.

Chapter 4 reviews recent developments related to non-financial information (NFI) reporting encourage the adoption of a long-term vision approach to sustainable development. In turn, the self-determination theory (SDT) describes which elements explain the students' motivation and how their skills can be better developed from their choices. Using NFI as the subject and the SDT as the theoretical framework, this chapter links both topics aiming to identify the types of students' motivation and for what specific interests are accounting students motivated to learn topics related to NFI. Data were gathered from a questionnaire. The results, using frequency and textual analyses, indicate a higher level of intrinsic motivation. Environmental and social matters are the topics of concern, while governance issues are absent. As an exploratory analysis, this chapter provides insights into how students of an accounting course are motivated to acquire skills in NFI reporting, which is particularly relevant to higher education institutions, professors, students, and organizations related to accountancy education.

Chapter 5 presents a logical discussion on Sustainable Development Goals (SDGs). How it is being treated as an incorrect concept in the academic world and the Ethnic community, the Santal is one of the examples from Bangladesh. Methodologically, this chapter follows the 'Capability approach' by Amartya Sen to understand the changing trend in the Santal community of Bangladesh. The discussion shows that despite being a global phenomenon, Sustainable Development is not an ideal coupling phrase to combat global issues because it falls into the global trap within. Based on secondary data from the literature and the first author's reflections, the study of versatile literature for conduit the policy in the local arena has been intended to be noted in this chapter.

Chapter 6 argues that we are in an age of upheaval, accelerating change, and global fragility. The increasing complexity of problems we are facing and the discontinuity we have been experiencing are only likely to escalate as we proceed into the new millennium. These challenges are the more daunting when one considers dwindling resources, potential conflict, and environmental vulnerability. Less clear is what we can better do to prepare the next generation of leaders to guide and support engaged employees and citizenry to work together to solve immense problems and exploit opportunities as they arise. A vexing problem itself is how to prepare people for the atypical and, possibly, the unknown and unexpected nature of problems and opportunities. Organisations and educational institutions that focus on discontinuity, sustainability and critical learnership may prove to remain the most viable through tumultuous times. This article explains these concepts and highlights their importance in preparing for uncertainty, essentially through a dynamic systems model. The place, function, and interdependent nature of key elements of the system are depicted and explained. This is the first time that the linkages amongst these important concepts and disciplines have been drawn, thus this article represents an advance in understanding how learning and professional development can be enhanced in keeping with the demands (and limitations) of the 21st Century. The article subtext is that conventional education and professional development are insufficient—if not counterproductive—to equipping current and future generations with the skills and dispositions to contend with the chaos and complexity of the emerging millennium. To the degree this is true, approaches to learning and professional development need to change. But how? To this end, readers might benefit most from the practical and realistic recommendations outlined herein for schools, organisations, and communities.

Chapter 7 discusses that a traditional classroom approach focuses on teacher-centric learning and theoretical knowledge transition is often reinforcing spoon-feeding education. To this end, it leads to demotivating students' learning and failing to fulfill the employers' expectations. The business simula-

## Preface

tion game is a new, innovative educational tool for students to enjoy in an interactive learning classroom. The use of support tools can help students to improve their professionalization. This study mainly uses an illustrative real-life case study, Macro Business Simulation, as the target study area. In response, the study invited 64 university students to complete both pre-activity and post-activity surveys, along with 10 semi-structured, in-depth interviews with relevant parties including teachers, students, Macro Business Simulation operators, and business enterprises. Implications of the findings are also discussed.

Chapter 8 focuses on the purpose and objectives of this case study which are to explore the effective use of mobile technologies by first year students amid the COVID-19 coronavirus pandemic, using a situational analysis and active theory. Moreover, this study will unveil intersectional problems and educational inequality among 'digital natives' and 'digital immigrants' at the Rundu campus of the University of Namibia (UNAM). The study aims at examining how the interventions of distance and/or online learning are exclusive, exposing many, especially first year, students to educational inequality. Finally, the implications of sustainable development in higher education in terms of teaching, learning, and assessment will be considered.

Chapter 9 acknowledges that online learners have diverse backgrounds, skills, learning styles etc. Among all the attributes, learning styles play a significant role and has a major impact on academic performance. Learning style denotes the individual differences exists among individuals and their capacity in learning. The success in teaching depends on various factors, preferably adapting teaching pedagogy to individual's learning style. The instructor should create a favorable environment where the needs of the learners can be met. This chapter is divided into three segments. Segment one discusses about the dimensions of learning which includes cognitive, affective, physiological and psychological types. Segment two covers the strategies for meeting the needs of various online learners. Segment three covers managing diverse learners and different online teaching pedagogies and creating learner engagement.

Chapter 10 investigates how we expanded our teaching and learning beyond the classroom at Big University in the UK. It puts forward the theoretical concept of the "exploding university" as a way to help develop a critical yet hopeful understanding of our collective problems at local and global scales. This helps us explore three interrelated initiatives that brought teachers, students and communities together; namely a sustainability festival, research project on animal rehoming, and community tree-planting drive. The chapter illuminates how exploding our work beyond the classroom enabled everyone involved to take action on the challenges that matter to them, while also developing a "collective intelligence" about their underlying causes. The exploding university thus emerges as a theoretical and practical model through which we can inspire students to actively critique, reimagine and reconstruct the world around them. We conclude by encouraging and supporting others who might wish to embark on similar journeys themselves.

Chapter 11 discusses that one of the main purposes of multicultural education is to approach all individuals at an equal distance in educational environments, provide a sense of belonging by ensuring unity and integrity, and eliminate the gap in academic achievement among diverse groups by ensuring equal opportunities for all. In this regard, the present study intends to contribute to the existing research by providing a rich amount of evidence as to the challenges posed by linguistic and cultural diversity, and the strategies employed by the instructors to effectively overcome those challenges. The data of the study were collected through video-stimulated interviews with four instructors and semi-structured interviews with 20 lecturers. The study revealed that the EFL instructors most frequently experienced challenges in regards to language and communication and they develop numerous strategies to overcome these challenges. Considering the research process and its results, the current research study provided various pedagogical implications and suggestions for the main stakeholders of education.

Chapter 12 aims at exploring teachers' perceptions of using Arabic (L1) as a pedagogical tool to mediate teaching English in higher education. It further investigates the reasons for abstaining from using Arabic and its functions and attempts to determine the factors that affect teachers' decisions on whether or not to use L1. Forty (40) teachers from different universities responded to an online questionnaire. The results revealed that the teachers had positive perspectives toward the selective use of students' L1 (M= 2.89; SD= 0.39). The results showed a moderate positive correlation between the respondents' perceptions of using L1 and their classroom practices (r=0. 498; p=0.001). The results suggested that the teachers were hesitant about using students' L1 because of the misconception about its role in learning the target language. The chapter concludes with implications on functions for utilizing L1, its determining factors, and the reasons for abstaining from it explicated.

Chapter 13 foregrounds the important role of teaching and learning in the age of climate change. The author shows that education for sustainable development needs to promote communication practices that not only emphasize transition and betweenness, but that transcend current definitions of disciplines to create sustainable solutions to existing problems. Such writing and communication practices are necessary to contribute to 21st century solutions to such monumental issues as increased migration due to conflict, persecution, and natural disasters; food insecurity across the globe; the erasure of economic, social, cultural, gender, civil, and political rights; and pandemics that know no borders. The chapter concludes by emphasizing the importance of encouraging students to practice transdisciplinary writing and communication skills to ensure that they can participate successfully in a world where disciplinary boundaries often hinder new and innovative approaches to finding solutions to the pressing issues raised by the current climate emergency.

Chapter 14 admits that few scholarly studies have addressed SDL in HE. Competency improvement and curriculum change are important HE learning opportunities. Curricula should emphasize knowledge acquisition, future-oriented evaluation, and global accountability to meet HE's SDGs. Sustainable learning, living, and working must be explored alongside HE for sustainable development. New learning strategies and cultures are needed. It should be sustainable, open-minded, self-directed, and participatory. CSDL is essential for sustained capabilities and HE's growth. HE must promote SDL to engage pupils. This chapter claims that SDL skills are vital for HE's progress. Participatory learning builds these skills, which needs a university-wide approach. Using explicit, null, and hidden curricula creates meaningful learning experiences, linking theory and practice. Self-directed, sustained learning ought to be HE's focus. SDL should replace directed learning in HESD. Lastly, participatory learning might generate independently responsible and accountable thinkers who respect sustainable development.

Chapter 15 explores how, during this pandemic, authors have been volunteering among the Bangladeshi migrant workers in Malaysia, concomitantly finding that marginal people are unsecured for the severe food crisis. In doing this volunteering, a few questions were raised. What is the state's responsibility for the marginal people's food supply? Why does the state ignore its presence? Is there any philosophical reason? And how can these activities be theorized? Finally, how can these people survive? How can be theorized? We endeavoured to answer these questions from the Critical paradigm by adopting the Philanthropic Accountability Model. In this empirical study, we argue by applying or testing the Ubuntu for politics and policy as well a practical way forward in this New Normal for a happier, sustainable, and healthier community.

# Preface

Chapter 16 elaborates on inequality which still exists despite outstanding economic growth and a significant decline in poverty over the past 20 years. Quality education is regarded as one of the most powerful and successful methods, among others, for achieving sustainable development to address myriad difficulties. It is generally accepted that the development of a country is more heavily influenced by highly educated individuals than by the mere number of educated individuals. United nations sustainable development goals 4 and quality education go hand in hand, ensuring that all learners get the information and abilities necessary to advance sustainable development (UN, 2015). In order to produce trained people resources who will immediately contribute to improved and higher-quality output and ultimately Bangladesh's sustainable growth, it is crucial to guarantee quality higher education. However, the nation is behind in this area. This study has explored the issues against these depressing backdrops, concentrating on institutional deficiencies at the nation's tertiary level education sector.

*Eleni Meletiadou*
*London Metropolitan University, UK*

## REFERENCES

Aleixo, A. M., Azeiteiro, U. M., & Leal, S. (2018). The implementation of sustainability practices in Portuguese higher education institutions. *International Journal of Sustainability in Higher Education*, *19*(1), 146–178. doi:10.1108/IJSHE-02-2017-0016

Borg, C., Gericke, N., Höglund, H.-O., & Bergman, E. (2014). Subject-and experience-bound differences in teachers' conceptual understanding of sustainable development. *Environmental Education Research*, *20*(4), 526–551. doi:10.1080/13504622.2013.833584

Englund, T. (2006). Deliberative communication: A pragmatist proposal. *Journal of Curriculum Studies*, *38*(5), 503–520. doi:10.1080/00220270600670775

Farinha, C. S., Azeiteiro, U., & Caeiro, S. S. (2018). Education for sustainable development in Portuguese universities. *International Journal of Sustainability in Higher Education*, *19*(5), 912–941. doi:10.1108/IJSHE-09-2017-0168

Holden, E., Linnerud, K., & Banister, D. (2017). The imperatives of sustainable development: Needs, justice, limits. *Sustainable Development*, *25*(3), 213–226. doi:10.1002d.1647

Hopkins, C., & Mckeown, R. (2002). Education for sustainable development: an international perspective. In D. Tilbury, R. B. Stevenson, J. Fien, & D. Shreuder (Eds.), *Education and Sustainability: Responding to the Global Challenge*. IUCN.

Leal Filho, W., Brandli, L. L., Becker, D., Skanavis, C., Kounani, A., Sardi, C., Papaioannidou, D., Paço, A., Azeiteiro, U., de Sousa, L. O., Raath, S., Pretorius, R. W., Shiel, C., Vargas, V., Trencher, G., & Marans, R. W. (2018). Sustainable development policies as indicators and pre-conditions for sustainability efforts at universities. *International Journal of Sustainability in Higher Education*, *19*(1), 85–113. doi:10.1108/IJSHE-01-2017-0002

Öhman, J. (2008). Environmental ethics and democratic responsibility. *Values Democracy in Education for Sustainable Development: Contributions from Swedish Research*, 17-32.

Rieckmann, M. (2018). Learning to transform the world: key competencies in education for sustainable development. In A. Leicht, J. Heiss, & W. J. Byun (Eds.), *Issues and Trends in Education for Sustainable Development*. UNESCO.

Rudsberg, K., & Öhman, J. (2010). Pluralism in practice–experiences from Swedish evaluation, school development and research. *Environmental Education Research*, 16(1), 95–111. doi:10.1080/13504620903504073

Sinakou, E., Boeve-De Pauw, J., Goossens, M., & Van Petegem, P. (2018). Academics in the field of education for sustainable development: Their conceptions of sustainable development. *Journal of Cleaner Production*, 184, 321–332. doi:10.1016/j.jclepro.2018.02.279

Sterling, S. (2010). Living in the earth: Towards an education for our time. *Journal of Education for Sustainable Development*, 4(2), 213–218. doi:10.1177/097340821000400208

Summers, M., & Childs, A. (2007). Student science teachers' conceptions of sustainable development: An empirical study of three postgraduate training cohorts. *Research in Science & Technological Education*, 25(3), 307–327. doi:10.1080/02635140701535067

UNESCO. (2005). *United Nations Decade of Education for Sustainable Development (2005-2014): Draft International Implementation Scheme*. UNESCO.

UNESCO. (2014). *UNESCO Roadmap for Implementing the Global Action Programme on Education for Sustainable Development*. UNESCO.

Vare, P., & Scott, W. (2007). Learning for a change: Exploring the relationship between education and sustainable development. *Journal of Education for Sustainable Development*, 1(2), 191–198. doi:10.1177/097340820700100209

Vargas, V. R., Lawthom, R., Prowse, A., Randles, S., & Tzoulas, K. (2019). Sustainable development stakeholder networks for organisational change in higher education institutions: A case study from the UK. *Journal of Cleaner Production*, 208, 470–478. doi:10.1016/j.jclepro.2018.10.078

Venkataraman, B. (2009). Education for sustainable development. *Environment*, 51(2), 8–10. doi:10.3200/ENVT.51.2.08-10

Wals, A. E. (2012). *Shaping the Education of Tomorrow: 2012 Full-Length Report on the UN Decade of Education for Sustainable Development*. UNESCO.

Wals, A. E. (2014). Sustainability in higher education in the context of the UN DESD: A review of learning and institutionalization processes. *Journal of Cleaner Production*, 62, 8–15. doi:10.1016/j.jclepro.2013.06.007

# Chapter 1
# Leadership for Sustainability in Higher Education Amidst the COVID-19 Crisis:
## Exploring Female Educational Leaders' Strategies for Transformation

**Eleni Meletiadou**
https://orcid.org/0000-0003-4833-1450
*London Metropolitan University, UK*

## ABSTRACT

*Through assisted thematic content analyses of 40 female educational leaders' interviews, the chapter investigates the crisis management and leadership practices which foster sustainable development in higher education from their perspective. Drawing on diversity, gender, and upper echelon theories, the authors propose that the addition of unique female perspectives and leadership styles will afford gender-diverse senior leadership teams (SLTs) a leadership capability advantage over equally talented yet homogeneous male teams. This link between gender diversity and leadership capability is more pronounced in times of crisis such as the current pandemic. The study suggests that increasing female representation in SLTs may have a substantial and direct impact on overall leadership capabilities and elicit positive performance effects in times of crisis. Notably, and unique to this study, they show that feminine traits and inclusive leadership styles may be more efficacious in contemporary leadership contexts than generally believed.*

## INTRODUCTION

Although fifty nine percent of graduates within the EU-28 are women, only eighteen percent of female academics hold full professorship at universities (EP, 2015) and even less become assistant professors according to the Netherlands Organization for Scientific Research (2013, p. 5). Aspiring female educa-

DOI: 10.4018/978-1-6684-6172-3.ch001

tional leaders' career advancement has been slow despite support provided by programmes, such as the Athena Swan Charter, enhancing women marginalization (Carnes et al., 2008). Male-friendly organizational practices still dominate HEI and women are not supported due to lack of programmes which aim to develop their leadership skills (Correll, 2017).

Although there is ample research focusing on gendered barriers for women in the academy, relatively little attention has been paid to whether women academics are inclusive leaders amidst a major crisis such as the Covid-19 pandemic (Stefani & Blessinger 2017). This article contributes to the debate on how IL can help organisations face crises effectively by shedding light on how inclusive female leaders, who act as role-models (in line with the social information processing theory developed by Salancik & Pfeffer, 1978), may improve organisational performance and increase employees' positive response when faced with crisis-induced challenges. From a Human Resource Development (HRD) perspective, there are many issues that remain unanswered and are worth exploring in the crisis literature. Some of these issues, that are highlighted in this article, focus on how to minimize the negative impact of crisis by leveraging it to the organisation's advantage through consistent involvement of all stakeholders (e.g., leaders and followers) at each stage of the crisis (Bhaduri, 2019).

According to Garikipati and Kambhampati (2021), Covid-19 outcomes are systematically better in countries led by women due to the proactive and coordinated policy responses they adopt. Zenger and Folkman (2020) report that according to an analysis of 360-degree assessments, women were rated by their colleagues as more effective. Previous research indicates that female leaders tend to perform better in a crisis in terms of overall leadership effectiveness because employees need leaders who are honest, truthful, and mindful of their colleagues' feelings and frustration (Branson et al., 2016), can pivot new skills and focus on employee development even during major crises (Dirani et al., 2020).

To sum up, the current chapter reports on how female educational leaders in HEI in the UK perceive themselves as leaders during major crises such as the Covid-19 pandemic. It aims to explore whether they confirm previous studies claiming that women are effective leaders in crises (Aldrich & Lotito, 2020; Soares & Sidun, 2021) and unfold how female educational leaders in HEI in the UK are facing the Covid-19 pandemic. Based on the findings of this study, recommendations will be provided as to how all relevant stakeholders in HEI can promote gender equity, help female (and male) educational leaders enhance their crisis management (CM) skills and become more inclusive leaders responding to challenges associated with IL, i.e., leaders' anxiety (Choi et al., 2015).

## BACKGROUND

### Gender Diversity, Gender Inclusion and Inclusive Leadership in HEI

Gender diversity, broadly defined, is "any significant difference that distinguishes one individual from another" (Kreitz, 2008, p. 102). Research indicates that women still struggle to attain their goals in their chosen ðelds of study and are unlikely to be promoted to senior leadership positions (Winchester & Browning, 2015). By adopting critical gender theory as my theoretical framework, I regard gender as socially constructed (Kolb, 2000) acknowledging that it is reproduced regularly in daily negotiation sustaining structured inequalities between men and women and leading to the existing gender discrimination in their employment status (Morley 2013) highlighting a favouritism towards men within the academy (Knights & Richards, 2003). Savigny (2014) reports that female educational leaders feel as the 'other' not belonging within the academy. This leads to marginalisation of women, their contributions, and ideas (Savigny 2014). HEI are learning organizations, but according to Senge (1990), 'for a learning organization, it is not enough to survive, but to enhance capacity to create'. Therefore, their leaders have responsibilities for their successes and failures (Kareem, 2016) and a decision-making role for their increasingly diverse cohorts. Unless there is some deliberate adjustment to rules and organizational requirements, female leaders in HEI will still be unable to reach their full potential due to gendered inequalities in family obligations and life experiences (Gouthro et al., 2018). Having encountered discrimination in their lives, one of those characteristics, that female leaders often show, is inclusivity as they strive to support all their followers irrespective of their background (Cundiflr & Stockdale, 2013).

The impact of gender diversity in the upper echelons has received a lot of attention recently (Moreno-Gómez et al. 2018). Drawing on diversity, gender, and upper echelons theories we believe that in organisations where SLTs are disproportionately composed of males (Cataylst, 2019), the addition of female ideas, decision-making, and leadership styles (Perryman et al., 2016) will afford gender diverse SLTs, a managerial capability advantage over equally talented yet homogenous males teams. Moreover, social pressures and legal requirements have triggered a shift towards prioritizing gender diversity on SLTs (WEF 2018). A recent study found 38% of firms set targets for gender representation (Lean In and McKinsey & Company 2018). Women's inclusive leadership style combined with their stereotypically feminine traits are seen as particularly apt in crisis (Ryan et al. 2011).

According to Nembhard and Edmondson (2006, p. 947), IL has been defined as "words and deeds by a leader or leaders that indicate an invitation and appreciation for others' contributions". IL denotes leaders who demonstrate their visibility, accessibility, and availability during interaction with subordinates (Carmeli et al., 2010). Hassan and Jiang (2019) stress that inclusive leaders ensure that subordinates are given credit for their input and contribution as this seems to enhance workplace engagement (Wang et al., 2019) and creativity (Mikyoung & Moon, 2019).

IL is a cooperative and collaborative process which presupposes that all employees participate in decisions and processes. Moreover, leaders show altruistic behaviour to enhance employees' feelings of belongingness (Mitchell et al., 2015; Northouse, 2016; Prime & Salib, 2014). It is also perceived as a set of positive leader behaviours that promote group members' uniqueness as they are encouraged to fully contribute to group processes and outcomes (Randel et al., 2018). Inclusion is closely linked to top-down leadership and bottom-up engagement allowing leaders to interact with their group members to pursue the organisational goals. Likewise, leaders enable the organization to continuously grow and respond rapidly and effectively to change in response to the threats it encounters (Senge, 1990).

Diversity researchers also value inclusion, which stems from sociopsychological theories that describe humans' vital need to affiliate with others, such as human motivation (Maslow, 1943), social comparison (Festinger, 1954), and the belongingness hypothesis (Baumeister & Leary, 1995). These theories portray that their tendency to create and maintain meaningful relationships with others is fundamental to people's physical and psychological well-being as individuals use such relationships as an indication of whether they belong to or are accepted by various social groups.

Taking into consideration the optimal distinctiveness theory (Brewer, 1991), which claims that people try to balance their basic human need to belong to larger social groups with their need to retain a separate self-concept, certain diversity scholars define inclusion in terms of the tension between human need for association with a group and differentiation that control whether an individual can become member of a specific group. For instance, inclusion has been described as people's wholehearted engagement at their workplace, including equal access to decision-making and leadership positions, but also as being asked to form part due to their differences (Shore et al., 2011). Therefore, to promote female leaders in HEI, their multi-layered expertise should be unveiled and praised by HEI (Pillay, 2009).

IL is also defined as a special form of "relational" leadership in terms of which leaders are inclined to pay attention to employees' needs and opinions and value their contributions so that organizations and employees can share common goals and achieve win-win results promoting an open, available, and accessible relationship between leaders and subordinates (Carmeli et al., 2010; Choi et al., 2016; Hollander, 2009). Yanping et al. (2012) focused on balanced empowerment to achieve management, dynamic balance, and inclusive development. Finally, Minghui et al. (2014) proposed a four-degree model of IL based on affinity, tolerance, and support focusing on treating employees equally and fairly, recognizing their efforts, and encouraging their active participation.

While diversity scholars have conceptualized IL, our understanding of leader behaviours to facilitate an inclusive environment is relatively limited (Randel et al., 2018) and little attention has been paid to whether these behaviours are enacted by leaders in learning organizations. In this study, we examine leaders' recollections of the behaviours in which they engaged to create and retain inclusive environments. Taking into consideration the Social exchange theory (Blau, 1964) and the rules of reciprocity (Gouldner, 1960), we claim that when subordinates perceive that their leaders are genuinely interested in their well-being and provide socio-psychological support, they are likely to reciprocate by improving on their job/task performance (Walumbwa et al., 2011) especially in terms of a crisis showing high commitment to achieving set organizational goals and objectives. This paper wishes to explore whether female leaders perceive themselves as open, available, and accessible which in turn triggers employees' positive response (Carmeli et al., 2010).

## Crisis Management in HEI

Rosenthal, Boin and Comfort (2001) claim that "crisis is a serious threat to the basic structures or the fundamental values and norms of a social system, which - under time pressure and highly uncertain circumstances - necessitates making critical decisions" (p. 10). As a mainly human crisis, the Covid-19 crisis has been incredibly disruptive for leaders as it was exceedingly stressful for employees urging HR professionals to support them in their efforts to exit the crisis successfully (Harney & Collings, 2021). According to Hutchins and Wang (2008, p. 315), five elements are inherent in a crisis system: "technology, organizational structure, human factors, organizational culture, and top management psychology". Of these, organizational culture and human aspects can be thought as the most significant elements during a crisis. Sun (2008) noted, "culture provides better (or the best) ways of thinking, feeling, and reacting that could help managers to make decision and arrange activities of organization" (p. 137).

Organizational culture plays an undeniable role in shaping an organization's reaction to crisis situations, both positively and negatively (Elsubbaugh et al., 2004). Moreover, human characteristics like efficient leadership, coordinated teams and motivated followers can also have a significant impact on averting and managing crisis. Effective leadership is undeniably fostered by the organizational culture. A leader who "understands his/her organizational culture and takes it seriously is capable of predicting the outcome of his/her decisions in preventing any anticipated consequences" (Madu, 2012, p. 2). Nevertheless, not all leaders are equally equipped to manage crisis situations. Efficient leaders whose styles can align with the organizational culture and the crisis can be a good fit for addressing the situation (Bowers et al., 2017). Consequently, to enhance a proactive organizational culture, where employees appreciate, and actively take part in CM, efficient leaders can be an indispensable resource. Human resource development efforts should support leadership development and creation of a proactive, crisis-prepared organizational culture (Elsubbaugh et al., 2004).

However, there is very little research on human competencies required to prevent and control crisis situations (Wooten & James, 2008). "Crises often drive organizations to predictable mitigation strategies focused on managing distractions rather than prioritized actions targeted at crisis response" (Bowers et al., 2017, p. 553). In other words, there are very few studies on how leaders can assist and prepare learning organizations to confront, tackle and manage crises efficiently. Further research is necessary to reveal organizational culture and leadership competencies and values that are necessary for CM in the pre- and post-crisis phases. The current study is a step forward to fill some of the gaps in the literature.

Moreover, due to the current Covid-19 crisis, the psychological toll in terms of job demands has increased considerably. IL is a highly recommended remedy because it provides employees with psychological relief as they can confide their thoughts and fears in their inclusive leaders who provide comfort when their followers feel overwhelmed by interacting with them regularly (Ahmed et al., 2021). Their help and support help reduce the uncertainty, work-related stress, and job anxiety.

The theory of shattered assumptions by Janoff-Bulman (2010) clearly demonstrates that crises, such as the Covid-19, bring trauma and shatter the employee perceptions of the world being a secure place. IL supports the re-creation of a safety climate through its inherent characteristics. IL promotes a culture of openness, accessibility, and availability of the leaders who are continuously willing to support employees (Nembhard & Edmondson, 2006). This also fosters group members' psychological safety (PS) (Jiang et al., 2019). This study contributes to the context of traumatic events such as the Covid-19 pandemic as it wishes to explore whether female leaders use IL to reduce employees' crisis-related stress and promote PS which often leads to positive outcomes such as a positive mindset with lower levels of crisis-related distress.

Additionally, contingency theories include intervening variables to account for the change in the outcome behaviour across situational contexts (Yukl & Becker, 2006). Many scholars claim that, in terms of crisis leadership, learning organizations need to work "under magnified organizational issues" that are rarely encountered under usual circumstances (French & Niculae, 2005). The literature clearly indicates that leadership, in times of organizational crisis, is imperative to organizational survival (Borodzicz & van Haperen, 2002). However, senior leaders, adept at handling normal issues, are sometimes not as skilled and well-prepared to handle crisis situations.

Crisis leadership involves prevention and management, consistency and clarity, trust, and transparency - with communication playing a significant role during every phase (Gigliotti, 2019). As claimed by DuBrin (2013), crisis leaders show charisma, strategic thinking, and an ability to inspire and demonstrate sadness and compassion. By creating and retaining a reservoir of goodwill at the individual and collective level, they set the scene for authentic, values-centred dialogue when crises strike. CM and crisis prevention and preparedness are included in what we call crisis leadership in HEI. As Birnbaum (1992) claims, "universities are exceptionally complex systems that interact with even more complex environments" (p. 12).

Moreover, during times of organizational crisis, there is clear evidence by various researchers that female leaders are often appointed to high-ranking leadership posts (Bruckmüller et al., 2014; Ryan et al., 2016; Glass & Cook, 2016). Glass and Cook (2016) called this barrier the glass cliff. This is because CM requires leadership characteristics often associated with females such as collaborative traits and other interpersonal abilities (Gartzia et al., 2012).

Previous scholars have described the leadership in HEI under normal circumstances (BlackChen, 2015; Tran & Nguyen, 2020) rather than in crisis situations such as a pandemic. Findings indicate that inclusive leaders create a more open and psychologically safe environment for employees which also helps maintain and enhance employees' vitality, contribution, and focus on work by minimising crisis-related psychological distress. Therefore, this study compensates for the IL in crises gap in the literature.

Additionally, the relationship between the two constructs of leadership and crisis is well-documented in the CM literature. By maintaining effective communication, and building trust, leaders play a huge role during crisis times (Lockwood, 2005). Consequently, leadership competencies determine the success or failure of CM efforts. Lockwood (2005, p. 3) stressed how significant it is for leaders to have emotional intelligence competencies, such as "empathy, self-awareness, persuasion, teamwork skills and the ability to manage relationships" during CM. Wooten and James (2008, p. 354) increased the number of items in the list of competencies for crisis leadership by adding, "decision making, communication, creating organizational capabilities, sustaining an effective organizational culture, managing multiple constituencies, and developing human capital".

To sum up, crisis situations contradict normal organization operation in significant ways. Taking into consideration the disruption crisis situations bring to an organization, the emphasis on competent and adequate leadership is self-evident. The current study will explore female educational leaders' perceptions of their CM skills and examine whether they demonstrate IL characteristics.

## MAIN FOCUS OF THE CHAPTER

### Methodology

### Data Collection and Methods

To explore female educational leaders' CM skills and reactions to the Covid-19 crisis and examine how inclusive leaders they are, the researcher interviewed 40 leaders (for demographic data see Table 1) from 4 HEI in London, UK. Using opportunity and snowball sampling processes (Sharma, 2017), only a small number of women participated in this study as there were time, money, and access constraints (Vasileiou et al., 2018). Interviewees were found by tapping into the researcher's professional network. These were publicly funded universities and the researcher started collecting data as soon as the Covid-19 crisis emerged.

*Table 1. Characteristics of the participating female leaders (N=40)*

| Measure and Items | N |
|---|---|
| **Age** | |
| 25-34 | 2 |
| 35-44 | 15 |
| 45-54 | 16 |
| 55+ | 7 |
| **Ethnicity** | |
| White | 23 |
| Asian | 2 |
| Black | 7 |
| Mixed | 8 |
| **Years of employment** | |
| 11-20 | 10 |
| 21-30 | 23 |
| 30+ | 7 |
| **Years in a leadership position** | |
| 0-10 | 15 |
| 11-20 | 20 |
| 21-30 | 5 |
| **Marital status** | |
| Single | 4 |
| Married/in civil partnership | 27 |
| Divorced | 7 |
| Widowed | 2 |
| **Children** | |
| 0 | 3 |
| 1-2 | 33 |
| 3-4 | 4 |
| **Disability** | |
| Yes | 2 |
| No | 38 |

The researcher chose a qualitative research design and conducted lengthy semi-structured interviews with senior educational leaders (senior lecturers, heads of divisions, members of the senior management team). All interviews were conducted through MS Teams due to the Covid-19 restrictions. Each interview lasted for approximately fifty minutes in length. For data analysis, the interviews were transcribed verbatim. The aim of the current study was to address the following research questions:

- How inclusive leaders are female educational leader in HEI in the UK?

- How have female educational leaders in HEI in the UK reacted to the Covid-19 crisis?

## Data Analysis

Qualitative research data was collected from non-standardised interviews and was analysed using a prominent approach, thematic content analysis (King & Brooks, 2018). The themes that the researcher tried to identify during data analysis were closely linked to the theoretical background of IL and CM and were reflected in the questionnaire she used to interview the participants. The aim was to determine whether the participants in the current study perceived that they were inclusive leaders and explore their Covid-19 CM skills.

In terms of inter-coder reliability, two independent raters coded interviews into themes and subthemes. The level of agreement was calculated between raters using Cohen's Kappa (K). The value of Cohen's Kappa ranged from 0.18 to 0.86. A commonly used scale to determine the acceptability of Kappa values (Landis & Koch, 1977) considers Kappa values between .21 and .40 as indicating fair agreement, between .41 and .60 as indicating moderate agreement, between .61 and .80 indicating substantial agreement, and between .81 and .99 as indicating near perfect agreement. Interview instances on which coders did not agree were discussed until an agreement was reached, though sometimes some instances were omitted from the coding process. A detailed description of the themes and subthemes is provided in Table 2.

The interview data were analysed using thematic content analysis (Neuendorf, 2018). The researcher and her assistant independently identified main themes and subthemes that were joined by the researcher into a report. The researchers were responsible for identifying and interpreting the themes and subthemes as these emerged from the data keeping in mind the original research questions. A term was identified by more than half of the participants to be labelled as a sub-theme. Inter-validation processes were used (Yin, 2009). This procedure certified that the final report was explicit and coherent. They both recommended and examined interview themes and sub-themes. Quotations were selected to illustrate the sub-themes succinctly (Table 3).

The current study employed an exploratory multiple case study qualitative approach to explore female educational leaders' experiences of leadership in HEI at four HEI in London, UK (Gustafsson, 2017). It aimed to examine a modern real-life phenomenon within a particular context (Yin, 2013). The study used a qualitative interviewing data collection method, which is more suitable for exploratory studies that attempt to gain rich insights into a complicated phenomenon like female educational leadership in HEI (Punch, 2013). In the current study, a semi-structured interview technique was deployed as it matches this exploratory study that implements interpretive philosophy (Saunders, 2016). Its structure allows the researcher to "probe answers and allows a balance between focus and flexibility" (Saunders et al., 2016).

The researcher created different types of open-ended questions that comprised descriptive, structural, contrast and evaluative content to explore the participants' perspective and get valid information (Elo et al., 2014). To avoid reflexivity error and response bias, the researcher chose to initiate the interview with a brief discussion to explain the scope of the study in detail and develop intimacy as a strategy to lessen such biases. Case studies have been criticized because they offer little basis for scientific generalization (Yin, 2013). The current study has limitations because it was a qualitative study which used only a specific number of interviewees. It is closely related to the phenomenological and hermeneutical research approach which points to an internal and thorough awareness of the essence of research, not at generating generalizable outcomes.

## Data Collection

Using opportunity and snowball sampling processes (Naderifar et al., 2017), forty women from four HEI in London, UK (see their demographic data in Table 1) were invited to participate in this study as a small sample was sufficient for the current qualitative study which employed a lengthy questionnaire (Vasileiou et al., 2018). Interviewees were found by tapping into the researcher's professional network. All female leaders were reassured that the information they provided would be kept confidential and they gave us permission to have the interview recorded. The researcher asked them to provide demographic information via an online survey before the interview to save time. Exploratory interviews were conducted online through Microsoft Teams due to the Covid-19 pandemic. Social cues, e.g., body language, were also recorded. The research was conducted only at four universities due to time and access constraints. The researcher collected the data and tried to eliminate biases, which are frequently encountered in qualitative studies (Clark & Vealé, 2018).

*Table 2. Demographic data*

| Age | 35-44 | 45-54 | 55+ |
|---|---|---|---|
|  | 20% | 40% | 40% |
| **Ethnicity** | **Black** | **White** | **Mixed** |
|  | 80% | 10% | 10% |
| **Years of service** | **10-20** | **20-30** | **30+** |
|  | 70% | 10% | 20% |
| **Marital status** | **Married** | **Divorced** | **Single** |
|  | 70% | 20% | 10% |
| **Children** | **0** | **1-2** | **3-4** |
|  | 20% | 50% | 30% |
| **Disability** | **Yes** | **No** |  |
|  | 90% | 10% |  |

The interviews were recorded and transcribed verbatim, based on predetermined semi-structured questions (Yin, 2013). These questions were further elaborated to probe deep into the interviewee's experiences. They aimed to examine their opinions from both a social and an organizational perspective. The semi-structured interview questions were scrutinized taking into consideration an extensive literature review of women leading HEI and included a list of basic questions and some prompts (e.g., exploratory) to promote further discussion. Introductory, barrier and closing questions were used to allow for a certain kind of progression in the interview procedure and included background demographic questions, experience/behavior questions, opinion/value questions and feeling questions (Collis & Hussey, 2013). Each interview lasted approximately fifty minutes.

## Data Analysis

Qualitative research data was collected from non-standardized interviews and analyzed using a prominent approach, thematic analysis (Thornhill et al., 2015). Thematic analysis is adjustable and can provide an insight into major resemblances and contrasts on the current topic depending on how these are observed by the interviewees. The interview data were inductively analyzed, according to Braun and Clarke (2006, p. 87) six-step procedure of thematic analysis: a) becoming familiar with the data, b) forming codes, c) looking for themes, d) revising the themes, e) naming the themes and f) creating a report.

The research team (the researcher and an assistant) employed a constructivist grounded theory method to analyse the interviews (Ramalho, 2015). They independently identified main themes that were joined by the researcher into one report. The researcher named the different codes depending on the actual terms the participants used ('in vivo' codes) and on terms derived from related research and theories ('a priori' codes). The research team was responsible for identifying and interpreting the themes as these emerged from the data keeping in mind the original research questions. A term should have been identified by more than half of the participants to be labelled as a theme. Each researcher separately employed the constant comparison method when coding and revising themes (Vaismoradi et al., 2016). Consequently, they correlated the data several times through coding and recoding to locate prominent common themes and structures (Punch, 2013). After that, their outcomes were compared and synthesised. Inter-validation processes were also used.

This procedure certified that the final report would be explicit and coherent. They both recommended and examined interview themes. Based on those themes, the research team developed an introductory codebook. Two individual coders coded every interview. Researchers individually examined interviews to identify parts of speech relevant to the themes. Inter-rater agreement was determined to be considerably high. Using a comparative approach, the first-order themes were joined into several second-order subthemes which will be presented in the next section.

As soon as the initial coding was finalized, the researcher located themes based on the level of inter-rater compliance and the researcher's willingness to adopt a balanced perspective (e.g., positive and negative themes). Moreover, the researcher clarified the portrayal of these areas and re-evaluated the interviews to ensure that all related parts of speech were located. Interview passages linked to these themes were individually evaluated by two researchers and subthemes were located and negotiated. An elaborate codebook was formed for every theme. Consensus between raters was assessed using Cohen's Kappa (K). Its value ranged from 0.17 to 0.83. Interview instances on which coders disagreed were negotiated until a consensus was reached, although in some cases some parts were not included in the coding procedure. Quotations were selected to illustrate the points succinctly.

The study had some obvious limitations because it was a qualitative study which used only a specific number of interviewees. It is closely related to the phenomenological and hermeneutical research approach which points to an internal and thorough awareness of the essence of research, not at generating generalizable outcomes. Although case studies are not credible and have low reliability, validity, and replicability (Cohen et al., 2013), this research study showed meticulousness and precision but admitting the uncommon context of this case; the research findings will probably not be generalizable. Finally, the study admits that selecting a qualitative interview approach for data collection undoubtedly carries interviewer and participant biases (Punch, 2013).

## FINDINGS AND DISCUSSION

The study yielded rich data. The subthemes which address the main research questions of the study can be seen in Table 3.

*Table 3. Frequency counts for subthemes*

| Themes | Inclusive Leadership | F (N=40) | Crisis Management | F (N=40) |
|---|---|---|---|---|
| Subthemes | Collaboration/participation | 35 | Support/active listening | 36 |
| | Compassion | 34 | Management (short-term) | 30 |
| | Authenticity | 30 | Leadership (long-term) | 24 |
| | Flexibility | 26 | Scenario planning & adaptability | 36 |
| | Open communication | 36 | Shared responsibility | 35 |
| | Fairness | 33 | Fast, value-driven decision making | 37 |
| | No blaming | 22 | Individual Responsibility | 21 |
| | Inclusivity | 22 | Remedy | 28 |
| | Provide coaching/mentoring | 21 | Accountability | 22 |
| | Availability | 38 | Balance | 21 |
| | Respect & discretion | 37 | Psychological safety | 35 |
| | Employee development | 32 | Diplomacy | 21 |
| | Transparency | 32 | Bonding | 27 |
| | Approachability | 34 | | |

Female leaders' quotes were also used to highlight how inclusive female educational leaders really were and their response to the Covid-19 crisis (Table 4).

*Table 4. Frequency count for major subthemes and related quotes*

| Themes | Inclusive leadership | F (N=40) | Crisis management | F (N=40) |
|---|---|---|---|---|
| Subthemes | Collaboration/participation | 35 | Support/active listening | 36 |
| | Compassion | 34 | Management (short-term) | 30 |
| | Authenticity | 30 | Leadership (long-term) | 24 |
| | Flexibility | 26 | Scenario planning & adaptability | 36 |
| | Open communication | 36 | Shared responsibility | 35 |
| | Fairness | 33 | Fast, value-driven decision making | 37 |
| | No blaming | 22 | Individual Responsibility | 21 |
| | Inclusivity | 22 | Remedy | 28 |
| | Provide coaching/mentoring | 21 | Accountability | 22 |
| | Availability | 38 | Balance | 21 |
| | Respect & discretion | 37 | Psychological safety | 35 |
| | Employee development | 32 | Diplomacy | 21 |
| | Transparency | 32 | Bonding | 27 |
| | Approachability | 34 | | |

## Discussion

### Inclusive Leadership and Female Leaders

Responding to various questions, participants emphasized the importance of having a personal relationship with their followers (Table 2) showing respect and consideration which aligns perfectly with the core characteristics of inclusive leaders as these were described in the literature (Gartzia et al., 2012; Nembhard & Edmondson, 2006). They offered support during the crisis when needed, as they were facing similar challenges, i.e., caring responsibilities. This confirms previous research findings and supports the critical gender theory which discusses the gendered inequalities women often face (Cundiflr & Stockdale, 2013; Kolb, 2000).

Some leaders also referred to the sensitive issue of showing appreciation and recognition and being fair (Table 2 & 3) at the same time (Nembhard & Edmondson, 2006). Their aim was to encourage their followers to continue contributing to the university goals in their own unique way fostering a positive and supportive organisational culture in which they felt they belonged in line with the theories of human motivation (Maslow, 1943), optimal distinctiveness (Brewer, 1991), social comparison (Festinger, 1954), social exchange (Blau, 1964), the rules of reciprocity theory (Gouldner, 1960) and the belongingness hypothesis (Baumeister & Leary, 1995).

Those leaders stressed that they were available and easily accessible for their followers offering support or advice if they faced any challenges (Tables 2 & 3). Our participants felt that team members had to feel psychologically safe to approach their leaders and share any concerns (Şahin et al., 2014). More core values mentioned by the female leaders in this study included mentoring, and coaching followers (Beechler & Javidan, 2007), sharing responsibilities, and encouraging participation (Tables 2 & 3). Through these initiatives, female leaders tried to deal with experiences of bias, gender inequity and challenges in their personal career trajectories (Table 3, subtheme 3), as presented in the literature (Good & Sherrod, 2001) and promote inclusion for their followers irrespective of their background. When leaders show admiration for others' contributions and involve group members to offer input (Table 2 & 3), they reflect their inclusive behaviour towards diversified people as the leader has a central role in promoting IL.

Women leaders also avoided putting the blame on people, opted for finding solutions and remedies to problems and challenges (Table 2 & 3). They were willing to assume responsibility for any mistakes and chose to be diplomatic and discrete when dealing with their followers' mistakes. They tried to be fair and transparent encouraging people in their teams and promoting them in every possible way (Table 2 & 3), especially during the Covid-19 crisis.

Our participants seemed to be inclusive leaders as they ensured that their employees were overall satisfied with their working conditions (Table 3) in line with the theory of work adjustment (Dawis & Lofquist, 1984) which claims that inclusive leaders develop an ideal working environment in which employees feel supported and therefore formulate suitable coping strategies when faced with a crisis (Heatherton & Wyland, 2003). Aspiring female leaders also turned to them for advice. were available and approachable, and always managed to find time for everyone (Tables 2 & 3). This aligns perfectly with the core characteristics of IL as these were described in the literature (Carmeli et al., 2010; Choi et al., 2016).

## Crisis Management and Female Leaders

Our findings in terms of CM revealed that female educational leaders' response to the Covid-19 pandemic was dual since leaders were asked to manage and lead simultaneously. They had to change the mode of delivery at a very short notice promoting a proactive, crisis-prepared organizational culture (Elsubbaugh et al., 2004) and support their members of staff (Tables 2 & 3), especially those who had caring responsibilities minimizing the side-effects of the Covid-19 trauma (see theory of shattered assumptions - Janoff-Bulman, 2010). Other leaders stressed the fact that they tried to find alternative ways to protect and support their team members although some of them were particularly difficult to manage at times (DuBrin, 2013), increasing their anxiety as leaders (Choi et al., 2015).

Thinking long-term was one of the priorities for some of our leaders who were worried about the impact of the pandemic on the long-term plans of their department (Table 3) and wanted to include this parameter in all conversations that they had with their colleagues (Lockwood, 2005). As true selfless leaders (Glass & Cook, 2016), they wanted to be present during the crisis and support their university and colleagues in every possible way putting their personal and professional plans on hold until the pandemic was over.

These leaders had established guidelines to follow and often worked through crisis planning steps (Table 3) as part of their regular planning cycles (Zdziarski, 2006). They believed that HEI needed to adapt to different changes to ensure they supported students and staff especially in terms of mental health (Burrell & Heiselt, 2012). They believed that dealing with the crisis was a shared responsibility (Table 3 & 4), so they involved everyone in the decision-making and made sure everyone's opinion was heard and valued (Vroom & Jago, 2007). Finally, they were also ready to make tough decisions to ensure sustainability for the university and well-being for various stakeholders (Table 3).

To sum up, our findings suggest that female educational leaders demonstrate core characteristics of inclusive educational leadership and have good CM skills. The current study clearly indicates that they tend to reap the benefits of their diverse group members' contributions as they include them in the decision making (Northouse, 2016) and ensure their participation in overcoming various challenges HEI face amidst unprecedented crises such as the Covid-19 pandemic (Tables 2 & 3). Our results clearly highlight the need to discuss how female educational leaders can be supported to enhance their CM skills and possibly provide an example to their male counterparts in terms of how IL can be the key to unlocking their group members' potential at the outbreak of a crisis that may threaten the viability of every learning organisation and their employees' health and well-being. IL in HEI should therefore be considered as a central pillar of the global response to crises like the Covid-19 pandemic.

## LIMITATIONS OF THE STUDY AND RESEARCH, THEORY, AND PRACTICAL IMPLICATIONS

### Limitations of the Study and Research Implications

Literature suggests that studies which link IL, female leadership and CM have been neglected to a large extent by researchers (Meagher et al., 2020; Stefani & Blessinger, 2017). Therefore, it is expected that this article will not only stimulate more scholarly interest in understanding CM, but also prompt some actions towards empirical studies that examine the relationship of IL and gender on crisis outcomes. Unlike many culture studies, this article provided a close examination of different characteristics of female leaders and aspects of the IL style to establish the link with CM (Table 2). The current study provided insights into female leaders' thoughts on their leadership practices and their CM skills. However, it would also be interesting to see how their male colleagues view them as leaders.

The current study used a relatively small sample which was not representative of female educational leaders in the UK or even in London. Moreover, it did not include their team members' perceptions of them as leaders. More research is needed to explore how changing demographics and global markets are influencing the nature of learning organizations, particularly in the context of leadership and culture. The current study was conducted in the UK; thus, the results cannot be generalized across other countries. Moreover, a nation's culture and values shape diversity, thus cross-cultural and comparative studies can also be conducted by aspiring researchers in the field. Finally, our study was confined to studying the female leaders' perceptions. Future researchers can incorporate various other dimensions of diversity, like age or sexual orientation.

### Theory Implications

The current study extends the upper echelons framework beyond age, education, and experience related demographic characteristics to incorporate gender as a key feature. Moreover, taking into consideration the findings of the current study, we propose a new theoretical framework. This framework intends to guide female (and male) educational leaders in HEI in creating and maintaining an environment that fosters IL during a crisis (see Figure 1). HR professionals and senior leaders in HEI should take it into consideration and offer relevant training to their educational leaders to help them become more inclusive leaders and face severe crises such as the Covid-19 pandemic.

*Figure 1. Key values of inclusive (female) leaders amidst major crises*

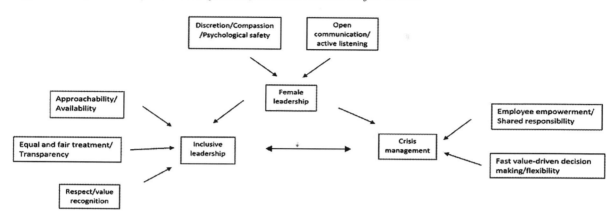

## Practical Implications

Taking into consideration the findings of this study which indicates that female leaders still score low in terms of some aspects of IL and CM i.e., perceiving themselves as inclusive (see Table 2), and their own wishes for more support, we conclude that they should receive some training in IL and CM skills and have the necessary resources to face unexpected situations (Coombs, 2007). Therefore, genuine IL interventions should be encouraged to trigger events that stimulate an important behavioural change in leadership style and include an explicit focus on ethical decision-making processes (Cooper et al., 2005). Undeniably, leaders must use their authentic selves to promote an inclusive climate by role modelling inclusive behaviours for their followers which is in line with the social information processing theory (Salancik & Pfeffer, 1978).

Training efforts should include large and small-scale incidents where senior leaders both men and women, who are responsible for the coordination of services across units, should be educated on protocols for crisis response (Miser & Cherrey, 2009). HEI should also sensitize and train senior leadership teams and HR professionals in HEI on the gender dimensions of crises and stress the importance of female educational leaders' contribution to managing major crises such as the Covid-19 pandemic. These training sessions could also help develop openness, availability, and accessibility as part of the organizational culture (see Table 3 & Figure 1) as they will include: (a) meeting crucial everyday needs of the employees; (b) improving the level of communication to ensure delivering valid and reliable messages in a comforting way; and (c) the need to build a set of robust measures to emphasize mental health and psycho-social support. This aligns perfectly with the literature related to the benefits of IL for an organisation in traumatic events (Choi et al., 2016).

Moreover, there are various significant insights for managers and human resource (HR) professionals. The recruitment and selection process should focus on the identification of inclusive leaders based on the key features of self-awareness, relational transparency (see Table 3), balanced processing, and an internalized moral perspective (Walumbwa et al., 2008). Cooper, Scandura, and Schriesheim (2005) claim that IL can be detected using survey-based methods, experiential exercises, and scenario-based exercises (e.g., presenting an ethical dilemma to potential job candidates to assess their ethical decision-making abilities). Finally, HEI should make continuous and systematic efforts to minimize inclusive leaders' uncertainty and anxiety by offering support and professional development sessions.

## CONCLUSION

Advancements in gender equality internationally are being derailed by the Covid-19 pandemic. Consequently, advocating for more women as leaders and decision makers at all levels in HEI settings is important to adequately address the gendered complexities of pandemics to better support vulnerable group members (Meagher et al., 2020). This study stresses theoretical underpinnings of IL style which is characterized by supportive behaviour towards employees. The inclusive environment with open behaviour, where leaders are accessible, promotes psychological safety among followers. This in turn makes the employees more proactive, sharing, and helpful. Knowing that their leaders will support and actively listen to them in times of need, helps reduce work-related stress. It is of outmost importance not just for employees, but for students as well. The psychological well-being of HEI employees brings about benefits for the students because psychologically safe employees are less likely to make mistakes. It also reduces adverse events.

This article indicates that inclusion should be institutionalized in HEI by drawing on social information processing theory as an overarching theoretical framework (Salancik & Pfeffer, 1978). Moreover, the integration-and-learning paradigm (Ely & Thomas, 2001) also supports the findings of the current study. This paradigm claims that when organizations sincerely value and embrace diversity by linking it to work processes, tasks, and strategies, the outcome is a significant improvement in terms of group functioning. Nevertheless, employees will only use their individual differences if they feel at ease in the workplace.

Consequently, it is important to understand how a climate for inclusion can be institutionalized. This article revealed that the participating female educational leaders were inclusive leaders and were able to significantly influence the formation of a climate for inclusion. Inclusive leaders can help their group members understand the value of individual differences by using their elevated status to look for opportunities to support and encourage employees to apply their individual differences to improve work processes. HR departments and University governing boards should consider taking these recommendations into consideration and try to implement as many of them as possible to foster gender equity, IL, and effective CM.

## REFERENCES

Ahmed, F., Zhao, F., Faraz, N. A., & Qin, Y. J. (2021). How inclusive leadership paves way for psychological well-being of employees during trauma and crisis: A three-wave longitudinal mediation study. *Journal of Advanced Nursing*, *77*(2), 819–831. doi:10.1111/jan.14637 PMID:33231300

Aldrich, A. S., & Lotito, N. J. (2020). Pandemic performance: Women leaders in the Covid-19 crisis. *Politics & Gender*, *16*(4), 960–967. doi:10.1017/S1743923X20000549

Baumeister, R. F., & Leary, M. R. (1995). The need to belong: Desire for interpersonal attachments as a fundamental human motivation. *Psychological Bulletin, 117*(3), 497–529. doi:10.1037/0033-2909.117.3.497 PMID:7777651

Beechler, S., & Javidan, M. (2007). Leading with a global mindset. In M. Javidan, R. M. Steers, & M. A. Hitt (Eds.), *The Global Mindset* (pp. 131–169). Elsevier. doi:10.1016/S1571-5027(07)19006-9

Bhaduri, R. M. (2019). Leveraging culture and leadership in crisis management. *European Journal of Training and Development, 43*(5/6), 554–556. doi:10.1108/EJTD-10-2018-0109

Birnbaum, R. (1992). *How academic leadership works: Understanding success and failure in the college presidency.* Jossey-Bass.

BlackChen, M. (2015). To lead or not to lead: Women achieving leadership status in higher education. *Advancing Women in Leadership Journal, 35*, 153–159.

Blau, P. M. (1964). *Exchange and power in social life.* John Wiley.

Borodzicz, E., & Van Haperen, K. (2002). Individual and group learning in crisis simulations. *Journal of Contingencies and Crisis Management, 10*(3), 139–147. doi:10.1111/1468-5973.00190

Bowers, M. R., Hall, J. R., & Srinivasan, M. M. (2017). Organizational culture and leadership style: The missing combination for selecting the right leader for effective crisis management. *Business Horizons, 60*(4), 551–563. doi:10.1016/j.bushor.2017.04.001

Branson, C. M., Franken, M., & Penney, D. (2016). Middle leadership in higher education: A relational analysis. *Educational Management Administration & Leadership, 44*(1), 128–145. doi:10.1177/1741143214558575

Brewer, M. B. (1991). The social self: On being the same and different at the same time. *Personality and Social Psychology Bulletin, 17*(5), 475–482. doi:10.1177/0146167291175001

Bruckmüller, S., Ryan, M. K., Rink, F., & Haslam, S. A. (2014). Beyond the glass ceiling: The glass cliff and its lessons for organizational policy. *Social Issues and Policy Review, 8*(1), 202–232. doi:10.1111ipr.12006

Burrell, S. M., & Heiselt, A. K. (2012). Presidential perspectives of crisis preparedness at Christian higher education institutions. *Christian Higher Education, 11*(4), 260–271. doi:10.1080/15363759.2010.544614

Carmeli, A., Reiter-Palmon, R., & Ziv, E. (2010). Inclusive leadership and employee involvement in creative tasks in the workplace: The mediating role of psychological safety. *Creativity Research Journal, 22*(3), 250–260. doi:10.1080/10400419.2010.504654

Carnes, M., Morrissey, C., & Geller, S. (2008). Women's health and women's leadership in academic medicine: Hitting the same glass ceiling? *Journal of Women's Health, 17*(9), 1453–1462. doi:10.1089/jwh.2007.0688 PMID:18954235

Cataylst. (2019). *Pyramid: Women in S&P 500 Companies.* https://www.catalyst.org/ research/ women-in-sp-500-companies/

Choi, S. B., Tran, T. B. H., & Kang, S. W. (2016). Inclusive leadership and employee well-being: The mediating role of person-job fit. *Journal of Happiness Studies*, *18*(6), 1877–1901. doi:10.100710902-016-9801-6

Choi, S. B., Tran, T. B. H., & Park, B. I. (2015). Inclusive leadership and work engagement: Mediating roles of affective organizational commitment and creativity. *Social Behavior and Personality*, *43*(6), 931–943. doi:10.2224bp.2015.43.6.931

Correll, S. (2017). Reducing gender biases in modern workplaces: A small wins approach to organisational change. *Gender & Society*, *31*(6), 725–750. doi:10.1177/0891243217738518

Coombs, W. T. (2007). Protecting organization reputations during a crisis: The development and application of situational crisis communication theory. *Corporate Reputation Review*, *10*(3), 163–176. doi:10.1057/palgrave.crr.1550049

Cooper, C. D., Scandura, T. A., & Schriesheim, C. A. (2005). Looking forward but learning from our past: Potential challenges to developing authentic leadership theory and authentic leaders. *The Leadership Quarterly*, *16*(3), 475–493. doi:10.1016/j.leaqua.2005.03.008

Cundiñr, N. L., & Stockdale, M. S. (2013). Social psychological perspectives on discrimination against women leaders. Women and Management: Global Issues and Promising Solutions [2 volumes]: Global Issues and Promising Solutions, 155.

Dawis, R. V., & Lofquist, L. H. (1984). *A psychological theory of work adjustment*. University of Minnesota Press.

Dirani, K. M., Abadi, M., Alizadeh, A., Barhate, B., Garza, R. C., Gunasekara, N., Ibrahim, G., & Majzun, Z. (2020). Leadership competencies and the essential role of human resource development in times of crisis: A response to Covid-19 pandemic. *Human Resource Development International*, *23*(4), 380–394. doi:10.1080/13678868.2020.1780078

DuBrin, A. J. (2013). *Handbook of research on crisis leadership in organizations*. Edward Elgar Publishing. doi:10.4337/9781781006405

Elsubbaugh, S., Fildes, R., & Rose, M. B. (2004). Preparation for crisis management: A proposed model and empirical evidence. *Journal of Contingencies and Crisis Management*, *12*(3), 112–127. doi:10.1111/j.0966-0879.2004.00441.x

Ely, R. J., & Thomas, D. A. (2001). Cultural diversity at work: The effects of diversity perspectives on work group processes and outcomes. *Administrative Science Quarterly*, *46*(2), 229–273. doi:10.2307/2667087

European Parliament (EP). (2015). *Report on women's careers in science and universities, and glass ceiling encountered*.

Festinger, L. (1954). A theory of social comparison processes. *Human Relations*, *1*(2), 117–140. doi:10.1177/001872675400700202

French, S., & Niculae, C. (2005). Believe in the model: Mishandle the emergency. *Journal of Homeland Security and Emergency Management*, *2*(1), 24–35. doi:10.2202/1547-7355.1108

Garikipati, S., & Kambhampati, U. (2021). Leading the fight against the pandemic: Does gender really matter? *Feminist Economics, 27*(1-2), 401–418. doi:10.1080/13545701.2021.1874614

Gartzia, L., Ryan, M. K., Balluerka, N., & Aritzeta, A. (2012). Think crisis–think female: Further evidence. *European Journal of Work and Organizational Psychology, 21*(4), 603–628. doi:10.1080/1359432X.2011.591572

Gigliotti, R. A. (2019). *Crisis leadership in higher education: Theory and practice*. Rutgers University Press.

Glass, C., & Cook, A. (2016). Leading at the top: Understanding women's challenges above the glass ceiling. *The Leadership Quarterly, 27*(1), 51–63. doi:10.1016/j.leaqua.2015.09.003

Good, G. E., & Sherrod, N. (2001). The psychology of men and masculinity: Research status and future directions. In R. Unger (Ed.), *Handbook of the Psychology of Women and Gender* (pp. 201–214). Wiley.

Gouldner, A. W. (1960). The norm of reciprocity: A preliminary statement. *American Sociological Review, 25*(2), 161–178. doi:10.2307/2092623

Gouthro, P., Taber, N., & Brazil, A. (2018). Universities as inclusive learning organizations for women? *The Learning Organization, 25*(1), 29–39. doi:10.1108/TLO-05-2017-0049

Harney, B., & Collings, D. G. (2021). Navigating the shifting landscapes of HRM. *Human Resource Management Journal*. Advance online publication. doi:10.1111/1748-8583.12343

Hassan, S., & Jiang, Z. (2021). Facilitating learning to improve performance of law enforcement workgroups: The role of inclusive leadership behaviour. *International Public Management Journal, 24*(1), 106–130. doi:10.1080/10967494.2019.1680465

Heatherton, T. F., & Wyland, C. L. (2003). Assessing self-esteem. In S. J. Lopez & C. R. Snyder (Eds.), *Positive psychological assessment: A handbook of models and measures* (pp. 219–233). American Psychological Association. doi:10.1037/10612-014

Hollander, E. (2009). *Inclusive leadership: The essential leader-follower relationship*. Routledge.

Hutchins, H. M., & Wang, J. (2008). Organizational crisis management and human resource development: A review of the literature and implications to HRD research and practice. *Advances in Developing Human Resources, 10*(3), 310–330. doi:10.1177/1523422308316183

Janoff-Bulman, R. (2010). *Shattered assumptions*. Simon and Schuster.

Jiang, Z., Hu, X., Wang, Z., & Jiang, X. (2019). Knowledge hiding as a barrier to thriving: The mediating role of psychological safety and moderating role of organizational cynicism. *Journal of Organizational Behavior, 40*(7), 800–818. doi:10.1002/job.2358

Kareem, J. (2016). The influence of leadership in building a learning organization. *IUP Journal of Organizational Behaviour, 15*(1), 7–18.

King, N., & Brooks, J. (2018). Thematic analysis in organisational research. In C. Cassell, A. L. Cunliffe, & G. Grandy (Eds.), *The Sage handbook of qualitative business and management research methods* (pp. 219–236). Sage.

Knights, D., & Richards, W. (2003). Sex discrimination in UK academia. *Gender, Work and Organization, 10*(2), 213–238.

Kreitz, P. A. (2008). Best practices for managing organizational diversity. *Journal of Academic Librarianship, 34*(2), 101–120.

Kolb, D. M. (2000). More than just a footnote: Constructing a theoretical framework for teaching about gender in negotiation. *Negotiation Journal, 16*(4), 347–356. doi:10.1111/j.1571-9979.2000.tb00763.x

Landis, J. R., & Koch, G. G. (1977). An application of hierarchical kappa-type statistics in the assessment of majority agreement among multiple observers. *Biometrics, 33*(2), 363–374. doi:10.2307/2529786 PMID:884196

Lean In and McKinsey & Company. (2018). *Women are Doing Their Part. Now Companies Need to do Their Part, Too*. Available at: https://womenintheworkplace.com/2018#!

Lockwood, N. R. (2005). Crisis management in today's business environment. *SHRM Research Quarterly, 4*, 1–9.

Madu, B. C. (2012). Organization culture as driver of competitive advantage. *Journal of Academic and Business Ethics, 5*, 1.

Maslow, A. H. (1943). A theory of human motivation. *Psychological Review, 50*(4), 370–396. doi:10.1037/h0054346

Mikyoung, K., & Moon, J. (2019). Inclusive leadership and creative performance: The role of psychological safety, feedback-seeking behaviour, and power-distance. *Korean Journal of Human Resource Development, 22*(4), 181–205. doi:10.24991/KJHRD.2019.12.22.4.181

Minghui, Y., & Yuanxu, L. (2014). Research on the mechanism of inclusive leadership on employees' innovative behaviour [J]. *Scientific Progress and Countermeasures, 31*(10), 6–9.

Miser, K. M., & Cherrey, C. (2009). Responding to campus crisis. In G.S. McClellan, J. Stringer, & Associates (Eds.), The handbook of student affairs administration (3rd ed., pp. 602-622). Jossey-Bass.

Mitchell, R., Boyle, B., Parker, V., Giles, M., Chiang, V., & Joyce, P. (2015). Managing inclusiveness and diversity in teams: How leader inclusiveness affects performance through status and team identity. *Human Resource Management, 54*(2), 217–239. doi:10.1002/hrm.21658

Moreno-Gómez, J., Lafuente, E., & Vaillant, Y. (2018). Gender diversity in the board, women's leadership and business performance. *Gender in Management, 33*(2), 104–122. doi:10.1108/GM-05-2017-0058

Morley, L. (2013). The rules of the game: Women and the leaderist turn in higher education. *Gender and Education, 25*(1), 116–131. doi:10.1080/09540253.2012.740888

Nembhard, I. M., & Edmondson, A. C. (2006). Making it safe: The effects of leader inclusiveness and professional status on psychological safety and improvement efforts in health care teams. Journal of Organizational Behaviour: *The International Journal of Industrial, Occupational and Organizational Psychology and Behaviour, 27*(7), 941–966. doi:10.1002/job.413

Netherlands Organization for Scientific Research. (2013). *Researchers' report*. Country Profile.

Neuendorf, K. A. (2018). Content analysis and thematic analysis. In P. Brough (Ed.), Advanced research methods for applied psychology (pp. 211-223). Routledge. doi:10.4324/9781315517971-21

Northouse, P. G. (2016). *Leadership: theory and practice* (7th ed.). Sage.

Perryman, A., Fernando, G., & Tripathy, A. (2016). Do gender differences persist? An examination of gender diversity on firm performance, risk, executive compensation. *Journal of Business Research*, 69(2), 579–586. doi:10.1016/j.jbusres.2015.05.013

Pillay, N. (2009). Human rights in United Nations action: Norms, institutions, and leadership. *European Human Rights Law Review*, 1, 1–7.

Randel, A. E., Galvin, B. M., Shore, L. M., Ehrhart, K. H., Chung, B. G., Dean, M. A., & Kedharnath, U. (2018). Inclusive leadership: Realizing positive outcomes through belongingness and being valued for uniqueness. *Human Resource Management Review*, 28(2), 190–203. doi:10.1016/j.hrmr.2017.07.002

Rosenthal, U., Boin, A., & Comfort, L. K. (2001). *Managing crises: Threats, dilemmas, opportunities*. Charles C. Thomas.

Ryan, M. K., Haslam, S. A., Morgenroth, T., Rink, F., Stoker, J., & Peters, K. (2016). Getting on top of the glass cliff: Reviewing a decade of evidence, explanations, and impact. *The Leadership Quarterly*, 27(3), 446–455. doi:10.1016/j.leaqua.2015.10.008

Şahin, D. R., Çubuk, D., & Uslu, T. (2014). The effect of organizational support, transformational leadership, personnel empowerment, work engagement, performance, and demographical variables on the factors of psychological capital. *EMAJ*, 3(3), 1–18. doi:10.5195/EMAJ.2014.49

Salancik, G. R., & Pfeffer, J. (1978). A social information processing approach to job attitudes and task design. *Administrative Science Quarterly*, 23(2), 224–253. doi:10.2307/2392563 PMID:10307892

Savigny, H. (2014). Women, know your limits: Cultural sexism in academia. *Gender and Education*, 26(7), 794–809. doi:10.1080/09540253.2014.970977

Senge, P. M. (1990). *The fifth discipline: The art and practice of the learning organization*. Doubleday.

Shore, L. M., Randel, A. E., Chung, B. G., Dean, M. A., Holcombe Ehrhart, K., & Singh, G. (2011). Inclusion and diversity in work groups: A review and model for future research. *Journal of Management*, 37(4), 1262–1289. doi:10.1177/0149206310385943

Soares, S. E., & Sidun, N. M. (2021). Women leaders during a global crisis: Challenges, characteristics, and strengths. *International Perspectives in Psychology: Research, Practice, Consultation*, 10(3), 130–137. doi:10.1027/2157-3891/a000020

Stefani, L., & Blessinger, P. (Eds.). (2017). *Inclusive leadership in higher education: International perspectives and approaches*. Routledge. doi:10.4324/9781315466095

Sharma, G. (2017). Pros and cons of different sampling techniques. *International Journal of Applied Research*, 3(7), 749–752.

Sun, S. (2008). Organizational culture and its themes. *International Journal of Business and Management*, 3(12), 137–141.

Tran, T. T. T., & Nguyen, H. V. (2020). Gender preference in higher education leadership: Insights from gender distribution and subordinate perceptions and expectations in Vietnam universities. *International Journal of Leadership in Education*, 1–22.

Vasileiou, K., Barnett, J., Thorpe, S., & Young, T. (2018). Characterising and justifying sample size sufficiency in interview-based studies: Systematic analysis of qualitative health research over a 15-year period. *BMC Medical Research Methodology*, *18*(1), 1–18. doi:10.118612874-018-0594-7 PMID:30463515

Vroom, V. H., & Jago, A. G. (2007). The role of the situation in leadership. *The American Psychologist*, *62*(1), 17–24. doi:10.1037/0003-066X.62.1.17 PMID:17209676

Walumbwa, F. O., Cropanzano, R., & Goldman, B. M. (2011). How leader-member exchange influences effective work behaviours: Social exchange and internal-external efficacy perspectives. *Personnel Psychology*, *64*(3), 739–770. doi:10.1111/j.1744-6570.2011.01224.x

Wang, L., Law, K. S., Zhang, M. J., Li, Y. N., & Liang, Y. (2019). It's mine! Psychological ownership of one's job explains positive and negative workplace outcomes of job engagement. *The Journal of Applied Psychology*, *104*(2), 229–246. doi:10.1037/apl0000337 PMID:30211569

WEF. (2018). *The global gender gap report 2018*. https://www.weforum.org/reports/theglobal-gender-gap-report-2018/

Winchester, H. P., & Browning, L. (2015). Gender equality in academia: A critical reflection. *Journal of Higher Education Policy and Management*, *37*(3), 269–281. doi:10.1080/1360080X.2015.1034427

Wooten, L. P., & James, E. H. (2008). Linking crisis management and leadership competencies: The role of human resource development. *Advances in Developing Human Resources*, *10*(3), 352–379. doi:10.1177/1523422308316450

Yanping, L., Yang, T., & Pan, Y. J. (2012). Building and implementing inclusive leadership based on the perspective of new generation employee management. *China Human Resources Development*, *3*, 31–35.

Yin, R. K. (2009). Case study research: Design and methods. *Sage (Atlanta, Ga.)*.

Yukl, G. A., & Becker, W. S. (2006). Effective empowerment in organizations. *Organizational Management Journal*, *3*(3), 210–231. doi:10.1057/omj.2006.20

Zdziarski, E. L. (2006). Crisis in the context of Higher Education. In K. S. Harper, B. G. Paterson, & E. L. Zdziarski (Eds.), *Crisis management: Responding from the heart* (pp. 3–24). NASPA.

Zenger, J., & Folkman, J. (2019). *Women score higher than men in most leadership skill. Harvard Business Review*.

## ADDITIONAL READING

Meletiadou, E. (2022). Learners' perceptions of peer assessment: Implications for their willingness to write in an EFL classroom. *International Journal of Teacher Education and Professional Development*.

Meletiadou, E. (2022). The use of peer assessment as an inclusive learning strategy in Higher Education Institutions. In E. Meletiadou (Ed.), *Policies and Practices for Assessing Inclusive Teaching and Learning*. IGI Global Publishers. doi:10.4018/978-1-7998-8579-5.ch001

Meletiadou, E. (2022). Nurturing students' writing knowledge, self-regulation, and attitudes in Higher Education. In E. Meletiadou (Ed.), *Policies and Practices for Assessing Inclusive Teaching and Learning*. IGI Global Publishers. doi:10.4018/978-1-7998-8579-5.ch002

Meletiadou, E. (2022). *Policies and Practices for Assessing Inclusive Teaching and Learning*. IGI Global Publishers.

Meletiadou, E. (2021a). Exploring the impact of peer assessment on EFL students' writing performance. *IAFOR Journal of Education*, *9*(3), 77–95. doi:10.22492/ije.9.3.05

Meletiadou, E. (2021b). Opening Pandora's box: How does peer assessment affect EFL students' writing quality? *Languages*, *6*(3), 115. doi:10.3390/languages6030115

Meletiadou, E. (2021c). Using Padlets as e-portfolios to develop undergraduate students' writing skills and motivation. *IAFOR Journal of Undergraduate Education*, *9*(4), 67–83. doi:10.22492/ije.9.5.04

Meletiadou, E. (2012). The impact of training adolescent EFL learners on their perceptions of peer assessment of writing. *RPLTL*, *3*(1), 240–251.

Meletiadou, E. (2011). *Peer assessment of writing in secondary education: Its impact on learners' performance and attitudes*. M.A. in Applied Linguistics. University of Cyprus.

Meletiadou, E., & Tsagari, D. (2016). The washback effect of peer assessment on adolescent EFL learners in Cyprus. In D. Tsagari (Ed.), *Classroom-based assessment in L2 contexts*. Cambridge Scholars Publishing.

Meletiadou, E., & Tsagari, D. (2014). An exploration of the reliability and validity of peer assessment of writing in secondary education. In D. Tsagari (Ed.), *Major trends in theoretical and applied linguistics 3* (pp. 235–250). De Gruyter Open Poland. doi:10.2478/9788376560915.p14

Meletiadou, E., & Tsagari, D. (2012). Investigating the attitudes of adolescent EFL learners towards peer assessment of writing. In D. Tsagari (Ed.), *Research on English as a foreign language in Cyprus* (Vol. 2, pp. 225–245). University of Nicosia Press.

## KEY TERMS AND DEFINITIONS

**Crisis Management:** The process by which a business or other organization deals with a sudden emergency situation.

**Leadership:** The ability of an individual or a group of individuals to influence and guide followers or other members of an organization.

**Sustainability:** Ability to maintain or support a process continuously over time. In business and policy contexts, sustainability seeks to prevent the depletion of natural or physical resources, so that they will remain available for the long term.

# Chapter 2
# Using Virtual Professional Learning Communities to Foster Sustainable Learning and Close the Awarding Gap in Higher Education Amidst the COVID-19 Pandemic

**Eleni Meletiadou**
https://orcid.org/0000-0003-4833-1450
*London Metropolitan University, UK*

## ABSTRACT

*In the current study, a combination of synchronous and asynchronous online strategies has been used to support undergraduate students at a University in the UK, as VPLC embraces individual students' needs for learning development and professional growth through peer support building community among the student population. The intent of this research study was to unravel students' perceptions of the benefits and the challenges that VPLC may have amid the pandemic. An exploratory anonymous survey design was employed to explore their impact. Students were also asked to provide anonymous feedback at regular intervals during the implementation using Mentimeter. Descriptive statistics and thematic analysis were used to examine the data. Findings suggest that VPLCs can be used as a means to support students through collaboration, peer mentoring/coaching, networking, and sharing of resources.*

## INTRODUCTION

Challenges to Management Education have been pervasive during the COVID-19 crisis, and Human Resource Management (HRM) students, in particular, have faced numerous obstacles as a result. One of the most unfortunate losses for management students was the impossibility to meet their peers and a lost

DOI: 10.4018/978-1-6684-6172-3.ch002

sense of community. In terms of the current study, a Virtual Professional Learning Community (VPLC) program was implemented by the researcher, who was the Programme Leader of a student cohort of Human Resource Management (HRM) students in an effort to expand the university offerings through the use of its virtual learning platform to increase a sense of connectedness among HRM students. It enabled students to share their pandemic challenges, their professional worries while also connecting with HRM professionals on the COVID-19 frontlines. Moreover, it seemed to be extremely beneficial for BAME students as VPLCs increased their opportunities for networking and finding peer support which helped them increase their performance and close the awarding gap which still persists in HE in the UK.

Students were offered one two-hour online session every week of the two academic semesters (autumn and spring) with their Course Leader and a guest speaker each week. The aim was to enable students to share insights regarding: (1) how to succeed as an HRM student during COVID-19, (2) potential implications of the pandemic on students' learning and professional development, (3) development of learning and professional skills, (4) tips for securing career-enhancing positions and internships, and (5) realities of serving as remote HRM professionals during a global crisis.

To sum up, the current chapter reports on HRM students' attitudes towards the use of a VPLC scheme during the Covid-19 pandemic when this is used to improve students' learning and professional skills and help them face crisis-related challenges during the Covid-19 crisis. It aims to explore whether VPLCs can effectively support diverse cohorts with multilingual and multicultural students fostering intercultural awareness and promoting a sense of community and psychological safety amidst the Covid-19 pandemic. Based on the findings of this study, recommendations will be provided as to how all relevant stakeholders in HEI can promote the use of VPLCs to support Management students effectively and minimize the harmful impact of crises such as the Covid-19 pandemic.

## BACKGROUND

COVID-19 pandemic's impact on HEI has been widespread and fast-moving. While e-learning has been used in some educational settings for several years (Rodrigues et al., 2019), many universities began transitioning to virtual learning in record time while still having to continue to meet their student populations' educational, digital, mental, and emotional needs. Classes moved quickly from in-person to virtual instruction with little time for training and development; staff and students had to adapt to new technological learning platforms, learning and teaching styles, study techniques, strategies and challenges while still mastering the content being taught and studied. Researchers have exhaustively discussed learning structures (Bloom et al., 1956; Krathwohl, 2002) and theories about communities of practice and the learning environment across disciplines and subjects (Lave & Wenger, 1991; Roberts, 2006). However, during the pandemic, students and staff faced incredible challenges and emotional and menta health issues due to constant change, transitions, and numerous uncertainties, including factors impacting learning, teaching and assessment that have not been widely explored. This was undeniably true for Business schools, where tightly packed and in-person reliant curricula shifted to being taught through hybrid or online learning with stricter testing and assessment procedures and fewer chances for in-person experience, peer support and meaningful interaction with lecturers and peers.

Covid-19 changes, challenges and stressors affected Business students' mental, emotional, and physical well-being (Krishnamurthy, 2020) in addition to the normal rigors of Business schools. To address these realities, Business schools must respond to the needs of their students through the implementation of strategies to enhance student coping, emotional well-being, and mental preparedness (Peltier et al., 2022). One education structure to consider for working on supporting student learning, emotional welfare and mental preparedness is the learning community (LC). An LC can be defined as a group of people (students in this case) sharing common goals, values, interests, and ideas that actively engage in learning with and from each other. LCs, an iteration of small group learning, offer opportunities for students to engage in mentoring, coaching and wellness activities with support from both their peers and staff (Shochet et al., 2019). LCs intentionally focus on enhancing student engagement, interaction and communication, not only with staff, the syllabus and the curriculum but also with peers and through self-reflection and other-awareness (Ferguson et al., 2009). This is frequently accomplished through a perceived increase in social, peer and community support. The purpose of this case study is to describe the approach of a Business School in the UK to adapting management (HRM) education training through LCs during the COVID-19 pandemic.

Community Learning is thought of as a social process based on interactions and communication within groups (Swan & Shea, 2005; Vygotsky, 1986). The interactions and engagement among group members lead to the formation of community, the construction of knowledge, the enhancement of valuable learning and professional skills and student learning and development (Cobb, 1994; Vygotsky, 1986). The participation of all members (both students and members of staff) plays a fundamental role in the development, support, and maintenance of any learning community. A crucial task for Business and Management and more specifically for HRM educators is to consistently teach, develop and engage students within the sociocultural practices of the discipline (Kelly, 2007; Leach & Scott, 2003). Nevertheless, examining learning through this perspective necessitates a unit of analysis that is larger than an individual student or a small group of students. As an alternative, it calls for an expanded framework that captures an entire HRM learning community, which could be recognized as a community of practice (Vickers & Fox, 2010).

An HRM learning community circumscribes the social and physical environment that offers a context for participation and engagement. The community itself is constituted by the acting students and members of staff, the tools, both conceptual, virtual, and physical, used in community practices, and the cultural and linguistic norms that guide practice, engagement, and interactions within the community (Sadler, 2009). The boundaries of a community are defined by a central focus, goal or aim. For instance, learning communities in HRM education tend to coalesce around the teaching and learning of HRM and the development of vital professional skills. Since the practices promoted in terms of an HRM course of an academic department of a Business and Management discipline (or briefly a Business and Management department) are inherently learning and sociocultural activities (Ranga & Etzkowitz, 2015), their exploration requires investigating the different ways and circumstances under which students engage with HRM learning communities' practices (Turner, Christensen, Kackar-Cam, Fulmer, & Trucano, 2018). Therefore, conceptualizing the members of an HRM course as a learning community offers a powerful lens through which to explore students' learning and development of professional skills as they interact in the context of an HRM discipline. The idea of the course as a learning community can be traced back to the works of Dewey (1938) and Vygotsky (1986) who claimed that the process of learning is facilitated through individual participation in social interactions. Thus, the learning activities based on this social-constructivism perspective stress learner–learner interactions within a group engaged in constructing a culture of shared understanding. Conceiving HRM courses as communities emphasizes participating in learning activities, developing professional skills, sharing experiences, and communicating the meaning and value of these experiences. Thus, applying a sociocultural conceptual framework allows lecturers to estimate learning and development by analyzing students' experiences in relation to HRM (Redmond et al., 2018). A key aspect of understanding learning through this lens is that members of an HRM learning community acquire the skills to perform practices by interacting with educational tools, digital tools, peers, and more knowledgeable members of the community (instructors and guest speakers) (Lave & Wenger, 1991). As such, this conceptual framework highlights the importance of identifying the kinds of engagement and interactions that provide a context for learning and professional development to take place for an entire HRM community.

The present study is grounded on a sociocultural perspective which assumes that students' learning is social and, therefore, highly affected by their interactions with others (Vygotsky, 1986). In formal educational contexts, students' interactions are determined by sociocultural practices that account for ways of talking, reading, writing, knowing, and doing (Gee, 2008). The community of learning framework also includes various types of behavior such as interactions between members of a community and how these interactions can explain the degree of human members' engagement in community goals (Lave & Wenger, 1991). Jan & Vlachopoulos (2018) found that the type of interaction between the participants of a learning community is a key influential factor in the formation of the community. Some of the original views about interaction in education focused mainly on human–human interaction. Wagner (1994) characterized interaction as "reciprocal events that require at least two objects and two actions. Interactions occur when these objects and events mutually influence one another" (Wagner, 1994, p. 8). Other definitions of interaction (Beard & Harper, 2002) refer to the social purpose and processes of interaction, particularly regarding student–student and student–instructor interactions. Moore (1989) distinguished among three forms of interaction: (a) student–student interaction among individual students or among students working in small groups; (b) student–lecturer interaction that traditionally focused on classroom-based dialogue between students and the lecturer; and (c) student–content interaction which refers to students interacting with the subject matter under study to construct meaning, relate it to personal knowledge, and apply it to problem solving. According to social theories of learning and distributed cognition (Salomon, 2000), student–student interaction is desirable both for cognitive purposes and motivational support. However, student–lecturer interaction is valued by both students and teachers and has been found to be associated with positive perceptions of learning (Wu & Hiltz, 2004). Recent studies have also utilized the framework of communities of practice to examine how learning communities engage in learning practices. For instance, González–Howard & McNeill (2016) found that the interactions between students (working in smaller group structures, such as pairs) and the interactions between students and tools (linguistic resource for engaging in science discourse) promoted students' engagement in argumentation. Students' engagement in practices, like argumentation, by using scientific models to build explanations or framing issues in their social context, depends on lecturer's knowledge and practices (Chen, 2020; Jiménez-Aleixandre, 2014; Pierson et al., 2019).

On the other hand, distance education is an instruction that occurs when the lecturer and student are separated by distance, time, or both (Mupinga, 2005). The communication and interaction between lecturers and students can be either "synchronous" when they are present at the same time during lectures or "asynchronous" when lecturers and students do not have onsite face-to-face direct interaction at the same time or place (Cannon, 2002). Online learning is a subset of distance education embracing a wide set of technology applications and learning processes including computer-based learning, web-based learning, virtual classrooms, and digital communication and collaboration. Therefore, it is employed as an umbrella term that covers various types of teaching, learning and assessment as web-based training, e-learning, distributed learning, Internet-based learning, web-based instruction, cyber learning, virtual learning, or net-based learning (Keengwe & Kidd, 2010). Taking into consideration OECD (2005), "E-learning refers to the use of information and communications technology (ICT) to enhance and/or support learning in post-secondary education. This implies that "e-learning" refers to both wholly online provision and campus-based or other distance-based provision supplemented with ICT in some way." Blended learning (b-learning) is a teaching, learning and assessment approach that combines both online and face-to-face modalities to create a cohesive learning and assessment experience and provides students the benefit of flexibility in shifting time and space, among other advantages (Shu & Gu, 2018). Distance learning with various forms, from fully online courses to blended courses, takes place outside the traditional classroom. Various factors closely linked to the features of the learning community have been identified by lecturers as important concerns within the distance learning environments. The role of participants within distance learning environments is key to the development of the community. Interactions and communication among participants are vital and may be supported by an effective technological infrastructure which must create a context of social activities sufficiently robust to ensure that each student has a voice (Hodge et al., 2006). In courses taught and assessed fully online, the lecturer is not physically present.

On synchronous online teaching, all participants in the learning environment are present at the same time, but not necessarily at the same place. Special platforms can be employed that try to replicate the experience of a traditional classroom with live video streaming, screen sharing, and a live chat feature that supports the communication and the interaction among students and lecturers in real time. On asynchronous online teaching, the teaching materials are posted online, and students work through them in their own time and at their own pace, communicating with each other and the lecturer via discussion boards or forums or even by e-mail. Pallof & Pratt (2007) suggest that "there is one element that sets online distance learning apart from the traditional classroom setting": the central role of student–student and lecturer–student interactions in the learning process. In addition, online environments, particularly the asynchronous courses, require more responsibility from students. A responsible student employs course material when he/she has sufficient self-regulation skills. Self-regulated students take control of their own learning, by developing suitable metacognitive strategies such as planning, correcting their mistakes and staying organized and motivated (Kaufman, 2015). Varying levels of online experience result in different levels of motivation and self-regulation to online learning; as a result, graduate students show more adaptive self-regulated learning profiles than undergraduates (Artino & Stephens, 2009). Crucial barriers linked with distance learning are reported (Dietrich et al., 2020) including issues of communication between student, lecturers and institution, isolation, tutoring, access to books, development of valuable skills, i.e., interpersonal skills, and informatics issues, including training of lecturers and the need for technical support and the development of students' digital skills, or even difficulties of access to a sufficiently high-performance internet connection.

To sum up, the current chapter will explore how VPLCs can support undergraduate students during a major crisis such as the Covid-19 pandemic both in terms of promoting sustainable learning and developing their professional skills but also in providing emotional support and a sense of community when they are threatened by isolation and some of them face mental health issues due to challenges related to the pandemic. This may also support BAME students who are particularly disadvantaged due to the crisis and allow HEI to close the awarding gap.

# MAIN FOCUS OF THE CHAPTER

## Methodology

### Data Collection and Methods

The present study examined the implementation of Virtual Professional Learning Communities (VPLC) with 120 undergraduate HRM students who joined two-hour long VPLC sessions once a week for one academic year at a University in the UK. All undergraduate HRM students participated in their respective VPLC sessions, one per year of study. During these VPLC sessions, students had the opportunity to become involved in workshops which helped them develop their professional (i.e., negotiation, team working) and academic skills (i.e., time management, presentation skills) and interact with guest speakers who shared their experience and responded to students' questions. The researcher asked students to fill in a survey at the end of the academic year and provide anonymous feedback - using Mentimeter - on the sessions regularly (every 3 weeks) responding to the lecturer's questions. The study took place during the Covid-19 pandemic as the Course Director and lecturer wanted to support her students during this unprecedented crisis.

An online questionnaire of two sections was utilized to collect data. Section one collected biographic information (see Table 1). Section two consisted of 10 closed-end statements in total. The statements were graded on a five-point Likert scale ranging from strongly agree to strongly disagree. Section two gathered data on the respondents' perception regarding the use of VPLCs by students in higher education. At the end of each of the two sections, an open-ended field was provided to elicit other perspectives that the respondents might have. The questionnaire was shared through Google Forms.

*Table 1. Characteristics of the participating students (N=100)*

| Measure and Items | N |
|---|---|
| **Age** | |
| 18-25 | 72 |
| 26-35 | 22 |
| 35+ | 6 |
| **Ethnicity** | |
| White | 38 |
| Asian | 3 |
| Black | 43 |
| Mixed | 16 |
| **Year of study** | |
| 1st | 38 |
| 2nd | 36 |
| 3rd | 26 |
| **Disability** | |
| Yes | 4 |
| No | 96 |

The researcher chose a mixed-methods approach and used a survey with closed and open items and anonymous feedback with the students who accepted to provide feedback. Surveys which are "subjective" methods frequently used in learning and teaching research (Hoepfl, 1997, pp. 6-8) were also employed to answer the research questions. According to Watanabe (2004, p. 23) surveys can help researchers gather public opinions which otherwise could not be identified. Additional information was also provided by the anonymous feedback provided by the students in response to the questions. VPLC sessions were offered to all students, but participation was voluntary. The researcher informed the students about the study and asked them to provide feedback. Students who accepted to participate signed an informed consent form. Only 100 from 120 students completed the survey. We do not know how many students provided anonymous feedback for obvious reasons. It was impossible to monitor which of the students provided feedback each time. Descriptive statistics were also used to analyse the closed items of the survey and thematic analysis was used to analyse the recurring themes from the open questions of the survey and the anonymous feedback.

The aim of the current study was to address the following research questions:

- What were students' attitudes towards the VPLCs during the Covid-19 crisis?
- What were students' perceived benefits of participating in the VPLCs?
- What were the challenges students encountered while participating in the VPLCs?

## Data Analysis

Quantitative data was collected from the closed-ended part of the questionnaire. Furthermore, questions (in the survey and to elicit anonymous feedback from the students) which are "subjective" methods frequently used in teaching research (Hoepfl, 1997, pp. 6-8) were also employed to answer the third and the fourth research questions (see Section 6.2). According to Watanabe (2004, p. 23) questionnaires are valuable ways for gathering public opinions which otherwise could not be identified. The data analysis utilized descriptive statistics to report the findings using SPSS. Descriptive statistics such as means and standard deviations were calculated.

Qualitative research data was collected from students' responses to the open-ended questions of the survey and the anonymous feedback they provided via Mentimeter every 3 weeks. Data was analysed using a prominent approach, thematic content analysis (King & Brooks, 2018). The themes that the researcher identified were related to the perceived benefits and challenges students encountered when participating in VPLCs. The aim was to determine the participants' overall attitudes towards VPLCs amid the Covid-19 crisis.

In terms of inter-coder reliability, two independent raters coded the data into themes and subthemes. The level of agreement was calculated between raters using Cohen's Kappa (K). The value of Cohen's Kappa ranged from 0.30 to 0.82. A commonly used scale to determine the acceptability of Kappa values (Landis & Koch, 1977) considers Kappa values between .21 and .40 as indicating fair agreement, between .41 and .60 as indicating moderate agreement, between .61 and .80 indicating substantial agreement, and between .81 and .99 as indicating near perfect agreement. Data instances on which coders did not agree were discussed until an agreement was reached, though sometimes some instances were omitted from the coding process. A detailed description of the major themes and sub-themes is provided in Table 3.

The qualitative data were analysed using thematic content analysis (Neuendorf, 2018). The researcher and her assistant independently identified main themes and subthemes that were joined by the researcher into a report. The researchers were responsible for identifying and interpreting the themes and subthemes as these emerged from the data keeping in mind the original research questions. A term was identified by more than half of the participants to be labelled as a sub-theme. Inter-validation processes were used (Yin, 2009). This procedure certified that the final report was explicit and coherent. They both recommended and examined qualitative data themes and sub-themes. Quotations were selected to illustrate the sub-themes succinctly (see the section on Findings).

To sum up, the current study employed a mixed-methods approach which combined features of an exploratory case study qualitative approach (students' anonymous feedback) and a quantitative approach since a survey with closed and open-ended items (Gustafsson, 2017) were used to examine HRM students' attitudes towards VPLCs during the Covid-19 crisis in a HEI in the UK. The researcher created different types of open-ended questions and closed-ended items (in the survey) that comprised descriptive, structural, contrast and evaluative content to explore the participants' perspective and get valid information (Elo et al., 2014). Case studies have been criticized because they offer little basis for scientific generalization (Yin, 2013). The current study has limitations because it was study which used only a specific number of students in one Business School. It is closely related to the phenomenological and hermeneutical research approach which points to an internal and thorough awareness of the essence of research, not at generating generalizable outcomes. Although case studies are not credible and have low reliability, validity, and replicability (Cohen et al., 2013), this research study showed meticulousness and precision but admitting the uncommon context of this case; the research findings will probably not be generalizable. Finally, the study admits that selecting a qualitative approach for data collection undoubtedly carries participant biases (Punch, 2013).

## FINDINGS AND DISCUSSION

The study yielded rich data. Both quantitative and qualitative findings can be seen in the next two subsections.

## Quantitative Data

*Table 2. Students' attitudes toward VPLCs amid the Covid-19 crisis*

| Statements (Using a Five-point Likert Scale) | M | SD | Responses |
|---|---|---|---|
| 1. VPLCs develop students' academic skills. | 4.75 | .98 | Agree |
| 2. VPLCs develop students' professional skills. | 4.60 | 1.00 | Agree |
| 3. VPLCs promote collaboration. | 4.17 | .67 | Agree |
| 4. VPLCs take collective responsibility for student learning. | 3.60 | .84 | Agree |
| 5. VPLCs necessitate a shared vision and shared values. | 3.20 | .61 | Agree |
| 6. VPLCs promote inclusive and sustainable learning. | 4.22 | .94 | Agree |
| 7. 'Reflective dialogue' is a crucial component of VPLCs. | 3.45 | .93 | Agree |
| 8. VPLCs promote intercultural awareness. | 3.82 | .90 | Agree |
| 9. VPLCs offer opportunities of networking with peers and professionals. | 4.47 | .84 | Agree |
| 10. VPLCs ensure learning at all levels (for students, lecturers, and guest speakers). | 3.05 | .67 | Agree |
| Overall | 3.93 | | Agree |

Table 2 displays the participating students' perceptions of engaging in VPLCs with their peers in terms of their HRM Course amid the pandemic. As indicated in Table 2, the respondents had overall positive attitudes towards the use of VPLCs in higher education (M= 3.93). The results indicated that the respondents believed that VPLCs were valuable for the development of their academic and professional skills as it helped them develop their writing skills and improve their academic performance considerably. They also confessed that they helped them network, find a mentor and develop their digital skills. They felt less isolated and found their interactions with their peers, lecturer, and guest speakers meaningful. Finally, BAME students reported that it helped them even more since otherwise they would have had no opportunities to get to know their peers better, communicate with them regularly and receive additional support when necessary as they felt they needed that. Ultimately, they allowed them to ask for help when necessary and share their concerns and challenges. Their lecturer and speakers listened actively and then provided precious advice which they thought helped them immensely. They were then able to improve their academic performance and achieve their personal and professional goals (Nieto, 2015).

## Qualitative Data

The themes which address the main research questions of the study can be seen in Table 3. These derived from the analysis of the qualitative data (anonymous feedback and open-ended questions of the survey).

*Table 3. Frequency counts for subthemes*

| Major Themes | Benefits of VPLCs | | Challenges of VPLCs | |
|---|---|---|---|---|
| | (N=100) | | (N=100) | |
| | Collaboration/participation | 88 | Equality of access to internet | 21 |
| | Compassion/emotional support | 93 | Training to develop digital skills | 30 |
| Major | Development of professional skills | 90 | On-going support | 24 |
| subthemes | Intercultural awareness | 59 | Access to laptop and equipment | 20 |
| | Sustainable learning | 78 | Lack of support from technicians | 35 |
| | Development of academic skills | 98 | Lack of face-to-face interaction | 37 |
| | Networking | 93 | Feeling of isolation (mature students) | 21 |
| | Inclusivity | 88 | Lack of bonding | 22 |
| | Provide coaching/mentoring | 78 | | |
| | Psychological safety | 89 | | |

Findings revealed a number of benefits that students thought they gained when involved in VPLC sessions. Students reported that VPLCs allowed students to feel psychologically safe as they were able to receive and provide support to their peers regarding challenging aspects of their learning and ultimately felt more included since they were not able to meet their peers face-to-face. BAME students also felt that they were also able to improve their performance significantly.

*"At the beginning I thought that would be a waste of time but soon I realized that was an opportunity to network with my peers and ask them to help me develop my writing skills. I could also help them with the development of their digital skills. This was basically a 'give and take' relationship which was mutually beneficial. It also helped us feel safe as there was someone we could talk to if we were in trouble." (Participant 29)*

Other students talked about the opportunity to talk openly about their concerns and receive adequate support by their lecturers. This helped them – especially BAME students - voice their concerns, communicate openly with their peers and enhance valuable professional skills while listening to a different speaker every week. This promoted sustainable learning for the whole cohort and allowed them to make progress at their own pace.

*"I am Asian, and I find it difficult to voice my concerns…It is cultural…Therefore, I cannot improve my performance and achieve my goals. VPLCs allowed me to talk openly and ask for help. Our lecturer provided remedial teaching to help me develop my presentations skills. I needed that. I was so grateful, and I attended the sessions every week without fail." (Participant 73)*

The kind of emotional support students received in terms of the VPLCs was also highlighted by some students as some of them faced considerable mental health issues and had to support their families during the pandemic. Being unable to interact with their peers, made them feel isolated and lost.

*"My mother is vulnerable. Therefore, I have to be careful and isolate. This drives me crazy as I cannot get to know new people and share my concerns and fears. During the VPLC sessions, I was able to exchange ideas and work on interesting tasks with my peers. We could then meet online after the sessions to work on our projects and help each other. VPLCs were an amazing opportunity to meet HRM professionals and get valuable insights into the profession as well." (Participant 12)*

On the other hand, some students faced considerable challenges as they did not have reliable connection to the internet and missed some sessions. They also requested support from academic mentors and training to develop their digital skills and participate more actively in the sessions.

*"I love VPLCs, but I missed a couple of them. I need a better laptop and more stable internet connection. I do not know who can help me. I am also a mature student. I need training and support to develop my digital and technical skills. My peers helped me but that is not enough..." (Participant 33)*

All in all, the findings indicated that VPLCs supported students during the Covid-19 pandemic as they allowed them to share their values and vision, develop their reflective professional skills, build collaborative networks, and develop their skills through group and individual learning as previously stated in the literature (Stoll et al., 2003).

## Discussion

During the Covid-19 pandemic, VPLCs helped the course leader share information, promote student leadership and peer mentoring/coaching, identify support systems, and foster deeper relationships between faculty and students as well as peer to peer. It allowed her to create links among students and professionals and challenge student uncertainties as they feared they would be unable to secure a career-enhancing position when they graduated due to the pandemic. There were several lessons learned during this experience. First, there were certainly some differences in VPLC experiences by year. Students who had just started the School in a fully virtual environment, hence their perspectives differed from final year students who have had a much greater level of face-to-face interaction and education in prior years. However, they were intimidated by the thought of not finding a job after graduation. The uncertainty affected their mental health, and they needed additional support which was provided through VPLCs. The findings from this study also suggested that the support role of VPLCs may have been less necessary for those students who had previously experienced in-person learning and had the opportunity to build additional supportive relationships outside of the VPLC structure. Most students rated their experience as excellent and thanked their course leader for taking this initiative amid the isolation of the Covid-19 crisis.

The findings also indicated that HEI need to regularly remind faculty and students to stay flexible, adaptable and open to change in the face of numerous unknowns-especially amid crises. This is helpful in decreasing anxiety for situations outside of their control. VPLCs served as a vehicle to deliver information to students with immediate student feedback to said information. VPLC sessions often began with "Roses and Thorns," an assessment of student experiences, successes, and challenges since the last session. This portion of the session enabled students to voice their concerns in a safe space, giving peers the opportunity to support each other in agreement. They also promoted sustainable learning (Hays & Reinders, 2020) as students were able to develop various academic skills over the course of the academic semester and improve their performance closing the awarding gap, especially for BAME students (Hubbard, 2021) as they confessed in the survey and anonymous feedback they provided. Moreover, they developed students' intercultural awareness (Barker & Mak, 2013) as students were asked to work in multicultural groups to discuss the different issues raised by the speakers and develop their academic skills.

However, the virtual learning environment and the in-person physical learning environment function differently. A 90-min, large group in-person session does not necessarily transfer minute for minute in the virtual learning environment. Verbal and nonverbal communication strategies look and feel different in the virtual environment compared to in-person learning; numerous online distractions lead to decreased focus and increased fatigue. During the 90- min VPLC sessions held via the online virtual platform, students were required to engage by having their cameras on (i.e., Join with Video). This was essential in order to both give and receive verbal/nonverbal feedback from others and simulate "in person" as much as possible to support a sense of belonging. Students being completely aware that VPLCs are a safe space and that "what is said in VPLC, stays in VPLC" began to express specific concerns, such as not being in a quiet space at their fully "occupied" homes, some with multigenerational families; others were living alone and felt isolated while others were embarrassed of their homes, which now were clearly visible on Zoom calls. Nonetheless, amidst these hardships, a sense of companionship emerged when "survival skills," new learning techniques and self-care tips were shared via peer feedback. Yet the one thing that surfaced at the top of the gnawing list of concerns was sustaining and possibly improving their academic grades.

In a HE environment in the UK, which already tended to be a highly competitive academic arena, the pandemic only heightened academic anxieties. When changes happen rapidly, such as those seen during the COVID-19 pandemic, and education is forced to go virtual without adequate planning time, courses may lead to Zoom/ virtual learning burnout for both the faculty and students. According to Taylor and Frechette (2022), similar pedagogical challenges have been experienced in Business education in the UK as well as around the world. This may be more acute in student final years as their curriculum is more heavily focused on experiential and professional learning often through internships.

Virtual VPLCs may help students connect with their classmates when other modes are not readily available. However, VPLCs must continue to be relevant and timely or they risk being seen as an "add-on." With a tightly packed curriculum, VPLCs can potentially become just another time commitment. Some students may find the loosely structured, conversation-focused VPLC sessions less critical in comparison to other coursework. It is important for faculty, student leaders and student participants to commit to the sessions. This engagement includes equal and active participation from all members of the VPLC. The relevance of the session should also be included in the discussion guide and explained during the conversation. A focus on the importance of self-reflection, peer mentoring/coaching, active listening and student engagement can enhance positive student perceptions of VPLCs.

This time in Business and Management education history calls for systematic innovation and ingenuity to continue training future HRM professionals (Hamouche, 2021). The call for innovation is particularly important in light of COVID-19's and numerous other health disparities' disproportionate impact on BAME (CDC, 2020). The Business School student body is comprised of more than 60% racial and/or ethnic minority students. HRM VPLCs should continue to evolve and change based on faculty and student feedback to address the needs of an increasingly diverse student body. This allows for streamlined and effective programming in service to future HRM students and in future challenging times. As the UK approaches a "quasi normal" post-pandemic, the impact that virtual learning had on current students' experiences needs to be monitored over the entirety of their time in Business school. Assessment of the cohorts affected by the COVID-19 pandemic will be essential to identify if unusual struggles or needs for resources arise. Underrepresented students often come into Business school with lower grades compared to their counterparts (Winkle-Wagner & McCoy, 2016). Students that are underrepresented in Business Schools may also experience different external pressures, cultural norms and realities that could be affected by an event like a pandemic. However, producing a competent and diverse workforce in HRM is essential in the quest for equity in Business and combating social disparities (Thevanes & Arulrajah, 2017). To retain and support a diverse Management student body, there must be consideration for the social determinants of health that may affect the global and national student population differently and focus on mentoring and relationship building (Gasman and Nguyen, 2015).

This chapter describes using VPLCs as a vehicle to create and maintain relationships, receive real-time feedback from students and monitor student well-being in the absence of in-person experiences. This institution's values and mission attract students who are interested in equity, service to the community and the importance of diversity in providing culturally appropriate HRM professionals, particularly for people of color and underserved urban and rural populations. Leadership, faculty, and staff work together to recruit students who align with this culture and mission. This process creates an HRM student body with a diverse set of backgrounds, cultural and social representations, and community affiliations.

The abruptness of the COVID-19 pandemic ushered in panic and insecurities. By utilizing the already established VPLC structure intrinsically built into this Business school curriculum, the cohesive small groups easily connected and were able to address concerns as a team. Navigating uncharted territories together brought a sense of security and further bonded the small VPLCs. Mentors and students alike voiced their uncertainties of the future, all while being supportive of one another. The VPLC structure was a forum to process academic anxieties, emotional concerns, COVID-19 losses and insecurities.

During the pandemic, students were fearful of losing their academic momentum. Utilizing the VPLC model, peers began receiving academic assistance from each other. The sharp edge of competitiveness was replaced with collaborative efforts to see each other not only survive but also succeed. The VPLC students began to lean on each other and share what academic techniques worked and did not work for them. Additionally, this Business school has institutional resources that offer Student Learning Support Services, of which VPLC mentors frequently and intentionally remind the students to utilize. The Student Learning Support Services reported that many students utilized tutoring services during the pandemic, and some participated in the workshops. This VPLC structure was already robust and impactful but became helpful as both a mode of teaching and of support for students during the pandemic. Students were able to interact with each other in a safe space that fostered validation and a sense of security. The faculty mentor involvement and relationship with the students were strong and worth the effort and investment. The students received assistance from their VPLC mentors, but perhaps, most importantly, they learned to be resilient from one another in these times of uncertainty.

## CONCLUSION

The current study used a relatively small sample which was not representative of HRM students in the UK or even in London. More research is needed to explore the impact of VPLCs on students' academic and professional development as well as especially in the post-Covid-19 era. The current study was conducted in the UK; thus, the results cannot be generalized across other countries. Moreover, a nation's culture and values shape diversity, thus cross-cultural and comparative studies can also be conducted by aspiring researchers in the field.

The COVID-19 pandemic has created both challenges and opportunities for HRM education. It is clear from this case study that finding ways to continue to create a sense of safety and community during times of stress and unpredictability are key for faculty and students in HEI. VPLCs appears to be an advantageous curricular component for adapting HRM education during a pandemic, as well as creating a sense of safety and community. As time goes by, and space is intentionally made for reflection, curricular change may need to occur to assess what modes of HRM education can remain virtual as opposed to in-person, as well as increase or decrease learning sessions based on student need. O'Byrne et al. (2020) call for pandemic preparedness content to be added to Business education curricula. As HRM practices continue to evolve, pandemic preparedness HRM education will need to include not only the digital learning and research aspects of COVID-19, but also the psychosocial components for managing the lived realities of future HRM practitioners.

# REFERENCES

Artino, A. R., Jr., & Stephens, J. M. (2009). Academic motivation and self-regulation: A comparative analysis of undergraduate and graduate students learning online. *The Internet and Higher Education, 12*(3–4), 146–151.

Barker, M. C., & Mak, A. S. (2013). From classroom to boardroom and ward: Developing generic intercultural skills in diverse disciplines. *Journal of Studies in International Education, 17*(5), 573–589. doi:10.1177/1028315313490200

Beard, L. A., & Harper, C. (2002). Student perceptions of online versus on campus instruction. *Education, 122*(4), 658–663.

Bloom, B. S. (1956). Taxonomy of educational objectives: the classification of educational goals. In M. D. Engelhart, E. J. Furst, W. H. Hill, & D. R. Krathwohl (Eds.), *Handbook 1: Cognitive Domain*. David McKay.

Bratton, J., Gold, J., Bratton, A., & Steele, L. (2021). *Human resource management*. Bloomsbury Publishing.

Cannon, J. R. (2002). Distance learning in science education. In J. W. Altschuld & D. D. Kumar (Eds.), *Evaluation of Science and Technology Education at the Dawn of a New Millennium* (pp. 243–265). Kluwer Academic/Plenum Publishers. doi:10.1007/0-306-47560-X_10

Centers for Disease Control and Prevention. (2020). *COVID-19 hospitalization and death by race/ethnicity*. Available at: https://www.cdc.gov/coronavirus/2019-ncov/covid-data/ investigations-discovery/hospitalization-death-by-race-ethnicity.html

Chen, Y. C. (2020). Dialogic pathways to manage uncertainty for productive engagement in scientifc argumentation. *Science & Education, 29*(2), 331–375. doi:10.100711191-020-00111-z

Cobb, P. (1994). Where is the mind? Constructivist and sociocultural perspectives on mathematical development. *Educational Researcher, 23*(7), 13–19. doi:10.3102/0013189X023007013

Cohen, A. S., Morrison, S. C., & Callaway, D. A. (2013). Computerized facial analysis for understanding constricted/blunted affect: Initial feasibility, reliability, and validity data. *Schizophrenia Research*, *148*(1-3), 111–116. doi:10.1016/j.schres.2013.05.003 PMID:23726720

Dewey, J. (1938). *Experience and education*. Macmillan Publishing Company.

Dietrich, N., Kentheswaran, K., Ahmadi, A., Teychené, J., Bessière, Y., Alfenore, S., Laborie, S., Bastoul, D., Loubière, K., Guigui, C., Sperandio, M., Barna, L., Paul, E., Cabassud, C., Liné, A., & Hébrard, G. (2020). Attempts, successes, and failures of distance learning in the time of COVID-19. *Journal of Chemical Education*, *97*(9), 2448–2457. doi:10.1021/acs.jchemed.0c00717

Elo, S., Kääriäinen, M., Kanste, O., Pölkki, T., Utriainen, K., & Kyngäs, H. (2014). Qualitative content analysis: A focus on trustworthiness. *SAGE Open*, *4*(1). doi:10.1177/2158244014522633

Ferguson, K. J., Wolter, E. M., Yarbrough, D. B., Carline, J. D., & Krupat, E. (2009). Defining and describing medical learning communities: Results of a national survey. *Academic Medicine*, *84*(11), 1549–1556. doi:10.1097/ACM.0b013e3181bf5183 PMID:19858814

Gasman, M., & Nguyen, T. H. (2015). Myths dispelled: A historical account of diversity and inclusion at HBCUs. *New Directions for Higher Education*, *2015*(170), 5–15. doi:10.1002/he.20128

Gee, J. P. (2008). A sociocultural perspective on opportunity to learn. In P. A. Moss, D. C. Pullin, J. P. Gee, E. H. Haertel, & L. J. Young (Eds.), *Assessment, equity, and opportunity to learn* (pp. 76–108). Cambridge University Press. doi:10.1017/CBO9780511802157.006

González-Howard, M., & McNeill, K. L. (2016). Learning in a community of practice: Factors impacting English-learning students' engagement in scientific argumentation. *Journal of Research in Science Teaching*, *53*(4), 527–553. doi:10.1002/tea.21310

Gustafsson, J. (2017). *Single case studies vs. multiple case studies: A comparative study*. Academic Press.

Hamouche, S. (2021). Human resource management and the COVID-19 crisis: Implications, challenges, opportunities, and future organizational directions. *Journal of Management & Organization*, *1*, 1–16. doi:10.1017/jmo.2021.15

Hays, J., & Reinders, H. (2020). Sustainable learning and education: A curriculum for the future. *International Review of Education*, *66*(1), 29–52. doi:10.100711159-020-09820-7

Hodge, E., Bossé, M. J., Faulconer, J., & Fewell, M. (2006). Mimicking proximity: The role of distance education in forming communities of learning. *International Journal of Instructional Technology and Distance Learning*, *3*(12), 3–12.

Hoepfl, M. C. (1997). Choosing qualitative research: A primer for technology education researchers. *Journal of Technology Education*, *9*(1), 47–63. doi:10.21061/jte.v9i1.a.4

Hubbard, K. (2021). Using Data-Driven Approaches to Address Systematic Awarding Gaps. In *Doing Equity and Diversity for Success in Higher Education* (pp. 215–226). Palgrave Macmillan. doi:10.1007/978-3-030-65668-3_16

Jan, S. K., & Vlachopoulos, P. (2018). Infuence of learning design of the formation of online communities of learning. *International Review of Research in Open and Distributed Learning.* . doi:10.19173/irrodl.v19i4.3620

Jiménez-Aleixandre, M. P. (2014). Determinism and underdetermination in genetics: Implications for students' engagement in argumentation and epistemic practices. *Science & Education, 23*(2), 465–484. doi:10.100711191-012-9561-6

Kaufman, H. (2015). A review of predictive factors of student success in and satisfaction with online learning. *Research in Learning Technology, 23*. Advance online publication. doi:10.3402/rlt.v23.26507

Keengwe, J., & Kidd, T. T. (2010). Towards best practices in online learning and teaching in higher education. *Journal of Online Learning and Teaching, 6*(2), 533–541.

Kelly, G. J. (2007). Discourse in science classrooms. In S. K. Abell & N. G. Lederman (Eds.), *Handbook of research on science education* (pp. 443–469). Lawrence Erlbaum.

King, N., & Brooks, J. (2018). Thematic analysis in organisational research. In C. Cassell, A. L. Cunliffe, & G. Grandy (Eds.), *The Sage handbook of qualitative business and management research methods* (pp. 219–236). Sage.

Krathwohl, D. (2002). A revision of bloom's taxonomy: An overview. *Theory into Practice, 41*(4), 212–218. doi:10.120715430421tip4104_2

Krishnamurthy, S. (2020). The future of business education: A commentary in the shadow of the Covid-19 pandemic. *Journal of Business Research, 117*, 1–5. doi:10.1016/j.jbusres.2020.05.034 PMID:32501309

Landis, J. R., & Koch, G. G. (1977). An application of hierarchical kappa-type statistics in the assessment of majority agreement among multiple observers. *Biometrics, 33*(2), 363–374. doi:10.2307/2529786 PMID:884196

Lave, J., & Wenger, E. (1991). *Situated Learning: Legitimate Peripheral Participation*. Cambridge University Press. doi:10.1017/CBO9780511815355

Leach, J., & Scott, P. (2003). Individual and sociocultural views of learning in science education. *Science & education, 12*(1), 91–113. doi:10.1023/A:1022665519862

Moore, M. G. (1989). Three types of interaction. *American Journal of Distance Education, 3*(2), 1–6. doi:10.1080/08923648909526659

Mupinga, D. M. (2005). Distance education in high schools: Benefts, challenges, and suggestions. *The Clearing House: A Journal of Educational Strategies, Issues and Ideas, 78*(3), 105–109. doi:10.3200/TCHS.78.3.105-109

Neuendorf, K. A. (2018). Content analysis and thematic analysis. In P. Brough (Ed.), Advanced research methods for applied psychology (pp. 211-223). Routledge. doi:10.4324/9781315517971-21

Nieto, S. (2015). *The light in their eyes: Creating multicultural learning communities*. Teachers College Press.

O'Byrne, L., Gavin, B., & McNicholas, F. (2020). Medical students and COVID-19: The need for pandemic preparedness. *Journal of Medical Ethics*, *46*(9), 623–626. doi:10.1136/medethics-2020-106353 PMID:32493713

OECD. (2005). *E-learning in tertiary education*. Available at http://www.cumex.org.mx/archivos/ACERVO/ElearningPolicybriefenglish.pdf

Pallof, R. M., & Pratt, K. (2007). *Building online learning communities: Effective strategies for the virtual classroom*. John Wiley & Sons.

Peltier, J. W., Chennamaneni, P. R., & Barber, K. N. (2022). Student anxiety, preparation, and learning framework for responding to external crises: The moderating role of self-efficacy as a coping mechanism. *Journal of Marketing Education*, *44*(2), 149–165. doi:10.1177/02734753211036500

Pierson, A. E., Clark, D. B., & Kelly, G. J. (2019). Learning Progressions and science practices. *Science & Education*, *28*(8), 833–841. doi:10.100711191-019-00070-0

Punch, K. F. (2013). *Introduction to social research: Quantitative and qualitative approaches*. Sage.

Ranga, M., & Etzkowitz, H. (2015). Triple Helix systems: an analytical framework for innovation policy and practice in the Knowledge Society. *Entrepreneurship and knowledge exchange*, 117-158.

Rastegar Kazerooni, A., Amini, M., Tabari, P., & Moosavi, M. (2020). Peer mentoring for medical students during COVID-19 pandemic via a social media platform. *Medical Education*, *54*(8), 762–763. doi:10.1111/medu.14206 PMID:32353893

Redmond, P., Heffernan, A., Abawi, L., Brown, A., & Henderson, R. (2018). An online engagement framework for higher education. *Online Learning*, *22*(1), 183-204.

Roberts, J. (2006). Limits to communities of practice. *Journal of Management Studies*, *43*(3), 623–639. doi:10.1111/j.1467-6486.2006.00618.x

Rodrigues, H., Almeida, F., Figueiredo, V., & Lopes, S. (2019). Tracking e-learning through published papers: A systematic review. *Computers & Education*, *136*, 87–98. doi:10.1016/j.compedu.2019.03.007

Sadler, T. D. (2009). Situated learning in science education: Socio-scientifc issues as contexts for practice. *Studies in Science Education*, *45*(1), 1–42. doi:10.1080/03057260802681839

Salomon, G. (2000). *E-moderating the key to teaching and learning online*. Kogan Page.

Shochet, R., Fleming, A., Wagner, J., Colbert-Getz, J., Bhutiani, M., Moynahan, K., & Keeley, M. (2019). Defining learning communities in undergraduate medical education: A national study. *Journal of Medical Education and Curricular Development*, *6*, 2382120519827911. doi:10.1177/2382120519827911 PMID:30937385

Shu, H., & Gu, X. (2018). Determining the diferences between online and face-to-face student–group interactions in a blended learning course. *The Internet and Higher Education*, *39*, 13–21. doi:10.1016/j.iheduc.2018.05.003

Stoll, L., & Earl, L. (2003). Making it last: Building capacity for sustainability. In B. Davies & J. West-Burham (Eds.), *Handbook of Educational Leadership and Management*. Pearson/Longman.

Swan, K., & Shea, P. (2005). The development of virtual learning communities. In S. R. Hiltz & R. Goldman (Eds.), *Asynchronous Learning Networks: The Research Frontier* (pp. 239–260). Hampton Press.

Taylor, D. G., & Frechette, M. (2022). The impact of workload, productivity, and social support on burnout among marketing faculty during the COVID-19 pandemic. *Journal of Marketing Education*, *44*(2), 02734753221074284. doi:10.1177/02734753221074284

Thevanes, N., & Arulrajah, A. A. (2017). The search for sustainable human resource management practices: A review and reflections. In *Proceedings of Fourteenth International Conference on Business Management (ICBM)* (pp. 606-634). Academic Press.

Turner, J. C., Christensen, A., Kackar-Cam, H. Z., Fulmer, S. M., & Trucano, M. (2018). The development of professional learning communities and their teacher leaders: An activity systems analysis. *Journal of the Learning Sciences*, *27*(1), 49–88. doi:10.1080/10508406.2017.1381962

Vickers, D., & Fox, S. (2010). Towards practice-based studies of HRM: An actor-network and communities of practice informed approach. *International Journal of Human Resource Management*, *21*(6), 899–914. doi:10.1080/09585191003729366

Vygotsky, L. S. (1986). *Thought and language*. MIT Press.

Wagner, E. D. (1994). In support of a functional defnition of interaction. *American Journal of Distance Education*, *8*(2), 6–29. doi:10.1080/08923649409526852

Watanabe, Y. (2004). Methodology in washback studies. In Washback in Language Testing: Research Context and Methods (pp. 19-36). Laurence Erlbaum & Associates.

Winkle-Wagner, R., & McCoy, D. L. (2016). Entering the (postgraduate) field: Underrepresented students' acquisition of cultural and social capital in graduate school preparation programs. *The Journal of Higher Education*, *87*(2), 178–205.

Wu, D., & Hiltz, S. R. (2004). Predicting learning from asynchronous online discussions. *Journal of Asynchronous Learning Networks*, *8*(2), 139–152.

Yin, R. K. (2009). Case study research: Design and methods. *Sage (Atlanta, Ga.)*.

Yin, R. K. (2013). Validity and generalization in future case study evaluations. *Evaluation*, *19*(3), 321–332. doi:10.1177/1356389013497081

## ADDITIONAL READING

Meletiadou, E. (2012). The impact of training adolescent EFL learners on their perceptions of peer assessment of writing. *RPLTL*, *3*(1), 240–251.

Meletiadou, E. (2021a). Exploring the impact of peer assessment on EFL students' writing performance. *IAFOR Journal of Education*, *9*(3), 77–95. doi:10.22492/ije.9.3.05

Meletiadou, E. (2021b). Opening Pandora's box: How does peer assessment affect EFL students' writing quality? *Languages*, *6*(3), 115. doi:10.3390/languages6030115

Meletiadou, E. (2021c). Using Padlets as e-portfolios to develop undergraduate students' writing skills and motivation. *IAFOR Journal of Undergraduate Education*, *9*(4), 67–83. doi:10.22492/ije.9.5.04

Meletiadou, E. (2022). Learners' perceptions of peer assessment: Implications for their willingness to write in an EFL classroom. *International Journal of Teacher Education and Professional Development*.

Meletiadou, E. (2022). The use of peer assessment as an inclusive learning strategy in Higher Education Institutions. In E. Meletiadou (Ed.), *Policies and Practices for Assessing Inclusive Teaching and Learning*. IGI Global Publishers. doi:10.4018/978-1-7998-8579-5.ch001

Meletiadou, E. (2022). Nurturing students' writing knowledge, self-regulation, and attitudes in Higher Education. In E. Meletiadou (Ed.), *Policies and Practices for Assessing Inclusive Teaching and Learning*. IGI Global Publishers. doi:10.4018/978-1-7998-8579-5.ch002

Meletiadou, E. (2022). *Policies and Practices for Assessing Inclusive Teaching and Learning*. IGI Global Publishers.

Meletiadou, E., & Tsagari, D. (2012). Investigating the attitudes of adolescent EFL learners towards peer assessment of writing. In D. Tsagari (Ed.), *Research on English as a foreign language in Cyprus* (Vol. 2, pp. 225–245). University of Nicosia Press.

Meletiadou, E., & Tsagari, D. (2014). An exploration of the reliability and validity of peer assessment of writing in secondary education. In D. Tsagari (Ed.), *Major trends in theoretical and applied linguistics 3* (pp. 235–250). De Gruyter Open Poland. doi:10.2478/9788376560915.p14

Meletiadou, E., & Tsagari, D. (2016). The washback effect of peer assessment on adolescent EFL learners in Cyprus. In D. Tsagari (Ed.), *Classroom-based assessment in L2 contexts*. Cambridge Scholars Publishing.

## KEY TERMS AND DEFINITIONS

**Intercultural Awareness:** It is, quite simply, having an understanding of both your own and other cultures, and particularly the similarities and differences between them.

**Learning Communities:** They connect people, organizations, and systems that are eager to learn and work across boundaries in pursuit of a shared goal.

**Sustainable Learning:** It is the practice of giving students the skills they need for life-long learning outside of the classroom.

# Chapter 3
# Facilitating an Online and Sustainable Learning Environment for Cloud Computing Using an Action Research Methodology

**Sukhpal Singh Gill**
https://orcid.org/0000-0002-3913-0369
*Queen Mary University of London, UK*

**Ana Cabral**
*Queen Mary University of London, UK*

**Stephanie Fuller**
*Queen Mary University of London, UK*

**Yue Chen**
*Queen Mary University of London, UK*

**Steve Uhlig**
*Queen Mary University of London, UK*

## ABSTRACT

*In this chapter, a research plan is presented to investigate online teaching and evaluation analysis for cloud computing using an action research methodology to enable sustainable learning environment. Using online teaching, the authors planned to conduct a thorough evaluation of student learning implementation in order to identify both merits and challenges. An investigation of the authors' own teaching and learners' understanding while working together as a team on a cloud computing project has assisted in finding the perfect methods for improving both. Further, the authors used action research methodology to analyze the literature and scholarship critically and designed best practices for action plan to facilitate an online and sustainable learning environment for cloud computing. Moreover, possible ethical concerns have been considered as students worked in a team for a group project. Finally, they have discussed the plans for monitoring and evaluation of the action and impact assessment.*

DOI: 10.4018/978-1-6684-6172-3.ch003

## INTRODUCTION

In the wake of the Covid-19 pandemic, preliminary evidence from the Queen Mary University of London (QMUL) Cloud Computing module reveals that students are less engaged, more reluctant to participate, and less willing to attend classes delivered online due to the module's in-person delivery relative to the online delivery. According to the analysis findings, just 30% of participants have completed and submitted their assignments by the deadline in the year 2020, when the module was taught in-person. According to the students' feedback, it is very difficult to complete the project individually which is also very time consuming. In addition, it required considerable technical skills that some students lacked due to their diverse academic backgrounds and experiences, such as professional cloud experts, software engineers, or continuing students (Singhal et al., 2021). Several alumni acknowledged the necessity of working together to build innovative skills useful in their future career opportunities (Holtzman & Kraft, 2011). Based on informal observations of practice and consultations with colleagues teaching similar modules at other universities (Imperial College London, University of Melbourne, Cardiff University and the University of Manchester), there is a need to enhance the students' involvement and participation along with their teamwork and leadership, which are extremely important for their professional success (Kashefi et al., 2012). Achieving the goals of this action plan will aid in the creation of an online and sustainable learning environment for cloud computing (Gill et al., 2022a).

### Motivation and Contributions

Due to the good educational quality and career opportunities at Queen Mary University of London (QMUL), the number of students are increasing every year, which also contributes towards an increase in the number of students for the cloud computing module as well (Gill et al., 2023a). Therefore, it is challenging to enable engagement, primarily when students work individually on their projects. The problem emerged when students were working on their projects individually during the Covid-19 pandemic and resulted in a reduction in students' satisfaction rate by 10%. An addition of teamwork activity in this module should have improved students' engagement and technical skills and help the school and staff to manage the students' projects more effectively. We have been involved in designing a similar approach for another Indian university module, implemented successfully for teaching virtually (Singhal et al., 2021). With this approach, a lecturer can manage the workload easily with fewer administrative tasks and utilize more time to provide feedback to different groups, which assists them in completing their assignment on time and enables an online and sustainable learning environment for cloud computing to be established (Gill et al., 2023b).

The module's quality was evaluated by various stakeholders, including the discipline, employers, and students as customers following professional frameworks such as "Frameworks for Higher Education Qualifications (FHEQ)" (Qi, 2012) and "Quality Assurance Agency (QAA) benchmark statements" . They are connected to the cloud computing module's Intended Learning Outcomes (ILOs), which includes "Computing (2019)" and "Engineering (2020)." Credit Level Descriptors for Higher Education (2016) and the QMUL Statement of Graduate Attributes (QMUL, 2009) are considered to form a cloud computing module. The proposed action plan has included the following new disciplinary skills and attributes in ILOs of this module to enable a sustainable learning environment:

*Facilitating an Online and Sustainable Learning Environment for Cloud Computing*

- Review modern cloud computing research concepts and become familiar with computing platform (Amazon Web Services (AWS) cloud) for corporate leadership.
- Apply AWS cloud to manage web services, practice what you've learned in class.
- Create an AWS-based cloud application utilising RESTful Application Programming Interface (API) services to improve your teamwork skills.
- Develop an application using AWS cloud and exhibit their capability to work with other people to know about the spirit of collaboration.

Lab activities have been updated to reflect the most current professional standards by including the latest software tools. Teamwork activities were included in this course to understand the essential teamwork skills they would need for career advancement. On the first day of cloud computing module, students choice regarding coursework was asked using Mentimeter. 196 students have participated in this survey and 81.1% students preferred group based lab project while only 18.9% voted for individual lab project. It also indicates that teamwork is an important activity which must be included to improve students teamwork skills while working in a team, which offers more sustainable learning environment (Gill et al., 2023c). To further motivate learners to participate in online contests, compete in MSc research, join internship programs, and unlock the doors to career prospects, the module allows learners to undertake numerous online courses and certifications on these tools.

The rest of the chapter is structured as follows: Second section gives the background to discuss use of an action research methodology to offer an online and sustainable learning environment. Further, we discuss the evaluation of existing practice in third section. Fourth section presents the review of literature. Fifth section gives the details of methods to inform and evaluate the action. Sixth section discuss the limitations and ethical constraints. Seventh section presents an approach for monitoring and evaluation of the action along with impact assessment. Eighth section shows the preliminary results. Nineth section gives the discussions and offers recommendations for potential readers. Finally, last section concludes the chapter. The detailed description of data gathering tools is given in Appendix 1. Appendix 2 gives the procedure used for addressing ethical concerns.

## ADOPTING AN ACTION RESEARCH METHODOLOGY AND BACKGROUND

By adopting an Action Research (AR) methodology to investigate practice, educational practitioners can investigate their practice, solve problems and generate change to enable an online and sustainable learning environment for cloud computing. In the context of Higher Education, this methodology gives academics a tool to address concerns like, "How do I enhance my practice?" and develop small-scale context-driven initiatives that are established to solve particular challenges related to the requirements of students and staff advancement and institutional goals or explore an area of interest or concern for sustainable future (Carr & Kemmis, 1986) (Elliott, 1991) (Lewin, 1946) (Stenhouse, 1975). AR encompasses a cycle involving: reflection on practice and collection of information to inform the design of the action, action planning, implementation of the action, collection of data, reflection on the outcomes and results and consideration of the need to start new cycles. According to Lambirth & Cabral (2017), action research can be regarded as a tool for professional learning due to its ability to integrate systematic research into the daily work of practitioners.

Collaborating with peers, exchanging thoughts, discussing viewpoints, and engaging in genuine conversations with students are all essential components of action research (Naeem et al., 2022). This collaboration in knowledge development is continuously challenged by the restrictions and limitations of power relations. However, action research can become a transformative strategy in terms of professional learning with practitioners using it to (re)claim agency and tailor their practice to their own needs, the needs of their students and the contexts in which they work (Lambirth et al., 2019).

In the field of education and information technology, action research can help practitioners answer the particular demands of the 21st century to develop more sustainable learning environment. As argued by Glassman (2020) 'education must take new approaches to meet the social opportunities and challenges brought about through the information revolution, in particular access to new information, capabilities for new types of communities that can challenge place-based agendas, and distributed power and voice' (Amstelveen, 2019). In this article, authors have discussed how action research was used to investigate the use of a flipped classroom in college-level Mathematics (Amstelveen, 2019) and analyzed the post-graduate information systems module's communication skills (Isaias & Issa, 2014).

Furthermore, we have tested and developed strategies to improve classroom design and teaching methods for teaching critical transferable skills to computer science and engineering students in a sustainable learning environment (Burrows & Borowczak, 2019). Based on students' feedback, assessment results, informed observations and considering the role of other stakeholders, we have identified various critical challenges (Figure 1) that motivate us to design a new research plan for cloud computing and enable sustainable learning environment for cloud computing. To address these issues, we have studied the effectiveness of a novel team-based virtual lab activity on the learning process of students enrolled in a Cloud Computing course as an outcome of this research (Junco, 2012). Through this approach, students can acquire the required benefit and support from the staff, school, university and Higher Education (HE) to improve their careers (HEA, 2015).

*Figure 1. Important challenges in practice to enable sustainable learning environment for cloud computing*

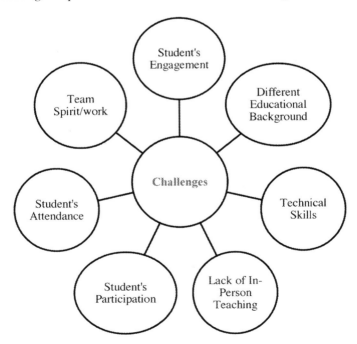

## EVALUATION OF THE EXISTING PRACTICE

We have applied the action research model to the cloud computing module through different steps: i) plan, ii) act, iii) observe and iv) reflect (Zuber-Skerritt, 2021). The first step is "Plan" for action research to evaluate existing practice by considering various important factors. These factors include students' feedback, evaluation results, reflection log, informal discussions with students, observations by focus groups and colleagues and review of the literature and scholarship (Figure 2).

*Figure 2. Important factors are considered for evaluation of practice*

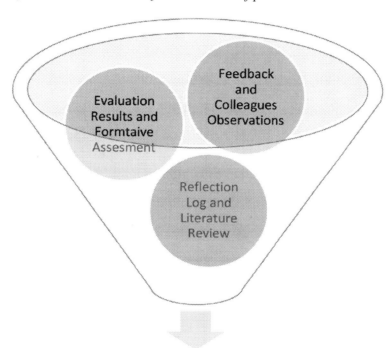

Through this action research, we have implemented (act) the above discussed plan by delivering this module using various well-proven active learning activities. These activities include online webinars, H5P-based interactive videos for each topic (Homanová & Havlásková, 2019), problem-based learning (PBL) pedagogy (think-pair and share) to enable teamwork (Alves, 2012), group discussion through drop-in sessions (Giannini, 1999), lab quizzes (Geiger & Bostow, 1976), and interactive Q/A sessions using web-based tools such as Mentimeter and Kahoot (Gokbulut, 2020). Students have given feedback after each online session through Google survey forms, which helped us adapt the teaching practice as needed during the module delivery. This module has been delivered by lecturers and four senior demonstrators using a virtual environment which improves learner engagement as seen in law education (Brooman, 2011) and microbiology (Sancho, 2006). Figure 3 illustrates how Bloom's taxonomy (Sosniak, 1994) (shown at several levels) was allocated resources effectively to implement a research plan. Bloom's Taxonomy is a valuable tool for improving the ability to think critically and tackling real-world issues with innovation, which has been utilised successfully in many disciplines such as science and engineering (Hager et al., 1994), sustainability (Pappas et al., 2013) and music education (Hanna, 2007) to enable a sustainable learning environment. The first two lower levels (**Remember and Understand**) of Bloom's taxonomy have explored essential ideas by reading the research papers and viewing the interactive videos.

Further, participation in the Mentimeter/Kahoot quiz during the online session and answering questions on QMPlus (Virtual Learning Environment (VLE) at QMUL) after the online session have improved understanding of the current topic (Gill et al. 2023a). While working through the lab tasks, the demonstrators have supported Bloom's taxonomy's third level (**Apply**), including learning about the newest cloud computing and software solutions, such as AWS (Gill et al., 2022b). Demonstrators helped learners diagnose errors while doing activities, creating very dynamic laboratory sessions for online learning (**Analyse**). Lab quizzes for self-learning are designed to assess students' understanding of various lab tasks (**Evaluate**). Four drop-in sessions was used to clear students' doubts, including group discussions, real-world applications, and forming teams (Gill et al. 2023b). The students then analyzed their mini-projects utilizing the think-pair-share activity. Students can choose the domain/area/programming tool they want to work in (**Evaluate**). To develop a cloud application, the team must come up with original ideas based on group conversation and prior experience in similar projects (**Create**).

*Figure 3. Applying Bloom's taxonomy to learn Cloud Computing*

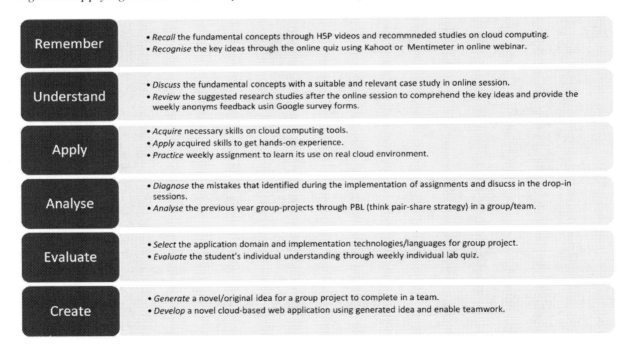

We have **observed** the impact of action research on students' learning through feedback, formative and summative assessments. Finally, we have **reflected** based on students' feedback, evaluation results, informal discussions with students, observations by focus groups and colleagues, and reviewing the literature and scholarship, which helped us improve teaching practice to enable an online and sustainable learning environment for cloud computing.

## ANALYSIS OF LITERATURE

On the basis of current research, we have developed an action approach to allow an online and long-term learning environment for cloud computing (Gill et al. 2023c). For example, during the COVID19 pandemic, a digital device-based active learning strategy for online education was developed (Singhal et al., 2021). Academics form QMUL were on a research team. Teamwork activities were used to execute this task at the University of Petroleum and Energy Studies (UPES) in India. This method boosted students' learning ability and increased average scores in two engineering disciplines by 66.9%. The success of this strategy in an Indian institution inspired us to use it for our cloud computing module to offer an online and sustainable learning environment.

Also, at Indiana University, a collaborative exercise to improve student interest, involvement, and attention was examined (Cavinato et al., 2021). The feedback of 6,000 undergraduate students showed teamwork-based practical learning activities enhance students' enthusiasm and willingness to study. Students believed it was more interactive, which increased attention, attendance, technical abilities, and favourable student relationships. The research also shows that students are more likely to succeed when given a flexible deadline for their projects and assignments. This evidence helped us increase student teamwork, involvement, and attendance in cloud computing module. Another study (Kapilan et al., 2021) may lead to a new instructional approach for completing virtual laboratory experiments in mechanical engineering courses. According to participant feedback collected through questionnaires, focus groups, and interviews, the learning process and student involvement increased across nine courses. Effective utilization of problem-based learning (PBL) for teamwork skills improved student engagement and was useful for our research plan to offer a sustainable learning environment. According to student comments, online learning is also less participatory and impairs students' capacity to self-learn. Another piece of research (Pazos et al., 2020) looked at the impact of interdisciplinary undergraduate partnerships on teamwork efficiency. The authors observed that performance in terms of problem-solving and technical abilities improved considerably due to using a start-stop-continue feedback strategy. Another study (Gunawan et al., 2017) glanced at how learning electricity online affects problem-solving skills and recommended that trained demonstrators improve students' learning. We have used this for our action research to improve teamwork skills. Further, AWS cloud-based training was provided to cloud computing demonstrators under AWS Programs for Research and Education which improved their knowledge and enabled long-term students' learning.

Another study (Gerstenhaber, & Har-El, 2021) used virtual laboratories for a biomaterials course, and students were examined individually and in groups. They assessed the module's effectiveness across ethnic and cultural groups using web-based questionnaires and laboratory data (Luse & Rursch, 2021). The student opinions reveal that working individually and in teams was advantageous when implementing our action plan for coping with diversity. Pre-recorded videos must be uploaded on each topic to provide them better understanding of important concepts before participating in the lab. Another study (García-Peñalvo et al., 2021) from four Spanish institutions discusses enhancing online assessments—an exciting vision for ongoing assessment during the delivery of the cloud computing module. The researchers say that to administer the evaluation method properly, students must be informed beforehand about evaluation criteria. Another piece of research (Yusuf & Widyaningsih, 2020) acknowledged participants' metacognitive talents while doing online Physics activities. These skills were assessed qualitatively using video recordings of classroom discussions and quizzes. Students could ask and answer questions in a customizable virtual classroom, and 97.6% of the students took online quizzes. Their feedback indicates that weekly quizzes reduce stress and increase cognitive, psychological, and interpersonal engagement, which suggested that this was worthy of adoption in our research plan to make more sustainable module (Hughes et al., 2020).

Learning chemistry in a virtual environment can help students better comprehend key ideas by employing simulations, videos, animations, and images (Achuthan, & Murali, 2017). 524 undergrads were assessed online and in-person using evaluation questionnaires which shows its effectiveness for student engagement and also help dyslexic students the most. Therefore, we have included active learning tools and approaches into cloud computing curriculum to make this module more sustainable in terms of learning and teaching. Similarly, another study (Achuthan et al., 2017) assessed various aspects such as knowledge transfer, analogical reasoning, and metacognition. They used multiple-choice questions (MCQs), questions and answers (Q/A), and True or False (T/F) statements. Using an H5P based interactive video pre-lab fosters active learning, which was included in our strategic plan. According to the feedback of 145 students who participated in this research, studying in a virtual classroom is superior to learning in a physical lab, and incorporating these learning elements improves critical thinking. Uncovering an online computer networking lesson to increase students' awareness of 'business' configuration settings is examined in another research article (Gerstenhaber, & Har-El, 2021). It appears that this technique improves students' technical skills, which in turn improves their deliberate process at the highest levels of Bloom's taxonomy, allowing them to produce creative solutions to the problem at hand. This study was helpful for cloud computing students to improve technical skills using Bloom's taxonomy to create innovative ideas for their team projects, which assisted to sustain this teaching practice for long time. Similar studies (Hoegl & Parboteeah, 2007) (Baker et al., 2016) examined learners' creative and critical thinking abilities while collaborating to achieve a common objective, but we have applied this study to cloud computing cautiously, given a negative correlation between team performance and creative thinking.

## Critical Analysis

Table 1 compared the proposed action plan with existing literature. It has been noted that all the above-mentioned works presented approaches for an online and sustainable learning environment except the work done by García-Peñalvo et al. (2021), which is for in-person teaching. Investigation of the published literature (Singhal et al., 2021) (Gerstenhaber, & Har-El, 2021) (García-Peñalvo et al., 2021) (Hughes et al., 2020) indicated that different kinds of feedback (weekly questionnaires based and mid module feedback) and formative assessments (Q/A and Kahoot or Mentimeter based quizzes) during the delivery of module could improve students' engagement, participation, attendance and performance in the virtual environment (Gill et al. 2023a). It has been clearly shown that authors considered summative and formative assessments and multiple feedback forms (García-Peñalvo et al., 2021). However, the inclusion of various activities for feedback and formative assessments reduces students' interaction (Naeem et al., 2022). It hinders their ability to self-learn, according to the feedback collected from the students in another study (Kapilan et al., 2021). Various studies (Singhal et al., 2021) (Cavinato et al., 2021) (Kapilan et al., 2021) (Pazos et al., 2020) showed that teamwork is an important activity to improve student engagement and enable an online and sustainable learning environment. Problem Based Learning (PBL) pedagogy can be used for teamwork activities to enhance problem-solving abilities (Kapilan et al., 2021). However, the impact of teamwork on students' attendance, participation and performance is missing in the literature (Gill et al. 2023b), which is most important component to enable sustainable learning environment for cloud computing.

Further, no study has identified the impact of students' learning technical skills in a team with their different culture, nationality, educational background or experience, age of students, ethnicity, race and gender (Gill et al. 2023c). Various drop-in sessions can be organised for helping the students to complete their group projects in a team. Further, active learning activities such as H5P based interactive videos, online quizzes, group discussion activities and interactive Q/A sessions can be used for formative assessments to improve students' engagement (Gerstenhaber, & Har-El, 2021) (García-Peñalvo et al., 2021) (Hughes et al., 2020) (Achuthan, & Murali, 2017) (Achuthan et al., 2017). Literature also reported that implementing multiple active learning activities for large classes is very challenging, requiring effective time management and planning in advance. Further, it needs a substantial amount of time to mark these assessments. Integration of these activities with online teaching platforms such as QMPLUS have saved the tutor's time and offer easy marking. The regular utilisation of these teaching tools can improve the personal and professional development of the lecturer. We were inspired to use Mentimeter based quizzes (formative assessment) during the online session, enhancing student engagement. Later, it will help students do their weekly individual quizzes (summative assessment) effectively after every lab to evaluate their individual performance (Geiger & Bostow, 1976). The utilisation of Mentimeter-based quizzes can further improve students' attendance and participation (Gill et al. 2023a). Most of the above-mentioned literature used written exams and individual projects as summative assessments for student's evaluation, which are the main reasons for lacking student engagement. The utilisation of formative and summative assessments and other active learning activities can improve students' engagement, participation, attendance, and performance in a virtual environment (Gill et al. 2023b). This research plan adopted the evidence from the literature and scholarship to improve the students' learning for the cloud computing module to facilitate an online and sustainable learning environment.

*Table 1. Comparison of proposed action research study with existing works*

| Work | Online | Drop-in Sessions | Teamwork | Focus of Study (Sustainable Development) ||| Assessment | Feedback | Evaluation Approach |
|---|---|---|---|---|---|---|---|---|---|
| | | | | Engagement | Attendance | Participation | | | |
| (Singhal et al., 2021) | ü | | ü | ü | ü | ü | Summative | Online quizzes based feedback | Group Project |
| (Gerstenhaber, & Har-El, 2021) | ü | | | ü | | | Summative | Final Module Feedback | Written Exam and Individual lab viva |
| (Cavinato et al., 2021) | ü | | ü | ü | ü | ü | Summative | Final Module Feedback | Group Project |
| (García-Peñalvo et al., 2021) | ü | | | | | | Summative and Formative | Weekly Questionnaires based, Mid Module and Final Module Feedback | Written Exam |
| (Kapilan et al., 2021) | ü | | ü | ü | | | Summative | Final Module Feedback | Group Project |
| (Yusuf & Widyaningsih, 2020) | ü | | | | | | Summative | Final Module Feedback | Written Exam |
| (Hughes et al., 2020) | ü | | | ü | | ü | Summative | Online quizzes based feedback | Written Exam and Individual lab viva |
| (Achuthan, & Murali, 2017) | ü | | | | | | Summative | Final Module Feedback | Written Exam and Individual lab viva |
| (Achuthan et al., 2017) | ü | | | | | | Summative | Final Module Feedback | Written Exam |
| (Luse & Rursch, 2021) | ü | | | | | | Summative | Final Module Feedback | Individual lab viva |
| (Pazos et al., 2020) | | | ü | | | | Summative | Final Module Feedback | Group Project |
| (Zeni, 1998) | ü | | | | | | Summative | Final Module Feedback | Written Exam |
| (Gunawan et al., 2017) | ü | | | | | | Summative | Final Module Feedback | Individual lab viva |
| (Hoegl & Parboteeah, 2007) | | | | | | | Summative | Final Module Feedback | Written Exam |
| (Baker et al., 2016) | ü | | | | | | Summative | Final Module Feedback | Individual lab Project |
| **Our Proposed Action Plan** | ü | ü | ü | ü | ü | ü | **Summative and Formative** | **Weekly Google Forms Survey, Mid Module and Final Module Feedback** | **Individual Lab Quiz and Group Project** |

## METHODS TO INFORM AND EVALUATE THE ACTION

In light of our previous experiences from teaching, we have defined methodologies which were used

*Facilitating an Online and Sustainable Learning Environment for Cloud Computing*

to inform and assess out action to facilitate an online and sustainable learning environment for cloud computing module at QMUL (Gill et al., 2022).

**Evidence 1:** We have used the following methods to inform our action:

- For questions such as i) how can we improve student engagement and teamwork skills during online delivery of module; ii) how can we evaluate student performance using different types of tools, and iii) what are the different types of feedback that we can use to understand the student's learning, an **academic literature review** will be used to inform questions.
- **Professional frameworks** such as "Quality Assurance Agency (QAA) benchmark statements", "QMUL Statement of Graduate Attributes", and "Frameworks for Higher Education Qualifications (FHEQ)" were used to determine the appropriate level of disciplinary skills & attributes, and then designing activities in line with this to attain the ILOs.
- We have kept a **reflective log** of our practice to highlight problems we have discovered with the present assessment system. These problems include gaps in our knowledge about managing teamwork; and practical problems in students' understanding.
- Data from prior **assessments and evaluations** also utilised to identify problems with the current assessment from the students' viewpoints, such as whether or not they reported issues with it and whether or not they did satisfactorily on them.
- Another method is to engage in debates on most effective methods for engagement (including teamwork) with colleagues from other institutions teaching the same module at QMUL and other universities (Manchester University, Melbourne University and Imperial College London). Further, teaching observations and informal conversations with colleagues about the **assessments and feedback** were used to inform action.
- We intended to use student **feedback** to identify areas where we can improve. The insights obtained will help improve the delivery of online labs and lecturers in the future.

**Evidence 2:** We have identified the following methods to evaluate the action:

- The **academic literature** is providing a benchmark against which our results may be evaluated and a guide to the methodologies used in conducting this evaluation. Using a **literature review** on active learning approaches, we are tracking students' performance and determine what influences team members' learning.
- For **Virtual Learning Environment (VLE)** reports and analytics, we intended to provide lab quizzes, project reports from the previous year, interactive videos based on H5P and presentations using QMPLUS to the students in order to aid them in completing the lab exercise. This also provide us with the opportunity to do engagement analytics on QMPLUS. For the aim of achieving the action plan to make it more sustainable, this module was delivered through a combination of online video lectures and active learning activities, which has included Problem Based Learning (PBL) pedagogy using MS Teams or Zoom, group discussion sessions, lab quizzes, and interactive Q/A sessions using web-based tools such as Mentimeter, Kahoot and Google forms. These active learning tools and techniques will provide statistical data of students' engagement, participation, attendance and performance.
- Statistics from assessments and evaluations are used, compared the findings to those in prior years. We used **summative assessments** (individual lab quiz and group project) and formative

assessments (Mentimeter or Kahoot based quiz during online session and weekly Google survey forms after the online session) to evaluate the cloud computing module. Data collected from students, assessment results, grades, and interactions with colleagues who teach cloud computing courses also considered. Learners' presence and test performances (individual assessment grades and the overall grades) have also taken into account when determining their ILO success.

- For example, a **reflective log** of our experience running the assessment helped note how many students interact during drop-in sessions. It was necessary to keep a reflection record during the project's duration to identify barriers in teaching practice and put countermeasures in place. Our existing teaching practice was evaluated, and development opportunities were identified through action research. We were also able to experiment and gather data that will aid us in discovering the most successful and sustainable techniques to enhance teaching and students' learning for long-term. **Formative assessments** were used to evaluate the participants' involvement. Further, we were tracked their performance by conducting a literature review on active learning methods to identify the participants' learning factors.
- Another method that has been identified in the literature is a **focus group**. This allowed for more in-depth qualitative research of students' learning both in teams and individually. To assess and examine participation following the intervention, we used the opinions of our colleagues as well as inputs from the interview session of the focus group.
- Through the use of **external observers** (colleagues from QMUL or other institutions), we assessed our research activities, and the comments we have received assisted us to enhance our teaching practice for facilitating sustainable and online learning environment for cloud computing module.
- A variety of **feedback** methods were used to assess the performance of ILOs, including a weekly Google Forms survey, mid-module and final-module feedback, and alumni input from students who have progressed on to successful careers. Google surveys was used to get anonymous student feedback on weekly material. A Traffic Light Model have assessed students' remarks and improve our teaching approach and methods when it comes to this feedback. Reflective action have boosted student engagement when students find it challenging to learn a particular topic. Semi-structured Data and Advanced Data Modelling module in semester A at QMUL noticed an improvement in student satisfaction when we used the same method. Aside from that, we have collected mid-module input from students using QMPlus-based mid-module feedback. This feedback was used to monitor and track the development of ILOs, which was beneficial to students working on lab assignments and other course-related concerns. In the second session, students' final remarks were used to evaluate their overall satisfaction with the way the course was delivered.

The detailed description of data gathering tools is given in **Appendix 1**. Our action study was implemented following a timeline for feedback and assessments (Figure 4), which we developed in accordance with the methodologies for evaluating the action (Gill et al., 2023b).

*Facilitating an Online and Sustainable Learning Environment for Cloud Computing*

*Figure 4. Timeline for Assessment and Feedback*

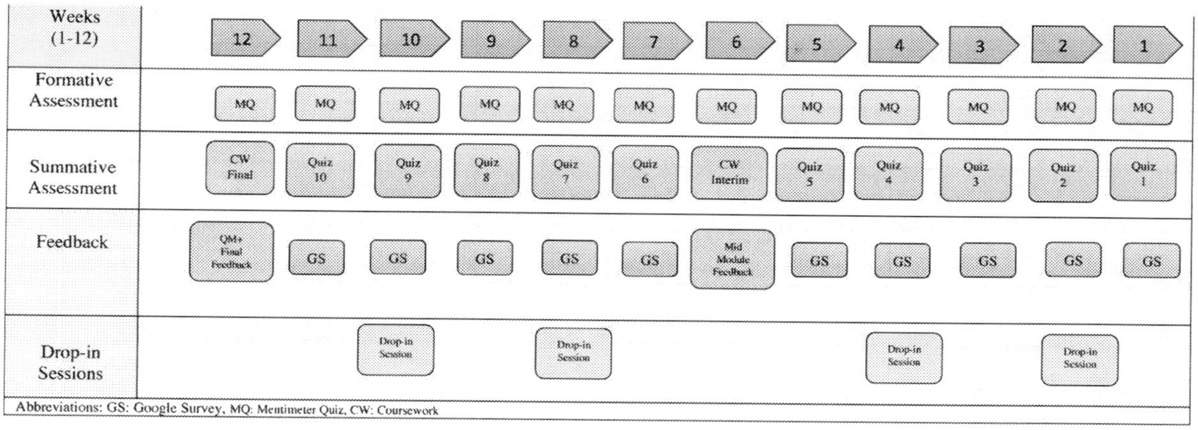

| Weeks (1-12) | 12 | 11 | 10 | 9 | 8 | 7 | 6 | 5 | 4 | 3 | 2 | 1 |
|---|---|---|---|---|---|---|---|---|---|---|---|---|
| Formative Assessment | MQ | MQ | MQ | MQ | MQ | MQ | MQ | MQ | MQ | MQ | MQ | MQ |
| Summative Assessment | CW Final | Quiz 10 | Quiz 9 | Quiz 8 | Quiz 7 | Quiz 6 | CW Interim | Quiz 5 | Quiz 4 | Quiz 3 | Quiz 2 | Quiz 1 |
| Feedback | QM+ Final Feedback | GS | GS | GS | GS | GS | Mid Module Feedback | GS | GS | GS | GS | GS |
| Drop-in Sessions | | | Drop-in Session | | Drop-in Session | | | | Drop-in Session | | Drop-in Session | |

Abbreviations: GS: Google Survey, MQ: Mentimeter Quiz, CW: Coursework

## LIMITATIONS AND ETHICAL CONSTRAINTS

We have considered moral standards specified in the QMUL ethical policy (QMUL, 2022) and the BERA principles (BERA 2018) in this action research. It is critical to think about ethical concerns daily, in addition to undergoing formal ethical evaluation and approval, as advocated by Kemmis and McTaggart (1988). We intended to carry out our study plan according to the ethical standards outlined by Zeni (1998), engage students only with their consent, and treat them all equally and with respect as recommended by Cohen et al. (2011). During the implementation of our study plan, we have looked out for ethical challenges that can occur in our everyday activities (Gill et al. 2023c). Following the findings of our action study, students collaborated to accomplish their group projects (Naeem et al., 2022). The collection of data regarding participants' experiences working in groups have faced various ethical and moral problems, such as the confidentiality of students' data and their anonymity and the possibility of victimisation.

- Loss of anonymity: For this project, every student was required to disclose their interests and skills on a shared platform (for example, Google forms) to build online groups based on their interests and programming skills.
- Loss of confidentiality: All of the other students' data, including their personal and academic information, were available to all of the other students in the class.
- Potential victimization: When there was more considerable diversity in terms of culture, nationality, educational background or experience, the age of students, ethnicity, race, and gender, internal disagreements or conflicts were emerged due to this greater diversity.

Among the steps we were taken to mitigate these ethical risks is to make announcements at the beginning of each lab session about crucial topics, such as accepting responsibility by all participants to maintain confidentiality (Kemmis, & McTaggart, 1988). As a researcher and a teacher, our role in this action plan was multifaceted. However, we have proceeded with utmost caution and ensured that all data was maintained securely and acceptably (BERA Guidelines (BERA 2018)). Additionally, we have used information sheets to clarify the terms and conditions and written consent to guarantee that recognized practice standards are maintained while adhering to the QMUL ethical policy (QMUL, 2022). Following the General Data Protection Regulation (GDPR), a password and the participant's right to withdraw were used to protect the confidentiality of the information gathered throughout the study (UK GDPR, 2018). We have wished to study the action plan for the cloud computing module (BERA Guidelines (BERA 2018)) mainly because our primary goal was to evaluate the module's delivery and improve our teaching practice (Zeni, 1998). A weekly evaluation of each group's progress was conducted to verify that they are on track to meet their objectives (Kemmis & McTaggart, 1988). A student who were not feeling comfortable in a group because of greater diversity were allowed to work alone or join another group with our prior agreement if they so want. Data confidentiality, student permission, and the ability to join or quit a group have been highlighted in the literature (Gunawan et al., 2017) to boost students' performance and participation in a project, which made this module more sustainable. **Appendix 2** gives the procedure which were used for addressing ethical concerns.

## MONITORING AND EVALUATION OF THE ACTION

As a result of the intervention, we anticipate that students' attendance, participation and engagement have improved. Figure 5 shows the sequence of steps that were used to implement the action plan to facilitate an online and sustainable learning environment. Research plan pathways was divided into five main parts: 1) inputs, 2) activities, 3) outputs, 4) outcomes, and 5) impacts. In addition, we have considered feedback (Google survey forms data, mid-module and final QMPLUS feedback, colleagues observations and feedback from alumni and previous year students), formative assessment (Mentimeter or Kahoot-based quizzes during the lecturers), summative assessment (lab quiz and coursework marks) and prior evaluations (grades and results from previous year students) as **inputs** to the research.

The next part of the research plan pathway was **activities** that included students watching H5P-based Interactive videos to understand basic concepts, attempting lab quizzes after each lab (from week 1 to week 10), working on group projects in a team, participating in the Mentimeter quizzes during the online session to check the understanding of concepts, Q/A on QMPLUS and drop-in sessions to discuss concepts and clearing students doubts. The third part was **outputs** of an implemented research plan, which included evaluation results including students' grades, assessment marks including lab quizzes marks and group project marks, statistical data which showed the interaction of students with H5P based videos, quality of group project report including format, structure, figures, tables & references and working prototype of a group project. We have monitored the action through the first three parts of the research plan pathways (inputs, activities and outputs) and which can be controlled based on the mid module feedback and formative assessment during the module.

The fourth part of the research plan pathway will be an **outcome** in learning teamwork skills, technical skills, and how teamwork can improve students' careers. Then, we will consider the outputs and outcome of the research plan pathway to evaluate the action plan. The final part of the research plan pathway will be impacts, including student engagement, attendance, participation, and performance. Further, impact analysis will be done by using both **outcome** and **impacts**, while outcome gets direct influence and impacts gets indirect consequence of the research plan.

*Figure 5. Research Plan Pathway*

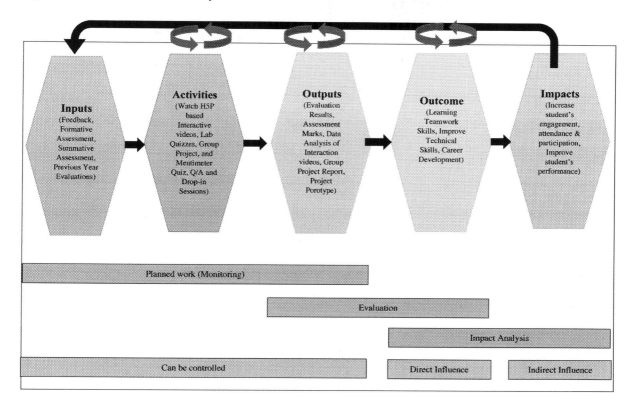

## PRELIMINARY RESULTS: DATA ANALYSIS AND FINDINGS

This section highlights the important findings in the form of preliminary results to show the effectiveness of our research plan.

### Formative Assessments

In every online session, we have used Mentimeter quizzes for two different purposes: 1) first quiz to test the previous knowledge of students before starting the lecture and 2) second quiz to check the gained knowledge after this session. For the academic year 2021–2022, 190 students at QMUL were enrolled in the Cloud Computing module and we have tested our action research plan by teaching cloud computing to these students. Statistics revealed that every week, at least 152 students took the Mentimeter questionnaire, demonstrating that the use of web-based tools order to increase student participation in virtual learning.

### Feedback

We have collected anonymous feedback using Google surveys and QMPLUS, where 50% students have participated to share their views on the online delivery of cloud computing module. This feedback shows that most of the students were very satisfied with this action research plan. Students have mentioned that the use of various active learning tools helped them to connect with the course content. It has been stated that use of web-based quizzes assisted students to maintain their attention during the online session. We have received important suggestions including the utilisation of video tutorials for every laboratory activity, lab-specific practical exercises, and a reduced number of learners partaking within every laboratory activity. Each of the laboratory assignments will have pre-recorded videos available the following academic year (2022-23), and learners will be able to make a start on them straightaway. There will be review meetings for the labs during reading week (after completing the 50% delivery of module), and we will give one more supporting session to the students to finish any incomplete assignments at the end of the module. The majority of learners were happy with this teamwork activity for their profession, according to comments that were collected to better understand individuals' perspectives on teamwork, career, and teaching methodology. Students also highlighted how valuable the modern tools and technology they learned in this module were for their careers. According to further input on the learning ideas, the majority of students considered them to be extremely beneficial for their career. Students are extremely satisfied with the teaching approach adopted to deliver lessons through this action research plan, according to their overall analysis on the teaching and learning process.

## Analysis

Based on the formative assessments and collected feedback, it is clearly shows that this action research plan has enhanced students' teamwork and technical skills, increased engagement and participation of students and also helped them to find the jobs in the area of cloud computing. Further, this research plan has assisted us to deal with diversity in an efficient manner.

### Positive Aspects of The Action Research Plan

Comparatively to the last year, when significant modifications were made as a result of virtual teaching, the action plan has developed. On the whole, the lessons and offered material were better organized. In order to give learners practical exposure, laboratory activities and assignments are now designed on a AWS Cloud to give real time cloud experience to the students. Each student has learned how to collaborate with others through the group project. Each group turned in their assignments on time, and the majority of learners completed their laboratory tests in a timely manner. The answers to the practice queries have been submitted by certain students each week.

### Negative Aspects of the Action Research Plan

For the team work activity, several participants' collaboration was incredibly lacking. A few students failed to participate in the laboratory quizzes based on weekly lab exercises, which had an impact on their overall scores obtained in this module. A tiny but vocal number of students without an education in computer science often objected that this action research plan was too advanced and too challenging for them. We set up five drop-in sessions for everybody in different weeks, but a few participants were unwilling to listen to our instructions and persisted in having this attitude throughout the whole semester.

The majority of comments were really favourable, which clearly shows the effectiveness of research plan. The majority of learners strongly complimented the material and viewed it as being really helpful for their future careers. Since working with others during teamwork/group project is challenging owing to online learning, the group project received a number of critiques. We would take into account different group project-based comprehensive case studies for dealing with diversity in the next year. We have provided a thorough study of how the modifications made during action research plan have affected the input from students. While we continue using this strategy in the next year, we will consider feedback when analysing the impact of action research plan on learners' employability.

## DISCUSSIONS AND RECOMMENDATIONS

This investigation helped us to gain much insight into our practice as a teacher and researcher and how to better help students with a teamwork-based project in their preparation for the future. During the implementation of this plan, we have analysed how students' involvement, performance, and attendance affected their careers and how working in a team has helped these students to develop their abilities (Gill et al., 2023b). We have implemented this action research plan at Queen Mary University of London (QMUL) for Cloud Computing module successfully and it will serve as an example for promoting teamwork at the school and institution levels in the future. This work will act as a benchmark for other schools at QMUL and other institutes to facilitate an online and sustainable learning environment for other modules of Computer Science and other disciplines (Gill et al., 2022).

This action plan have improved teaching practices for our personal, academic and professional development as shown in Figure 6.

Based on students' feedback and assessment results, we have identified the important areas of development to improve research plan for cloud computing and other modules of Computer Science and Engineering for making robust and sustainable learning environment. Further, we have created focus groups to study the direct and indirect impact of a novel team-based virtual lab activity on the learning process of students, and their feedback showed that teamwork is very useful to develop their teamwork and technical skills. Further. this study helped postgraduate students to get the necessary assistance and support from the staff, school, university and Higher Education (HE), which has improved their personal and professional development.

*Figure 6. Improved key development areas during Action Plan*

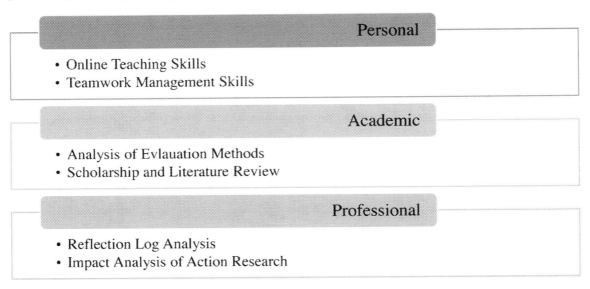

We have noted that the implementation of this research plan at QMUL has helped students of Computer Science and Engineering directly for the improvement of their thoughts on engagement, their opinions on what Computer science education is presently giving them, and their recommendations on how we can further promote student participation in the future. The successful implementation of this action research plan have encouraged students to share their own opinions with others throughout the process through various types of formative assessments and feedback types. Further, this action research plan will be implemented for face to face teaching in the post-Covid era. Prospective researchers and teachers can use this effective research plan for teaching other modules of Computer Science and other disciplines to understand its effectiveness and identify the further areas of improvements.

## CONCLUSION

In this chapter, we outlined our action research plan for investigating cloud computing-based online laboratory assessment analysis to facilitate an online and sustainable learning environment. This proposal has been designed to evaluate how well students have learnt using virtual laboratories to see where they were succeeding and where they were failing. While working on a cloud computing project together, we understood our own teaching and the comprehension of our students to offer sustainable learning and teaching environment. To come up with the finest strategies for action, we studied the literature and scholarship rigorously in this study to build a foundation for the development of sustainable environment for online learning. As students collaborate on a group project, potential ethical issues have been taken into account. Lastly, we have discussed about the strategies for monitoring and evaluation and impact assessment.

## ACKNOWLEDGMENT

We are thankful to faculty members and colleagues who have given their valuable comments to improve the quality of this work. We declare that this work is an updated version of the assignment which has been submitted for the module "Action (practitioner) Research Design" in partial fulfilment of the requirements for the award of degree of *Postgraduate Certificate Academic Practice (PGCAP) – UK Teaching Qualification* submitted in *QM Academy* of Queen Mary University of London, UK is an authentic record of research work carried out by *Sukhpal Singh Gill (First Author)* under the supervision of *Ana Cabral (Second Author)* and refers other researcher's work which are duly listed in the reference section. This *Assignment* has been checked using Tutnitin at Queen Mary University of London, UK and submitted assignment has been stored in repository for university record.

## REFERENCES

Achuthan, K., Francis, S. P., & Diwakar, S. (2017). Augmented reflective learning and knowledge retention perceived among students in classrooms involving virtual laboratories. *Education and Information Technologies*, *22*(6), 2825–2855. doi:10.100710639-017-9626-x

Achuthan, K., & Murali, S. S. (2017). Virtual lab: An adequate multi-modality learning channel for enhancing students' perception in chemistry. In Computer Science On-line Conference. Springer. doi:10.1007/978-3-319-57264-2_42

Alves, A. C., Mesquita, D., Moreira, F., & Fernandes, S. (2012). Teamwork in Project-Based Learning: engineering students' perceptions of strengths and weaknesses. *Third International Symposium on Project Approaches in Engineering Education (PAEE'2011): Aligning Engineering Education With Engineering Challenges*, 1-13.

Amstelveen, R. (2019). Flipping a college mathematics classroom: An action research project. *Education and Information Technologies*, *24*(2), 1337–1350. doi:10.100710639-018-9834-z

Baker, R. S., Clarke-Midura, J., & Ocumpaugh, J. (2016). Towards general models of effective science inquiry in virtual performance assessments. *Journal of Computer Assisted Learning*, *32*(3), 267–280. doi:10.1111/jcal.12128

British Educational Research Association Guidelines. (2018). *BERA Ethical Guidelines for Educational Research*. Available at: https://www.bera.ac.uk/wp-content/uploads/2018/06/BERA-Ethical-Guidelines-for-EducationalResearch_4thEdn_2018.pdf?noredirect=1

Brooman, S. (2011). Enhancing Student Engagement by Building upon the 'Tectonic Plates' of Legal Education. *The Liverpool Law Review*, *32*(2), 109–112. doi:10.100710991-011-9097-x

Burrows, A., & Borowczak, M. (2019). Computer science and engineering: Utilizing action research and lesson study. *Educational Action Research*, *27*(4), 631–646. doi:10.1080/09650792.2019.1566082

Carr, F., & Kemmis, S. (1986). *Becoming Critical: Education, Knowledge and Action Research*. Falmer Press.

Cavinato, A. G., Hunter, R. A., Ott, L. S., & Robinson, J. K. (2021). Promoting student interaction, engagement, and success in an online environment. *Analytical and Bioanalytical Chemistry*, *413*(6), 1513–1520. doi:10.100700216-021-03178-x PMID:33479816

Cohen, L., Manion, L., & Morrison, K. (2011). *Research methods in education*. Rutledge Flamer.

Elliott, J. (1991). *Action Research for Educational Change*. Open University Press.

García-Peñalvo, F. J., Corell, A., Abella-García, V., & Grande-de-Prado, M. (2021). Recommendations for Mandatory Online Assessment in Higher Education During the COVID-19 Pandemic. In *Radical Solutions for Education in a Crisis Context* (pp. 85–98). Springer. doi:10.1007/978-981-15-7869-4_6

Geiger, O. G., & Bostow, D. E. (1976). Contingency-managed college instruction: Effects of weekly quizzes on performance on examination. *Psychological Reports*, *39*(3), 707–710. doi:10.2466/pr0.1976.39.3.707

Gerstenhaber, J. A., & Har-El, Y. E. (2021). Virtual biomaterials lab during COVID-19 pandemic. *Biomedical Engineering Education*, *1*(2), 353-358.

Giannini, G. (1999). 'Drop-in' sessions: Information literacy responding to student needs. *Australian Academic and Research Libraries*, *30*(3), 212–218. doi:10.1080/00048623.1999.10755094

Gill, S. S., Fuller, S., Cabral, A., Chen, Y., & Uhlig, S. (2023a). An Operating System Session Plan Towards Social Justice and Intercultural Development in Microteaching for Higher Education. In E. Meletiadou (Ed.), *Handbook of Research on Fostering Social Justice Through Intercultural and Multilingual Communication* (pp. 1–15). IGI Global.

Gill, S. S., Fuller, S., Cabral, A., Chen, Y., & Uhlig, S. (2023b). Curriculum Redesign for Cloud Computing to Enhance Social Justice and Intercultural Development in Higher Education. In E. Meletiadou (Ed.), *Handbook of Research on Fostering Social Justice Through Intercultural and Multilingual Communication* (pp. 44–61). IGI Global.

Gill, S. S., Naeem, U., Fuller, S. Chen, Y., & Uhlig, S. (2022a). How Covid-19 Changed Computer Science Education. *ITNOW*, *64*(2), 60–61.

Gill, S. S., Thibodeau, D., Kaur, R., Naeem, U., & Stockman, T. (2023c). Reflection on Teaching Observation for Computer Science and Engineering to Design Effective Teaching Resources in Transnational Higher Education. In G. R. Morris & L. Li (Eds.), *Handbook of Research on Developments and Future Trends in Transnational Higher Education* (pp. 62–80). IGI Global.

Gill, S. S., Xu, M., Ottaviani, C., Patros, P., Bahsoon, R., Shaghaghi, A., & Uhlig, S. (2022b). AI for next generation computing: Emerging trends and future directions. *Internet of Things*, *19*, 100514. doi:10.1016/j.iot.2022.100514

Glassman, M. (2020). The internet as a context for participatory action research. *Education and Information Technologies*, *25*(3), 1891–191. doi:10.100710639-019-10033-1

Gokbulut, B. (2020). The effect of Mentimeter and Kahoot applications on university students'-learning. World Journal on Educational Technology. *Current Issues*, *12*(2), 107–116.

Gunawan, G., Harjono, A., Sahidu, H., & Herayanti, L. (2017). Virtual laboratory to improve students' problem-solving skills on electricity concept. *Journal Pendidikan IPA Indonesia, 6*(2), 257–264. doi:10.15294/jpii.v6i2.9481

Hager, P., Sleet, R., & Kaye, M. (1994). The relation between critical thinking abilities and student study strategies. *Higher Education Research & Development, 13*(2), 179–188. doi:10.1080/0729436940130208

Hanna, W. (2007). The new Bloom's taxonomy: Implications for music education. *Arts Education Policy Review, 108*(4), 7–16. doi:10.3200/AEPR.108.4.7-16

HEA. (2015). *Framework for student engagement through partnership*. Available: https://www.heacademy.ac.uk/sites/default/files/downloads/studentenagagement-through-partnership-new.pdf

Hoegl, M., & Parboteeah, K. P. (2007). Creativity in innovative projects: How teamwork matters. *Journal of Engineering and Technology Management, 24*(1-2), 148–166. doi:10.1016/j.jengtecman.2007.01.008

Holtzman, D. M., & Kraft, E. M. (2011). A comparison of qualitative feedback from alumni and employers with a national study for assessment of business curricula. *American Institute of Higher Education 6th International Conference Proceedings, 4*, 173-179.

Homanová, Z., & Havlásková, T. (2019). H5P interactive didactic tools in education. *11th International Conference on Education and New Learning Technologies*, 1-6.

Hughes, M., Salamonson, Y., & Metcalfe, L. (2020). Student engagement using multiple-attempt 'Weekly Participation Task' quizzes with undergraduate nursing students. *Nurse Education in Practice, 46*, 22–36. doi:10.1016/j.nepr.2020.102803 PMID:32526682

Isaias, P., & Issa, T. (2014). Promoting communication skills for information systems students in Australian and Portuguese higher education: Action research study. *Education and Information Technologies, 19*(4), 841–861. doi:10.100710639-013-9257-9

Junco, R. (2012). The relationship between frequency of Facebook use, participation in Facebook activities, and student engagement. *Computers & Education, 58*(1), 162–171. doi:10.1016/j.compedu.2011.08.004

Kapilan, N., Vidhya, P., & Gao, X. Z. (2021). Virtual laboratory: A boon to the mechanical engineering education during covid-19 pandemic. *Higher Education for the Future, 8*(1), 31–46. doi:10.1177/2347631120970757

Kashefi, H., Ismail, Z., & Yusof, Y. M. (2012). The impact of blended learning on communication skills and teamwork of engineering students in multivariable calculus. *Procedia: Social and Behavioral Sciences, 56*, 341–347. doi:10.1016/j.sbspro.2012.09.662

Kemmis, S., & McTaggart, R. (1988). *The action research planner*. Deakin University.

Lambirth, A., & Cabral, A. (2017). Issues of Agency, Discipline and Criticality: An Interplay of Challenges Involved in Teachers Engaging in Research in a Performative School Context. *Educational Action Research, 25*(4), 650–666. doi:10.1080/09650792.2016.1218350

Lambirth, A., Cabral, A., & McDonald, R. (2019). Transformational professional development: (re) claiming agency and change (in the margins). *Teacher Development*, *23*(3), 387–405. doi:10.1080/13664530.2019.1605407

Lewin, K. (1946). Action research and minority problems. *The Journal of Social Issues*, *2*(4), 4–46. doi:10.1111/j.1540-4560.1946.tb02295.x

Luse, A., & Rursch, J. (2021). Using a virtual lab network testbed to facilitate real-world hands-on learning in a networking course. *British Journal of Educational Technology*, *52*(3), 1244–1261. doi:10.1111/bjet.13070

Naeem, U., Bosman, L., & Gill, S. S. (2022, March). Teaching and Facilitating an Online Learning Environment for a Web Programming Module. In *2022 IEEE Global Engineering Education Conference (EDUCON)* (pp. 769-774). IEEE. 10.1109/EDUCON52537.2022.9766757

Pappas, E., Pierrakos, O., & Nagel, R. (2013). Using Bloom's Taxonomy to teach sustainability in multiple contexts. *Journal of Cleaner Production*, *48*, 54–64. doi:10.1016/j.jclepro.2012.09.039

Pazos, P., Cima, F., Kidd, J., Ringleb, S., Ayala, O., Gutierrez, K., & Kaipa, K. (2020). Enhancing Teamwork Skills Through an Engineering Service-learning Collaboration. *2020 ASEE Virtual Annual Conference Content Access, Virtual Online*, 1-6. 10.18260/1-2--34577

Qi, W. (2012). On the New Development of the Framework of Higher Education Qualifications in England, Wales and Northern Ireland (FHEQ) and Its Enlightenment. *China Higher Education Research*, *3*, 1–20.

QMUL. (2009). *The Queen Mary Statement of Graduate Attributes*. Available at http://www.arcs.qmul.ac.uk/media/arcs/docs/quality-assurance/QMULGraduate-Attributes.pdf

Quality Assurance agency (QAA). (2018). *The UK quality code for higher education*, https://www.qaa.ac.uk/en/quality-code

Sancho, P., Corral, R., Rivas, T., González, M. J., Chordi, A., & Tejedor, C. (2006). A blended learning experience for teaching microbiology. *American Journal of Pharmaceutical Education*, *70*(5), 1–16. doi:10.5688/aj7005120 PMID:17149449

Singhal, R., Kumar, A., Singh, H., Fuller, S., & Gill, S. S. (2021). Digital device-based active learning approach using virtual community classroom during the COVID-19 pandemic. *Computer Applications in Engineering Education*, *29*(5), 1007–1033. doi:10.1002/cae.22355

Sosniak, L. A. (1994). *Bloom's taxonomy* (L. W. Anderson, Ed.). Univ. Chicago Press.

Stenhouse, L. (1975). *Introduction to curriculum research and development*. Heinemann Educational.

UK GDPR. (2018). *The General Data Protection Regulation (GDPR) Guidance for members*. Available at: https://www.local.gov.uk/sites/default/files/documents/The%2BGeneral%2BProtection%2BData%2BRegulation%2B%28GDPR%29%2B-%2BGuidance%2Bfor%2BMembers.pdf

Yusuf, I., & Widyaningsih, S. W. (2020). Implementing E-Learning-Based Virtual Laboratory Media to Students' Metacognitive Skills. *International Journal of Emerging Technologies in Learning*, *15*(5), 1–12. doi:10.3991/ijet.v15i05.12029

Zeni, J. (1998). A guide to ethical issues and action research. *Educational Action Research*, *6*(1), 9–19. doi:10.1080/09650799800200053

Zuber-Skerritt, O. (Ed.). (2021). *Action research for change and development*. Routledge. doi:10.4324/9781003248491

## ADDITIONAL READING

Marinescu, D. C. (2022). *Cloud computing: Theory and practice*. Morgan Kaufmann.

Meletiadou, E. (2012). The impact of training adolescent EFL learners on their perceptions of peer assessment of writing. *RPLTL*, *3*(1), 240–251.

Meletiadou, E. (2021a). Exploring the impact of peer assessment on EFL students' writing performance. *IAFOR Journal of Education*, *9*(3), 77–95. doi:10.22492/ije.9.3.05

Meletiadou, E. (2021b). Opening Pandora's box: How does peer assessment affect EFL students' writing quality? *Languages*, *6*(3), 115. doi:10.3390/languages6030115

Meletiadou, E. (Ed.). (2023). *Handbook of Research on Fostering Social Justice Through Intercultural and Multilingual Communication*. IGI Global.

Meletiadou, E., & Tsagari, D. (2012). Investigating the attitudes of adolescent EFL learners towards peer assessment of writing. In D. Tsagari (Ed.), *Research on English as a foreign language in Cyprus* (Vol. 2, pp. 225–245). University of Nicosia Press.

Meletiadou, E., & Tsagari, D. (2014). An exploration of the reliability and validity of peer assessment of writing in secondary education. In D. Tsagari (Ed.), *Major trends in theoretical and applied linguistics 3* (pp. 235–250). De Gruyter Open Poland. doi:10.2478/9788376560915.p14

Meletiadou, E., & Tsagari, D. (2016). The washback effect of peer assessment on adolescent EFL learners in Cyprus. In D. Tsagari (Ed.), *Classroom-based assessment in L2 contexts*. Cambridge Scholars Publishing.

Wang, L., Ranjan, R., Chen, J., & Benatallah, B. (Eds.). (2017). *Cloud computing: methodology, systems, and applications*. CRC Press. doi:10.1201/b11149

## KEY TERMS AND DEFINITIONS

**Action Research:** Instructors uses this methodology to conduct investigations into their own professional practises to learn more about how students learn and how to better educate them.

**Cloud Computing:** Pay-as-you-go IT resources are made available on-demand over the Internet.

**Formative Assessment:** Monitor student learning to offer feedback that may be utilised by instructors to enhance their instruction as well as the student's learning, the purpose of formative assessment.

**Learner:** This word is used interchangeably with "student" and "participant."

**QMPLUS:** It is the online learning environment (OLE) used across the university (Queen Mary University of London) and is based on Moodle.

**Sustainable Learning:** With this approach to life and education students, teachers, schools as well as their surrounding communities may work together to create a more just, sustainable, and equal society.

**Think-Pair-Share:** Students work together to solve an issue or answer a question on a text they've been assigned.

## APPENDIX 1: DETAILED DESCRIPTION OF DATA GATHERING TOOLS

We have collected data using the various intervention tools described below to evaluate this action plan.

1. **Feedback:** We used different types of feedback: 1) weekly google survey form-based feedback after every lecture, 2) QMPlus-based mid-module feedback, 3) QMPlus-based final module feedback, and 4) alumni feedback. The following questions were included in the weekly Google survey form-based feedback (Questionnaire):

    a. Are you satisfied with the ideas presented in the online session that can be applied to your profession? (Please answer on a scale of 1-5)
    b. Is there anything more should say during this online session?
    c. Is there anything should remove from this session?

For this feedback, we have utilised the Traffic Light Model, which assisted us in evaluating teaching throughout the course's delivery and improve teaching practice in the future. Next, we used the following three questions for QMPlus-based mid-module feedback:

    a. What are the most beneficial aspects of this module?
    b. What changes could be made to this module to make it more helpful?
    c. Rate the module so far: (1 - Very dissatisfied, 2 - Dissatisfied, 3- Neutral, 4 - Satisfied, 5 - Very Satisfied)

QMPlus-based final module feedback have contained the standard questions as per QMUL norms. Alumni Feedback: This is a semester B module, which means that most students started work, internships, completing online certificates, or applying for a PhD in May or June. Through the cloud computing module, we have collected their opinions on how to improve their chances of achieving professional success. The questions on the Alumni Feedback form are as follows:

    a. Do you believe that the cloud computing module that has been made available to you includes beneficial ideas that may be applied to your professional success? (Please answer on a scale of 1-5)
    b. Have you completed online certifications in the most recent cloud computing tools and technologies with good scores?
    c. Have you successfully gained employment skills that will be beneficial to you in your future employment?
    d. Have you been offered the position, employment, or a research opportunity (PhD)?
    2. **Formative Assessments:** For each topic, we have utilised a QMPlus-based Q/A format, and students must respond to these questions within one week after receiving them. The quizzes we utilised throughout the online session were Mentimeter- or Kahoot-based and used for various objectives, including activating past knowledge and checking students' understanding to determine their level of knowledge, involvement, attendance and engagement. The following two examples (Figure 7 and Figure 8) show the use of Mentimeter or Kahoot-based quizzes for cloud computing module:

*Figure 7. An example shows the use of Kahoot-based quiz*

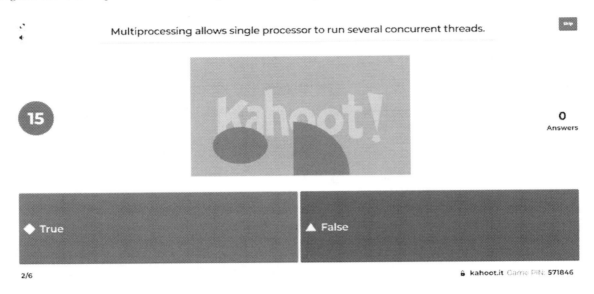

*Figure 8. An example shows the use of Mentimeter-based quiz*

3. **External Observations:** We have requested one of our colleagues to act as an external observer for online session and lab. The comments were collected using the usual teaching observation

Pro-forma, which we utilised in the second module of Postgraduate Certificate Academic Practice (PGCAP) at QMUL. i.e. Learning and Teaching in the Disciplines (Gill et al., 2023c).

4. **Summative Assessments:** We have evaluated the students individually (lab quiz after every lab) and in a group (to check their teamwork skills while doing a group project in a team).
5. **Reflective Log:** When implementing this action plan, we wanted to maintain a reflective log that will provide with the data we needed to enhance teaching practice in the future.
6. **VLE report and Analysis:** There are a variety of active learning activities that we have deployed on QMplus, including H5P-based videos, Blackboard-based online sessions, Q/A, lab quizzes, and different types of feedback (more details given in the assignment). We used this information to learn more about students' involvement, attendance, and engagement.
7. **Interview with Focus Groups:** Following the delivery of the module, we have done some interviews with focus groups to learn more about the areas that need to be improved.
8. **Give presentations and discussions with colleagues:** To showcase our findings inside the school, we have conducted presentations and seminars, as well as engage in discussions with colleagues who are teaching the same module at other institutions such as Imperial College London, University of Manchester and the University of Melbourne. These presentations & discussions have provided us with valuable feedback on this action research, which has helped to improve teaching practice for its sustainable future.

## APPENDIX 2: ADDRESSING ETHICAL CONCERNS

What are the risks?

- **Loss of anonymity:** Using a shared platform (such as Google Forms), students forms online groups depending on their preferences and programming skills.
- **Loss of confidentiality:** Every one of the class participants accesses to the participant's data, including both personal and educational information to make groups.
- **Potential victimization:** For example, a learner can decline to work in a team because of their differing educational backgrounds or cultures.
- **Distress:** Working in a team might cause stress or anxiety.
- **Embarrassment:** Keep an eye out for certain teams or members of specific teams.

How will you reduce these risks?
Gaining the informed consent of participants using:

- **Verbal information provided:** Every lab should begin with an ethical announcement outlining essential aspects, such as everyone accepting responsibility for preserving confidentiality. Every team's performance should be assessed weekly to ensure that they are on track to meet their goal. Individual work or the formation of new teams may be an option for students who are uncomfortable working in teams because of their academic qualifications, ethnicity or religion.

- **Information sheet:** All of the information on ethical challenges, data protection & confidentiality, and fair assignment of responsibilities is contained in this document. As part of the Data Protection and Confidentiality policy (GDPR), the information sheet specified that data records are handled in accordance with this policy. Only members of the team are able to view the details of other group mates as mentioned in BERA Guidelines. Following QMUL's research integrity standards, all individual data is maintained in accordance with the local ethical policy, and all acquired data is safeguarded using credentials (such as username and passwords).
- **Signed consent form:** In order to keep the zone of recognized behaviour intact, adhere to the instructions provided in the information sheet and join a specific group only if the individual has consented to do so.
- **Verbal consent:** All members of the group should get full equality.
- Participants will be informed about their right to withdraw at any time.

# Chapter 4
# Exploring Drivers and Barriers of Accounting Students' Motivation for Non-Financial Information

**Alexandra Domingos**
*Lisbon Accounting and Business School, Portugal & Instituto Politécnico de Lisboa, Portugal*

**Fábio Albuquerque**
https://orcid.org/0000-0001-8877-9634
*Lisbon Accounting and Business School, Portugal & Instituto Politécnico de Lisboa, Portugal*

**Ana Isabel Dias**
*Lisbon Accounting and Business School, Portugal & Instituto Politécnico de Lisboa, Portugal*

## ABSTRACT

*Recent developments related to non-financial information (NFI) reporting encourage the adoption of a long-term vision approach to sustainable development. In turn, the self-determination theory (SDT) describes which elements explain the students' motivation and how their skills can be better developed from their choices. Using NFI as the subject and the SDT as the theoretical framework, this chapter links both topics aiming to identify the types of students' motivation and for what specific interests are accounting students motivated to learn topics related to NFI. Data were gathered from a questionnaire. The results, using frequency and textual analyses, indicate a higher level of intrinsic motivation. Environmental and social matters are the topics of concern, while governance issues are absent. As an exploratory analysis, this chapter provides insights into how students of an accounting course are motivated to acquire skills in NFI reporting, which is particularly relevant to higher education institutions, professors, students, and organizations related to accountancy education.*

DOI: 10.4018/978-1-6684-6172-3.ch004

## INTRODUCTION

Recent efforts taken by the European Union (EU) and internationally recognised standard-setting bodies indicate that non-financial information (NFI) is of increasing relevance in the accounting field. For the EU case, we can point out the examples of the Non-Financial Reporting Directive (NFRD) and the Corporate Sustainability Reporting Directive (CSRD), in 2014 and 2021, respectively, with which the European Financial Reporting Advisory Group (EFRAG) has been providing support for the implementation of the EU legislation requirements. Furthermore, the recent work by the International Financial Reporting Standards (IFRS) Foundation, which led to the creation of the International Sustainability Standards Board (ISSB) and the first set of standards (in progress), the IFRS Sustainability Disclosure Standards, can illustrate the international developments in this area.

Therefore, the assessment of the motivational types and the subjects of interest related to the NFI may contribute to reinforcing and encouraging the relevant aspects seen as relevant from the students' perspective, as a path to improve the learning activities and environment in higher education institutions (HEIs). The self-determination theory (SDT) provides explanations behind the students' intrinsic and extrinsic motivations, as well as the reasons for their possible amotivation.

Considering the above-mentioned elements, the present chapter uses the NFI as the subject and the SDT as the theoretical framework to assess the types of students' motivation and for what specific interests are accounting students motivated to learn topics related to NFI in a Portuguese public HEI. There are two related objectives in linking these topics:

1. firstly, to identify the motivational types underlying this relevant theory in the educational context.
2. secondly, and considering the emergence of the NFI reporting in the accounting area, to identify the NFI subjects that are seen as relevant from the students' perspective.

The research is an exploratory analysis. To conduct this research, students were previously invited to attend an online conference on NFI reporting. Then, they were requested to answer a questionnaire, comprised of demographic variables and an open question on the students' motivation regarding the learning of topics related to the NFI reporting. To assess students' answers, frequency data complemented with textual analysis were performed.

The findings from this chapter indicate a higher level of intrinsic motivation for the learning of NFI topics. In this context, environmental and social matters are the specified topics of concern, due to personal and non-specified interests. Another finding to be highlighted is the absence of governance issues in the students' answers. Furthermore, some demographic characteristics seem to be also relevant for a better understanding of students' motivation and their main topics of interest.

The relevance of this research is associated with its scientific contribution to the accounting area since it has epistemological peculiarities that should be considered in the teaching and learning process. In addition, it is important to highlight the relevance of the understanding of the motivational types of students for the learning of NFI topics, which is still a research gap in this area. This has an important social and practical implication since this research allows HEIs, in general, and professors to plan the contents and learning strategies to encourage and explore the students' motivation for NFI learning in the academic environment. Despite specifically assessing accounting students, some findings may be used in other scientific areas. Furthermore, the analysis performed in this research can be replicated in the future.

In the development of this research, it was not found evidence of previous research that linked the accounting students' motivation to topics related to NFI reporting. Then, the main contribution of this chapter is to provide HEIs which offer accounting courses with some understanding of how their students are motivated to acquire skills in the NFI topics. In addition, accounting students may also benefit from the findings provided by this research, with the knowledge of their actions taken by HEIs to improve their motivations for the learning of topics related to NFI reporting, as a topic of increasing importance for the accounting profession.

The structure of this chapter is as follows. The next section presents the background with definitions and a brief discussion on the topic. Section three develops relevant literature. Section four presents the objectives and the proposed methodology, from which the analysis for this chapter was performed and the main findings discussed. Finally, the last section presents the conclusions from this research.

## BACKGROUND

In recent years, the role of accounting has been the target of several transformations, which required more than mere technical knowledge to the accounting professionals (Arquero & Fernández-Polvillo, 2019). The NFI reporting in the accounting area has gained growing relevance, being the object of some recent investigations (Carmo & Ribeiro, 2022; Kristofík et al., 2016; La Torre et al., 2018; Oberrauch, et al., 2021; Tarquinio & Posadas, 2020). The NFI reporting ensures complementarity with financial reporting, involving the dissemination of non-financial indicators (Cenar, 2020). Thus, it provides stakeholders with further information for decision-making, providing transparency and improving the development of a responsible approach to business (Esser et al., 2020). These responsible approaches, part of the sustainable development perspectives including social and corporate responsibility, can only be embedded in our societies through education and learning (UNESCO, 2014).

Cenar (2020) argues that the improvement of public services in education is a part of the organizational development. The author proposes the inclusion of sustainable reporting matters by ensuring the complementarity of financial reporting, which involves the connection of schools with the evolution of educational systems, as well as the dissemination of both financial and non-financial indicators. For instance, the environmental education provided by HEIs has been seen with an important impact on the training and preparation of future generations for a "green society" (Boca & Saraçlı, 2019; Saraite-Sariene et al., 2020). One of the HEIs' missions usually involves the development of sustainability skills, which enable students to act as "agents of change" in the future professional environment (Oberrauch et al., 2021).

Students' progression to higher education occurs for a variety of reasons. These reasons influence how and why individuals learn, as well as their academic performance (Byrne & Flood, 2005). Motivation may become an important indicator of all the factors that should be considered in the teaching-learning process (Teixeira et al., 2015) as it has a significant impact on students' learning behaviour (Byrne & Flood, 2005). The knowledge of these factors can promote changes for what needs to be improved and maintain what is being done correctly (Steinmayr et al., 2019). Teixeira et al. (2015) state that the literature reports that extrinsic motivations such as career and academic reasons are often at the top of students' motivations to enter higher education.

The motivation of higher education students has been increasing its relevance not only in the scientific and academic context but also in the organizational one (Ribeiro et al., 2019). The literature review also shows some research that has been specifically assessing the motivations of students enrolled in accounting courses (Arquero & Fernández-Polvillo, 2019; Byrne & Flood, 2005; Byrne et al., 2012; Colares & Amorim, 2020; Ho et al., 2021; Leal et al., 2013; Souza & Miranda, 2019; Teixeira et al., 2015; Yudi et al., 2020). In the higher education context, the self-determination theory (SDT) is one of the theories commonly used to study and explain students' motivation (Deci & Ryan, 2008; Howard et al., 2021).

Developed by Deci and Ryan (1985), the SDT considers motivation as intrinsically or extrinsically oriented, a *continuum* that ranges from lack of motivation to external and internal motivation. According to these authors, students develop their skills better when they derive pleasure and are satisfied with their choices. Despite the existence of various theories about motivation and, more specifically, academic motivation, researchers all over the world have been using the SDT theoretical framework to measure intrinsic and extrinsic students' motivation with different samples and educational contexts (Colares & Amorim, 2020; Ho et al., 2021; Leal et al., 2013; Souza & Miranda, 2019).

To support the objectives initially proposed, the literature review presented in the next section was divided into two subsections. The first provides an overview of the NFI through its recent developments, as well as from the researchers' perspectives on its relevance and the main elements incorporated by this concept. The second one is specifically dedicated to the theoretical aspects behind the students' motivations to learn and, more specifically, the SDT.

## LITERATURE REVIEW

### Non-Financial Information and Agents Involved

The NFI reporting is an ongoing concept, particularly developed in the latest years (EFRAG, 2021; Erkens et al., 2015; European Comission, 2014; Kristofík et al., 2016; La Torre et al., 2018; Tarquinio & Posadas, 2020; UNCTAD, 2019). NFI presents itself with a special role because it promotes respect for human rights, is focused on creating value with the optimal use of human, material, financial and natural capital, and supports the reliability of financial reporting (Cenar, 2020).

In the literature, expressions such as "non-financial information", "corporate social reporting", "corporate sustainability reporting" or "environmental, social and governance (ESG)" are commonly used to describe types of disclosures or reporting that differ from the traditional financial measures and/or are released through non-traditional channels of communication (Erkens et al., 2015; Tarquinio & Posadas, 2020). Tarquinio and Posadas (2020) found 28 definitions of NFI, provided mostly by researchers from Europe and the United States of America, due to the lack of common legal regulation. ESG is particularly viewed as the companies' engagement in environmental, social, and ethical action, as part of their corporate social responsibility and ethical behaviour (Chouaibi et al., 2022), generally combined to shape the meaning of NFI (Tarquinio & Posadas, 2020). The distinction between financial and NFI is also not consensual, given that financial reporting also includes environmental information (IFRS Foundation, 2020). On the other hand, NFI embraces topics on the impact that the businesses' activities may have on the environment and society, as well as how companies are reacting to the risks of climate change and using the related opportunities (Demaria & Rigot, 2021; Haller et al., 2017; Melloni et al., 2017; Santos & Rodrigues, 2021; TCFD, 2017).

Historically, the literature has simply evidenced two main types of reporting, mandatory and voluntary (Bushman et al., 2004; Cho & Patten, 2007; Erkens et al., 2015; Francis et al., 2008; Larrinaga et al.,

2008; La Torre et al., 2018; Mata et al., 2018; Mohammed, 2018; Santos & Rodrigues, 2021). However, the inclusion of NFI as voluntary information is not consensual (Cormier & Magnan, 2007; Sullivan & Gouldson, 2012). ESG components, for instance, usually mentioned as NIF, have been included as part of both types of reporting, with the information regarding environmental and social aspects mostly disclosed as part of voluntary reporting (La Torre et al., 2018; Tarquinio & Posadas, 2020), and the governance information is generally seen as a mandatory one given it is more regulated than the previous topics (Melloni et al., 2017). In the same sense, the distinction between financial and NFI is also controversial, given that financial reporting also includes environmental information (IFRS Foundation, 2020) and, on the other hand, NFI embraces topics on the impact that the businesses' activities may have on the environment and society, and how companies are reacting to the risks of climate change and using the related opportunities. Notwithstanding, this characterization may be important in terms of presentation to stakeholders. Since financial reporting is traditionally presented as mandatory financial reporting, NFI is being presented in one or more reports, such as in financial (including management), sustainability, environmental, separate or integrated reports, as well as in the entities' websites (Carmo & Ribeiro, 2022; Smith, 2014).

Despite the nature of voluntary reporting, some working groups have been contributing to global efforts to promote the reliability and comparability of reports, through organizations that are traditionally linked to financial reporting such as the IFRS Foundation, which supports and oversees the International Accounting Standards Board (IASB), Financial Accounting Foundation (FAF), which supports and oversees the Financial Accounting Standards Board (FASB), Securities Exchange Commission (SEC), and the G20 Financial Stability Board (FSB) (United Nations Conference on Trade and Development [UNCTAD], 2020). Through these organizations or even independently, some guidance to report NFI has been issued, within frameworks or sets of standards. Examples include the frameworks by the Integrated Reporting Council (IIRC), as well as the standards by the Global Reporting Initiative (GRI) and the Climate Disclosure Standards Board (CDSB), which is based on the recommendations of the Task Force on Climate-related Financial Disclosures (TCFD), as well as the standards by the Sustainability Accounting Standards Board (SASB) and the International Sustainability Standards Board (ISSB), which are supported and overseen by the Value Reporting Foundation (VRF) and the IFRS Foundation, respectively. In 2021, VRF and CDSB were consolidated into the IFRS Foundation.

In the context of the EU, companies are more prominently encouraged to disclose NFI since 2014, with the issuance of the NFRD 2014/95/EU, which amends the Accounting Directive 2013/34/EU. EU (2014) states the need to improve undertakings' disclosure of social and environmental information and exposes the rules on disclosure of non-financial and diversity information. These disclosures are of mandatory compliance by large public-interest companies with more than 500 employees, to periods that had its beginning in 2018, for the information relating to the 2017 financial year. Under the requirements of the NFRD, those companies must publish a non-financial statement, which should be included in the management report, with information related to, at least, environmental matters, social and employee-related matters, respect for human rights, anti-corruption, and bribery matters, following for each matter a description of the policies, outcomes, and risks.

In Portugal, the NFRD was transposed in the Decree-law 89/2017 and follows the alternative approaches to the NFI reporting provided in that Directive. This flexibility of the NFRD to use alternative frameworks or set of standards for the NFI reporting, presented in multiple channels, allows companies to act, disclose and report what may be considered as an artefact of managerial actions (Dumay, 2016; La Torre et al., 2018).

Accounting education has been changing over the last decades to be focused less on rules and more on principles and concepts (Heffes, 2008). Nowadays, educators and professionals of accounting are facing new challenges as NFI is taking its place in the world of businesses. The students' perceptions about topics of NFI may influence their willingness to accept NFI reporting as part of their academic curriculum.

More recently, the European Commission (2021) adopted a proposal for a CSRD, which would amend the requirements of the NFRD. The proposal extends the scope to all large companies and all companies listed on regulated markets (except listed micro-enterprises), requires the assurance of reported information, introduces more detailed reporting requirements, and a requirement to report according to mandatory EU sustainability reporting standards. The proposal for CSRD aims to build on and contribute to international sustainability reporting initiatives, such as GRI, IIRC, SASB, CDSB and CDP, and TCFD. With this development, the EFRAG has widened its scope of action and incorporated EFRAG Sustainability Reporting Board, to develop European Sustainability Reporting Standards, which will have to be applied by those companies.

As previously mentioned, alongside the developments within the EU, the IFRS Foundation created the ISSB, which will work with the IASB to develop IFRS Sustainability Disclosure Standards. Together with the VRF, the CDSB, and the World Economic Forum, supported by IOSCO, ISSB will publish the requirements related to general sustainability and climate-related disclosures. These initiatives are intended to create a global sustainability disclosure standard-setter to solve this lack in the financial markets (International Financial Reporting Standards [IFRS] Foundation, 2021). Following, in 2022 it was announced that IASB and ISSB, which integrate the IFRS Foundation, will use the principles and concepts from the integrated reporting framework in their standard setting.

The recent changes related to NFI reporting suggest that accounting students have important challenges and a role in improving entities' reporting (Cenar, 2020) since they represent future accountants. Liu et al. (2018), for instance, studied the latest developments in this field from the perspective of accounting professionals and underlined the need for preparers to review their approach to environmental accounting practices to encourage the adoption of a long-term vision approach to sustainable development. An individual characteristic that Krasodomska et al. (2020) identified as distinctive in accountant professionals is that corporate social reporting significantly differs between those who had participated and those who did not, in training related to non-financial reporting. In the education area, Vukelic (2022) also determined that student teachers who have attended courses of education for sustainable development express higher levels of intention to implement it. As an element of Sustainable Development Goals (SDG), the principles of responsible management education (PRME) would suggest that a key challenge for business schools is to prepare students to engage with and drive this changing context (Pizzi et al. 2022; Storey et al., 2017; Tyran, 2017).

## Motivation to Learn and the Self-Determination Theory

Motivation refers to the energy, persistence, and intention that an individual has, i.e., what mobilizes a person to perform a certain activity (Deci & Ryan, 2008; Ryan & Deci, 2000). In academic terms, motivation is a concept that encompasses different connotations or constructs significantly related to learning and educational development and which has generated several research perspectives.

Deci and Ryan's (1985) SDT is one of the best-known theories about human motivation and personality, being based on social psychology and it has been applied and validated in diverse ways and domains (Ryan & Deci, 2000) namely in an academic environment of traditional/face-to-face learning. SDT supports the idea that individuals, in addition to being guided by their needs for autonomy and thus determining their behaviour, also seek ways to acquire skills and positive relationships in social relationships. This theory proposes that all individuals have an innate propensity to develop their determination and that they engage in activities that provide them with the satisfaction of basic psychological needs: competence, autonomy, and relationship.

The SDT's taxonomy of motivation presents a *continuum* of development of self-determination (Ryan & Deci, 2020), subdivided into three categories: (i) amotivation; (ii) regulations by extrinsic motivation (external regulation, introjection, identification, integration); and (iii) regulations by intrinsic motivation. There is a passage from a more self-determined motivation (intrinsic motivation) to partially self-determined (e.g., introjection) and finally to an absence of self-determination (amotivation). Thus, according to SDT theory, motivation should not be viewed from a unidimensional perspective. Instead, the above three dimensions of motivation need to be examined as a multidimensional concept, as illustrated in Figure 1 (Ryan & Deci, 2000).

*Figure 1. SDT's Taxonomy of Motivation*
Source: Ryan and Deci (2020, p. 2)

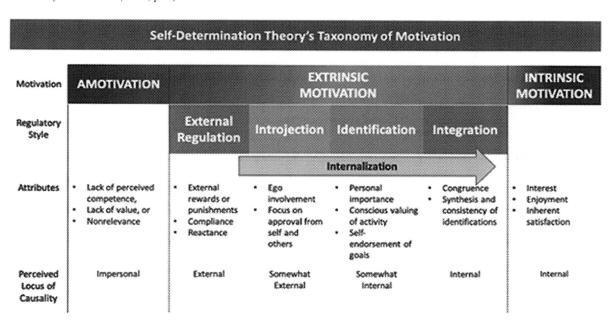

Intrinsic motivation drives actions for personal interest, positive experience, and satisfaction. In the context of learning it is affected by the student's satisfaction and enjoyment of studying. Intrinsically motivated individuals voluntarily participate in an activity without experiencing external or internal pressures to do so and without expecting rewards (Deci & Ryan, 1985). In contrast, extrinsic motivation stimulates actions due to external sources, such as obtaining rewards or pressures arising from work, competition or even obtaining the approval of others. When compared to intrinsic motivation, extrinsic motivation is less autonomous because it is driven by internally defined goals related to external reward or punishment (Ryan & Deci, 2000). Deci and Ryan (1985) view extrinsic motivation as a multidimensional construct, as well. Four types of extrinsic motivation are defined in the SDT theory (Ryan & Deci, 2020): *external regulation, introjection, identification,* and *integration.*

*External regulation* is the most representative type of extrinsic motivation. It refers to the involvement in an activity to gain rewards or to avoid punishment. This is the least autonomous form of motivation, guided by external contingencies. The second type of extrinsic motivation, *introjection* corresponds to doing something because you pressure yourself to do it. Behavior is regulated by the internal rewards of self-esteem, success, and avoidance of anxiety, shame, or guilt over failure. In academic activities, this type of regulation often takes the form of ego involvement (Ryan & Deci, 2020), in which self-esteem depends on outcomes, resulting in "internally controlled" regulation. At this stage, behavior is not yet self-determined, but the individual is beginning to internalize the reasons for her/his actions. *Identification* refers to doing something because you decided to do it, with the individual showing a high degree of willingness to act. In *Integration*, the individual does not recognize and identify only with the value of the activity but also considers it coherent with other interests. It refers to the most autonomous form of extrinsic motivation.

Although intrinsic motivation, amotivation, and extrinsic motivations – external, introjection, and identification – are the most applied in SDT investigations (Howard et al., 2021) another type of extrinsic motivation (integration) has also been developed in the literature.

When a person does not have either intrinsic or extrinsic motivation, is considered amotivated (Ryan & Deci, 2020). The authors present the concept of amotivation when individuals do not seem to have specific purposes and goals. Amotivated individuals simply do not demonstrate the intent to engage in an activity.

According to Ryan and Deci (2020), autonomous extrinsic motivations (identification and integration) share with intrinsic motivation the quality of being highly volitional but differ particularly in the fact that intrinsic motivation is based on interest and pleasure (people adopt the behaviors because they find them engaging or even fun) while both extrinsic motivations are based on a sense of worth – people see activities as valuable even if they are not enjoyable.

Linking these types of motivation to the academic environment, on one hand, an intrinsically motivated student engages in activities that interest him freely and spontaneously, without the need for rewards, engaging simply because that activity is enjoyable and satisfying to him/her. On the other hand, an extrinsically motivated student will perform an activity not out of interest but because has to achieve a goal, earn a reward, or even avoid a punishment (Leal et al., 2013). Amotivation, which is quite common in classroom environments, can result from a lack of interest and perceived competence to perform. According to Ryan and Deci (2020), amotivation has been a strong negative predictor of engagement, learning, and well-being.

Therefore, as motivation can be perceived as an internal and/or external stimulus that drives the desire to act, a more specific discussion can be found in the literature about why students are motivated to study accounting, to create a successful educational and professional environment (Ho et al., 2021).

Previous studies suggest that students are motivated by intrinsic motivational factors, such as personal development through increased knowledge (Arquero et al., 2009; Byrne & Flood, 2005; Byrne et al., 2012; Leal et al., 2013), the broadening of horizons and new challenges (Arquero et al., 2009), intellectual and personal development (Byrne & Flood, 2005; Byrne et al., 2012; Colares & Amorim, 2020; Teixeira et al., 2015; Yudi et al., 2020), personal interest (Colares & Amorim, 2020; Umar, 2014; Yudi et al., 2020), as well as a desire for better education and vocational interest (Arquero et al., 2009).

Other studies have concluded that higher education accounting students were largely motivated by extrinsic motivations of prestige and job security (Umar, 2014; Yudi et al., 2020), future financial rewards, and career prospects (Arquero et al., 2009; Arquero & Fernández-Polvillo, 2019; Byrne & Flood, 2005; Byrne et al., 2012), career focus (Teixeira et al., 2015) and obtaining a diploma (Ho et al., 2021; Leal et al., 2013) and a better salary (Umar, 2014; Yudi et al. 2020).

Third parties may influence accounting learning such as parents, however, other relatives or the employer were also extrinsic motivational influencers found in Colares and Amorim (2020), Ho et al. (2021), and Umar (2014). These findings are not aligned with those by Yudi et al. (2020), which have not identified this influence.

It seems that most studies have pointed out that both intrinsic and extrinsic motivation are responsible for motivating students to learn accounting (Arquero et al., 2009; Byrne & Flood, 2005; Colares & Amorim, 2020; Leal et al., 2013; Umar, 2014), contrary to what was found by Arquero and Fernández-Polvillo (2019), who concluded that students in this area are substantially less vocational and much more attracted to external factors than others in different areas.

Regarding greater or lesser motivational autonomy, studies have concluded that there is a decrease in motivation by accounting students that is shown throughout the course (Carmo et al., 2012; Colares & Amorim, 2020; Leal et al., 2013; Souza & Miranda, 2019). On the other hand, Souza and Miranda (2019) found that "student and worker" are more motivated than "only students".

Ho et al. (2021) found that the intrinsic motivation of altruism is positively correlated with the extrinsic motivation of social pleasure, indicating that those who enjoy a social life, as well as the social environment, are willing to help others and contribute to society.

As for the influence of age and gender, previous studies have shown that a higher level of intrinsic motivation is associated with students in older age groups, females and in the initial periods of the course (Colares & Amorim, 2020). For the authors, this conclusion makes sense, since more experienced and older people usually already have greater knowledge and certainty about their decisions, which would lead to a higher level of intrinsic motivation, while young people often make decisions in an incipient way. In this line of reasoning, Ho et al. (2021) concluded that female students have greater intrinsic motivation and external regulation, while men have a higher level of amotivation. On the other hand, Yudi et al. (2020) conclude that gender does not have a significant relationship with accounting professional qualification.

The students' perceptions from different areas of specialization related to sustainability have also been an object of investigation, considering the students' attitudes and behaviour towards the environment. Some related factors found are environmental importance, concerns, and culture, as well as participation, voluntary action, and recycling influence (Boca & Saraçlı. 2019). Thus, the main reasons that lead students to enter courses related to sustainability are intrinsic factors (Oberrauch et al., 2021).

The next section presents the empirical study proposed for this chapter, including the objectives, methodology, as well as results analysis and discussion of the main findings.

## EMPIRICAL STUDY

### Objectives and Methodology

This chapter aims to identify the types of motivation and for what specific interests are accounting students motivated when learning topics of NFI. More specifically, this research intends to provide the answers to the following research questions (RQ):

- **RQ1**: What types of motivation explain the accounting students' interest in the topics related to NFI?
- **RQ2**: What are the specific interests in the topics related to ESG that motivate accounting students to learn more about it?

For this purpose, this research explores the answers provided by accounting students to an open question, included in a questionnaire, on their motivation for NFI, taking the opportunity from the latest development in the EU on this matter. Despite the absence of consensus in the literature, the UN General Assembly adopted a new global sustainable development framework: the 2030 Agenda for Sustainable Development, in which the ESG underlying elements were proposed as a reference for classifying the main topics of NFI. Additionally, the term ESG is frequently used as a proxy for both that concept and the overall voluntary information (Arif et al., 2021; Mariia Evdokimova & Kuzubov, 2021; Turzo et al., 2022).

To identify the elements behind the RQ1, the open answers were read and subsequently classified, through a previously proposed codification, into one of the following types of motivation, as a summary of the SDT:

- "**0**" (**no answer cases**).
- "**1**" (**amotivation**): this classification was proposed for those cases in which students presented none or low levels of motivation to learn more about the topics related to NFI.
- "**2**" (**extrinsic motivation**): this classification was proposed for those cases in which the main concern with learning presented by students was centred on professional development motivated by the new reporting requirements related to NFI.
- "**3**" (**intrinsic motivation**): this classification was proposed for those cases in which the main concern was the specific content of matters related to NFI, including the residual cases in which students also mentioned some concerns, but not as the central one, regarding the learning of reporting requirements.

It is worth mentioning that, according to the SDT, extrinsic motivation could be divided into more categories since some aspects are somewhat internal, such as identification and integration, but not classified as intrinsic motivation. Notwithstanding, and considering the significant difficulty of properly distinguishing those specific classifications through the students' answers based on an open question, as proposed in the questionnaire object of this research, this research has only classified the students' answers into two types of motivations, namely into extrinsic and intrinsic ones.

Whenever the answers were classified as "3" (**intrinsic motivation**), the next step was to classify them into additional subgroups, to accomplish the objective behind the RQ2:

- **E (environmental)**: this classification was proposed for those cases in which students expressed concerns regarding **the environmental aspects of NFI**, through the possible use of words and expressions such as "environment", "resources", "climate change", "planet Earth", "save the world", "pollution", and similar.
- **S (social)**: this classification was proposed for those cases in which students expressed concerns regarding **the social aspects of NFI**, through the possible use of words and expressions such as "people", "culture", "poverty", "inequalities", "gender"; "opportunities"; "immigrants", "refugees", and similar.
- **G (governance)**: this classification was proposed for those cases in which students expressed concerns regarding **the governance aspects of NFI**, using words and expressions such as "management"; "board", "executives", "auditing", "control systems", "processes"; "companies", and similar.
- **O (others/not specified)**: as a residual codification, this classification was proposed for those cases in which students did not express any specific concerns regarding the previous topics besides their interests.

A combination of these classifications is possible for those cases in which students mentioned more than one issue of ESG matters.

The sample for this research, subsequently detailed, was comprised of students in the second and third (last) year of the accounting degree at the Lisbon Accounting and Business School (ISCAL). ISCAL is a faculty of the Polytechnic Institute of Lisbon. ISCAL is a highly traditional school of accounting in Portugal. Its history can be found in the Trade Class ("Aula do Comércio", in the Portuguese language), launched by the Marquis of Pombal more than 260 years ago (Estatutos da Aula do Comércio, 1759).

Previously to the survey distribution, students were invited to attend an online conference within the last quarter of the Spring semester of the academic year 2021/2022 (more specifically, on 30 April 2022). At this conference, the topic of NFI was lectured by two specialists: a professor at ISCAL with a recent Ph.D. in this area of investigation and an Audit and Assurance partner of a Big-4 audit firm. The intention was to provide two presentations of about thirty minutes by each invited speaker covering this topic with different approaches: a more academic (by the Ph.D. professor) and a more professional one (by the partner auditor).

The conference was entitled "Reporting: An integrated thinking", and the presentations by the invited speakers were specifically entitled as follows: "A look at the past and future of reporting" and "From voluntary to mandatory information: From Nice to Must-Have in Europe", respectively. To sum up, the past, present, as well as perspectives of the accounting profession as regards NFI, including the latest developments on this subject within the EU, were discussed during the conference. The following link provides further details on the conference:

https://www.iscal.ipl.pt/eventos/seminario-reporting-integrated-thinking

The conference was organised by a group of professors from ISCAL, including the accounting course director, and moderated by a professor at ISCAL. During the conference session, students were encouraged to ask questions to the invited speakers. Based on the zoom report, 188 students attended the session. Subsequently, an online survey was created on Google Docs and the link was distributed to the students via Moodle, and 103 valid answers were obtained, which represents 55% of the students who attended the conference.

When providing the answers to RQ1 and RQ2, demographic variables were also included in the questionnaire and will be used to potentially identify different patterns amongst students concerning the following five characteristics:

- **By gender**: male, female, and other options/I would rather not answer.
- **By age**: younger than (or equal to) 21 years old *versus* older than 21 years old.
- **By students' occupation**: only student *versus* student and worker simultaneously.
- **By stage in the course**: second-year student *versus* third-year student.

As an exploratory analysis, this research will provide the results through frequency analysis.

Additionally, for the assessment of RQ2, a textual analysis tool (the {L}exos) is used to identify the most frequent words mentioned by students to express their main concerns regarding the topics related to NFI. Besides providing the counting of the words and the most frequent ones, the {L}exos builds word clouds. As usual in these processes, some of the most frequent words have no meaning for research purposes. Then, those words must be classified as "stop words" and, subsequently, removed from the analysis. The {L}exos has no automatic process, requesting users to identify those words. Therefore, a judgment must be made to exclude them. For this research, the most common abbreviations were excluded, such as articles, adverbs (mostly, conjunctive adverbs), determiners, numbers, prepositions, pronouns, and the verb "to be" and "to have" in their different forms, and modal verbs. On the other hand, adjectives and some adverbs were kept, as they could express different feelings of students as regards the topics on NFI.

It is also worth mentioning that students' answers were previously translated into the English language for this analysis, having in mind the importance of preserving the feelings and, simultaneously, the consistency amongst the words used in the students' original statements. 824 words and 4,926 characters (including spaces) were assessed through the {L}exos. After excluding the "stop words", 386 words and 3,149 characters (excluding spaces) were kept, which means that less than half of the words, but almost two-thirds of the characters, remained.

Following, the next subsection presents the analysis of the results obtained, based on the methodological approach proposed for this research.

## Results Analysis

The purpose of this subsection is to present the obtained results.

Table 1 provides the figures on the types of motivations in number and percentage, with a breakdown by gender, age, location of residence, students' occupation, and stage in the course, aiming to provide answers to RQ1.

*Table 1. Types of motivations in number and percentages by total and subgroups (RQ1)*

| Types of Motivations | In Number | | | | | In Percentage | | | | |
|---|---|---|---|---|---|---|---|---|---|---|
| | 0 | 1 | 2 | 3 | Total | 0 | 1 | 2 | 3 | Total |
| Total | 6 | 9 | 21 | 67 | 103 | 6 | 9 | 20 | 65 | 100 |
| **By gender** | | | | | | | | | | |
| Male | 0 | 1 | 10 | 20 | 31 | 0 | 3 | 32 | 65 | 100 |
| Female | 5 | 8 | 10 | 46 | 69 | 7 | 12 | 14 | 67 | 100 |
| Other options/I would rather not answer* | 1 | 0 | 1 | 1 | 3 | 33 | 0 | 33 | 33 | 100 |
| **By age** | | | | | | | | | | |
| Younger than (or equal to) 21 years old | 2 | 2 | 16 | 44 | 64 | 3 | 3 | 25 | 69 | 100 |
| Older than 21 years old | 4 | 7 | 5 | 23 | 39 | 10 | 18 | 13 | 59 | 100 |
| **By students' occupation** | | | | | | | | | | |
| Only students | 2 | 5 | 13 | 45 | 65 | 3 | 8 | 20 | 69 | 100 |
| Student and worker | 4 | 4 | 8 | 22 | 38 | 11 | 11 | 21 | 58 | 100 |
| **By stage in the course** | | | | | | | | | | |
| Second-year student | 3 | 5 | 8 | 23 | 39 | 8 | 13 | 21 | 59 | 100 |
| Third-year student | 3 | 4 | 13 | 44 | 64 | 5 | 6 | 20 | 69 | 100 |

Note: (1) Considering the low representativeness, this will not be assessed.

Globally, non-answers and amotivations represent the lowest level of cases, with 15% of the total, followed by extrinsic motivation (20%) and, finally, intrinsic motivation (65%). This means that about two-thirds of students are intrinsically interested in matters related to NFI. Some examples of phrases that indicate extrinsic and intrinsic motivations based on the students' answers are provided below:

- Extrinsic motivations:
    - *"For professional reasons"*
    - *"To finish the course"*
    - *"Be up to date and on top of changes made to financial reporting"*
    - *"Importance that financial reporting will have in the professional area"*
    - *"I believe it is a new responsibility of the accountant, and for the difficult job market it is important to be informed to make a difference."*
    - *"The world is increasingly global, and more and more users of financial information want to know the company's non-financial information in order to align values, etc."*
- Intrinsic motivations:
    - *"My desire to learn"*
    - *"Improve my personal character"*
    - *"Interest in new cultures"*
    - *"I think all the additional information we learn is important"*
    - *"For the sake of global equality, the discussion of these issues leads to global equality thinking and looking for solutions to this."*

- *"I think this subject is quite important. I endorse these themes and I think it fits in well with my philosophy of life."*
- *"As the latest generations care about the common good, between communities and between communities and the environment, I am no exception. Have a huge concern for the next and the environment. Since companies are the entities most responsible for the consumption of natural resources and consequently for pollution, it makes perfect sense to report information related to these topics."*

However, some relevant differences may be found when the groups of analysis are assessed.

The non-answers and amotivations cases reach the maximum of 28% for students older than 21 years old, followed by the students that work and study simultaneously (22%), in the middle of the course (21%) and female students (19%).

By gender, the difference in percentage points (16) between males (3%) and females (19%) students for the non-answers and amotivations cases are significantly compensated by the figures for extrinsic motivations, where males reached almost one-third of cases (32%) *versus* the 14% found for the females. Therefore, there were no relevant differences to point out by gender for the analysis of intrinsic motivation (65% and 67%, respectively).

By age, the 22 percentage points of difference between younger (6%) and older students (28%) have a two-fold explanation: the higher level of both extrinsic and intrinsic motivations identified for younger students, who presented 25% and 69% of answers recorded for those cases, respectively. This may be compared with 13% and 59% of answers, respectively, found for older students.

By students' occupation and stage in the course, the differences in percentage points (10) observed between subgroups for the non-answers and amotivations cases are almost totally compensated within the intrinsic motivations. In this context, students who do not work and at the end of the course (69% in both cases) present a higher level of answers for this type of motivation when compared with the opposite group, namely those students who simultaneously work and are in the middle of the course (58% and 59%, respectively).

The answers classified as intrinsic motivation were subsequently assessed to identify the students' specific interests in the topics related to ESG. Table 2 provides the figures on these matters in number and percentage, with a breakdown by gender, age, place of residence, students' occupation, and stage in the course, aiming to provide answers to RQ2.

*Table 2. Specific interests in the topics related to ESG in number and percentages by total and subgroups (RQ2)*

| Interests in the Topics Related to ESG | In Number ||||| In Percentage |||||
|---|---|---|---|---|---|---|---|---|---|---|
|  | E | S | E-S | O | Total | E | S | E-S | O | Total |
| **Total** | 7 | 7 | 9 | 44 | 67 | 10 | 10 | 13 | 66 | 100 |
| **By gender** | | | | | | | | | | |
| Male | 2 | 2 | 1 | 15 | 20 | 10 | 10 | 5 | 75 | 100 |
| Female | 5 | 5 | 8 | 28 | 46 | 11 | 11 | 17 | 61 | 100 |
| Other options/I would rather not answer* | 0 | 0 | 0 | 1 | 1 | 0 | 0 | 0 | 100 | 100 |
| **By age** | | | | | | | | | | |
| Younger than (or equal to) 21 years old | 1 | 6 | 5 | 32 | 44 | 2 | 14 | 11 | 73 | 100 |
| Older than 21 years old | 6 | 1 | 4 | 12 | 23 | 26 | 4 | 17 | 52 | 100 |
| **By students' occupation** | | | | | | | | | | |
| Only students | 2 | 6 | 4 | 33 | 45 | 4 | 13 | 9 | 73 | 100 |
| Student and worker | 5 | 1 | 5 | 11 | 22 | 23 | 5 | 23 | 50 | 100 |
| **By stage in the course** | | | | | | | | | | |
| Second-year student | 2 | 1 | 1 | 19 | 23 | 9 | 4 | 4 | 83 | 100 |
| Third-year student | 5 | 6 | 8 | 25 | 44 | 11 | 14 | 18 | 57 | 100 |

**Note**: (1) Considering the low representativeness, this will not be assessed.

Globally, personal reasons or no specific interests were indicated by about two-thirds of students (66%).

Regarding the concepts that underly the acronym ESG, both the social and environmental issues component comprises 10% of the answers (or 20% of the total answers at total), which can be summed to 13% of the answers when those concepts are considered together. Then, one-third of the answers were specifically related to these themes in the context of intrinsic motivation, which means that none of the answers indicated specific interests in the issues related to governance.

By students' characteristics, a non-specific interest was particularly identified in the subgroup of students in the middle of the course, reaching 83%. Oppositely, the students who are also workers, older, and at the end of the course were the ones that provided information as regards specific interests in their answers, which may indicate a higher level of knowledge of the issues related to ESG matters associated with these characteristics. Further, there is a slight difference between females (61%) and males (75%), which is also interesting to highlight, suggesting a stronger attitude toward taking a position by female students. Some examples of intrinsic motivation phrases with no-specific interest are provided below:

- *"My motivations are linked to greater learning of various topics and acquisition of knowledge for the future."*
- *"My will to learn"*
- *"Improve my personal character"*
- *"Gain knowledge in different areas"*
- *"It is enriching"*
- *"I'm interested in this area"*

- *"It is an important subject for learning"*

Finally, regarding specific interest cases, environmental issues are of relevance for older students as well as workers, reaching about 25% of the cases. Some examples of phrases that indicate specific interest in social and environmental issues, including both at the same time, are provided below:

- **Social issues**:
    - *"Learn more about the world and the various cultures and facts about these cultures"*
    - *"I am interested in new cultures"*
    - *"It is important that everyone has the basic needs"*
    - *"I think it's important for our culture and personal training. We are not all the same, and the knowledge of the difference between equity and equality is essential."*
- **Environmental issues:**
    - *"I think it's important for companies to be sustainable and act in a way that minimizes their environmental impact."*
    - *"Environmental issues"*
    - *"Sustainability"*
    - *"The motivation that led me to want to learn more about topics related to the reporting of non-financial information is the fact that, at this moment, non-financial information is essential due to the little time that human beings still have to be able to reverse climate change and the negative environmental impact that it has had on the planet."*
- **Social and environmental issues together**:
    - *"My motivations are linked to better learning about non-financial information such as the environment and being a global citizen."*
    - *"Environmental and social issues are extremely important and there should be more interest in this subject for a long time."*
    - *"More and more younger generations are concerned about the common good, between communities and between communities and the environment, I am no exception. I have a huge concern for others and the environment. Since companies are the entities most responsible for the consumption of natural resources and consequently for pollution, it makes perfect sense to report information related to these topics."*
    - *"We have to think about future generations."*
    - *"Non-financial information is very important for us to understand where a company contributes to the world. What motivates me is the fact that we see it every day as a different catastrophe, and those who have everything they need must be aware that they are very privileged and that they need to help."*

Following, Figure 2 provides a word cloud to illustrate the words commonly used by the students regarding their motivations for learning topics related to NFI. Four interactions were performed and subsequently selected to include a major number of more frequent words identified.

*Figure 2. Word cloud based on the students' answers to the open question*

The words "more" and "important" were the most used, followed by "world" and "information", with 12 and 9 cases, respectively. Then, "learn" and "non-financial" appeared 8 times. As related to the previous ones, the terms "social" (6), "importance" (5), "know" (5), "knowledge" (4), "growing" (4), "future" (4), learning" (3), and "understand" (3) may be used as complementary. The same is applied for the set of words, such as "issues" (5), "topic" (4), "topics" (4), as well as "area" (3), and "part" (3), usually included in the same context by students to justify their motivation.

As previously evidenced, most of the words previously mentioned were used to explain both extrinsic and intrinsic motivation in a general way (in most of the cases) or to express social and/or environmental concerns, which is particularly evidenced by the words "social" and "world". On the matters of ESG, additional words such as "global" (4), "sustainability" (4), "environment" (4), "environmental" (4), "impact" (3), "person" (3), as well as "cultures" (3) / "culture" (2), "planet" (2) and "climate" (2), must be also stressed, as they are specifically related to these topics. The extrinsic motivation is also evident with the use of words such as "reporting" (3) / "report" (2), and "decisions" (3), with lower levels of occurrence, however.

Following, the next subsection provides a discussion of the main findings.

## DISCUSSION OF THE MAIN FINDINGS

The purpose of this subsection is to discuss the obtained results based on the literature review.

This research has found important differences when assessing the students' motivations by groups (RQ1). To sum up, for the non-answers and amotivations cases, the highest levels of differences was found for older students and those who work and study simultaneously. A possible explanation for that, based on the answers received for the amotivations cases only from the second before-mentioned group, may be related to the feeling expressed by those students of being overwhelmed. Some of the indications provided by them can be read as follows:

- *"I don't have great motivation on the subject, because also in terms of personal time availability, I don't have much time for that".*
- *"Regardless of my motivation, I don't have enough time to learn more about this topic."*

This might probably explain the difference between younger and older students since this last subgroup is mostly comprised of students that are workers too. However, there were no specific indications that may explain the figures for the remaining groups.

Considering both types of motivation under assessment (intrinsic and extrinsic motivation), the differences by gender are more evident at the level of extrinsic motivation, with female students being less extrinsically motivated, but equally intrinsically motivated in comparison to male students. On the other hand, by students' occupation and stage in the course, the differences can be observed for intrinsic motivation, with students who also work and in the middle of the course the less motivated. Finally, the differences are partially shared between the subgroups by age, with older students less extrinsically and intrinsically motivated.

The findings by gender, which indicated a higher (lower) level of amotivation (extrinsic motivation) for female students, do not corroborate the study by Ho et al. (2021), who found that this subgroup of students have greater intrinsic motivation and external regulation, while male students have a higher level of amotivation. Also, the research by Teixeira et al. (2015) evidenced differences by gender as regards the reasons, expectations, and preparation of higher education students, finding a more prominent sense of duties and responsibilities associated with higher education for female students, in comparison to the male ones. From a different perspective, it is also contrary to the findings by Yudi et al. (2020), who concluded that gender does not have a significant relationship with accounting professional qualification, which is a concept related to extrinsic motivation. There is no indication, however, based on the students' answers, of possible explanations for the differences found by gender.

This research has found, by age, that younger students seem to be more motivated than older students, regardless of the type of motivation under assessment, which is also partially not aligned with the results by Colares and Amorim (2020), who identified that intrinsic motivation is associated with older students. An idea that seems to illustrate the answers of younger students for extrinsic motivation is related to the "future", as the examples provided below:

- *"The future depends a lot on sustainability, hence the motivation to learn more about reporting non-financial information, since it is increasingly important to disclose environmental actions."*
- *"It will help in my future work"*
- *"I think it will help me in my professional future"*
- *"Because it will be the new reality in the coming years in accounting"*

Finally, the figures did not evidence relevant differences in what concerns extrinsic motivation between the subgroups regarding students' occupation, and stage in the course, which may be an indication that, based on these characteristics, amotivation and intrinsic motivation have more evident signs of inverse relationship. Therefore, students who also work and those who are in the middle of the course the less intrinsically motivated. These results, however, are not aligned with a study conducted by Souza and Miranda (2019), who found that students who work are generally more motivated than those who do not.

Considering the specific interests in the topics related to ESG that motivate accounting students to learn (RQ2), no personal reasons or no specific interests were mostly expressed by them from the answers gathered. This finding suggests that environmental education provided in HEIs should be reinforced, aiming to impact the consciousness of future generations for a "green society" (Boca & Saraçlı, 2019; Saraite-Sariene et al., 2020). This reinforcement can also promote the development of sustainability skills, which allow students to act as "agents of change" in the future professional environment (Oberrauch et al., 2021).

Issues specifically related to the aspect of governance were not mentioned at all. This is a finding that matters to stress given that the research sample is composed of accounting students. As previously discussed, this probably means that, from these students' perspective, the concept of NFI does not incorporate "governance issues" since this topic is possibly associated with financial information matters. Additionally, this finding is also aligned with Oberrauch et al. (2021) and Ho et al. (2021), who pointed out that extrinsic motivation may be linked with social and sustainability concerns.

By students' characteristics, a non-specific, and interest was particularly identified in the subgroup of students in the middle of the course, reaching 83%. Oppositely, the students who are also workers, older, and at the end of the course were the ones that provided information as regards specific interests in their answers. This may indicate a higher level of knowledge of the issues related to ESG matters associated with these characteristics. Further, there is a slight difference between females (61%) and males (75%), which is also interesting to highlight, suggesting a stronger attitude toward taking a position by female students.

Regarding intrinsic reasons with no specific interests, the topics found from the assessment of students' statements are aligned with the literature review regarding accounting learning in matters such as either personal development and increased knowledge (Arquero et al., 2009; Byrne & Flood, 2005; Byrne et al., 2012; Leal et al., 2013) or students' personal interests (Colares & Amorim, 2020; Umar, 2014; Yudi et al., 2020).

Finally, regarding specific interest cases, older students and those who are also workers expressed more concerns regarding environmental issues, which is an interesting finding given that the concerns with these matters are usually associated with younger generations. Even so, Colares and Amorim's (2020) research may provide insight into this finding by revealing that more experienced and older people are usually more knowledgeable and certain about their decisions, leading to a higher degree of intrinsic motivation, whereas young people tend to make incipient decisions.

Following, the next section presents a summary of the main conclusions obtained during the development of this analysis.

## CONCLUSION

This chapter proposes to assess the accounting students' answers on their motivation regarding the topics of NFI, with a two-fold objective: to identify the type of motivation that is behind their interest and what specific interest they have to learn more about this issue.

In what concerns the first objective, the findings indicate a higher level of intrinsic motivation. Assessing the specific reasons behind this motivation, personal and non-specified interests were the most common justification. Governance issues were absent from the students' answers. The analysis also found some different patterns by demographic variables. Therefore, some demographic characteristics should be seen as relevant for a better understanding of students' motivation and their main topics of interest.

An important limitation regarding this research relates to the subjectivity of the method chosen for data collection, based on phrasal interpretations of the answers provided by students. Consequently, some options had to be considered to overcome some constraints, as mentioned in the section on the empirical study. Notwithstanding, the process has the advantage of gathering their thoughts and feelings about the issues under assessment without the barriers that are inherent to a closed and structured survey. Furthermore, the previous conclusions considered data that were exclusively obtained from the accounting students of a single Portuguese HEI, Lisbon-based. This represents another relevant limitation of this study it may not be representative of accounting students in Portugal.

Overcoming the previous aspects, further analysis may use different explanatory factors, including different social, economic, and cultural variables, that may be useful to explain the differences of opinion from the students' perspective, exploring more robust statistical methods, such as factor analysis, regression techniques, as well as equation structural modelling. Accountants (professionals) could be also considered as an avenue for future research, as well as the comparison between the students' and professionals' perspectives from different areas regarding the elements that underly non-financial information.

Besides, it can be also relevant to consider, in similar studies, differences that may arise from previous knowledge and expositions to different pedagogical methods (by accounting students), as well as from experience with different frameworks and organisational environments (by accounting professionals). An international comparison amongst professionals or students inserted in business courses for which NFI might be seen as relevant would also allow concluding on the possible differences from contextual or cultural reasons behind their perspectives.

Finally, the analysis from the users' perspective, including a breakdown by the type of stakeholder, would be also relevant to finding their specific interests and perceived usefulness from NFI reported by entities.

The main contribution of this chapter is to provide some insights into how students of an accounting course are motivated to acquire skills in NFI reporting. This is particularly relevant and has practical implications for HEIs, professors, students, and organizations related to accountancy education. In addition, this research can contribute to promoting new activities and/or triggering curricular changes in HEIs by linking the motivational factors mentioned in the literature review with students' interest in NFI. This can be useful for students to develop all the sustainability knowledge and skills they need to be successful in their careers, also playing a relevant role in the non-financial reporting challenges entities face as these issues have an increasing relevance.

## REFERENCES

Arif, M., Gan, C., & Nadeem, M. (2021). Regulating non-financial reporting: evidence from European firms' environmental, social and governance disclosures and earnings risk. *Meditari Accountancy Research, 30*(3). doi:10.1108/MEDAR-11-2020-1086

Arquero, J. L., Byrne, M., Flood, B., & Gonzalez, J. M. (2009). Motives, expectations, preparedness, and academic performance: A study of students of accounting at a Spanish university. *Revista de Contabilidad-Spanish Accounting Review*, *12*(2), 279–299. doi:10.1016/S1138-4891(09)70009-3

Arquero, J. L., & Fernández Polvillo, C. (2019). Estereotipos contables. Motivaciones y percepciones sobre la contabilidad de los estudiantes universitarios de Administración de Empresas y Finanzas y Contabilidad. *Revista de Contabilidad-Spanish Accounting Review*, *22*(1), 88–99. doi:10.6018/rc-sar.22.1.354341

Boca, G. D., & Saraçlı, S. (2019). Environmental Education and Student's Perception, for Sustainability. *Sustainability*, *11*(6), 1553. doi:10.3390u11061553

Bushman, R. M., Piotroski, J. D., & Smith, A. J. (2004). What Determines Corporate Transparency? *Journal of Accounting Research*, *42*(2), 207–252. doi:10.1111/j.1475-679X.2004.00136.x

Byrne, M., & Flood, B. (2005). A study of accounting students' motives, expectations, and preparedness for higher education. *Journal of Further and Higher Education*, *29*(2), 111–124. doi:10.1080/03098770500103176

Byrne, M., Flood, B., Hassall, T., Joyce, J., Montano, J. L. A., Gonzalez, J. M. G., & Tourna-Germanou, E. (2012). Motivations, expectations, and preparedness for higher education: A study of accounting students in Ireland, the UK, Spain, and Greece. *Accounting Forum*, *36*(2), 134–144. doi:10.1016/j.accfor.2011.12.001

Carmo, C., & Ribeiro, C. (2022). Mandatory Non-Financial Information Disclosure under European Directive 95/2014/EU: Evidence from Portuguese Listed Companies. *Sustainability*, *14*(8), 4860. Advance online publication. doi:10.3390u14084860

Cenar, I. (2020). Non-financial Reporting and Performance in Pre-university Education. *Ovidius University Annals, Economic Sciences Series*, *20*(2), 830-836. https://stec.univ-ovidius.ro/html/anale/RO/wp-content/uploads/2021/03/Section%205/5.pdf

Cho, C. H., & Patten, D. M. (2007). The role of environmental disclosures as tools of legitimacy: A research note. *Accounting, Organizations and Society*, *32*(7–8), 639–647. doi:10.1016/j.aos.2006.09.009

Colares, A. C., & Amorim, N. B. (2020). Motivação dos discentes em ciências contábeis na ótica da teoria da autodeterminação. *International Journal of Accounting and Reporting*, *14*, 1–18. doi:10.34629/ric.v14i0.e-020008

Cormier, D., & Magnan, M. (2007). The revisited contribution of environmental reporting to investors' valuation of a firm's earnings: An international perspective. *Ecological Economics*, *62*(3–4), 613–626. doi:10.1016/j.ecolecon.2006.07.030

Deci, E. L., & Ryan, R. M. (1985). Conceptualizations of Intrinsic Motivation and Self-Determination. In *Intrinsic Motivation and Self-Determination in Human Behavior. Perspectives in Social Psychology*. Springer. doi:10.1007/978-1-4899-2271-7_2

Deci, E. L., & Ryan, R. M. (2008). Self-determination theory: A macrotheory of human motivation, development, and health. *Canadian Psychology*, *49*(3), 182–185. https://psycnet.apa.org/doi/10.1037/a0012801. doi:10.1037/a0012801

Dumay, J. (2016). A critical reflection on the future of intellectual capital : From reporting to disclosure. *Journal of Intellectual Capital, 17*(1), 168–184. doi:10.1108/JIC-08-2015-0072

EFRAG. (2021). *Conceptual Framework for Non-Financial Information Standard Setting.* Retrieved from https://www.efrag.org/Assets/Download?assetUrl=%2Fsites%2Fwebpublishing%2FSiteAssets%2FEFRAG%2520PTF-NFRS_A3_FINAL.pdf

Erkens, M., Paugam, L., & Stolowy, H. (2015). Non-financial information: State of the art and research perspectives based on a bibliometric study. Comptabilite Controle Audit, 21(3), 15-92. doi:10.3917/cca.213.0015

Erkens, M., Paugam, L., & Stolowy, H. (2015). Non-financial information: State of the art and research perspectives based on a bibliometric study. Comptabilite Controle Audit, 21. doi:10.3917/cca.213.0015

Esser, I.-M., MacNeil, I., & Chalaczkiewicz-Ladna, K. (2020). Engaging stakeholders in corporate decision-making through strategic reporting: An empirical study of FTSE 100 companies (Part 2). *European Business Law Review, 31*(2), 209–242. http://eprints.gla.ac.uk/177301/

Estatutos da Aula do Comércio. (1759). Série Preta Nº 2193/9. Instituto dos Arquivos Nacionais/Torre do Tombo.

European Commission. (2014). *Directive of the European Parliament and of the Council of 22 October 2014 amending Directive 2013/34/EU as regards disclosure of non-financial and diversity information by certain large undertakings and groups.* https://eur-lex.europa.eu/legal-content/EN/TXT/PDF/?uri=CELEX:32014L0095&from=EN

European Commission. (2019). *Communication from the Commission Guidelines on non-financial reporting: Supplement on reporting climate-related information (2019/C 209/01).* https://eur-lex.europa.eu/legal-content/EN/TXT/PDF/?uri=CELEX:52019XC0620(01)&from=EN

European Commission. (2021). *Proposal for a Directive of the European Parliament and of the Council amending Directive 2013/34/EU, Directive 2004/109/EC, Directive 2006/43/EC, and Regulation (EU) N. 537/2014, as regards Corporate Sustainability Reporting.* https://eur-lex.europa.eu/legal-content/EN/TXT/PDF/?uri=CELEX:52021PC0189&from=EN

Evdokimova, M., & Kuzubov, S. (2021). Non-Financial Reporting And The Cost Of Capital In BRICS Countries. *Higher School of Economics Research Paper No. WP BRP, 83.* https://wp.hse.ru/data/2021/06/25/1430000555/83FE2021.pdf

Francis, J., Nanda, D., & Olsson, P. (2008). Voluntary disclosure, earnings quality, and cost of capital. *Journal of Accounting Research, 46*(1), 53–99. doi:10.1111/j.1475-679X.2008.00267.x

Heffes, E. M. (2008). FASB chairman advocates 'improving and adopting' IFRS for U.S. companies. *Financial Executive, 24*(7). https://link.gale.com/apps/doc/A185460066/AONE?u=anon~976de3b9&sid=googleScholar&xid=32f32333

Ho, M. H., Fido, D., & Simonovic, B. (2021). An investigation of the Learning Motivation of Student Studying Accounting Courses in China. *International Journal of Learning and Teaching, 7*(3), 219–225. doi:10.18178/ijlt.7.3.219-225

Howard, J. L., Bureau, J., Guay, F., Chong, J., & Ryan, R. (2021). Student Motivation and Associated Outcomes: A meta-Analysis from Self-Determination Theory. *Perspectives on Psychological Science*, *16*(6), 1300–1323. doi:10.1177/1745691620966789 PMID:33593153

IFRS Foundation. (2020). *Effects of climate-related matters on financial statements*. https://www.ifrs.org/content/dam/ifrs/supporting-implementation/documents/effects-of-climate-related-matters-on-financial-statements.pdf

IFRS Foundation. (2021, November 3). *Global sustainability disclosure standards for the financial markets*. https://www.ifrs.org/news-and-events/news/2021/11/global-sustainability-disclosure-standards-for-the-financial-markets/

Krasodomska, J., Michalak, J., & Świetla, K. (2020). Directive 2014/95/EU: Accountants' understanding and attitude towards mandatory non-financial disclosures in corporate reporting Directive 2014 / 95 / EU disclosures incorporate reporting. *Meditari Accountancy Research*, *28*(5), 751–779. doi:10.1108/MEDAR-06-2019-0504

Kristofík, P., Lament, M., & Musa, H. (2016). The Reporting of Non-Financial Information and the rationale for its standardisation. *Business Administration and Management*, (2), 157–175. doi:10.1016/j.jaci.2012.05.050

La Torre, M., Sabelfeld, S., Blomkvist, M., Tarquinio, L., & Dumay, J. (2018). Harmonising non-financial reporting regulation in Europe: Practical forces and projections for future research. *Meditari Accountancy Research*, *26*(4), 598–621. doi:10.1108/MEDAR-02-2018-0290

Larrinaga, C., Carrasco, F., Correa, C., Llena, F., & Moneva, J. (2002). Accountability and accounting regulation: The case of the Spanish environmental disclosure standard. *European Accounting Review*, *11*(4), 723–740. doi:10.1080/0963818022000001000

Leal, E. A., Miranda, G. J., & Carmo, C. R. S. (2013). Teoria da autodeterminação: Uma análise da motivação dos estudantes do curso de ciências contábeis. *Revista Contabilidade & Finanças*, *24*(62), 162–173. doi:10.1590/S1519-70772013000200007

Liu, G., Yin, X., Pengue, W., Benetto, E., Huisingh, D., Schnitzer, H., Wang, Y., & Casazza, M. (2018). Environmental accounting : In between raw data and information use for management practices. *Journal of Cleaner Production*, *197*, 1056–1068. doi:10.1016/j.jclepro.2018.06.194

Mata, C., Fialho, A., & Eugénio, T. (2018). A decade of environmental accounting reporting: What we know? *Journal of Cleaner Production*, *198*, 1198–1209. doi:10.1016/j.jclepro.2018.07.087

Melloni, G., Caglio, A., & Perego, P. (2017). Saying more with less? Disclosure conciseness, completeness and balance in Integrated Reports. *Journal of Accounting and Public Policy*, *36*(3), 220–238. doi:10.1016/j.jaccpubpol.2017.03.001

Mohammed, S. D. (2018). Mandatory Social and Environmental Disclosure : A Performance Evaluation of Listed Nigerian Oil and Gas Companies Pre- and Post-Mandatory Disclosure Requirements. *Journal of Finance and Accounting*, *6*(2), 56–68. doi:10.11648/j.jfa.20180602.12

Pizzi, S., Caputo, A., Corvino, A., & Venturelli, A. (2020). Management research and the UN sustainable development goals (SDGs): A bibliometric investigation and systematic review. *Journal of Cleaner Production, 276*, 124033. doi:10.1016/j.jclepro.2020.124033

Ribeiro, M. F., Saraiva, V., Pereira, P., & Ribeiro, C. (2019). Escala de Motivação Académica: Validação no Ensino Superior Público Português. *Revista de Administração Contemporânea, 23*(3), 288–310. doi:10.1590/1982-7849rac2019180190

Ryan, R. M., & Deci, E. L. (2000). Self-determination theory and the facilitation of intrinsic motivation, social development, and well-being. *The American Psychologist, 55*(1), 68–78. doi:10.1037/0003-066X.55.1.68 PMID:11392867

Ryan, R. M., & Deci, E. L. (2020). Intrinsic and extrinsic motivation from a self-determination theory perspective: Definitions, theory, practices, and future directions. *Contemporary Educational Psychology, 61*, 101860. doi:10.1016/j.cedpsych.2020.101860

Santos, A. L., & Rodrigues, L. L. (2021). Banks and climate-related information: The case of Portugal. *Sustainability (Switzerland), 13*(21), 12215. Advance online publication. doi:10.3390u132112215

Smith, L. M. (2014). The benefits of sustainability and integrated reporting. *Journal of Legal, Ethical and Regulatory Issues, 17*(2), 93–113. https://www.proquest.com/openview/bcb70ca0b973d8fbea1cdcd76a9bdcff/1?pq-origsite=gscholar&cbl=38868

Souza, Z. A., & Miranda, G. J. (2019). Motivação de alunos de graduação em Ciências Contábeis ao longo do curso. *Enfoque: Reflexão Contábil, 38*(2), 49–65. doi:10.4025/enfoque.v38i2.41079

Steinmayr, R., Weidinger, A. F., Schwinger, M., & Spinath, B. (2019). The importance of students' motivation for their academic achievement–replicating and extending previous findings. *Frontiers in Psychology, 10*, 1730. doi:10.3389/fpsyg.2019.01730 PMID:31417459

Storey, M., Killian, S., & O'Regan, P. (2017). Responsible management education: Mapping the field in the context of the SDGs. *International Journal of Management Education, 15*(2), 93–103. doi:10.1016/j.ijme.2017.02.009

Sullivan, R., & Gouldson, A. (2012). Does voluntary carbon reporting meet investors' needs? *Journal of Cleaner Production, 36*(January), 60–67. doi:10.1016/j.jclepro.2012.02.020

Tarquinio, L., & Posadas, S. C. (2020). Exploring the term "non-financial information": An academics' view. *Meditari Accountancy Research, 28*(5), 727–749. doi:10.1108/MEDAR-11-2019-0602

TCFD. (2017). *Final Report: Recommendations of the Task Force on Climate-Related Financial Disclosures.* https://www.fsb-tcfd.org/wp-content/ uploads/2017/06/

Teixeira, C., Gomes, D., & Borges, J. (2015). Introductory accounting students' motives, expectations, and preparedness for higher education: Some Portuguese evidence. *Accounting Education, 24*(2), 123–145. doi:10.1080/09639284.2015.1018284

Turzo, T., Marzi, G., Favino, C., & Terzani, S. (2022). Non-financial reporting research and practice: Lessons from the last decade. *Journal of Cleaner Production, 345*(February), 131154. doi:10.1016/j.jclepro.2022.131154

Tyran, K. L. (2017). Transforming students into global citizens : International service learning and PRME. *International Journal of Management Education, 15*(2), 162–171. doi:10.1016/j.ijme.2017.03.007

Umar, I. (2014). Factors influencing students' career choice in accounting: The case of Yobe State University. *Research Journal of Finance and Accounting, 5*(17), 59-62. https://core.ac.uk/download/pdf/234630127.pdf

UNCTAD. (2020, October 29). *International Accounting and Reporting Issues: 2019 Review.* https://isar.unctad.org/annual-review/

UNESCO. (2014). *Education for Sustainable Development.* doi:10.4324/9781315876573

Yudi, M. M., Ibrahim, N. N., Kamaruzaman, S. A., Haron, N. Q. A., Hamid, N. S., & Hambali, S. S. (2020). Accounting Students' Motivation for Getting Professionally Qualified. *Environment-Behaviour Proceedings Journal, 5*(15), 41–48. doi:10.21834/ebpj.v5i15.2454

## ADDITIONAL READING

Breijer, R., & Orij, R. (2022). The Comparability of Non-Financial Information: An Exploration of the Impact of the Non-Financial Reporting Directive (NFRD, 2014/95/EU). *Accounting in Europe, 19*(May), 332–361. Advance online publication. doi:10.1080/17449480.2022.2065645

Ekundayo, G., & Josiah, M. (2020). Environmental accounting disclosure: A critical examination of the literature. *British Journal of Economics, Finance and Management Science, 17*(2), 34–45.

Eng, L. L., Fikru, M., & Vichitsarawong, T. (2022). Comparing the informativeness of sustainability disclosures versus ESG disclosure ratings. *Sustainability Accounting, Management and Policy Journal, 13*(2), 494–518. doi:10.1108/SAMPJ-03-2021-0095

Fırat, M., Kılınç, H., & Yüzer, T. V. (2018). Level of intrinsic motivation of distance education students in e-learning environments. *Journal of Computer Assisted Learning, 34*(1), 63–70. doi:10.1111/jcal.12214

Hatane, S. E., Gunawan, F. A., & Pratama, S. W. (2021). Intrinsic Motivation, Career Exposure, and Quality of Life: How Do They Influence the Accounting Students' Career Choice? *Journal of Education and Learning, 15*(3), 335–345. doi:10.11591/edulearn.v15i3.19870

Hortigüela-Alcalá, D., Sánchez-Santamaría, J., Pérez-Pueyo, Á., & Abella-García, V. (2019). Social networks to promote motivation and learning in higher education from the students' perspective. *Innovations in Education and Teaching International, 56*(4), 412–422. doi:10.1080/14703297.2019.1579665

IFRS Foundation. (2021a, November 3). *IFRS Foundation announces International Sustainability Standards Board, consolidation with CDSB and VRF, and publication of prototype disclosure requirements.* https://www.ifrs.org/news-and-events/news/2021/11/ifrs-foundation-announces-issb-consolidation-with-cdsb-vrf-publication-of-prototypes/

Iraola-Real, I., Matos, L., & Gargurevich, R. (2022). *The type of motivation does matter for university preparation.* Estudos de Psicologia. doi:10.1590/1982-0275202239e190177

Jeno, L. M., Nylehn, J., Hole, T. N., Raaheim, A., Velle, G., & Vandvik, V. (2021). Motivational Determinants of Students' Academic Functioning: The Role of Autonomy-support, Autonomous Motivation, and Perceived Competence. *Scandinavian Journal of Educational Research*, 1–18. doi:10.1080/00313831.2021.1990125

Karsten, I., Steenekamp, K., & Van der Merwe, M. (2020). Empowering accounting students to enhance the self-determination skills demanded by the fourth industrial revolution. *South African Journal of Higher Education*, *34*(2), 36–58. doi:10.20853/34-2-3487

Saraite-Sariene, L., Alonso-Cañadas, J., Galán-Valdivieso, F., & Caba-Pérez, C. (2019). Non-financial information versus financial as a key to the stakeholder engagement: A higher education perspective. *Sustainability*, *12*(1), 331. doi:10.3390u12010331

UNCTAD. (2019). *International Accounting and Reporting Issues 2019 Review*. Retrieved from https://unctad.org/webflyer/international-accounting-and-reporting-issues-2019

## KEY TERMS AND DEFINITIONS

**Accounting Course:** The skills provided by higher education institutions to report, traditionally, financial information and, more recently, non-financial information.

**Amotivation:** The absence of what drives a person to do something or a certain activity.

**Extrinsic Motivation:** The actions driven by external factors.

**Intrinsic Motivation:** The actions driven by personal interest and/or satisfaction.

**Motivation:** What drives a person to do something or a certain activity.

**Non-Financial Information:** Topics that are typically related to the environment and society, more recently known as environmental, social, and governance, thus embracing information on the administration of businesses.

**Reporting:** The act of giving and/or describing the information.

**Self-Determination Theory:** One theory about human motivation and personality.

**Skills:** The competence to do something or a certain activity.

## Chapter 5
# A Philosophical Discussion of Sustainable Development:
## A Case From the Bangladeshi Santal Community

**Parimal Roy**
https://orcid.org/0000-0002-0461-2587
*Universiti Malaya, Malaysia*

**Haris Abd Wahab**
https://orcid.org/0000-0001-9834-3797
*Universiti Malaya, Malaysia*

**Mashitah Hamidi**
*Universiti Malaya, Malaysia*

## ABSTRACT

*This chapter aims to present a logical discussion on the Sustainable Development Goals (SDGs) and how they are being treated as incorrect concepts in the academic world and the ethnic community. The Santal is one of the examples from Bangladesh. Methodologically, this chapter follows the 'capability approach' by Amartya Sen to understand the changing trend in the Santal community of Bangladesh. The discussion shows that despite being a global phenomenon, sustainable development is not an ideal coupling phrase to combat global issues because it falls into the global trap within. Based on secondary data from the literature and the first author's reflections, the study of versatile literature has been noted in this chapter.*

DOI: 10.4018/978-1-6684-6172-3.ch005

## INTRODUCTION

This chapter intends to provide a concise philosophical argument on the history of 'Sustainable Development and as this term bears the 'double standard' meaning in the scholarship and academic world (Parris et al., 2003;Paul, 2008). So, it is discerning to be cognizant of practicing the term Sustainable Development.. We also used logical connotations; examples from life had been taken to prove the philosophical arguments in the case of Sustainable Development. The term 'Development' has not come directly from western society and its generated philosophical root (Grober,2007;Pissani, 2006; Rist,2014). However, we can compare its emergence to an evolutionary concept. The evolutionary conceptual process is *Progress—Economic Growth—Development—Environmental protection—Sustainable Development*. While there is an established discourse on Sustainable Development all around what we see reflections on theory in nineteenth century (Majumder, 1948). The authors believe in going out from this discursive discussion to start a philosophical conversion like 'Sustainable Development: A Zero Concept.' [The authors intend to develop an article on that issue to prove mathematically Sustainable Development is a Zero Concept]. However, European colonization spread differently according to the metropolis' and the colonies' interests. We can assume as examples in this chapter,

*France, for its part, had two groups of territories: (a) Guyana, Guadeloupe, and Martinique in the Americas; and the 'historic' colonies of St Pierre and Miquelon; St Louis and Gorey in Senegal, Reunion Island and trading stations in Gabon and India; (b) Algeria (1830), Marquesas Islands and Tahiti (1845), New Caledonia (1853), Cambodia (1865), the more recent possessions of Cochin-China (1867) and Senegal (1854–65) (see Paul, 2008, p. 48).*

The second world war paved the way for 'Development' in this sense, and Brundtland Report 1987 is the journey point of today's Sustainable Development discussion as a popular concept in a sense-making to discursive text. Before describing that Sustainable Development voyage, we should understand our Development in the light of our social position where the authors' thoughts, consciousness, and actions are embedded.

Sustainable, we mean here, in the sense that it is localizing though its journey started globally. When the Sustainable concept is mixed with corporate profit, it does not bring any meaning to the small ethnic groups. Instead, it pushed into a multi-facet crisis; the Santal community is one of them in Bangladesh. Keeping sustainability in mind, if the people never deem ethnic communities actively for Research on Implications of Sustainable Development in Higher Education of entire human race, like the ethnic groups, will fall into an existential crisis once upon. Those days are far from throwing a stone at the crisis, herein is the purpose and motivation of this chapter to explore the SD in higher education and research. Because we can refer finally " in order to overcome the limitations of the rights discourse, new strategies are needed to shift indigenous political mobilization efforts from rights to responsibilities.--- indigenous self- determination needs to be rearticulated on indigenous terms as part of a sustainable, community-based process rather than as narrowly constructed political/legal entitlements(Corntassel, 2008, p.116)."

*A Philosophical Discussion of Sustainable Development*

## WHERE EMBEDDED OUR THOUGHTS, ACTIONS, CONSCIOUSNESS

One of the first authors studied Anthropology and claims still now a learner; in connection with this subject matter, he also have an avid interest in small ethnic groups; and his eyes stare at the ethnic people's cascading catastrophic sorrows what he sees from his childhood memory in a poverty prone remote village to global development politics over the world. The first author spent his childhood till youth in a remote village that is a poverty-prone district of Bangladesh, where small ethnic groups such as Santal, Kol, Bhim, Munda, and Rajbangshi are all popularly known to live in the vicinity. He indeed had the opportunity to commemorate their culture, customs, and socio-economic conditions; His father's best friend belongs to the Santal community and recently retired as a college principal— he does not know how to ensure SDGs will act for them.

Another concomitant example is to conduit the Sustainable Developemnt decision in this connection. One of the female Santal classmates of the first author got a child married after the Secondary School Certificate exam and turned into like grandmother's physical appearance just two years after marriage. From the ethnic lens, what this Sustainable Development brings or has brought to them—such thoughts and experiences inspired us to note down in black and white in this chapter—Sustainable Development is indeed an incorrect concept or mismatch coupling word to the ethnic community. Most readers would call this auto-reflexive ethnographic writing, but to us, it seems to be the accountability of academic knowledge practice—where our thoughts, consciousness, and actions are alive.

However, Victor Hugo said—Europe realized that Africa was already colonized in the nineteenth century, and Europe tried to make them civilized; in the 20th century, Europe would create an Africa called a better world; where the old Africa is to be made to fit for civilization.' This process was candid but made a glitch while joining America after the second world war. The capitalist world wanted to maximize profit, and the 'Club of Rome' (1968) indicated the threat by saying we have a limit to growth and environmental exploitation. The capitalist countries realized the peril after the second world war. When the colonized areas became Independent states, they delimited the markets. The colonial power thought of alternative strategies to sustain the economic power to uphold disguised colonialism.

So, the goods market narrowed down, but economic growth or production never stopped but instead increased. Market searching strategy is, on the one hand, another international Organizations such as the World Bank (1945), the United Nations (1945), and IMF 1945) are created - led by the United States of America. Therefore, it indicates that Sustainable Development is the result of Development politics. Look at the Brundtland report of 1987, based on which we now converse about Sustainable Development Goals like hot cake—prepared with the financial and technical assistance of the World Bank (Soeftestad, 2004, 2009; Sneddon et al., 2006).

## WHOSE PROBLEM IS SOLVED BY WHOM?

After the independence of the colonies generally in the 1950s, not only the market of European products became compressed but also American products. As a result, on the one hand, the flow of goods became necessary. On the other hand, profit maximization for progress was taking reshaping in the industrialized countries. It became imperative to spread new strategies and concepts among underdeveloped countries for capital proliferation. The industrialized developed countries divided the world mainly into two parts by GDP indicators. Those countries' GDP is lower—called third world than Industrialized or western countries. When the honeymoon period did not finish the prior colonized State was due to achieve independence, and then they needed aid and loans to ensure people's welfare. The reality is also we can refer to all these countries that were lagging in the development journey.

Again, international organizations and industrialized countries came forward to help them, basically involving them in loan and aid traps. Now, when we gaze at Sustainable Development or international organizations, concomitantly, we see the glitch voice of trapped countries— it is a bottleneck of Development. As an upshot, we can undoubtedly articulate that Development and Sustainable Development for the Santal community does not mean to my [of the first author] classmate or the retired Principal to change their quality of life when the statistical indicators showed a worrying position comparing the national or mainstream people (Barkat,2016;Roy et al., 2022; Sarker et al., 2016). Whatever, it is a pertinent question 'whose problems who solve?

## METHOD

This study centers on secondary data with an extensive literature review of versatile books, journals, and articles. The first author interviewed ethnic leaders, Santal leaders, the Santal people of Dinajpur, Bangladesh to make understand their views, and a limited number of senior civil servants of Bangladesh. Furthermore, the authors also reviewed relevant literature, such as UNDRIP-2007 and ILO convention-169.

This study located in a remote Santal ethnic village in Biraganj Upazilla of Dinajpur district of northern Bangladesh; and the first author lived at least 20 springs in the village under Birol Upazilla of the same district and country where thoughts and consciousness bore for empathized with the Santal community. More in this point, this chapter basically reflects childhood memories with the Santal people's living standard of today and what was yesterday. So, the Gap has been depicted through philosophical conduits to contribute or at least raise a question for the Santal people's development. Methodologically, the authors were guided by the Indigenous Paradigm, where the first thing is for research to be 'Reciprocal' for either researcher or researched community (Chilisa, 2017; Chowdhury et al., 2022; Smith, 2021). In this sense, researchers want to give feedback to the community by referring the Santal community to the policymakers for concentration upon them (Chowdhury et al.,2022)

## HISTORY OF SUSTAINABLE DEVELOPMENT: A GLANCE

In a general sense, we can divide the history of Sustainable Development into three parts—

1. Pre-Stockholm (Covering the until WCED — 1972).
2. From Stockholm to WCED (1972 —1978)
3. Post WCED (1987—1997). The concept of Sustainable Development is categorized in the above three historical periods (Mebratu, year p.96). Nevertheless, we cannot deny the role of the "Club of Rome" in discussing Sustainable or Sustainable Development in a practical sense of SDGs discourse (Meadows et al. 1972). In this context, we can throw a light upon an equitably brief of history when the 'great powers' put then-dominant ideas into practice and, in mind, opened the way to 'Development' (Benjaminsen, 2021; Pissani, 2006; Sen, 2009). Western belief in 'Development' has ancient roots "the end of the last century, with a long history already behind it, European

colonization branched out in quite different forms according to the metropolis's pace and interests (Grober, 2007;Rist, 2014). Victor Hugo informs us "Men's destiny lies in the South. the moment has come to make Europe realize that it has Africa alongside it. In the nineteenth century, the White man civilized a black man; Europe civilized the rest of the world in the twentieth century. It was a fashion to make a new Africa amenable to civilization – that is the problem. This story is very relevant to the case of the Santal community in Bangladesh to make them Bangali by British East India Company, later the Independent State with the collaboration of global strategies like SDGs (Debnath, 2020, 2012, 2010;Tripura, 2020, 2018, 2016).

Nevertheless, in the immediate post-world war period, the most critical concerns seemed to be in the North rather than the South. First, there was the reconstruction of ruined Europe. On 5 June 1947, the Marshall Plan was launched to help the European economy and to provide America's colossal production capacity with the markets it needed for post-war conversion. But, there was also the looming breach between the wartime allies. Stalin's claims in Europe as Poland (1947), Romania (1948), Czechoslovakia (1948), and Hungary (1949) became 'people's democracies' – not forgetting the civil war in Greece between 1946 and 1949. By 1948, the Soviets were blockading berlin, and the Cold War called for serious preventive measures that led to the creation of NATO. The major powerful states were thus mainly preoccupied with events transforming European political relations. Concomitant, the changes in the South tended to be pushed into the background. In this hardly auspicious context, however, the concept of 'Development' entered the arena.

From 1949 onwards, often without realizing it, more than two billion inhabitants of the planet found themselves changing their name, being 'officially' regarded as they appeared in the eyes of others, called upon to deepen their Westernization by repudiating their own identity. No longer African, Latin American, or Asian. They were now simply 'underdeveloped.' Those who headed the independent State accepted this new 'definition.' Because it was a way of asserting their claim to benefit from the 'aid' that was supposed to lead to 'Development. For the colonized, it was a way of affirming the legal equality that was refused them. It looked as if they had everything to gain – respectability and prosperity. But their right to self-determination had been acquired in exchange for a right to self-definition. In gaining political independence, they forfeited their identity and economic autonomy and were now forced to travel the 'development path' mapped out for them by others. Whereas the world of colonization had been seen mainly as a political space to encompass ever larger empires, the 'Development age' was the period when economic space spread everywhere, with the raising of GDP as the number one imperative (Barkat, 2016; Paul, 2008).

Colonization is now one of the highest activities of societies that have reached an advanced stage of civilization. A society colonizes when it reaches a high degree of maturity and strength; it procreates, protects, places in good conditions for Development, and leads on to virility. This new society has emerged from its entrails. Colonization is one of the most intricate and sensitive processes in social physiology; the benefit of colonizing individuals is to situate the nascent society it has created. It is distressing that the East-India company did not motivate the local people in this sub-continent while they ruled over almost two hundreds year (1757-1947) even though their policy was divided and ruled the Indian people to prolong their power; moreover, they exploited Indian economy, and people labor to increase the GDP of the British empire. We see these scenarios in independent Bangladesh, Government did not ratify the UNDRIP-2007 and ILO convention 169 to strengthen the internal colonization in the job market (elope the quota system for ethnic communities), decreasing the Capability framework (Sen, 2009); for instance, Phulbari coal mine, Gobindoganj Police, Santal clash, violate human rights (Two Santals taken poisonous in daylight in front of people as protesting the injustice) and after all 'self-determination' (see the table 2 & 3) as who are they (Hasan, 2020;ILO-169; UNDRIP, 2007, ILO-169).

In the reports of Meadows et al. (1972), "Sustainable Development had two objectives and proposed sustainability to depict the limits of growth as sustainable without sudden and uncontrolled collapse; and capable of satisfying the basic requirements of all its people (Grober, 2007, p.6)." Environmental conservation is one of the critical global concerns that 'The Club of Rome,' a non-profit, unofficial group of versatile scholars, seeks to explore critically. In 1968, they established the Club of Rome in Rome, Italy's Accademia di Lincei. Current and former heads of State and government, UN administrators, senior politicians and government officials, diplomats, scientists, economists, and business executives worldwide comprise this group. The release of the Club of Rome's inaugural report, The Limits to Growth (Meadows et al.,1972), significantly boosted public awareness of Environmental protection. Further, this report became a hive to make sense of Sustainable Development. Now we can see the evolutionary trend of SDGs in the following table.

*Table 1. Year-based SDGs Interventions*

| Year | Organizations/ Individuals | Activities |
|---|---|---|
| 1968 | Club of Rome | Established |
| 1972 | Club of Rome | A report on 'The Limits to Growth ' was published to indicate the Growth & environmental limitations. |
| 1980 | IUCN, WWF/ UNEP | They tried to fix up a world conservation strategy 'living resources conservation for sustainable development. They gave priority of the Sustainability of natural protection. |
| 1981 | Brown | He elevated the concept of Sustainability within environmental discourse. |
| 1983 | WCED | It prioritized the concept of humans and the environment |
| 1987 | WCED | It used Sustainable Development in its naming Brundtland report mentioning our Common Future. This report emphasized Environment & Development. |
| 1992 | United Nations | UN conference on Environment & Development (Earth Summit or Rio Declaration) declared Agenda 21 to achieve global development. Human Development was highlighted by dephasing poverty. |
| 2002 | UN | Follow up Agenda 21– Poverty alleviation |
| 2005 | UN | Declared on MDGs (10 Goals) |
| 2015 | UN | Declared SDGs (17 Goals) |

Source: Authors' compilation

Now, SDGs are the hot cake for all politicians, policymakers, bureaucrats, professionals, students, business people, and academic researchers. In that case, the salient features of Sustainable Development we may offer from Yetunde Jeje (2006) like following—

1. It is a worldview concept
2. It is characterized as expressionist

*A Philosophical Discussion of Sustainable Development*

3. Multi-constructed or as a social construct concept.
4. It is a political act of power
5. Local to a global concept (Jeje, 2006).

## SUSTAINABLE DEVELOPMENT: WHY IMPERFECT COUPLING WORDS

Sustainability and Development are two opposite words and have an unhappy consciousness to lead the Development. By Sustainable, we mean to protect the environment or natural resources; And Development means making positive changes and exploiting those natural resources.

We can represent the unhappy relationship between the two by Figure 1.

*Figure 1. Representation*
*(Source: Author compilation)*

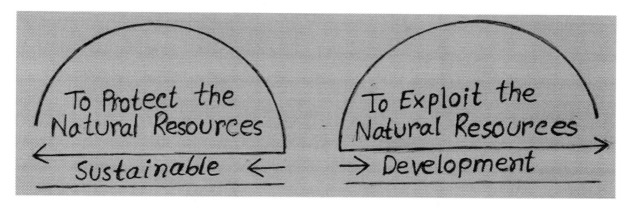

Figure 1 above reminds us, "Today the two paths of the two people have gone in two directions (Popular Bengali songs in 70-the 80s of twentieth centuries)." Therefore, if we put the two words together, we have to say, like another prominent Bengali literature critic Promoth Chowdhury, 'Language comes from the mouth to the pen; if you do the opposite, the ink falls on the mouth.' Therefore, before discussing and solving the relationship between these two words, we need to discuss the two words apiece.

We see Development as a positive change and interconnected with respective entities. Where the first position of it is progress, then the growth that we have explained above. When the UN launched the Human Development Index in 1991, before of the question of qualitative life changes was raised in the global context. We can consider the Brundtland Report of 1987 general as the basis of Development at the last stage of the continuum. This report under the title "our common future" indicates our Development course. See figure 2.

*Figure 2. Law and Order – Three components*
(*Source: author complation*)

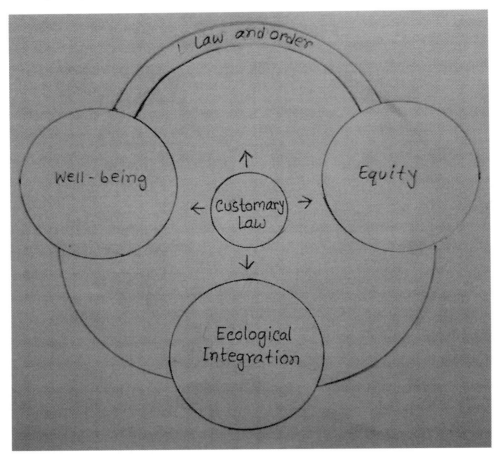

Figure 2 shows three components: *Well-being, Equity, and Ecological integration*. We can see law and order as a relation that connects both components— first and second elements to improve the general quality of life. Concomitantly, the third element becomes necessary for the first and second elements, and the area of interest of the report is the conservation of the environment. For these three elements, we suggest Customary Law. Customary Laws should be given importance for material implementation. However, this report does not mention the customs or customary laws. Yes, this is a limitation of this report. However, we are taking discussion this coordination for conducting policy on Sustainable Development.

Sustainable is now difficult to classify as a globalizing force because it falls (James Rosenau, 2003, p.16 cited in Sneddon, et al. 2006, p.257). Thus, the term Sustainability is endangered by the optimal and highest utilization rates of resources in industrialized societies. Because, more growth happens from exploiting natural resources, which would expose environmental damage. On the one hand, is the consumption of wealth, and on the other is the protection of wealth, this is a contradictory statement to make the understanding of Sustainable Development. In this case, we can draw a figure on Sustainable Development confronted relationship amid Progress, Growth, and Development as following the figure, the overlapping part is identified as Sustainable Development.

## A Philosophical Discussion of Sustainable Development

*Figure 3. Sustainable development*
(Source: Authors compilation)

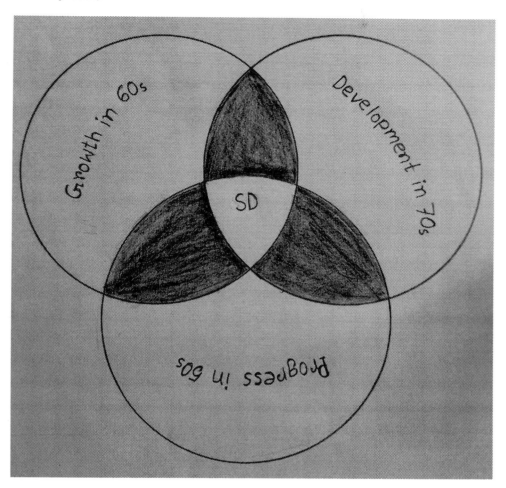

Culture is deeply related to the way we think and act the first author told his life story in aforesaid. The concept of Sustainability has a long European tradition, which seems to have matured over three centuries. Sustainability aims to treat ourselves to be more accountable and responsible for natural resources, which is also a moral obligation too to protect our milieu for our interest; Nature must be respected, meeting the basic needs of the next generation so as not to fall into any kind of crisis (Graber, 2007, p. 29). Graber suggests that this sustains the motto we found in other religious eras or doctrines. "it is the exciting debates on ecology basic human needs and global equity that sprang up in the 1960s and 1970s, inspired the design of sustainable development" (Graber, 2007, p. 29).

We have the natural quality to live with the environment, which helps us to adapt to life. The adaptive capacity is typical to all; we find such reflection in the Brundtland report of 1987, while the report title is - 'our common future.' Several international organizations brought it forward after the mid-term of the 20th century to address our expected future; like 'Club of Rome(1968)'; World Wide Life Fund (1961), and Social Democrat Norwegian former Prime Minister Brundtland also later figure in this movement, but a factor; These individual and organizations bring this Sustainable Development to a global discussion. After various discussions and criticisms, we see it being implemented by the UN, known as UN Agenda 2030 but widely known as SDGs 2030, consisting of 17 Goals and 169 targets to achieve this paramount.

## SUSTAINABLE DEVELOPMENT: A CASE FROM THE SANTAL COMMUNITY

Bangladesh achieved a flag and a constitution through a bloody war of nine months in 1971. If, the Constitution is a mirror of a nation-state, where the hopes and aspirations of all ethnic groups are reflected. To an extent, the Constitution is the mother-womb, that gives shelter to all her citizens, from street children to LGBT to far-reaching hill people. A debate, almost since the inception of the Constitution, started in the national assembly of Bangladesh on 31 October 1972, when all the small ethnic groups were advised to become 'Bengali' (Mohsin, 2002, 2001; Chakma & Maitrot, 2016). It is not only a painful, unpardonable phenomenon but is rather distressing to deal forebay-born nation-state. This debate originated from many blood-shaded occurrences in this country, and yet to date, is now a topic among the civil society, academicians, politicians, and ethnic leaders, particularly Barrister Raja Debashis Roy, Sanjeeb Drang, Prashanta Tripura, Advocate Gonesh Shoren, Rabindra Shoren all are notable. This debate is the point of the journey of the ethnic crisis in independent Bangladesh. We delve more into this issue with some solid facts. Later, when the ethnic leaders—*M.N Larma, Gyanenendu Bikash Chakma, Upendralal Chakma, Siddhartha Chakma* (https://www.parbattanews.com/) met with the father of the nation of Bangladesh, Sheikh Mujibur Rahman, boldly, advised them as "You become Bangali" (Roy et al., 2022; Azad, 2014). For our consideration, the fate was decided that day, the crisis of majority-minority. This statement is the core of the Government's political decision on what they would do in the case of Ethnic people. A good number (17 times during 1972-2022) of Constitution amendments happened over the last fifty years, but not only the Santals but also all the ethnic people were ignored regarding their communal identity, and respectful space, recognition of the Constitution. The two treaties, as said, GoB did not ratify yet, rather the state was called by different names from time to time (see table 2 &3). For example—Primitive, Tribal, Adivasi, and Indigenous. According to the Small Ethnic Groups Institutions Act 2010, Ethnic people have not been freed from the crisis of making their identity, even the 15th amendment of the constitution declared as the People of Bangladesh shall be as Bangali as a nation and citizens of Bangladesh shall be known as Bangladesh (the 15th Amendment of the Constitution, 2011).

*Table 2. Scholarly Debate on the total number of SEGs in Bangladesh*

| Organizations/Acts | Number |
| --- | --- |
| Small Ethnic Groups and Cultural Institutions Act-2010 (Amendment, 2019) | 50 |
| A Review Committee of Ministry of Cultural Affairs 2015 Census, 2011 | 50 |
| Poverty Reduction Strategy Paper, 2001 | 45 |
| Bangladesh Adivasi Forum | 45 |
| International Work Group of Indigenous Affairs, 2022 | 54 |

Source: Authors' compilation.

## A Philosophical Discussion of Sustainable Development

In table 2, we see scholarly debates on the total number of issues; indeed number is still not yet decided. However, in table 3, we see another academic debate about their collective name.

*Table 3. Scholarly Debate on Santal naming issue in Bangladesh*

| Authors | Referring to Santal Is - |
| --- | --- |
| Ali (1998), Besra (2014), Debnath (2010), Sur (1977) | Santal |
| O'Malley (1916) | The people are not all Bengalis, settlers |
| Sarker et al., (2017) | Not Indigenous but Tribal; Small Ethnic Group |
| Rahmatullah et al.(2012) | Tribal |
| Mehrab Ali (2002); Shafie and Kilby (2003) | *Adivasi* |

Source: Authors' compilation.

Tables 2 and 3 give us a complete puzzling scenario about the identity as well as their quantification. Identity takes down to the legal practice in Bangladesh to understand the logic of the self-determination claimed by Small Ethnic Groups for ensuring political participation and human rights. A blurred picture comes after reading tables 2 and 3.

We need to admit that International organizations can do nothing. The Santal people's self-identity crisis has now turned into a scream; because, the Bangladesh government did not intervene yet to ratify ILO-169 and UNDRIP on the other hand their human rights availing situation is becoming ailing day to day (Barkat, 2016; Chakma & Maitrot, 2016). Government and non-governmental organizations take various measures to facilitate the development of dialogue between the government and the ethnic people in this country, however, the paramount objectives of this dialogue are to protect and recognize the human rights of indigenous peoples, sustain the hopes and aspirations of those disadvantaged, improve their institutions, and ensure economic development and political participation, either in a collective or individual identity and dignity in the society. The reality is that the Santal people's identity crisis has now turned into a scream in Bangladesh that was started almost fifty years ago in the parliament (Chakma& Maitrot, 2016; Mohsin, 2002, 2001; Tripura, 2020). The next section is to take the Santal with the treaties.

ILO and UNDRIP are Directives documents that work to protect and enhance the quality of life of Indigenous peoples. The Sustainable Development Goals (SDGs) are one of the steps the United Nations has taken to make the enduring endeavor of Sustainable Development. Looking at the time frame, this is an ongoing international program. Among the SDGs, 'Sustainable Communities' is the eleventh goal out of 17 in the sustainable initiatives by the UN, which, along with Goal Four and others, obviously address the people. During implementing sustainable development goals from 2015, we need to make also the community sustainable, which UNDRIP—2007, and ILO—169 have been advocating for a long time across the world.

We can debrief that to sustain the community, it is wise to be allowed them to go its way, the rooted reason is that SDGs, UNDRIP, and ILO are not even a hundred years old, but the sustainability mechanism, practiced in this community has been time-tested. To us, this is the key to a Sustainable Community, or, true development. Denial the fact (Jahan, 2020, Besra, 2014) is to deny the local history. Taking the local into the legal participation may be seeded in the community Resource Pool, Common Property

Resources, and Political Participation. People of the Santal community, if we imagine, are involved in decision-making at the community level when developing or directing policies taken by the government of Bangladesh for this community, then, we may think of two direct outcomes, no rights violation, and no exclusion will be seen. Yet, in light of UNDRIP and ILO, as said, are legal dimensions to incorporate the peoples' knowledge, then the community [Santal] must continue to move towards political rights for sustainable community development.

All over the world, the ethnic community has a lifelong relationship with land and forest. The Santal community is not exceptional in Bangladesh. To grasp their land in Phulbari, Nawabganj, and Gobindoganj by State agency showed the disrespectful and inhumane relationship.! God gives the earth to men.! Where the kings brought war, bring concord! Take it, not for the cannon but the plow! Not for the service but for commerce! Not for battle but for the industry! Not for conquest but for fraternity! Go on, do it! Make roads, make ports, make towns! Grow, cultivate, colonize, multiply! And on this land, ever clearer of priests and princes, may the divine spirit assert itself through peace and the human spirit through liberty!" (Cited in Paul, 2008, p.51). While discussing the concept of Sustainability, we need to look at the back of western society. The New Science, this western society has a significant contribution; how advanced are we to measure developing countries like us or to measure ourselves by their standards? The Development of retired Santal Principal or Santal female classmates will be calculated on the scale of this new science or by western determined indicators- GDP, Per capita; how far will they go to make progress within the SDGs strategy (Roy,et.al., 2022; Rahman, et.al.,2022)?

In 1683, the French philosopher Bernard Le Bouyer de Fontenelle introduced the great concept of progress. With new science and advanced technology, humans have entered an era of necessary and boundless progress for the human species. After the age of Enlightenment (1750-1900), this idea reached its peak point. The works of August Comte, Hegel, Karl Marx, Herbert Spenser, and so forth, and their contribution to establishing new science, worked fantastically. As a result, a connection was established between progress, growth, Development, technological innovation, and empiricism; science controlled nature and mastery humankind to lead the progress. When the establishment of human authority over nature and the invention of science began, people began to collect raw materials from nature. As production increases, markets are also needed for profit expansion; in this association, colonization becomes a necessary part as we know it.

On the other hand, the tone of environmental disasters is rising globally. This environment protection tone is the tone of today's sustainability development. Suppose one thinks that the concept of Sustainable Development began to practice in the 1970s or 1980s. See the comments of Robert Allen (1980), "Sustainable Development as Development that is likely to achieve lasting satisfaction of human needs and improvement of quality of life" (Cited in Piassani, 2006, p. 92).

The colonial states spread the idea of progress in the colonized areas by talking about the change in the fate of the people in the 1950s. Although the colonies were at the very bottom of civilizational Development, the industrialized colonial powers were at the top of civilizational Development. Hence, growth became a powerful or popular indicator for distinguishing between the population of the industrialized states and the colonies. Although such ideas were in vogue until the 60s, in the 70s, they started facing challenges globally for the interest of the mainstream community but not for minority people like the Santal community.

During the 1960s, the mood had been optimistic. It had been assumed that the development problems of the underdevelopment world to be solved quickly as a result of worldwide economic growth, but in the 1970s, the optimism faded. Economic growth did not prove to be the hoped-for solution o global

### A Philosophical Discussion of Sustainable Development

inequalities. This realization necessitated a paradigm shift to a new notion of Development. We can think it is Sustainable Development, which became popular and widely used in the 1980s.

Sustainable Development is a western philosophy or technology imported to all countries, but the responsibility of financing is given to the respective countries. Think Globally but finance locally. If also there had been funding for development partners to implement the MDGs, it is not in the SDGs; As a result, the question naturally arises, will globalization-based strategies work? As a result, 'localizing SDGs' has emerged as a strategy for implementation in the developing world like ours. Donald Trump raised his chest and said, 'We will not fund for climate change. When the localization is done, there was no need to formulate this strategy globally. Because the nature and the local financing pattern are different, imposed from the top does not bring the benefits of Development, the history of Development has told us rightly long ago.

## CONCLUSION

We saw in this chapter, that since the birth of Bangladesh, when the highest level of authority of the state advised them "Become a Bengali"(Azad, 2014, p.18; Bhowmick, 1996, p.96), then the rest is, to us, an inherent phenomenon. The question of protection of human rights arose to us. It is required to know the minority groups' sensitivity to this issue of 'self-determination.' Otherwise, human rights will worst, already in danger. Establishing human rights for the ethnic people [Santal], we hope the proposed framework will work effectively to make ensure sustainable community development (Roy, et al., 2022).

This article is limited to philosophical discussions on Sustainable Development, we have explained, discussed with field evidence (Rahman et al., 2022), put inference, and finally proposed our opinions on the Santal-related issues. Known, these people have been faced as one of the small ethnic groups in Bangladesh. In this case, the proposed framework could only be one of the options for empowering the Santal community, not the only panacea, however. As discussed, whatever the procedure to deal with the problems, the government is the key role player, and it is the obligation of the nation-state, to ratify the treaties first. By the constitution, the government is the only one who is accountable for its implementation with the service of other agencies. We can see and say that the subject of tripartite relations will come to the local, rural and remote Santal village of the Northeastern part of Bangladesh. Yet, the unanswered question is, in a nation-state, can the government always give equal priority to all ethnic groups (including mainstream groups)? Our unquestioned answer is: No. Does not this mean that we are in favor of discrimination against the Santal community or self-determination? In this context, what is our way out of this issue? For this reason, another unquestioned answer is that, before implementing our proposed framework, the Government of Bangladesh must convey a fundamental structural reform, per se, a constitutional amendment for SEGs recognition. Like Cindy Holder (2004), we can optimistic by saying as concluding remarks—

*By recognizing the right to self-determination and multiple political authorities, Holder argues, indigenous people will receive the respect they deserve (Eisenberg & Halev eds, 2004, p.13)*

Since Sustainable Development is two contradictory terms or concepts, both concomitant terms cannot overstay closely. We should add a word like community or institution in the middle of two words. We indeed suggest the word Community in the case of the Santal people to improve their grassroots development. Authors firmly believe that a Sustainable Community will ensure Development without whipping and catastrophic situations. We, therefore, suggest that community should be added between both words (see figures1 and 2). "Development should be done by maintaining community resources. Furthermore, customary laws are adequate for maintaining or using resources because "Sustainable development is difficult to classify it falls" (James Rosennau, 2003, p.16 cited in Sneddon et al. 2006, p.257)." Again, we contemplate Customary laws when we see "Environmental issues are pervasively integrative in the sense that the value of preserving the environment and maintaining its viability is widely shared at every level of community (James Rosennau, 2003, p.16 cited in Sneddon et al. 2006, p.257).

If a donation or grant is related to Development, it gets the status of a political relationship. Fighting poverty with these donation weapons does not save the environment or develop. This process also leads to internal colonialization (Rist, 2008; Soeftestad, 2004), whereby ethnic minorities lose their self-identity/determination. Nowadays, Sustainable Development is as a process (Orebech et al.,2005) that is evolved with livelihoods, food security, community governance, relationships to homelands and the natural world, and ceremonial and spiritual life are practiced locally within a nation-state. When the Sustainable Development takes the accountability of enabling the transmission of these customary practices to future generations, then it would have brought unexpected (negatively for the ethnic group) result to the ethnic community. It should have operating strategies at multiple levels, Government of Bangladesh have to seek to regenerate the implementation of ethnic natural laws or customary laws on ethnic homelands and expand the scope of Sustainable Developement process. Otherwise, Sustainable Developent is a "captive mind" concept (Alatas, 1972) to the Santal People in Bangladesh.

## REFERENCES

Alatas, S. H. (1972). The Captive Mind In Development Studies. *International Social Science Journal, 24*(1), 9–25.

Ali, A. (1998). *Santals of Bangladesh*. Institute of Social Research & Applied Anthropology.

Ali, M. (2002). *Dinajpurer Adivasi*. Adivasi Academy.

Azad, H. (2014). *Parbbatya Chattogram: Sobuj Paharer Vitor Diye Hingsar Jharna Dhara*. Agami Prakashani.

Barkat, A. (2016). *Political economy of unpeopling of indigenous peoples: The case of Bangladesh*. Mukto Buddhi Prokasana.

Benjaminsen, T. A., & Svarstad, H. (2021). *Political ecology: A critical engagement with global environmental issues*. Springer Nature. doi:10.1007/978-3-030-56036-2

Besra, L. (2014). *A Critical Review of Democracy and Governance Challenges in Bangladesh with special refences to a human rights-based approach for the Development of marginalized indigenous people* [PhD thesis]. Flinders of Institute of Public Policy Management.

Chakma and Maitrot. (2016). *Working paper on – How Ethnic Minorities became poor and stay poor in Bangladesh: A Qualitative enquiry*. EEP/ Shiree.

Chilisa, B. (2017). Decolonising transdisciplinary research approaches: An African perspective for enhancing knowledge integration in sustainability science. *Sustainability Science, 12*(5), 813–827. doi:10.100711625-017-0461-1

Corntassel, J. (2008). Toward sustainable self-determination: Rethinking the contemporary Indigenous-rights discourse. *Alternatives, 33*(1), 105–132. doi:10.1177/030437540803300106

Debnath, M. K. (2010). *Living on the Edge: The predicament of a rural indigenous Santal community in Bangladesh* (Doctoral dissertation).

Debnath, M. K. (2012). The invisible agenda: Civilising mission or missionizing civilization. *International Journal of Human Rights, 16*(3), 461–473. doi:10.1080/13642987.2011.572550

Debnath, M. K. (2020). A community under siege: Exclusionary education policies and indigenous Santals* in the Bangladeshi context. *Third World Quarterly, 41*(3), 453–469. doi:10.1080/01436597.2019.1660634

Du Pisani, J. A. (2006). Sustainable development–historical roots of the concept. *Environmental Sciences, 3*(2), 83–96. doi:10.1080/15693430600688831

Grober, U. (2007). *Deep roots-A conceptual history of sustainable development*. Academic Press.

Hasan, M. M. (2020). *Mining Conflict, Indigenous Peoples and Environmental Justice: The Case of Phulbari Coal Project in Bangladesh* [PhD Thesis]. https://www.ilo.org/wcmsp5/groups/public/---ed_norm/ normes/documents/publication/wcms_205225.pdf https://www.un.org/development/desa/indigenouspeoples/declaration-on-the-rights-of-indigenous-peoples.html

Jahan, F. (2020). *The issue of identity: state denial, local controversies and everyday resistance among the Santal in Bangladesh* [PhD Thesis]. Hale University.

Jeje, Y. (2006). *Southern Alberta Landscapes: Meeting the Challenges Ahead: Export Coefficients for Total Phosphorus, Total Nitrogen and Total Suspended Solids in the Southern Alberta Region: a Review of Literature*. Alberta Environment.

Meadows, D. H., Meadows, D. L., Randers, J., & Behrens, W. W. (2018). The limits to growth. In *Green planet blues* (pp. 25–29). Routledge. doi:10.4324/9780429493744-3

Mohsin, A. (2001). *The state of "minority" rights in Bangladesh*. International Centre for Ethnic Studies.

Mohsin, A. (2002). *The Politics of Nationalism: The Case of the Chittagong Hill Tracts Bangladesh* (2nd ed.). The University Press Limited.

Orebech, P., Bosselman, F., Bjarup, J., Callies, D., Chanock, M., & Petersen, H. (2005). *The role of customary law in sustainable development*. Cambridge University Press.

Parris, T. M., & Kates, R. W. (2003). Characterizing and measuring sustainable development. *Annual Review of Environment and Resources, 28*(1), 559–586. doi:10.1146/annurev.energy.28.050302.105551

Paul, B. D. (2008). A history of the concept of sustainable development: Literature review. The Annals of the University of Oradea. *Economic Sciences Series, 17*(2), 576–580.

Rahman, M. M. (2020). *Organizational gap analysis in achieving SDGs in Bangladesh*. Academic Press.

Rist, G. (2014). *The history of development: from western origins to global faith*. Bloomsbury Publishing.

Roy, P., Chowdhury, J. S., Abd Wahab, H., & Saad, R. (2022). Social Justice Through BPATC in Bangladesh Under the Shadow of Colonialism: Prospects and Challenges. *Social Justice Research Methods for Doctoral Research*, 303-319.

Roy, P., Chowdhury, J. S., Abd Wahab, H., & Saad, R. B. M. (2022). Ethnic Tension of the Bangladeshi Santal: A CDA of the Constitutional Provision. In Handbook of Research on Ethnic, Racial, and Religious Conflicts and Their Impact on State and Social Security (pp. 208-226). IGI Global. doi:10.4018/978-1-7998-8911-3.ch013

Roy, P. K., Hamidi, M., & Roy, S. (2022). Internet as a Field: An Analysis of the Santal Online Communities. In *Practices, Challenges, and Prospects of Digital Ethnography as a Multidisciplinary Method* (pp. 124–137). IGI Global. doi:10.4018/978-1-6684-4190-9.ch009

Sarker, M. A. R., Khan, N. A., & Musarrat, K. M. (2016). Livelihood and vulnerability of the Santals community in Bangladesh. *The Malaysian Journal of Social Administration*, *12*(1), 38–55. doi:10.22452/mjsa.vol12no1.2

Sen, A. (2009). *The Idea of Justice*. Allan Lane Penguin Books.

Shafie, H., & Kilby, P. (2003). *Including the excluded: ethnic inequality and Development in Northwest Bangladesh*. Academic Press.

Smith, L. T. (2021). *Decolonizing methodologies: Research and indigenous peoples*. Bloomsbury Publishing. doi:10.5040/9781350225282

Sneddon, C., Howarth, R. B., & Norgaard, R. B. (2006). Sustainable development in a post-Brundtland world. *Ecological Economics*, *57*(2), 253–268. doi:10.1016/j.ecolecon.2005.04.013

Soeftestad, L. T. (1994). *Workshop on participatory development*. Academic Press.

Soeftestad, L. T. (2004). Biodiversity conservation, communication and language–is English a solution, a problem or both? *Policy Matters*, *13*, 281–283.

Tripura, J. (2016). Reflection of the Santal Rebellion and the Situations of the Indigenous Peoples of Bangladesh. *Unread Voice*.

Tripura, P. (2018). *Prantikotar Khaad Theke Mohaakashe*. Samhati Publication.

Tripura, P. (2020). *Colonial Shadow in Bangladesh (Bangla books)*. Sangbed.

## ADDITIONAL READING

Bodding, P. O. (1887). *Traditions and Institutions of Santals*. Bahumukhi Prakashan.

Bodding, P. O. (1925). *Studies in Santal Medicine and Connected Folklore: The Santals and Disease.* Royal Asiatic Society of Bengal.

Chowdhury, J. S., Wahab, H. A., Saad, R. M., Reza, H., & Ahmad, M. M. (Eds.). (2022). *Reciprocity and its practice in social research.* IGI Global. doi:10.4018/978-1-7998-9602-9

Day, A. (2015). An Ancient History: Ethnographic Study of the Santhal. *International Journal of Novel Research in Humanity and Social Sciences, 2*(4), 31–38.

Erueti, A. (2017). The Politics Of International Indigenous Rights. *University of Toronto Law Journal, 67*(4), 569–595. doi:10.3138/utlj.67.5

Erueti, A. (2022). *The UN Declaration on the Rights of Indigenous Peoples: A New Interpretative Approach.* Oxford University Press. doi:10.1093/oso/9780190068301.001.0001

Gilbert, J. (2017). Indigenous Peoples, Human Rights, and Cultural Heritage: Towards a Right to Cultural Integrity. In A. Xanthaki, S. Valkonen, L. Heinämäki, & P. Nuorgam (Eds.), *Indigenous Peoples' Cultural Heritage: Rights, Debates, Challenges* (pp. 20–38). Brill.

Hossain, K. T. (2000). *The Santals of Bangladesh: An ethnic minority in transition.* Works Shop Paper of ENBS.

Kais, S. M. (2021). Dying with dignity: Perception of good death among the Santals of Bangladesh. In *Death and Events* (pp. 26–47). Routledge. doi:10.4324/9781003155324-3

Kukutai, T., & Taylor, J. (2016). *Indigenous data sovereignty: Toward an agenda.* ANU Press. doi:10.22459/CAEPR38.11.2016

Myrdal, G. (1972). *Asian drama; an inquiry into the poverty of nations* (Vol. 1). Pantheon.

Rafi, M. (2017). *Small ethnic groups of Bangladesh: a mapping exercise.* Panjeree Publications.

Rostow, W. W. (1959). The stages of economic growth. *The Economic History Review, 12*(1), 1–16. doi:10.1111/j.1468-0289.1959.tb01829.x

Roy, P., Chowdhury, J. S., Abd Wahab, H., Saad, M. R. B., & Parahakaran, S. (2021). Christianity, COVID-19, and marginal people of Bangladesh: An experience from the Santal Community. In Handbook of Research on the Impact of COVID-19 on Marginalized Populations and Support for the Future (pp. 65-82). IGI Global.

Roy, P., Wahab, H., & Hamidi, M. (2022). *Achieving Sustainable Development Goals: A Case Study of Ministry ff Chittagong Hill Tracts Affairs.* IGI. doi:10.4018/978-1-6684-7499-0.ch010

Sen, A. (1976). Poverty: An ordinal approach to measurement. *Econometrica, 44*(2), 219–231. doi:10.2307/1912718

Sen, A. (1988). *The standard of living.* Cambridge University Press.

Sen, A. (2008). The idea of justice. *Journal of Human Development, 9*(3), 331–342. doi:10.1080/14649880802236540

## KEY TERMS AND DEFINITIONS

**Customary Law:** Is a long-standing practice among the community to guide their socio-economic life.The Santal community is habituated with their tradions to keep it for long term.

**Development:** When the community feels the positive change to smooth their life without making their traditions devasted is called Development in the Santal community.

**Santal:** Is one of the Ethnic groups amid 50 according to Government of Bangladesh. This community is the largest community in number in the norther part of Bangladesh; and the second largest of Bangladesh. But in this community, most of the people live with hand to mouth, and lots of sufferings to lead the life.

**Sustainable:** Whatever we have in the text regarding the meaning of Sustainable, we understand that it is the nurturing of nature based on community-based guidelines. So, the Santal community says they have Customary law to protect nature with love and humanity, which is called sustainability.

# Chapter 6
# Discontinuity, Sustainability, and Critical Learnership:
## Development, Dynamics, and Demand

**Jay Hays**
*Melbourne Institute of Technology, Australia*

**Hayo Reinders**
*King Mongkut's University of Technology, Thonburi, Thailand*

## ABSTRACT

*It is generally understood that we are in an age of upheaval, accelerating change, and global fragility. The increasing complexity of problems we are facing and the discontinuity we have been experiencing are only likely to escalate as we proceed into the new millennium. These challenges are more daunting when one considers dwindling resources, potential conflict, and environmental vulnerability. Less clear is what we can better do to prepare the next generation of leaders to guide and support engaged employees and citizenry to work together to solve immense problems. The chapter's subtext is that conventional education and professional development are insufficient—if not counterproductive—to equipping current and future generations with the skills and dispositions to contend with the chaos and complexity of the emerging millennium. To the degree this is true, approaches to learning and professional development need to change. To this end, readers might benefit most from the practical and realistic recommendations outlined herein for schools, organisations, and communities.*

## INTRODUCTION

### Context

It is generally understood that we are in an age of upheaval, accelerating change, and global fragility (See for example, Anderson, 2019; Bendell, 2016; Hays, 2015b). The increasing complexity of problems we are facing and the discontinuity we have been experiencing in our lives—social, political, economic—

DOI: 10.4018/978-1-6684-6172-3.ch006

are only likely to escalate as we proceed into the new millennium (Deudney, 2018; Smith, et al., 2017; Weber & Tarba, 2014). These challenges are the more daunting when one considers dwindling resources, potential conflict, and environmental vulnerability.* The coming decades will be fraught with wicked problems needing solution but also rich opportunities on which we might capitalize.

Less clear is what we can better do to prepare the next generation of leaders to guide and support engaged employees and citizenry to work together to solve immense problems and exploit opportunities as they arise. Becoming more evident is the fact that conventional approaches to learning and development are largely ineffective (if not counterproductive) at equipping individuals and, by extension organisations and society, to deal with problems and opportunities of global consequence, particularly when involving circumstances not before encountered (Berkes, 2007; Lotz-Sisitka, et al., 2015; Miceli, et al., 2021). Novel, unanticipated situations require different approaches than standard ones (Weick & Sutcliffe, 2011). Thus, a different kind of learning is needed to prepare individuals and teams to contend with them (Hays, 2015a; Lotz-Sisitka, et al., 2015). Again—and a vexing problem itself—is how to prepare people for the atypical and, possibly, the unknown and unexpected? As attributed to Albert Einstein, 'we can't solve problems by using the same kind of thinking we used when we created them'.

*Figure 1. Sustainability, discontinuity and critical learnership*

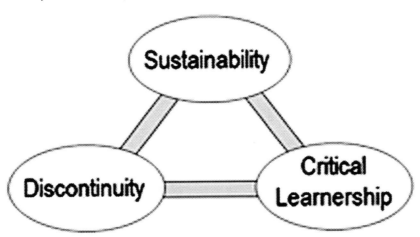

Unanticipated opportunities or problems of sufficient scope can make or break an organisation or a nation (Coaffee, 2019). The ill-equipped will likely fail; the resilient and ready will possibly prevail (Deffuant & Gilbert, 2011; Representing CSIRO, see Cork's (2010) edited volume on resilience and transformation). Organisations and educational institutions that understand and exploit (1) discontinuity, (2) sustainability, and (3) critical learnership may prove to remain the most viable through tumultuous times (Burnard & Bhamra, 2011. See, also, Fiksel (2015) and Kantur & Iseri-Say (2012). Hays & Reinders introduced the concept of "critical learnership" in their so-titled 2018 article). Thus, one purpose of this article is to explain these concepts and highlight their importance in preparing for uncertainty (Chapter 14 in Shuck, et al., (2018) is an engaging read on preparing for uncertainty and Stacey's (1992) book a watershed text on the subject applied to management and organisation). Understanding their interdependent nature is also critical. Because they operate in concert, knowing and applying the theory and

## Discontinuity, Sustainability, and Critical Learnership

principles of only one—say, sustainability—will be less productive than incorporating all three (Taken together, the references listed above lead to this conclusion, with Miceli, et al., (2021) particularly relevant). We suggest that there is a synergetic relationship amongst discontinuity, sustainability, and Critical Learnership[†].

At the same time, it should be realised that, while the title of this article, *Discontinuity, Sustainability and Critical Learnership,* provides a reasonable place to begin, each term is itself complex and there are many other associated elements needing explication. These terms are unpacked and shown, and other important elements are included in the dynamic model put forward as the centrepiece of the article (Figure 4). This model, representing the second part of the title, *Development, Dynamics, and Demand,* illustrates the relationships amongst, possible synergies, and potential value of integrating the core concepts, principles, and practices of discontinuity, sustainability, and critical learnership.

This is the first time that the linkages amongst these important concepts and disciplines have been drawn. Thus, this article represents an advance in understanding how learning and professional development can be enhanced in keeping with the demands (and limitations) of the 21$^{st}$ Century. That said, more research is needed to confirm the place, power, and lines of influence between and amongst the elements of the model, and under what conditions the complex system the model portrays (and designated parts of it works). In other words, how does the environment affect operation and how does system operation affect its surrounds? The model is, in the end, an ecological one, and thus how the system behaves in and interacts with the environment is an important consideration. The model (see Figure 4), attempts to represent and account for possible environment affects and their implications.

While largely a conceptual model based in theory and emerging empirical study, education and professional development are applied disciplines. If we accept that learning is about transforming lives, organisations, and societies and equipping individuals for possibilities still unfolding (ideas of unfolding and emergence are taken up in sources including Litiche, et al., (2011) and Peschl (2019). The authors entertain "learning forward" and anticipatory learning with respect to curricula for the future in Hays & Reinders, 2020) then we need to know what practical measures can be taken to achieve those ends. We also need to identify and eliminate practices that are impeding initiative, creativity, autonomy, and collective action within an ethical framework (Kostoulas-Makrakis (2012) provides useful background in this complex of interrelated variables). Our model attempts to do that by showing elements that impede positive transformation and those that promote it sustainably, and how and why those dynamics take place.

The new millennium is dramatic, ever-changing, and both exciting and threatening. Conventional education offers correspondingly little: it is conservative, staid, and slow to change, seemingly more concerned with replication and perpetuation than evolution and transformation (Hays, 2013b, 2015a; Lautensach, 2020). As the model at Figure 4 suggests, this tendency is mirrored in many of today's organisations. It appears that educational institutions and businesses unwittingly and unintentionally collude to dampen sustainable innovation. To the degree this is true, approaches to learning and professional development need to change by making them somewhat *unconventional.* Terms that might embody the kinds of change necessary include paradoxical, metaphorical, extemporaneous, inverted, even chaotic (Insightful background may be found in e Cunha, et al., (2212) and Lewis, 2014). But how? To this end, readers might benefit most from the practical and realistic recommendations outlined herein for schools, organisations, and communities.

## IMPORTANT TERMS, CONCEPTS, AND PRINCIPLES

**Critical Learnership** – Critical Learnership is a term coined in 2018 by Hays and Reinders, describing an emerging ecosystem perspective on sustainable and collaborative learning, innovation, and transformation. At its essence, it is a critical, active mindset towards finding sustainable solutions to everyday problems. As they have explained,

*Critical Learnership is a perspective of learning incorporating and governing strategies and values oriented toward sustainability, innovation, and transformation. It involves continual and deliberate critique and challenge of existing ways of thinking, doing, and being, and unlearning and supplanting these when found to limit our ability to solve problems and capitalise upon opportunities that arise.*

Later, these same authors added that,

*Critical Learnership is a way of thinking about and restructuring how we approach learning. It enables continual learning, unlearning, and reinvention through building certain skills and favourable dispositions and introducing strategies founded on paradoxical principles of sustainability and discontinuity (Hays & Reinders, 2020, p. 399).*

The notion of "paradoxical principles of sustainability and discontinuity" is key to the thesis put forward in this present article. Critical Learnership needs coexisting of both sustainability and discontinuity as the tensions produced by the dynamic relationship fuel continued learning and development.[1] At the same time, feedback loops operating in the system (primarily from Critical Learning) promote continued sustainability and discontinuity, as depicted in Figure 4 (See Perrin, 2012).

**Disruption** – Disruption implies a disturbance, interruption, unsettling, interference, or disorganisation in a task, activity, or normal flow of work. Responses include (1) efforts to return to the way things were (status quo) and (2) embrace or learn from the disruption, making the most of it. It is probably the result of some external force (and likely unanticipated), though might arise from within. Critical Learnership actively and intentionally promotes disruption in order to upset the status quo and keep organisational members "on their toes".

**Discontinuity** – In many respects, a discontinuity is a disruption in a steady and generally predictable stream of activity or process. Think of a break, disconnect, or gap. A discontinuity could be an altered or transformed state (a new or different way of being) than that previous and leading up to the discontinuity, probably unexpected.

As we demonstrate in Figure 4, a quality of both disruption and discontinuity may—for all the churn and turmoil they cause—be productive and constructive in leading to positive and beneficial learning and change; that is, leading to development. This is, however, not given. A framework for best handling disruption and discontinuity is needed to help organisation members channel and constructively use the tension. Such a framework provides systems and mechanisms for supporting organisational members through the process of converting disruption and discontinuity to learning and innovation. Suggestions on what this might entail are provided in Table 2.

**Development** – A development is both a process, such as maturing, and an event or activity. Synonyms for development include, for the former, evolution, progress, and advancement, and, for the latter, discovery, outcome, or phenomenon. For our purposes, here, the term "progress" is germane as discussions on innovation often imply progress as in *movement towards an improved or advanced capability*. With respect to sustainability, we will emphasise that an innovation may be neither necessary nor necessarily represent progress.

**Sustainability** – In a 2020 article, Hays and Reinders explain sustainability thusly:

*At its most basic level, [sustainability] means possessing an enduring quality. For human systems, this involves making the best use of available resources to support a healthy existence and ensure a viable future for all, neither depleting resources irreplaceably nor harming the environment. At the least, sustainability concerns continued maintenance (having enough or doing enough to survive). At its best, it is about thriving and flourishing now and into the future (Hays & Reinders, 2020, p. 37).*

Historically, sustainability was primarily thought to relate to the environment and natural resources, as in, *how much demand can the environment bear?* We use the term more broadly and apply it to any human endeavour, with questions such as:

- How sustainable is the current level of effort? (How much can an individual or team be expected to do given resources available?)
- How can we do more with what we have?
- Is our output worth the effort and cost? How can we reduce drain and increase desired output?
- How can we create and sustain a more enriching environment with reduced or no additional demand on resources?
- How are short-term benefits impacting our long-term quality of life?
- Do we really need that next innovation? How does it improve our long-term prospects?

In *Sustainable Learning and Education: A Curriculum for the Future* (Hays & Reinders, 2020, p. 37), we outlined 25 principles of sustainability and ecological thinking. A couple of the more germane here being:

- Design and build to solve more than one problem or requirement.
- Design and build for need and meaningful purpose, rather than for profit and consumerism.
- Accept responsibility for future generations and the welfare of the planet.
- Strive to become self-sustaining and self-sufficient (lessen dependence on external support and funding). Build internal capacity through learning.
- Always investigate and ascertain as far as possible the place of a new product or idea in the wider system and its long-term contributions and impacts.
- Strive for the flourishing of all, seeking equity and balance across stakeholders and generations.

And one we just made up: see every disruptive complex problem as an opportunity to collaborate across disciplines and around the globe to design and implement sustainable and innovative solutions.

Whilst not all-encompassing, these principles and guidelines touch on important aspects of relevance to our thesis here. We see reference to (a) the big picture and long-term viability, (b) innovate because there is a real problem to solve not merely an opportunity to capitalise on (or create) an indulgent demand, (c) the power of diversity, collaboration, and capability-building, and (d) the importance of inclusion and well-being for all.

**Innovation** – An innovation is basically a new product, service, method, or process. It is generally implied that innovation is a good thing, as if innovations assure a better future, easier or improved labour, or more pleasant lifestyle. Innovation is held to be necessary for the survival of businesses and, perhaps, following from this, good for societies. There is, however, nothing necessarily or inherently better in any given innovation, so a cost-benefit analysis is probably justified before a potential new product or way of doing things is released or implemented. In our opinion, to ensure a sustainable future, it is incumbent upon leaders to thoroughly investigate the potential contribution of an innovation to making the world a better place before deciding to promote it.

**Wicked Problems** – As the authors have explained in "Wicked Problem: Educating for Complexity and Wisdom" (Hays, 2013; Hays & Reinders, 2018; Hays & Reinders, 2020 and elsewhere), wicked problems are characterised by the facts that:

- There is seldom one right answer to solving a wicked problem, though there might be many partial solutions from which to choose.
- The problem may have been unyielding to attempts to solve it; or it may appear to have been solved only to later resurface.
- Solution attempts may also produce unintended, unexpected consequences or permit the arising of other latent problems.

Wicked problems have been described by other researchers as "tangles of complexity, controversy, and uncertainty" and as "webs of problems", (Carvalho & Mazzon, 2015; Ghuman & Olmstead, 2015; Walke et al., 2008) as such, they are complex, stubborn, and hard to fathom. Being able to work effectively within and upon complex systems requires more than intelligence, knowledge, and experience. Wicked problems require a different sort of mind, a new kind of thinking, generating creative, innovative solutions not before attempted. *Discontinuity, Sustainability and Critical Learnership: Development, Dynamics, and Demand* is not about wicked problems, per se, but they—along with Complex Adaptive Systems (CAS), in general—must be understood as any significant development or innovation will be deployed into a system where it will be integrated or rejected as determined by factors inherent in the system or operating on it already (Perrin (2012). The article by de Lourdes Machado-Taylor (2011) presents a relevant and accessible discussion of CAS and change).

For the same reasons, it is likewise important to understand the system for potential innovation (or creating a culture of innovation). System impediments, leverages, consequences / impacts, and implications can all be ascertained through system analysis, which will help determine whether or not a given innovation or strategy will be constructive and sustainable in the long run, and how it might be best implemented. Our model at Figure 4 exemplifies these types of dynamics and how systems analysis may be used to assess readiness for and implications of a given change, and determine likely points of impedance and opportunities for leverage.

**Sustainable Development (and Innovation)** – From the foregoing, sustainable development and innovation is a complex concept and set of strategies for productive transformation that is beneficial in the long run for the planet and all its inhabitants, today and into the future. Adhering to principles of sustainable development and innovation should increase the likelihood that potential development(s) and innovation(s) add more value in terms of resources and resourcefulness than they cost, that they are generative and build capability and capacity rather than depleting or undermining it. Sustainable development and innovation is long term and big picture. It may seem to slow progress and demand

## Discontinuity, Sustainability, and Critical Learnership

investment unnecessarily in the short term, but the payoff in the long run—the greater good—is worth it. If not, the potential development(s) and innovation(s) are not beneficial and advisable, even if presently attractive. Better understanding and weighing the drivers and dynamics of related decisions and courses of action is a major purpose behind *Discontinuity, Sustainability and Critical Learnership: Development, Dynamics, and Demand.*

## Dynamics

From Hays (2010b) and other sources, the following table presents background on dynamics.

*Table 1. Enumerated principles and characteristics of dynamics (as applicable in Complex Adaptive Systems (CAS)). (You can find sources exploring dynamics with respect to wisdom in Hays (2008) and to leadership in Hays (2015c).*

| Dynamics |
| --- |
| 1. Dynamic means characterised by continuous change, activity, or motion. It generally implies a positive movement such as progress, learning, or evolution; but may also be a downward, defeating, degrading, or devolving tendency. |
| 2. Dynamics have to do with forces and motions that characterise systems. As characterising, these forces and motions produces patterns. Patterns can be mapped. |
| 3. A system is a set of interacting or interdependent parts forming an integrated whole. How these parts interact amongst themselves and with their external environment are the patterns referred to above that can be mapped. |
| 4. Forces can be either internal or external to the system. That is, one element may influence another within the system, or an external force may influence one or more elements within the system. |
| 5. As one element is impacted, it varies. This means it raises or lowers, increases or diminishes. This variance causes elements linked to it to vary as well. Thus, whatever happens to one element will have impact on other elements in the system. |
| 6. Were it not dynamic, that is changing or moving, it would be static. Stasis means no movement, as in "status quo" (conditions remaining as they are). |
| 7. A key concept of dynamic systems is interaction between and amongst elements and between the system and its environment. Interaction implies mutual influence—elements interdepend. |
| 8. A system influences its environment, as well as being influenced by it. |
| 9. Elements influence one another: as one varies (as a response to some stimuli) it causes one or more other elements to vary. For this reason, elements can be called "variables." |
| 10. Influence on other elements is called flow. Flows have direction, but sometimes the direction of flow changes depending on which variables are being influenced by internal and external forces. |
| 11. All human groups are social systems—lovers, friends, families, teams, clubs, members of religious institutions, organisations of all types and sizes, communities, and so on—partners in a relationship. Negotiations occur between / across social systems. |
| 12. Influences (forces) on human systems such as teams, organisations, and communities, can come in diverse forms including social, political, moral, emotional, intellectual, and psychological, as well as a raft of physical forces (climate, economics). |
| 13. There are dynamics at work in all social endeavour and interaction: conflict, problem-solving and decision-making, leadership and influence, teamwork and collaboration, motivation, morale, spirit, etc. |

## Ecology / Ecosystem

Ample references exist covering ecology and ecosystems (literally in the millions), with Preiser et al., (2018) indicative and relevant to our thesis. However, for our purposes, here, we will consider the topics as discussed previously by us (e.g., Hays & Reinders, 2020, 2021) as they have established a conceptual and analytical framework for complex social systems and their dynamic behaviour.

Simply put, and drawing on Complex Adaptive Systems theory and systems thinking (See Thakore et al., 2022), this view holds that any given social system such as a team, partnership, or institution and any given phenomenon or behavior within a social system such as motivation, conflict, or innovation can only be understood by taking into consideration all the elements in the system, their interdependencies and interaction, and the co-influences between the system and its larger environment. The elements and their dynamic relationships can be "mapped"; and, to the degree this mapping complete and accurate, the behaviour of the system can be at least partly predicted, as has been shown in Hays & Reinders (2021) and Hays (2010b).

## Systems Thinking / Complex Adaptive Systems

As may be drawn from the discussion above with respect to ecosystem, dynamics, and wicked problems, Complex Adaptive Systems (CAS) are comprised of multiple elements or parts grouped (permeably bounded) together to serve a particular function or purpose, the parts dynamically interdependent and interacting (Hazy & Silberstang, 2009). There are likely subsystems (smaller groupings) within the CAS, each with its own defined structure, purpose, and function. Permeably, in this case, implies that the system or some of its parts interact with the external environment, exchanging information or other resources, influencing and, in turn, being influenced by it. Subtly (or not so) the system and the environment adapt and evolve together (or perish). There are mountains of useful resources on CAS (a handful included as background for this article include: Carvalho & Mazzon, 2020; de Lourdes Machado-Taylor, 2011; Dooley, 1997; Hays, 2010b; Holden, 2005); Levin et al., 2013; Perrin, 2012; Preiser et al., 2018) so only brief treatment is provided here.

As mentioned earlier, system behaviour can be predicted to a degree based on thorough knowledge of the cogent elements and their arrangements and relationships (Hays, 2010b). Patterns of behaviour will be consistent until the system is perturbed significantly, likely the result of some stimulus in the environment. This means that the system is designed perfectly to deliver what it does (like it or not). If something needs to happen or produce differently, then one or more operative parts of the system has to be modified, at what may be thought of as leverage points (Hays & Reinders, 2021). A key assumption regarding CASs is that their behaviour (and their composite identity) is greater than the simple sum of their parts, or what is called synergy (Hays, 2010a).

About systems thinking, Hays (2010a, p. 77) explained,

*Systems thinking helps us understand the complexity of problems and opportunities, and informs us where to intercede with the greatest probability of success. Systems thinking and its tools are clever, but not merely. Their use can elicit wisdom and if used wisely can promote elegant, ethical, and sustainable solutions to seemingly intractable problems.*

And as Arnold and Wade put it: 'Systems thinking is, literally, a *system of thinking about systems*' (2015; p. 670. Emphasis in the original).

Given the increasing recognition of the fragility of our planet, interconnectedness of all things, and nature of wicked problems (see Barnett & Jackson (2020) and Lehtonen et al., (2019) for rich and relevant discussions on these themes). thinking systemically and acting responsibly to solve problems and innovate sustainably within the context of Complex Adaptive Systems is imperative. One way to help us do that is modelling the problem or opportunity system, to which we now turn our attention.

## Modelling Complex Adaptive Systems

Understanding and effectively striving to solve complex, wicked problems or change Complex Adaptive Systems is as challenging as it is important. Toward the end of solving tenacious, multifaceted, and far-reaching problems and improving the performance of a given CAS, researchers, policymakers, and astute program executives develop and / or utilise various modelling tools and approaches (See Kazakov et al., (2021) or Sturmberg (2018) for recent examples, and Reynolds &Holwell (2010) for an accessible text on various modelling systems). The model we employ is a home-grown modification of soft systems modelling (Checkland, 2000; Checkland & Poulter, 2010), resembling the systems mapping techniques of Causal Loop and Relationship Diagrams (see Jia et al., (2021) for a timely article using causal loop and relationship diagramming), with our article, "Viability of the Sustainable Development Ecosystem" (Hays & Reinders, 2021), a recent example (the first author has explored a range of phenomena using this socioecological approach to understand and depict the dynamics of the respective Complex Adaptive Systems, with germane examples including Hays (2008, 2010b, 2012, 2015b, 2015c).

In the next section, we present causal loop-relationship diagrams depicting what we believe are key elements of a disruption, sustainability, and Critical Learnership ecosystem, Figures 1, 2, and 3, respectively. Figure 4 integrates these subsystems (herein referred to as domains) into an encompassing Complex Adaptive System model and characterises the elements of these domains and their dynamic interactions and co-influences. Envisaging and comprehending this ecosystem is vital due to the (a) degree we confront disruption and demands for adaptation, (b) increasing demand for sustainability, and (c) presumed requirement for Critical Learnership to enable sustainable response to disruption and adaptation.

Whilst we are relatively certain that disruption, sustainability, and Critical Learnership have not formerly been integrated and conceived of as an ecosystem, we draw on previous work by the authors who explored sustainable development as an ecosystem (Hays & Reinders, 2021). Their model emphasised the role and dynamics of learning from both success and failure, and the importance of motivation in driving the system. Though not presenting a dynamic model, Hays & Reinders (2020) developed an adaptive systems / ecological framework for sustainable learning and education. There they were concerned with:

*...innovation that constantly seeks to reduce harm to the environment and the planet's ecosystems and improve the quality of life for all Earth's inhabitants. Such innovation accepts that profit and efficiency can be achieved whilst simultaneously serving widespread interests and preserving long-term viability. It is innovation that is conscious of itself—a knowing innovation—responsive, responsible, and ethical, continually learning from and in its interaction with the world and improving upon itself (p. 42).*

Earlier, Hays (2015c) presented a detailed causal loop – relationship diagram of a Complex Adaptive System model he labelled citizenship, democracy, and professionalism for a sustainable future. Key aspects of that model include the building of empowered and agentic engagement in the community towards sustainability. Interestingly, Critical Reflection, was shown to be a crucial driver of learning and change (as shown in the model at Figure 4, Critical Reflection is a key factor of Critical Learnership) and enabling involvement, collaboration, and participation appeared essential to a productive ecosystem.

These subjects are taken up, again, from a different perspective in "Criticality and Creativity in Presencing" (Hays & Reinders, 2020). The authors note that Critical Presencing—an integration of presencing, Critical Learnership, and sustainable development—can lead to

*...individual, team, and organisational outcomes [(innovations)] that contribute to the greater good and long-term sustainability. It does this by increasing individuals' conscious engagement in the world while imposing a critical stance to what is known, what needs to be learned, and what must be unlearned, then reconstructed. Being always present and critically mindful, individuals are more likely to see objectively the merits and disadvantages of the way things are, why they may be so, and what needs to be done differently (p. 410).*

The model proposed here takes into account and builds upon this previous research, along with complementary sources such as Inigo &Albareda (2016) and Karakiewicz (2016).

## A WALK AROUND THE MODEL

Befitting the title of this article, the Causal Loop – Relationship Diagram presented here (Figure 4) comprises three main regions or domains, Discontinuity, Sustainability, and Critical Learnership. Note that each domain has its own internal elements, functions, operations, and dynamics, but, for the purposes of this portrayal of the real world, each region is relevant only insofar as it relates to the others in a comprehensive Complex Adaptive System (CAS) as discussed in the preceding sections. Each region may be thought of as a major subsystem of the larger Discontinuity, Sustainability, and Critical Learnership ecology.

Toward building a comprehensible dynamic model, we first present three simplified causal loop – relationship diagrams, one for each region of the Discontinuity, Sustainability, and Critical Learnership ecosystem, Figures, 1, 2, and 3 respectively. These are later elaborated in the encompassing model of the ecosystem presented in Figure 4.

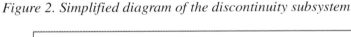

*Figure 2. Simplified diagram of the discontinuity subsystem*

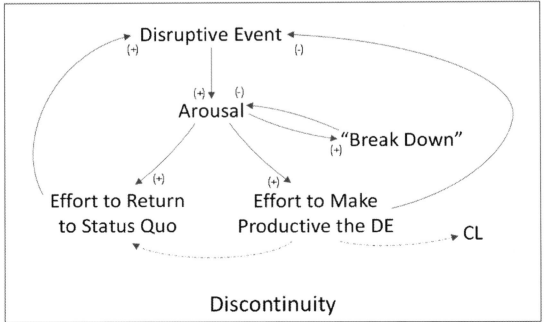

*Discontinuity, Sustainability, and Critical Learnership*

At left you see a causal loop - relationship diagram of the discontinuity subsystem. To simplify explanation, system elements are limited to a very few and no context is provided. The purpose of this and the two simplified diagrams to follow is to illustrate dynamic influence relationships amongst system elements and demonstrate how CLRDs function to model Complex Adaptive Systems.

We begin with a "disruptive event". Any given disruption is likely to produce arousal, as indicated by the positive symbol (+). Arousal may be thought of as a flight or fight response, stress or excitement (see Roelofs et al., (2010 and Schabracq et al., 2003). We see this as tension that seeks release, fuel that drives behaviour. Plus (+) and minus (-) symbols indicate the influence one element (variable) has on another: The plus sign indicates that as one variable increases, correspondingly so does the one that follows. A negative sign (-) indicates that the raising of one variable has a reverse or counter-influential role on the subsequent variable.

In this case, arousal has three possible routes depending on the individual or organisation (and, in fact, might affect different individuals in the same circumstances differently depending on their resilience, experience, attitudes, perceptions, and other factors). One route concerns efforts to maintain the status quo—the way things are, to get back to normal as soon as possible. This route reflects the view that disruption is bad, to be avoided, and can be prevented with sufficient skill, effort, and other resources.

The second possible route is attempt to make productive the disruptive event, either incorporating basic learnings from the experience in attempting to get back to normal, shown by the dashed line to the left, or to make the most of disruption from a learning point of view. We will find this second possible route to be potentially the most constructive from a learning, adaptation, and innovation perspective. The third route is to "freeze" as a result of heightened or continuous stress in the aroused state caused by disruption. This is effectively a paralysis or shut down, the "burn out" we sometimes hear of, basically a defense mechanism, which, whilst understandable, is not productive in organisational terms. It could represent turning a blind eye toward disruption and change or pretending it doesn't exist. As indicated by the (-), increased break down results in decreased arousal in the individual (though granted this may increase stress for other organisational members).

*Figure 3. Simplified diagram of the sustainability subsystem*

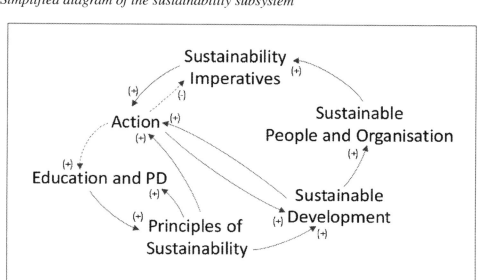

At right we see the simplified CLRD of the sustainability subsystem. We begin with Sustainability Imperatives. In organisational terms, these are the results of dramatic shifts in the external environment leading to perceived need for urgent action, increasing appreciation for the role of the organisation in demonstrating sustainability initiatives as part of Corporate Social Responsibility (CSR) (Moon, 2007; Montiel, 2008), or undertaking projects linked to sustainability principles (indicatively listed at Table 1) to remain viable in the long-term.

Imperatives imply action, as shown next. If action is perceived as effective, there will be a reduction in the challenge posed by Sustainability Imperatives, indicated by the (-). One action taken as a response to Sustainability Imperatives might be to increase Education and Professional Development for Sustainability, granted a strategic rather than operational response. If this happens, the flow-on affect ultimately leads to better Action and Sustainable Development, and further to Sustainable People and Organisation. This is a result of adoption of Principles of Sustainability, which, not coincidentally, improves Education and Professional Development, comprising a virtuous cycle. A virtuous cycle is basically a reinforcing loop across system elements that continually increase or improve performance in a desired, beneficial direction. Virtuous cycles are explained and illustrated in a series of articles by Hays (2010a), Neeley (2015), and many other sources, some included in the reference section.

Increasing Sustainable People and Organisation will have two affects on Sustainability Imperatives, as indicated by the (+ / -) reflecting that (a) the negative impact of external imperatives will be reduced as an outcome of better resilience and capability to deal with disruption—the (-) part—and the organisation's leadership may adopt a constructive and proactive approach to intentional disruption in order to promote continuous learning, adaptation, and innovation—the (+) aspect. Support for this portrayal may be found in Beabout (2012), Earl et al., (2018), and Hays (2015a).

*Figure 4. Simplified diagram of the Critical Learnership subsystem*

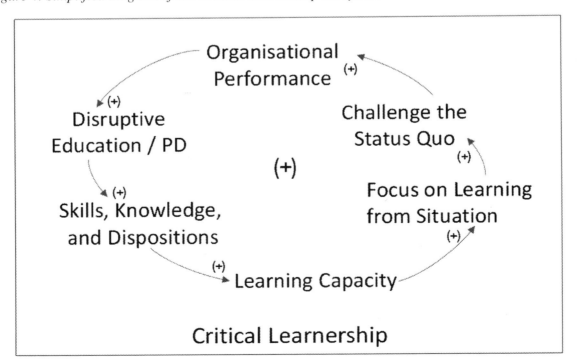

Moving to the third simplified CLRD, Critical Learnership (Hays & Reinders, 2018), we begin with Organisational Performance, assuming that it is a matter of high interest to organisations everywhere and presumably a key objective of learning. The performance in focus is with respect or in response to disruption, generally from the environment (market forces, technology).

The diagram (Figure 4) shows that Organisational Performance and Disruptive Education and Professional Development are positive linked. In this case, implied is that as performance drops (or is recognised as less than desirable) as a function of disruption, conventional education and professional development are increasingly deemed insufficient. (Not shown is a possible response being to increase conventional training, education, and professional development (as in *more is better*), but this will be proven to be wasteful and, perhaps, counterproductive, as has been demonstrated in Hays (2012, 2013b). The paradox of success applies here; see e Cunha & Putnam (2019) and Elsass (1993). As a result, the need for responsive and effective training, education, and professional development *in that context* is compelling and, thus, suitably designed and implemented. Suggestions of the nature of disruptive training, education, and professional development are provided at Table 2.

Continuing, we see that as Disruptive Education and Professional Development increase, so do relevant Skills, Knowledge, and Dispositions (showcased in Table 3). As these go up, so does organisational Learning Capacity, one aspect of which is Learning from Situation. With increased Learning Capacity and real-time learning, there is likely to be a corresponding increase in Challenging of the Status Quo—questioning how things are, how they need to be, and taking appropriate action to redress problems and weaknesses. As Challenging of the Status Quo increases (to some level of saturation and overload causing breakdown; see Figure 1), Organisational Performance improves, reinforcing the importance of Disruptive Education and Professional Development. This subsystem is largely a virtuous cycle, as indicated by the (+) in the centre of the diagram.

There is, of course, some danger that improved Organisational Performance might lead to less attention to and investment in Disruptive Education and Professional Development. Should this unfortunate outcome come to pass, each subsequent step in the cycle is likely to reduce, cycling back, ultimately, to diminished Organisational Performance.

The previous section presented simplified Causal Loop-Relationship Diagrams for the Discontinuity, Sustainability, and Critical Learnership subsystems respectively. Key points to take forward are that:

1. Disruption produces arousal. As we will see, arousal is inevitable and essential, potentially beneficial, and sometimes gravely problematic.
2. Sustainability can be driven by focused Education and Professional Development, what we will be referring to "disruptive education".
3. Disruptive Education and Professional Development is unconventional in its design and delivery, challenging long-held assumptions about teaching and learning, work-ready skills and knowledge, and organisational performance. As we will see, Disruptive Education and Professional Development plays an essential role in pathways to innovation and sustainability.

## It's Always a Little More Complicated Than It Appears on the Surface…

Figure 5, below, presents an integrated dynamic model incorporating the Discontinuity, Sustainability, and Critical learnership subsystems described in the previous section. Whilst a few variables have been added and a couple removed for clarity of display, the essence of those subsystems is retained. This integrated model is obviously more complex than the individual subsystems, befitting their merger and our attempt to explain and illustrate the more complicated dynamic interactions and influences. As many of these relationships were characterised above, we will focus on the new variables and linkages amongst the subsystems.

Table 2. New or relabeled elements

| § "Burn-Out" | § Management Push for Productivity |
|---|---|
| § Conventional Education and Professional Development | § Perceptions and Attitudes Favourable to Resilience and Adaptation |
| § Management Drive for Sustainability | § Sustainable Problem-Solving |

Each of these will be explained below, along with discussion of their implications for ecosystem operation.

Figure 5. The Discontinuity, Sustainability, Critical Learnership Ecosystem (Causal Loop-Relationship Diagram)

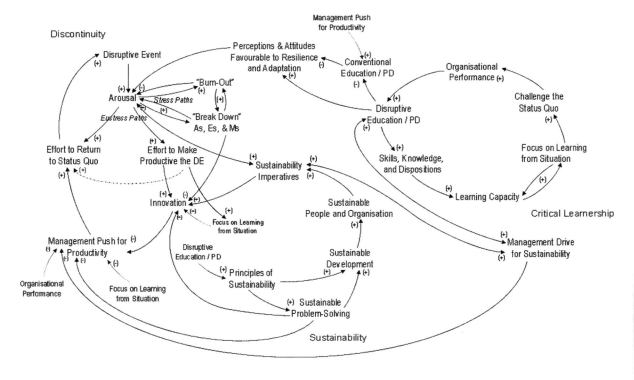

Before we begin our "walk around the model", a prime assumption we make is that disruptions and discontinuities from the environment of some order are inevitable, and that Complex Adaptive Socio-ecological Systems such as organisations are always attempting to adjust to these. Typical strategies

## Discontinuity, Sustainability, and Critical Learnership

for adjustment are depicted in Figure 5 as pathways from Arousal. Here, immediately, we see the first important additions in this diagram not included in the previous simplified diagrams: the depiction of eustress and stress (Mowbray, 2008; Schabracq, 2003) pathways around Arousal, and the unpacking of "Break Down", now showing "Burn-Out" and further defining "Break Down" as entailing Accidents (As), Errors (Es), and Misjudgements (Ms) (the dynamics and effects of stress are covered in Bagaji & Okhidemeh, 2014).

The concept of eustress is important with respect to response to disruption. It is a productive use of the energy resulting from Arousal. However, whilst generally better than either "Break Down" or "Burn-Out", the productive energy from Arousal—the eustress affect—can be used as either (a) Effort to Return to Status Quo or (b) Effort to Make Productive the Disruptive Event (DE). Both can feel rewarding or at least in service of practical and worthwhile endeavour, thus are likely to be reinforced. (See Meyer et al., (2004) for relevant insights on motivation and reinforcement.) The outcomes of the two paths, however, are very different. The former bringing a sense of order and control; the latter more likely leading to learning and innovation.

Also, a benefit of Causal Loop-Relationship Diagrams such as Figure 5 is that they highlight aspects of systems that play particularly significant roles in the system's function. This is often indicated by elements with the greatest number of connections, or relationships, to other elements in the system. These key nodes would be leverage points (Hays, 2010b). In our system, Arousal is a prime example. Other things equal, if we want to beneficially affect the discontinuity-innovation-sustainability ecosystem then we need to consider Arousal and its relationships. The major influence on Arousal that will likely increase the virtuous nature of our ecosystem—that is, lead to sustainability and innovation—is Perceptions & Attitudes Favourable to Resilience and Adaptation (see top, centre), arising from Disruptive Education and Professional Development (Critical Learnership Domain), another of our strategic elements.

Two additional key elements in our diagram are (a) Management Push for Productivity and (b) Management Drive for Sustainability, two factors that *may* be in opposition but *could* operate synergistically as we will later discuss. Such diagrams may also surface unexpected and subtle influence relationships and dynamic effects that aren't immediately apparent. Such is the impact of Management Push for Productivity, which, whilst a typical and understandable organisational behaviour, actually has counterproductive effects or downsides that reduce productivity in the long run.

There are numerous influences on Management Push for Productivity, some promoting and some inhibiting it. The push comes from

1. perceptions that organisational performance in terms of "productivity" could be better, coupled with a belief that it can be achieved by greater effort and that it is a manager's job to "push" employees to work harder, and
2. performance management and reward systems that promote achievement in productivity terms (*getting your numbers*).

This behaviour can result in greater stress for workers, feeding back into the Arousal—Break Down and Burn-Out dynamics, ultimately creating a vicious cycle of demand, try harder, and fail. According to Hays (2010b and elsewhere), a vicious cycle is a reinforcing loop across system elements that continues to increase (worsen). That is, in this case, as things fail, greater effort is expended to drive the system to improve performance, making a bad situation worse.

Moderating influences on Management Push for Productivity largely come from the sustainability and learning domains, which we will describe shortly. Meanwhile, a critical affect of Management Push for Productivity is increasing Effort to Return to the Status Quo (post disruption), the assumption being that the preexisting state was more accommodating to productivity or otherwise predictable, desirable, and manageable—*the devil you know*.... This involves bolstering the framework and systems to reduce impacts of disruption—insulate people from problems as much as possible, keep them doing what they are trained and supposed to do or get them back on track quickly.

An interesting aspect of this that may not be immediately apparent is the reinforcement of Conventional Education, Training, and Professional Development, which is largely rule-bound and designed to standardise and formalise, essentially reinforcing beliefs and practices that keep things as they are, including that managers (and teachers) know better (Hays, 2012, 2013b). Likewise, stronger Conventional Education and Professional Development reinforces Management Push for Productivity becoming a vicious cycle. Conventional Education and Professional Development also *reduce* Perceptions & Attitudes Favourable to Resilience and Adaptation contributing to the vicious cycle.

Moving on to Disruptive Education and Professional Development, we see that as it increases, Conventional Education and Professional Development *decreases,* with beneficial affects on Perceptions & Attitudes Favourable to Resilience and Adaptability, which is also directly influenced productively by Disruptive Education and Professional Development. The rest of the Critical Learnership domain essentially operates as described in Figure 3, but, here, with the addition of Management Drive for Sustainability, which is positively influenced by Disruptive Education and Professional Development whilst also being favourably influenced in return in a basic virtuous, mutually beneficial relationship.

Perceptions & Attitudes Favourable to Resilience and Adaptability, as suggested above, plays a critical role in Arousal (Discontinuity Domain) and the direction it takes. If organisational members believe disruption irregular, bad, or counterproductive, they will emerge from Arousal onto either (a) a stress path with ensuing problems or (b) the eustress path to Effort to Return to the Status Quo, both vicious cycles with respect to learning and change. If, on the other hand, they believe disruption is typical and may be beneficially positive and productive, then they will take the eustress path to Make Productive the Disruptive Event leading, possibly, to Innovation and flowing to Focus on Learning from the Situation (Critical Learning Domain), which feeds back to Innovation in a virtuous cycle.

Sustainable Imperatives (Sustainability Domain) plays a key role in the ecosystem. Whether imposed by external circumstances or championed internally, it increases Arousal, where, again, any of the three pathways might be taken by organisational members depending on the level of existing disruption and Arousal, support and response frameworks, scope and implications of the imperatives, and, of course, Perceptions and Attitudes Favourable to Resilience and Attitudes. (See Folke et al., (2002) for a thorough discussion of resilience and sustainable development.)

Sustainable Imperatives drive Innovation directly, but the nature of the Innovation and its success depend on a supportive environment, including Learning Capacity (Critical Learnership Domain), and leadership support, not shown, but implied by Management Drive for Sustainability. For instance, Focus on Learning from [and in] Situation enriches and enables relevant Innovation. Probability of productive Innovation is also aided by Sustainable Problem-Solving, which, whilst part of the Sustainability Domain, is a product of Disruptive Education and Professional Development, shown here through Principles of Sustainability, but involving considerable training in sustainability and complex and creative problem solving (Dörner & Funke, 2017) (Also see Hays & Reinders, 2020).

*Discontinuity, Sustainability, and Critical Learnership*

The line of influence connecting Management Drive for Sustainability and Sustainability Imperatives implies that the organisation's leadership may respond to environmental disruptions (and opportunities) as well as generate its own mandate for increasing sustainability, including sustainable innovations in products and services. This drive feeds and is fed by Disruptive Education and Professional Development (Critical Learnership Domain). And, as Management Drive for Sustainability increases, there is a corresponding decrease in Management Push for Productivity, as indicated by the (-) sign.

All that said, if and when the "productivity" in Management Push for Productivity embraces Sustainability in concept, principle, and practice, then existing vicious cycles will melt away. Thus, dimensions of sustainability, innovation, and learning should all be emphasised, measured, and reinforced as part of Organisational Performance (element located in the Critical Learnership domain presently).

## TAKEAWAYS FROM THE PORTRAYAL OF THE DISCONTINUITY, SUSTAINABILITY, AND CRITICAL LEARNERSHIP ECOSYSTEM

There is much to be gleaned from conceiving of disruption—normally thought to be annoying and problematic—as a naturally occurring phenomenon that holds within it the potential for driving sustainable innovation. This is, of course, not automatic as there are factors within the system, itself, that limit learning and productive adaptation. Accepting this is important because poor organisational performance is often blamed on circumstances beyond managers' control, and measures to respond are often based on flawed understanding of system dynamics. And, whilst disruptions cannot often be predicted or halted, it is how we deal with disruptive events that makes the difference between being a victim of circumstance and capitalising on opportunities posed by them.

How we deal with disruptions is a function of several factors, firstly our perception and interpretation of them and our capabilities to respond effectively, which largely come from a resilient culture promoted by what we refer to as Disruptive Education and Professional Development. The more organisational members accept that disruption is potentially valuable and understand how its affects can be channeled towards learning and innovation, the more resilient and adaptable the organisation will become. Accepting that one has a choice in how to use the tension and fuel of Arousal is empowering. Knowing it is a natural tendency to try to keep things as they are (or go back to better days) but that this is counterproductive in the long run can motivate individuals to learn new skills and knowledge, take on new roles, and develop their behavioural repertoire toward greater effectiveness.

It may be disconcerting to realise one has the power to decide as this responsibility is conferred and limited to managers in many organisations, a cultural phenomenon that restricts the organisation's inherent ability to respond to and learn from disruption and challenge. Thus, cultivating a disruptive culture may present many hurdles, but future-minded leaders will champion disruption and install systems that support employees to become resilient and self-sufficient.

One system that may have to be overhauled is Conventional Education and Professional Development, with the critical interrogatives being,

*What beliefs and assumptions do we hold that underpin what we teach or how we train, and are these really viable?*

*What have we been doing to trap our employees in assumptions and practices that no longer serve us?*

*How do we supplant these with skills, knowledge, and dispositions that will see us into a sustainable future?*

It is also quite possible that performance management and reward systems need to be revised to encourage behaviours that promote learning and innovation, *changing rather than reinforcing the status quo*. Here, we might ask,

*What have been the key performance indicators we seek and use to determine promotions, rewards, and raises in salary?*

*What behaviours are most productively beneficial in seeing us into a sustainable future, and how can we best reinforce them?*

Returning to the idea that it's always a little more complicated than it appears on the surface..., and to creating a more resilient, adaptable culture, one aspect of Disruptive Education and Professional Development that will benefit most managers and staff is training in systems thinking and mapping Complex Adaptive Systems. As our portrayal of the Discontinuity, Sustainability, and Critical Learnership Ecosystem reveals, there are many factors involved in any human endeavour, often with countervailing influences. Exploring factors that may be involved in a given situation and their dynamic relationships can help managers and staff understand why certain things stay as they are no matter what and why others things happen despite best intentions to prevent them. And, importantly, how we are all complicit in creating and perpetuating systems, procedures, and behaviours that impede our becoming the best we can be.

## Toward a Disruptive and Innovative Organisation

Supported by our dynamic ecosystem model and ample research from a range of disciplines, this article suggests that disruption and discontinuity are not necessarily bad, though may productively be conceived as a necessary evil. Whilst annoying and frustrating as they interfere with the accustomed flow of activity and expectations about how things *should* be, disruption and discontinuity can drive the organisation toward what it *could* be: what extraordinary levels of performance might be attained and how the organisation can remain viable long into the future. Deceptively simple, this shift begs release from the bonds of self-limiting beliefs and behaviours underlying orthodox management and conventional education and professional development.

The essential part in *necessary evil* is that disruption and discontinuity—whilst possibly impeding typical productivity—fuels action through the arousal process,[‡] action that is unlikely to arise other things equal (when the status quo is maintained). Chances are greater that the organisation will move towards learning and sustainable innovation when assumptions and beliefs about the current state (the status quo) are challenged. Enabling such challenge is Disruptive Education and Professional Development and, over time, creating a disruptive culture. Table 2 presents attributes of Disruptive Education and Professional Development and Table 3 outlines the skills, knowledge, and dispositions of individuals subject to disruptive learning. As the organisation's leaders and managers adopt disruptive philosophy and practice, the culture is likely to become more change-ready, always poised on the edge of learning and innovation, driven by disruptive tensions and supported by systems and mechanisms that channel those tensions constructively. The descriptors in Tables 2 and 3 may be used as guidelines for revising Disruptive Education and Professional Development and associated management practices.

We worry somewhat about the willingness and ability of higher and tertiary education to embrace disruptive philosophy and practice on a large scale. First of all, educational institutions are subject to the same dynamics portrayed in Figure 4. Additionally, they are bridled by governments, industry standards, and public demand, none of which necessarily accede to the necessity to do things differently, that is, engage in or allow paradoxical, metaphorical, extemporaneous, inverted, even chaotic "formal" learning experiences we depicted as *unconventional* education in the introduction. Here, we note in particular the increasingly insidious emphasis in higher and tertiary education to produce "work-ready graduates" who may, in some measure, possess generic skills of value to industry, but are essentially replicants of the conventional institutions that spawned them. They may know how things "are" (or more likely "were"), but are not equipped with skill and authority (sense of personal power and obligation) to challenge the systems and practices that unintentionally strive to maintain the status quo. Trepidations aside, academic faculty and staff are in a position to challenge beliefs and assumptions about their work and should be supported and rewarded for doing so, just as their industry counterparts.

*Table 3. Attributes of Disruptive Education and Professional Development*

**Disruptive Education and Professional Development**

Anti-conventional. Any characteristic of typical training and education technique is called into question and revised wherever possible to make instruction different, breaking learners' expectations about the nature of teaching and learning, including who teaches and how, where learning takes place and how it is assessed.

Lerner-Centred. Learners are required to take a bigger role in the learning process and assume more responsibility for their own learning and that of their colleagues. This spans needs assessment, setting objectives, developing learning strategies, gathering resources, developing and delivering content (lessons), and evaluating learning.

Organic. Learning is real-time, practical, targeted, and applied making use of genuine problems and opportunities rather than creating and sticking to a set curriculum.

Holistic. Learning strategies employ / tap multiple modalities to engage diverse learners and involve them fully in learning. As much variety as possible is encouraged in instructional methods in order that learners themselves develop a wider and more-flexible portfolio of problem-solving, learning, adapting, and innovating strategies.

Metamorphic DNA. Disruptive Education and Professional Development are programmed to continually adapt to the environment, reinvent themselves, and transform to remain viable. They are resilient with high plasticity, "born" to sustain themselves over time in changing circumstances.

Complex and "Wicked". The KISS Principle (Elsenbroich and Gilbert, 2014; Giezen, 2012) is done away with in favour of a more-realistic and useful view of the dynamic complexity of problems, opportunities, and existence in ecosystems. Instruction is not simplified in order to make it easier for learners or facilitators but purposely complicated in keeping with the richness of real life and requiring all concerned to get beneath the surface and consider wider and longer-range implications.

By design, Disruptive Education and Professional Development foster:
Independence and initiative
Self-Directed Learning
Teamwork and Collaboration
Adaptability and resilience—appreciation and capacity to deal effectively with *and promote* disruption, innovation, and change
Understanding and appreciation of Complex Adaptive Systems and ecosystem thinking
Effectiveness in complex and creative problem-solving, and in design thinking (Buhl et al., 2019).

*Table 4. Disruptive Skills, Knowledge, and Dispositions.*

| Disruptive Skills, Knowledge, and Dispositions |
|---|
| Understand and apply principles of sustainability (refer to Table 1). |
| Understand and apply systems thinking, including concepts and principles of Complex Adaptive Systems and ecologies / ecosystems. Proficiency in Complex Problem Solving. |
| Superior teamwork and collaboration skills and orientations. The ability to work within and make the most of diversity in skills, perspectives, ways of working, and roles / functions. |
| Flexibility and willingness to take on various roles, including assuming leadership when needed. |
| Critical Thinking (Hays & Reinders, 2018) and application of PABBAVEM# in problem-solving, decision-making, action planning. |
| Creative and divergent thinking (Hays & Reinders, 2020), possessing and utilising a repertoire of creative thinking tools and approaches, including design thinking and facilitating creative group problem-solving. |
| Courage and capability to challenge the Status Quo. Knowing when things aren't right or could be better, and taking a stand and / or taking action to change things for the better. |
| Keen Performance Management skills enabling assessment of performance and analysis of contributors and inhibitors to performance; knowing where and how to intervene to improve performance. |
| Be uncomfortable with comfort: adhering to a philosophy and practice of "If it ain't broke, break it!" Understanding that factors such as ease, stability, harmony, and predictability may indicate system weakness such as inability to scan the environment, neglecting the significance of available evidence of performance, threat, or opportunity, resting on past laurels, burn out, or lack of initiative. |
| Self-Directed Learning and anticipatory learning. Knowing that whilst processes or methods may be working at the moment, circumstances could change at any moment necessitating change. Preparedness for such eventualities may be vital for survival, and resilience and adaptability depend on planning for a range of possibilities as well as the improbable! What do we need to know and be able to do to navigate whatever problems and opportunities might arise? |
| Self-leadership, autonomy, and citizenship behaviour. A stance of self-reliance and lack of dependence on leaders who can and will solve major problems and make the important decisions. Acceptance of the responsibility that individuals must play key roles in ensuring organisational effectiveness and success and share responsibility for failing. |
| Ability and disposition to debate and argue for the greater good in problem-solving and decision-making, whilst divorcing oneself from ego needs to win. Commitment to fairly considering all stakeholder views before committing to a course of action. |

See https://www.google.com/search?q=<author>+PABBAVEM&rlz=1C1CHBF_enSG879SG879&oq=<author>+PABBAVEM&aqs=chrome..69i57j69i60.8213j0j15&sourceid=chrome&ie=UTF-8n for background on PABBAVEM.

## CONCLUSION

Figure 5, a causal loop-relationship diagram, presents 20-some elements comprising the Discontinuity, Sustainability, and Critical Learnership Ecosystem and describes many of the dynamic relationships amongst those elements. The diagram attempts to model aspects of organisational behaviour of considerable importance to learning, innovation, and sustainability. Whilst no doubt educational and organisational researchers and practitioners could identify other salient elements involved in each of these phenomena, the model integrates for the first time three distinct arenas—Disruption, Sustainability, and Critical Learnership. As our model illustrates, these domains can operate synergetically to enable sustainable development. Unfortunately, they can also work in subtle and insidious ways to maintain conventional practice and perpetuate the status quo.

## Discontinuity, Sustainability, and Critical Learnership

As we have argued, people in organisations respond to disruption in predictable ways that represent beliefs and assumptions about the nature of productivity and what drives it. In an effort to minimise the impact of disruption, managers attempt to insulate workers from disruption and drive to return to the "normal" state as soon as possible. Despite feeling that this is the right thing to do, the result is of short-term value and may be counterproductive in the long run. Not realising the potential value of the energy (Arousal) from disruption and what can be learnt from it or unable to channel and capitalise upon it lacking suitable mechanisms, tools, and skills attempts to reduce the effects of disruption make sense. This behaviour results, in part, from conventional management practice and the platforms that support it, including education and professional development and performance management and reward systems.

To counter conventionality, we suggest creating a disruptive culture that can undo or at least balance conventional thinking and practice. Our model refers to this alternative approach as Disruptive Education and Professional Development, which essentially calls into question existing patterns of behaviour and the systems and mechanisms that support it, and emphasising principles of sustainability, provides training in complex and creative problem-solving. On the whole, such education and professional development builds workers able and disposed to challenge the status quo, make the most of learning, and sustainably innovate.

The dynamics described in our ecosystem model, if sometimes counterintuitive, appear reasonable when following the lines and directions of influence between and amongst elements, and are generally supported by the extant literature. Further research might attempt to ascertain and further define the salient elements in the ecosystem and their dynamic relationships. Which are most important, are others needed to more completely explain behaviour, and what affects do context and circumstances have on the dynamics? It would also be productive to determine if the dynamics operate similarly in diverse organisations and at different levels of organisation. Actual case examples would elucidate the theoretical dynamics and provide more grounding for organisational interventions. For example, how do managers really help constructively channel the energy from arousal, reducing the stress pathways and capitalising on eustress?

In final analysis, we are confident that disruption may be a necessary evil, as conflict can be constructive (Dyer and Song, 1998; Tjosvold, 2008). How to make the most of this, however, has yet to be determined. Drawing from research in positive psychology (Froman, 2010; Kour, El-Den, and Sriratanaviriyakul, 2019), what is certain is that optimistic and favourable perceptions and interpretations of disruption and discontinuity can go a long way in reducing conventional practices and promoting sustainable innovation.

Before putting this issue to bed, and having emphasised the potency of disruption throughout, we raise a provocative point. Organisational Development subscribes to a belief or philosophy of stability in motion (Perrin, 2012), that is, organisations need to be always adapting and changing, but to evolve smoothly and effectively, some stability is necessary to reduce stress and change-resistance and build resilience.[§] Already in 1964, Gardner wrote in *Self-Renewal: The Individual and the Innovative Society* that "the only stability possible is stability in motion" (p. 7).

This tenet of Organisational Development seems to contradict our thesis that continual disruption is a good thing. Perhaps a productive way out of this conundrum can be achieved by redefining stability. It seems that employees and other stakeholders may always need some measure of certainty. Perhaps it is assurance that they are doing something that matters they want, rather than a need to keep things as they are? If organisational purpose, meaning, key principles, and fundamental values are clear and unwavering, then disruptions in the flow of work and ensuing demands to change processes, methods, tools, and roles should be much easier to bear. This would especially be the case in a disruptive culture committed to learning and change for the better.

## REFERENCES

Anderson, W. (2019). *All Connected Now: Life in the First Global Civilization.* Routledge. doi:10.4324/9780429037122

Arnold, R. D., & Wade, J. P. (2015). A definition of systems thinking: A systems approach. *Procedia Computer Science*, *44*, 669–678. doi:10.1016/j.procs.2015.03.050

Bagaji, A., & Okhidemeh, E. (2014). Perspectives on stress and its management for individual well-being and organisational productivity. *International Journal of Public Administration and Management Research*, *2*(2), 129–147.

Barnett, R., & Jackson, N. (Eds.). (2020). *Ecologies for learning and practice: Emerging ideas, sightings, and possibilities.* Routledge.

Beabout, B. (2012). Turbulence, Perturbance, and Educational Change. Complicity. *An International Journal of Complexity and Education.*, *9*(2). Advance online publication. doi:10.29173/cmplct17984

Bendell, T. (2016). *Building anti-fragile organisations: Risk, opportunity and governance in a turbulent world.* Routledge. doi:10.4324/9781315570426

Berkes, F. (2007). Understanding uncertainty and reducing vulnerability: Lessons from resilience thinking. *Natural Hazards*, *41*(2), 283–295. doi:10.100711069-006-9036-7

Bousquet, F., Botta, A., Alinovi, L., Barreteau, O., Bossio, D., Brown, K., Caron, P., Cury, P., D'Errico, M., DeClerck, F., Dessard, H., Enfors Kautsky, E., Fabricius, C., Folke, C., Fortmann, L., Hubert, B., Magda, D., Mathevet, R., Norgaard, R. B., ... Staver, C. (2016). Resilience and development: Mobilizing for transformation. *Ecology and Society*, *21*(3), 40. doi:10.5751/ES-08754-210340

Bradshaw, D. (1999). *Transforming lives, Transforming communities: A conceptual framework for further education.* Adult Education Resource and Information Service (ARIS), Language Australia.

Buhl, A., Schmidt-Keilich, M., Muster, V., Blazejewski, S., Schrader, U., Harrach, C., Schäfer, M., & Süßbauer, E. (2019). Design thinking for sustainability: Why and how design thinking can foster sustainability-oriented innovation development. *Journal of Cleaner Production*, *231*, 1248–1257. doi:10.1016/j.jclepro.2019.05.259

Burchell, N., & Kolb, D. (2006). Stability and change for sustainability. *University of Auckland Business Review*, *8*(2), 33–41.

Burnard, K., & Bhamra, R. (2011). Organisational resilience: Development of a conceptual framework for organisational responses. *International Journal of Production Research*, *49*(18), 5581–5599. doi:10.1080/00207543.2011.563827

Camillus, J. C. (2008). Strategy as a wicked problem. *Harvard Business Review*, *86*(5), 98–101.

Carvalho, H. C., & Mazzon, J. A. (2019). Embracing complex social problems. *Journal of Social Marketing, 10*(1), 54–80. doi:10.1108/JSOCM-03-2019-0049

Checkland, P. (2000). Soft systems methodology: A thirty year retrospective. *Systems Research and Behavioral Science, 17*(1), 11–58. doi:10.1002/1099-1743(200011)17:1+<::AID-SRES374>3.0.CO;2-O

Checkland, P., & Poulter, J. (2010). Soft systems methodology. In M. Reynolds & S. Holwell (Eds.), *Systems approaches to managing change: A practical guide* (pp. 191–242). Springer. doi:10.1007/978-1-84882-809-4_5

Coaffee, J. (2019). *Futureproof: How to build resilience in an uncertain world.* Yale University Press.

Cork, S. (Ed.). (2010). *Resilience and transformation: Preparing Australia for uncertain futures.* CSIRO Publishing. doi:10.1071/9780643098138

Cunha, M. P. E., & Putnam, L. L. (2019). Paradox theory and the paradox of success. *Strategic Organization, 17*(1), 95–106.

Deffuant, G., & Gilbert, N. (Eds.). (2011). *Viability and resilience of complex systems: Concepts, methods and case studies from ecology and society.* Springer Science & Business Media. doi:10.1007/978-3-642-20423-4

Deudney, D. (2018). Turbo change: Accelerating technological disruption, planetary geopolitics, and architectonic metaphors. *International Studies Review, 20*(2), 223–231. doi:10.1093/isr/viy033

Dooley, K. J. (1997). A complex adaptive systems model of organization change. *Nonlinear Dynamics Psychology and Life Sciences, 1*(1), 69–97. doi:10.1023/A:1022375910940

Dörner, D., & Funke, J. (2017). Complex problem solving: What it is and what it is not. *Frontiers in Psychology, 8*, 1153.

Dyer, B., & Song, X. M. (1998). Innovation strategy and sanctioned conflict: A new edge in innovation? *Journal of Product Innovation Management, 15*(6), 505–519. doi:10.1111/1540-5885.1560505

Earl, A., VanWynsberghe, R., Walter, P., & Straka, T. (2018). Adaptive education applied to higher education for sustainability. *International Journal of Sustainability in Higher Education.* e Cunha, M. P., Clegg, S. R., & Kamoche, K. (2012). Improvisation as "real time foresight". *Futures, 44*(3), 265–272.

Elsass, P. M. (1993). The paradox of success: Too much of a good thing? *The Academy of Management Perspectives, 7*(3), 84–85.

Elsenbroich, C., & Gilbert, N. (2014). *Modelling norms.* Springer.

Farjoun, M. (2010). Beyond dualism: Stability and change as a duality. *Academy of Management Review, 35*(2), 202–225.

Fiksel, J. (2015). *Resilient by design: Creating businesses that adapt and flourish in a changing world.* Island Press.

Folke, C., Carpenter, S., Elmqvist, T., Gunderson, L., Holling, C. S., & Walker, B. (2002). Resilience and sustainable development: Building adaptive capacity in a world of transformations. *Ambio, 31*(5), 437–440.

Friend, M. (2018). Remarks of a philosopher of mathematics and science. In A. Riegler, K. Muller, & S. Umpleby (Eds.), *New horizons for second-order cybernetics* (Vol. 60, pp. 327–332). World Scientific.

Froman, L. (2010). Positive psychology in the workplace. *Journal of Adult Development, 17*(2), 59–69.

Gardner, J. (1963). *Self-renewal: The individual and the lnnovative society*. Harper and Row.

Ghuman, U., & Olmstead, W. (2015). Utilizing flux and chaos: A case study of wicked problems in environmental management. *International Journal of Organization Theory and Behavior, 18*(4), 379–404. https://doi.org/10.1108/IJOTB-18-04-2015-B001

Giezen, M. (2012). Keeping it simple? A case study into the advantages and disadvantages of reducing complexity in mega project planning. *International Journal of Project Management, 30*(7), 781–790.

Haski-Leventhal, D. (2020). *The purpose-driven university: Transforming lives and creating impact through academic social responsibility*. Emerald Group Publishing.

Hawick, L., Cleland, J., & Kitto, S. (2017). Getting off the carousel: Exploring the wicked problem of curriculum reform. *Perspectives on Medical Education, 6*(5), 337–343.

Hays, J. (2008). Dynamics of organisational wisdom. *The Business Renaissance Quarterly, 2*(4), 77–122.

Hays, J. (2012). *Wicked problem: Educating for complexity and wisdom* [Paper presention]. The Wise Management in Organisational Complexity Conference, Shanghai, China.

Hays, J. (2013a). The team learning pyramid. *Journal of Leadership, Management & Organization Studies, 3*(1), 1–19.

Hays, J. (2013b). Wicked problem: educating for complexity and wisdom. In M. Thompson & D. Bevan (Eds.), *Wise management in organisational complexity* (pp. 134–150). Palgrave Macmillan.

Hays, J. (2015a). *Chaos to capability: Educating professionals for the 21st century*. Unitec Press.

Hays, J. (2015b). *Privilege, proviso, and paradox: Leadership in—and for—a changing world*. Available at: https://www.researchgate.net/publication/323424440_Privilege_Proviso_and_Paradox_Leadership_in-and_for-a_Changing_World

Hays, J. (2015c). *Citizenship, democracy, and professionalism for a sustainable future* [paper presentation]. *The Unitec Community Development Conference*, Auckland, New Zealand.

Hays, J. (2017). A wise course: educating for wisdom in the 21$^{st}$ century. In W. Küpers & O. Gunnlaugson (Eds.), *Wisdom learning: Perspectives on wising-up business and management education* (pp. 185–210). Routledge.

Hays, J., & Reinders, H. (2018). Critical learnership: A new perspective on learning. *International Journal of Learning. Teaching and Educational Research, 17*(1), 1–25.

Hays, J., & Reinders, H. (2020). Sustainable learning and education: A curriculum for the future. *International Review of Education*, *66*(1), 29–52.

Hays, J., & Reinders, H. (2021). Viability of the sustainable development ecosystem. In M. Khosrow-Pour (Ed.), *Encyclopedia of organizational knowledge, administration, and technologies* (pp. 812–830). IGI.

Hays, J. M. (2010). The ecology of wisdom. *Management & Marketing*, *5*(1).

Hays, J. M. (2010). Mapping wisdom as a complex adaptive system. *Management & Marketing*, *5*(2).

Hazy, J., & Silberstang, J. (2009). Leadership within emergent events in complex systems: Micro-enactments and the mechanisms of organisational learning and change. *International Journal of Learning and Change*, *3*(3), 230–247.

Heinberg, R. (2015). *Afterburn: Society beyond fossil fuels*. New Society Publishers.

Holden, L. M. (2005). Complex adaptive systems: Concept analysis. *Journal of Advanced Nursing*, *52*(6), 651–657.

Inigo, E. A., & Albareda, L. (2016). Understanding sustainable innovation as a complex adaptive system: A systemic approach to the firm. *Journal of Cleaner Production*, *126*, 1–20.

Jia, S., Li, Y., & Fang, T. (2022). System dynamics analysis of COVID-19 prevention and control strategies. *Environmental Science and Pollution Research International*, *29*(3), 3944–3957.

Kantur, D., & İşeri-Say, A. (2012). Organizational resilience: A conceptual integrative framework. *Journal of Management & Organization*, *18*(6), 762–773.

Karakiewicz, J. (2016). Interventions in complex urban systems: how to Eenable modeling to account for disruptive innovation. In Understanding complex urban systems (pp. 113-127). Springer.

Kazakov, R., Howick, S., & Morton, A. (2021). Managing complex adaptive systems: A resource/agent qualitative modelling perspective. *European Journal of Operational Research*, *290*(1), 386–400.

Kostoulas-Makrakis, N. (2012). *The earth charter's integrated ethical approach to learning to live together sustainably: An example of an international master course* [Paper presentation]. *16th UNESCO-APEID International Conference*, Bangkok, Thailand.

Kour, J., El-Den, J., & Sriratanaviriyakul, N. (2019). The role of positive psychology in improving employees' performance and organizational productivity: An experimental study. *Procedia Computer Science*, *161*, 226–232.

Lautensach, A. (2018). Educating as if sustainability mattered. In Proceedings of the 11th Annual International Conference of Education. Research and Innovation. https://doi.org/10.21125/iceri.2018.0352.

Leana, C. R., & Barry, B. (2000). Stability and change as simultaneous experiences in organizational life. *Academy of Management Review*, *25*(4), 753–759.

Lehtonen, A., & Salonen, A. & Cantell, H. (2019). Climate change education: A new approach for a world of wicked problems. In C. Cook (Ed.), Sustainability, human well-being, and the future of education (pp. 339-374). Palgrave Macmillan.

Letiche, H., Lissack, M., & Schultz, R. (2011). *Coherence in the midst of complexity: Advances in social complexity theory*. Springer.

Levin, S., Xepapadeas, T., Crépin, A. S., Norberg, J., De Zeeuw, A., Folke, C., Hughes, T., Arrow, K., Barrett, S., Daily, G., Ehrlich, P., Kautsky, N., Mäler, K., Polasky, S., Troell, M., Vincent, J., & Walker, B. (2013). Social-ecological systems as complex adaptive systems: Modeling and policy implications. *Environment and Development Economics*, *18*(2), 111–132.

Lewis, T. G. (2014). *Book of extremes: Why the 21st century isn't like the 20th century*. Springer.

Lotz-Sisitka, H., Wals, A. E., Kronlid, D., & McGarry, D. (2015). Transformative, transgressive social learning: Rethinking higher education pedagogy in times of systemic global dysfunction. *Current Opinion in Environmental Sustainability*, *16*, 73–80.

Lukashova, L. (2020). Evaluation of the synergetic effect from implementation of economic activity by small business entities. *Technology Audit and Production Reserves*, *1*(4), 51.

Malcolm, M. (2013). Transforming lives and 'the measure of their states'. *Journal of Pedagogic Development*, *3*(3).

Maria, D. (2011). Complex adaptive systems: A trans-cultural undercurrent obstructing change in higher education. *International Journal of Vocational and Technical Education*, *3*(2), 9–19.

McGann, M., Wells, T., & Blomkamp, E. (2021). Innovation labs and co-production in public problem solving. *Public Management Review*, *23*(2), 297–316.

Meyer, J. P., Becker, T. E., & Vandenberghe, C. (2004). Employee commitment and motivation: A conceptual analysis and integrative model. *The Journal of Applied Psychology*, *89*(6), 991.

Miceli, A., Hagen, B., Riccardi, M. P., Sotti, F., & Settembre-Blundo, D. (2021). Thriving, not just surviving in changing times: How sustainability, agility and digitalization intertwine with organizational resilience. *Sustainability*, *13*(4), 2052.

Montiel, I. (2008). Corporate social responsibility and corporate sustainability: Separate pasts, common futures. *Organization & Environment*, *21*(3), 245–269.

Moon, J. (2007). The contribution of corporate social responsibility to sustainable development. *Sustainable Development*, *15*(5), 296–306.

Mowbray, D. (2008). Building resilience–an organisational cultural approach to mental health and wellbeing at work: a primary prevention programme. In A. Kinder, R. Hughes, & C. Cooper (Eds.), *Employee well-being support: A workplace resource* (pp. 309–321). John Wiley & Sons.

Neely, K. (2015). Complex adaptive systems as a valid framework for understanding community level development. *Development in Practice*, *25*(6), 785–797.

Perrin, D. (2012). Coming to grips with complexity: dynamic systems theory in the research of newswriting. In C. Bazerman, C. Dean, J. Early, K. Lunsford, S. Null, P. Rogers, & A. Stansell (Eds.), *International advances in writing research: Culture, places, measures* (pp. 539–558). Parlor Press.

Peschl, M. F. (2019). Design and innovation as co-creating and co-becoming with the Future. *Design Management Journal*, *14*(1), 4–14.

Preiser, R., Biggs, R., De Vos, A., & Folke, C. (2018). Social-ecological systems as complex adaptive systems. *Ecology and Society*, *23*(4), 46.

Reinders, H., & Hays, J. (2020). Creativity and criticality in presencing. In O. Gunnlaugson & W. Brendel (Eds.), *Advances in presencing vol II: Individual approaches in theory u* (pp. 393–420). Trifoss Business Press.

Roelofs, K., Hagenaars, M., & Stins, J. (2010). Facing freeze: Social threat induces bodily freeze in humans. *Psychological Science*, *21*(11), 1575–1581.

Schabracq, M. (2003). Everyday well-being and stress in work and organisations. In M. Schabracq, J. Winnubst, & C. Cooper (Eds.), *The Handbook of work and health psychology* (pp. 7–36). John Wiley & Sons.

Schuck, S., Aubusson, P., Burden, K., & Brindley, S. (2018). Future—always coming never comes: embracing imagination and learning from uncertainty. In S. Schuck, P. Aubusson, K. Burden, & S. Brindley (Eds.), *Uncertainty in teacher education futures* (pp. 253–264). Springer.

Smith, W., Erez, M., Jarvenpaa, S., Lewis, M. W., & Tracey, P. (2017). Adding complexity to theories of paradox, tensions, and dualities of innovation and change: Introduction to organization studies special issue on paradox, tensions, and dualities of innovation and change. *Organization Studies*, *38*(3-4), 303–317.

Stacey, R. (1992). *Managing the unknowable: Strategic boundaries between order and chaos in organizations*. John Wiley & Sons.

Sturmberg, J. (2018). *Health System Redesign*. Springer. doi:10.1007/978-3-319-64605-3_3

Thakore, R., Kavantera, A., & Whitehall, G. (2022). Systems-thinking theory: Decision-making for sustainable workplace transformations. In V. Danivska & R. Appel-Meulenbroek (Eds.), *A handbook of management theories and models for office environments and services* (pp. 25–35). Routledge.

Tjosvold, D. (2008). The conflict-positive organization: It depends upon us. *Journal of Organizational Behavior: The International Journal of Industrial. Occupational and Organizational Psychology and Behavior*, *29*(1), 19–28.

Varney, S. (2013). *A complexity perspective on organisational change: making sense of emerging patterns in self-organising systems* [Unpublished doctoral dissertation]. University of Reading, UK.

Walker, G., Daniels, S., & Emborg, J. (2008). Tackling the tangle of environmental conflict: Complexity, controversy, and collaborative learning. *Emergence*, *10*(4), 17–27.

Waterman, R. (1987). *The renewal factor*. Bantam.

Weber, Y., and Tarba, S. (2014). Strategic agility: A state of the art introduction to the special section on strategic agility. *California Management Review*, *56*(30), 5-12.

Weick, K. E., & Sutcliffe, K. M. (2011). *Managing the unexpected: Resilient performance in an age of uncertainty* (Vol. 8). John Wiley & Sons.

## ADDITIONAL READING

Arnold, R. D., & Wade, J. P. (2015). A definition of systems thinking: A systems approach. *Procedia Computer Science, 44*, 669–678. doi:10.1016/j.procs.2015.03.050

Barnett, R., & Jackson, N. (Eds.). (2020). *Ecologies for learning and practice: Emerging ideas, sightings, and possibilities*. Routledge.

Coaffee, J. (2019). *Futureproof: How to build resilience in an uncertain world*. Yale University Press.

Dooley, K. J. (1997). A complex adaptive systems model of organization change. *Nonlinear Dynamics Psychology and Life Sciences, 1*(1), 69–97. doi:10.1023/A:1022375910940

Hays, J., & Reinders, H. (2020). Sustainable learning and education: A curriculum for the future. *International Review of Education, 66*(1), 29–52. doi:10.100711159-020-09820-7

Hays, J., & Reinders, H. (2021). Viability of the sustainable development ecosystem. In M. Khosrow-Pour (Ed.), *Encyclopedia of organizational knowledge, administration, and technologies* (pp. 812–829). IGI. doi:10.4018/978-1-7998-3473-1.ch058

Montiel, I. (2008). Corporate social responsibility and corporate sustainability: Separate pasts, common futures. *Organization & Environment, 21*(3), 245–269. doi:10.1177/1086026608321329

Moon, J. (2007). The contribution of corporate social responsibility to sustainable development. *Sustainable Development, 15*(5), 296–306. doi:10.1002d.346

## KEY TERMS AND DEFINITIONS

**Critical Learnership:** A way of thinking about and restructuring how we approach learning. It enables continual learning, unlearning, and reinvention through building certain skills and favourable dispositions and introducing strategies founded on paradoxical principles of sustainability and discontinuity).

**Discontinuity:** A disruption in a steady and generally predictable stream of activity or process. Think of a break, disconnect, or gap. A discontinuity could be an altered or transformed state (a new or different way of being) than that previous and leading up to the discontinuity, probably unexpected.

**Disruption:** Disturbance, interruption, unsettling, interference, or disorganisation in a task, activity, or normal flow of work.

## ENDNOTES

* Heinberg's work on the innovation lab / co-production strategy reported in McGann, et al., (2021), appears to offer promise.
† Lukashova, L. (2020) provides a helpful perspective on synergy in her study on economic activites in small to medium enterprises. Earlier, Hays (2013a) explained synergy with respect to teamwork and the "multiplier effect". The central idea in synergy is that interactions between or amongst

‡ elements in a system produce effects greater than could be accounted for by a simple sum of the effects of individual elements.

‡ See the Discontinuity Domain Figure 1 and on Figure 4.

§ Various aspects of stability in motion are covered in Burchell and Kolb (2006), Farjourn (200), Friend (2017), Leana & Barry (2000). See, also, Waterman (1987), drawing on Gardner's (1964) earlier work.

ǀ Whilst possible, given certain circumstances, this is not always the result. The tensions resulting from the paradox of simultaneous sustainability and discontinuity can result in two possible streams, one counterproductive and one desirable. This type of dynamic is discussed in Hays (2012) and other sources by the author.

# Chapter 7
# Enhancing Student Professionalization Through Business Simulation Games

**Yui-Yip Lau**
*College of Professional and Continuing Education, The Hong Kong Polytechnic University, China*

**Macy Wong**
*College of Professional and Continuing Education, The Hong Kong Polytechnic University, China*

**Zhuang Yang**
*The Hong Kong Polytechnic University, China*

**Chan Kwai Nam**
*Icetech Education, China*

**Hsiao Arthur Shih-Kuei**
*Top-BOSS International Corporation, Taiwan*

## ABSTRACT

*A traditional classroom approach focuses on teacher-centric learning, and theoretical knowledge transition is often reinforcing spoon-feeding education. To this end, it leads to demotivating students' learning and failing to fulfill the employers' expectations. The business simulation game is a new, innovative educational tool for students to enjoy in an interactive learning classroom. The use of support tools can help students to improve their professionalization. This study mainly uses an illustrative real-life case study, Macro Business Simulation, as the target study area. In response, the study invited 64 university students to complete both pre-activity and post-activity surveys, along with 10 semi-structured, in-depth interviews with relevant parties including teachers, students, Macro Business Simulation operators, and business enterprises. Implications of the findings are also discussed.*

DOI: 10.4018/978-1-6684-6172-3.ch007

*Enhancing Student Professionalization Through Business Simulation Games*

## BACKGROUND

The United Nations addressed that education needs to encourage intercultural dialogue and sustainable development after the second world war (Dale and Robertson, 2014). The United Nations General Assembly asserted its Universal Declaration of Human Rights in Paris on 10 December 1948. Article 26 mentioned that 'Everyone has the right to education. Education shall be free, at least in the elementary and fundamental stages. Since the United Nations announced Article 13 of the International Covenant on Economic, Social, and Cultural Rights on 16 December 1996, the right to education was officially identified worldwide (United Nations, 2016). To a certain extent, education may reinforce national economic competitiveness by producing human capital (Lau, Ng, Tam & Chan, 2018; Fawns, Mulherin, Hounsell & Aitken, 2021).

Hong Kong's higher education system has been wholly based on the English model since the first Opium War (1839-1842). To a certain extent, Hong Kong higher education has performed tremendous growth and significant transformation in the past 180 years. Since the 1980s, Hong Kong has undergone two primary waves of educational reforms. The first was inclined toward enhancing internal effectiveness, like teaching and learning in schools, while the second mainly focused on increasing interface effectiveness, like quality, market competitiveness, and accountability. A series of educational reforms led Hong Kong has experienced a paradigm shift from a local to a global basis (Cheng, 2009). In general, the traditional classroom approach is mainly adopted by Hong Kong higher education institutions. Nevertheless, the conventional classroom method concentrates on theoretical knowledge transition, and teacher-centric learning usually addresses spoon-feeding education. That is the process of directly telling students what they need to know and, thus, requires little independent thought on their part. As such, it demotivates students' learning and fails to fulfil employers' expectations. Now, most of Hong Kong's higher education institutions strive toward ranking on league tables (e.g., QS and Times Higher Education). Graduates' employability, teaching pedagogy, and learning context are one of the key performance indicators affecting the ranking. Also, several of Hong Kong's higher education institutions prefer to obtain internationally renowned accreditations (e.g., AACSB, EQUIS, AMBA) to boost the number of student enrolment and improve their reputation in the academic world. Innovative teaching pedagogy is one of the evaluation items by such international accreditation bodies. To a certain extent, a business simulation game is one of the essential vehicles to sustain the Hong Kong higher education institutions' competitive position. In the dynamic business environment, most business firms and government bodies desire to recruit preferable graduates to perform high levels of professionalisation. In response, higher education institutions are increasingly striving to create innovative learning contexts and improve existing learning pedagogies (Lau and Ng, 2015; Lau et al., 2018). From an educational viewpoint, business simulation games are vital learning and motivational tools, an interconnection between practical problems and abstract concepts, 'hands-on' and 'learning by doing' method of learning. Based on a technical viewpoint, business simulation games provide education's long-last solution to support collaborative and online learning (Ben-Zvi, 2010). Educators incline toward working with advanced technology to produce more considerable learning experiences. Thus, investigating innovative methods for technology-friendly business simulation games for learning and teaching is specifically sensible (Tang, Chen, Law, Wu, Lau, Guan, He & Ho, 2021).

Broadly speaking, business simulation games generate an extremely complicated man-made context. Its purpose is to give students the chance to learn by doing, participating in a simulated experience of reality, and engage them in an original management scenario (Zulfiqar, Al-reshidi, Moteri, Feroz, Yahya

& Al-Rahmi, 2021). The adoption of business simulation games as a key learning tool is sometimes discussed in various literature. Draijer and Schenk (2004) employed a business simulation game to educate students on Enterprise Resource Planning concepts; Yeo and Tan (1999) applied a simulation game in delivering a decision technology course; Parker and Swatman (1999) investigated an online business simulation game simulating an electronic commerce context. In general, the adoption of business simulation games performs a vital role in learning and teaching, although it has been employed for over six decades. Most past research studies have shown the effectiveness of business simulation games in learning and teaching. But the key concerns that require to be highlighted are relevant to sustainability issues. This study helps to narrow the gap between industry-required skills and possessed skills, as well as discuss how to integrate the concept of employability into the learning context (Goi, 2019). This study also addresses the design process of a business simulation game and explores the student learning experiences from the pre-activity to the post-activity stage. To this end, it may give valuable insights for the educators to improve the teaching pedagogies and identify the future research direction.

This book chapter has mainly been divided into six main sections. The research context and settings are provided in Section 1. In Section 2, the literature review includes employability, sustainable development through employability in higher education, employability in professional education, and the use of business simulation games in professional education development. Then, Macro Business Simulation development and elements are described in Section 3. The research methodology is elaborated in Section 4. Empirical results and insights from interviewees are discussed in Section 5. Finally, the conclusion section is summarised in Section 6.

## LITERATURE REVIEW

### Employability

As a complex, multi-dimensional, and competence-based construct (Römgens, Scoupe & Beausaert, 2020), the existing definitions of employability can be broadly grouped into three main categories (Cheng, Adekola, Albia & Cai, 2021). The first category interprets employability as an absolute dimension of individual capabilities. Personal assets and intrinsic characteristics contribute to one's employability, and job success depends on whether an individual possesses the appropriate skills, attitudes, and capabilities that fit the needs of employers (König and Ribaric, 2019). The second category of definition focuses on the contextual nature and relative dimensions of employability, drawing attention to the interaction between social structures (such as gender, ethnicity, social class, and disability) with labour market opportunities and the influence of broader external factors (such as social, political, institutional, and economic factors) on employability (Jackson and Tomlinson, 2022). The third category's definition adopts a more holistic view of understanding the concept of employability, which emphasizes the dual dimension of employability and recognizes the need to understand the interplay of personal characteristics and the influence of external factors on employment opportunities (Cheng, et al., 2021). Small, Shacklock & Marchant (2018, p.4) conceived employability as the "capacity to be self-reliant in navigating the labour market, utilising knowledge, individual skills and attributes, and adapting them to the employment context, showcasing them to employers, while taking into account external and other constraints". Individuals are expected to possess industry/discipline-specific attributes and transferable skills that can be applied to a wide range of jobs and occupations to be relevant in the dynamic and competitive job market (Williams,

Karypidou, Steele & Dodd, 2019). In addition, employers often rated transferable graduate skills more highly than technical skills as transferable skills have broader applications in the workplace (Morgan, Yazdanparast & Rawski, 2018).

As employability is a contested issue, Small and others (2018) recognized the importance of having an agreed conceptual understanding of employability shared by all key stakeholders to achieve and enhance employability effectively. Studies were conducted to examine key stakeholders' perceptions of individual and contextual factors relating to promoting one's employability. For example, Clarke (2018) developed a comprehensive graduate employability model, drawing attention to how graduates' human capital (such as problem-solving skills, analytical thinking skills, communication skills), social capital, and individual behaviours influence their perceived employability and how perceived employability affects graduates' engagement in job search, job retention, and job transformation. Meanwhile, external factors such as economic and labour market conditions should be considered as they may also influence one's perceived employability and employment opportunities (Tan, Laswad & Chua, 2022).

Employability is a complex and multifaceted concept. Studies have examined individual and contextual factors relating to the promotion of one's employability. Indeed, the notion of 'employability capital' has been introduced recently. It refers to the various personal skills and resources needed to enhance the opportunity in one's employment (i.e., obtaining and retaining employment) (Römgens et al., 2020). Personal resources, considered the building blocks of employability, are comprised of knowledge, skills, and attitudes that can facilitate one's entry into the job market and support lifelong learning. Peeters, Nelissen, De Cuyper, Forrier, Verbruggen & De Witte (2019) further differentiated the concept of employability into four dimensions: job-related attitudes, job-related expertise, career-related employability capital, and development-related capital.

Apart from understanding the different categories in defining employability, the conceptualisations of employability can also be explained by two major perspectives, i.e., learning in higher education and the workplace. Both contexts share the same lifelong learning continuum in which higher education is commonly perceived as the preparatory phase for subsequent occurrences of workplace learning. Research findings from both fields (higher education and workplace learning) complement each other in defining employability competencies and offer an enriched understanding of the conceptualisation of employability (Jackson and Tomlinson, 2020).

In the past decade, a 'hot' topic has been discussed on how higher education achieves Sustainable Development Goal 4 (SDG 4). Higher education institutions expect to provide lifelong learning opportunities for young generations to enrich their skills and employability via comprehensive vocational education and training (United Nations, 2022).

## Sustainable Development Through Employability in Higher Education

Employability is a key concept in higher education worldwide. Graduates' employability has been a key performance indicator for higher education institutions (Fraccascia, Sabato & Yazan, 2021). The discourse of graduate employability has by far dominated the agenda of higher education, with employers urging higher education institutions to equip graduating students with work-ready skill sets that can harness the market changes arising from the rapid technological advancement in the 21st-century workplace and develop their capabilities to survive in an intensely competitive working environment. Graduate employment in higher education is of prime importance as these alumni form the future workforce. According to Kinash and Crane (2015), graduate employability means higher education institutions and employers have supported the student knowledge, attributes, skills, identity, and reflective disposition that graduates need to be career ready and succeed in the workforce.

While the graduate employment rate is often regarded as the key indicator of employability in the higher education sector, criticisms have been received about using such measurement. For example, while employment statistics may reflect actual percentages of graduates' job acquisition, employability encompasses more than that and measures a graduate's potential and capacity to obtain and retain a job (Cheng et al., 2021). Employability is more than a set of knowledge and skills, and it should be treated as a dialogue (Boffo, 2019). In addition, Ferns, Dawson & Howitt (2019) and Williams et al. (2019) commented that employability is a collaborative process engaging job seekers/holders and various stakeholders (e.g., policymakers, employers, higher education institutions) in the world of work aiming to maximise the chances of success in the employment sector. As suggested by Ng, Chan, Wut, Lo & Szeto (2021), both higher education institutions (supply side) and organisations (demand side) identify the required and acquired employability skill standards to maximise employment outcomes and ensure graduates are employable, work-ready, and adaptable to the workforce. This idea further reiterates that the promotion of employability is a collective responsibility amongst various stakeholders.

Cheng et al. (2021) discovered that employers often perceive employability as work readiness and emphasise capabilities beyond subject knowledge. It is not uncommon for employers to complain about graduates lacking the required skills and competencies for their organisations (Prikshat, Kumar & Nankervis, 2018). A study by Suleman and Laranjeiro (2018) in Portugal revealed that graduates' soft skills, such as teamworking and leadership skills, are most frequently criticised by employers as insufficient. Although Andreas (2018) argued that soft skill deficiency among students might be due to their preoccupation with social media, and hence, a decline in face-to-face contact and social interaction, and the use of virtual platforms for multiple purposes is inevitable in the digital era. Moreover, Chhinzer and Russo (2018) noticed that employers tend to evaluate graduate employability mostly based on generic skills (such as teamwork, communication, problem-solving), general mental ability (i.e., IQ), discipline-specific knowledge, etc. In addition, Williams et al. (2019) found that employers also tend to place importance on indicators of values and commitment of candidates. For example, whether candidates show a keen interest in the industry and company, as well as possess shared organisational goals and values with employers. Employers' emphasis on soft skills and attitudes further implies that employers are assessing candidates more subjectively, contradicting the focus of higher education institutions on imparting discipline-based knowledge and skills.

To address the diverse needs of employers and the skill deficiencies in graduating students, higher education institutions are therefore placing employability enhancement as a priority and passively taking on the responsibility for producing work-ready graduates for the highly competitive labour market, emphasising more the development of transferable generic skills, which can also be referred to as employability skills. Apart from imparting subject knowledge, educators were called upon to offer students training on employability skills, such as critical and analytical thinking, and competent reasoning to produce employable graduates who fit the needs of employers and the labour market (Osmani, Hindi & Weerakkody, 2018).

To keep up with the emergence of globalisation, internationalisation, and digitisation in the ever-changing labour market (Jackson and Tomlinson, 2020), employability is unquestionably core to higher education, and an upsurge of interest in employability has been observed in higher education studies (Mawson and Haworth, 2018). A study conducted by Cheng et al. (2021) found that although students are aware that they are responsible for their employability, they still perceive higher education institutions as responsible for developing and enhancing their general employability. While higher education institutions primarily focus on gaining employment, students believe that employability goes beyond gaining employment and involves the long-term plan of growing and developing a career.

Although diverging views have been observed among educational institutions, employers, and students on the relative importance of employability skills, the employers' perspectives are often used as a benchmark to inform educators and provide evidence for the development of employability enhancement programmes in higher education institutions. To increase students' competitiveness in the dynamic job market, higher education institutions have carefully planned and implemented various employability strategies and initiatives to enhance the required employability skills of their students (Winterton and Turner, 2019).

Higher education takes on a dual role in contributing to the sustainability of economic growth and development. Apart from promoting whole person development, facilitating access to employment has become another essential objective in higher education (Zulfiqar et al., 2021). Besides deploying resources on increasing employment-based training to students to prepare them for the world of work, higher education institutions are also working to establish and grow linkages between higher education institutions and various industries to improve graduate labour market prospects. For instance, Work-integrated learning, such as practicum, internship, and coop, is a popular method to enhance and increase graduate employability in higher education (English, De Villiers Scheepers & Fleischman, Burgess & Crimmins, 2021). Work-integrated learning provides students with practical employment experiences relevant to their field of study. They can apply the theoretical knowledge they learned during lectures to an actual workplace during their studies (Ng et al., 2021). By merging work experience with academic learning, work-integrated learning opportunities can enhance students' connection to the job market and encourage them to engage in a comparable employment context. These work experiences can undoubtedly strengthen their employability profile. The inclusion of work-integrated learning into the formal education curricula allows students to develop attributes and skills essential to obtaining and securing a job (Bilsland, Carter & Wood, 2019). To support employability, work-integrated learning also provides valuable opportunities for students to 'try on' job roles and professional identities and understand the norms, protocols, and codes at work that may not have been taught in academic learning (Bowen, 2018). A qualitative longitudinal study by Reddy and Shaw (2019) found that the experiences psychology students gained from work-integrated learning internships helped develop professionalism in their prospective careers.

## Employability in Professional Education

Professional education is known as the formal specialised training in a particular professional occupation. To prepare individuals for their chosen profession, professional education aims to foster learners' acquisition of necessary vocational and professional competencies for proper practice in actual work settings. In addition to learning about the core concepts, principles, and practical techniques, learners must also understand the application of relevant knowledge and skills in real practice (Gondwe, 2020).

Although graduate employability has been high on the higher education agenda, Stoten (2018) pointed out that technical and vocational education institutions may be more concerned about their graduates' employability than academically oriented higher education institutions. Thus, a well-planned employability enhancement programme is crucial for these professionally oriented higher education institutions. For example, the 'five-dimensional quality view' adopted by China's higher vocational education system, which comprises students' growth and achievement, institution's ability in management, development opportunity, global impact, and social contribution, reflected that higher professional education had been designated the responsibility for preparing and supplying employable, qualified, and high-value graduates who are matching the needs of both local and international labour market (Higher Technical Vocational Education in China, 2019). Furthermore, *the Annual Report on Vocational Education Quality in China 2019* (Higher Technical Vocational Education in China, 2019) revealed that the employment rate of graduates who received vocational and professional education in higher education institutions remains stable at 92% within six months from graduation. Since professional education focuses on strengthening and accrediting graduates' professional qualifications, this relatively high employment figure suggests that professional education greatly facilitates graduates' employment.

Indeed, a quantitative study by Huang, Cao, Zhao, Long, Han & Cai (2022a) examining factors affecting the employability and career development of finance and business graduates from higher vocational colleges in China found that professional education significantly influences the development of specific employability skills. This study investigates how educational practices, such as learning conditions, opportunities, and resources offered by higher professional education institutions, may contribute to graduates' development of employability through a questionnaire survey. One of the independent variables, educational practice, is categorised into three groups, i.e., professional education, transferable education, and teaching resources support (Huang et al., 2022a). In particular, professional education is about learning professional knowledge, cultivating professional skills, participating in actual work tasks or projects relevant to their discipline, and gaining opportunities for hands-on professional practices. Meanwhile, the dependent variable, employability development, is operationalised and classified into three domains, namely, the development of basic skills (i.e., general knowledge, professional knowledge, methodological knowledge, foreign language skills, computing skills, financial literacy, and understanding of the complex social, organisational, and technological system), professional skills (i.e., planning and coordination skills, statistical and data processing skills, learning skills, innovation skills, critical thinking skills, negotiation and decision-making skills, ability to work under pressure, attention to details, time management skills, relevance of work, and manipulative skills), and soft skills (i.e., ability to work independently, flexibility, the concentration of attention, loyalty and integrity, worldwide vision, language competent, written communication skills, reading comprehension skills, teamwork ability, leadership skills, and responsibility) (Fawns, Mulherin, Hounsell & Aitken, 2021). Results from multivariable linear regression analysis indicated that professional education significantly and positively affects graduates' basic skills development. Researchers from this study believed that the substantial improvement in basic skills could be explained by the quality social and practical skills offered through professional education (Perusso, van der Sijde, Leal & Blankesteijn, 2021). Besides, it was found that other variables, such as internship engagement, positively impact professional skills development. As work-integrated learning such as internships and practicum are often incorporated into professional education programmes, these practical work opportunities could reinforce students' development of professional skills and career competency (Huang, Silitonga & Wu, 2022b). Bonnard (2020) also commented that students participating in work placement had enhanced employability and value-added professional skills that can be applied in the workplace.

## The Use of Business Simulation Games in Professional Education Development

To cultivate graduate employability, higher education institutions are responsible for providing various flexible education pathways for students with different aspirations and abilities. Through professional education and training, students will acquire the necessary skills and knowledge for employment and lifelong learning. It is especially vital to understand and prepare 21st-century learners and graduates. This generation of learners is created by their lifelong access to the internet (Kinash, 2011; Zulfiqar et al., 2021). Thus, 21st-century learners are more connected and empowered than previous student generations, so they tend to feel entitled to quality education and insist that learning should be more relevant, practical, and efficient (Kinash, Wood & Knight, 2013; Freeman and Wash, 2013; Perusso et al., 2021).

One way to prepare students for their intended profession is through professional education. In response, there is an increasing trend of higher education institutions striving to create innovative learning contexts, improve existing learning pedagogies, recruit good quality teaching staff, and upgrade learning facilities. Indeed, a business simulation game is a new, innovative educational tool for students to enjoy in an interactive learning classroom. The use of support tools can help students to develop and improve their competencies, skills, and knowledge (Brazhkin and Zimmerman, 2019; Goi, 2019).

As experiential learning theory suggests, the use of business simulation games includes reflective observation and experimentation through complexity, learning by trial and error, and iterative decision-making (Vij and Sharma, 2018). As proposed by Kolb (1984 in 2014), experiential learning theory defines learning as a continuous process grounded in experience, not in terms of outcomes.

The present millennial generation of students is technology-driven and would expect some form of learning through technology than traditional models of teaching and learning (Bhavani, Mehta & Dubey, 2020). A game, like a business simulation game, can challenge students mentally and help to engage students constructively (Kinzie and Joseph, 2008; Carenys, Moya & Perramon, 2017). It is believed that higher education needs to adapt to the current pedagogic trends and student demands in order to enhance and sustain their learning capabilities and derive better results (Bhavani et al., 2020). To improve the understanding of the design and implementation of business simulation games, the real case study 'Top-BOSS' is described in the next section.

## OVERVIEW OF MACRO BUSINESS SIMULATION – TOP-BOSS

With the era of e-learning getting popular, learners started to move their interest from classroom learning to online learning with the benefit of privacy and convenience, being said that Top-BOSS is evolved to develop a series of management learning content to cope with this education trend by providing a new breed of the learning experience for students to arouse their interest in business management learning and teacher with interactive learning content with artificial intelligence (AI) algorithms through a business simulation game. The learner is encouraged to immerse in the virtual dynamic marketplace where comprehensive financial reports/ratios and business intelligence (BI) will be delivered with tangible results following their management decision (Top-BOSS, 2022).

This study mainly adopts a real-world case study, Macro Business Simulation, as the target research area. Top-BOSS International Corporation designs Macro Business Simulation. Macro Business Simulation is a cloud-based platform that gives micro and macro-economic contexts in business management simulation with in-depth financial reports in which tangible results are delivered every quarter and aligned with the intended learning objectives. Macro Business Simulation is an academic interactive learning platform being adopted in 136 China universities, 138 Taiwan universities, and some other universities where they are situated in Hong Kong, Vietnam, Japan, and Indonesia. Macro Business Simulation generates a practical learning experience to manage and operate a virtual business in a challenging and dynamic context, as well as being responsible for the overall performance of the business in finance, manufacturing, product development, supply chain management, marketing, and sales. Students will form a small group to perform as a manager to make daily strategic decisions in a simulated business context.

Macro Business Simulation develops a series of platforms/tools to integrate business, management, mathematics, and information. Theories, technologies, and professionals in various fields of science and technology develop a diversified teaching system for simulation business competitions to meet the needs of teaching in business management with the revolution of technology.

## Teaching System of Simulated Business Competition

The learning method of business simulation competition is to train students by simulating the situation of business operation and the problems generated and derived from inspiring students to analyse environmental information, deal with group relations and make decisions. This teaching system, which emphasises interactive learning and self-growth, is quite different from most current digital learning products combined with multimedia or network applications. However, it is still static teaching content (Pando-Garcia, Perianez-Canadillas & Charterina, 2016). The simulation business competition teaching system is widely used in various courses, including strategic management, production, marketing, innovation management, supply chain management, financial accounting, agricultural economics, etc. (Roser, Sato & Nakano, 2021). More than a quarter of management departments in the United States use business simulation competitions in various types of courses; at least more than 60% of large companies use business simulations as in-house training courses; Research shows that business simulation learning is the method to improve the learning effect more than the traditional business management teaching method (Subhash and Cudney, 2018). At present, there are only a few simulated business teaching materials applied on the Internet in Hong Kong or China. Most of them are modified by imitating foreign designs. It is rare to have completely self-developed products, as developing a complete set of business simulation games is rather difficult and risky. It consists of high technology and resources that must be combined in the form of complexity and flexibility (Tang et al., 2021).

The final business management simulation starts with a conceptual framework, prototype system structure, software programs by a professional software development team, and numerous tests by teachers and students. These groups of people must have the above-basic capabilities for software development or application tools. During the development period, they communicate and cooperate closely with each other. If any part of the process quits or fails, the whole game will be ruined; however, the communication gap between script developers and programmers is a crucial cause of slow or failed development. At present, the development of various countries still adopts the ad-hoc method. Complete development work takes several years, plus several years of evaluation and testing. The development funds and human investment consumed during the period are substantial; however, it will take years to know its teaching value or market reflection. Of course, there are also a few outstanding people who can complete system development independently, but most of them can only be used by developers personally. In the internet world, teamwork will be an inevitable trend of work, especially the high-value-added cross-industry integration that is the trend of the times (Top-BOSS, 2022).

## BLOM: Rapid Molding Technology of Business Operation Learning Components

The rapid molding technology developed by Top-BOSS International uses business learning object modelling to create a simulation business competition in a teaching system (hereinafter referred to as BLOM) based on the concept of value chain division of work to establish a set of development and production simulation business competitions with a systematic methodology for application by institutions or individuals interested in developing online interactive teaching materials for management.

Take the development of the 'Circulation Master' simulation game as an example to demonstrate the feasibility of the development. The realisation of this idea can significantly improve the development threshold, with faster speed (within one year) and lower cost (according to the complexity of the content will be different) to develop a simulation competition system that is suitable for teaching needs. At the same time, in conjunction with other software tool products and software development engineering methods, during the development process, on one end, different modules can be tested on a small scale and synchronously, and on the other end, part of the work can be outsourced. In the long run, through the division of labor, various business management competitions will be developed and used as teaching or competition activities for various types of management education.

The design of BLOM's software development technology is aimed at an integrated and open architecture, allowing individual new technologies to be added to ensure that the efficiency and precision of development work can keep pace with the times, and after long-term accumulation of experience, the accumulated advantages developed will also meet the essential characteristics of the teaching system of business management learning.

BLOM's method of making a simulation business competition teaching system is roughly divided into seven steps, which are (1) script compilation; (2) presentation method and Top-BOSS presentation Method EMBG; (3) business scenario generation; (4) internet access; (5) LMS (learning management system) platform connection; (6) product packaging and testing; and (7) operation analyzer (Top-BOSS, 2022). Its related process is shown in Figure 1.

*Figure 1. BLOM Process*

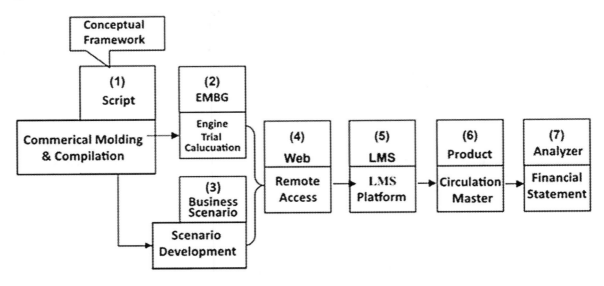

After investigating the key elements and implementation processes of the 'Top-BOSS' simulation game, the details of the research methodology are given in the next section. The adoption of a robust research methodology aims to respond to the key research objectives, describe the research design or processes, and prepare for the data collection.

## RESEARCH METHODOLOGY

To explore the integration of Macro Business Simulation in the educational process, the study invited 64 university students to complete both pre-activity and post-activity surveys in 2020. To this end, it can be easy for the researchers to understand the students' perceptions, learning experiences, and improvements. Such preliminary study provides valuable insights for educators to improve the teaching pedagogy, assists the researchers in producing the subsequent research, and provides the educational product designers to enrich the product quality in the future. The pre-activity survey focuses on nine main survey questionnaire questions provided in Table 1.

## Enhancing Student Professionalization Through Business Simulation Games

*Table 1. Pre-activity Survey Questions*

| S/N | Survey Questionnaire Questions |
|---|---|
| 1 | Have you ever heard about business simulation? |
| 2 | Do you want to know more about real-life business apart from the learning in the textbook? |
| 3 | Are you in favor of pursuing comprehensive data analysis before decision-making? |
| 4 | Do you understand what is the mission statement and vision of a company? |
| 5 | Do you know why management needs to work out the financial budget before the next quarter or year's business? |
| 6 | Do you know how business intelligence can help management to drive business decisions with a competitive market advantage? |
| 7 | Do you think your soft skill is to interact with other people effectively and harmoniously? |
| 8 | Do you want to know more about basic corporate performance and identify the cause-and-effect relationship between the drivers and business performance? |
| 9 | Do you want to understand more about simulation training? |

During this stage, the instructors could understand the students' backgrounds, expectations, and business simulation game knowledge level. Accordingly, the instructors may adjust the business simulation game level, the learning pace, and teaching approaches.

After completing the business simulation game, the instructors invited the participants to fill in the post-activity survey to evaluate their learning effectiveness and experiences. The post-activity survey questions are given in Table 2.

*Table 2. Post-activity Survey Questions*

| S/N | Survey Questionnaire Questions |
|---|---|
| 1 | Over six rounds of business simulation workshops, do you find MBS provides you a basic understanding of how the business operation is being run in a marketplace? |
| 2 | Do you agree business simulation provides you with a dynamic business experience with your competitors apart from textbook learning? |
| 3 | Do you agree the comprehensive data and diagram in MBS can help your team to form evidence of decision-making by way of alternative solutions? |
| 4 | Do you agree a profitable business requires a holistic understanding of potential demand & supply through production planning & inventory? |
| 5 | Do you think management by objective (forecast) is viable for management to review the progress towards the target and make necessary adjustments periodically? |
| 6 | Do you agree business intelligence can help management to drive business decisions in a competitive market advantage? |
| 7 | Do you think your soft skill to interact with your teammates can be enhanced effectively through the business simulation process? |
| 8 | Do you find yourself understanding more about the cause-and-effect relationship between the driver of potential demand and production vs business performance? |
| 9 | Do you find that financial statements, cost structure, breakdown point, sales trend financial analysis, and sales/ production analysis can enrich your learning of accounting and finance principles? |

To supplement the research findings, 10 semi-structured, in-depth interviews were conducted with relevant parties including teachers, students, and business simulation operators. The interviewees provide valuable insight to promote business simulation games as the primary learning tool in the forthcoming years. The key findings are given and summarised in the next section.

## FINDINGS

### Empirical Results

Before joining the business simulation games, participants were invited to participate in pre-activity surveys. Only 57.81% of participants have heard about business simulation. Simulation games are not popular in adopting university learning materials and teaching pedagogy. Most university students are young and more eager to accept the new learning environment and manner. As a result, 98.44% of participants said they would like to understand more about simulation training. Students generally obtain fundamental business knowledge from compulsory subjects like financial accounting, managing organisations, statistics, and business communication. In response, over 75% of students said they have confidence in participating in the business simulation game relevant to data analysis, the mission statement and vision of a company, the financial budget, and communication skills. However, only 51.56% of students reflected that they understood how business intelligence could help management to drive business decisions with a competitive market advantage. It implies that the educators may design training materials and workshops related to the business intelligence concept in the business simulation game context. To the best of the authors' knowledge, the business simulation game fosters the students to reinforce their basic business knowledge. It encourages them to strengthen their soft skills such as analytical, problem-solving, critical thinking, and tech. As a result, 90.63% of students expressed that they wanted to know more about basic corporate performance and the cause-and-effect relationship between the drivers and business performance, and 96.88% of students expected to know more about real-life business apart from learning in the textbook. The key findings are summarised in Table 3.

*Table 3. Pre-activity Survey Results*

| Items | Percentages (%) |
|---|---|
| I have heard about business simulation | 57.81 |
| I would like to understand more about simulation training | 98.44 |
| I have confidence in participating in the business simulation game relevant to data analysis, mission statement and vision of a company, the financial budget, and communication skills | 75.01 |
| I understood how business intelligence could help management to drive business decisions with a competitive market advantage | 51.56 |
| I want to know more about basic corporate performance and the cause-and-effect relationship between the drivers and business performance | 90.63 |
| I want to know more about real-life business apart from learning in the textbook | 96.88 |

After taking six rounds of the business simulation workshops, participants were invited to engage in post-activity surveys. Most students expressed that they were satisfied with the learning experience, and the programme outcome fits their initial expectations. 87.5% of participants found business simulation workshops provide them with a basic understanding of how the business operation is being run in a marketplace; 92.19% of participants agreed business simulation workshops provide them with a dynamic business experience apart from textbook learning; 85.94% of participants agreed that the comprehensive data and diagram in business simulation workshops can help their team to form evidence of decision-making by way of alternative solutions; 92.19% of participants agreed that a profitable business requires a holistic understanding of potential demand and supply through production planning and inventory; 82.81% of participants addressed that management by objective (forecast) is viable for management to review the progress towards the target and make necessary adjustments periodically; 93.75% of participants agreed business intelligence can help management to drive business decisions in a competitive market advantage; 82.81% of participants indicated that the soft skill to interact with their teammates can be enhanced effectively through the business simulation process; 87.5% of participants pointed out they performed understanding more about the cause-and-effect relationship between the driver of potential demand and production vs business performance; and 90.63% of participants perceived that financial statements, cost structure, breakdown point, sales trend financial analysis, and sales/production analysis can enrich their learning of accounting and finance principles. The main findings are shown in Table 4.

*Table 4. Post-activity Survey Results*

| Items | Percentages (%) |
|---|---|
| I found that business simulation workshops provide them with a basic understanding of how the business operation is being run in a marketplace | 87.50 |
| I agreed that business simulation workshops provide them with a dynamic business experience apart from textbook learning | 92.19 |
| I agreed that the comprehensive data and diagram in business simulation workshops could help their team to form evidence of decision-making by way of alternative solutions | 85.94 |
| I agreed that a profitable business requires a holistic understanding of potential demand and supply through production planning and inventory | 92.19 |
| I agreed that management by objective (forecast) is viable for management to review the progress towards the target and make necessary adjustments periodically | 82.18 |
| I agreed that business intelligence could help management to drive business decisions in a competitive market advantage | 93.75 |
| I agreed that the soft skill of interacting with their teammates could be enhanced effectively through the business simulation process | 82.81 |
| I performed understanding more about the cause-and-effect relationship between the driver of potential demand and production vs business performance | 87.50 |
| I agreed that financial statements, cost structure, breakdown point, sales trend financial analysis, and sales/production analysis could enrich their learning of accounting and finance principles | 90.63 |

## INSIGHTS FROM THE INTERVIEWEES

### Macro Business Simulation Operators

One of the most challenging jobs in developing a management game is creating the scenario; the application of this situation in teaching not only needs to provide a feeling close to reality and be challenging enough. As proposed by Goi (2019), the sustainability of business simulation games in learning and teaching is a challenging task. To elaborate on the situation, the Macro Business Simulation operators provided a real-life example:

*"Take 'Burger King Simulation Management' as an example, assuming that we can provide several sets of business management. The company's marketing management situation allows teachers to inspire through the simulated business action learning teaching system. Student's ability to analyse environmental information, manage group relationships, and make marketing decisions".*

Although a variety of business theories and models are often cited in the design of many business management games to improve the suitability and success rate of the invention, there may be conflicts or incomplete theoretical foundations among the many theories or models. that start from initialization, design, construction to operation stage (van der Zee and Slomp, 2009). Otherwise, students may exhibit demotivation because of difficulties with the game (Hernández-Lara and Serradell-López, 2018). In response, the Macro Business Simulation operators addressed that:

*"Consistent, resulting in different calculation results, how to select the most suitable part as the core model of the management game, of course, because of our bias may also affect the final product or the learning effect of the product, this part is difficult to avoid but should pay special attention".*

### Students

Business simulation games expect to learn how to run a company and make realistic business decisions. For example, analysing the market result and solving the current business problem. To create effective learning in business simulation games, the quality of the platform is crucial. Evaluating the effectiveness of business simulation games could be included the outcomes, meaning what the students learned from the games. And it is the main advantage of business simulation games since it provides an authentic environment for the students to operate the business. Yet, it might not accurately represent the real world since there are more challenges and changes in the real world. As supported by Sugahara and Lau (2019), business simulation games can help students achieve self-interested goals. In doing so, one student expressed that:

*"We can catch up on various learning opportunities which may help us to enrich our articulation and job opportunities in the future".*

To create effective learning in business simulation games, the game's design is important since a good design for the game can increase students' immersion and encourage active participation in the activities. This induces interactivity among learners (Hernández-Lara and Serradell-López, 2018). Measuring the results is a valuable technique for assessing the efficiency of business simulation games. By having students share what they have learned, they can gauge the effectiveness of the project. The students can modify the business simulation games for the future and increase their efficacy after gathering their feedback. Indeed, the benefit of playing business simulation games is that it gives students a chance to practice managing a firm in a completely risk-free, virtual setting, observe the effects of their actions throughout the entire organisation, and learn from their mistakes in a safe environment. Students can connect with other students from different parts of the world (Goi, 2019). Hence, one student perceived satisfaction with participating in joining the business simulation game:

*"This business simulation game can provide a new, innovative learning pedagogy. Such business simulation game enriches our learning process, like the decision-making process, big data analysis, and critical thinking skills. Also, we can have a chance to communicate with various students via the comprehensive platform without risk exposure and time zone limitation".*

## Teachers

Business simulation games offer a unique opportunity for students to integrate their knowledge in different business areas such as accounting, finance, production planning, logistics, marketing, etc. Students not only practice their entrepreneurial skills but also apply the theoretical knowledge they obtained in the classroom to a dynamic and competitive marketplace. (Zulfiqar, Al-reshidi, Moteri, Feroz, Yahya & Al-Rahmi, 2021). One teacher appreciated the business simulation game as follows:

*"The business simulation game enables my students to broaden their entrepreneurial perspectives and expand their level of knowledge and the ability to feel and perceive the dynamics of the international business environment via the eLearning platform".*

Also, business simulation games enhanced the students' problem-solving and analytical skills, creativity, communication, time management, and presentation skills. This skill set is invaluable in the workplace regardless of the industry (Hernández-Lara and Serradell-López, 2018). Additionally, learning how to provide a high-level overview of complex ideas and strategies to a panel of experts would be the most beneficial to personal employment prospects. This is confirmed by Tan, Laswad & Chua (2022). To reflect this point, one teacher reinforced the business simulation game:

*"The learning objective was met through the business simulation game and students were led to the virtual marketplace where they were able to manage their business with comprehensive financial statements and the BI graph to drive their company's growth with objective measurement. They can apply theory learned from the book to play with other teams in the dynamic economic development and see the consequences after each quarter of financial result".*

In addition, business simulation games provide students with a cross-border business platform where students can demonstrate their business skills in business strategy, marketing, business economics, and accounting through teamwork. The company's market share and profitability can be maximised through mutual discussion and critical thinking among group members. Business simulation games truly realise the participatory learning mode of linking theory with practice, allowing students to expand and enrich classroom learning into virtual enterprise management, providing sufficient preparation for students to enter the real business environment in the future. Business simulation game provides an excellent teaching tool for students to enjoy the learning process (Beltrão and Barcante, 2016). To this end, one teacher agreed on the business simulation game:

*"To a certain extent, business simulation game trains our students as the preferred graduates in the future".*

The following section mainly addresses the implications of the research study and identifies future research directions. The keynotes are well summarised in the conclusion section.

## CONCLUSION

Valuable insights and constructive comments provide a blueprint for supplying business simulation games in higher education as vehicles to equip students with professional knowledge and skills in a practical workplace. It is believed that increasing participatory learning and reducing spoon-feeding education will enhance sustainable development in higher education in terms of teaching and learning in the 21st century. Nevertheless, the COVID-19 pandemic has affected human lives and learning practices since early 2020. The COVID-19 pandemic has fundamentally changed from a traditional classroom to an online learning approach. In doing so, a business simulation game is considered an important learning tool in response to a new learning environment. The next research will use the community of inquiry framework to investigate the students' learning experience in the business simulation game competition. Also, this study only focused on Hong Kong undergraduate students. To improve the generalisation, it may consider enlarging the scale of the sample size considering different educational levels of students like sub-degree (i.e., associate degree and higher diploma) and other countries like China, Taiwan, and Japan, to name but a few. Furthermore, the students' fixed and growth mindsets may determine the student learning experience and expectation in the engagement of business simulation games. To this end, future research may add the personality test of students before joining the business simulation games. As expected, it may improve the reliability and validity of research findings.

## REFERENCES

Andreas, S. (2018). Effects of the decline in social capital on college graduates' soft skills. *Industry and Higher Education*, *32*(1), 47–56. doi:10.1177/0950422217749277

Beltrão, K. L., & Barcante, L. C. (2016). Teaching principles and fundamentals of business excellence to undergraduate students through a game. *Total Quality Management & Business Excellence*, *27*(5), 681–698. doi:10.1080/14783363.2015.1043116

Ben-Zvi, T. (2010). The efficacy of business simulation games in creating decision support systems: An experimental investigation. *Decision Support Systems*, *49*(1), 61–69. doi:10.1016/j.dss.2010.01.002

Bhavani, G., Mehta, A., & Dubey, S. (2020). Literature review: Game-based pedagogy in accounting education. *International Journal of Financial Research*, *11*(6), 165–176. doi:10.5430/ijfr.v11n6p165

Bilsland, C., Carter, L., & Wood, L. N. (2019). Work integrated learning internships in transnational education: Alumni perspectives from Vietnam. *Education + Training*, *61*(3), 359–373. doi:10.1108/ET-07-2017-0094

Boffo, V. (2019). Employability and higher education: A category for the future. *New Directions for Adult and Continuing Education*, *2019*(163), 11–23. doi:10.1002/ace.20338

Bonnard, C. (2020). What is employability for higher education students? *Journal of Education and Work*, *33*(5-6), 425–445. doi:10.1080/13639080.2020.1842866

Bowen, T. (2018). Becoming professional: Examining how WIL students learn to construct and perform their professional identities. *Studies in Higher Education*, *43*(7), 1148–1159. doi:10.1080/03075079.2016.1231803

Brazhkin, V., & Zimmerman, H. (2019). Students' perceptions of learning in an online multiround business simulation game: What can we learn from them? *Decision Sciences*, *17*(4), 363–386.

Carenys, J., Moya, S., & Perramon, J. (2017). Is it worth it to consider videogames in accounting education? A comparison of a simulation and a videogame in attributes, motivation and learning outcomes. *Revista de Contabilidad-Spanish Accounting Review*, *20*(2), 118–130. doi:10.1016/j.rcsar.2016.07.003

Cheng, M., Adekola, O., Albia, J., & Cai, S. (2021). Employability in higher education: A review of key stakeholders' perspectives. *Higher Education Evaluation and Development*, *16*(1), 16–31. doi:10.1108/HEED-03-2021-0025

Cheng, Y. C. (2009). Hong Kong educational reforms in the last decade: Reform syndrome and new developments. *International Journal of Educational Management*, *23*(1), 65–86. doi:10.1108/09513540910926439

Chhinzer, N., & Russo, A. M. (2018). An exploration of employer perceptions of graduate student employability. *Education + Training*, *60*(1), 104–120. doi:10.1108/ET-06-2016-0111

Clarke, M. (2018). Rethinking graduate employability: The role of capital, individual attributes and context. *Studies in Higher Education*, *43*(11), 1923–1937. doi:10.1080/03075079.2017.1294152

Dale, R., & Robertson, S. (2014). Global education policy. In N. Yeates (Ed.), *Global Social Policy*. Policy Press.

Draijer, C., & Schenk, D. J. (2004). Best practices of business simulation with SAP R/3. *Journal of Information Systems Education*, *15*(3), 244–261.

English, P., De Villiers Scheepers, M. J., Fleischman, D., Burgess, J., & Crimmins, G. (2021). Developing professional networks: The missing link to graduate employability. *Education + Training*, *63*(4), 647–661. doi:10.1108/ET-10-2020-0309

Fawns, T., Mulherin, T., Hounsell, D., & Aitken, G. (2021). Seamful learning and professional education. *Studies in Continuing Education*, *43*(3), 360–376. doi:10.1080/0158037X.2021.1920383

Ferns, S., Dawson, V., & Howitt, C. (2019). A collaborative framework for enhancing graduate employability. *International Journal of Work - Integrated Learning*, *20*(2), 99-111.

Fraccascia, L., Sabato, A., & Yazan, D. M. (2021). An industrial symbiosis simulation game: Evidence from the circular sustainable business development class. *Journal of Industrial Ecology, 25*(6), 1688–1706. doi:10.1111/jiec.13183

Freeman, G., & Wash, P. (2013). You can lead students to the classroom, and you can make them think: Ten brain-based strategies for college teaching and learning success. *Journal on Excellence in College Teaching, 24*(3), 99–120.

Goi, C. L. (2019). The use of business simulation games in teaching and learning. *Journal of Education for Business, 94*(5), 342–349. doi:10.1080/08832323.2018.1536028

Gondwe, S. S. (2020). Archival education and training opportunities in Malawi: After 50 years, why have we not done well? In S. Keakopa & T. Mosweu (Eds.), *Cases on electronic record management in the ESARBICA region* (pp. 277–297). IGI Global. doi:10.4018/978-1-7998-2527-2.ch015

Hernández-Lara, A., & Serradell-López, E. (2018). Student interactions in online discussion forums: Their perception on learning with business simulation games. *Behaviour & Information Technology, 37*(4), 419–429. doi:10.1080/0144929X.2018.1441326

Higher Technical and Vocational Education in China. (2019, June 20). *Annual Conference of China Higher Vocational Education Quality Report in Beijing 2019.* https://www.tech.net.cn/news/show-66627.html

Huang, X., Cao, J., Zhao, G., Long, Z., Han, G., & Cai, X. (2022a). The employability and career development of finance and trade college graduates. *Frontiers in Psychology, 12*, 719336. doi:10.3389/fpsyg.2021.719336 PMID:35082712

Huang, Y. M., Silitonga, L. M., & Wu, T. T. (2022b). Applying a business simulation game in a flipped classroom to enhance engagement, learning achievement, and higher-order thinking skills. *Computers & Education, 183*, 104494. doi:10.1016/j.compedu.2022.104494

Jackson, D., & Tomlinson, M. (2020). Investigating the relationship between career planning, proactivity and employability perceptions among higher education students in uncertain labour market conditions. *Higher Education, 80*(3), 435–455. doi:10.100710734-019-00490-5

Jackson, D., & Tomlinson, M. (2022). The relative importance of work experience, extra-curricular and university-based activities on student employability. *Higher Education Research & Development, 41*(4), 1119–1135. doi:10.1080/07294360.2021.1901663

Kinash, S. (2011). Next generation of what. *Education Technology Solutions, 44*, 52–54.

Kinash, S., & Crane, L. (2015). Enhancing graduate employability of the 21st century learner. *Proceedings of the International Mobile Learning Festival 2015: Mobile Learning, MOOCs and 21st Century Learning.*

Kinash, S., Wood, K., & Knight, D. (2013). Digital immigrant teachers and digital native students: What happens to teaching? *Education Technology Solutions, 54*, 56–58.

Kinzie, M. B., & Joseph, D. R. D. (2008). Gender differences in game preferences of middle school children: Implications for educational game design. *Educational Technology Research and Development, 56*(5-6), 643–663. doi:10.100711423-007-9076-z

Kolb, D. A. (2014). *Experiential learning: Experience as the source of learning and development.* Prentice Hall.

König, L. S., & Ribarić, H. M. (2019). Is there a mismatch between employers' and university teachers' perceptions on graduate employability in Croatia? *Journal of Managerial Issues, 24*(1), 87–102.

Lau, Y. Y., & Ng, A. K. Y. (2015). The motivations and expectations of students pursuing maritime education. *WMU Journal of Maritime Affairs, 14*(2), 313–331. doi:10.100713437-015-0075-3

Lau, Y. Y., Ng, A. K. Y., Tam, K. C., & Chan, E. K. K. (2018). An investigation on the professionalization of education in maritime logistics and supply chains. *Maritime Business Review, 3*(4), 394–413. doi:10.1108/MABR-08-2018-0029

Mawson, M., & Haworth, A. C. (2018). Supporting the employability agenda in university libraries. *Information and Learning Science, 119*(1/2), 101–108. doi:10.1108/ILS-04-2017-0027

Morgan, S., Yazdanparast, A., & Rawski, G. (2018). Creating a distinctive business career outcome programme. *Journal of Vocational Education and Training, 70*(2), 251–277. doi:10.1080/13636820.2017.1394356

Ng, P. M., Chan, J. K., Wut, T. M., Lo, M. F., & Szeto, I. (2021). What makes better career opportunities for young graduates? Examining acquired employability skills in higher education institutions. *Education + Training, 63*(6), 852–871. doi:10.1108/ET-08-2020-0231

Osmani, M., Hindi, N. M., & Weerakkody, V. (2018). Developing employability skills in information system graduates: Traditional vs. innovative teaching methods. *International Journal of Information and Communication Technology Education, 14*(2), 17–29. doi:10.4018/IJICTE.2018040102

Pando-Garcia, J., Perianez-Canadillas, I., & Charterina, J. (2016). Business simulation games with and without supervision: An analysis based on the TAM model. *Journal of Business Research, 69*(5), 1731–1736. doi:10.1016/j.jbusres.2015.10.046

Parker, C. M., & Swatman, P. M. C. (1999). An Internet-mediated electronic commerce business simulation: Experiences developing and using TRECS. *Simulation & Gaming: An Interdisciplinary Journal, 30*(1), 51–69. doi:10.1177/104687819903000107

Peeters, E., Nelissen, J., De Cuyper, N., Forrier, A., Verbruggen, M., & De Witte, H. (2019). Employability capital: A conceptual framework tested through expert analysis. *Journal of Career Development, 46*(2), 79–93. doi:10.1177/0894845317731865

Perusso, A., van der Sijde, P., Leal, R., & Blankesteijn, M. (2021). The effectiveness and impact of action learning on business graduates' professional practice. *Journal of Management Education, 45*(2), 177–205. doi:10.1177/1052562920940374

Prikshat, V., Kumar, S., & Nankervis, A. (2018). Work-readiness integrated competence model. *Education + Training, 61*(5), 568–589. doi:10.1108/ET-05-2018-0114

Reddy, P., & Shaw, R. (2019). Becoming a professional: A longitudinal qualitative study of the graduate transition in BSc Psychology. *Education + Training, 61*(2), 272–288. doi:10.1108/ET-10-2018-0210

Römgens, I., Scoupe, R., & Beausaert, S. (2020). Unraveling the concept of employability, bringing together research on employability in higher education and the workplace. *Studies in Higher Education*, *45*(12), 2588–2603. doi:10.1080/03075079.2019.1623770

Roser, C., Sato, M., & Nakano, M. (2021). Would you like some wine? Introducing variants to the beer game. *Production Planning and Control*, *32*(6), 454–462. doi:10.1080/09537287.2020.1742370

Small, L., Shacklock, K., & Marchant, T. (2018). Employability: A contemporary review for higher education stakeholders. *Journal of Vocational Education and Training*, *70*(1), 148–166. doi:10.1080/13636820.2017.1394355

Stoten, D. (2018). Employability: A contested concept in higher education. *Journal of Pedagogic Development*, *8*(1), 9–17.

Subhash, S., & Cudney, E. A. (2018). Gamified learning in higher education: A systematic review of the literature. *Computers in Human Behavior*, *87*, 192–206. doi:10.1016/j.chb.2018.05.028

Sugahara, S., & Lau, D. (2019). The effect of game-based learning as the experiential learning tool for business and accounting training: A study of management game. *Journal of Education for Business*, *94*(5), 297–305. doi:10.1080/08832323.2018.1527751

Suleman, F., & Laranjeiro, A. M. (2018). The employability skills of graduates and employers' options in Portugal: An explorative study of anticipative and remedial strategies. *Education + Training*, *60*(9), 1097–1111. doi:10.1108/ET-10-2017-0158

Tan, L. M., Laswad, F., & Chua, F. (2022). Bridging the employability skills gap: Going beyond classroom walls. *Pacific Accounting Review*, *34*(2), 225–248. doi:10.1108/PAR-04-2021-0050

Tang, Y. M., Chen, P. C., Law, K. M. Y., Wu, C. H., Lau, Y. Y., Guan, J., He, D., & Ho, G. T. S. (2021). Comparative studies for students readiness in live online learning during the coronavirus (COVID-19) outbreak in higher education sector. *Computers & Education*, *168*, 104211. doi:10.1016/j.compedu.2021.104211 PMID:33879955

The United Nations. (2016). Retrieved from https://www.un.org/en/universal-declaration-human-rights/index.html

Top-BOSS. (2022). Retrieved from https://www.top-boss.com/mbs-macro-business-simulation/

United Nations. (2022). Retrieved from https://www.un.org/en/transforming-education-summit?gclid=EAIaIQobChMI6PDkzs-d-gIV6cIWBR0G_wsgEAAYAiAAEgKPFfD_BwE

Verma, P., Nankervis, A., Priyono, S., Mohd Salleh, N., Connell, J., & Burgess, J. (2018). Graduate work-readiness challenges in the Asia-Pacific region and the role of HRM. *Equality, Diversity and Inclusion*, *37*(2), 121–137. doi:10.1108/EDI-01-2017-0015

Vij, S., & Sharma, R. (2018). Experiential learning through business simulation game in strategic management. *20th Annual Convention of Strategic Management Forum, "Strategy, Innovation and Entrepreneurship Curriculum in the Era of Disruption"*.

Williams, S., Karypidou, A., Steele, C., & Dodd, L. (2019). A personal construct approach to employability: Comparing stakeholders' implicit theories. *Education + Training*, *61*(4), 390–412. doi:10.1108/ET-08-2017-0112

Winterton, J., & Turner, J. J. (2019). Preparing graduates for work readiness: An overview and agenda. *Education + Training*, *61*(5), 536–551. doi:10.1108/ET-03-2019-0044

Yeo, G. K., & Tan, S. T. (1999). Toward a multilingual experiential environment for learning decision technology. *Simulation & Gaming: An Interdisciplinary Journal*, *30*(1), 70–83. doi:10.1177/104687819903000108

Zulfiqar, S. (2021). Understanding and predicting students' entrepreneurial intention through business simulation games: A perspective of COVID-19. *Sustainability (New Rochelle, N.Y.)*, *13*(4).

## ADDITIONAL READING

Ferreira, C. P., Gonzalez-Gonzalez, C. S., & Adamatti, D. F. (2021). Business simulation games analysis supported by human-computer interfaces: A systematic review. *Sustainability*, *21*(14), 4810. PMID:34300549

Lau, Y. Y., Tang, Y. M., Chau, K. Y., Vyas, L., Hernandez, S. H., & Wong, S. (2021). COVID-19 Crisis: Exploring community of inquiry in online learning for sub-degree students. *Frontiers in Psychology*, *12*, 679197. doi:10.3389/fpsyg.2021.679197 PMID:34366999

Tang, Y. M., Chau, K. Y., Lau, Y. Y., & Ho, G. T. S. (2022). Impact of mobile learning in engineering mathematics under 4-year undergraduate curriculum. *Asia Pacific Journal of Education*, 1–17. Advance online publication. doi:10.1080/02188791.2022.2082379

Tang, Y. M., Lau, Y. Y., & Chau, K. Y. (2022). Towards a sustainable online peer learning model based on students' perspectives. *Education and Information Technologies*. Advance online publication. doi:10.100710639-022-11136-y PMID:35668899

## KEY TERMS AND DEFINITIONS

**Innovative Educational Tool:** Innovative educational tools foster the teachers to create classes more educative, fun, and interactive. Also, innovative educational tools foster students' and teachers' easier access to learning materials and faster.

**Interactive Learning:** Interactive learning is an emerging pedagogical approach that integrates urban computing and social network into course design and delivery. The advancement of virtual communication devices and digital technology stimulates the growth of interactive learning.

**Macro Business Simulation Game:** Macro business simulation game refers to developing a series of platforms/tools to integrate business, management, mathematics, and information. Theories, technologies, and professionals in various fields of science and technology develop a diversified teaching system for simulation business competitions, to meet the needs of teaching in business management with the revolution of technology.

**Professionalization:** The process of professionalization refers to the occupational groups and industry themselves prefer to become more selective and self-motivated, that they are willing to improve the quantity and quality of their work and continue their relevant work learning area.

**Spoon-Feeding Education:** Spoon-feeding education describes treating the student like a baby. In other words, teachers must fill in with their knowledge. Such a process 'tells' the student what they require to understand and is more teacher oriented.

**Students:** Students are primarily a person enrolled in an educational institution.

**Teacher:** A teacher is a person whose job is to teach in a college or school.

**Traditional Classroom:** Traditional classroom in which a teacher regulates and moderates the key flow of knowledge and information. As expected, students develop their knowledge of a subject outside of school via various homework exercises. Thus, students' key resource is their teachers who only teach them face-to-face mode.

# Chapter 8
# Implications of Using Mobile Technologies in Higher Education Amidst the COVID-19 Pandemic:
## Accessing Teaching, Online Learning, and Assessment

**Patrick Nghuulondo**
*University of South Africa, South Africa*

**Leila Goosen**
https://orcid.org/0000-0003-4948-2699
*University of South Africa, South Africa*

## ABSTRACT

*The purpose and objectives of this case study are to explore the effective use of mobile technologies by first year students amid the COVID-19 coronavirus pandemic, using a situational analysis and active theory. Moreover, this study will unveil intersectional problems and educational inequality among 'digital natives' and 'digital immigrants' at the Rundu campus of the University of Namibia (UNAM). The study aims at examining how the interventions of distance and/or online learning are exclusive, exposing many, especially first year, students to educational inequality. Finally, the implications of sustainable development in higher education in terms of teaching, learning, and assessment will be considered.*

DOI: 10.4018/978-1-6684-6172-3.ch008

# INTRODUCTION

## Implications of Sustainable Development in Higher Education: Teaching, Learning, and Assessment

This section will describe the general perspective of the chapter and end by specifically stating the objective. As part of the edited volume 'Implications of Sustainable Development in Higher Education: Teaching, Learning and Assessment', this chapter will form part of a collection of research that will provide insights regarding the implications of Education for Sustainable Development (ESD) for educational practice of the applied developmental science of teaching, learning, and assessment in higher education (Darling-Hammond, Flook, Cook-Harvey, Barron, & Osher, 2020). ESD empowers learners to make informed decisions and take responsible actions for environmental integrity, economic viability, and a just society for present and future generations, promoting *equality*, diversity, and inclusion, which, according to Meletiadou (2022f), "are at the forefront of current" discussions, as these issues had "become an international concern for" e.g., politicians, government agencies and social activists. ESD aims at developing competencies that foster reflective thinking, taking into account current and future social, cultural, economic, and environmental impacts, from local and global perspectives. ESD has to be understood as an integral part of quality education that promotes lifelong learning. Higher Education Institutions (HEIs) can and should consider it their responsibility to deal intensively with issues in, for example, distance education and foster the development of educational sustainability competencies (Sherry, 1995). ESD provides an education that matters and is truly relevant to every student in the light of the challenges related to e-learning systems from higher educational institutions' perspective (Shahmoradi, et al., 2018). The purpose and objectives of this chapter, as part of the edited volume, are to respond to the needs of learners of any context and background, practitioners, educators, teacher educators, policymakers, administrators, program planners, educational managers, educational leaders, and researchers through a relevant case study that includes sound pedagogical and content knowledge. As one of the chapters of this book, it will explore the impact of the effective use of mobile technologies by first year students amid the Covid-19 coronavirus pandemic, using a situational analysis and active theory, on learning in Africa (United Nations Educational, Scientific and Cultural Organization (UNESCO), 2021). Moreover, this study will unveil intersectional problems and educational inequality between 'digital natives' and 'digital immigrants' at the Rundu campus of the University of Namibia (UNAM), as these higher education students are moving from disruption to recovery (UNESCO, 2020). The study aims at examining how the interventions of distance and/or online learning are exclusive, exposing many, especially first year, students to educational inequality (Belay, 2022). The study reported on by the latter author was situated in rural Ethiopia against the background of global risk and contingency management research in times of crisis.

In the proceedings of the 26th Conference of the Southern African Association for Research in Mathematics, Science and Technology Education (SAARMSTE), Goosen (2018a) argued that sustainable and *inclusive* quality education can be achieved through research-informed practice on Information and communication Technologies (ICTs). Therefore, the socio-cultural implications of sustainable development in higher education in terms of linking theoretical understanding and practical experiences of using ESD-informed teaching, learning and assessment practices in cyberspace will be considered towards making a valuable contribution in terms of new directions to the fields of higher, adult and continuing education (Conceição, 2002).

## Target Audience

Like the target audience of this book, that of the chapter consists of researchers, practitioners, educators, teacher educators, policymakers, administrators, program planners, educational managers, and educational leaders in higher education, who are interested in the fields of teaching, learning, assessment, and sustainability in higher education at large.

## Recommended Topics

Based on the recommended topics provided for the book, this chapter will focus on the use of game-based and especially mobile-assisted assessment, teaching and learning, and ESD. Attention will also be paid to the following:

- Collaboration as a learning tool for societal transformation (peer assessment)
- ESD and inclusive assessment practices and policies
- Ethical global issues in pedagogy
- ESD, globalization, equity, inclusion and inclusive assessment and teaching in higher education
- Sustainable development in higher education and crisis management (i.e., Covid-19 pandemic)
- Global frameworks for assessment, teaching, and learning with migrant learners, multilingual learners, English as a Foreign Language (EFL)/ English as a Second Language (ESL) learners fostering ESD
- Entrepreneurship Education and ESD
- Sustainable development in higher education and leadership as well as
- New technologies and assessment, teaching and learning fostering ESD
- Content and curriculum in terms of assessment, teaching, and learning fostering ESD
- Gender Gap in the Digital Age and ESD
- Community Development and ESD

## Objective

Journal articles on teacher education and research in the field of ESD show growing concern in terms of addressing the implications of meeting needs and attitudes towards computer use of the diverse student population exposed to emerging technology implementation at various higher education institutions nowadays (Mehra, 2007). In an Asia Pacific journal article on contemporary education and communication technology, Ali (2018) pointed out that people around the world recognize that current and emerging economic development trends are not sustainable and that public awareness of the influence of evolving technologies in their emerging online lives, as well as 'digital native' university students undergoing education and training, are key to moving society toward sustainability.

The UNESCO (2014) roadmap for implementing the global action program on education for sustainable development placed SD on the global agenda in order to improve actions towards a more sustainable future. ESD has grown from an idea into a global movement. Although ESD continues to grow both in content and pedagogy and its visibility and respect have grown in parallel, education officials, policymakers, educators, curriculum developers and others are called upon to rethink education in order to contribute to the achievement of the goals of sustainable development in higher education. As part of this book, the aim of the chapter is to demonstrate the value of adopting an ESD lens in higher education, by broadening and strengthening the evidence base of the impact that this can have on students, educators, and society as a whole. Educators, researchers and policymakers must develop the specific learning outcomes related to all Sustainable Development Goals (SDGs), promoting sustainability in higher education. Therefore, it is vital that educators promote whole-institution trans- and cross-disciplinary approaches to action research and action learning for e-schools, community engagement, and Information and Communication Technologies for Development (ICT4D) towards fostering interactive, integrative, and critical forms of learning; that is, an action-oriented transformative pedagogy (Goosen, 2018b). As part of the current edited volume, the chapter intends to encourage higher education institutions to see themselves as places of learning and experiences for sustainable development and orient all processes towards the principles of sustainability. After all, for ESD to be more effective, higher education institutions have to be transformed by mainstreaming sustainability into all their aspects. This involves rethinking the curriculum, campus operations, organizational culture, student participation, leadership and management, community relationships, as well as research. Along with the main goal of this book, that of the chapter is to promote sustainable learning environments, such as eco-universities or green campuses, allow educators and learners to integrate sustainability principles into their daily practices and facilitate capacity-building, competency development and value education in a comprehensive manner. As part of the present book, this chapter will focus on various perspectives aiming to make a scholarly contribution to the literature in the field of higher education for sustainable development, teaching, learning and assessment with efficient practices, approaches and ideas for professional development.

## BACKGROUND

This section of the chapter will provide broad definitions and discussions of the topic, on the implications of using mobile technologies in higher education amid the Covid-19 pandemic towards accessing teaching, online learning and assessment. It will also incorporate the views of others (in the form of a *literature review*) into the discussion to support, refute, or demonstrate the authors' position on the topic.

### Use of Game-Based and Mobile-Assisted Assessment, Teaching and Learning

The use of game-based learning and 21st century learning skills through the lens of cyber safety awareness were discussed in the lecture notes on Computer Science of Kritzinger, Loock and Goosen (2019).

### Collaboration as a Learning Tool for Societal Transformation (Peer Assessment)

Collaboration as a tool for the digital transformation of an automotive enterprise, as part of an empirical study of the impact on innovation and productivity, was discussed in the chapter by Bolton, Goosen and Kritzinger (2021). Peer assessment, "a process by which students' oral or written work is assessed by peers, has received a lot of attention recently", e.g., in the context of peer assessment of *adolescent* learners' writing performance and pedagogy (Tsagari & Meletiadou, 2015, p. 305). Peer Assessment (PA) "is one of the most popular forms of alternative assessment currently used in higher education institutions worldwide. In the" study reported on by Meletiadou (2022c, p. 1), "PA was used as an" *inclusive* learning strategy at higher education institutions towards enhancing student writing skills and *motivation*.

The unpublished MA thesis of Meletiadou (2011) discussed the peer assessment of writing in secondary education in terms of its impact on *learners'* performance and *attitudes*. One of the selected papers featured in the book 'Language Testing and Assessment around the Globe—Achievement and Experiences' by Meletiadou (2013) looked at EFL *learners' attitudes* towards peer assessment, teacher assessment and the process of writing. Against the background of languages and in answer to the question 'How does peer assessment affect EFL students' writing quality?', Meletiadou (2021a, p. 1) pointed out that recent research had "underlined the *benefits* of peer assessment ... as it helps learners write high-quality essays and increases their confidence as writers." When exploring the impact of peer assessment on EFL students' writing performance, the International Academic Forum (IAFOR) journal article on education by Meletiadou (2021b, p. 77) pointed out that lately, researchers had "expressed their *concern* for EFL students' poor writing performance and" examination failure. The latter author had "indicated that peer assessment" can be successfully implemented.

"In the past two decades, several researchers" had also "expressed their *concern* regarding students' attitudes towards writing". Learners' perceptions of peer assessment and the implications of these for their willingness to write in an EFL context were therefore addressed in an international journal article on teacher education and professional development by Meletiadou (2022a, p. 1). Several studies on peer assessment had highlighted the "significant *benefits* for the learning process such as increased student *motivation*" and enhanced collaborative learning. Meletiadou and Tsagari (2022, p. 1) were therefore exploring EFL teachers' perceptions of the use of peer assessment in external examination-dominated writing classes. In research on English as a Foreign Language *in Cyprus*, while investigating the attitudes of *adolescent* EFL learners towards the peer assessment of writing, Meletiadou and Tsagari (2012, p. 225) indicated that the use of peer assessment "as an alternative form of evaluation is reported to be helpful in learning and is increasingly being adopted in secondary education settings". Meletiadou and Tsagari (2016) also considered the washback effect of peer assessment on *adolescent* EFL learners *in Cyprus*.

## ESD and Inclusive Assessment Practices and Policies

According to Meletiadou (2022i), the internationalization or globalization of education (also see next section of this chapter) worldwide had "broadened student diversity in educational institutions in recent years. Inclusive assessment or" assessment for fostering social justice in education is therefore needed. The handbook of research on practices and policies for assessing inclusive teaching and learning edited by Meletiadou (2022b) similarly indicated that *inclusivity* "is a crucial factor in assessment design, as fair assessment must reflect the needs of a diverse student body. Assessment practices should also be culturally inclusive". "Self-assessment (SA) is regarded as a prestigious method of formative assessment in higher education. The" study reported on in the chapter by Meletiadou (2022d, p. 27) "explored the use of SA as an inclusive practice" aimed at helping to nurture students' writing knowledge, self-regulation, and attitudes in higher education.

## New Technologies, Community Development and ESD

In the proceedings of the South Africa International Conference on Educational Technologies (SAICET), Goosen (2015) showed how new technologies are being used for growing innovative e-schools in the

21st century in a community development project, while Goosen and Mukasa-Lwanga (2017) were using new technologies in distance education, going beyond the horizon with qualitative perspectives. In a similar context, Goosen and van der Merwe (2015) reported on e-learners, teachers and managers at e-schools in South Africa.

## MAIN FOCUS OF THE CHAPTER

### Issues, Problems, Challenges, Barriers

This section of the chapter will present the authors' perspective on the issues, problems, challenges, barriers, etc., as these relate to the main theme of the book, Implications of Sustainable Development in Higher Education: Teaching, Learning, and Assessment, and arguments supporting the authors' position. It will also compare and contrast with what has been, or is currently being, done as it relates to the specific topic of the chapter: the implications of using mobile technologies in higher education amid the Covid-19 pandemic towards accessing teaching, online learning and assessment.

People would have gone extinct if inventors had not created amazing breakthroughs to address daily issues (Bruner, 1997). Lifting weights, traveling quickly over great distances, and building cozy shelters that would guard from all types of vulnerabilities and calamities have all gotten easier because of the improvement in mental faculties through enhanced thinking. The development of audio-visual technologies, according to Lefrancois (2019), increased sensory capacity. The idea of employing technologies to improve human intelligence through the use of computer systems theories and symbols has now been integrated into the field of mental growth (Bruner, 1997). Newell (1981) claimed that symbolic representation is necessary for the sharing of knowledge among individuals. This symbolic representation may be achieved through online learning. The use of e-learning platforms by UNAM during the global pandemic may be a way of attaining symbolic representation (Quainoo & Pasawano, 2022).

Through the social constructivist paradigm, online learning can encourage higher thinking. According to social constructivists, learning happens through collaboration and interaction between students, their peers, and their instructors. This paradigm is seen to be a practical way to reach a large number of marginalized students with high-quality education (Martin, Ritzhaupt, Kumar, & Budhrani, 2019; Richards & Tangney, 2008). Online learning as a component of blended learning has the potential to produce learning results. Despite the potential educational benefits of online learning, there are issues with its implementation that prevent students from achieving their learning objectives.

According to Beans, et al. (2020, pp. 271-272), Ajzen (2002) postulated "that as a general rule, the more" favorable "the attitude and subjective norm toward a" behavior, "and the greater the perceived" behavioral control, the stronger "a person's intention to perform the" behavior under consideration should be. "Intention, in turn, is viewed as" a direct precursor of actual behavior. "However, the level of success will depend not only on one's intention, but also on such partly non-motivational factors as (the) availability of requisite opportunities and resources that represent people's actual control over the" behavior. This theory aided in comprehending how organizations, professors, and students behave and act in response to the change from in-person "to online teaching and learning in the context of the Covid-19 pandemic" (Beans, et al., 2020, p. 272). Tertiary institutions needed a multifaceted strategy to combat issues brought on by the Covid-19 epidemic. They had to maintain high standards of instruction for students in their learning environment in order to prevent disruptions of the students' learning and promote continuity of learning (Mukeredzi, 2013). During and after the Covid-19 pandemic, they also had to protect every student's access to high-quality education, which strongly depended on the ability of teachers to effectively meet students' learning needs.

e-Learning is accessing educational content outside of a traditional classroom by using electronic devices (Rennert-Ariev, 2008). The term 'e-learning' typically "refers to a course, program or degree" that is entirely online (Chellammal, 2021, p. 11). Distance education, "computerized electronic learning, online learning, internet learning, and many more words are used to describe learning that is given online" or via the internet (Rani, 2021, p. 18). The "significance of e-learning lies in" addressing the issue of the knowledge explosion, the rising demand for education, and expanding opportunities for admission to education (Al-Shammari, 2021, p. 3621). Additionally, it enables workers to receive training and education without having to leave their jobs, helps to "break down psychological barriers between" the teacher and the learner, and satisfies the needs and wants of both parties (LaPorta, 2020, p. 44).

The phrase 'digital gap' is becoming more frequently used to describe the social effects of some segments of the community having unequal access to information and communications technologies and to acquiring essential skills (Everitt, Neary, Delgardo Fuentes, & Clark, 2008). For full involvement in economic, political and social life, access to computers, the internet, and the ability to successfully use these technologies are becoming increasingly crucial (de Moraes Sarmento Rego, 2015). According to Bolt and Crawford (2000), the digital divide is a social issue brought on by "disparities in access to and use of information and communication technologies" (Senne, 2021, p. 1). Therefore, the digital gap endangers both education and social and economic justice. A criterion for guaranteeing equity in access to information is having access to online technologies.

The gap between people, households, businesses, and geographical areas at various "socioeconomic levels with regard to their opportunities to access information and communication technologies ... and their use of the Internet for a wide" range of activities is referred to as the 'digital divide', according to Boswell (2011). The digital divide is a reflection of numerous regional and national inequalities. In the Organization for Economic Co-operation and Development (OECD) region, as well as between OECD and non-member nations, there are considerable differences in how well-equipped people and businesses are to utilize the Internet. Burd and Buchanan (2004), as well as Light (2001), made the point that because it comes before and is more generally "available than access to and use of the internet", access to basic telecommunications facilities is crucial to any study of the issue (Aissaoui, 2021, p. 4). The alleged 'digital divide' thus presents several issues.

The digital divide, according to Light (2001), is the discrepancy in the access that people have to technologies. Two factors, income and education, appear to be the main drivers of the digital divide across households. Other factors that are significant include "household size and type, age, gender, racial and" ethnic background, and location (Aissaoui, 2021, p. 4). Access by household income varies greatly and is growing, although it is becoming more widely available to those with lower incomes. The likelihood that someone will have access to ICTs increases with education level, primarily due to its effects on income.

According to a literate review on related issues by Garrison and Arbaugh (2007), a community of inquiry, in this case UNAM, must include a variety of presences that are appropriate for any institution of higher education. These should primarily consist of teaching presences, social presences, and cognitive presences. Such presences typically take shape in online learning environments where conversations occur while learning. Because of the fact that the other two presences play supportive roles, Garrison and Arbaugh (2007) considered the cognitive presence to be the most significant one. However, it is also believed that social presence is critical to achieving teaching and learning objectives.

According to Guri-Rosenblit and Gros (2011), as well as Richardson, et al. (2012), the direct communication process in a distance education or online learning setting is typically mediated by mobile technologies, like laptops or mobile phones, among other devices. Social presence has a significant impact on learning outcomes because it raises students' levels of *motivation* and happiness by enhancing the affective learning domain. Students must make a conscious effort to be treated as individuals "in a virtual learning environment. According to" de Moraes Sarmento Rego (2015, p. 709), the ability of students to express themselves in an emotional and social sense as actual beings through the mobile technologies employed for communication processes is a definition of the social presence in an inquiry community (Garrison, 2000). The method of instruction and learning can only be regarded as open when it is well-structured and indicates a clear direction to take so that educational goals will be achieved. In an international review of research in open and distributed learning, Garrison (2000) also discussed theoretical challenges for distance education in the 21st century and a shift from structural to transactional issues.

From a higher educational institutions perspective, according to the findings of the study reported on in the journal article on education by Shahmoradi, et al. (2018, p. 1), almost "half of the participants (40%) had problems accessing the technology, and only 26.4% of the participants" were well-prepared for the challenges related to the use of the e-learning "system. Furthermore, a significant difference was found between the challenges of skill and culture of the participants (P value= 0.01)."

## Ethical Global Issues in Pedagogy

In terms of ensuring the ethical management of data and research integrity, the context of e-schools and community engagement (Goosen, 2018c) and ethical ICT4D solutions for Massive Open Online Courses (MOOCs) (Goosen, 2018d) could be considered.

## ESD, Globalization, Equity, Inclusion and Inclusive Assessment and Teaching in Higher Education

In the handbook of research on practices for advancing diversity and inclusion in higher education edited by Meletiadou (2022f), according to Meletiadou (2022h, p. 20), higher education students from "Black, Asian, and Minority Ethnic (BAME) backgrounds tend to withdraw from their undergraduate degree in the United Kingdom (UK)." There was therefore a need for profiling the writing competency of such BAME undergraduate students towards fostering inclusion and academic success to improve retention in tertiary education.

## Sustainable Development in Higher Education and Crisis Management (i.e., Covid-19 Pandemic)

In the Handbook of Research on Entrepreneurship, Innovation, Sustainability, and ICTs in the Post-Covid-19 Era, both the chapters by Bolton, et al. (2021) and Ngugi and Goosen (2021) provided perspectives towards the post-Covid-19 pandemic era, while in the proceedings of the 29th conference of SAARMSTE, Van Heerden and lGoosen (2021) reported on students' perceptions of e-assessment with regard to the Covid-19 pandemic in a case study of the University of South Africa (UNISA).

## Global Frameworks for Assessment, Teaching, and Learning With Migrant Learners, Multilingual Learners, EFL/ESL Learners Fostering ESD

Meletiadou (2021d) indicated that adopting a "multilingual approach towards comprehension in assessment" at higher education institutions in the UK amidst the Covid-19 pandemic focused "on the presumption that multilingual learners may face incredible challenges when" their teachers are using ICTs to facilitate multilingual teaching and learning (Libbrecht & Goosen, 2015) in the context of Mathematics education and *language diversity*.

## Entrepreneurship Education and ESD

In a scholarly compendium for teaching and learning, Du Toit and Kempen (2018, p. 186) considered "the current South African Consumer Studies curriculum, with the" aim of enhancing the value of Consumer Studies in South African secondary schools through entrepreneurship education to create economic value. Although "Consumer Studies could create social value", "the focus of the Consumer Studies curriculum" is not necessarily on addressing this. Du Toit (2018, p. iv) indicated that the subject included "significant entrepreneurship education. Despite this potential of Consumer Studies", the "intended and enacted curriculum for Consumer Studies" was not adequately developed with regard to a framework for the effective structuring and implementation of entrepreneurship education in Consumer Studies.

The journal article on Consumer Sciences by Du Toit (2021, p. 1) indicated that the subject "has the advantage of potentially" harnessing education through entrepreneurship in consumer studies to address youth unemployment in South Africa. "Most Consumer Studies teachers, however, face several challenges in their efforts to ensure that this advantage reaches their learners. These challenges impair teaching and learning in Consumer Studies," demoralize "teachers and diminish the potential advantage of the entrepreneurship education embedded in the subject." The foundations in the South African senior phase curriculum for entrepreneurship education in Consumer Studies were "described and linked to the prior knowledge required for learning in" the subject (Du Toit, 2016, p. 12).

Both the chapter by Bolton, et al. (2021) mentioned earlier in this chapter, as well as the chapter by Ngugi and Goosen (2021) on innovation, entrepreneurship, and sustainability for ICT students appeared in the Handbook of Research on Entrepreneurship, Innovation, Sustainability, and ICTs.

## Sustainable Development in Higher Education and Leadership

The multiple case study presented by Meletiadou (2022e, p. 85) explored forty *"female educational leaders'* current experiences" at higher education institutions in the UK "to unravel both barriers and facilitators using semi-structured interviews', as well as opportunity and snowball sampling. In the Handbook of Research on Practices for Advancing diversity and inclusion in higher education, the chapter by Meletiadou (2022g, p. 1) also discussed the lived experiences of *female educational* leaders "and their main guiding principles in leading as advancing women in leadership roles is in the best interest of the society" in the context of academic resilience and gender.

## SOLUTIONS AND RECOMMENDATIONS

This section of the chapter will discuss solutions and recommendations in dealing with the issues, problems, challenges, barriers, etc., presented in the preceding section.

### Solutions

The teaching and learning process in any educational setting is a phenomenon that is both complicated and interactive between teachers and students (Vygotsky, 1978). It is believed that learning is a process of "problem-solving and that the social" creation of solutions to issues forms the basis of learning (Cifuentes, 2021, p. 83). In addition, Vygotsky (1978) described the learning process as involving the creation of a 'zone of proximal growth' that will include "the teacher, the student, and" a problem that needs to be solved (Novakowski, 2019, p. 85). The solutions to problems that need to be solved can be put together or constructed by students and peers in a social context that is facilitated by an instructor.

### Recommendations

"In the last two decades, teachers, researchers and educational authorities" have expressed their concerns about English as a Foreign Language students' poor writing performance. In line with one of the recommended topics discussed earlier, Collaboration as a Learning Tool for Societal Transformation (Peer Assessment), Meletiadou (2017, p. v) recommended peer assessment as a dynamic learning-oriented tool for the development of such writing skills.

## FUTURE RESEARCH DIRECTIONS

This section of the chapter will discuss future and emerging trends and provide insight about the future of the theme of the book, Implications of Sustainable Development in Higher Education: Teaching, Learning, and Assessment, from the perspective of the chapter focus. The viability of a paradigm, model, implementation issues of proposed programs, etc., may also be included in this section. Future research directions within the domain of the topic, the implications of using mobile technologies in higher education amid the Covid-19 pandemic towards accessing teaching, online learning and assessment, will finally be suggested. Despite "increasing support for the use of e-portfolios, research on its utility is just beginning to" register as emerging trends. In the journal article on education reporting on the study by Meletiadou (2021c, p. 68), two hundred undergraduate students were asked to use padlets as e-portfolios to enhance their writing skills and motivation. While researching the community of inquiry framework, Garrison and Arbaugh (2007) also suggested future research directions in the context of the Internet and higher education.

## CONCLUSION

This section of the chapter will provide a discussion of the overall coverage of the chapter and concluding remarks. The chapter reviewed various theoretical and conceptual frameworks, which the study adopted to provide a better understanding of the phenomenon being investigated. Some of the major issues derived from the reviewed theories were that online learning enables both asynchronous and synchronous collaboration through a variety of platforms, including video conferencing, chat rooms, blogs, and discussion boards. Given the kind of students, who attend educational institutions nowadays, this style of education is seen as essential. These students frequently use online social networking to connect with one another and to stay up-to-date on the latest news and emerging trends. In line with Goosen (2004), this chapter comes to the conclusion that successful criteria and guidelines for the selection and implementation of an e-learning educational system is "one of the main approaches in managing (the) knowledge and educational needs of higher education" institutions (Shahmoradi, et al., 2018, p. 1).

## REFERENCES

Aissaoui, N. (2021). *The digital divide: A literature review and some directions for future research in light of COVID-19*. Global Knowledge, Memory and Communication. doi:10.1108/GKMC-06-2020-0075

Ajzen, I. (2002). Perceived behavioural control, self-efficacy, locus of control, and the theory of planned behaviour. *Journal of Applied Social Psychology, 32*(4), 665–683. doi:10.1111/j.1559-1816.2002.tb00236.x

Ali, W. (2018). Influence of evolving technology in emerging online lives of the digital native university students. *Asia Pacific Journal of Contemporary Education and Communication Technology, 4*(2), 141–155. doi:10.25275/apjcectv4i2edu15

Al-Shammari, H. T. (2021). The extent to which teachers of social curriculum at the intermediate stage possess e-learning skills. *Turkish Journal of Computer and Mathematics Education, 12*(13), 3619–3626.

Beans, H., Maireva, C., & Muza, C. (2020). Zimbabwe higher education institutions' preparedness in responding to Covid-19 induced disruptions to education. *Journal of New Vision in Educational Research, 1*(2), 267–282.

Belay, D. G. (2022). COVID-19 Pandemic, Distance Learning, and Educational Inequality in Rural Ethiopia. In Global Risk and Contingency Management Research in Times of Crisis (pp. 244-262). IGI Global.

Bolt, D. B., & Crawford, R. A. (2000). *Digital divide: Computers and our children's failure*. Bantam.

Bolton, A., Goosen, L., & Kritzinger, E. (2021). An Empirical Study into the Impact on Innovation and Productivity Towards the Post-COVID-19 Era: Digital Transformation of an Automotive Enterprise. In L. C. Carvalho, L. Reis, & C. Silveira (Eds.), *Handbook of Research on Entrepreneurship, Innovation, Sustainability, and ICTs in the Post-COVID-19 Era* (pp. 133–159). IGI Global. doi:10.4018/978-1-7998-6776-0.ch007

Boswell, S. W. (2011, Nov 1). *Digital Divide Definition*. Retrieved from https://wiki.uiowa.edu/display/edtech/Digital+Divide+Definition

Bruner, E. M. (1997). Ethnography as narrative. In *Memory, identity, community: The idea of narrative in the human sciences* (pp. 264–280). State University of New York Press.

Burd, B. A., & Buchanan, L. E. (2004). Teaching the teachers: Teaching and learning online. *RSR. Reference Services Review*, *32*(4), 404–412. doi:10.1108/00907320410569761

Chellammal, T. (2021). A Study of Students Perspective on E-Learning. *International Journal of Advanced Research in Commerce Management and Finance*, *1*(1), 11–16.

Cifuentes, L. (2021). *A guide to administering distance learning*. Brill. doi:10.1163/9789004471382

Conceição, S. (2002). The sociocultural implications of learning and teaching in cyberspace. *New Directions for Adult and Continuing Education*, *2002*(96), 37–46. doi:10.1002/ace.77

Darling-Hammond, L., Flook, L., Cook-Harvey, C., Barron, B., & Osher, D. (2020). Implications for educational practice of the science of learning and development. *Applied Developmental Science*, *24*(2), 97–140. doi:10.1080/10888691.2018.1537791

de Moraes Sarmento Rego, I. (2015). Mobile Language Learning: How Gamification Improves the Experience. In Y. Zhang (Ed.), *Handbook of Mobile Teaching and Learning* (pp. 705–720). Springer., doi:10.1007/978-3-642-54146-9_76

Du Toit, A. (2016). Foundations in the South African senior phase curriculum for entrepreneurship education in consumer studies. *Journal of Consumer Sciences*, *44*, 11–20. https://www.ajol.info/index.php/jfecs/article/download/143699/133413/0

Du Toit, A. (2018). *Developing a framework for the effective structuring and implementation of entrepreneurship education in Consumer Studies* (Doctoral dissertation). University of South Africa. Retrieved from http://hdl.handle.net/10500/24948

Du Toit, A. (2021). Harnessing education through entrepreneurship in consumer studies to address youth unemployment in South Africa. *Journal of Consumer Sciences*, *49*, 1–14. https://www.ajol.info/index.php/jfecs/article/download/210186/198144

Du Toit, A., & Kempen, E. L. (2018). Entrepreneurship education: Enhancing the value of Consumer Studies in South African secondary schools. In A scholarly compendium for teaching and learning (Vol. 1, pp. 185-212). Academic Press.

Everitt, J., Neary, S., Delgardo Fuentes, M. A., & Clark, L. (2008, November). *Personal guidance: What works?* London: The Careers & Enterprise Company.

Garrison, D. R., & Arbaugh, J. B. (2007). Researching the community of inquiry framework: Review, issues, and future directions. *The Internet and Higher Education*, *10*(3), 157–172. doi:10.1016/j.iheduc.2007.04.001

Garrison, R. (2000). Theoretical challenges for distance education in the 21st century: A shift from structural to transactional issues. *International Review of Research in Open and Distributed Learning*, *1*(1), 1–17. doi:10.19173/irrodl.v1i1.2

Goosen, L. (2004). *Criteria and Guidelines for the Selection and Implementation of a First Programming Language in High Schools*. Potchefstroom Campus: North West University. Retrieved from http://hdl.handle.net/10394/226

Goosen, L. (2015). Educational Technologies for Growing Innovative e-Schools in the 21st Century: A Community Engagement Project. In D. Nwaozuzu, & S. Mnisi (Ed.), *Proceedings of the South Africa International Conference on Educational Technologies* (pp. 49 - 61). Pretoria: African Academic Research Forum.

Goosen, L. (2018a). Sustainable and Inclusive Quality Education Through Research Informed Practice on Information and Communication Technologies in Education. In L. Webb (Ed.), *Proceedings of the 26th Conference of the Southern African Association for Research in Mathematics, Science and Technology Education (SAARMSTE)* (pp. 215 - 228). Gabarone: University of Botswana.

Goosen, L. (2018b). Trans-Disciplinary Approaches to Action Research for e-Schools, Community Engagement, and ICT4D. In T. A. Mapotse (Ed.), *Cross-Disciplinary Approaches to Action Research and Action Learning* (pp. 97–110). IGI Global. doi:10.4018/978-1-5225-2642-1.ch006

Goosen, L. (2018c). Ethical Data Management and Research Integrity in the Context of e-Schools and Community Engagement. In C. Sibinga (Ed.), *Ensuring Research Integrity and the Ethical Management of Data* (pp. 14–45). IGI Global. doi:10.4018/978-1-5225-2730-5.ch002

Goosen, L. (2018d). Ethical Information and Communication Technologies for Development Solutions: Research Integrity for Massive Open Online Courses. In C. Sibinga (Ed.), *Ensuring Research Integrity and the Ethical Management of Data* (pp. 155–173). IGI Global. doi:10.4018/978-1-5225-2730-5.ch009

Goosen, L., & Mukasa-Lwanga, T. (2017). Educational Technologies in Distance Education: Beyond the Horizon with Qualitative Perspectives. In U. I. Ogbonnaya, & S. Simelane-Mnisi (Ed.), *Proceedings of the South Africa International Conference on Educational Technologies* (pp. 41 - 54). Pretoria: African Academic Research Forum.

Goosen, L., & Van der Merwe, R. (2015). e-Learners, Teachers and Managers at e-Schools in South Africa. In C. Watson (Ed.), *Proceedings of the 10th International Conference on e-Learning (ICEL)* (pp. 127 - 134). Nassau: Academic Conferences and Publishing International.

Guri-Rosenblit, S., & Gros, B. (2011). E-learning: Confusing terminology, research gaps and inherent challenges. *International Journal of E-Learning & Distance Education/Revue internationale du e-learning et la formation à distance, 25*(1). Retrieved from https://www.ijede.ca/index.php/jde/article/view/729

Kritzinger, E., Loock, M., & Goosen, L. (2019). Cyber Safety Awareness – Through the Lens of 21st Century Learning Skills and Game-Based Learning. *Lecture Notes in Computer Science, 11937*, 477–485. doi:10.1007/978-3-030-35343-8_51

LaPorta, P. J. (2020). *The Psychological Effects of Patriarchy and Courtship: Eighteenth Century Women's Mentalities in Pamela and Clarissa.* State University at New York.

Lefrancois, G. R. (2019). *Theories of human learning.* Cambridge University Press.

Libbrecht, P., & Goosen, L. (2015). Using ICTs to Facilitate Multilingual Mathematics Teaching and Learning. In R. Barwell, P. Clarkson, A. Halai, M. Kazima, J. Moschkovich, N. Planas, & M. Villavicencio Ubillús (Eds.), *Mathematics Education and Language Diversity* (pp. 217–235). Springer. doi:10.1007/978-3-319-14511-2_12

Light, J. (2001). Rethinking the digital divide. *Harvard Educational Review*, *71*(4), 709–734. doi:10.17763/haer.71.4.342x36742j2w4q82

Martin, F., Ritzhaupt, A., Kumar, S., & Budhrani, K. (2019). Award-winning faculty online teaching practices: Course design, assessment and evaluation, and facilitation. *The Internet and Higher Education*, *42*, 34–43. doi:10.1016/j.iheduc.2019.04.001

Mehra, V. (2007). Teachers' attitude towards computer use Implications for Emerging Technology Implementation in Educational Institutions. *Journal of Teacher Education and Research*, *2*(2), 1–13.

Meletiadou, E. (2011). *Peer assessment of writing in secondary education: its impact on learners' performance and attitudes* (Unpublished MA thesis). University of Cyprus.

Meletiadou, E. (2013). EFL learners' attitudes towards peer assessment, teacher assessment and the process writing. In Selected Papers in Memory of Dr Pavlos Pavlou: Language Testing and Assessment around the Globe—Achievement and Experiences (pp. 312-32). Frankfurt am Main: Peter Lang GmbH.

Meletiadou, E. (2021a, July). Opening Pandora's box: How does peer assessment affect EFL students' writing quality? *Languages*, *6*(3), 115. Advance online publication. doi:10.3390/languages6030115

Meletiadou, E. (2021b, September). Exploring the impact of peer assessment on EFL students' writing performance. *IAFOR Journal of Education*, *9*(3), 77–95. doi:10.22492/ije.9.3.05

Meletiadou, E. (2021c, October). Using Padlets as E-Portfolios to Enhance Undergraduate Students' Writing Skills and Motivation. *IAFOR Journal of Education*, *9*(5), 67–83. doi:10.22492/ije.9.5.04

Meletiadou, E. (2021d, November). Adopting a multilingual approach towards comprehension in assessment in Higher Education Institutions in the UK amidst the Covid-19 pandemic. *The Association for Assessment (AEA)-Europe Conference.* Retrieved from https://www.aea-europe.net/conferences/22nd-annual-conference/

Meletiadou, E. (2022a, January 1). Learners' Perceptions of Peer Assessment: Implications for Their Willingness to Write in an EFL Context. *International Journal of Teacher Education and Professional Development*, *5*(1), 1–14. doi:10.4018/IJTEPD.295539

Meletiadou, E. (Ed.). (2022b, January 14). *Handbook of Research on Policies and Practices for Assessing Inclusive Teaching and Learning*. IGI Global. doi:10.4018/978-1-7998-8579-5

Meletiadou, E. (2022c). The Use of Peer Assessment as an Inclusive Learning Strategy in Higher Education Institutions: Enhancing Student Writing Skills and Motivation. In *Handbook of Research on Policies and Practices for Assessing Inclusive Teaching and Learning* (pp. 1–26). IGI Global. doi:10.4018/978-1-7998-8579-5.ch001

Meletiadou, E. (2022d). Nurturing Student Writing Knowledge, Self-Regulation, and Attitudes in Higher Education: The Use of Self-Assessment as an Inclusive Practice. In Handbook of Research on Policies and Practices for Assessing Inclusive Teaching and Learning (pp. 27-53). IGI Global.

Meletiadou, E. (2022e, January 26-27). Iron fists in velvet gloves: exploring female educational leaders' experiences in Higher Education in the UK. *Applied Research Conference* (pp. 85-88). Chartered Institute of Personnel and Development (CIPD).

Meletiadou, E. (Ed.). (2022f, June). *Handbook of research on practices for advancing diversity and inclusion in higher education*. IGI Global. doi:10.4018/978-1-7998-9628-9

Meletiadou, E. (2022g). The Lived Experiences of Female Educational Leaders in Higher Education in the UK: Academic Resilience and Gender. In Handbook of Research on Practices for Advancing Diversity and Inclusion in Higher Education (pp. 1-19). IGI Global.

Meletiadou, E. (2022h). Profiling the Writing Competency of BAME Undergraduate Students: Fostering Inclusion and Academic Success to Improve Retention in Tertiary Education. In Handbook of Research on Practices for Advancing Diversity and Inclusion in Higher Education (pp. 20-48). IGI Global.

Meletiadou, E. (2022i). *Inclusive assessment: fostering social justice in education*. Retrieved from European Association for Educational Assessment: https://www.aea-europe.net/inclusive-assessment-fostering-social-justice-in-education/

Meletiadou, E. I. (2017). *Peer assessment: a dynamic learning-oriented tool for the development of writing skills* (PhD dissertation). University of Cyprus. Retrieved from https://gnosis.library.ucy.ac.cy/bitstream/handle/7/38983/Eleni_I_Meletiadou_PhD.pdf?sequence=5&isAllowed=y

Meletiadou, E., & Tsagari, D. (2012). Investigating the attitudes of adolescent EFL learners towards peer assessment of writing. *Research in English as a Foreign Language in Cyprus*, 2, 225–245.

Meletiadou, E., & Tsagari, D. (2016). The washback effect of peer assessment on adolescent EFL learners in Cyprus. In *Classroom-based assessment in L2 contexts* (pp. 138–160). Cambridge Scholars Publishing.

Meletiadou, E., & Tsagari, D. (2022). Exploring EFL teachers' perceptions of the use of peer assessment in external exam-dominated writing classes. *Languages*, 7(1), 16. Advance online publication. doi:10.3390/languages7010016

Mukeredzi, T. G. (2013). Professional Development Through Teacher Roles: Conceptions of Professionally Unqualified Teachers in Rural South Africa and Zimbabwe. *Journal of Research in Rural Education*, 28(11). https://citeseerx.ist.psu.edu/viewdoc/download?doi=10.1.1.398.2997&rep=rep1&type=pdf

Newell, R. W. (1981). Skepticism and Cognitivism: A Study in the Foundations of Knowledge. *Mind*, 90(357), 137–139. doi:10.1093/mind/XC.357.137

Nghuulondo, P., Kanyimba, A. T., & Haipinge, E. (n.d.). *The use of smart phones and mobile devices to access learning support services for distance education students at University of Namibia*. Retrieved from https://www.academia.edu/download/62292616/Patrick_Nghuulondo_Article_201920200306-79049-j26pb.pdf

Ngugi, J. K., & Goosen, L. (2021). Innovation, Entrepreneurship, and Sustainability for ICT Students Towards the Post-COVID-19 Era. In L. C. Carvalho, L. Reis, & C. Silveira (Eds.), *Handbook of Research on Entrepreneurship, Innovation, Sustainability, and ICTs in the Post-COVID-19 Era* (pp. 110–131). IGI Global. doi:10.4018/978-1-7998-6776-0.ch006

Novakowski, J. T. (2019). *Analyzing Teacher-Student Relationships in the Life and Thought of William James to Inform Educators Today*. Ohio State University.

Quainoo, M. A., & Pasawano, T. (2022, April 22). *A Study of Blended E-Learning Platforms for Continuing Education During the Covid-19 Pandemic in Ghana.* doi:10.21203/rs.3.rs-1566095/v1

Rani, N. (2021). *Impact of mobile technology on students' achievements in higher education.* Waikato Institute of Technology. Retrieved from http://researcharchive.wintec.ac.nz/7810/

Rennert-Ariev, P. (2008). The hidden curriculum of performance-based teacher education. *Teachers College Record, 110*(1), 105–138. doi:10.1177/016146810811000105

Richards, D., & Tangney, B. (2008). An informal online learning community for student mental health at university: A preliminary investigation. *British Journal of Guidance & Counselling, 36*(1), 81–97. doi:10.1080/03069880701715671

Richardson, J. C., Arbaugh, J. B., Cleveland-Innes, M., Ice, P., Swan, K. P., & Garrison, D. R. (2012). Using the community of inquiry framework to inform effective instructional design. In L. Moller & J. B. Heuett (Eds.), *The Next Generation of Distance Education* (pp. 97–125). Springer. doi:10.1007/978-1-4614-1785-9_7

Senne, F. (2021, June). Beyond connectivity: Internet for all. *Internet Sectoral Overview, 13*(2), 1–10.

Shahmoradi, L., Changizi, V., Mehraeen, E., Bashiri, A., Jannat, B., & Hosseini, M. (2018, September). The challenges of E-learning system: Higher educational institutions perspective. *Journal of Education and Health Promotion, 7*. Advance online publication. doi:10.4103/jehp.jehp_39_18 PMID:30271801

Sherry, L. (1995). Issues in distance learning. *International Journal of Educational Telecommunications, 1*(4), 337–365.

Tsagari, D., & Meletiadou, E. (2015). Peer Assessment of Adolescent Learners' Writing Performance. *Writing & Pedagogy, 7*(2/3), 305–328. doi:10.1558/wap.v7i2-3.26457

United Nations Educational, Scientific and Cultural Organization (UNESCO). (2014). *UNESCO roadmap for implementing the global action programme on education for sustainable development.* Retrieved from https://unesdoc.unesco.org/images/0023/002305/230514e.pdf

UNESCO. (2020). *Education: From disruption to recovery.* Retrieved November 1, 2021, from https://en.unesco.org/covid19/educationresponse

UNESCO. (2021). *Exploring the impact of COVID-19 in Learning in Africa.* Retrieved from https://en.unesco.org/news/exploring-impact-covid-19-learning-africa

Van Heerden, D., & Goosen, L. (2021). Students' Perceptions of e-Assessment in the Context of Covid-19: The Case of UNISA. In M. Qhobela, M. M. Ntsohi, & L. G. Mohafa (Ed.), *Proceedings of the 29th Conference of the Southern African Association for Research in Mathematics, Science and Technology Education (SAARMSTE)* (pp. 291-305). SAARMSTE.

Vygotsky, L. S. (1978). *Mind in Society: The development of higher mental processes* (M. Cole, V. John-Steiner, S. Scribner, & E. Souberman, Eds.). Harvard University Press.

# Chapter 9
# Learning Styles and Enhancing Learner Engagement in Online Platform Strategies for Sustainable Development in Higher Education

**Therasa C.**
https://orcid.org/0000-0001-7052-9805
*SASTRA University (Deemed), India*

## ABSTRACT

*Online learning replacing face-to-face interactions is a preferred medium now and gained popularity especially after pandemic. The success in online learning would depend upon different learning styles, and it is highly necessary to understand the strategies to handle Gen Z for developing learner engagement. The purpose of this paper is to throw light on the inter-relationships between different learning styles and learner engagement and also to understand the characteristics of Gen Z and the strategies used to create engagement with Gen Z. The suggestions from this chapter insist that the different learning style require different pedagogies to create engagement among learners. The sociability skills and care about sustainability are incredibly more for Gen Z than previous generations, and hence, the learning environment can be carefully structured using these strategies, which brings in sustainable development.*

## INTRODUCTION

Adoption of online learning poses many challenges that developing countries has to confront than developed countries. E-learning was stunning in the digitally advanced economies nevertheless it is not in developing economies due to several problems Basilaia and Kvavadze (2020). This chapter provides the reader an extensive view of problems due to different learning styles, personality and macro level

DOI: 10.4018/978-1-6684-6172-3.ch009

variables and most effective strategies in online teaching and learning to achieve sustainable development in Higher Education.

Online learning has gained its fame only very recently. The popularity of online and hybrid learning amongst Indians is very high that was found by the survey by Pearson India, and it was conducted across five counties. The participants were adult learners between 18-65 years of age from Australia, India, Malaysia, UAE, UK. From the survey, it has been observed that India is in its headway in Online education. The majority (49%) of the Indian learners show a green signal to blended learning, whereas 32% of the adults prefer complete online courses. Another exciting aspect of this survey is about different types of learning among Indians, including social, emotional, and experiential learning that is viewed as very significant as they are the current job market requirements.

Online learners have diverse backgrounds, skills, learning styles, etc. Among all the attributes, learning styles play a significant role and significantly impact academic performance. Learning style denotes the individual differences that exist among individuals and their capacity in learning. Success in teaching depends on various factors, preferably adapting teaching pedagogy to an individual's learning style. The instructor should create a favorable environment where the needs of the learners can be met.

This chapter is divided into three parts. Part one discusses different dimensions of learning, including cognitive, affective, physiological, and psychological types. Part two covers the needs, expectation and barriers of various online learners in online education. Part three covers managing diverse learners and different online teaching pedagogies and creating learner engagement.

## Defining Sustainability in the Context of E-Learning

The term "sustainability" has multiple connotations. The following definitions highlight the meaning of sustainability as follows:

UNESCO (2005) defined it as: "Education for Sustainable Development means including key sustainable development issues into teaching and learning; for example, climate change, disaster risk reduction, biodiversity, poverty reduction, and sustainable consumption. It also requires participatory teaching and learning methods that motivate and empower learners to change their behavior and take action for sustainable development. Education for Sustainable Development consequently promotes competencies like critical thinking, imagining future scenarios and making decisions in a collaborative way". Based on the meaning defined above the following research aims and questions were framed to structure the chapter.

The current study will explore the following dimensions:

- What is the relationship between learning styles and effective online learning in achieving sustainable development through student engagement?
- What is the relationship between individual (personality) and macro dimensions (socio-economic status) and learning styles in attaining sustainable development among students in higher education?
- What are the effective strategies for efficacious online learning in accomplishing sustainable development in higher education?

*Learning Styles and Enhancing Learner Engagement in Online Platform Strategies*

## LEARNING STYLES AND ONLINE LEARNING

Online education is the topmost priority for various institutions today, especially in this COVID-19 pandemic (Organisation for Economic Co-operation and Development, 2020). But to ensure quality education online, it is very much necessary to investigate different learning styles, and hence this segment covers this aspect. Many research supported the fact that students have a diverse set of learning techniques. The instructors must design the course to meet learners' needs and expectations, depending upon the learning style. Specifically, this study had taken the VARK model, which includes four different kinds of learning styles, namely, visual, aural, read-write, and kinesthetic styles, and analyzed the perception of course effectiveness by the individuals who have different learning styles. It concluded that students taking online education possess a high score in visual and read/write learning styles. It had found that students who are good at read/write learning style and all types of learning style was found lacking in evaluating the course effectiveness, whereas students who possess aural style and read/write style and doesn't possess any other learning styles was found to be good at evaluating course effectiveness. This finding seemed to be an exciting finding which stimulated the author to understand the literature related to different learning styles and student performance during online learning.

The four general dimensions of learning styles (Dunn, Beaudry & Klavas, 1989) are listed as follows:

1. Cognitive – the way in which an individual's processes information when they see, think, remember, solve problems, and relate with other concepts.
2. Affective – learning associated with individual's characteristics such as personality, motivation, anxiety, and frustration.
3. Physiological – learning related to biological characteristics which are expressed as VARK model (Visual, Auditory, Reading, and Kinaesthetic)
4. Psychological – learning is associated with the inner strength of the individual and their individuality.

*Figure 1. Learning styles, characteristics, and Strategies*

| Learning Style | Characteristics | Teaching Strategies |
|---|---|---|
| Visual | • Preference for written instructions, photographs and illustrations to view | • Variety of interesting options<br>• Attractive, easy-to-read handouts<br>• Use of technological variety |
| Aural (Auditory) | • Preference for listening to instruction and discussion<br>• Remembers through verbal repetition | • Variations in presentations of tone, pitch, and speed<br>• Multimedia that uses speech and sounds such as audio recordings |
| Reading | • Preference for written instructions and materials | • Provide handouts<br>• Required and suggested readings |
| Kinesthetic/Tactile | • Preference for getting physically involved<br>• Remembers by doing or experiencing | • Encourage movement<br>• Use of multimedia<br>• Tactile activities<br>• Return demonstrations |

*From* Russell S. An overview of adult-learning processes. Uro Nurs 2006;26:349–52, 370; with permission.

The above figure discusses different learning styles, characteristics of different learners, and teaching strategies. The visual learning styles prefer written instructions, photographs, and illustrations. The strategies which could be used to engage learners who possess visual learning style are attractive handouts and flashcards, mind mapping diagrams and pictures, etc. The aural learners will be interested in listening to instructions and actively participate in discussion forums, and remembers texts through verbal repetition. The strategies for aural learners include mnemonics, rhymes, and jingles, which help them memorize the text. The reading style prefers for handwritten instructions and materials, and the strategies include handouts, required, and suggested reading. Finally, Kinesthetic learners look for activity-based and experiential learning. The strategies include the usage of multimedia tools, tactile activities, etc.

To figure out the potential barriers of online learners it is very much necessary to understand the basic characteristics and demographic information of the individuals (Galusha, 2008). Sadeghi et al. (2012) analyzed the relationship between the characteristics or traits of the students with their preferred learning styles. They studied its impact on academic success among students studying in school and University. The study found a significant correlation between different personality traits of the learners and their learning styles and also a significant impact on learner performance. Another study by (Kruck et al. 2014) confirmed that learning styles had significant impact on student success, and it found that active learners are better performers than reflective learners.

Bazier (2015), with the samples of 302 college students and instructors working at a community college in Texas, US had conducted a study to scrutinize the relationship between teacher's trait of extraversion and student's learning styles and the results found that the factors teacher's extraversion personality and learner's visual learning style was correlated significantly. In contrast, the student's auditory and kinesthetic learning was found a negative correlation with the personality trait of extraversion of the teacher.

A study conducted by Urval et al. (2014) had taken 415 medical students as samples who did under graduation in Karnataka. The study highlighted that most of the students were multimodal learners, and the study had taken the VARK learning style to measure the impact of a demographic variable, namely gender and the outcome factor academic performance. It was found that the learner who was high in aural and kinesthetic learning style was found to be highly seen among learners and the demographic variables like gender and outcome factor, academic performance did not have a significant relationship with any of the learning styles. Another study by Erdal et al. (2014) conducted a study on 224 participants who possess an assimilating learning style. Nearly 46% of the total sample having assimilating learning style are good at idea generation, and concept development and the study found that the majority of the respondents have agreeableness as a trait, and this study had also confirmed that there was no significant relationship between personality traits and learning styles.

Another vital learning style's framework includes Kolb's learning style framework, which includes assimilative style, accommodative style, convergent style, and divergent style. These different styles of learning are associated with one particular learning mode where assimilative type is associated with Abstract conceptualization (Logic, Ideas & Concepts) and Reflective Observation (Understand the meaning of ideas). The second learning style accommodative style, is associated with Concrete Experiences (Involved Interpersonal experiences) & Active Experimentation (Influencing people & changing situations). The third learning style, convergent, includes Abstract conceptualization and Active Experimentation, and the last learning style, Divergent include Reflective observation and concrete experiences.

Despite many researches, a study which stressed on Kolb learning styles comprising four varieties of learning environment namely affective, symbolic, perceptual and behavioral learning environment is a unique study. An affective learning environment puts emphasize on concrete experiences through

## Learning Styles and Enhancing Learner Engagement in Online Platform Strategies

activities like practical tasks, simulations, field study. The symbolic environment makes the learners involved in solving problems that have a unique solution. Information will usually be in the form of raw data, readings, pictorial representation, lectures. The third type called perceptual environment, also emphasize problem-solving but the solution to the problem is not concrete or the best solution unlike the previous learning environment called symbolic learning environment and its aim to identify and understand the concepts with the help of available information for formulating research questions and probing the research area with the help of opinion survey method, expert opinion or literature reviews and also by listening, field study, collecting and synthesizing the information and personally drafting as a report. In the behavioral environment, the application of previously acquired knowledge and skills solve a practical problem. The learners could acquire intrinsic rewards which would be psychological rewards and values. Small group activities and interactive project works will suit this environment (Richmond & Cummings, 2005).

Apart from these learning styles, the strategies which include Project –based learning is a distinctive method which helps achieve sustainable development by taking intricate real-world scenarios, applying cross-curricular methodologies, and appropriate stakeholders who needs particular attention. We summarize other strategies that develop higher-order skills embrace self-directed learning [23], collaborative learning [23], problem-based learning [16,23], experiential learning [54], and in-service learning [14].

*Figure 2. Kolb's theoretical framework – Learning styles*
*Source: Richmond, A. S., & Cummings, R. (2005)*

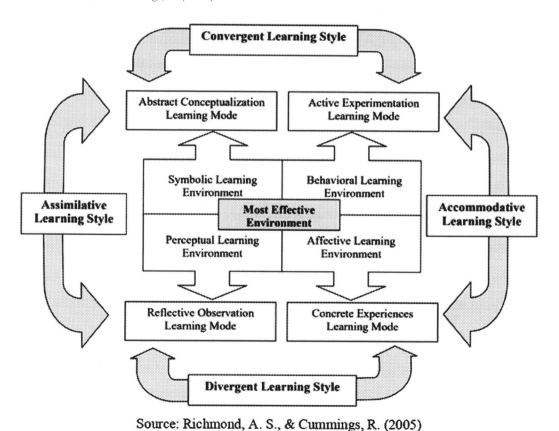

Source: Richmond, A. S., & Cummings, R. (2005)

## INDIVIDUAL DIMENSIONS AND MACRO DIMENSIONS AND LEARNING STYLES

Research had defined various aspects of digital inequality in terms of access, time of usage, skill sets of individuals, and individual perceptions and lighted on future elements. Learning and understanding digital inequality is significant by taking all individual-specific variables that include demographic factors such as gender, race, class, marital status, level of education, etc. and macro-level factors such as health care, organization, economic aspects, politics, cultural, social factors, etc. In this part let us understand the role of individual level and macro level variables and different frameworks of learning styles since inequities in online learning might be due to the individual differences like personality traits, learning styles etc.

There exists a body of literature which explored the correlation between personality traits and different learning styles and also its impact on educational outputs specifically academic performance and academic achievement (Chamorro-Premuzic & Furnham, 2008; Furnham, Monsen & Ahmetoglu, 2009; Komarraju et al. 2011; Marcela, 2015; Stojanovska et al. 2015). A study by Furnham, Jackson & Miller (1999) conducted three important studies that made use of different learning style models and studied the relationship with personality traits. The first study had taken learning style inventory developed by Honey & Mumford (1992) and also cognitive style scale developed by Whettsen & Cameron (1984) was analyzed with Kolb's (1984) learning style scale. In most cases, he found that extraversion personality traits and psychoticism have shown a strong correlation with the learning styles. Another research by Komarraju et al. (2011) with a sample of 308 UG holders tested the correlation between different personality traits and learning styles. He had taken the Big Five Personality measure and he observed that "conscientiousness and agreeableness have a positive relationship with all types of learning styles." Neuroticism personality type showed a negative correlation between the VARK learning styles. Sadeghi et al. (2012) scrutinized the relationship between different learning styles, personality traits and reading ability performance and another study by Salehi et al. (2014) analyzed the influence of other personality traits on different styles of learning of students. He also reported that there exists a positive correlation with all the learning styles. A cross cultural study by Wu and Lai (2010) included college students who are undergraduates in Taiwan and the US. From the results, it can be observed that there exists a slight variation in relationships between variables between two countries and specifically, a strong correlation was found in Taiwan than the US.

Moorman & Clark (2012) conducted a study using Big Five Personality traits and different learning styles. The results showed that extroverted individuals possess auditory and visual learning style. Individuals who are high in agreeableness are highly related to auditory, tactile and visual styles of learning. Learners who are highly conscience exhibited auditory, tactile and visual styles. Individuals who score high in neuroticism fall on auditory and tactile learning styles.

A study which was conducted in Malaysia have tested the influence of personality traits and different learning styles on academic achievement and the results highlighted that the traits openness and conscientiousness were found to be commonly associated with different learning styles whereas converger style on Kolb's framework (thinking & doing) was found to be common among all the samples and the study results showed that there was no statistical relationship among three factors namely personality traits, learning styles and academic achievement. Apart from this, gender didn't have statistical significance with personality and academic achievement. The research conducted by Siddiquei & Khalid (2018) found that the personality trait extraversion was found to be positively correlated with all the learning styles and neuroticism found to have a negative relationship with the learning styles. Here also, gender didn't have a significant relationship with personality and learning styles. Boyd (2004) found that technical skills relating to email communications, filtering relevant and required information available online, knowledge of software installation play a significant role in a successful online education.

The education industry has started to undergo unprecedented change due to new technological innovations. Even though these breakthroughs have changed the functioning of the educational sector, the predominant problem of stopping many students is the availability of access to the internet. This is creating a huge "digital split" between the poor and the rich people. The widening factors would be due to several socio-economic factors.

Socioeconomic status has been found to be a very important variable that is more closely associated with internet usage, especially while searching for information during online education. The pandemic time had introduced the term "digital divide" and capturing much of the attention because of inequalities due to a shortage of necessary skills, low-income group people, etc. Some more fueling factors are poverty, poor infrastructure, malpractices in government, corruption, bureaucracy, etc.

The digital split can be minimized by following these ways in the educational sector:

- New ways for developing and expanding information infrastructure, equip access by market improvisation, reduction in service cost particularly internet cost.
- Implementing cost-effective solutions by keeping the affordability of the people.
- Assigning each student, a laptop, tablet or related devices for free.
- Providing free wi-fi facilities in certain areas like libraries, study areas etc.
- Making student community digitally literate and mastery by conducting necessary campaigns or providing attractive incentives
- Build and strengthen a robust network and establishing partnerships with related successful bodies

## NEEDS OF ONLINE LEARNERS

This part fully covers the needs of various students regarding online education. It is very much needed to understand the learner's expectations and needs and the barriers they face during online education. Understanding the barriers and expectations clearly by the instructors who could create student engagement. Every individual follows a unique learning style and it depends upon the characteristics and traits of every individual and it is affirmed that "personal qualities that influence the ability to acquire information, to interact with peers … and to otherwise participate in learning experiences" (Grasha 1996, 41). The needs and expectations also vary from person to person and it depends upon various factors of learning styles. The factors include active and interactive learning, Visual learning and written and spoken form of learning etc. Therefore, irrespective of any course, student's preference and factors may differ. The themes listed below were revealed by the student community which highlighted the needs of learners in online education. 1) Best input from the instructors throughout the program; 2) trust should have to be developed between learners and instructors related to the process of advising 3) teachers are expected to provide individualized advice and treat every student as an individual 4) instructors should realize that advising play a major role and also significant for the success of every student 5) instructors should be available all the time for clarification purposes and immediate response also is very important (Schroeder & Terras, 2015). A study which had thrown light on the necessities of University concerning online education includes well-crafted handbook for self-study, frequent workshops for the learners, simplified online learning process, enhancing system attractiveness, public relations efforts to efficiently promote online learning are considered to be significant needs of students towards online learning (Srichanyachon, 2014). Another study of qualitative type had identified certain factors as very significant with respect to online learning namely full time job, flexible learning and all time accessibility, the responsibility of individual, efficient time management, physical distancing, the brand power of the institutions and disability are the general factors for UG and graduate students with respect to online learning (Ilgaz & Gulbahar, 2017).

Duncan, Range, and Hvidston (2013) have highlighted a rigorous curriculum as a significant motivating factor in online learning. A rigorous curriculum refers to a clear representation of goals and a clear learning outcome. Literatures have also pointed out that, instructors with different methods than in those conservative approach should be used to create an engagement among learners in online learning (Brocato, Bonanno, & Ulbig, 2015).

A study which has found an answer for a paradox between increasing online classes and decreasing retention rate among the students who are attending online classes. This study had better handled the situation and studied the barriers during their online education. The second important aspect this study had dealt with is whether there is any difference between students who are interested in online classes and the students who did not have an interest in attending online classes. The study had made an attempt to find the answer for the second part with the help of the Mann-Whitney Test and also it found mean and standard deviation to see the difference between the two groups. In this stage, the barriers were also summarized which includes, perception about the online education, interaction/collaboration, confused layout, etc. in online as well as in blended education. The study also found that, to improve the mindset of the students and to motivate them, use of the asynchronous method and proper collaborative tools should be used and the reason behind the group which belongs to "majority enrolled students" and are not interested to take online classes felt that the course layout should be very simple. Proper collaboration tools like email and text messaging should be adopted and in addition to this the instructor should give high priority to the course layout and increased response time to students (Abramenka, 2015).

A study by Mupinga, Nora & Yaw (2006) used the personality indicator MBTI and learning style and it had not targeted one group of student who has a particular learning style. However overall, from the data, the majority of the students belong to an introvert, sensing and judging type of personality. From the results, an interesting finding that learning styles are not having significant relationship with the mode of learning (face-to-face or online mode) and it seemed to no difference among the students who have enrolled in online education and on-campus students. The most significant benefit in online learning was perceived to be interaction with the online instructors and this study found that if there is the highest level of interaction between learners and instructors, then there would be the highest level of learning Frederickson et al. (2000). The study further quoted that frequent quizzes, regular feedback on their assignments also would do great among online learners and various asynchronous tools like email, discussion boards, LMS (assignments) were recommended (Mupinga, 2003). This study also found that communication between learners and instructors through prompt feedback was found vital. Another important aspect was the 24-7 availability of instructors and clear communication regarding their availability would reduce learner disappointment, anxiety and confusion and increase satisfaction and learning among students.

E-education seemed to be an inevitable one especially during a crisis that is happening globally. Now it has become the main agent for education. Even though, e-education has given importance nowadays, many research was conducted before. The researchers showed interest in finding out the quality of learning and learning outcomes from different perspectives. With the help of many literature reviews and data, a study was conducted by (Assareh & Bidokht, 2011) which threw light on the barriers aspect to e-learning. The perspectives about four different kinds of barriers were taken in the study namely, Learners, Teacher, Curriculum and The School. Through this study we can come to know about various variables which made the study an interesting one. The variables included under learners include problems related to financial aspects, motivation, the progress of the assessments, peer isolation, lack of skills and nature of experience in distance mode of learning, social aspects related to affection, and social domain. The second dimension from teachers included the following aspects, namely, lack of knowledge due to very less exposure to the teaching environment, assessment difficulties in all the components. The third dimension of curriculum includes ambiguous nature, quality, resources, the process of teaching and evaluation methods. The final dimension namely, the school includes two aspects which provides for organizational and structural factors. This study was attempted to understand the barriers aspects fully on these dimensons (Assareh & Bidokht, 2011).

E-learning can occur in two ways namely synchronous way or asynchronous way. The synchronous method ensures that the learning and the teaching process occur simultaneously at the same time. Asynchronous style is the other way and learning and teaching occur at different times. Overall, we have both advantages and disadvantages in both types and it should be decided before implementing the course of study (Egan & Akdere, 2004).

## GENERATIONS AND ONLINE LEARNING

*Figure 3. Generations characteristics and attributes*

| Generation | Period | Other Names | Typical Characteristics/ Behavioural Patterns |
|---|---|---|---|
| Traditionalists | 1945 & before | Veterans, Silent, Radio Boomers, The Forgotten Generation | Conformers, dedication, sacrifice, duty before pleasure, discipline, patience, loyalty |
| Baby Boomers | 1946 to 1964 | Moral Authority, "Me" Generation | Anti-government, equal opportunities and rights, personal gratification |
| Gen X | 1965 to 1981 | The Doers, Post Boomers | Balance, diversity, entrepreneurial, fun, highly educated |
| **Millennials** | **1982 to 2000** | **Gen Y, Gen Next, Echo Boomers. Digital Natives, Net Generation** | Self-confident, sociability, diversity, extreme fun, extremely techno savvy, instant gratification |
| Centennials | 2001 onwards | iGen, Gen Z, Gen Zee | Vigilant outlook, tempered expectations, less self-absorbed, more self-assured |

**Source:** Dutta & Jain (2016).

Dutta & Jain had classified the current generation into different categories according to different lifetime period. The generation between 1900 to 1946 was called "Matures," and between (1946-1964) were called "Baby Boomers," "Generation X" were between 1965 to 1982 and Net Generation or Millennials were between (1982-1991).

Since the Millennials are the most important demographic and it would be interesting if we compare the last two generations' characteristics and their learning perspectives. First let us understand the attributes of the Millennials.

*Table 1. Characteristics of Millennial generations*

| | |
|---|---|
| Digitally literate | Living up with technologies |
| | The usage of several IT devices is inborn. |
| | Visually literate compared with other previous generations |
| | Usage of contemporary tools like the internet rather than using the library for research purpose. |
| Connected | Seeing the world as a connected place as long as they are alive |
| | Prefer to be mobile and are always connected |
| | Capable of using all digital devices for connecting with people |
| Immediate | Likely to get immediate responses and quick in getting information |
| | Efficient in multitasking and experts in carrying out activities parallel |
| | Concentrated on performing activities in an agile manner rather than accurate |
| Experiential | They prefer learning by doing rather than following what superiors are dictating to them. |
| | Very much attached to video games perhaps, they prefer to learn everything through discovery. |
| | Ability to remember every information and using it later creatively |
| Social | Excellent in communication and love social interaction. |
| | Open to interaction and love sharing, professionally manage diversity and differences. |
| | Collaborative learning is of high priority |

Source: Author

The learning journey of millennials from 1991 has started with getting and learning almost everything from their teachers and parents since there was no technology like the internet at that time period. Cellular phones just entered markets and they used their black and white cellphones and some period later when the markets grow, they learned everything starting from the internet, digital tools like social media, e-education, tech savvy mobile phones and all the upcoming technological development without any boundary by throwing away all their skeptical notions of complexities.

Whenever effective learning is in place, it means e-learning which has proven to be the most cost effective method. There are several advantages in e-learning which gives a rich learning experience and many companies are showing great interest in creating intuitive e-learning programmes that match their organization requirements. It was also found that, the e-learning models like custom training programmes are much effective than traditional teaching methods and it has become a mandate to live in this technologically strong environment which forces both Gen Y and Z to adapt to it smartly.

## Generation Z and Their Characteristics

Mostly, current faculty members who work for universities could either belong to Baby Boomers or Generation X who teaches for Generation Y and Generation Z. The need of hour is to bridge the gap between the generations of instructors and learners and this require a proper understanding of the current generation student's characteristics and the learners needs and wants (Mohr, & Mohr, 2017). There has been several research that unearthed the characteristics of Gen Z characteristics and their learning attitude. Apparently Gen Z has a high preference for flipped methods of learning and YouTube as a preferred medium to learn the concepts and consider as a primary source (Seemiller & Grace, 2016). GenZ is born and brought up with the technology and it rests in their blood. They are highly tech savvy and digital centric (Postolov, Sopova, & Iliev (2017). It is highly necessary to scrutinize and collect information about this fresh blood to understand their needs and wants in education.

Gen –Z has the characteristics which seem to be good at problem-solving, perform the work individually, give preference to jigsaw formats where they would be capable of contributing the right piece of information to the whole block of a large project. Their unique feature of being interested in 24/7 access to know what is happening around the globe, they tend to show less interest to know about current events.

Gen Z is shortly called Digital Natives since they are born in the Information age and they highly feel comfortable working with technologies and they require minimum guidance in knowing how to filter the information, sort and to mobilize related information from the massive amount of information available, checking for accuracy and also evaluating the information. Due to the extreme level of addiction on the internet and favorite shows by Gen Xers, it would be challenging for the instructors to understand the behavior of Gen Xers with regard to internet usage and it may make the instructors think the level of assignments that require internet support. Hence if assignments that are given to students require information online, instructors could specify standard rules which insist on goals, sources and how to get the information, and evaluation methods. These efforts can minimize the binge mentality among GenZ students who waste time unnecessarily and lose their focus.

## Strategies Which May Work Out With Gen Z

- Give autonomy and freedom which means motivating them to participate freely
- Sharing their creative ideas
- Establishing a collaborative learning environment
- Giving them challenging tasks and enforcing control at required times
- Formulate lesson plans which incorporate these elements whichever is suitable and create some impact
- The role of assignments could be explained to the student community to understand how this is going to create an impact on their daily lives and in their social communities.

**Suggestions:** Gen z are digital natives and they tend to use video platforms like YouTube. Flipping classroom is also an effective methodology which enhances self-paced learning which paves way for an active learning environment. Making our lectures short can also be followed, as the attention span of Gen Z learners are very low. Social Media approaches to learning could be used as they are fond of networking with others. As Gen Z learners show interest to deal with challenging problems, they can conduct research on their own, deduce results and take action. The sociability skills and care about sustainability are incredibly more for Gen Z than previous generations, and hence, the learning about environment can be carefully structured using these strategies which brings in a sustainable development.

- Importance of Group Tasks and its Objective.

The rationale behind every task whether it is a team or group activity should be clearly explained and also their individual responsibilities

- The significance of how to synthesize the information which can solve a particular problem.
- In an online environment, it would be advisable to practice a collaborative learning methodology before conducting any group or team activity for strong participation.
- Inculcate a higher order thinking to make the learners demonstrate skills and strategies to create new models and they can create an entirely new thing which might be an extended form of the concepts they already learned.
- **Foster information literacy**: they may be educated on how the information could be filtered, sorted out, critically analyze, summarize and consolidate content from the sea of information. Make them understand the importance of authentic information, appropriate sites and solid sources of information, comparing the reliability of the information which should be unbiased in nature.
- Autonomy to frame assignments called "destiny assignments" of their preference can be carried out.

## EFFECTIVE STRATEGIES FOR EFFECTIVE ONLINE LEARNING

Even though there are inequities in there are several potential solutions to minimize the effect of these inequities in online learning and enrich the degree of interest, attention, curiosity, passion and optimism levels by adopting various learning models as listed below.

### Blending With Pedagogical Purpose Model

The best way to attract students using online as the medium is by giving attractive 'content. There exist many ways to present and deliver content. The linguistic delivery of content sharing is entirely different from sharing the content through an online platform. Mayer (2009) through his extensive collection of literature reviews has concluded the visualization matters a lot and highly significant in effective learning. Representing the concepts by the use of digital images could be used for subjects like humanities and visual simulations could be the best tool that will work out in science related subjects. For blended learning, LMS (Learning Management Systems) like Moodle, Canvas could be adopted which help the teachers to better represent the content by using media tools like text, video and audio. Nowadays, Games are also developed and are found effective in this space. This blending with the pedagogical purpose model works out with the help of multiple technologies and effective use of media tools.

The second most important aspect next to the content is social and emotional support to the students. The constructivists of research affirmed that teaching and learning is a social activity and the physical presence of a teacher would create comfort and would make both teacher and student familiar with each other. Education at all levels require social and emotional development and hence teachers spend sufficient time to speak with their students informally by advising them about career and professional opportunities. This will give promised results especially in fully online courses if the teacher provides sufficient importance to social and emotional support wherever possible and appropriate. A study has recommended that for the development of online communities it is highly necessary to evaluate learner intellectual, social and emotional development (Khoo, Forret, 2011). Another study had confirmed that the affective domain is highly needed in asynchronous learning. The pedagogical strategy that brings a sense of community between a teacher and students could augment cognition by creating affective engagement among learners (Reilly, Gallagher-Lepak & Killion, 2012).

The third most important in effective online learning is Dialectics otherwise called questioning could also be an effective way by probing the students to know their receptivity and refining their knowledge. Socratic method is a recognized method used to stimulate discussion by throwing "right" questions which can kindle their analytical and critical thinking. These right questions will help to converge all the concepts related to the topic or issue and enhance a good level of understanding of the concepts rather than an open-ended activity give. These kind of activities require a threaded electronic discussion board where students may share their ideas and it is suggested that VoiceThread is an appropriate one. The well organized activity would definitely help the students to better understand the topic and the visualization of the thread equip the students with how the topic has evolved by seeing the entire discussion. Hence, this electronic discussion board can help massively in online learning to get a better understanding of the topic.

Another powerful pedagogy is "Reflection" and this is not a new concept as this had captured its attention during the early 20th century (Dewey (1916), Schon (1983). There exists literature that focuses on "reflective learner" and "reflective teacher" and its importance in effective online learning. The reflection on what we learn is extremely important and at the next level sharing their reflections is even more important to enrich our understanding through writing blogs and blogging. Hence the appropriate tools for refection are writing blogs and it is proved to be a successful technique for both students and teachers and it is viewed as a powerful pedagogical strategy.

Collaborative learning has grown as a powerful medium. It includes all sorts of activities ranging from informal discussions to highly structured discussion conducted in groups. It is one of the exercises where they can know about others in the class. Online learners could acquire a higher order thinking through collaborative learning and this activity as such is quite a difficult one for the instructor and can be a successful one if the teacher following the instructor centered approach. The strategy that might be adapted for this collaborative learning would be a group of minimal members and this more intimate groupings make the instructors find even a reserved student. It can also make the participant an active learner. Collaborative learning is seen as an important vehicle for developing knowledge and content by following a peer review and peer discussions (Fredericksen, 2015). Wikis have been an excellent tool for conducting activities like group projects and assignment. A research has affirmed that collaboration in online learning was highly in use among students, but there seemed to be enormous differences between synchronous learning and an asynchronous learning (Curtis & Lawson, 2001).

The last important component is the evaluation of learning. In this regard, Content Management Systems or Learning Management System plays a key role in evaluating the learner and learning. Methods that are highly used are tests, assignment, quizzes which can be done electronically. The regular classroom discussions on discussion boards and other blogs can be reviewed to assess the student's participation and progress over time. This can also help the instructors to find out the most effective mechanism and help them to assess the teaching efficiency. All these put together, learning analytics are seemed to be a technology that improves learning and teaching. And the online tools and technology have enabled the best sharing of information and could also create a permanent anytime accessible record for both instructors and learners.

The above six components namely, content, social and emotional support, dialectics, reflection, collaborative learning and evaluation form into a holistic model which is called as "integrated community of learning." This model irrespective of any mode, whether it is a face to face or online or blended learning has proved to be a successful one. It is not mandatory to use all the six components for every course, rather it could be used based on the pedagogical objectives.

## CONCLUSION

Online learners have diverse backgrounds, skills, learning styles, etc. Among all the attributes, learning styles play a significant role and significantly impact academic performance. Learning style denotes the individual differences that exist among individuals and their capacity in learning. Success in teaching depends on various factors, preferably adapting teaching pedagogy to an individual's learning style. Some studies have also explained the role of cognitive emotions (D'Errico, Paciello, De Carolis, Vattanid, Palestra, & Anzivino, 2018), affective component (Sandanayake, Madurapperuma & Dias, 2011), psychological impacts (Irawan, Dwisona & Lestari, 2020; Tellakat, Boyd, & Pennebaker, 2019) on academic achievements and especially effective online learning. Hence this chapter covers the all individual level variables and its impact on effectiveness of online learning. Next part, covers all the needs, expectations and mainly the barriers of online learning to better understand the learners which create a better student engagement in online courses. Perception about online education is extremely important in determining the success of online education. Hence this part stressed on the importance of needs and expectations of learners. Mostly, the faculty members who work for universities could either belong to Baby Boomers or Generation X who teaches for Generation Y and Generation Z. The need of hour is to bridge the gap between the generations of instructors and learners and this require a proper understanding of the current generation student's characteristics and the learners needs and wants (Mohr, & Mohr, 2017). This part is structured by dealing with the characteristics of the learners who belong to different generations specifically, GenY called Millennials and GenZ called Digital Natives. The equities in online education might also arise due to generational differences. Hence this part rightly pointed out the characteristics and their change in preferences with respect to online education. This part also discusses the strategies that can be used according to the generations needs and expectations. It synthesized the ideas, strategies and learning methods (Nicholas, 2020) that could be used especially to Gen Z learners like short quizzes, small group and team activities, "one minute papers" – active learning, Games, Storytelling, caring & consistent feedback (Carmen Miranda, 2020). This part also discusses some good theoretical frameworks that better create an amazing learning environment. The models Blending with Pedagogical Purpose Model (Bosch, 2016) & Integrated model is discussed with the strategies.

Learning frameworks mostly give importance to certain parameters of which "Content" occupy first. The linguistic delivery of content sharing is entirely different from sharing the content through an online platform. Mayer (2009) through his extensive collection of literature reviews has concluded the visualization matters a lot and highly significant in effective learning. Content is followed by "social and emotional support" to the students. The constructivists of research affirmed that teaching and learning is a social activity and the physical presence of a teacher would create comfort and would make both teacher and student familiar with each other. The third important aspect is "Dialectics" otherwise called questioning could also be an effective way by probing the students to know their receptivity and refining their knowledge. This is followed by "reflection" on what we learn is extremely important and at the next level sharing their reflections is even more important to enrich our understanding through writing blogs and blogging. "collaborative learning" is the next strategy where intimate groupings were formed and this make the instructors find even a reserved student. The last important component is the "evaluation of learning". In this regard, Content Management Systems or Learning Management System plays a key role in evaluating the learner and learning. These learning frameworks help instructors to find which is necessary for a successful online learning minimizing the inequities in online education.

# REFERENCES

Abramenka, V. (2015). *Students' motivations and barriers to online education*. Academic Press.

Basilaia, G., & Kvavadze, D. (2020). Transition to online education in schools during a SARSCoV-2 coronavirus (COVID-19) pandemic in Georgia. *Pedagogical Research*, *5*(4). Advance online publication. doi:10.29333/pr/7937

Bazier, C. C. (2015). *An analysis of instructor extraversion and student learning style* [Doctoral dissertation]. Walden University.

Bosch, C. (2016). *Promoting Self-Directed Learning through the Implementation of Cooperative Learning in a Higher Education Blended Learning Environment* [Doctoral dissertation]. North-West University.

Boyd, D. (2004). The characteristics of successful online students. *New Horizons in Adult Education and Human Resource Development*, *18*(2), 31–39. doi:10.1002/nha3.10184

Brocato, B. R., Bonanno, A., & Ulbig, S. (2015). Student perceptions and instructional evaluations: A multivariate analysis of online and face-to-face classroom settings. *Education and Information Technologies*, *20*(1), 37–55. doi:10.100710639-013-9268-6

Chamorro-Premuzic, T., & Furnham, A. (2008). Personality, intelligence and approaches to learning as predictors of academic performance. *Personality and Individual Differences*, *44*(7), 1596–1603. doi:10.1016/j.paid.2008.01.003

Clark, R. E. (1983, Winter). Reconsidering research on learning from media. *Review of Educational Research*, *53*(4), 445–459. doi:10.3102/00346543053004445

Curtis, D. D., & Lawson, M. J. (2001). Exploring collaborative online learning. *Journal of Asynchronous Learning Networks*, *5*(1), 21–34.

D'Errico, F., Paciello, M., De Carolis, B., Vattanid, A., Palestra, G., & Anzivino, G. (2018). *Cognitive emotions in e-learning processes and their potential relationship with students' academic adjustment*. Academic Press.

Duncan, H. E., Range, B., & Hvidston, D. (2013). Exploring student perceptions of rigor online: Toward a definition of rigorous learning. *Journal on Excellence in College Teaching*, *24*(4), 5–28.

Dunn, R., Beaudry, J., & Klavas, A. (1989). *Survey on Research on Learning Styles Educational Leadership*. Academic Press.

Egan, T. M., & Akdere, M. (2004). *Distance learning roles and competencies*. Academy of Human Resource Development.

Erdal, Y., Kiziltepe, Z., Seggie, F. N., & Sekerler, S. A. (2014). The Learning styles and personalities traits of undergraduate: A case at a state university in Istanbul. *The Anthropologist*, *18*(2), 591–600. doi:10.1080/09720073.2014.11891577

Fredericksen, E., Pickett, A., Shea, P., Pelz, W., & Swan, K. (2000). Student satisfaction and perceived learning with online courses: Principles and examples from the SUNY learning network. *Journal of Asynchronous Learning Networks*, *4*(2), 1–29.

Furnham, A., Jackson, C. J., & Miller, T. (1999). Personality, learning style and work performance. *Personality and Individual Differences*, *27*(6), 1113–1122. doi:10.1016/S0191-8869(99)00053-7

Furnham, A., Monsen, J., & Ahmetoglu, G. (2009). Typical intellectual engagement, Big Five personality traits, approaches to learning and cognitive ability predictors of academic performance. *The British Journal of Educational Psychology*, *79*(4), 769–782. doi:10.1348/978185409X412147 PMID:19245744

Galusha, J. M. (2008). *Barriers to Learning in Distance Education*. Retrieved from http://www.infrastruction.com/barriers.htm

Grasha, A. (1996). *Teaching with style*. Alliance.

Honey, P., & Mumford, A. (1992). *The manual of learning styles*. Academic Press.

Ilgaz, H., & Gulbahar, Y. (2017). *Why Do Learners Choose Online Learning: The Learners' Voices*. International Association for Development of the Information Society.

Irawan, A. W., Dwisona, D., & Lestari, M. (2020). Psychological Impacts of Students on Online Learning During the Pandemic COVID-19. *KONSELI: Jurnal Bimbingan dan Konseling (E-Journal)*, *7*(1), 53-60.

Khoo, E., & Forret, M. (2011). Evaluating an online learning community: Intellectual, social and emotional development and transformations. *Waikato Journal of Education*, *16*(1).

Kolb, D. A. (1984). *Experiential Learning: Experience as the Source of Learning and Development*. Prentice-Hall, Inc.

Komarraju, M., Karau, S. J., Schmeck, R. R., & Avdic, A. (2011). The Big Five personality traits, learning styles, and academic achievement. *Personality and Individual Differences*, *51*(4), 472–477. doi:10.1016/j.paid.2011.04.019

Kruck, S. E., Sendall, P., Ceccucci, W., Peslak, A., & Hunsiger, S. (2014). Does personality play a role in computer information systems course performance? *Issues in Information Systems*, *15*(2), 383–392.

Marcela, V. (2015). Learning strategy, personality traits and academic achievement of university students. *Procedia: Social and Behavioral Sciences*, *174*, 3473–3478. doi:10.1016/j.sbspro.2015.01.1021

Miranda, C. (2020). *Generation Z: Re-thinking Teaching and Learning Strategies*. Retrieved from: https://www.facultyfocus.com/articles/teaching-and-learning/generation-z-re-thinking-teaching-and-learning-strategies/

Mohr, K. A., & Mohr, E. S. (2017). Understanding Generation Z students to promote a contemporary learning environment. *Journal on Empowering Teaching Excellence*, *1*(1), 9.

Moorman, D., & Clark, K. (2012). *Student learning style and personality types: Their implications for teaching*. SOTL-Commons conference paper 33. http://digitalcommons.georgiasouthern.edu

Mupinga, D. M. (2003). Communicating with online students. *Sketches of Innovators in Education*.

Mupinga, D. M., Nora, R. T., & Yaw, D. C. (2006). The learning styles, expectations, and needs of online students. *College Teaching*, *54*(1), 185–189. doi:10.3200/CTCH.54.1.185-189

Nicholas, A. J. (2020). *Preferred Learning Methods of Generation Z*. Academic Press.

Organisation for Economic Co-operation and Development. (2020). *The potential of online learning for adults: early lessons from the COVID-19 crisis*. OECD Publishing.

Postolov, K., Magdinceva Sopova, M., & Janeska-Iliev, A. (2017). *E-learning in the hands of generation Y and Z*. Academic Press.

Reilly, J. R., Gallagher-Lepak, S., & Killion, C. (2012). "Me and my computer": Emotional factors in online learning. *Nursing Education Perspectives*, *33*(2), 100–105. doi:10.5480/1536-5026-33.2.100 PMID:22616408

Richmond, A. S., & Cummings, R. (2005). Implementing Kolb's learning styles into online distance education. *International Journal of Technology in Teaching and Learning*, *1*(1), 45–54.

Russell, T. L. (1999). *The "no significant difference phenomenon."* North Carolina State University. Retrieved September 30, 2004, from: http://nt.media.hku.hk/no_sig_diff/ phenom1.html

Sadeghi, N., Kasim, Z. M., Tan, B. H., & Abdullah, F. S. (2012). Learning styles, personality types and reading comprehension performance. *English Language Teaching*, *5*(4), 116–123. doi:10.5539/elt.v5n4p116

Salehi, Z., Mokhtari Nouri, J., Khademolhoseyni, S. M., & Ebadi, A. (2014). Studying the effect of education and implementation of Evidence-Based Nursing Guidelines on parents' satisfaction in NICU. *Journal of Applied Environmental and Biological Sciences*, *4*(8), 176–182.

Sandanayake, T. C., Madurapperuma, A. P., & Dias, D. (2011). Affective E learning model for Recognising learner emotions. *International Journal of Information and Education Technology (IJIET)*, *1*(4), 315–320. doi:10.7763/IJIET.2011.V1.51

Schroeder, S. M., & Terras, K. L. (2015). Advising experiences and needs of online, cohort, and classroom adult graduate learners. *The Journal of the National Academic Advising Association*, *35*(1), 42–55. doi:10.12930/NACADA-13-044

Siddiquei, N. L., & Khalid, R. (2018). The relationship between personality traits, learning styles and academic performance of E-Learner. *Open Praxis*, *10*(3), 1–20. doi:10.5944/openpraxis.10.3.870

Srichanyachon, N. (2014). The barriers and needs of online learners. *Turkish Online Journal of Distance Education*, *15*(3), 50–59. doi:10.17718/tojde.08799

Tellakat, M., Boyd, R. L., & Pennebaker, J. W. (2019). How do online learners study? The psychometrics of students' clicking patterns in online courses. *PLoS One*, *14*(3), e0213863. doi:10.1371/journal.pone.0213863 PMID:30908503

Urval, R., Kamath, A., Ullal, S., Shenoy, A., Shenoy, N., & Udupa, L. (2014). Assessment of learning styles of undergraduate medical students using the VARK questionnaire and the influence of sex and academic performance. *Advances in Physiology Education, 38*(3), 216–220. Advance online publication. doi:10.1152/advan.00024.2014 PMID:25179610

Vasileva-Stojanovska, T., Malinovski, T., Vasileva, M., Jovevski, D., & Trajkovik, V. (2015). Impact of satisfaction, personality and learning style on educational outcomes in a blended learning environment. *Learning and Individual Differences, 38*, 127–135. doi:10.1016/j.lindif.2015.01.018

Whetten, D. A., & Cameron, K. S. (1984). *Instructors Manual for Developing Management Skills*. Scott, Foresman.

Wu, C. K., & Lai, H. S. (2010). Learning style and personality type profiles of hospitality undergraduate students of Taiwan and the United States. *Airity Library, 6*, 111-139. http://ge.cyut.edu.tw

## ADDITIONAL READING

Cilliers, E. J. (2021). Reflecting on social learning tools to enhance the teaching-learning experience of generation Z learners. In *Frontiers in education* (p. 286). Frontiers. doi:10.3389/feduc.2020.606533

El-Sabagh, H. A. (2021). Adaptive e-learning environment based on learning styles and its impact on development students' engagement. *International Journal of Educational Technology in Higher Education, 18*(1), 1–24. doi:10.118641239-021-00289-4

Seemiller, C., Grace, M., Dal Bo Campagnolo, P., Mara Da Rosa Alves, I., & Severo De Borba, G. (2019). How generation Z college students prefer to learn: a comparison of US and Brazil students. *Journal of Educational Research and Practice, 9*(1), 25.

## KEY TERMS AND DEFINITIONS

**Learner Engagement:** Learning engagement is the ability to motivationally and behaviorally engage in an effective learning process.

**Learning Style:** A style of learning refers to an individual's preferred way to absorb, process, comprehend and retain information.

**Sustainable Development:** SD is 'development that meets the needs of the present without compromising the ability of future generations to meet their own needs' (Our Common Future, 1987, 43).

# Chapter 10
# Sustainability Education Beyond the Classroom:
## How the "Exploding University" Nurtures Collective Intelligence Across Local and Global Communities

**Helen Wadham**
*Manchester Metropolitan University, UK*

**Clare Hart**
*Manchester Metropolitan University, UK*

**Anita Hashmi**
 https://orcid.org/0000-0001-5176-6266
*Manchester Metropolitan University, UK*

**Helena Mary Kettleborough**
*Manchester Metropolitan University, UK*

**Roz Marron**
*Manchester Metropolitan University, UK*

**Sally Randles**
*Manchester Metropolitan University, UK*

**Konstantina Skritsovali**
*Liverpool John Moores University, UK*

**Megan Tucker**
*Manchester Metropolitan University, UK*

## ABSTRACT

*This chapter explores how the authors expanded their teaching and learning beyond the classroom at Manchester Metropolitan University in the UK. It puts forward the theoretical concept of the "exploding university" as a way to help develop a critical yet hopeful understanding of collective problems at local and global scales. This helps them explore three interrelated initiatives that brought teachers, students, and communities together, namely a sustainability festival, research project on animal rehoming, and community tree-planting drive. The chapter illuminates how exploding the work beyond the classroom enabled everyone involved to take action on the challenges that matter to them, while also developing a "collective intelligence" about their underlying causes. The exploding university thus emerges as a theoretical and practical model, which we can use to inspire students to actively critique, reimagine, and reconstruct the world around them. The authors conclude by encouraging and supporting others who might wish to embark on similar journeys themselves.*

DOI: 10.4018/978-1-6684-6172-3.ch010

*Sustainability Education Beyond the Classroom*

## INTRODUCTION

How can we enable our students to engage critically with the thorny and contradictory concept of sustainability, while actively imagining a more liveable future at both local and global scales? Our chapter explores this question by sharing the experiences of a group of academics, support staff and students based at Manchester Metropolitan University Business School in the UK. Our focus is on how we experimented with and learnt from three interrelated initiatives that enabled us to "explode" our sustainability teaching and learning beyond the classroom.

Inspired by a critical approach to the United Nations' Sustainable Development Goals (SDGs), our chapter has three aims. First, it develops a theoretical contribution to the ESD literature by developing the concept of the "exploding university," which might help students and communities alike develop a critical yet hopeful understanding of our collective problems at local and global scales. Second, it provides three empirical examples of how this shared action can help students, communities and others address those challenges and - as importantly - build a shared understanding of (or "collective intelligence" about) their underlying causes. Third, by way of a reflection on our theoretical and empirical analysis, we consider how we might encourage and support others wishing to embark on similar journeys themselves.

### Context

A focus on teaching and learning about sustainability seems more necessary than ever. Alongside existing and deepening concerns about climate change, the Covid-19 pandemic has brought other global challenges into sharp relief. Its deeply negative impact on health and well-being, unemployment and social inequality threatens the achievement of the United Nations' Sustainable Development Goals more broadly (UN, 2021). However, the pandemic also demonstrated the power of collaboration, as the drive to develop and roll out coronavirus vaccines led to unprecedented levels of local, national and international collaboration between government, industry and civil society actors (Guimon & Narula, 2020).

These contemporary global challenges thus offer us an opportunity to redefine our future and develop a more "meaningful" understanding of sustainability (Tsing, 2017, p. 51). As teachers and learners, we seek to explore how we might balance economic wellbeing, social justice and environmental stewardship now and in the future. But the sheer number of underlying challenges - climate change, protecting biodiversity, addressing socioeconomic inequity - makes it hard to prioritise among them (Washington, 2015). Such challenges are highly complex, deeply uncertain and the subject of significant conflict among diverse stakeholders (Sediri et al., 2020). Thus, the very notion of sustainability can give rise to a paralysing sense of helplessness (Murphy, 2012).

The starting point for our chapter, then, is to ask how we – as teachers, learners and citizens – might recognise the complex, system-level challenges to which we are all subject, while also acknowledging and leveraging our individual and collective agency to bring about some kind of change. We are aware of how threatened the natural-social world is and we seek to discuss this with our students and coursemates in ways that are meaningful for them. For example, we all engage in first-person practice of finding news stories each week and finding out what is happening – bearing witness – so that together we can reflect on the challenges and begin to imagine potential solutions (Kettleborough, 2019). All the authors are committed to teaching and learning about these issues to the very best of our ability, seeking at the same time to encourage ourselves and others to reflect on our own behaviour and professional/personal lives.

Our institutional home, Manchester Metropolitan University, has a long history of engaging with sustainability issues. We are all based or engaged with the Faculty of Business and Law (FoBL), specifically the Department of Strategy, Enterprise and Sustainability (SES). There have been two main phases in the Business School's own sustainability journey. From around 1992-2011, the roots of sustainability teaching and learning were established, led by impassioned but lone champions (Christian & Walley, 2016). Then, starting in 2012, we became part of a critical mass of people - researchers, teachers, professionals and students - who are motivated by a wide range of sustainability cares and concerns. Together we have supported the university-wide embedding of sustainability into the curricular and extra-curricular experiences of students (Randles et al., forthcoming).

Today, Manchester Met in general – and our faculty and department specifically – are widely recognised as particularly active with regards to the sustainability agenda. The university has ranked in the top three of the People and Planet University League for its environmental and ethical performance since 2013. The Business School has been a signatory to the United Nations' Principles of Responsible Management Education (PRME) since 2012. Our department (SES) has been key to university and faculty efforts to develop sustainability teaching and strategy throughout that time. For example, its Young Enterprise programme was recognised in 2020 with a Green Gown Award by the UK and Ireland Environmental Association of Universities and Colleges (EAUC). Likewise, in 2018 the authors and others piloted a scheme with the Carbon Literacy Project to enable students to measure and reduce their environmental footprint. This has now been rolled out to all first-year undergraduates in the Business School and will be extended across the university over the next three years.

## Our Aspirations for This Chapter

Our contribution is concerned with several overlapping themes that arise throughout the book, particularly those of global citizenship and sustainability, reflective practices in education for sustainable development (ESD) and the possibilities of management and business education for a sustainable world. The purpose of our chapter is to explore how we can help our students to engage critically with the multiple often terrifying challenges we face, while (more positively) imagining a more liveable future. We agree that sustainability can potentially be a limiting concept, authored and defined by those who have power and privilege, while excluding the voices of those on the margins (Barnett, 2018; Kayumova & Tippins, 2021). Thus, we focus on the value of taking our teaching and learning activities beyond the confines of the university, in order to relocate them within the communities that surround us locally and beyond. In so doing, our chapter theoretically extends Colin Ward's notion of the "exploding school" into the higher education (HE) context (Ward & Fyson, 1973).

Our chapter proceeds as follows. We will begin by reviewing the existing literature on sustainability as collective intelligence, and explore how we might build that intelligence through transformative learning and effectively rethinking the role of the university itself. We will then set out our theoretical framework, namely the "exploding university." We then briefly introduce our methodology, before turning to our findings and discussion. These centre on how our three chosen examples enabled us to "explode" our sustainability teaching into the local community, and the consequences of this for our students and the communities themselves. Finally, we offer up some tentative conclusions, along with concrete suggestions for action that may prove helpful to other teachers and learners.

*Sustainability Education Beyond the Classroom*

## BACKGROUND

Our introduction above indicates that we might usefully describe sustainability as a "wicked problem," namely one that appears intractable because the interdependencies between different actors and systems make it hard to articulate goals and manage potential solutions (Rittel & Webber, 1973). It is difficult to apportion responsibility, for example, when the respective causes and consequences of unsustainable practices may be geographically distant (Murphy, 2012). Likewise, temporal complexities arise, as the changes required – to cultural, physical and social structures – are urgent yet simultaneously slow-moving (Wadham, 2020). Our understanding of sustainability, then, is necessarily incomplete, fragmented and contradictory: This can lead to a reluctance to engage with the concept altogether (Longo et al., 2016).

The particular contradiction that concerns us in this chapter is the dichotomy between what might be called top-down and bottom-up approaches. The SDGs reveal sustainability as a global process, leading to a focus on universal and top-down approaches (Dymitrow & Halfacree, 2018). For example, Murphy (2012) suggests that it is "wishful thinking" to hope that systemic challenges might be addressed via small-scale, organic solutions. Yet exogenous, large-scale initiatives are more likely to render individuals and communities mere passive receptors of change, rather than active agents (Mazon et al., 2020). If the future is to be more liveable, then, we must combine top-down leadership with bottom-up participatory approaches. Ravetz suggests this requires us to develop our "collective intelligence," via a step-change that draws on both "collaborative 'know-how' and 'know-*why*'" (Ravetz, 2020, pp. 3 – our emphasis).

Universities – and perhaps business schools in particular – can play a key role in helping us develop this collective intelligence: They can effectively serve as catalysts and agents of social and economic transformation (Akrivou & Bradbury-Huang, 2015). The origins of this idea date back more than 80 years, when Whitehead pointed out that the "task of a university is the creation of the future…[which is] big with every possibility of achievement and of tragedy" (Whitehead, 1938, p. 171).

Stengers (2018, p.110) finds it particularly compelling that Whitehead associates the future "neither with the advancement of knowledge nor with progress, but rather with radical uncertainty." However, she suggests that the longstanding purpose of universities is being compromised by "fast science." That is, just as we should be seeking out ever more opportunities to articulate and engage with complex challenges in the world around us in meaningful and thoughtful ways, our ability to do so is constrained by the same forces that exacerbate the economic, social and environmental crises discussed above. Market-driven values like economic rationalism, massification and internationalisation have radically reconstituted the HE sector in the UK and elsewhere, reaching into our teaching and research (Sandel, 2012). Universities have been transformed into corporate enterprises characterised by conformism, competitiveness, and opportunism (Lewis & Shore, 2019; Whelan et al., 2013). Yet, even as we acknowledge the challenges within our education system and beyond, we remain hopeful for the future. The remainder of this section will give some insight into our reasons for optimism.

### Sustainability as a Form of Collective Intelligence

As outlined above, the coronavirus pandemic disrupted life as usual on a global scale that we are yet to fully comprehend. This leads Roy (2020) to reflect that this shared global experience represents "a portal, a gateway between one world and the next." That is, it offers an opportunity to leave behind dead ideas and a chance to redefine our future and develop a more meaningful understanding of sustainability (Tsing, 2017). As we have explained above, imagining this more liveable future will require a more active, bottom-up approach that will develop our "collective intelligence" and make us wiser in all possible ways (Black et al, 2017).

Collective intelligence across communities and societies comprises both shared know-how and - more importantly - shared *"know-why."* Yet, when it comes to sustainability teaching and practice, what Ravetz (2020, pp. 3) calls the "human dimension" is often overlooked in favour of clever technological solutions. A more bottom-up approach, by contrast, acknowledges that our understandings of sustainability and its possibilities are inherently and necessarily grounded in our own everyday experiences. We therefore find it helpful to reflect on Sayer's (2011) work on "why things matter" to people. Humans are sentient beings whose relation to the world is one of concern, which is experienced through practical everyday events, acts and moments of care and caring (Sayer, 2011; Nilsson, 2015). With this in mind, students, teachers and communities are all embedded within a host of different time/place-situated cares and concerns. Sustainability education thereby represents an opportunity to understand what matters to us, what changes we might like to see in the world, and how we might come together to help bring them about. That is, ESD becomes a means to social change through community engagement, an encounter that is at once practical, aspirational and playfully subversive.

## Building Collective Intelligence Through Transformative Learning

Our own previous research suggests that the kind of transformative learning that is required to build collective intelligence overlaps with and reinforces related notions of "transformative communities" and "transformative leadership," which are traditionally explored within the literature as separate concepts (Randles et al., forthcoming). We will briefly discuss each before illustrating how they are indeed better understood as co-constitutive and mutually reinforcing. According to Southern (2007), *transformative learning* is always *for* something, such as learning for community and sense of place, for communities of practice, for civic culture, or for the biosphere and biocentric diversity. As such, transformative learning appreciates universal needs of subsistence, protection, affection, understanding, participation, idleness, creation, identity and freedom (Taylor, 2008). In addition, transformative learning always invites us to consider who we are in relation to others (Southern, 2007, p. 334). It engages us in shared efforts at both sense-making and practical action, and thus requires us to cultivate relations of trust, truth, shared values and shared understanding. Southern (2007) therefore suggests that transformative learning passes through various steps, namely invitation, participation, engagement, commitment and collaboration.

This in turn highlights the link between transformative learning and *transformative communities*. The latter unfold when transformative learning moves beyond the classroom and into community engagement via an organised, systematic and problem-centred teleological process (Souza et al., 2019). Blay-Palmer et al. (2013) suggest that bringing communities together around a common interest/concern could foster the formation of democratic learning communities of inquiry and practice. And through social discourse, these communities of interest in turn themselves generate new knowledge, while at the same time critically examining this knowledge in relation to existing social practices.

Finally, there is a smaller yet not less important stream of literature that explores the intersections between transformative learning and *transformative leadership* (e.g. Astin and Astin, 2000; Shields, 2011; 2017; 2020; Haddock-Fraser et al., 2018). Taking a critical and normative approach, transformative leadership aims to bring about social change, and asks questions about social justice and democracy (Shields, 2011). The above writers and others explore what kind of approaches and actions are most likely to nurture collaboration, capitalise on members' diverse talents and support a shared purpose.

*Sustainability Education Beyond the Classroom*

Our own research (Randles et al., forthcoming) explored theoretically the intersections between these three concepts. Co-authored between staff and students, our paper reflected on how our bottom-up approach to sustainability teaching and learning enabled us all to learn from each other, build communities of trust with others beyond the university and share leadership across a wide and diverse group. We thereby showed how transformative learning, communities and leadership overlap and function as a single composite, integrated and mutually reinforcing model for change. This in turn requires that we rethink the social and institutional purpose of the university.

## Reimagining the Role of the University

Our previous research (Randles et al., forthcoming) indicated the usefulness of Barnett's (2011; 2018) model of the "ecological university." According to his definition, the ecological university uses its resources to create a more sustainable future that is structured around interconnectedness and a critique of the world order. Its aim is to play an active role in making the world – in which it is organically embedded itself – a better place. The ecological university is a "feasible utopia," which he believes could "just about" be realised. However, he goes on to suggest that this model of HE is most needed at the precise moment when it is most in peril. Stengers (2018) agrees, suggesting that - despite the constraints to which they are subject - academics need to engage and negotiate with the broader public and appreciate their questions: To refer back to the earlier discussion, we could say that academics need to respect and attend to people's own "matters of concern" as well as their own. As Stengers (2018) suggests, this more relational approach requires us all to slow down, in order to become capable of learning again, to reacquaint ourselves with things again, and to recognise our interdependence with other people, beings and places:

*It means thinking and imagining, and in the process creating relationships with others that are not those of capture. (Stengers, 2018, p. 82)*

For theoretical inspiration about how we might go about doing this, we turn to an provocative yet overlooked book by the British anarchist writer Colin Ward.

## Our Theoretical Framework: Introducing the "Exploding University"

Ward is perhaps best known for documenting the history of peculiarly English institutions like holiday camps and allotments. Citing anarchist predecessors such as Kropotkin and Bakunin, he highlights that people are fundamentally cooperative (Ward, 1973). A humane and forward-thinking society will enable people and communities to discover – *for themselves* – interim-if-imperfect solutions to the challenges they face (Ward, 1997). Ward's geographically specific interests, together with an unassuming and pragmatic writing style, mean his work is often overlooked (Wilbert & White, 2011). Yet his emphasis on self-help in everyday life has a powerful contemporary resonance for our exploration of how we might encourage our students to engage critically, actively and (often) prosaically with the "wicked" problems that we face as a society.

"Streetwork: The exploding school" (Ward & Fyson, 1973) is a kind of manifesto for environmental education, written while the authors were education officers at the UK's Town and Country Planning Association. They advocated taking children out of the classroom in order to learn about the world around them. That is, teachers should take an issue of importance to the local community – such as traffic congestion, antisocial behaviour, or consumerism (to add a more recent example) – and tackle it from "whatever angle strikes some response from the class" (Ward & Fyson 1973, p. 12). Exchanging the constraints of the classroom for streets and public spaces, the child becomes purposeful and energetic, and understands and takes part willingly in processes of community decision-making and development

This is not just about increasing the amount of local study or formalising what is already part of the child's experience. Rather it demands a fundamentally different (less top-down) approach to education altogether. For example, returning to the issue of traffic congestion mentioned just now, an "exploding" approach would require pupils to engage with the challenge first-hand. As a starting point they might undertake a survey of traffic blackspots and try to devise solutions. Next, they could consider if sufficient weight is being given to interests that conflicted with the prevailing "traffic-centric/efficiency" standpoint. Third, they could consider how they and the public at large should act in order that their views be noticed.

By developing young people's habits of evaluating and questioning, so we can effectively give them the tools to actively reshape their world, rather than consigning them to "a lifetime of resigned indifference" (Ward & Fyson, 1973, p. 32). This kind of approach requires careful and meticulous planning, but will reward children, teachers and society alike.

Even as the book prefigures current theories and practices around pupil participation, consultation and place-based education, it is consistently more radical in its agenda. In particular, it imagines school communities as resources for bringing about social change:

*It offers a view of the natural inclination of children and young people to not only have a view and a voice when adults deem to consult them, but also to critique, re-imagine and reconstruct their world for themselves with and for the communities [to which they belong.] (Burke, 2014, p. 437)*

Streetwork thus envisaged children and young people as positive resources of and for their communities. Understood as relational sites of interaction between people, places and things, these communities are in turn acknowledged as inherently subject to continual negotiation and change. Children are freed up to determine their own learning path (literally) through peripatetic wandering, but always within what Burke (2014, p. 440) calls a "purposeful and structured framing of pedagogic intent."

Our findings show how this model can effectively be expanded from schools into universities, while our discussion considers some of the consequences and implications of doing so. Before introducing our own experiences, however, it is useful to reflect briefly on three key characteristics of Ward and Fyson's (1973) work that we found particularly useful.

First, the model is built on the assumption that effective learning requires that people take action themselves. There is no substitute for experiencing an environment at first hand: As young people encounter life beyond the classroom, they learn to both observe and interpret what they encounter, and the immediacy of this experience deepens their understanding of it. Yet, just as 50 years ago Ward and Fyson (1977, p. 6) were responding to complaints that children were leaving school "unprepared for any kind of useful role in society," so contemporary employers suggest that today's young graduates lack critical thinking, creativity and problem-solving skills (ISE, 2022). We suggest that the "exploding university" offers a way to better prepare students for the life they will build for themselves and others, by offering them deeper insight and multiple perspectives into the challenges they (and future generations) are likely to encounter.

Second, the model recognises and embraces diversity and disorder. It underlines that concern for the wellbeing of society (and nature) does not and should not be equated with a search for universal agreement: "Consensus is not something to be invoked like a spiritual cement to stick something together that would otherwise be broken apart" (Ward & Fyson, 1973, p.14). Rather, seeking out the dissenting group and examining the validity of their views can be a profoundly insightful experience.

Again, this is of particular relevance in the context of ESD. For example, Ravetz (2020) suggests that large-scale challenges like climate change and rising inequality demand us to think synergistically: Such is their complexity that any consensus around how to understand and act on them will always be temporary and fragile. Rather, we should aim at wider and deeper forms of decision-making. The exploding university would enable students and communities to take part in these kinds of deliberative and reflexive experiments.

Third, the goal of the model is to create both community feeling and global awareness. This is achieved through an emphasis on "unofficial" culture, which is concerned with what actually happens, and what people really do or enjoy doing, rather than the "official" culture of what ought to be happening or what "top" people think:

*Irreverent, boisterous and subversive as it usually is… it is this culture which binds us to a place, which gives us those subtle ties of concern for [the world around us.] (Ward & Fyson, 1973, p. 28)*

This perspective is helpful in the context of ESD. By exploding our work beyond the classroom, we are effectively asking our students to shift their focus: Rather than concentrate on general or abstract "principles" (such as those that lie behind the SDGs, for example), we suggest they take the time to open their imagination and consider this particular occasion with these people, in this place (Stengers, 2018; Taylor, 2020). This represents a normative as well as a tactical choice. That is, by exposing students to "other" ways of knowing, we are effectively encouraging them to challenge (perhaps fundamentally) their understanding of what sustainability "is" and what it could be.

As well as expanding into the HE context, we seek to make our own theoretical contribution to Ward's work by bringing his ideas into conversation with those of James Lovelock, namely his "Gaia hypothesis." This suggests that the earth and its biological systems interact and co-evolve as a single, synergistic and self-regulating entity (Lovelock, 1995). Lovelock brings to our attention that exploding processes are a fundamental part not only of education but of life itself, enabling us to more fully recognise how our efforts as individuals and communities are in turn embedded and interconnected with the natural-social world around us. Indeed, Ward himself uses the term "seeds beneath the snow" to describe the myriad everyday but often unseen acts of solidarity and inventiveness through which people try to find new ways of living differently. Thus, it is not only people who explode out into the world. Even plants like dandelions and bulrushes are simultaneously settled and itinerant beings. Their seeds need to travel. For example, as David Attenborough explains in his enchanting Plant World documentary (2021), the "squirting cucumber" (echallium elaterium) store its seeds in a pod and - when the pod is ripe – they explode into the air and get carried miles away. By bringing Ward's ideas into conversation with those of Lovelock and other ecological thinkers, then, we hope to bring added nuance and significance to his underlying metaphor: Our students are themselves seeds beneath the snow, who explode out into the community while they are with us but more importantly will continue to do so long after graduation, in ways that will help our society and the planet.

## METHODOLOGY: AN APPROACH INSPIRED BY ACTION RESEARCH

First-person action research develops practical knowing and pursues workable solutions to issues of pressing concern to people (Reason & Bradbury, 2001). It is a dynamic and evolving form of reflective practice. The specific form of action research adopted is that of co-operative inquiry, which invites groups of people to use the full range of their sensibilities to inquire together into any aspect of the human condition, with the aim of both reframing our understanding of the world and transforming practice within it. Co-operative inquiry appealed to us because of its humanistic beginnings, and its variety of forms and potential participants (Bradbury, 2015). It has been used all across the world, by students to explore ideas of deep ecology (Maughan & Reason, 2001), by social workers to learn together about tensions between reflection and following policy (Baldwin, 2001) and by leaders of social justice-based organisations exploring issues of leadership and empowerment (Duncan, 2015; Yorks et al., 2008).

Key to co-operative inquiry is its focus on extended ways of knowing. These include experiential (lived) knowing, presentational knowing, the knowing of art, story, music and expression, propositional knowing, the knowing of science, academia and policy and finally practical knowing that is the sum of all of the others and takes place out in the world. The method has been explored with great value and enthusiasm in Columbia for example (Fals Borda, 2006; Rappaport, 2020). During the pandemic, co-operative inquiry has gone virtual. For example, the Schumacher College Living Waters course has used online meetings as a way to undertake two such inquiries into how we might acknowledge and respond to rivers as sentient beings (Kurio & Reason, 2021).

Our own earlier work was based on an online experiment in co-operative inquiry (Randles et al, forthcoming). Through a series of nine online meetings involving the present authors and others, we together developed a composite model of transformative learning, communities and leadership (mentioned above). But, as significant, we also resolved to continue working together in order to take practical steps towards addressing our own matters of concern: Three of the initiatives that resulted are documented in the present chapter. Our original experiment was just one example of a wider effort to bring action research into the work of our own institution, as a way of creating a sense of agency and engagement among staff and students within what is a large and busy metropolitan university. Action research is now integrated into the training for our faculty's PhD students, and on the MBA programme, as well as within a reflective postgraduate unit on professional practice.

In collecting and analysing the data for this chapter, we have used elements of both co-operative inquiry and first-person practice. The data comes from our shared reflections of our experiences on three projects, namely the Action for Sustainability Festival, a research project on animal rehoming, and tree-planting in south Manchester. Along with members of the local community, we and dozens of other colleagues and students worked together under the auspices of the Staff Student Sustainability Group to shape, organise and implement these initiatives. This organic approach enabled us to co-develop them through action and inquiry, aiming for equality between all members, whether from staff, student or community. Our data comprised the field notes, posters and questionnaires produced as part of the initiatives themselves. We also drew on notes from research and working meetings we held online and in person before and after the events, and our research diaries and email exchanges.

Table 1 provides more information, after which we will introduce our findings and discussion. In summary, we are excited by the possibilities of continuing to grow action research within our institution and have many plans for the future, to which we will return in the conclusion.

*Table 1. Summary of pilot ESD initiatives and data collected*

| Initiative | Participants | Data Collected |
| --- | --- | --- |
| 1 Action for Sustainability Festival (June 2022) | 5 academic/ professional staff & 12 students co-developed the event. Total of 180 staff, students & community members attended the event | Participant observation at event. Questionnaires completed by organisers & participants (N=18). Notes from 20 research & working meetings. Academic posters prepared by participants. Email exchanges between the organisers |
| 2 Animal rehoming in a post-pandemic world (research project) (March-July 2022) | 1 academic led the project. 1 member of professional staff & 7 students acted as research assistants, engaging with staff/ volunteers from 6 nonprofit organisations | 6 research visits to participating organisations & subsequent fieldnotes/ research diaries. Notes from 6 research & working meetings. Academic posters/conference abstracts prepared by participants. Email exchanges between the organisers |
| 3 Tree-planting in south Manchester (March 2022-) | 1 academic led the project, in consultation with 4 members of local community groups. Planting sessions attended by 9 staff, 7 students & 15 members of local communities | Participant observation at event. Questionnaires completed by organisers & participants (N=12). Notes from 5 research & working meetings. Conference abstracts prepared by participants. Email exchanges between the organisers |

# FINDINGS

## Initiative 1: Action for Sustainability Festival

Held in the atrium of Manchester Met Business School, this mid-summer event brought students and staff together with communities and organisations from the local, national and international community in which the university is embedded. The aim was to provide a platform for students to connect and exchange ideas with other people who were also passionate about creating positive change. It would also enable them to make sense of their cares, concerns, stories and experiences, build their knowledge of underlying sustainability challenges, and identify ways they might help contribute to ongoing efforts to overcome them. As one of the students said:

*"Planning this has made me think more about everything…if my generation can see what I can see and appreciate [our world]…we could create possibilities to act."*

Speakers included writer and broadcaster Jonathon Porritt, and representatives from Greenpeace and Steady State Manchester, as well as Manchester Met students. The atrium was packed with 24 stands from organisations like Amnesty International, Slave Free Alliance and Friends of the Earth, along with a wide variety of ethical businesses. Huge colourful posters enabled students, academics and organisations to share their research and their ideas and concerns for living on a healthy and just planet. Other participants included children from two local primary schools and a golden retriever, who was co-hosting the animal rehoming stand. In total, over 180 people joined in with the event, with plans underway to make it into an annual fixture on the university calendar.

## Connecting and Galvanising People

*"What has been most striking about the whole day,"* reflected one of the organisers as she tucked questionnaires, cables and reusable coffee mugs into an already overflowing cardboard box, *"are all the elements of interconnectedness."*

The festival was an opportunity to build a community of people between seemingly disparate groups and initiatives, to engage in meaningful conversations, to celebrate many small (but not insignificant) successes and to plan how to move to a life-enhancing flourishing future. As one of the students later commented, this required some determination on their part:

*"[Although] my nerves were in overdrive…I made the decision to meet some of the different organisations…I was glad I did, as I would not normally interact with these organisations and I learnt so much about them. Later, I exchanged contact details with the representative from Amnesty UK who would like me to be involved in some of their work."*

It was also a day to meet old and new friends. As the self-organised Staff Student Sustainability Group, we had been working together for over a year, first on our previous book chapter and more recently on organising this event. But many of us had never met in person:

*"Woooah – your beard is so long in real life!"* exclaimed one of the students as another walked in.

It was immediately clear that regular online meetings were no replacement for the sheer pleasure of seeing each other face-to-face. Throughout the morning as people arrived to set up, there were waves, hugs and laughter around the venue.

The festival represented a defining moment for the organisers, a way for like-minded and passionate individuals to act upon their commitment to sustainability in a visible and holistic way. The event provided an emotional and immersive bookend to our theoretical and online efforts to date. As the day went on, there was an almost overwhelming sense of pride and accomplishment that a small group of students and staff had managed to pull off such an inspirational event, especially at the tail-end of the academic year when many students were heading off for the summer and staff were buried in marking.

*"The event was amazing,"* reflected one participant afterwards. *"Full of encouragement and ideas."*

From invitations to join a student-led sustainability consultancy, a hands-on demonstration of 3D printing, to enthusiastic debates around fast fashion and the future of food, the festival was intended to galvanise people into action. Participants commented on the mixture of emotions they experienced throughout. This was reflected too in the keynote session with Jonathon Porritt, in which he expressed admiration for young climate strikers while voicing impatience at current political developments. One of the students later reflected:

*"He provided a perfect example of accepting that it is okay to feel frustrated but be happy at the same time."*

## The Joys and Risks of an Organic Approach

Students found that by engaging with diverse people, experiences and views, they were able to complement the more mainstream and business-focused approaches to sustainability they had encountered in their studies to date:

*"I learnt so much throughout my [course],'"* reflected one undergraduate. *"But having personal conversations and learning everyone's stories has inspired me more to make a pledge towards making a difference [to climate change]."*

Over lunch, the visiting children were given a platform to tell us about their school and community environmental projects. They brought their learning to life as they explained to this large group of largely unfamiliar adults how and why they work together to minimise waste, grow their own food and so on. This was what Lawson et al. (2018) call "intergenerational learning" at its best! At the end of the day, one of the teachers quietly commented on the impact this had on the children themselves:

*"The pupils felt they were listened to and made a contribution to the day - for them that is a big thing!"*

In another corner of the atrium, a local artist was recreating an existing artwork of endangered macaws. The picture had been cut up into dozens of pieces, which participants then reimagined on their own paper-covered tiles. Throughout the day, even those initially reluctant to pick up a paintbrush were unable to resist joining in – with skill, enthusiasm and occasionally both – as the Andy Warhol-esque mosaic gradually took shape. This collaborative activity was a particular hit with the children, who had joined us midmorning and brought a new energy to the atrium:

*"I want to come here when I'm older!"* one of them enthused.

While the plan had been to walk them around the poster displays, they were waylaid by Chata, the rescue dog. Their teachers found it impossible to round them up off the floor as several of them had never stroked a dog before and were keen to make the most of the experience. They never got to see the posters, but did join us for the keynote presentation with Jonathon Porritt. After sitting patiently for 45 minutes, they were rewarded with an invitation to ask the first questions. Many participants commented delightedly on how Jonathon had clearly adapted the content and tone of his presentation to enable the children to follow along. A relaxed approach thus demands that you cede an element of control over events: It is never quite clear who will arrive and when, and what they might do when they get there.

## Taking Up Space

*"It really looks like a sustainable building now!"* said one of the students, waving towards the multicolour bunting, stands of recycled books, and trays of vegan food on offer.

The organisers had created a diverse and inspiring programme of talks, and despite all the distractions on offer, the lecture theatre remained well-populated all day. Yet many students commented on the learning that was going on "around the edges," enabling them to make meaningful connections:

*"Actually speaking to some of the speakers in the atrium allowed a more in-depth look into their particular work and created a deeper understanding."*

The posters provided a range of great talking points too. Most reflected initiatives in progress at the university or within the local community. However, one display board highlighted sustainability efforts underway by staff and students at a partner institution, the Autonomous University of Mexico State. Interestingly, the projects featured showed a remarkable symmetry with those outlined here, including a focus on tree-planting and community enterprise.

## Initiative 2: Animal Rehoming in a Post-Pandemic World

This co-created research project aimed to empower small organisations to respond more effectively to the reported "perfect storm" of increased demand versus decreased funding for their services (BBC, 2021). Seven students and two staff undertook pilot research to explore how these changing patterns of dog ownership/relinquishment and fundraising have impacted upon six local rescue/rehoming organisations and the communities of which they are part. Our starting point was that society extends beyond the human world. By exploring our relations with other species, we might help students adopt a more critical approach to sustainability, while also enabling them to use their developing consultancy skills to benefit the organisations and the people/animals they work with.

The project explored the underlying challenges from three different perspectives. First, we focused on the social and economic sustainability of the "business" of animal rescue through interviews with staff and volunteers. Second, through a range of innovative and collaborative research methods, we wanted to help students apply what they have learnt in the classroom to better understand and address organisations' actual sustainability challenges. Finally, we tried to consider those same challenges from an animal perspective, by focusing on welfare and caseloads.

### The Pandemic and Organisational Sustainability

Our literature review led us to anticipate that the pandemic and its aftermath would represent a major (possibly existential) threat to already overstretched animal welfare organisations. Our interviews revealed there had indeed been disruption. Lockdown restrictions prevented volunteers coming to clean kennels and walk the dogs, for example. There were also concerns about staff welfare and its impact on operations:

*"We were worried that…we've not got many staff. If two or three were knocked out with Covid we would have been in a mess."*

But we found surprisingly little impact on the financial bottom line, despite the inherently precarious economic situation of the organisations:

*"We're quite lucky in that we have a committee that keeps a firm eye on the finances," said one participant.*

This particular organisation (and others) noted that they kept afloat during and after Covid – as at other times – thanks to stable income from legacies. Thus, despite losing two income streams when its

## Sustainability Education Beyond the Classroom

town centre charity shop and onsite café were forced to close for several months, the organisation itself continued to function.

Non-financial donations also play a key role in keeping expenditure under control. And here, by contrast, it is the emerging cost-of-living crisis that is having a negative effect:

*"We've noticed...that we've been receiving less donations of animal food,"* observed one participant.

We were quickly realising that the very premise of our project needed to be revisited: If we wanted to help these organisations, we needed to recognise that the threat to their continued survival was not being caused by Covid and its aftermath, so much as the cost-of-living crisis that – ominously – had barely begun.

### Learning on the Ground and at the Kennels

With regards to pedagogy, students were able to try out and refine their practical research and consulting skills, bringing benefits to themselves and the participating organisations. Going out into the local community allowed students to gain valuable experience and witness the direct impact of their work. Importantly, they were paid for taking part: This enabled a wider range of students to participate, enabled them to dedicate more time to the project, but also unequivocally signalled that their involvement was valued:

*"It gave the project credibility...It felt like real paid work and not an academic exercise."*

This helped the project subvert traditional academic hierarchies:

*"We were all researchers, we weren't lecturers and students,"* said one member of the team. *"We were doing stuff that we loved so we were able to connect on that level...around our common values and interests."*

We posted links on WhatsApp to useful research and supported each other as we secured, carried out and wrote up field visits. But we also shared weekend plans, new-to-us memes and homemade videos of impossibly tiny terriers.

### A Dog-centred View of Sustainability

Our assumptions were quickly challenged again. We expected that animal welfare would be compromised by Covid and its aftermath. Certainly some dogs spent more time in kennels when adoptions ground to an abrupt halt. But many found themselves better off when people on furlough stepped in as temporary fosterers. In an unexpected but delightful turn of events, some of those dogs are still there, having now become part of the family.

Similarly, once kerbside and appointment-only visits enabled rehoming to open up, it became apparent that the dogs liked this model better. At one centre, a poster in reception explains to any disappointed visitors why animals were no longer on view:

*"We have noticed a marked improvement on our animals' stress levels...the animals are calmer...and get more quality time [with staff and volunteers]"*

Students realised that for this and other organisations, the animals always come first. Research visits took place in cramped kitchens as kibble was being measured out, or in the open air where we were handed a brush and invited to make ourselves useful. Some visits were cancelled as people just didn't have time to meet with us.

In terms of caseload more broadly, bigger rescues are experiencing (or anticipating) a sizable increase in relinquishment: The "new normal" is driving people back into offices and the rising cost of living means they have less money for pet food and vets' bills (Dogs Trust 2022). But, with their long experience of achieving so much with so little, our participants are quietly prepared for what the future may bring:

*"There's just an unrelenting flow of animals,"* said one. *"There always has been."*

## Initiative 3: Tree Planting in South Manchester

This brought together staff, students, their friends and families, along with Friends of Platt Fields and communities in south Manchester. Starting in the spring, about 40 people came along to community planting and watering days, in a shared effort to enhance the biodiversity of the local area and encourage students and others to spend more time outdoors. The initial project (2017-2021) was to plant 47 trees in honour of the late MP, Sir Gerald Kaufman, at different sites all around his constituency. The next stage of the tree planting initiative saw 73 trees – yew, beech and fruit trees – planted in Platt Fields, a 15-acre park close to the university campus, which provides valuable breathing space in the heart of Manchester's urban landscape. Now seeking funding for additional trees, the Staff Student Sustainability Group plans to run events at the start of each academic year to encourage future generations of students to get involved. We will briefly reflect on three key aspects of our shared experience, namely the way it brought people together, facilitated practical and higher order learning, and illuminated the challenges inherent to leading this kind of co-created initiative.

### Bringing Communities and Generations Together Through Shared Purpose

The first tree-planting session took place on a clear and crisp Saturday morning in March. Everyone met in the outdoor cafe at Platt Fields Market Garden. People wandered in, uncertainly at first, looking around for familiar faces:

*"I didn't recognise you with a pram in tow!"* said one academic happily flopping down next to a colleague.

*"I thought I must be in the wrong place,"* the other answered. *"I wasn't expecting so many people!"*

The clusters of staff, students and neighbours gradually intermingled, especially when the tools were handed out and we were invited to choose which of the hessian-overcoated saplings we would like to plant.

The event had gradually taken form in our collective minds during the isolation of the pandemic (Randles et al., forthcoming). But it built on relationships that were established long before. Sustainability-related efforts within the local community started 15 years ago, while those involving Manchester Met staff and students date back even further, perhaps 20 years (Christian & Walley, 2016; Kettleborough et al., 2018).

Three staff members brought their children with them, a neighbour brought her son, and a grandmother and granddaughter were among those excitedly choosing the best spot for their chosen tree. For the children, this was an opportunity to run around and get dirty. It was also a chance to do something practical to make their world a better place, rather than just listening to older people lamenting how badly things are going. With four generations gathered together, so we inched our way towards the "seventh generation principle" of the Haudenosaunee First Nation, which urges us to think of the future beyond even our great great grandchildren (Lyons, 2004). It was also a time to remember people who are no longer with us, or living in distant places: We dedicated yew trees to the people of Afghanistan, communities in Ukraine and to a colleague who had died very recently.

## Transformational Learning at Multiple Levels

This was practical learning in action. Students had been introduced to the United Nations SDGs in the classroom. Now they were being asked to combine their learning from academic journal articles with the learning of stories and the learning of simply living, in order to bring it altogether and put it into practice in everyday life. As we planted, people reflected on how trees provide a focal point for everyone using the park, not only the people but also birds, insects and other plants and shrubs, for whom the trees offer up shade in the summer and their leaves in the winter.

*"Have you heard of the Green Belt Movement?" one of the academics asks as we walk back towards the café.*

She tells us about Kenyan activist Wangari Maathai, who effectively pioneered the idea that we might make improve our world through the simple action of planting trees. This leads to an animated discussion of all the other tree-planting projects going on around the world at this very moment - in Pakistan, Saudi Arabia and elsewhere - and how they help us on our journey towards meeting the SDGs. Here in the UK, we have much to learn from initiatives all around the planet.

The trees also help us learn about place. Most of our students' learning happens within the sterile environment of the business school. Today they are outside. They have to consider where to plant the trees so they won't be accidentally crushed by council mowers. They have to work out how best to dig a hole in long grass, gently putting the sapling in, filling with soil and stamping down. Then we must cover them with bark chippings to retain moisture for the roots. The chippings are fetched in from some distance away, balanced precariously on a hefty wheelbarrow.

## Transformative Leadership Requires Time and Attention to Detail

The success of the event demanded leadership and negotiation on all sides. The Friends of Platt Fields is a totally voluntary organisation, and its members had to source the trees (70 plus on this particular day) and bring spades and wheelbarrows to the event. The volunteers and staff members worked together on the health and safety audit for the event. So many people gave freely of their time, in effect reciprocating what Irish theologian Anne Primavesi (2013) describes as "Gaia's Gifts" to humanity.

Within Manchester Met, the initiative was led by a group of female staff. With its emphasis on mutual support and engaging students and communities, this represented an important and visible model of collaborative leadership. It was an example of the kind of solidarity needed to genuinely address our multidisciplinary challenges together (UNDP, 2022).

In our euphoria, we did not pay sufficient attention to the effects of climate change. That summer saw the hottest temperatures ever recorded in the UK (Booth & Abdul, 2022). It was a month later that we came together again, trudging across the park with bottles and makeshift containers. Members of the local community continue to water the trees as often as they can during dry spells. We will plant more later in the year when we hope to have children from our local school with us. And this time we will plant the trees in the autumn: Our hope is that Gaia herself will keep them safe and watered, watching over them for future generations both human and more-than-human.

Table 2 summarises our findings, in order to set the scene for the discussion that follows below.

*Table 2. Summary of findings*

| Initiatives and Their Value From an ESD Perspective | Key Themes Identified Within the Data |
|---|---|
| 1 Action for Sustainability Festival Platform for students & others to build shared knowledge of underlying sustainability challenges, and identify ways they might help contribute to ongoing efforts to overcome them | Connecting & galvanising people<br>• Interconnectedness of diverse groups & initiatives<br>• Focus on celebrating small but important successes<br>• Emotional & immersive complement to theoretical & online efforts<br><br>Organic approaches bring joys & risks<br>• Diversity of views & experiences complements classroom learning<br>• Intergenerational learning reverses hierarchies<br>• Presence of artists & animals encourages spontaneity<br><br>Taking up space<br>• Learning takes places in formal spaces & "around the edges"<br>• Posters enable distant people to participate also |
| 2 Animal Rehoming in a Post-Pandemic World Consultancy with rehoming organisations opens up a critical & more-than-human understanding of sustainability. Also enables students to play practical role in supporting charities & people/animals they work with. | Pandemic reveals organisational vulnerability but also resilience<br>• Lockdown disrupted care of animals but less impact than expected on financial bottom-line<br>• Greater threat to organisations comes from cost-of-living crisis<br><br>Learning on the ground & in the kennels<br>• Paying students enabled wider participation & signalled that their role was valued<br>• Unconventional approach subverted academic hierarchies & built warmer relationships<br><br>A dog-centred view of sustainability<br>• Students saw animals being prioritised within organisations & research process |
| 3 Tree Planting in South Manchester Staff, students, friends, families, & local communities came together to plant & water trees in Platt Fields park. Focus on enhancing biodiversity & spending time together outdoors. | Communities & generations brought together through shared purpose<br>• People arrived separately but join together on practical tasks<br>• Event was more than a year in the making, but also depended on relationships established over many years<br>• Wide range of ages & backgrounds gathered together<br><br>Learning takes place at multiple levels<br>• Practical learning focuses on the trees in front of us but ties us in to wider global conversation<br>• Trees also help us learn about place & biodiversity<br><br>Transformative leadership requires time & attention to detail<br>• Even a comparatively small event requires tools & extensive paperwork<br>• Female staff team offered an important & visible model of collaborative leadership in action for our students & others |

## DISCUSSION

How did the three initiatives outlined above enable our students to engage critically with the contested concept of sustainability? And, perhaps more positively, how did these initiatives enable them to come together with others to actively imagine a more liveable future at both local and global scales? In the following discussion, we will address these questions by drawing on the theoretical framework developed earlier in the chapter. That is, we will consider how the Action for Sustainability Festival, research project on animal rehoming, and community tree-planting enabled us to "explode" our sustainability teaching into the local community. We will also reflect on some of the consequences for staff, students and communities, and our collective understanding of ESD more broadly. We do so via a focus on three themes that emerged throughout, namely relationality, hierarchy, and scaling up.

### Sustainability Is about Everyday Relationality as Much as Extraordinary Technological Solutions

The scale of the challenges that confront us lead to a tendency to focus on sustainability as a series of technical fixes, big dreams and grand schemes (Longo et al., 2016; Taylor, 2021) Yet, as Moore (2015, p. 899) reminds us, "the substance of the ordinary and everyday" is as useful to our analysis as "the epic, the extraordinary or the catastrophic." The "fresh educational techniques" that we adopted (Ward & Fyson, 1973) centred these matters of concern and encouraged us to engage with others. Even fifty years ago, the use of simulations, off-site work, playful engagement and so on were often neither technologically innovative nor complex. Rather, they are simple (if time-consuming) approaches. However, by enabling us to build our relationships to each other and the world around us, such techniques can effectively change our perceptions of both.

Unlike the abstract thinking that is the privilege of academic practice, then, the concrete things about which people care are situated in the day-to-day (Sayer, 2011). Thus the three initiatives outlined in our findings captured the imagination of our students and others precisely because they resonated with their own everyday matters of concern. They thereby galvanised the students into action and enabled them to deepen their understanding of the SDGs and associated academic concepts in a way that was meaningful to them.

The exploding university effectively foregrounds these matters of concern, whether that is supporting a friend under threat of eviction, caring for a family member who is taken ill, or seeing trees being cut down to make way for new buildings or a cycle way. It thus helps build our relationships and networks with others who share our interests (Blay-Palmer et al., 2013). Crucially, by serving as an intermediary in bringing us together over what really matters to us, the exploding university helps us maintain these relations over time. For example, Johnathon Porritt's relationship with Manchester Met goes back to 2014, when he officially launched our Social and Ethical Enterprise Group. The legacy of that visit has continued: Jonathon's work is required reading for final-year Business Management undergraduates and a shelf in the west wing of the library is turned bright yellow by a dozen copies of his inspirational but out-of-print book "The world we made."

Through such relationships, we can effectively shift our understanding of many different challenges. In turn, from the perspective of the exploding university itself, its ties to communities and other actors become part - over time - of what the organisation does but also what it *is*. Our focus on the exploding university thus indicates that Manchester Met can be a flourishing institution, a true community of peoples rather than a closed system. As Capra and Luisi (2016) and Sterling (2021) argue, the university should be an open system where "co-evolutionary interactions" and "living networks" can thrive, enabling us to address the system failures and wicked problems discussed earlier in the chapter.

## The Exploding University Collapses Hierarchies and Barriers

We began our chapter by highlighting that sustainability tends to privilege top-down approaches (Dymitrow & Halfacree, 2018; Kayumova & Tippins, 2021). That is, as a universalising concept, it disallows for differences in culture, geography and socioeconomic circumstances (Chassagne, 2018). Similarly, ESD – like any institutionalised form of education – is infused with power relations that tend to reproduce hegemonic and often problematic values, such as prioritising human needs above all else, or emphasising individual over collective responsibility (Kopnina, 2015). This feels uncomfortably close to Ward and Fyson's (1973) long-ago critique that curriculum-based approaches can effectively discourage people from educating themselves. Similarly, schools (or in our case universities) are imagined as expensive structures for containing these sanctioned forms of education, which are in turn delivered by special people licensed to accomplish this process.

In contrast, by exploding beyond the classroom, whether we mean to or not, we collapse the academic hierarchy in all its forms. Student, teacher and local resident alike come together, joyfully recreating a colourful painting, sharing thoughts about how dogs experience life on the streets, or wheeling a squeaky barrow across the park. We are learning together sometimes without realising. This is education as a meaningful disturbance (Wahl, 2017). The lecturer herself can no longer hold tight to her specialist knowledge as though it represents an objective consensus view (Ward & Fyson, 1973). Rather, all participants share an "emotional contact" with our subject matter: Our understanding of the SDGs is brought to life as we make our first attempt at visible mending, or listen to a poem written just for us. Together, we are helping each other build the shared "know-how" and "know-why" that will be fundamental to our collective flourishing in future (Ravetz, 2020).

As regards where all this might unfold, Ward and Fyson (1973) suggest fieldwork should take place away from the school (university). We are sympathetic to their concern that we can be intimidated by these costly installations, in turn constraining our collective imaginings. Manchester Met's buildings dominate the local skyline, communicating our socio-cultural authority like the cathedrals of old (Campbell, 1988). However, things are of course more complex than this. Our Business School, for example, has won multiple awards for its sustainable design. Yet even our own students are sometimes unaware of this, confounded by its austere grey walls and lack of greenery. By working with people who might otherwise take our imposing demeanour at face value, or who have perhaps never set foot in a university at all, we might bring the institution – and what it represents – down to a more human scale. In other words, we can help revise our mental maps of who we are and create a transformative process that really enables people to shift the way that they see their role and their future, both inside and outside of the institution (Wahl, 2017). The festival in particular demonstrated that an effective way of breaking down barriers is not just to go *out* (as Ward and Fyson suggest), but to invite people *in*, bringing the institution alive through living, dynamic networks and communities of practice (Capra & Luisi, 2016).

## The Exploding University Embeds the Local in the Global

By exploding ESD beyond the university, staff, students and communities worked together to effectively explore the relationship between the "personal troubles of the milieu" and the "public issues of social structure," which lie at the heart of all social research (Wright Mills, 1959, p. 8). Through our action research-inspired approach, our students were invited to place their own matters of concern within a wider context, and take practical steps to articulate and address them. First, in class, we introduced students to the SDGs and the global policy framework for sustainability. Then we explored their own matters of concern through our initial project to develop a theoretical model of transformative learning, communities and leadership (Randles et al., forthcoming). From this, we developed the three projects outlined here (and others), which the students played a key role in shaping and implementing. Finally, back in the classroom – and in the writing of this chapter and other outputs – we reflected together on the wider significance of our collective endeavours. Across this process, then, we enable students to effectively track back and forth between the global and the local.

In so doing, according to Ward and Fyson (1973), we enable students to absorb from the experience the things that are meaningful and interesting to *them*. This in turn awakens participants to alternative possibilities and enables them to communicate those alternatives. We can only imagine what we have seen, so this concrete action and modelling is important for students and communities alike, as it enables people to reimagine and articulate what a more liveable future might look like (Tsing, 2017). By basing our interventions around what matters to the students and communities themselves, we are effectively heeding Ward and Fyson's invocation that we plan *for* not *against*. By bringing people together to take practical action on things about which they care, our approach is thus based on an appreciation of the positive core of what works (Cooperrider & Godwin, 2022). This perhaps contrasts with a prevailing (and less galvanising) focus on deficiency, which can often characterise our collective discussions about sustainability.

We started our chapter by stating that, like many in this field, we have a particular interest in the dichotomy between top-down and bottom-up approaches. Like Murphy (2012) quoted above, Monbiot (2022) is doubtful about the power of this kind of small-scale action for change:

*Incrementalism is too small an ask…to drive transformation…Only a demand for system change, directly confronting the power driving us to planetary destruction, has the potential to match the scale of the problem and to inspire and mobilise the millions of people required to generate effective action.*

Monbiot is right that small changes alone won't save the world. And, of course, we are not denying the need for structural, system-level change. But we take comfort from Ward's anarchism, which suggests that the prevailing global order that is ravaging our natural and social worlds is not a "thing" to be overthrown. Rather, it is a "condition," a particular relationship between human beings: We destroy it by behaving differently, by reinventing daily life in the here and now (Ward, 2004). Teachers and learners have to believe that we can help bring about that change because hopelessness is not an acceptable academic position: As Deutsch (2011, p. 446) eloquently reminds us "no one is creative in fields in which they are pessimistic." Rather, as students and academics, we believe that are working for a new form of action that will transform learning, communities and leadership alike.

## TENTATIVE CONCLUSIONS AND AN INVITATION TO ACTION

Inspired by a critical approach to the UN SDGs, our chapter has developed the theoretical concept of the "exploding university," reflecting on how such an approach might enrich the understanding and practice of sustainability for students, staff and communities. Through a focus on three related initiatives, we have reflected on our own experience, and how it built our collective intelligence, enabling us to become capable of deeper learning and address our varied matters of concern. Collective intelligence encourages us to consciously reflect, care-for, nurture and put into practice through positive action our relationships with each other and - by extension – with all of these communities. It is a slow and purposeful process because it takes time to nourish these relationships, and fully experience and care for them. They unfold across multiple sites and in multiple individual moments, combining the urgency of the present with the imperative of long-term time horizons, and guardianship across and within each of our cases. In these and other multiple examples across the world, we see people coming together, transforming their communities by putting sustainability into action. In this final section, we will first reflect on our contribution to theory. We will then share some practical lessons that may help others explode their own organic, non-hierarchical and enduring approaches beyond the classroom.

### Contribution to Knowledge

Ward and Fyson's (1973) book proposes that we can empower the next generation to become agents for change within the community by taking them outside the classroom and giving them concrete opportunities to actively critique, re-imagine and reconstruct the world around them. We have expanded the reach of this work by illuminating its usefulness within the higher education context, specifically within the framework of ESD. In so doing, we have also demonstrated the value of recognising that the "exploding" metaphor is found well beyond the confines of the human world within nature itself: By bringing Ward's ideas into conversation with those of Lovelock and other ecological thinkers, we have demonstrated that our efforts as students, staff and communities are in turn embedded and interconnected with the natural-social world around us. In so doing, we have also provided an empirical extension of our own theoretical ideas about the integrated nature of transformative learning, communities and leadership (Randles et al., forthcoming): Our chapter demonstrates that hope work and the exploding university depend in turn upon commitment and relationships of trust.

Our chapter has also illuminated how the success and reach of important top-down initiatives such as the Principles for Responsible Management Education (UN PRME) and the Civic University Network depends crucially upon our ability to effectively ground them within the everyday cares and concerns of students, staff and communities. As our analysis has ranged back and forth across global and local levels, so we have foregrounded the relationships that are crucial to developing collective intelligence, and reflected on how these might be reconfigured in ways that subvert prevailing power relationships within and beyond the classroom. These three themes also inform our practical suggestions below.

## Practical Lessons That Might Be Useful to Others

### 1. Relationality Takes Time: Embrace It

Exploding our teaching beyond the classroom requires time and effort. Rooted in care and caring, the temporal scales involved in our relational, reflective and experiential approach clearly contrast with the ever-faster pace of university life (Stengers, 2018; Taylor, 2020). We do not wish to downplay the extraordinary pressures that we are all under. And we agree with Barnett (2018) that the "feasible utopia" of a more embedded and forward-thinking university is needed most urgently at the precise moment when it is most in peril. Yet we take heart from Ward's (2004, p. 8) idea that change depends – somewhat prosaically – on "contracting other relationships [and] behaving differently." We are *already* making a difference just by doing what we do. So, our advice to others is simply to keep the faith: Even if the gains seem small now, over time they will add up.

### 2. Ceding Control Leads to Unpredicted (and Sometimes Useful) Outcomes: Be Ready

We acknowledge that our approach can be risky: By exploding outwards, we engage with a range of people and issues, and effectively cede our control of both the wider agenda and how specific encounters might unfold. At the festival, for example, a representative of Extinction Rebellion joined in a session about greenwashing, and asked some uncomfortable questions about how the university aligned its own messaging and actions. But if we play it safe, we risk meeting with what Ward and Fyson (1973, pp. 22) call the "same boredom and indifference that [we hope] to overcome." Their suggestion is that – before embarking on this approach – we should find allies among our colleagues. We would add that some of these should include people with leadership roles across the organisation: The risks of discomfort and censure will diminish considerably if there is high-level buy-in to the countervailing and longer-term benefits.

### 3. Global Ambition Through Local Action: Think Big and Small at Once

Ward and Fyson (1973, p. 11) suggest that educators (and others) worry that a focus on local issues may be considered parochial, in that "this particular sample of reality may [be seen to] lack any general significance." At the same time, they highlight that people – of whatever age – find it hard to engage with big issues that are presented to them at an "inhuman" scale. This is reminiscent of Taylor's (2020, p. 255) emphasis on the "slow singularities" that underpin "collective mattering." Ward and Fyson (1973, p. 11) recommend that we counter potential parochialism by developing "carefully balanced courses [and] syllabuses." The key here is making a clear and explicit link between our on-the-ground work with students and communities, the wider global sustainability agenda (SDGs, PRME) and our own institution's strategic efforts to deliver on them. Our recommendation to others, then, is that you consider how to "plan *for* not against" within your own institution: How can you frame what you are doing within these university-level and global frameworks? In so doing, the matters of concern arising within informal and participatory processes can be brought into conversation with – and potentially help shape – more formal, objectives within your own institution and far beyond.

To conclude, this chapter has offered up and developed the concept of the exploding university as a way to build the collective intelligence that might help us understand and tackle contemporary wicked problems. We recognise that such challenges – social injustice, migration, biodiversity loss and the climate emergency – require structural and system changes. But, in the meantime, we can build mutual understanding of their myriad iterations and seek out interim-if-imperfect solutions. Imagined as seeds of constructive action and dedicated work, impelled by an outpouring of energy, care and positive ideas, students, staff and communities themselves can begin to take our own small and tentative steps towards imagining and building a better world in the future but also in the here and now.

## ACKNOWLEDGMENT

We would like to thank all the people who took part in the initiatives on which this research is based, and who generously shared their time, energy and ideas with us.

## REFERENCES

Akrivou, K., & Bradbury-Huang, H. (2015). Educating integrated catalysts: Transforming business schools toward ethics and sustainability. *Academy of Management Learning & Education*, *14*(2), 222–240. doi:10.5465/amle.2012.0343

Astin, A. W., & Astin, H. S. (2000). *Leadership reconsidered: Engaging higher education in social change*. The Kellogg Foundation.

Baldwin, M. (2001). Working together, learning together, co-operative inquiry in the development of complex practice by teams of social workers. In P. Reason & H. Bradbury (Eds.), *The Sage handbook of action research* (pp. 287–293). Sage.

Barnett, R. (2011). The coming of the ecological university. *Oxford Review of Education*, *37*(4), 439–455. doi:10.1080/03054985.2011.595550

Barnett, R. (2018). *The ecological university. A feasible utopia*. Routledge.

Black, A. L. (2018). Responding to longings for slow scholarship: Writing ourselves into being. In A. Black & S. Garvis (Eds.), *Women activating agency in academia: Metaphors, manifestos and memoir* (pp. 23–34). Routledge. doi:10.4324/9781315147451-3

Black, A. L., Crimmins, G., & Jones, J. K. (2017). Reducing the drag: Creating v formations through slow scholarship and story. In S. Riddle, M. Harmes, & P. A. Danaher (Eds.), *Producing pleasure in the contemporary university*. Sense. doi:10.1007/978-94-6351-179-7_11

Blay-Palmer, A., Landman, K., Knezevic, I., & Hayhurst, R. (2013). Constructing resilient transformative communities through sustainable food hubs. *Local Environment*, *18*(5), 521–528. doi:10.1080/13549839.2013.797156

Booth, R., & Abdul, G. (2022, July 19). UK reaches hottest ever temperature as 40.2C recorded at Heathrow. *The Guardian*. https://www.theguardian.com/uk-news/2022/jul/19/uk-weather-record-hottest-day-ever-heatwave

British Broadcasting Corporation (BBC). (2021, September 10). *More people trying to give up their lockdown dogs, says charity*. https://www.bbc.co.uk/news/uk-58518892

Burke, C. (2014). Fleeting pockets of anarchy. Streetwork. The exploding school. *Paedagogica Historica*, *50*(4), 433–442. doi:10.1080/00309230.2014.899376

Campbell, J. (1988). *The power of myth*. Random House.

Capra, F., & Luisi, P. L. (2016). *A systems view of life: A unifying vision*. Cambridge University Press.

Chassagne, N. (2018). Sustaining the good life: Buen vivir as an alternative to sustainable development. *Community Development Journal: An International Forum*, *54*(3), 482–500. doi:10.1093/cdj/bsx062

Christian, J., & Walley, L. (2016). Termite tales: Organisational change – A personal view of sustainable development in a university – As seen from the "tunnels.". In W. Leal Filho, L. Brandli, O. Kuznetsova, & A. Paco (Eds.), *Integrative approaches to sustainable development at university level* (pp. 525–538). Springer.

Cooperrider, D., & Godwin, L. (2022). Strengths-based megacommunities and the appreciative inquiry's complete convention: Creating wholepower, willpower and waypower for our world's Earthshot moment. *AI Practitioner*, *24*(1), 94–106. doi:10.12781/978-1-907549-50-2-8

Dogs Trust. (2022, July 14). *Cost-of-living crisis starts to bite dog owners, shows new poll*. https://www.dogstrust.org.uk/latest/2022/dogs-trust-cost-of-living

Duncan, G. (2015). Innovations in appreciative inquiry: Critical appreciative inquiry with excluded Pakistani women. In P. Reason & H. Bradbury (Eds.), *The Sage handbook of action research* (pp. 107–123). Sage. doi:10.4135/9781473921290.n6

Dymitrow, M., & Halfacree, K. (2018). Sustainability – differently. *Bulletin of Geography. Socio-Economic Series*, *40*(40), 7–16. doi:10.2478/bog-2018-0011

Guimon, J., & Narula, R. (2020, April 22) A happy exception: The pandemic is driving global scientific collaboration. *Issues in Science and Technology*. https://ingsa.org/covidtag/covid-19-commentary/guimon-collaboration/

Haddock-Fraser, J., Rands, P., & Scoffham, S. (2018). *Leadership for sustainability in higher education*. Bloomsbury Publishing.

Institute of Student Employers (ISE). (2022). *ISE Development Survey*. https://ise.org.uk/page/ise-development-survey-22

Kayumova, S., & Tippins, D. J. (2021). The quest for sustainable futures: Designing transformative learning spaces with multilingual black, brown, and Latinx young people through critical response-ability. *Cultural Studies of Science Education*, *16*(3), 821–839. doi:10.100711422-021-10030-2 PMID:34484464

Kettleborough, H. (2019). Gaia's graveyards: Bearing witness as first-person inquiry. *Action Research Journal*, *17*(3), 292–322.

Kopnina, H. (2015). Neoliberalism, pluralism and environmental education: The call for radical re-orientation. *Environmental Development*, *15*, 120–130. doi:10.1016/j.envdev.2015.03.005

Kurio, J., & Reason, P. (2021). Voicing rivers through ontopoetics: A co-operative inquiry. *River Research and Applications*, *38*(3), 376–384. doi:10.1002/rra.3817

Lawson, D., Stevenson, K. T., Peterson, M. M., Carrier, S. J., Strnad, R., & Seekampa, E. (2018). Intergenerational learning: Are children key in spurring climate action? *Global Environmental Change*, *53*, 204–208. doi:10.1016/j.gloenvcha.2018.10.002

Lewis, N., & Shore, C. (2019). From unbundling to market making: Reimagining, reassembling and reinventing the public university. *Globalisation, Societies and Education*, *17*(1), 11–27. doi:10.1080/14767724.2018.1524287

Longo, S., Clark, B., Shriver, T., & Clausen, R. (2016). Sustainability and environmental sociology: Putting the economy in its place and moving toward an integrative socio-ecology. *Journal of Sustainability*, *8*(5), 437–454. doi:10.3390u8050437

Lovelock, J. (1995). *The ages of Gaia: A biography of our living earth*. Norton.

Lyons, O. (2004). *The ice is melting* [Paper presentation]. 24th Annual E. F. Schumacher lectures. https://centerforneweconomics.org/publications/the-ice-is-melting/

Maughan, E., & Reason, P. (2001). A co-operative inquiry into deep ecology. *ReVision*, *23*(4), 18–24.

Mazon, G., Pereira Ribeiro, J. M., Montenegro de Lima, C. R., Castro, B. C. G., & Guerra, J. B. (2020). The promotion of sustainable development in higher education institutions: Top-down bottom-up or neither? *International Journal of Sustainability in Higher Education*, *21*(7), 1429–1450. doi:10.1108/IJSHE-02-2020-0061

Monbiot, G. (2022, July 18). Heatwave extreme weather climate crisis. *The Guardian*. https://www.theguardian.com/commentisfree/2022/jul/18/heatwave-extreme-weather-uk-climate-crisis

Moore, L. (2015). A day at the beach: Rising sea levels, horseshoe crabs, and traffic jams. *Sociology*, *49*(5), 886–902. doi:10.1177/0038038515573474

Murphy, R. (2012). Sustainability: A wicked problem. *Sociologica*, *2*, 1–23.

Nilsson, W. (2015). Positive institutional work: Exploring institutional work through the lens of positive organizational scholarship. *Academy of Management Review*, *40*(3), 370–398. doi:10.5465/amr.2013.0188

Primavesi, A. (2013). *Exploring earthiness*. Cascade Books.

Randles, S., Wadham, H., Skritsovali, K., Hart, C., Hoque, S., Kettleborough, H., Klapper, R., Marron, R., Taylor, T., & Walley, L. (forthcoming). Leveraging hope & experience: Towards an integrated model of transformative learning, community & leadership for sustainability action & change. In W. Purcell & J. Haddock-Fraser (Eds.), The Bloomsbury handbook of sustainability in higher education. London: Bloomsbury.

Rappaport, J. (2020). *Cowards don't make history: Orlando Fals Borda and the origins of participatory action research.* Duke University Press.

Ravetz, J. (2020). *Deeper city: Collective intelligence and the pathways from smart to wise.* Routledge. doi:10.4324/9781315765860

Reason, P., & Bradbury, H. (Eds.). (2001). *The Sage handbook of action research.* Sage.

Rittel, H., & Webber, M. (1973). Dilemmas in a general theory of planning. *Policy Sciences, 2*(2), 155–169. doi:10.1007/BF01405730

Roy, A. (2020, April 3). The pandemic is a portal. *Financial Times.* https://www.ft.com/content/10d8f5e8-74eb-11ea-95fe-fcd274e920ca

Sandel, M. (2012). *What money can't buy: The moral limits of markets.* Allen Lane.

Sayer, A. (2011). *Why things matter to people: Social sciences, values and ethical life.* Cambridge University Press. doi:10.1017/CBO9780511734779

Sediri, S., Trommetter, M., Frascaria-Lacoste, N., & Fernandez-Manjarrés, J. (2020). Transformability as a wicked problem: A cautionary tale? *Sustainability, 12*(15), 5895. doi:10.3390u12155895

Shields, C. (2020). Transformative leadership. *Oxford research encyclopedia of education.* https://oxfordre.com/education/view/10.1093/acrefore/9780190264093.001.0001/acrefore-9780190264093-e-632

Shields, C. M. (2011). Transformative leadership: An introduction. In C. M. Shields (Ed.), *Transformative leadership: A reader.* Peter Lang.

Shields, C. M. (2017). *Transformative leadership in education: Equitable and socially just change in an uncertain and complex world.* Routledge. doi:10.4324/9781315207148

Simon, E., Dormer, K., & Hartshorne, J. (1971). *Lowson's textbook of botany.* University Tutorial Press.

Southern, N. (2007). Mentoring for transformative learning: The importance of relationship in creating learning communities of care. *Journal of Transformative Education, 5*(4), 329–338. doi:10.1177/1541344607310576

Souza, D. T., Jacobi, P. R., & Wal, A. E. J. (2019). Learning based transformations towards sustainability: A relational approach based on Humberto Maturna and Paulo Freire. *Environmental Education Research, 25*(11), 1605–1619. doi:10.1080/13504622.2019.1641183

Stengers, I. (2018). *Another science is possible: A manifesto for slow science.* Polity.

Sterling, S. (2021). Concern, conception, and consequence: Re-thinking the paradigm of higher education in dangerous times. *Frontiers in Sustainability, 2,* 743806. doi:10.3389/frsus.2021.743806

Taylor, C. (2020). Slow singularities for collective mattering: New material feminist praxis in the accelerated academy. *Irish Educational Studies, 39*(2), 255–272. doi:10.1080/03323315.2020.1734045

Taylor, D. (2021). On damaged and regenerating life: Spinoza and mentalities of climate catastrophe. *Crisis and Critique*, *8*(1), 476–501.

Taylor, E. W. (2008). Transformative learning theory. *New Directions for Adult and Continuing Education*, *2008*(119), 5–15. doi:10.1002/ace.301

Tsing, A. (2017). A threat to holocene resurgence is a threat to liveability. In M. Brightman & J. Lewis (Eds.), *The anthropology of sustainability* (pp. 51–65). Palgrave. doi:10.1057/978-1-137-56636-2_3

United Nations (UN). (2021, July 15). *Deeply negative impact of COVID pandemic, reverses SDG progress*. https://news.un.org/en/story/2021/07/1095942

Wadham, H. (2020). Horse matters: Re-examining sustainability through human-domestic animal relationships. *Sociologia Ruralis*, *60*(3), 530–550. doi:10.1111oru.12293

Wahl, D. C. (2017). *Regeneration: A webinar with Fritjof Capra, Simon Robinson and Daniel Christian Wahl*. https://www.youtube.com/watch?v=DU699CwJiv4&ab_channel=Simon Robins

Ward, C. (1973). *Anarchy in action*. Freedom Press.

Ward, C. (2004). *Anarchism: A very short introduction*. Oxford University Press. doi:10.1093/actrade/9780192804778.001.0001

Ward, C., & Fyson, A. (1973). *Streetwork: The exploding school*. Routledge.

Washington, H. (2015). *Demystifying sustainability: Towards real solutions*. Routledge. doi:10.4324/9781315748641

Wegener, D. T., & Petty, R. E. (1994). Mood management across affective states: The hedonic contingency hypothesis. *Journal of Personality and Social Psychology*, *66*(6), 1034–1048. doi:10.1037/0022-3514.66.6.1034 PMID:8046576

Whelan, A., Walker, R., & Moore, C. (2013). *Zombies in the academy: Living death in higher education*. Intellect Books.

Whitehead, A. N. (1938/1968). *Modes of thought*. Free Press.

Wilbert, C., & White, D. (2011). *Autonomy solidarity possibility: The Colin Ward reader*. AK Press.

Wright Mills, C. (1959/2000). *The sociological imagination*. Oxford University Press.

Yorks, L., Arnold, A., James, L., Rees, A., Hoffman-Pinilla, H., & Ospina, S. (2008). *The tapestry of leadership: lessons from six co-operative inquiry groups of social justice leaders*.

## ADDITIONAL READING

Barnett, R. (2011). The coming of the ecological university. *Oxford Review of Education*, *37*(4), 439–455. doi:10.1080/03054985.2011.595550

Black, A. L. (2018). Responding to longings for slow scholarship: Writing ourselves into being. In A. Black & S. Garvis (Eds.), *Women activating agency in academia: Metaphors, manifestos and memoir* (pp. 23–34). Routledge. doi:10.4324/9781315147451-3

Haddock-Fraser, J., Rands, P., & Scoffham, S. (2018). *Leadership for sustainability in higher education.* Bloomsbury Publishing.

Kettleborough, H. (2019). Gaia's graveyards: Bearing witness as first-person inquiry. *Action Research Journal, 17*(3), 292–322.

Lovelock, J. (1995). *The ages of Gaia: A biography of our living earth.* Norton.

Ravetz, J. (2020). *Deeper city: Collective intelligence and the pathways from smart to wise.* Routledge. doi:10.4324/9781315765860

Sayer, A. (2011). *Why things matter to people: Social sciences, values and ethical life.* Cambridge University Press. doi:10.1017/CBO9780511734779

## KEY TERMS AND DEFINITIONS

**Action Research:** A dynamic, evolving, and reflective research methodology that develops practical knowing and pursues solutions to issues that matter to people.

**Collaborative Approaches:** A diversity of actions and techniques that enable people to work together, by capitalising on their diverse talents and supporting a shared purpose.

**Ecological University:** A higher education institution that aims to make the world a better place by recognising its interconnectedness with the outside world and using its resources to create a more sustainable future. The concept was developed by Ronald Barnett.

**Education for Sustainable Development (ESD):** An approach to education that focuses on bringing global challenges such as climate change, economic inequality and biodiversity decline into teaching and learning. It requires participatory approaches and far-reaching changes to the curriculum.

**Participatory Research:** Research strategies that explicitly and actively aim to include local communities and others within the research process. Such approaches subvert the power relations that are inherent to the experience and practice of research.

**Slow Science:** Like other manifestations of the broader slow movement, this advocates a steady, thoughtful, and more measured approach to academic research. Proponents are critical of the encroachment of neoliberal practices and values within academia, such as performance and funding targets.

**Systemic Change:** Global or societal transformation that demands far-reaching changes to policies, practices, power relations and social norms. This in turn depends upon collaboration between a wide range of local, national, and international stakeholders.

**Transformative Learning:** An approach to education that invites us to consider who we are in relation to others and to pursue positive change on behalf of these known and unknown others. Focused on shared sense-making and practical action, it requires us to build relations of mutual trust, truth, values and understanding.

# Chapter 11
# Tackling the Challenges Posed by Linguistic and Cultural Diversity in EFL Classrooms

**Akin Gurbuz**
https://orcid.org/0000-0003-4868-5152
*Mugla Sitki Kocman University, Turkey*

**Rana Yildirim**
https://orcid.org/0000-0002-9959-6769
*Çukurova University, Turkey*

## ABSTRACT

*One of the main purposes of multicultural education is to approach all individuals at an equal distance in educational environments, provide a sense of belonging by ensuring unity and integrity, and eliminate the gap in academic achievement among diverse groups by ensuring equal opportunities for all. In this regard, the present study intends to contribute to the existing research by providing a rich amount of evidence as to the challenges posed by linguistic and cultural diversity, and the strategies employed by the instructors to effectively overcome those challenges. The data of the study were collected through video-stimulated interviews with four instructors and semi-structured interviews with 20 lecturers. The study revealed that the EFL instructors most frequently experienced challenges in regards to language and communication, and they developed numerous strategies to overcome these challenges. Considering the research process and its results, the current research study provided various pedagogical implications and suggestions for the main stakeholders of education.*

## INTRODUCTION

Based on the standards found in the Council of Europe's Common European Framework of Reference for Languages (2001), scholars underline the fact that teachers need to be equipped with the necessary skills to create an environment of curiosity and inquiry and guide learners toward building a multicul-

DOI: 10.4018/978-1-6684-6172-3.ch011

## Tackling the Challenges Posed by Linguistic and Cultural Diversity in EFL Classrooms

tural mindset due to the ever-changing nature and force of culture (Byram, Gribkova, & Starkey, 2002). Attitudes toward linguistic and cultural diversity need to be considered in the classroom context and teachers have a leading role in the transformation of this context. Concerning the changing landscape of educational institutions, there is ample unanimity among numerous scholars that it has been essential for teaching professionals to acquire the necessary skills and competencies to address the needs of diverse populations effectively (e.g. Ameny-Dixon, 2004; Kucuktas, 2016; Marina, 2004; Miranda, 2002; Pratt-Johnson, 2006; Yang & Montgomery, 2011).

Due to the political and social instability beyond its borders, the population of immigrants and refugees in Turkey has reached a vast number. The United Nations International Migrant Stock report indicates that this number reached around 6 million by 2019, and it has been increasing constantly. According to the United Nations Department of Economic and Social Affairs (UNDESA) report, the rate of refugee population growth in the world has exceeded the general population growth. The report further indicates that the number of migrants and refugees, which was 221 million in 2010, reached 272 million in 2019. On the other hand, while international immigrants comprised only 2.2% of the total share of the population in 1990 in Turkey, it rose to 7% by 2019. The cultural and linguistic mobility within the populations of the countries around the world is bound to sustain henceforward.

*Figure 1. The number of international students in tertiary education in Turkey (2013-2019)*

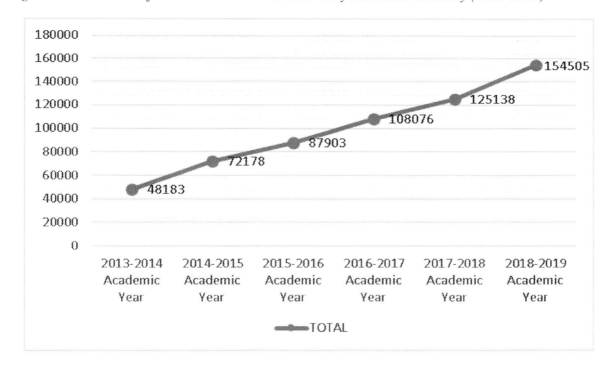

Deeming the population structure and the distribution of international populations in Turkey, a radical change has been monitored in the last decade (Republic of Turkey Ministry of Interior Directorate General of Migration Management, 2017). Accordingly, there has been a significant rise in the number of international students both in the earlier levels of National Education and in higher education institutions (the Council of Higher Education, 2019; Ministry of National Education, 2019). The number of students by nationality report submitted by the Council of Higher Education indicates a considerable rise in the population of international students in tertiary education in Turkey. The report illustrates that the diversity in tertiary education has tripled from about 50 thousand to over 150 thousand from 2013 to 2019 (see Chart 1). Due to the vast change in their populations and already-existing nationwide diversity, higher education institutions are bound to be reorganized and adapted to the doctrines of multicultural education.

Some higher education institutions in Europe have their strategies for the internationalization of higher education (e.g. the Ministry of Education in Finland, 2009) by actively taking part in supporting the multicultural higher education community and civil society. Villegas and Lucas (2002) point out that it is necessary to prepare tomorrow's teachers to be ready to deal responsibly with the needs of diverse student bodies and possible challenges raised by diversity in classrooms. In a similar line, Gay and Howard (2000) point out that teaching practitioners already working in the field and teacher candidates enrolled in education faculties will further be affected by the rising distribution of diverse students in schools in the future. The question at this point is to what extent teaching professionals are ready to teach students from diverse backgrounds. Another important question concerns the amount of research on multicultural education in Turkey and the provision needed for designing and implementing courses geared to improve the skills of teaching professionals to meet the challenges in diverse classrooms. Recent studies highlight the compelling need for the provision of multicultural teaching competencies in pre-service teacher education programs as a subject course (Aydın & Acar-Çiftçi, 2014; Aydın & Tonbuloğlu, 2014; Çoban, Karaman, & Dogan, 2010; Erbas, 2019; Kaya & Aydın, 2014; Ünlü & Örten, 2013; Yavuz & Anil, 2010). In line with this, Erbaş (2019) concludes that it is notable to introduce multicultural education into teacher education programs and encourage teachers to adopt its principles. He further suggests that teachers should be educated and/or trained and the number of studies on the issue needs to be increased. Likewise, concerning necessary acts for the realization of multicultural education, Aydın and Acar-Çiftçi (2014) suggest that there is a need for legal regulations, the inclusion of courses on multicultural education in teacher education programs, and the provision of in-service training programs for teaching professionals.

With the motive to address the gap in the literature, this study has been conducted as part of a larger study that aimed to reveal the multicultural competences of English as a Foreign Language (EFL) instructors about the four dimensions of multicultural teaching competency, namely *awareness, knowledge, attitude,* and *skill*, the challenges experienced and the strategies used. In this sense, the initial focus of the present study is on EFL instructors' challenges posed by linguistic and cultural diversity in language classrooms, and the strategies they employ to tackle these challenges. In line with the purpose of the study, the following research questions guided the investigation:

- Do EFL instructors face any challenges due to the linguistic and cultural diversity in their language classrooms?
- What kinds of strategies do EFL instructors implement to overcome these challenges?

In this regard, the present study is significant as it aimed to extend the scope of the current literature and research on multicultural teaching competencies by providing a rich amount of evidence as to the challenges posed by cultural and linguistic diversity and the strategies employed by the instructors to face those challenges effectively. Furthermore, the research design of the study enabled the researchers to carry out an in-depth exploration of the problems the EFL instructors experience and the strategies they use by engaging in actual classroom practices through video-stimulated recall interviews and semi-structured interviews.

## BACKGROUND

The continuous and dynamic shift in demographic structures and population characteristics of countries has forced governments to make reforms in their policies to promote multiculturalism, and societies to adopt multicultural approaches in almost every scope of life (Grant & Khurshid, 2009; Sutton, 2005). Although multicultural education is a concept that is highly discussed with definitional differences across countries (Banks, 2009; Gundara, 2015), it is broadly described as socially just and equal education for all children who come from different cultural groups (Cha, Gundara, Ham & Lee, 2017). In this manner, the aim is to raise citizens of the future equipped with the necessary knowledge and skills, and able to live in a new form of a democratic society that embraces multiculturalism (Sutton, 2005).

To understand how multicultural education was inaugurated and influenced educational reforms, the historical foundations should be well understood. Gorski (1999) asserts that the history of multicultural education was commenced by civil rights movements that go back to the 1960s. The first movements were initiated by especially those African Americans who shook the United States of America to its core at the time (Davidman & Davidman, 1997). The United States is a highly integrated society which is accommodating populations from various nations in itself. However, as Patterson (2000) asserts, it has suffered from noticeable issues in eliminating discrimination in many aspects such as law, economics, and education. A cornerstone of the civil rights movement was 'Brown v. Board of Education which helped to authorize the precedent for 'separate-but-equal' education and endorse educational reforms to enhance equality among racial groups in schools (Sunstein, 2004). The Brown case prompted the schooling of African Americans and European Americans together in the same school environment (Patterson, 2000).

Bringing two racial groups together in a school environment launched attempts to change the curriculum, but it was soon realized that this physical togetherness was not adequate to decrease segregation. According to Gay (2004), the first initiative was very simplistic compared to today's perspective, yet it tried to enhance the representation of different ethnic and racial groups in instructional materials and content. However, there was a huge conflict even in this first attempt due to the diversity of the racial groups consisting of Asian Americans, Latinos, Natives, and African Americans (Gay, 2004) and each group's struggle to take its place in the curricula. This conflict resulted in the emergence of a race-specific educational model -the application of educational studies for each ethnic group (Gay, 1990).

Changes in curriculum and school context stimulated research on the effects of a multicultural school environment on students in various fields (Harring, 1992; Nishimura, 1995; Sue, Arredondo & McDavis, 1992). The result of these studies showed that the representation of different racial groups in school materials was even deepening segregation by implementing prejudicial thoughts and damaging the self-concepts and learning achievement of minorities (Gordy & Pritchard, 1995; Healey, 1974). This development further supported the enhancement of the curriculum to encourage a more positive approach and information in the educational content.

In a broad sense, multicultural teaching is regarded as an instructional pattern that calls for the inclusion of learners' cultural strengths in the curriculum (Gay, 2000; Ladson-Billings, 1992). The overall purpose of multicultural education is to create a homogenous class environment for all students from different cultural and ethnic backgrounds (Banks, 1995a). In this sense, Banks devised five dimensions of multicultural education which could also be used in teacher training programs: (a) *content integration* (b) *the knowledge construction process,* (c) *prejudice reduction,* (d) *equity pedagogy, and* (e) *empowering school culture and social structure* (p. 20).

The dimension of content integration refers to the usage of examples from different cultural contexts. In this way, key principles, theories, and concepts of the discipline could be illustrated. The knowledge construction dimension refers to classroom activities and teaching methods that teachers used to make students understand and question the assumptions, biases, and perspectives of cultures. Teachers also try to teach how these implicit essences of cultures affect the knowledge construction about those cultures (Banks, 1995a). In this way, it also aims to help students understand how knowledge about cultures is influenced by individuals' and groups' race and ethnicity (Collins, 1990).

Another indication of multicultural responsiveness is the reduction of prejudice and biases which suggests that teachers should help students from various cultural and linguistic backgrounds to improve their values and attitudes democratically. One of the important aspects of this dimension is that democratic values and attitude development interventions should start at an early age to obtain efficient results because it becomes harder to change students' misconceptions as they grow older (Banks, 1995b).

A further purpose of multicultural education is to increase the academic achievement level of students who have different ethnic and cultural backgrounds. In equity pedagogy, teachers are to reconsider their instructional methods in a way to enhance students' academic achievement. For this purpose, teachers should use the cultural and linguistic strengths of students in their teaching methods, especially for multicultural students and those who have low socioeconomic status. To effectively create equality among students, teachers are anticipated to be 'warm demanders' and have high expectations from their students no matter what social groups they belong to (Cohen & Lotan, 1995).

Despite the recent increase in theoretical research on school reforms, instruction, and curriculum, the educational needs that stem from increasingly culturally diverse classrooms have not comprehensively been addressed yet. Learners necessarily carry their multiple social group identities such as gender, race/ethnicity, immigration status, sexual orientation, dis/ability, age, socioeconomic status, and religion into the classroom environment (Garibay, 2015). Studies indicate that there is a significant relationship between student achievement and a positive classroom climate where students are encouraged (Gurin, 1999; Terenzini, Cabrera & Bernal, 2001; Gurin, Dey, Hurtado & Gurin, 2002). Antonio and colleagues (2004) revealed that classrooms with an average level of heterogeneity (where students from diverse groups compose about 35% of enrolled students) illustrate constructive effects on learners' problem-solving and group skills (Antonio, Chang, Hakuta, Kenny, Levin & Milem, 2004). They further observed that there was a higher integrative complexity in the group discussions when viewpoints from diverse students were included. Moreover, Gurin et al. (2002) suggest that learners demonstrate better commitment to exercises that require active thinking when they collaborate with diverse peers. According to Gorham (2001), although teachers may not sufficiently hold the required skills, it will be necessary to be equipped with the necessary knowledge, skills, and attitudes to meet the demands of the broad array of students from different cultural backgrounds.

Research in the field provides ample evidence indicating that students from diverse backgrounds are disadvantaged in terms of academic achievement. For instance, Horm (2003) assert that teachers' paucity of multicultural knowledge and awareness leads to lower academic achievement for minority groups in their classes. When teachers do not display the required multicultural responsiveness, students from different ethnic and cultural backgrounds tend to fail in social and academic attainments (Townsend, 2002).

Concerning the demands of learners from minority groups, Bowman (1994) reported that children from poor families and those from diverse ethnic backgrounds such as African, Latin, and Native Americans were more prone to fail at school or required to get special-needs education compared to other students at school. He further asserts that these children might not be expected to participate in social life and contribute to the economic development of the country unless there is a change in their performance at school. In line with this, Gay (2004) claims that instructional quality is much more important than the curriculum itself; hence, there needs to be an improvement not only in the curriculum but also in the way teachers deliver instruction.

In their study on multicultural teaching in preschool, Leung and Hue (2017) state that one focus of teacher development programs in Hong Kong preschool education is multicultural teaching competence. The presence of those students from diverse ethnic, linguistic, and cultural backgrounds such as Indian, Indonesian, Nepalese, Pakistani, Filipinos, and Thai was ignored in the education system until the Hong Kong Racial Discrimination Ordinance was issued in 2008 and these children suffered from low academic success, low family income, lack of social support and orientation (Chong, 2005; Hue, 2011; Hue & Kennedy, 2012; Kennedy & Hue, 2011). Hence, Leung and Hue (2017) claim that it is essential for teachers working with linguistically and culturally diverse populations to have competence in multicultural teaching to provide proper learning climates for all.

A final aspect suggested by Banks (1995a) regarding multicultural education is 'empowering school culture and social structure' which was concerned with the social system in the school as a whole rather than referring to separate aspects of the educational process. This dimension suggests that the school is a larger system than a mere physical structure of teachers and students. Therefore, educational reform in line with the purposes of multicultural education should be operational throughout the entire system and a new structure of diversity is expected to be constructed (Banks, 1995a).

According to NCATE standard 4 (2008), a good understanding of diversity is to be reflected in the curriculum and prospective teachers need to be aware of various learning styles and be able to adapt instruction suitably for students. They are supposed to possess the required awareness, knowledge, attitudes, and skills to effectively teach diverse classrooms. They are further expected to be able to associate the content with learners' cultures and backgrounds and create a classroom climate that values diversity. Finally, candidate teachers are required to show attitudes in the classroom that are compatible with equity and the belief that all students have the potential to learn.

## METHOD

The participants and the setting of the research inquiry have been purposefully and prudently chosen so that it promotes the chance of collecting deep, rich, and meaningful data from various aspects. The semi-structured interviews were conducted with 20 participant instructors, and the video-stimulated interviews were conducted by recording the lessons of four participant instructors. The interviews were conducted in English. The participant instructors who were asked to participate in the semi-structured interviews (N=20) and video-stimulated recall interviews (N=4) were purposefully selected because they were expected to provide significant information that might not be obtained from other options (Patton, 1990; Maxwell, 1998). Nunan (1992) asserts that the selection of participants based on *typicality* is essential for purposeful sampling. In a similar line, Patton (1990) states that "most sampling in qualitative research neither falls into probability sampling nor convenience sampling, but falls into a third category: purposeful sampling", a strategy by which particular settings, persons, or events are intentionally selected (p. 169). In regards to the conveniences of purposeful sampling, Leavy (2014) notes that nonprobability sampling suits qualitative content analysis for several reasons because it allows the researcher to determine who best to study without missing the critical persons needed in the sample; it increases the chance to collect deep, rich, and meaningful data; and it allows the researcher to refine and adapt the sample as one enters the study (pp. 541-542).

The breadth and depth of understanding and corroboration were ensured by an in-depth qualitative content analysis of the data obtained from semi-structured interviews and video-stimulated recall interviews. As Weber (1990) states "content analysis is a research method that uses a set of procedures to make valid inferences from the text", and it holds several benefits in comparison with other research methods (p. 117). First, content analysis is administered directly to texts or transcripts, which are the productions of human communication and the basis of social interaction. Next, high-quality studies merge both qualitative and quantitative analyses of texts, and mixing methods are broadly considered an efficient way of ensuring the credibility of the research inquiry regarding validity and reliability. Additionally, using different kinds of documents grant a reliable source of information for a longer course of time, since the "lifespan" of these documents might last for several decades or even centuries. Finally, the nature of the data is ensured to be conserved due to the unobtrusive characteristic of this research method; hence, there is little risk that the participants react under the influence of certain assumptions (Cohen et al., 2007; Stemler, 2001; Weber, 1990). In this respect, the coding of raw data was carried out in a cyclical process with a colleague in a cross-referencing method to ensure interrater reliability to achieve the highest levels of accuracy in agreement in coding. At the initial step, the researcher and the interrater agreed on codes that were based on the dimensions of the study. After codes were defined, raw data from the interviews were clustered into themes and subthemes by the researcher and interrater independently. Following the completion of each step in the coding process, the categorization of extracts under relevant themes and subthemes was reviewed and reformulated by referring back to raw data and finalized in the third step.

## FINDINGS

The qualitative content analysis of the interviews revealed the following themes pertaining to the challenges the participating instructors' experience and the strategies they employ in their classrooms, as displayed in Table 1.

*Tackling the Challenges Posed by Linguistic and Cultural Diversity in EFL Classrooms*

*Table 1. Challenges posed by diversity and strategies used*

| Challenges | f | Strategies | f |
|---|---|---|---|
| Instructors' lacking the necessary multicultural teaching competencies | 32 | Essential role of experience | 21 |
| | | Cooperating with colleagues | 12 |
| | | Demand for in-service training | 11 |
| Learners' lack of proficiency in the target (English) and local (Turkish) languages | 32 | Strategies used for facilitating learners' comprehension: use of non-verbal language, and translation | 29 |
| Isolation of diverse students | 16 | Encouraging peer support | 19 |
| Conflicts regarding cultural, religious, and political issues | 13 | Acting proactively | 16 |
| Diverse students' lack of classroom participation | 9 | Encouraging classroom participation | 11 |
| Diverse students' difficulties improving English language skills | 7 | Paying extra attention to students' difficulties and assigning remedial tasks | 22 |

The study revealed that the instructors considered *lacking the necessary multicultural competencies* (cited 32 times) as one of the main challenges posed by linguistic and cultural diversity in their language classrooms. This incompetence mainly consists of a lack of necessary *knowledge* and *skill* in dealing with learners from diverse backgrounds. To illustrate, one of the instructors stated that she did not find herself knowledgeable enough and that they needed support to improve knowledge and the teaching in linguistically and culturally diverse classrooms. Another instructor claimed that teaching in such a diverse environment included lots of risky circumstances in its nature and he was trying to improve himself as an instructor.

In addition to lacking the necessary *knowledge*, some instructors claimed that they did not find themselves *skilled* enough to deal with linguistic and cultural diversity. For instance, an instructor shared her experience with a diverse group, in which she claimed to have realized that she did not find herself competent enough to deal with multicultural groups. She described the group as being disobedient and resistant to the institutional regulations and that they drove her crazy as she did not know how to handle the situation. She stated that those students from diverse backgrounds were unfamiliar with local culture and persistent in behaving the way they did in their home culture. She even asserted that the learners needed professional help and that the effort she had put in was inadequate to tackle the challenge. Another instructor stated that:

## Example 1

*"It is really difficult to deal with those students outside, so I feel like that it's not my responsibility, after some point. I feel a little bit different I don't know."*

Concerning their competence, the majority of the instructors emphasized the *essential role of experience* in the construction of *knowledge* as the majority claimed to have not received any prior instruction during pre-service teacher education and/or in-service training programs. Although some stated that they *cooperated with colleagues* in cases of need, they also *demanded in-service training* to more professionally manage the linguistic and cultural diversity in their classrooms. For example, one stated that:

## Example 2

*"...it would be nice to have this as a separate course. Because this is what we are experiencing in a real teaching environment. We have lots of students from different backgrounds, so it would be nice to have a course in the undergraduate program."*

When inquired whether they had previously engaged in any training focused on multicultural teaching, one of the instructors stated that:

## Example 3

*Unfortunately, not. ...er, but I would find such kind of training helpful because we have lots of students from different cultures and countries. I think it will be helpful. Of course, we try to solve our problems, but sometimes we can have a block [stuck]. That's why they can help us how to solve these problems.*

The interviews also displayed challenges pertaining to *diverse students' linguistic incompetency*, which some of the participating instructors perceive as the possible source of some further complications such as academic failure and lack of participation. For instance, one of the participants stated that she considered "the learners from diverse backgrounds who speak poorly either in local or in the target language" as a serious challenge because it "raises a barrier in communication". Another instructor mentioned that linguistic challenges further caused problems concerning time management for the teacher as it slowed down the pace of teaching and loss of concentration and motivation for other learners.

Interestingly enough, one of the participants cited that she found linguistic diversity more challenging than cultural diversity because she was stuck on the language barrier. She emphasized the importance of switching to her mother tongue, which she could not do with linguistically diverse students. As some strategies to tackle this challenge, the participant instructors claimed to have provided *non-verbal language strategies* that might facilitate learner comprehension and/or used *translation* into diverse learners' mother tongues with the help of a student from the same linguistic background. For example, some of the instructors stated that they receive help from those international students who were more competent in the target language to assist those from the same linguistic background and face serious problems in understanding instructions for classroom practices.

In EFL classrooms, it is a conventional phenomenon that most teachers systematically and deliberately switch to L1 to check comprehension, give feedback, explain difficult concepts, or give instructions and explanations in a short-cut where necessary. It seems evident that besides addressing the needs of local learners in their mother tongue, the participant instructors put ample effort to deliver the instruction in direct or indirect ways for those learners from diverse linguistic backgrounds.

Another significant challenge that emerged from interviews was found to be the *isolation of linguistically and culturally diverse students*. In the interviews, some instructors remarked (16 citations) that students from diverse linguistic and cultural backgrounds feel isolated and lose connection with the local students in their classrooms. One of the instructors defined this as an unfavorable aspect of diversity and a reason for the loss of motivation. Another instructor claimed that local students treated those students from diverse linguistic and cultural backgrounds as if they were outsiders in the classroom. He asserted that it was a problem that was to be coped with by the instructor as the mediator of the class.

## Example 4

*"And then our X [country] students feel alienated. They feel the isolation. This is a problem but as a teacher, your responsibility is here: You need to solve the alienation problem by creating a good atmosphere in the class."*

The instructors cited that they *encourage peer support* (19 citations) to prevent the exclusion of these learners. They claimed that this forms a consensus among students and promotes mutual benefit for both local and diverse students. It seems evident that engaging learners from different cultural and linguistic backgrounds promotes cooperation and positive interaction among learners and helps to create a positive classroom atmosphere for all. On the other hand, putting individual learners on the spot might make them feel insecure or intimidated.

A further remarkable challenge that the study revealed respects *conflicts regarding cultural, religious, and political issues* (13 citations) among learners. Particularly with regards to learners' engagements in religious or political debates, it seems evident that most instructors favored *acting proactively* (16 citations) and avoiding addressing these issues in the classroom as these topics are considered to be contradictory and delicate. For instance, a participant instructor highlighted the importance of paying attention to using appropriate language not to humiliate learners and refrained from making comments on political or religious issues.

## Example 5

*"I think, it is also important to use the proper language in order not to hurt them in the classroom. I don't want to talk about politics and religion. They're critical [sensitive] issues in classes, and I want to focus on teaching English only."*

One of the instructors stated that they experience *cultural conflicts among students* and identified this as the most challenging aspect of diversity in language classrooms. Another instructor mentioned the problems related to the political backgrounds of the students and that she found it challenging to keep the balance between the groups.

## Example 6

*"About the challenges, sometimes in my classroom, I have some problems with international students. They had some relationship problems with other Turkish students, not with the teacher but with the other students because of some political backgrounds also, they had some problems. It was difficult for me because as a teacher you should remain neutral but you should also solve the problem. You should also learn to keep your opinion to yourself, so it was a difficult balance for me sometimes."*

Although some emphasized the impact of being a positive role model or the importance of remaining neutral in managing these conflicts as a teacher, some stated that they restrain learners from holding debates on these issues as they could be problematic. Conflicts undoubtedly have an ambivalent function, they can either be disruptive in case of poor management and loss of control or worthwhile and transformative when properly managed.

Some other challenges the participants claimed to experience in their language classrooms were found to be *diverse students' lack of classroom participation* (9 citations), and *diverse students' difficulties improving English language skills* (7 citations). In the interviews, one of the instructors claimed to fail to ensure classroom participation despite all the effort she puts in. Another participant remarked the *lack of classroom participation* was the most challenging in teaching linguistically and culturally diverse groups. She asserted that the hesitancy of these students might stem from the anxiety of being embarrassed. To raise learners' participation, the instructors stated that they *encouraged participation* (11 citations) by embracing cultural topics that might appeal to all, discussing cultural aspects, and giving place to cultural identities, norms, traditions, and backgrounds of learners so that they might participate by presenting examples from their own cultural identities.

With respect to the challenges in improving the English language skills of learners from diverse backgrounds, the participating instructors claimed to have used such strategies as *paying extra attention to students' difficulties and assigning remedial tasks* (22 citations) to overcome the challenges that they encountered in their language classrooms. For example, a participating instructor stated that she had difficulties in teaching *writing*, especially in terms of spelling and using punctuation marks, in which students made a lot of mistakes in the spelling of words and linked sentences without using proper punctuation marks. The instructors frequently cited that they put extra effort to raise learners' motivation and participation by closely monitoring learners' progress and providing them with additional tasks inside or outside the classroom. Despite the load and variety of challenges posed by linguistic and cultural diversity, it seems evident that the participating instructors have an overall positive attitude to overcome the challenges and provide a safe and caring environment for all.

## DISCUSSION

The study proved evidence for several challenges posed by linguistic and cultural diversity in EFL classrooms. One of these challenges that the instructors most frequently stated to experience is the *lack of necessary multicultural teaching competencies*. In tackling this challenge, the instructors were found to heavily depend on previous experiences and cooperation with colleagues as well as demanding in-service training. With respect to this, Pope, Reynolds, and Mueller (2019) assert that it is necessary to implement multicultural teaching into teaching and training programs, and incorporate it into pre-service teacher education programs, in which the knowledge and values of professionals are formed as the lack of multiculturalism in educational interventions leads to an incomplete and more markedly deficient education.

In a similar line, Polat (2009) asserts that personality can be developed through education and the dissemination of multicultural education in the courses of education faculties will provide an opportunity for students to develop their multicultural personalities, which will help to equip candidate teachers with the essential needs of the modern age. In his study on teachers' attitudes towards refugee students, Dolapçı (2019) concluded that the supportive school climate and in-service training played a significant role in teachers' positive attitudes. In another study, Polat and Kılıç (2013) argue that Turkey is seen to have a serious deficiency compared to most other countries considering teacher education concerning multicultural context. They emphasize that the absence of training or course in the context of multiculturalism in teacher education programs can be regarded as a major drawback despite the presence of numerous ethnic, linguistic, and cultural groups in the country. It is obvious that to effectively meet the demands of diversified learner populations in contemporary educational institutions, teachers essentially need to obtain the necessary multicultural teaching competencies.

Another conspicuous challenge that is encountered in language classrooms concerns communication breakdowns with linguistically diverse students due to their *poor linguistic competency either in the target or the local language*, which leads the learners to the incapability of comprehending classroom instructions and a *sense of isolation* inducing the *lack of classroom participation*. The linguistic challenges in multicultural classrooms stand as one of the focal drawbacks that EFL instructors face (Ippolito, 2007; Mena & Rogers, 2017). For example, with regard to the challenges posed by the lack of proficiency in the target language at a multicultural university, Ippolito (2007) found that language was perceived as a barrier that made communication slower and led to misunderstandings and inequality of contribution (p. 758).

As to the strategies that the instructors articulated to use, the findings proved evidence that most of the instructors who asserted that they faced challenges in regards to language and communication also affirmed to have used *strategies for facilitating learners' comprehension* such as the *use of non-verbal language and translation*. They stated that they frequently made use of non-verbal language when there is a breakdown in the interaction with linguistically and culturally diverse students. Tarone (1983) considers these attempts as the solutions to communication problems when there is a gap between the linguistic knowledge of second-language learners and that of the target language interlocutors in real communication situations. She further adds that individuals use such strategies when their interactional problems become apparent. Similarly, Poulisse (1990) asserts that compensatory interaction strategies are used by language users as alternative means of expression when it becomes impossible for them to convey their intended meanings due to linguistic shortcomings. On the other hand, despite the effort the instructors put forward, it is not as easy as it looks because research further says that the use and function of nonverbal communication can vary (Wintergerst and McVeigh, (2011). Nonverbal communication neither occurs in a vacuum nor exists independently of meaning, in which the message might vary for people from different cultures. Hence, the instructors' intentional use of nonverbal communication might help the learners from diverse linguistic and cultural backgrounds on one hand but is prone to misunderstandings on the other hand.

With respect to the *isolation of diverse students* as a challenge, the instructors stated that linguistically and culturally diverse students were demotivated because they felt isolated or alienated in the classroom. Some even asserted that this was because of local students' discriminatory attitudes and behaviors towards students from different cultural backgrounds who were treated as if they were outsiders in the classroom.

In a recent study on the challenges of diverse students in Greece, Paraskevi and Nikolaos (2017) found that participating teachers considered the integration and acceptance of diverse students as a significant challenge and that students from different cultural backgrounds faced the risk of being isolated from other students and had difficulty in communication. Those from dominant culture might consider being a part of a minority group as a negative attribute and hence, individuals from diverse backgrounds might be neglected, treated disrespectfully, and treated in a passive way (Achkovska-Leshkovska and Davchev, 2013). In this regard, the findings revealed that the learners were encouraged to *support* each other to get rid of the *isolation* of their peers from diverse linguistic and cultural backgrounds. The instructors asserted to have mixed the students from various backgrounds and encouraged them to help and benefit from each other so that they might ensure harmony and unity in the classroom.

It seems evident that the instructors paid special attention to putting local and diverse students together in a group and pair-work activities so that they could cooperate and work together. In that sense, studies indicate that there is a significant relationship between student achievement and positive classroom climates where students are encouraged (Gurin, 1999; Terenzini, Cabrera & Bernal, 2001; Gurin, Dey, Hurtado & Gurin, 2002). Antonio and colleagues (2004) revealed that classrooms with an average level of heterogeneity (where students from diverse groups composed about 35% of enrolled students) illustrate constructive effects on learners' problem-solving and group skills (Antonio, Chang, Hakuta, Kenny, Levin & Milem, 2004). They further suggested that there was a higher integrative complexity in the group discussions when they included viewpoints from diverse students. Moreover, Gurin et al. (2002) suggest that learners demonstrate better commitment in exercises that require active thinking when they collaborate with peers from diverse backgrounds.

The study revealed further evidence indicating that the instructors encounter challenges due to *conflicts regarding cultural, religious, and political issues* among learners from different backgrounds. While some of the learners from diverse backgrounds tended to experience culture shock, difficulties in relationships with local students, and conflicts due to political or religious differences, some challenged the instructors due to the difficulties in adapting to school policies and showing resistance to obeying the rules in their classrooms. In some cases, the participant instructors were found to have felt almost helpless as they believed teaching such classes was relatively challenging and demanded the necessary professional support to cope with diverse populations. As Çoban and colleagues (2010) state, teachers need to be aware of the religious, social, political, and ideological variety the students possess and should encourage respecting and reconciling diverse beliefs, views, and ideologies as an essential characteristic of culture-sensitive individuals.

In establishing social cohesion, the European Commission (2001) stressed the significance of education systems in the inclusion of students not only in the school environment but also in social life was seen to be feasible only by the improvements in education. According to the Council of the European Union (2006), education is the promoting power that helps raise active citizens who "fully participate in the civic life", based on knowledge of social and political concepts and structures, and a commitment to active and democratic participation. On the grounds of this view, the council declared the decision number 1904/2006, which underpins the establishment of a program called *Europe for Citizens* that would last for a period between 2007 and 2013 and intended to create a 'civic education curricula' that would help to fulfill the commitment of active citizenship (Faas, Hajisoteriou & Angelides, 2014, p. 310). Consequently, multiculturally responsive teachers need to recognize that education is quite a complex process in terms of the political and moral aspects of its nature and attempt to handle these social, institutional, professional, and personal drawbacks they encounter in their classrooms (Acar-Çiftçi & Gürol, 2015).

On the other hand, the findings revealed that some instructors stated to have taken *necessary precautions* as a strategy for *conflicts regarding cultural, religious, and political issues*. Some consider this the instructors' responsibility to create a safe zone of learning and encourage students to show tolerance and understanding towards differences. To maintain this safe zone of learning, some of the instructors were found to have avoided discussing political and religious issues in the class as a precautionary approach and remained neutral toward students' diverse political views by keeping a balance in case of a debate among students. Behaving proactively and avoiding the discussion of such fragile issues in the classroom context might appeal to most instructors but Milem (1992, 1994) asserts that students extend their levels of understanding and awareness towards ethnic and cultural diversity, and hold liberal views when they commit to more debates on socio-political issues, express their opinions about ethnic and cultural diversity, interact with students from various backgrounds, participate in workshops focusing on raising awareness towards ethnic diversity, and engaged in courses on ethnic studies. In a similar line, Pascarella and colleagues (1996) found that students valued ethnic and cultural variety and become more open to differences when they participated in workshops aimed at raising cultural awareness (Pascarella, Whitt, Nora, Edison, Hagedorn & Terenzini, 1996).

This study also revealed that *lack of classroom participation* and *difficulties improving English language skills* arouse linguistically and culturally diverse students as a challenge for some of the instructors. Although some stated that they tried to encourage these students to participate, they were unable to efficiently raise their motivation. In their study on multicultural teacher education, Gay and Howard (2000) reported that teachers were reluctant to teach in diverse classrooms since they were worried about handling the diversity in their classrooms responsively and anxious about humiliating students from diverse backgrounds unintentionally. Although none of the participating EFL instructors showed any reluctance, some affirmed to have felt insufficient or despaired after several inept attempts. Some further asserted that the lack of classroom participation among minority groups could stem from the anxiety of being embarrassed or humiliated. In a similar line, the relevant literature suggests that learners from minority groups tend to attain lower academic achievement because they are more sensitive when teachers do not provide the required multicultural responsiveness (Horm, 2003; Townsend, 2002). In addition, the findings further proved that some of the participating instructors were posed by the challenges in teaching certain language skills such as writing, grammar, and vocabulary to linguistically and culturally diverse students. The participating instructors voiced to have used strategies like *encouraging classroom participation,* and *paying extra attention to students' difficulties, and assigning remedial tasks* by including cultural aspects of diverse students. All these efforts indicate that the participating EFL instructors demonstrate multiculturally responsive teaching attitudes and behaviors.

In the globalized world, diversity in educational institutions has been a conventional phenomenon in many countries. Despite the benefits like reducing social inequalities and conflicts, preparing students for work-life, and increasing social harmony and unity committed by diversity at the tertiary level, as Bergan and Damian indicate (2010), the present study provides compelling evidence that it has brought about challenges for the teaching staff due to the increase in the number of individuals from diverse ethnic, cultural, and linguistic backgrounds over the years. Hence, those working in multicultural contexts are supposed to deal with social, institutional, professional, and personal challenges (Acar-Çiftçi & Gürol, 2015).

## CONCLUSION

This study aimed to explore likely *challenges* posed by linguistic and cultural diversity the EFL instructors experience in language classrooms, and the *strategies* that are engaged to overcome these challenges. In this regard, the study proved evidence showing that the instructors put ample effort to bring learners from diverse backgrounds together, integrate the elements of diverse learners' cultures into their teaching, treat and assess diverse learners equally, and provide a safe and caring environment for learners from diverse backgrounds. Cooperating with colleagues was also found to be a way to tackle the challenges posed by diversity.

Another significant indication of the study regards the essential role of experience. As the participant EFL instructors claimed not to have had any formal education or training on the issue, they attributed the construction of knowledge regarding multicultural teaching to their experiences in teaching classrooms with learners from diverse backgrounds. Considering the needs of those instructors who claimed to have insufficient knowledge, and those who stated that they needed expert support to be able to teach in these classrooms, it can be concluded that there is a noteworthy demand for in-service training to acquire the essential competencies for multicultural teaching. Another implication can be made about pre-service teacher education, in which teacher competencies in multicultural teaching can be provided as a separate course. Therefore, further research might be conducted on the competency perceptions of prospective teachers and the effectiveness of in-service teacher training on the issue.

With respect to the challenges posed by the linguistic and cultural diversity in language classrooms, the study revealed that communication breakdown due to the learners' lack of proficiency in the target and local language stood as a major challenge the EFL instructors claimed to encounter. Non-verbal language and translation (by learners from the same linguistic background) can be utilized to facilitate learners' comprehension to overcome these challenges. The study also revealed that the instructors inspire peer support when learners from diverse backgrounds felt isolated and lacked classroom participation. Another concluding remark of the study is the instructors' choice of acting proactively to avoid disrupting the consequences of conflicts regarding cultural, religious, and political issues. The instructors' preference of staying in their comfort zone and not showing a sign of poor management is can be regarded as acceptable, but the constructive and transformative role of the discussion of these issues is beyond doubt. On the other hand, the provision of remedial tasks and paying extra attention to support the academic achievements of learners from diverse backgrounds indicate the multicultural responsiveness of the majority of the instructors. In conclusion, the study unveiled that challenges regarding language and communication are imminent in linguistically and culturally diverse classrooms, but the teaching practitioners in these classrooms should be able to employ effective strategies to tackle these challenges.

## REFERENCES

Acar-Çiftçi, Y., & Gürol, M. (2015). A conceptual framework regarding the multicultural education competencies of Teachers. *Hacettepe University Journal of Education, 30*(1), 1-14.

Achkovska-Leshkovska, E., & Davchev, V. (2013). Intercultural Education: Analysis of the primary school textbooks in the Republic of Macedonia. *International Journal of Cognitive Research in Science, Engineering and Education, 1*(2), 51–56.

Ameny-Dixon, G. M. (2004). Why multicultural education is more important in higher education now than ever: A global perspective. *International Journal of Scholarly Academic Intellectual Diversity, 6,* 1–12.

Antonio, A. L., Chang, M. J., Hakuta, K., Kenny, D. A., Levin, S., & Milem, J. F. (2004). Effects of racial diversity on complex thinking in college students. *Psychological Science, 15*(8), 507–510. doi:10.1111/j.0956-7976.2004.00710.x PMID:15270993

Aydın, H., & Acar-Çiftçi, Y. (2014). A study on the necessity of multicultural education in Turkey. *SDU Journal of Social Sciences., 33*(1), 197–218.

Aydın, H., & Tonbuloğlu, B. (2014). Graduate students' perceptions on multicultural education: A qualitative case study. *Eurasian Journal of Educational Research, 0*(57), 29–50. doi:10.14689/ejer.2014.57.3

Banks, J. A. (1995a). Multicultural Education and Curriculum Transformation. *The Journal of Negro Education, 64*(4), 390–400. doi:10.2307/2967262

Banks, J. A. (1995b). Multicultural Education: Its effects on students' racial and gender role attitudes. In J. A. Banks & C. Banks (Eds.), *Handbook of research on multicultural education* (pp. 617–627). Macmillan.

Banks, J. A. (2009). *The Routledge International Companion to Multicultural Education*. Routledge. doi:10.4324/9780203881514

Bergan, S., & Damian, R. (2010). Higher Education for Modern Societies – Competences and Values. Publishing Council of Europe Higher Education Series No. 15, Council of Europe Publishing.

Bowman, B. T. (1994). Cultural diversity and academic achievement. Urban Education Program. Urban Monograph Series, 10-22.

Byram, M., Gribkova, B., & Starkey, H. (2002). *Developing the intercultural dimension in language teaching: A Practical introduction for teachers*. Council of Europe Publishing.

Cha, Y. K., Gundara, J., Ham, S. H., & Lee, M. (2017). *Multicultural Education in Glocal Perspectives: Policy and Institutionalization*. Springer. doi:10.1007/978-981-10-2222-7

Chong, S. (2005). The logic of Hong Kong teachers: An exploratory study of their teaching culturally diverse students. *Teaching Education, 16*(2), 117–129. doi:10.1080/10476210500122691

Coban, A. E., Karaman, N. G., & Doğan, T. (2010). Investigation of preservice teachers' perspectives on cultural diversity in terms of various demographic variables. *Abant Izzet Baysal University Journal of Faculty of, 10*(1), 125-131.

Cohen, E. G., & Lotan, R. A. (1995). Producing equal-status interactions in the heterogeneous classroom. *American Educational Research Journal, 32*(1), 99–120. doi:10.3102/00028312032001099

Cohen, L., Manion, L., & Morrison, K. (2007). *Research Methods in Education* (6th ed.). Routledge Falmer. doi:10.4324/9780203029053

Collins, P. H. (1990). *Black feminist thought: feminist theory and the construction of knowledge*. Routledge.

Davidman, L., & Davidman, P. (1997). *Teaching with a multicultural perspective: A practical guide*. Longman.

Dolapçı, E. (2019, Spring). *The examination of the relationships among teachers' multicultural self-efficacy, school climate, and teachers' attitudes towards refugee students* [Master's thesis]. Kastamonu University.

Erbas, Y. (2019). A qualitative case study of multicultural education in Turkey: Definitions of multiculturalism and multicultural education. *International Journal of Progressive Education, 15*(1), 23–43. doi:10.29329/ijpe.2019.184.2

Faas, D., Hajisoteriou, C., & Angelides, P. (2014). Intercultural education in Europe: Policies, practices, and trends. *British Educational Research Journal, 40*(2), 300–318. doi:10.1002/berj.3080

Garibay, J. C. (2015). *Creating a positive classroom climate for diversity*. UCLA Diversity & Faculty Development.

Gay, G. (1990). Achieving educational equality through curriculum desegregation. *Phi Delta Kappan, 72*, 56–62.

Gay, G. (2000). *Culturally responsive teaching*. Teachers College Press.

Gay, G. (2004). Beyond Brown: Promoting equality through multicultural education. *Journal of Curriculum and Supervision, 19*(3), 193–216.

Gay, G., & Howard, T. C. (2000). Multicultural teacher education for the 21st century. *Teacher Educator, 36*(1), 1–16. doi:10.1080/08878730009555246

Gordy, L. L., & Pritchard, A. M. (1995). Redirecting our voyage through history: A content analysis of social studies textbooks. *Urban Education, 30*(2), 195–218. doi:10.1177/0042085995030002005

Gorham, E. (2001). *Multicultural teaching competence as perceived by elementary school teachers* (Order No. 3106783). Available from ProQuest Dissertations & Theses Global. (304729078). Retrieved from https://www.proquest.com/dissertations-theses/multicultural-teaching-competence-as-perceived/docview/304729078/se-2

Gorski, P. C. (1999). *A brief history of multicultural education*. Available online also at: http://www.edchange.org/multicultural/papers/edchange_history.html

Grant, C. A., & Khurshid, A. (2009). Multicultural education in a global context: Addressing the varied perspectives and themes. In R. Cowen & A. M. Kazamias (Eds.), *Second international handbook of comparative education* (pp. 403–416). Springer. doi:10.1007/978-1-4020-6403-6_26

Gundara, J. S. (2015). *The case of international education in a multicultural world*. Mosaic Press.

Gurin, P. (1999). *The compelling need for diversity in education*. Expert report. http://www.umich.edu/~urel/admissions/legal/expert/gurintoc.html

Gurin, P., Dey, E., Hurtado, S., & Gurin, G. (2002). Diversity and Higher Education: Theory and Impact on Educational Outcomes. *Harvard Educational Review, 72*(3), 330–367. doi:10.17763/haer.72.3.01151786u134n051

Harring, R. D. (1992). Biracial children: An increasing concern for elementary and middle school counselors. *Elementary School Guidance & Counselling*, 123-130.

Healey, G. W. (1974). *Self-concept: a comparison of Negro-, Anglo-, and Spanish-American students across ethnic, sex, and socioeconomic variables*. R & E Research Associates.

Horm, D. M. (2003). Preparing early childhood educators to work in diverse urban settings. *Teachers College Record, 105*(2), 226–244. doi:10.1111/1467-9620.00237

Hue, M. T. (2011). Developing resiliency in students with behavioral problems in Hong Kong secondary schools: Teachers' narratives from a school guidance perspective. *Pastoral Care in Education, 29*(4), 261–272. doi:10.1080/02643944.2011.626067

Hue, M. T., & Kennedy, K. J. (2012). Creation of culturally responsive classrooms: Teachers' conceptualization of a new rationale for cultural responsiveness and management of diversity in Hong Kong secondary schools. *Intercultural Education, 23*(2), 119–132. doi:10.1080/14675986.2012.686021

Ippolito, K. (2007). Promoting intercultural learning in a multicultural university: Ideals and realities. *Teaching in Higher Education*, *12*(5–6), 749–763. doi:10.1080/13562510701596356

Kennedy, K. J., & Hue, M. T. (2011). Researching ethnic minority students in a Chinese context: Mixed methods design for cross cultural understandings. *Comparative Education*, *47*(3), 343–354. doi:10.1080/03050068.2011.586766

Kucuktas, S. (2016). *Examination of faculty members' multicultural teaching competencies at a four-year institution* [Ph.D. Thesis]. Auburn University.

Ladson-Billings, G. (1992). Culturally relevant teaching: The key to making multicultural education work. In C. A. Grant (Ed.), *Research and Multicultural Education* (pp. 106–121). The Falmer Press.

Leavy, P. (Ed.). (2014). *Oxford library of psychology. The Oxford handbook of qualitative research*. Oxford University Press. doi:10.1093/oxfordhb/9780199811755.001.0001

Leung, C.-H., & Hue, M.-T. (2017). Understanding and enhancing multicultural teaching in preschool. *Early Child Development and Care*, *187*(12), 2002–2014. doi:10.1080/03004430.2016.1203308

Marina, B. L. H. (2004 February 16-20). *The multicultural competence among faculty and administrators in a predominantly white institution*. Paper presented at the 7th International Conference on The First-Year Experience, Maui, HI.

Maxwell, J. A. (1998). Designing a qualitative study. In L. Bickman & D. J. Rog (Eds.), *Handbook of Applied Social Research Methods* (pp. 69–100). Sage Publications, Inc.

Mena, J. A., & Rogers, M. R. (2017). Factors associated with multicultural teaching competence: Social justice orientation and multicultural environment. *Training and Education in Professional Psychology*, *11*(2), 61–68. doi:10.1037/tep0000143

Milem, J. F. (1992). *The Impact of College on Students' Racial Attitudes and Levels of Racial Awareness* [PhD Thesis, UCLA]. Ann Arbor: University Microforms International (UMI), Order Number 9301968.

Milem, J. F. (1994). College, students, and racial understanding. *Thought & Action*, *9*(2), 51–92.

Miranda, A. H. (2002). Best practices in increasing cross-cultural competence. In A. Thomas & J. Grimes (Eds.), *Best Practices in School Psychology IV* (Vol. 1, pp. 353–362). National Association of School Psychologists.

Nishimura, N. (1995). Addressing the Needs of Biracial Children: An Issue for Counsellors in a Multicultural School Environment. *The School Counsellor*, *43*(1), 52-57. Retrieved March 27, 2021, from http://www.jstor.org/stable/23901428

Nunan, D. (1992). *Research methods in language learning*. Cambridge University Press.

Paraskevi, A., & Nikolaos, M. (2017). Students from Different Cultural Backgrounds, Their Difficulties upon Elementary School Entry in Greece and Teachers' Intercultural Educational Practices. *Brock Journal of Education*, *5*(4), 2053–5813.

Pascarella, E. T., Whitt, E. J., Nora, A., Edison, M., Hagedorn, L. S., & Terenzini, P. T. (1996). What Have We Learned from the First Year of the National Study of Student Learning? *Journal of College Student Development, 37*(2), 182–192.

Patterson, J. T. (2000). *Brown V. Board of Education: A civil rights milestone and its troubled legacy.* Oxford University Press.

Patton, M. Q. (1990). *Qualitative evaluation and research methods* (2nd ed.). Sage Publications, Inc.

Polat, İ., & Kılıç, E. (2013). Multicultural education in Turkey and teachers' competencies in multicultural education. *Van Yuzuncu Yil University Journal of Faculty of Education, 10*(1), 352-372.

Polat, S. (2009). Determining the level of characteristics of pre-service teachers towards culturally responsive education. *International Online Journal of Educational Sciences, 1*(1), 154–164.

Pope, R. L., Reynolds, A. L., & Mueller, J. A. (2019). *Multicultural competence in student affairs: Advancing social justice and inclusion.* John Wiley & Sons.

Poulisse, N. (1990). The use of compensatory strategies by Dutch learners of English. Foris.

Pratt-Johnson, Y. (2006). Communicating cross-culturally: What teachers should know. *The Internet TESL Journal, 12*(2).

Republic of Turkey Ministry of Interior Presidency of Migration Management. (2017, June) *Residence permit data.* https://www.goc.gov.tr/kurumlar/goc.gov.tr/YillikGocRaporlari/2016_yiik_goc_raporu_haziran.pdf

Stemler, S. (2001). *An overview of content analysis. Practical assessment, research, and evaluation.* http://pareonline.net/getvn.asp?v=7&n=17

Sue, D. W., Arredondo, P., & McDavis, R. J. (1992). Multicultural counselling competencies and standards: A call to the profession. *Journal of Counseling and Development, 70*(4), 47. doi:10.1002/j.1556-6676.1992.tb01642.x

Sunstein, C. R. (2004, April 26). Did Brown Matter? On the fiftieth anniversary of the fabled desegregation case, not everyone is celebrating. *The New Yorker.* Retrieved from https://www.newyorker.com/magazine/2004/05/03/did-brown-matter

Sutton, M. (2005). The globalization of multicultural education. *Indiana Journal of International Legal Studies, 12*(1), 97–108.

Tarone, E. (1983). Some thoughts on the notion of 'communication strategy'. In C. Faerch & G. Kasper (Eds.), Strategies in Interlanguage Communication (pp. 61-74). Academic Press.

Townsend, B. L. (2002). Leave no teacher behind: A bold proposal for teacher education. *International Journal of Qualitative Studies in Education: QSE, 15*(6), 727–738. doi:10.1080/0951839022000014402

Ünlü, İ., & Örten, H. (2013). Investigation of the perception of teacher candidates about multiculturism and multicultural education. Dicle University Journal of Ziya Gokalp Education Faculty, 21.

Villegas, A. M., & Lucas, T. (2002). Preparing culturally responsive teachers: Rethinking the curriculum. *Journal of Teacher Education, 53*(1), 20–32. doi:10.1177/0022487102053001003

Weber, R. P. (1990). *Sage University paper series on quantitative applications in social sciences, No. 07-049. In Basic Content Analysis* (2nd ed.). Sage Publications, Inc.

Wintergerst, A. C., & McVeigh, J. (2011). *Tips for teaching culture: Practical approaches to intercultural communication.* Pearson Education.

Yang, Y., & Montgomery, D. (2011). Behind Cultural Competence: The Role of Causal Attribution in Multicultural Teacher Education. *The Australian Journal of Teacher Education, 36*(9). Advance online publication. doi:10.14221/ajte.2011v36n9.1

## ADDITIONAL READING

Banks, J. A. (2001). Multicultural education: characteristics and goals. In J. A. Banks & C. M. Banks (Eds.), Multicultural education: Issues and perspectives (4th ed., pp. 3-30). New York: Wiley.

Banks, J. A. (2004). *Diversity and citizenship education: Global perspectives.* Jossey-Bass.

Banks, J. A. (2006). *Cultural diversity and education: Foundations, curriculum, and teaching* (5th ed.). Pearson.

Banks, J. A. (2014). *An introduction to multicultural education.* Allyn and Bacon.

Banks, J. A., & Banks, C. A. M. (2007). *Multicultural education: Issues and perspectives* (6th ed.). Wiley.

## KEY TERMS AND DEFINITIONS

**Cultural Diversity:** It refers to a number of differences among groups of people from diverse cultural backgrounds (Arredondo, Toporek, Brown, Jones, Locke, Sanchez & Stadler, 1996).

**Culturally Responsive Teaching:** It can be defined as the multicultural competence of a teacher to hold the necessary awareness, knowledge, attitudes, and skills so as to teach learners from diverse backgrounds efficiently (Gay, 2010).

**Culture:** It can broadly be defined as an organized set of thoughts, beliefs, and norms for interaction and communication among people, which may influence perceptions, attitudes, and behaviors (Ingraham & Meyers, 2000).

**Dimension of Attitude:** It refers to the behavioural or emotional reactions that an individual creates based on his past experiences of other people, concepts, and events (İnceoğlu, 2010, p. 13).

**Dimension of Awareness:** It is comprised of those values, attitudes, and assumptions of self- and others that are crucial to working with students who are culturally different from a particular professional" (Pope, Annandale, & Morrison-Saunders, 2004).

**Dimension of Knowledge:** It refers to teachers' recognition of teaching in linguistically and culturally diverse environments, and teaching approaches in regards to diverse groups (Spanierman, Oh, Heppner, Neville, Mobley, Wright, Dillon, & Navarro, 2011).

**Dimension of Skills:** The capabilities of teachers to (a) generate, use, and assess strategies that promote learners' personal development and academic achievement, (b) implement culture-sensitive classroom management strategies, and (c) contribute to the school's policy in regards to cultural responsiveness (Spanierman et al., 2011).

**Diverse Students:** Learners that come from diverse linguistic and cultural backgrounds. Diverse students, and linguistically and culturally diverse students are used interchangeably throughout the thesis.

**Diversity:** It indicates to the groups represented in schools who are from various cultural, ethnic, and linguistic backgrounds, from different genders, and with special needs (Banks, 2014).

**Multicultural Education:** It is an educational reform that enables all students to benefit from education equally, regardless of differences such as religion, language, race, gender, age, social class, economic level, and so forth (Banks, 2008).

**Multicultural Teaching Competency:** It is a key term that defines a continuous process that teachers go through in order to (a) reflect on their own beliefs and attitudes toward diversity in their classrooms, (b) construct and raise their knowledge of learners from diverse backgrounds, (c) investigate the effect of this awareness and knowledge on the way and the content they teach, and the effects of these on interactions (Spanierman et al., 2011). The terms multicultural teaching competency and multicultural teaching competence are used interchangeably throughout the thesis.

# Chapter 12
# Teachers' Perceptions on Using Arabic L1 to Teach English in Higher Education in Yemen

**Abdullah Rajab Alfalagg**
*Hadhramout University, Yemen*

**Hassan Saeed Awadh Ba-Udhan**
*Seiyun University, Yemen*

## ABSTRACT

*This chapter aims at exploring teachers' perceptions of using Arabic (L1) as a pedagogical tool to mediate teaching English in higher education. It further investigates the reasons for abstaining from using Arabic and its functions and attempts to determine the factors that affect teachers' decisions on whether or not to use L1. Forty teachers from different universities responded to an online questionnaire. The results revealed that the teachers had positive perspectives toward the selective use of students' L1 (M= 2.89; SD= 0.39). The results showed a moderate positive correlation between the respondents' perceptions of using L1 and their classroom practices (r=0. 498; p=0.001). The results suggested that the teachers were hesitant about using students' L1 because of the misconception about its role in learning the target language. The chapter concludes with implications on functions for utilizing L1, its determining factors, and the reasons for abstaining from it.*

## INTRODUCTION

Recent studies point out that teachers and teacher trainers worldwide view the use of students' L1 positively (Kerr, 2019; Storch & Aldosari, 2010), and the monolingual principle has been questioned. Teachers' judicious use of students' mother tongue serves as a scaffolding artifact that aids learners' cognition to understand L2 profoundly (Wei & Garcia, 2017). However, utilizing students' L1 in higher education has not received due effort in Yemen. Also, there has not been a precise method delineating how it should be employed. Although it is a common practice in most EFL contexts (Wei & Garcia,

DOI: 10.4018/978-1-6684-6172-3.ch012

2017), making the best use of this resource has remained unexplored. In Yemen, teachers use their mother tongue intuitively while lecturing without even reflecting on how much Arabic they use and how to employ Arabic pedagogically in the classroom.

Investigations of teachers' perceptions of Arabic L1 in higher education gain further significance at the time of war in Yemen from two strands. Concerning students' language proficiency, Yemeni students' commitment to studying English has become weak due to the ongoing civil war. Consequently, their proficiency in the English language has deteriorated. Limited language proficiency in English could be one of the driving factors for using the students' mother tongue while teaching English. Second, the teaching faculty shares the same mother tongue with the students. Almost all the teaching faculty in English language programs are native speakers of Arabic. Unlike the pre-war crisis in 2010, the teaching staff in departments of English used to include non-Arabic speaking professors along with Yemenis. While Yemeni teaching faculty run the English language programs, they should seize any opportunity to enhance students' learning during wartime at any cost.

While some academicians believe that using students' mother tongue to teach English in higher education is taboo (Al Balushi, 2020), being so and being commonly used without investigation does not make the issue better understood. Turning a blind eye to the reality of students' struggling level to understand subject matters and instructions in the English language would highly unlikely to aid the students in learning English. On the contrary, it has detrimental effects on students' motivation and achievement. Moreover, separating students' L1 while teaching L2 in monolingual classes is unpractical and illogical (Littlewood & Yu, 2011). Principled employment of L1 can save enormous challenges EFL teachers and students encounter in mastering L2.

Several studies have explored L1 use in higher education in foreign language contexts in regions with richer resourced environments than Yemen. Al Blushi (2020) investigated teachers' beliefs and reasons for using Arabic L1 in higher education in Oman. Al-Amir (2017) explored EFL teachers' perceptions of using Arabic L1 in higher education in Saudi Arabia. Alomaim's (2018) doctoral dissertation examined the relationship between the language education policy, EFL teachers' perceptions of using Arabic in teaching L2, and teachers' classroom practices in Saudi Arabia. Alrabah, Wu, Alotaibi, and Aldaihani (2016) investigated the functions, the affective and psycholinguistic factors, and teachers' attitudes towards using Arabic in college classrooms in Kuwait. In Turkey, Inal and Turhanli (2019) and Kaymakamoglu and Yiltanlilar (2019) explored university teachers' perspectives on using Turkish L1 in teaching English at university. In Korea, Lee and Macaro (2013) investigated whether English-only instruction or teacher codeswitching was more beneficial f to for vocabulary learning and retention.

The present study explores university teachers' perceptions of utilizing Arabic L1 as a pedagogical tool while teaching English in an EFL context, with Yemen as a case in point. It further focuses on reasons for abstaining from using L1, the functions for incorporating the students' L1, and the key factors determining whether teachers use Arabic. This study can provide insights into teachers' selective utilization of Arabic L1 to teach English in higher education. It would help improve English language teaching in higher education in EFL contexts by raising awareness of the functions of using students' L1 while lecturing and the variables that might encourage using L1. This study can be helpful not only for the newly joined professors in departments of English but also for experienced professors of English to raise their awareness about why and how learners' mother tongue can be exploited to make the optimum use of it. Also, it can bring insights to policy-makers at quality assurance and heads of the departments in Yemeni universities. This study may attract them towards heeding vigilance to the feasibility of sanctioning the use of learners' mother tongue by departments of English and setting up regulations per recent advancements in English language education. This study could explain the purposes of utilizing students' mother tongue as an invaluable resource to aid in teaching English. On this basis, the following research questions are addressed:

1. What are the teachers' perspectives towards using Arabic purposefully in higher education?
2. Is there a relationship between the teachers' perspectives of using Arabic and their teaching practices?
3. What are the main reasons for abstaining from using Arabic in higher education?
4. What are the most common functions for using Arabic in higher education?
5. What are the main factors affecting whether a teacher uses Arabic in higher education?

## THE LANDSCAPE OF ENGLISH LANGUAGE PROGRAMS IN HIGHER EDUCATION IN YEMEN

As a foreign language, Yemeni learners of English get in contact with the English language mainly in universities for academic purposes. Classes are homogenous in terms of the student's mother tongue. All the students speak Arabic as their mother tongue. When students enroll in the department of English, they have about six years of exposure to English via formal schooling. However, classes are heterogeneous in terms of students' English language ability when they join the department of English.

There are two sets of students. The first set is the non-English-major students, and they study the English language as a required curriculum subject in their respective departments. The overarching goal of the syllabus is to enhance the students' general English language abilities, so it introduces the basics of the English language. It might be a core language course in the undergraduate or graduate program. For instance, students doing a B.A. in the departments of Islamic studies, Arabic language, and business administration take an English language course in their first year. Similarly, candidates for graduate studies in different departments take an English language proficiency program as a mandatory language requirement by the Ministry of Higher Studies to be exempt from TOEFL/IELTS.

The second set of students is English-major students. Depending on the college, they are conferred B.A. in English with a special focus on either literature, education, language, or translation. The curriculum of the English-major students contains general requirement courses taught in the Arabic language, courses on English language skills, and specialized content courses in literature, linguistics, English language teaching, and translation studies depending on the emphasis of their respective colleges. For instance, the undergraduate program in the department of English at the College of Arts, Hadhramout University, offers 120 credit hours through forty (40) core English courses, each of which carries three credit hours. The courses focus on language competencies and theory-based knowledge. They are sequenced to focus on language skills, and they become increasingly professionally oriented over the semesters (Mahwari, 2016). It is noteworthy that there are slight variations in the sequences of courses, their names, and numbers in the curricula of the different departments in Yemeni universities (Muthanna, 2016).

*Table 1. The curriculum of the B.A. English language courses of Department of English, College of Arts, Hadhramout University*

| | Freshman- Semester I | | Freshman- Semester II |
|---|---|---|---|
| 1. | Grammar I | 1. | Grammar II |
| 2. | Reading I | 2. | Reading II |
| 3. | Vocabulary Study | 3. | Vocabulary II |
| 4. | Speaking and Listening I | 4. | Speaking and Listening II |
| | **Sophomore- Semester I** | | **Sophomore - Semester II** |
| 1. | Writing I | 1. | Elizabethan Drama |
| 2. | Survey of English Literature I | 2. | Survey of English Literature II |
| 3. | Grammar III | 3. | Introduction to Linguistics |
| 4. | Study Skills | 4. | Writing II |
| | **Junior- Semester I** | | **Junior - Semester II** |
| 1. | Linguistics I | 1. | Linguistics II |
| 2. | Writing III | 2. | Short Stories |
| 3. | 18th and 19th Century Novel | 3. | 19th Century Poetry |
| 4. | Non-Fictional Prose | 4. | Psycholinguistics |
| 5. | Research Methods I | 5. | Research Methods II |
| 6. | Sociolinguistics | 6. | Translation |
| | **Senior- Semester I** | | **Senior - Semester II** |
| 1. | 20th Century American Literature I | 1. | 20th Century American Literature I |
| 2. | Advanced Composition | 2. | 20th Century Novel |
| 3. | 20th Century Poetry | 3. | Discourse Analysis |
| 4. | Applied Linguistics | 4. | 20th Century Drama |
| 5. | Translation II | 5. | Translation III |
| 6. | Practice and Theory of literary Criticism | 6. | Graduate Project Writing |

Source: Hadhramout University portal page. Retrieved at https://hu.edu.ye/lifac/en/english-language/

English-major students are enrolled in departments of English via three different enrollment schemes; general admission, specialized admission, or open-education admission. There is no clear policy of admission to the department of English. The essential criterion in the general admission mode is students' GPA in the high school exit examinations and an entrance examination. Applicants should obtain a minimum GPA of 75 percent. The entrance examination is conducted routinely, and it does not filter competent students (Muthanna, 2016). Enrollment in specialized admission allows high school graduates to obtain a higher degree irrespective of their high school GPA or level of proficiency. University administrators are interested in accepting as many students as possible since extra admission and tuition fees are charged every semester (Muthanna, 2016). Regular classes of the specialized admission mode are offered in the afternoon shift. The third mode of admission is open education. Students have much-limited interaction with professors compared with regular students. They have two to three sessions per course, each session is three to four hours long, and attendance is optional. Students raise any doubts about the prescribed course books that they have to study independently during the session. The professors answer their questions and discuss the course materials. Both the open education and specialized admission mostly attract household breadwinners who aspire to complete their higher education to get salary promotion and their social status. A common feature amongst English-major students in the specialized and open education admissions is the low proficiency in the English language. This phenomenon poses enormous challenges to lecturers in higher education.

The teaching faculty are native Yemeni assistants and associate professors with Ph.D. degrees obtained from different countries. Also, many master's degree holders and some instructors are graduates of the same colleges. The faculty share the same mother tongue Arabic henceforth referred to as (L1), with the students. Lecturing is the most preferred teaching method (Muthanna, 2016). The departments of English do not have a stated policy that dictates what language should be employed to regulate the use of the mother tongue while lecturing. It is left to the teachers' common sense to utilize the English language to the maximum.

Like primary education, higher education in Yemen suffers from the absence of highly needed facilities (Muthanna, 2016). It features a poor-resourced environment and frequent interruptions during the school calendar and large classes. The typical number of mainstream classes usually is not less than fifty students.

## Argument for L1 Exclusion in Higher Education in EFL Context

Using L1 in higher education is one of the most controversial issues. Some educators consider it seriously impedes language learning, and frequent use of the mother tongue can negatively affect learners' language competence (Ustunel, 2016). This perceptive draws support from the monolingual principle, i.e., using the target language exclusively to teach L2. The monolingual principle is based on three main arguments. First, it suggests that a teacher cannot be competent in all her/his students' L1 in a multilingual classroom. Second, it is argued that visual aids, body language, and modeling can help teach the most challenging aspects of language. Hence, they compensate for the use of L1, making it unnecessary. Third, the monolingual principle gained momentum by Krashen's Input Hypothesis (Ustunel, 2016). In other words, avoidance of L1 classroom is motivated by the hypothesis that L2 learners should be exposed to the target language as much as possible. On this basis, it is posited that classroom time spent using L1 is worth spending in immersing students to get exposed to the English language.

Furthermore, one of the main arguments advanced against using L1 while teaching English in higher education is that many professors feel that their professional ability is underestimated; thus, they view L1 use with a sense of skepticism and guilt (Atkinson, 1993; Littlewood & Yu, 2011; Tsagari & Giannikas, 2018). They feel confident about their proficiency in English, and they are highly qualified in their academic fields. Using L1 constrains their expertise and challenges their dogmatic belief in the English-only policy. Therefore, instructors abstained from using students' L1. Another justification for abstaining from using L1 is to differentiate the teaching approach at the university from what students are familiar with at high school (Kerr, 2019). Instructors feel the elephant in the room when they refer to students' L1, especially in the English department.

Besides, some instructors believe that using L1 in teaching is associated with the grammar-translation method. They unwittingly equate using L1 with this outdated teaching method. Moreover, many educators emphasize that learners should be taught to think in L2 to master it. This function is best accomplished by excluding L1 from the EFL classroom (Kerr, 2019; Littlewood & Yu, 2011). Instructors, reasonably, are concerned that if L1 is formally sanctioned in the teaching policy, some instructors might overuse it. Therefore, they believe it is more practical not to open this floodgate. Many argue that the instructor should be a role model for students using English for communication in the college environment. In other words, if the teacher uses Arabic in the classroom, the students cannot be expected to act differently (Kerr, 2019). While "there is no theoretical reason to exclude the L1 from the communicative classroom, its use undermines the communicative principle of CLT" (Lee & Macaro, 2013, p.888).

Despite the arguments stated above in favor of the monolingual principle, avoidance of students' L1 in EFL classroom "has no straightforward theoretical rationale (Cook, 2001, p. 410 as cited in Ustunel, 2016, p. 32)". Kerr (2019) garnered counter-arguments against the monolingual principle. Recent research studies demonstrated that L1 is an indispensable asset, to variant degrees, to learning a foreign language in a monolingual EFL context, in particular when the instructor shares the students' native language (Ustunel, 2016).

## Theoretical Underpinning of Principled Use of L1 at L2 Higher Education

Using students' L1 in EFL classrooms draws support from several theoretical paradigms of SLA. Recent developments in translanguaging research advocate the viability of using learners' native language to improve their academic engagement, outcomes, and illiteracy (Wei & Garcia, 2017). Cumming's (1978) Linguistic Interdependence Hypothesis, as cited in Ustunel (2016), acknowledges the contribution of L1 to Target Language (T.L.) developments. Every new language is learned based on an already existing L1. Efficiency in language teaching can be achieved if teachers draw on students' already existing linguistic repertoire. The assumed compartmentalization of L1 and L2 by the monolingual principle counters the nature of the Interdependence Hypothesis. Studies showed that students performed better when allowed to discuss in their native language (Wei & Garcia, 2017).

Similarly, Vygotsky (1962), as cited in Ustunel (2016, p. 33), stated that "success in learning a foreign language is contingent on a certain degree of maturity in the native language." Third, accommodation theory posits that speakers adapt their language use and strategically vary their language as a tool for communicating and negotiating in different environments (Ustunel, 2016). Fourth, research studies on code-switching in education demonstrated that L1 has sociocultural, linguistic, and educational functions (Wei & Garcia, 2017).

## Argument for L1 Inclusion at EFL Higher Education

Employing students' L1 as a teaching tool is commonplace in EFL, where students share the same mother tongue with the teacher. "There is now a very clear consensus, among applied linguists, that some use of L1 can support the learning of English (Kerr, 2019, p. 7)". The recent revision of the National Curriculum for foreign language teaching in the U.K. shows a gradual shift in English-only policy to a measured inclusion of students' mother tongue (Meiring & Norman 2002 as cited in Littlewood & You, 2011). In South Korea, L1 is used extensively in teaching English. Teachers' estimate shows 68% use of Korean L1. English L1 is used 28% to 76% of teaching French in Canadian high schools. In New Zealand high schools, native speakers teachers of Japanese, Korean, German, and French use English L1 about 12% to 77% of the time. In Hong Kong, students recall that L1 is used about 20% of the time to teach English in junior secondary schools. The Ministry of Education of Mainland China recognizes that L1 can be used for explaining grammar and translating English words and expressions. Students' perspectives show that L1 is used 64% of the time while teaching English to junior secondary schools in Mainland China (Littlewood & Yu, 2011). Furthermore, university-level English writing instruction in China often includes L1 during lectures (Reichelt, 2009).

Regionally, in many richer-resourced EFLenvironments compared to Yemen, the Arabic language is utilized in higher education. Al Balushi's (2020) study reveals that while Omani universities adopt an English-only teaching policy, the teachers hold positive attitudes toward using Arabic L1 in higher education. In Saudi Arabia, Al-Amir's (2017) study shows that college teachers acknowledge the benefits of using Arabic on certain classroom occasions. However, most of them do not feel comfortable using Arabic while teaching English. Similarly, Alomaim(2018) finds that EFL teachers at college preparatory programs are not at ease with the ban policy of L1, so they do not implement this rule. They use Arabic to serve particular goals. Alrabah et al. (2016) state that although college teachers in Kuwait do not have favorable attitudes towards using Arabic L1, they cannot avoid using it. They are compelled to use it when their needs call for it. In a similar vein, Al Balushi (2020) reveals that college teachers in Oman believe that using the students' Arabic L1 in the classroom is very important, and they use it as a last resort.

Moreover, Lasagabaster (2013) explores in-service teachers' perspectives on using Spanish L1 to teach Content and Language Integrated Learning (CLIL) context in Colombia. The study finds that the participants unanimously have positive perceptions towards the inclusion of Spanish in teaching CLIL, though to varying degrees. In Cyprus, Tsagari and Giannikas (2018) state that 75% of the teachers sometimes refer to Greek L1 to teach advanced students the English language, and 14.6% of the teachers hardly ever use the students' mother tongue. De la Campa and Nassaji (2009) report that two native speaker teachers of German as a foreign language in an Anglophone Canadian university utilize the students' L1 with an average of 11.3%. The data above demonstrate that while there is near consensus that the Target Language (T.L.) should be used to the maximum, students' L1 cannot be excluded. Littlewood and Yu (2011) state that total exclusion of the students' L1 in monolingual classes is impossible where the teacher speaks the students' mother tongue. Exclusive or near-exclusive use of the target language is rarely encountered in ESL or EFL context.

## The Paradox Unraveled: Negative Attitudes of L1, yet Utilized

Previous literature demonstrates mixed and often contradictory results about teachers' attitudes or perceptions towards the purposeful use of students' L1 while teaching English in a higher EFL context. Teachers might have negative attitudes towards the inclusion of L1, yet they use it while teaching. Inal and Turhanli (2019) conclude that while the quantitative results show the teachers have negative attitudes toward using L1 in the L2 classroom, "the qualitative data indicated that the teachers' general opinion about the use of L1 was positive, p.872". Likewise, Kaymakamoglu and Yiltanlilar (2019) state that Turkish university teachers hold neutral attitudes towards using Turkish L1 while teaching, but the majority of the participants acknowledge using Turkish while teaching. The authors interpret the neutral attitude on the ground of the multicultural learning setting since the program included international students. Alrabah et al. (2016) and AlBalushi (2020) showed that while the teachers show negative attitudes towards using Arabic L1, they utilize it for different purposes. Al-Amir (2017) arrives at the same result. She further adds that "over half of the teachers feel guilty whenever they use students' native language, whereas only a minority of them indicate that they feel comfortable p.16". These results demonstrate a valuable role for students' L1, but teachers do not understand how to exploit this resource best (Mahboob & Lin, 2016). The negative attitudes towards using students' L1 are attributed to the historical development of the ELT context and native speakers' negative attitudes. They result in the common fallacy that using

L1 in teaching is not pedagogically sound. Most language teaching approaches have been developed in the U.S. and the U.K., so local languages' contribution to ELT is not emphasized. Mahboob and Lin (2016) stated that Academics and researchers in English-speaking countries publish textbooks for English language teachers, and these textbooks are marketed as international. Teachers who accept such methods are considered 'progressive' while teachers who do not are considered 'traditional and backward.' Most EFL teachers have not been taught or trained to use their L1. However, they have been instructed explicitly to avoid it as a potential threat to L2 teaching. Western-trained educators propagate the idea of the threat L1 introduction to teaching L2. Mahboob and Lin (2016, p. 29) further add that the negative attitudes developed by native speakers are based on "theory building that occurred in inner-circle countries rather than by a careful non-consideration of the value and role of local languages in outer and expanding circle countries where teachers might share students' local language."

## Reasons/Functions for Using L1 While Teaching English

University instructors' use of the students' mother tongue in EFL classrooms is motivated by external and internal classroom factors. The former refers to students' proficiency in the T.L., teachers' perceptions of the distance between L1 and the T.L., the teachers' educational background, and the institution's policy of using the T.L. The latter factors are "related to features of language use or activities at a given time in the classroom (Polio & Duff, 1994, p. 315)". Socio-cognitive, affective, disciplinary, psychological, and pedagogic functions account for teachers' use of the students' mother tongue (Alrabah et al., 2016). Previous literature consistently reports several inevitable reasons for incorporating L1 in teaching T.L. The first commonly reported reason is the students' low proficiency in the T.L. (Littlewood & Yu, 2011). (De la Campa & Nassaji, 2009). Students' proficiency level is a crucial deciding factor in how much L1 might be used and whether or not to use it. L1 is used in advanced English language classes to help weak students comprehend the lesson in mixed ability classes (Tsagari & Giannikas, 2018). The second factor for using L1 is establishing constructive social relations with students (de la Campa & Nassaji, 2009; Kaymakamoglu & Yıltanlılar, 2019; Littlewood & Yu, 2011; Tsagari & Giannikas, 2018; Ustunel, 2016). This factor reduces the students' affective filter and helps them to feel comfortable engaging actively with teachers. It creates an anxiety-free environment, so it motivates the students to learn. A third common function is explaining cognitively-demanding vocabulary and concepts, especially abstract ones (Alrabah et al., 2016; Al-Amir, 2017; Canagarajah, 1999; Inal & Turhanli, 2019; Kaymakamoglu & Yıltanlılar, 2019; Lasagabaster, 2013). L1 uses the function to foster students' metalinguistic awareness (Lasagabaster, 2013; Ustunel, 2016). The teacher might utilize this function via providing single-word definitions, equivalent translation, explanation, clarification, reformulation, repetition, exemplification, and reinforcing the matters taught. Vocabulary learning and retention entail presenting L1 equivalents irrespective of students' age and proficiency. "University students learnt more words via the L1 equivalent method as compared to the L2 only method (Lee & Macaro, 2013, p. 897)". Exclusion of L1 reduces learners' cognitive and meta-cognitive opportunities to process the target language (Storch & Aldosari, 2010). The fourth commonly reported function is providing and explaining administrative information and disciplinary remarks for setting classroom rules (Al-Amir, 2017; Al Balushi, 2020; Alrabah et al., 2016; Canagarajah, 1999; Inal & Turhanli, 2019; Lasagabaster, 2013; Kaymakamoglu & Yıltanlılar, 2019). The task type of the classroom activity has a significant impact on the use of L1 (Storch & Aldosari, 2010). Teachers use L1 to give clarifying instructions related to activities directions. As a result, L1 inclusion saves the class time (Tsagari & Giannikas, 2018; Ustunel, 2016). Explanation of instructions is closely associated with students' cognitive level and the sufficient procedural knowledge it requires to be fulfilled successfully. In a similar vein, Yigzaw's (2012) study shows that L1 is fundamental for developing content for writing in English. The experimental group that was allowed to use the mother tongue (Amharic) to generate ideas outperformed the control group that was asked to generate content in English. The fifth function of incorporating students' L1 is to explain complex grammatical structures (Lasagabaster, 2013) and compare rules in the T.L. with rules in students' L1 to help them understand these rules (Al-Amir, 2017; Al Balushi, 2020; Alrabah et al., 2016; Inal & Turhanli, 2019; Kaymakamoglu & Yıltanlılar, 2019).

## METHOD

### The Study Design

The study followed a mixed-method design, where it utilized qualitative analysis at the phase of building the data collection instrument and quantitative analysis for the analysis of the data. During the instrument construction phase, seven associate professors of English who work in five public universities were interviewed about their perspectives on using Arabic while teaching English in higher education, especially with English-major students. Their interviews were analyzed verbally and considered the raw items for the questionnaire. Also, some of the questionnaire items were adapted from Tsagari and Giannikas (2018) and Littlewood and Yu (2011). The data analysis utilized descriptive statistics to report the findings using SPSS version twenty-one.

An online questionnaire of two sections was utilized to collect data. Section one collected biographic information. Section two consisted of five parts of 45 closed-end statements in total. The statements were graded on a four-point Likert scale ranging from strongly agree to strongly disagree. Part one gathered data on the respondents' perception of using Arabic as a facilitative tool to teach English to English and non-English major students in higher education. Part two elicited the participants' self-reported teaching practices about using Arabic while teaching English. Part three elicited perspectives on the reasons for abstaining from using Arabic, while part four gathered perspectives on the functions of using Arabic purposefully. At the end of each of the four parts, an open-ended field was provided to elicit other perspectives that the respondents might have. Part five asked the respondents to rank order six factors that determine teachers' utilization of Arabic. The questionnaire was shared through social media websites, and it was active accepting responses for two months.

### Population and Sampling

The electronic questionnaire was released in the English language on professional Facebook pages and WhatsApp groups of faculty members of different universities all over Yemen. They were recommended to fill out the questionnaire and share it with their colleagues. Therefore, a snowball sample of forty (40) university teachers of English filled it out. They were Yemeni native speakers of Arabic affiliated with thirteen public and private universities in Yemen. They teach English at different colleges with varying teaching experiences. The following table shows their demographic information.

*Table 2. Biographic information of the participants*

| Years of Experience of Teaching at College % (n) | Academic Title of the Participants % (n) | Latest Qualifications Obtained % (n) | Specialization % (n) |
|---|---|---|---|
| a) 1-3 years 35% (14) | a) Teaching assistants 47.5% (19) | a) B.A. 15% (6)<br>b) M.A. 30%(12) | a) General 20% (8) |
| b) 4-7 years 27.5% (11) | c) Assistant Professors 40% (16) |  | b) E.L.T./ Applied Linguistics 32.5% (13) |
| c) 8 years or more 37.5% (15) | d) Associate Professors 10% (4) | c) Ph.D. 55% (22) | c) Literature 12.5% (5) |
|  | e) Full Professor 2.5% (1) |  | d) Linguistics 30% (12) |
|  |  |  | e) Other 5% (2) |

Source: Field survey

## Data Analysis

The frequency of the closed-end responses in the questionnaire was analyzed using SPSS software program version 21 to calculate the descriptive statistics, i.e. Mean (M) and Standard deviation (SD) of agreement/disagreement. The four Likert scale levels of agreements were assigned the values ranging from 1 to 4 to demonstrate the extent to which the respondents agreed/disagreed with the statements as follows:

*Table 3. Four-point Likert scale items*

| Responses | Weight | Weighted M |
|---|---|---|
| Strongly Agree | 4 | ＜3.25 to 4 |
| Agree | 3 | ＜2.50 to 3.25 |
| Disagree | 2 | ＜1.75 to 2.50 |
| Strongly Disagree | 1 | 1 to 1.75 |

## RESULTS

Based on the research questions, the key findings were presented. Teachers' perspectives on the selective use of Arabic were offered first, followed by the relationship between perceptions and teaching practices. After that, the reasons for abstaining from using Arabic were discussed, followed by the functions for utilizing Arabic while teaching. Finally, the determining factors for using Arabic while teaching in higher education were provided.

## Teachers' Perceptions of Using Arabic in Higher Education

The first research question explored teachers' perceptions of using Arabic as a pedagogical tool with English-major students and non-English majors.

*Table 4. Teachers' perspectives on using Arabic in higher education*

| Statements | M | SD | Responses |
|---|---|---|---|
| 1. The teacher's use of Arabic while teaching English is necessary sometimes. | 2.75 | .98 | Agree |
| 2. It's natural for native Arabic-speaking teachers to use Arabic in classes with English majored students when needed. | 2.60 | 1.00 | Agree |
| 3. It's natural for native Arabic-speaking teachers to use Arabic in classes with non-English majored students when needed. | 3.17 | .67 | Agree |
| 4. A teacher who uses only English in class is less approachable than a teacher who uses Arabic sometimes | 2.60 | .84 | Agree |
| 5. Students feel more at ease when teachers use Arabic in class. | 3.02 | .61 | Agree |
| 6. The department of English should put a clear policy to regulate the use of Arabic while teaching English. | 3.22 | .94 | Agree |
| 7. Teacher's use of Arabic with English-majored students in classroom should be banned strictly | 2.45 | .93 | Disagree |
| 8. Using Arabic purposefully is an effective method for learning English. | 2.82 | .90 | Agree |
| 9. Using only English in the classroom makes students feel intimidated and less active. | 2.47 | .84 | Disagree |
| 10. Teacher's use of Arabic depends primarily on the students' proficiency in English. | 3.05 | .67 | Agree |
| Overall | 2.89 | 0.39 | Agree |

Table 4 displays the participating teachers' perceptions of using Arabic as a pedagogical tool with English-majored and non-English-majored students. As indicated in Table 4, the respondents had positive perceptions of using Arabic L1 in higher education (M= 2.89; SD= 0.39). The results showed that the respondents believed that teachers' use of Arabic is necessary. It is natural to use it with English-majored and non-English-majored students when needed. They stated that they disagreed with strictly banning teachers' use of Arabic with English-majored students. They also agreed that teachers' purposeful use of Arabic is an effective method for learning English. They agreed that teachers' use of Arabic during classes depends primarily on the students' proficiency in English. They supported the idea that the department of English should set up a clear policy to regulate the use of Arabic while teaching English.

## The Relationship Between Teachers' Perceptions and Their Teaching Practices

The second research question was about the relationship between the teachers' perspectives on using Arabic L1 and their classroom teaching practices.

*Table 5. Mean and standard deviation of the teaching practices*

| | Statements | M | SD | Responses |
|---|---|---|---|---|
| 11. | I use Arabic during classes while teaching English to English majored students. | 1.55 | .67 | Strongly Disagree |
| 12. | I use Arabic during classes while teaching English to non-English majored students. | 2.55 | .78 | Agree |
| 13. | I use Arabic sometimes with low proficiency students in particular. | 2.27 | .81 | Disagree |
| 14. | I don't allow English majored students to use Arabic in the classroom. | 2.85 | .92 | Agree |
| 15. | I encourage other teachers to use Arabic with English majored students. | 1.52 | .90 | Strongly Disagree |
| 16. | I encourage other teachers to use Arabic with non-English majored students. | 2.07 | .85 | Disagree |
| Overall | | 2.14 | 0.50 | Disagree |

Table 5 presents the teachers' responses to their self-reported classroom practices using Arabic during lectures. The overall result showed that they did not use Arabic (M=2.14; SD= 0.50). The results showed that they strongly disagreed with using Arabic during classes while teaching English in the department of English to English majors. However, they agreed with using it with non-English-major students who learn English as a requirement in departments other than English. The respondents stated that they did not use Arabic with low proficiency students in the department of English, and they did not allow the students to use it during classes. The respondents strongly discouraged other teachers from using Arabic with English-major students, and they did not encourage fellow teachers to use it with non-English major students.

*Table 6. Pearson coefficient correlation results between teachers' perspectives and classroom practices*

| | | Teachers' Perspectives | Teachers' Self-reported Practices |
|---|---|---|---|
| **Using of Arabic in L2 classroom** | Pearson Correlation | 1 | .498** |
| | Sig. (2-tailed) | | .001 |
| | N | 40 | 40 |

\*\* Correlation is significant at the 0.01 level (2-tailed)

Pearson (r) correlation coefficient was computed to investigate the relationship between the respondents' perceptions in Table 5 and their self-reported classroom practices in Table 6 about using Arabic. In Table 6, the results revealed a moderate positive correlation between the respondents' perceptions and their self-reported practices (r=0. 498; p=0.001). These results showed that the positive the perceptions of using Arabic, the more likely it is used as a pedagogical resource.

## The Reasons for Abstaining From Using Arabic in Higher Education

The third question addressed the main reasons for abstaining from the selective use of Arabic while teaching English in higher education from the respondents' perspectives.

## Teachers' Perceptions on Using Arabic L1 to Teach English in Higher Education in Yemen

*Table 7. Mean and standard deviation of reasons for abstaining from using Arabic in higher education in the department of English*

| Statements | M | SD | Responses |
|---|---|---|---|
| Teachers *should not* use Arabic in English classes because … | | | |
| 17. It deprives students of valuable input in English. | 3.05 | .84 | Agree |
| 18. It prevents students from trying hard to understand input in the English language. | 3.20 | .72 | Agree |
| 19. It doesn't help students learn English. | 2.75 | .86 | Agree |
| 20. It is equated with Grammar-translation Method, an infamous and outdated method for teaching. | 2.65 | .80 | Agree |
| 21. It gives the students the impression that they also can rely on Arabic to get their message across. | 3.07 | .82 | Agree |
| 22. It compromises teachers' academic professional knowledge. | 2.75 | .83 | Agree |
| 23. It hinders learning English successfully | 2.85 | .86 | Agree |
| 24. Methods of teaching in higher education should be differentiated from high school, so it should be in English | 3.00 | .751 | Agree |
| Overall | 2.92 | 0.61 | Agree |

Table 7 presents the reasons for abstaining from using Arabic in higher education in the department of English. Overall, the participants agreed that teachers should not use Arabic in English classes in the department of English (M= 2.92; SD= 0.61). They stated that teachers should not use Arabic in the department of English because it deprives students of valuable input in English; it does not help students learn English, and it hinders learning English successfully. The respondents agreed that teachers' use of Arabic prevents learners from trying hard to understand input in the English language, and they equated the use of Arabic with the grammar-translation method. The respondents stated that they abstained from using Arabic because it compromises teachers' academic and professional knowledge. They also stated that teaching methods in higher education should be differentiated from primary and secondary education.

## The Common Functions for Using Arabic in Higher Education

The fourth research question addressed the common functions of using Arabic in higher education from the respondents' perspectives.

*Table 8. Mean and standard deviation of the functions for using Arabic in higher education*

| Statements | M | SD | Response |
|---|---|---|---|
| 25. Teachers should use Arabic in English classes to encourage students to be active with the teacher. | 2.35 | .80 | Disagree |
| 26. Teachers should use Arabic in English classes to save much of the class time. | 2.42 | .81 | Disagree |
| 27. Teachers should use Arabic in English classes to cater knowledge/feedback to weak students in mixed-ability classes. | 2.67 | .79 | Agree |
| 28. Teachers should use Arabic in English classes to introduce new vocabulary/concepts when student don't understand them. | 2.87 | .79 | Agree |
| 29. Teachers should use Arabic in English classes to ensure that the material taught is understood properly by all students. | 2.62 | .95 | Agree |
| 30. Teachers should use Arabic in English classes to explain complex grammatical structures in the lesson. | 2.70 | .85 | Agree |
| 31. Teachers should use Arabic in English classes to give instructions of how to do activities and tasks. | 2.52 | .87 | Agree |
| 32. Teachers should use Arabic in English classes to build rapport with students. | 2.42 | .84 | Disagree |
| 33. Teachers should use Arabic in English classes to provide written feedback on students' compositions. | 2.25 | .84 | Disagree |
| 34. Teachers should use Arabic in English classes to announce administrative issues/rules like exam/assignment dates, and classroom code of conduct. | 2.67 | .76 | Agree |
| 35. Teachers should use Arabic in English classes to clarify complex concepts when students seem perplexed. | 3.02 | .76 | Agree |
| 36. Teachers should use Arabic in English classes to deal with discipline issues during classes. | 2.72 | .71 | Agree |
| 37. Teachers should use Arabic in English classes to present information about cross-cultural issues. | 2.80 | .75 | Agree |
| 38. Teachers should use Arabic in English classes to answer students' queries about the lesson. | 2.32 | .85 | Disagree |
| 39. Teachers should use Arabic in English classes to relieve the monotony of class. | 2.45 | .93 | Disagree |
| Overall | 2.59 | 0.62 | Agree |

Table 8 presents the results of the common functions for using Arabic in higher education in the department of English. Overall, the respondents agreed with the common functions for using Arabic (M=2.59; SD= 0.62). The participants agreed with nine out of fifteen of the most commonly addressed functions in the literature, but they disagreed with six functions, as shown in Table 8. They agreed that teachers should use Arabic in English classes to perform the following functions:

1. catering knowledge/feedback to weak students in mixed-ability classes;
2. introducing new vocabulary/concepts when students don't understand them;
3. ensuring that the material taught is understood properly by all students;
4. explaining complex grammatical structures in the lesson;
5. giving instructions on how to do activities and tasks;
6. announcing administrative issues/rules like exam/assignment dates and classroom code of conduct;
7. clarifying complex concepts when students seem perplexed;
8. dealing with discipline issues during classes;

9.  presenting information about cross-cultural issues;

## The Factors Determining Teachers' Use of Arabic in Higher Education

The final research question explored the main factors that affect whether or not a teacher uses Arabic with English-major students in higher education.

*Table 9. Rank order of the factors influencing the teachers' decision to use Arabic*

| | Statements | Rank | % |
|---|---|---|---|
| 40. | The students' proficiency in the English language | 1 | 40% |
| 41. | The students' specialization whether English or non-English major | 3 | 27.5% |
| 42. | The department policy | 5 | 22.5% |
| 43. | Large classes | 6 | 20% |
| 44. | The complexity of the subject content matter | 2 | 30% |
| 45. | The complexity of the classroom task/activity | 4 | 25.5% |

Table 9 presents the rank-order of the factors that affect the teachers' decision whether or not to use Arabic while lecturing in higher education. 40% of the respondents stated that students' proficiency level was the first decisive factor, followed by the complexity of the subject content matter (30%). Whether English or non-English major, the students' specialization came third in the rank order with 27.5%, and the complexity of the classroom task or activity to be accomplished comes as the fourth with 25.5%. Finally, the respondents indicated that the department policy ranked the fifth factor with 22.5%, and the class size ranked the last with 20%.

## Discussion and Interpretation of Results

The present study investigated university teachers' perceptions of the purposeful use of students' L1, reasons for abstaining from it, and the perceived functions of using. The study also examined the main factors that affect teachers' decision to use L1 or not while teaching English. The findings demonstrated that the teachers had positive perceptions of using Arabic purposefully. This finding was congruent with Inal and Turhanli (2019) and Lasagabaste (2013). The respondents agreed that it is necessary sometimes and natural for native Arabic-speaking teachers to use L1 while lecturing to both English-major students in the department of English and non-English major students in different departments. The respondents agreed that the students feel more at ease when teachers use some Arabic while teaching, making the teacher more approachable. They also agreed that using Arabic selectively is an effective method, and its utilization depends on the students' proficiency level in English. The respondents disagreed with strictly banning the use of Arabic. They stated that the departments of English should put a clear policy to regulate the use of Arabic while teaching. This finding means that principled use of students' L1 can be a great asset at teachers' disposal, and teachers can utilize it to deliver the content knowledge effectively.

The results showed a moderate positive correlation concerning the relationship between the classroom teaching practices and teachers' perceptions of using L1. This finding seems to suggest that the better the teachers understand how students' L1 can be employed, the more efficient they would use it. However, when asked about their teaching practice, the respondents replied that they strongly disagreed with using L1 during classes while teaching English to English-major students. They strongly discourage other teachers from using it, not even with low proficiency students of the department of English. The respondents agreed that they used Arabic while teaching English to non-English major students. The findings of teachers' teaching practices contradicted the respondents' positive perceptions. This finding corroborated previous research findings that teachers in EFL contexts have contradictions regarding perspectives of L1 inclusion and their teaching practices (Al-Amir, 2017; Al Balushi, 2020; Alrabah et al., 2016; Inal & Turhanli, 2019; Kaymakamoglu & Yıltanlılar, 2019). This contradiction might be interpreted as the teachers being unsure how and when to use the students' L1 while teaching. While they might hold positive perceptions of using L1, they did not use it, and they strongly discouraged using it selectively in the department of English. Mahboob and Lin (2016) explained that the historical development of ELT, negative perspectives of native English speakers, and Western instructed ELT specialists towards exploiting students' L1 while teaching English contributed to the negative attitudes towards utilizing local languages; labeling teachers who employ them as *'traditional and backward.'*

Western originated principles of pedagogies cannot be imported blindly to the EFL context. In the era of post-method, teachers should theorize their practices and practice their theories to solve local problems by exploiting local resources (Kumaravadivelu, 2006).

The second significant finding revealed that the respondents abstained from using Arabic in higher education for valid reasons. They emphasized that teachers should not use Arabic in English classes. Using L1 deprives students of valuable input, prevents students from trying hard to understand input in English, and gives the students the impression that they can also rely on Arabic to get their message across. In addition, the respondents clarified that they abstained from using Arabic because it hinders learning successfully and compromises the instructors' professional knowledge of English. They also equated using Arabic with the infamous grammar-translation method. They think that the teaching method in higher education should be differentiated from primary and secondary education and should be in English. While these reasons are understandably valid, adopting English-only in higher education in a monolingual EFL context might be impractical and quite unwise. Abstaining totally from using students' L1 is analogous to swimming against the current because L1 would exist, students would use it during the interaction, and some teachers might use it too. Significantly enough, however, the present study underscores the fact that using students' L1 can be the biggest danger to the T.L. development if it jeopardizes the primacy of the T.L. However, it can also be the most important ally a foreign language can have if used "systematically, selectively, and in judicious doses" (Littlewood & Yu, 2011, p.75). There is reasonable anxiety that L1 might be overused if little is allowed (Kerr, 2019).

The reported reasons for abstaining from Arabic completely in the EFL context are worth re-visiting. For instance, students in the department of English learn English for academic purposes. The efficacy of content knowledge delivery cannot be underestimated at the expense of exposure to language input. Several content courses such as *Research Methods, Semantics, Syntax, and Socio-linguistics* are taught. Adamantly insisting on excluding students' L1 amid students' poor language proficiency yields two worse situations. Teachers unnecessarily struggle in vain to deliver the content knowledge. Uncaring, teachers ignore students' current socioeconomic situations and Yemen's sociopolitical conditions. As a result, they unwittingly adopted an exclusive teaching method irrespective of the students' exacerbated socioeconomic conditions. The results showed that the teachers abstained from using Arabic because it gives the students the impression that they can also rely on Arabic to get their message across. However, the teachers' classroom practices refuted this concern. The teachers' practices showed that they did not allow the students to use Arabic in the classroom.

Moreover, equating the selective use of students' L1 with the grammar-translation method is a misconception. Some key features of the wider grammar-translation method from the 1900s to 2000s included grammatical explanation, bilingual vocabulary lists, and translation exercises. The negative stereotype for grammar-translation is attributed to the development of the Direct Method, which gave priority to oral skills, and grammar was taught inductively where examples were met in a meaningful context. However, using students' L1 to mediate teaching L2 in EFL higher education is different from grammar-translation. Nevertheless, translation is a discipline on its own and a sub-field of applied linguistics. It is an everyday activity and a pivotal job for many EFL students. Semantic, pragmatic, and functional translations across types of texts can be communicative activities, and translation proponents argue that translation can be included as a fifth skill (Jin & Cortazzi, 2011).

Methods of teaching in higher education should be differentiated from high school provided that the language ability of the incoming students in the departments of English encourages doing it. It is apparent that the war in Yemen has compounded all aspects of life, and higher education is not an exception. Although the students had been schooled for six years, the proficiency level of the majority is less than mediocre. The sudden transfer to an English-only policy might have counter effects on students' motivation and performance.

This study found that teachers' agreed to the inclusion of Arabic to perform the following commonly referred functions in the ELT literature:

1. catering knowledge/feedback to weak students in mixed-ability classes;
2. introducing new vocabulary/concepts when students don't understand them;
3. ensuring that the material taught is understood properly by all students;
4. explaining complex grammatical structures in the lesson;
5. giving instructions on how to do activities and tasks;
6. announcing administrative issues/rules like exam/assignment dates and classroom code of conduct;
7. clarifying complex concepts when students seem perplexed;
8. dealing with discipline issues during classes; and
9. presenting information about cross-cultural issues.

These findings are consistent with previous studies. However, the respondents disagreed with the following functions for using Arabic L1:

1. building rapport with students;
2. providing written feedback on students' compositions; and
3. answering students' queries about the lesson.

This study presents the following key factors to determine that instructors utilize students' L1 judiciously:

1. students' proficiency in the L2;
2. the complexity of the content matter;
3. specialization;

4. the complexity of the classroom task/activity;
5. the department policy; and
6. large classes.

Students' language proficiency in the T.L. is the first factor. Language mediates understanding, so teachers use L1 to scaffold students' understanding when they do not understand a construct. This finding is consistent with sociocultural theory (Vygotsky, 1986). The less competent the students in English are, the more likely teachers would resort to Arabic. In other words, teachers may code-switch to Arabic when they feel that the students do not understand and switch back to English when they feel students understand the construct. The complexity of the content matter ranks the second factor. The content courses taught in the departments of English introduce advanced knowledge. Therefore, a certain amount of students' L1 might be necessary to explain some constructs and terms as the following:

- in Research Methods, *reliability and validity of a research instrument, research design, dependent and independent research variables*;
- in Advanced Composition, *using the different styles of citations, the different scenarios of in-text citation, and argumentation strategies*;
- in Syntax, *transposition, complements, adjuncts, modifiers, mood, and aspect*;
- in Semantics, *subject, predicate, predicator, sense, and reference*;
- in poetry, *consonance and assonance alliteration'*.

Specialization is the third factor in striking a balance between using English and students' L1 in higher education. In other words, teachers are more likely to utilize Arabic when they teach non-English-major students and utilize much more English while teaching in the departments of English. Forth, teachers might resort to Arabic when they teach complex tasks rather than daily routine tasks. Teachers may use Arabic to demonstrate the analysis of the argumentation structure of a text in a particular genre. The department policy dictating what language teachers should use is ranked the fifth factor when they determine whether or not to use Arabic while teaching. This finding corroborates previous studies that, although the teaching policy dictates that teachers should use only English, they utilize Arabic (Al Balushi, 2020; Alomaim, 2018). Adopting an English-only policy cannot succeed in EFL monolingual context where teachers share the mother tongue with the students and realize that their students' linguistic competence is poor. If enforced, an English-only policy can backfire, thus the most vivid manifestations of which could be students' demotivation to attend classes. Sixth, the larger the classroom, the more likely the teacher might utilize Arabic to reach out to every student and manage the classroom.

## CONCLUSION AND IMPLICATIONS

Teachers' perceptions form a crucial rationale for their teaching philosophy. This study demonstrates that the respondents had positive perceptions of using Arabic judiciously in higher education in Yemen EFL context. However, their teaching practices contradicted their perceptions. They did not use it and did not recommend using it with English majors or non-English-major students. The present study attempted to raise teachers' awareness about exploiting Arabic while teaching English to serve pedagogical purposes in higher education. This conclusion by no means suggests or encourages the overuse of students' L1.

This study espouses striking a balance between using an English-only policy and Arabic. The six key factors explained above present the determinants for an apt balance of L1 and T.L. in higher education.

*It's always important to use as much English as possible, but the L1 can be a vital resource and there is certainly no reason why any teacher in a monolingual class should feel that it is somehow 'wrong' to make use of it (Atkinson, 1993, p.13).*

Adopting an English-only policy in a monolingual EFL environment seems impractical, particularly in poor-resourced educational environments. The ongoing war compounded the educational situation introducing new realities that should be addressed. Teachers should theorize their sound teaching practices using students' L1 and practice what they theorize to solve their day-to-day problems. Teachers' purposeful use of students' L1 can be a viable resource for embracing an inclusive approach to higher education. Judicious use of students' L1 can aptly address the deterioration in the students' proficiency level. The departments of English in Yemeni universities might sanction the use of the Arabic language to serve the pedagogical functions reported in this study, advanced content courses in particular. Based on a periodic diagnostic assessment of the student's proficiency in the T.L., departments might develop a clear policy that regulates procedures of how, when, and how much Arabic language might be allowed. Yemeni universities might introduce a one-year preparatory intensive English language program to engage students in procedural exposure to English before being streamed into the college specializations. Well-designed admission tests should be developed to diagnose the students' proficiency levels. The four language skills should be integrated into admission tests to filter students appropriately.

This study had some inevitable limitations that should be considered while interpreting the results. The present study utilized a questionnaire to explore the teachers' self-reported teaching practices. It is recommended that future studies collect data through classroom audio recordings and observation. Also, the study adopted a four-point Likert scale purposefully to encourage the respondents to take a stand on the issue of teachers' use of L1, one of the thorniest issues in EFL higher education. This study was a small-scale size, and the results obtained might not have the power of generalizability. It is recommended that future studies may investigate the students' and administrators' perspectives on the selective use of Arabic in higher education.

## ACKNOWLEDGMENT

The authors would like to extend sincere thanks to Prof. Ahmed Sheikh Al-Aidaroos of Ahgaff University for his assistance and expertise in handling the quantitative analysis of data. Further, our thanks go to the anonymous reviewers of the manuscript for spending their valuable time reading and commenting on the manuscript.

## REFERENCES

Al-Amir, B. (2017). Saudi female teachers' perspectives of the use of L1 in the EFL classrooms. *English Language Teaching*, *10*(6), 12–20. doi:10.5539/elt.v10n6p12

Al Balushi, H. (2020). The reasons of using L1 in ESL classrooms. *Language Teaching Research Quarterly, 16*, 56–70. doi:10.32038/ltrq.2020.16.04

Alomaim, T. (2018). *Language education policy and language practices in teaching English as a foreign language in a Saudi newly established university: An interpretive case study* [Unpublished thesis]. University of Birmingham.

Alrabah, S., Wu, S., Alotaibi, A., & Aldaihani, H. (2016). English teachers' use of learners' L1 (Arabic) in college classrooms in Kuwait. *English Language Teaching, 9*(1), 1–11. doi:10.5539/elt.v9n1p1

Atkinson, D. (1993). *Teaching monolingual classes*. Longman.

Canagarajah, S. (1999). *Resisting linguistic imperialism in English teaching*. Oxford University Press.

De la Campa, J., & Nassaji, H. (2009). The amount, purpose, and reasons for using L1 in L2 classrooms. *Foreign Language Annals, 42*(4), 742–759. doi:10.1111/j.1944-9720.2009.01052.x

Inal, S., & Turhanli, I. (2019). Teachers' opinions on the use of L1 in EFL classes. *Journal of Language and Linguistic Studies, 15*(3), 861–875. doi:10.17263/jlls.631526

Jin, L., & Cortazzi, M. (2011). Re-evaluating traditional approaches to second language teaching and learning. In E. Hinkel (Ed.), *Handbook of research in second language teaching and learning* (Vol. 2, pp. 558–575). Routledge.

Kaymakamoglu, S., & Yıltanlılar, A. (2019). Non-native English teachers' perceptions about using Turkish (L1) in EFL classrooms: A case study. *International Online Journal of Education & Teaching, 6*(2), 327–337. https://iojet.org/index.php/IOJET/article/view/614

Kerr, P. (2019). *The use of L1 in English language teachingPart of the Cambridge Papers in ELT series*. Cambridge University Press. Retrieved from cambridge.org/cambridge-papers-elt

Kumaravadivelu, B. (2006). *Understanding language teaching from method to postmethod*. Lawrence Erlbaum Associates. doi:10.4324/9781410615725

Lasagabaster, D. (2013). The use of L1 in CLIL classes: The teachers' perspective. *Latin American Journal of Content and Language Integrated Learning, 6*(2), 1–21. doi:10.5294/laclil.2013.6.2.1

Lee, J., & Macaro, E. (2013). Investigating age in the use of L1 or English-only instruction: Vocabulary acquisition by Korean EFL learners. *Modern Language Journal, 97*(4), 887–901. doi:10.1111/j.1540-4781.2013.12044.x

Littlewood, W., & Yu, B. (2011). First language and target language in the foreign language classroom. *Language Teaching, 44*(01), 64–77. doi:10.1017/S0261444809990310

Mahboob, A., & Lin, A. (2016). Using local languages in English language classroom. In W. Renandya & H. Widodo (Eds.), *English language teaching today:Linking theory to practice* (pp. 25–40). Springer Nature. doi:10.1007/978-3-319-38834-2_3

Mahwari, W. (2016). *Designing a model for pre-service EFL teacher education programs: An exploratory study in the Yemeni context*. Retrieved December 2016, from https://www.awej.org/index.php?option=com_content&view=article&id=1038

Polio, C., & Duff, P. (1994). Teacher's language use in university foreign language classrooms: A qualitative analysis of English and target language alternation. *Modern Language Journal, 78*(3), 313–326. doi:10.1111/j.1540-4781.1994.tb02045.x

Reichelt, M. (2009). A critical evaluation of writing teaching programmes in different foreign language settings. In R. Manchon (Ed.), *Writing in foreign language contexts. Learning, teaching and research* (pp. 183–206). Multilingual Matters. doi:10.21832/9781847691859-011

Storch, N., & Aldosari, A. (2010). Learners' use of first language (Arabic) in pair work in EFL class. *Language Teaching Research, 14*(4), 355–375. doi:10.1177/1362168810375362

Tsagari, D., & Giannikas, C. (2018). Re-evaluating the use of the L1 in the L2 classroom: students vs. teachers. *Applied Linguistics Review*, 1-31. doi:10.1515/applirev-2017-0104

Ustunel, E. (2016). *EFL classroom code-switching*. Palgrave Macmillan. doi:10.1057/978-1-137-55844-2

Vygotsky, L. (1986). *Thought and language*. The MIT Press.

Wei, L., & Garcia, O. (2017). From researching translanguaging to translaguaging research. In Research methods in language and education (pp. 227-240). Gewerbestrasse: Springer International Publishing.

Yigzaw, A. (2012). Impact of L1 use in L2 English writing classes. *Ethiop J. Educ. & Sc., 8*(1), 11–27.

# Chapter 13
# Teaching and Learning in the Age of Climate Change:
## Postcolonial Ecofeminism and the Rhetorics of Sustainability

**Sibylle Gruber**
*Northern Arizona University, USA*

## ABSTRACT

*The chapter foregrounds the important role of teaching and learning in the age of climate change. The author shows that education for sustainable development needs to promote communication practices that not only emphasize transition and betweenness, but that transcend current definitions of disciplines to create sustainable solutions to existing problems. Such writing and communication practices are necessary to contribute to 21st century solutions to such monumental issues as increased migration due to conflict, persecution, and natural disasters; food insecurity across the globe; the erasure of economic, social, cultural, gender, civil, and political rights; and pandemics that know no borders. The chapter concludes by emphasizing the importance of encouraging students to practice transdisciplinary writing and communication skills to ensure that they can participate successfully in a world where disciplinary boundaries often hinder new and innovative approaches to finding solutions to the pressing issues raised by the current climate emergency.*

## INTRODUCTION

Severe droughts have affected many countries during the last few decades and have increased in severity all across the globe over the last few years. In 2022, an out-of-control wildfire in the eastern part of Spain burned more than 47,000 acres, with strong winds making it difficult to control the fire. In August 2022, *The Associated Press (AP)* reports, "wildfires in Spain have burned four times more land than they did during the last decade" (AP, 2022). Western Europe's most important waterway, the Rhine river, has seen decreasing water levels that make it "too shallow for many ships to pass" which, according to Rob Schmitz (2022), is "a problem for a country that depends on the river for 80% of its water freight"

DOI: 10.4018/978-1-6684-6172-3.ch013

## Teaching and Learning in the Age of Climate Change

(Schmitz, 2022). Because of the drought in southwestern China, farmers have "lost half its vegetable crop in heat as high as 41 degrees Celsius (106 Fahrenheit)" and it "has shrunk the giant Yangtze River and wilted crops across central China" (Schiefelbein, 2022). In other parts of the world, flooding destroys lives and livelihoods, animals, and homes. South Korea's record rainfall in Seoul, for example, has led to several deaths, has devastated many neighborhoods and has left people homeless (Bae & Yeung, 2022). In addition, NASA's report on the driest place in North America, Death Valley, shows that a "thousand-year rainfall event dropped 75 percent of the local average annual rainfall" (NASA, 2022).

The many climate-related disasters, and the crisis surrounding environmental protection and justice efforts provided a starting point for exploring the important role of teaching and learning in the age of climate change. This chapter shows that education for sustainable development needs to move beyond traditional disciplinary boundaries in order to promote communication practices that not only emphasize transition and betweenness, but that transcend current definitions of disciplines to create sustainable solutions to existing problems. Such writing and communication practices are necessary, I show, to contribute to 21st century solutions to such monumental issues as increased migration due to conflict, persecution, and natural disasters; food insecurity across the globe; the erasure of economic, social, cultural, gender, civil, and political rights; and pandemics that know no borders.

I expand on Kenneth Burke's (1965, 1966, 1969) theory of transcendental redefinition to establish the importance of going beyond – transcending – "terministic screens" that determine how we see reality, or, in this case, how we see disciplinary fields and the communication strategies used in those fields. I include Javier Echeverría's (1999) concept of epistemopolis – a concept that takes into account new social spaces where "a plurality of diverse activities … overlap and interact with each other" – where the "third environment" moves beyond currently established communication frameworks and requires the transcendental redefinition discussed by Burke. I argue that an understanding of transcendental redefinition and epistemopolis is necessary to situate current discussions on transdisciplinarity (Alvargonzález, 2011; Angelstam, 2013; Bernstein, 2015; Hall, 2018; Klein, 2004; Mauser, 2013; Max-Neef, 2005; Nicolescu, 2010; Osborne, 2015) and postcolonialism and ecofeminism (Banerjee, 2016; Carlassare, 2000; Gaard, 2017; Huggan & Tiffin, 2015; Mies & Shiva, 1993; Plumwood, 2004) within the larger theoretical framework of how language constructs knowledge, limits knowledge, and, if we transcend the limitations of our terministic screens, pushes knowledge in new directions by redefining, blending, and expanding existing boundaries.

Situating teaching and learning in the age of climate change as part of an epistemopolis that requires a transdisciplinary approach grounded in postcolonial and ecofeminist theories to problem solving is especially important because, as Mauser et al. (2013) point out, "no definitive blueprint exists yet" for creating "new forms of learning and problem-solving" between "different parts of society and academia that have not traditionally been in close contact" (p. 427). After exploring past discussions on the concept of epistemopolis, transdisciplinarity, and postcolonial critical ecofeminism, I show the need for expanding current climate change discussions by expanding the epistemological frameworks of transdisciplinarity with a postcolonialist and ecofeminist grounding, emphasizing how an epistemopolis can take into account the complexities of climate change action. I provide an example of the beginnings of a new epistemopolis by bringing in examples from a course titled "Environmental Rhetoric in Public Spaces." This course transcended disciplinary boundaries and used postcolonial and ecofeminist tenets to suggest future directions for climate change discussions. I conclude by emphasizing the importance of encouraging students to practice transdisciplinary writing and communication skills grounded in postcolonial and ecofeminist theories to ensure that they can participate successfully in a world – an epistemopolis – that requires new and innovative approaches to finding solutions to the pressing issues raised by the current climate emergency.

## WHAT WE KNOW: DRAWING CONNECTIONS

### Knowledge Societies: Expanding Terministic Screens

In *Language as Symbolic Action*, Kenneth Burke (1966) argues that the language we use and the definitions we attribute to language are a "*reflection* of reality" as well as a "*selection* of reality" and a "*deflection* of reality" (p. 45). We use what Burke (1966) calls "terministic screens" (p. 50) that provide us with filters and with a specific frame through which to see the world. That means that we don't use language to reflect reality, but that we use it to construct knowledge and to construct our social realities by directing attention in specific directions. Burke explains this by pointing out that the difference between humans and animals is defined differently depending on the scientific, philosophical, or theological perspective employed by the author. Darwin, he points out, "views man [sic] as *continuous* with other animals," whereas "the theologian sees a difference in kind" (p. 50). As a further example, discussions about sustainability and the current climate crisis have been filtered through the terministic screens we use and have long been contentious, with climate change deniers insisting that climate change predictions are fabricated, and climate change activists pointing to scientific data to show that anthropogenic climate change is undeniable and is a reality that can no longer be ignored.

In order to go beyond the differences created by set frameworks and definitions, Burke (1965, 1966, 1969) explores the need for redefinitions to establish the importance of going beyond – transcending – "terministic screens" that determine how we see reality, or how we see political factions, cultural expressions, social conventions, religious communities, or disciplinary fields. Such redefinition is important because, as Burke (1969) puts it, "you persuade a man [sic] only insofar as you can talk his language by speech, gesture, tonality, order, image, attitude, idea, identifying your ways with his" (p. 55). To redefine reality, then, means to pay attention to the communication strategies used by members of the various discourse communities we encounter or engage with, and, in the case of the climate crisis, learn what causes fear, doubt, apprehension and unease on the one hand, and hopefulness, determination, and tenacity on the other hand.

To construct sustainable spaces for transcending terministic screens shaped by established and often entrenched frameworks on climate change, theorists and researchers have argued for a paradigm shift in how we address the climate crisis (see, e.g., Bagheri, A., & Hjorth, 2007; Burns, 2012; Edwards, 2005; Kuhn, 1970; Rao & Saul, 2021). Of particular interest for this discussion is the concept of communities of practice addressed by Lave and Wenger (1991) where "situated learning" (p. 98) takes place in a community that shares information and experiences. Such sharing, they point out, is an "intrinsic condition for the existence of knowledge" (p. 98). This mutual engagement and sharing of resources encourages members of specific communities to work together and develop common practices (Wenger, 1998, 1999). It is necessary in order to create new knowledge that, as Tennant (2019) points out, is transmitted to, revised, and rewritten in communities of practice.

Communities of practice, according to Wenger (1999), "are everywhere," "change over the course of our lives," and "are informal and so pervasive that they rarely come into explicit focus" (p. 6-7). This informality differentiates communities of practice from knowledge communities where "people in diverse positions collectively help the members of an enterprise shape their future" (Senge & Käufer, 2000). This distinction is further highlighted by Echeverría, Alonso, and Oiarzabal (2011) who argue that we need to introduce the notion of communities of knowledge "as a way to analyze the structure of the emergent knowledge societies" (pp. 8-9). This is especially important, they argue "if we believe that a complex society has to be integrated by various and heterogeneous communities" (p. 9). Therefore, they conclude, *"a knowledge society should be the plurality of communities of knowledge"* (p. 9, emphasis in original).

Echeverría's (2011) discussion of knowledge societies brings in the additional concept of knowledge cities which he defines as "complex forms of association that develop on a foundation of a plurality of shared knowledge among different communities, and that maintain public spaces for the free exchange of knowledge" (p. 23). This knowledge city, he continues, "must be capable of integrating diverse knowledge communities, each one of whom cultivates specific kinds of knowledge" (p. 24). In addition, a "knowledge city must also be able to maintain a specific space (*agora*) in which all these different types of knowledge can be expressed freely and accessed by any citizen" (p. 24). By "generating citizen spaces of knowledge," he points out, we arrive at an "*epistemopolis* or a knowledge republic" where "the boundaries of these spaces of knowledge are open or, if one prefers, endless" (p. 24, emphasis in original). The exchange of knowledge, or the transfer of knowledge, is integral to the successful functioning of an epistemopolis, especially because a knowledge republic must "promote, facilitate, and marshal knowledge flow among very different communities" (p. 27). With the promotion of public spaces for knowledge exchange, individuals and groups in knowledge cities can provide information on specific topics, learn from each other about different ideas and interpretations, and reevaluate the topic based on the knowledge exchange encouraged in an epistemopolis or knowledge society.

In addition to Echeverría's (1999, 2011) conceptual discussion of knowledge societies, Afgan and Carvalho (2010) incorporate the importance of developing a sustainability paradigm based on the principles of knowledge societies. As they point out, a knowledge society "is a human structured organisation based on contemporary developed knowledge and representing new quality of life support systems. It implies the need to fully understand distribution of knowledge, access to information and capability to transfer information into knowledge." Combined with sustainability, defined as "the dynamic state of a complex system characterised by the criteria comprising the social, institutional, and environmental contribution to global long term human welfare based on their specific and unique set of inherent goals and functions" (p.30), a knowledge society approach "emphasises the interacting characteristics of different facets of human development and how the failure or omission of one function can negatively affect the whole system" (p. 31). This then becomes "a potential frame for human society development leading to social cohesion, economic competitiveness and stability, use of resources and economic development, safeguarding biodiversity and the ecosystem" (p. 31).

The concept of knowledge cities and knowledge societies addressed by Echeverría (2011) encourages us to move beyond currently established communication frameworks and requires a transformative and transcendental redefinition discussed by Burke (1969). Current disciplinary discussions on climate change, for example, need to transform and transcend the limitations imposed by disciplinary fields and instead need to bring in Echeverría's (2011) concept of knowledge cities which "are based on the convergence of various (for example, disciplinary) communities and on the presentation, exchange, and evaluation of their respective knowledge in the public sphere" (p. 34).

## Transdisciplinarity: Transcending Boundaries

To move from current thinking and information distribution organized to a large extent by disciplines, industry sectors, national and international borders, politics, race, gender, sexuality, religion, and others, and to make future thinking possible – where systems are no longer organized in exclusive structures – the theoretical and epistemological concept of knowledge societies needs to be applied to complex empirical problems such as creating solutions to the current climate crisis. This means that the concept of a well-functioning epistemopolis is contingent on systems that expand what Burke called "terministic screens" and instead work towards transformative and transcendental redefinitions (Burke, 1969) of currently accepted procedures regulated by disciplinary control. In other words, we need to encourage the redefinition of long-held beliefs on how knowledge is created and circulated within disciplinary boundaries. It is, therefore, especially important to establish transdisciplinary spaces, defined by Piaget (1972) as a "higher stage succeeding interdisciplinary relationships" that "would not only cover interactions or reciprocities between specialized research projects, but would place these relationships within a total system without any firm boundaries between disciplines" (p. 138). With a "desire to actively apply knowledge to the betterment of man [sic] and society" (Mahan, 1970, p. 195), transdisciplinarity promotes "the interconnectedness of many seemingly disparate things" and "develops meaningful linkages between subjects superficially kept far apart" (Bernstein, p. 3). In such a system, knowledge is shared between and among many disciplines and many stakeholders. Current discussions on transdisciplinarity (Alvargonzález, 2011; Angelstam et.al., 2013; Bernstein, 2015; Klein, 2004; Mauser et al., 2013; Max-Neef, 2005; Nicolescu, 2010; Osborne, 2015; Pohl et al., 2021) are especially focused on how we can expand and possibly eliminate the restrictions of systematized boundaries and instead create new spaces where people can "learn together to create something additional to what they normally do" (Angelstam et al., 2013, p. 260).

Angelstam et al.'s (2013) discussion of how to address the problems in social-ecological systems revealed that transdisciplinarity cannot only be restricted to academic fields. Instead, they point out that transdisciplinary research has to include diverse research disciplines, researchers, and also practitioners and stakeholders if we want to create sustainable solutions to the climate crisis. As they point out, a traditional academic system "reinforces traditional disciplinary approaches" and "produces disciplinary trained researchers, who largely tend to focus on successfully solving disciplinary or applied pre-defined problems" within a system that is "self-reinforcing" (p. 258). They emphasize the importance of the "production of new knowledge and collaborative learning processes" (p. 255) in transdisciplinary research in order to create "adaptive governance" which focuses on "iterative learning that enables humans to cope with uncertainty and change, thus enabling institutions that guide stakeholder collaboration" (p. 255). Different participants are no longer passive recipients of information; instead, the "active inclusion and participation of stakeholders representing different societal sectors" encourages a new approach to "problem formulation, knowledge production, and learning" (p. 256). This will, according to Angelstam et al. (2013), "enhance integration of novel theoretical and innovative methodological perspectives from different disciplines, as well as including non-academic knowledge in the empirical problem-solving process" (p. 256). Such integrated knowledge creation is essential in discussions surrounding climate change when disciplinary solutions are no longer enough to find solutions for a continuously escalating environmental emergency.

Angelstam et al.'s (2013) argument for new spaces where people can "learn together to create something additional to what they normally do" (p. 260) allows for transdisciplinarity to be part of a knowledge society. The communication of knowledge in such an environment can contribute to solving issues related to sustainability and climate change that are, according to Mauser et al. (2013) "impossible to define or attempt to solve… within the boundaries of subjects or disciplines, or where one goes beyond such definitions" (p. 424). The complexities of climate change research, they point out, "calls for new research strategies, with a strong focus on joint efforts by researchers from the natural, social and human sciences and engineering to contribute to the co-design of a global sustainable future" (p. 421). This is especially important because "societal needs" reinforce that an "established set of scientific methodologies will need to be supplemented by newly structured and prioritized approaches and processes" because "their research results should assist societies to make informed decisions" (p. 422). Assisting society in finding solutions to the climate crisis is no longer a theoretical endeavor. The many climate disasters show that action and advocacy, supported by solid research, is the necessary next step in fighting climate change.

The importance of making informed decisions is reiterated in the research conducted by Pohl et al. (2021) who point out in their work on the multidimensionality of transdisciplinary integration that knowledge "must be reorganised and connected to be relevant for solving societal problems" (p. 18). In addition, they point out, knowledge must be co-produced in "collaborative processes" that involve "researchers of different disciplines, inter- and trans-disciplinary fields, and representatives of private and public sectors including civil society" (p. 18). They emphasize the "heterogeneity and relationality of knowledge" (p. 19) and argue that transdisciplinary stakeholders need to pay attention to the complexity of the research problem, the diverse perspectives of the participants, and the opportunities for developing "descriptive, normative and transformative knowledge" and that "link *abstract* and *case specific* knowledge" (p. 19, emphasis in original). Pohl et al.'s emphasis on the heterogeneity of knowledge and on the diverse perspectives of participants is imperative in climate change action and advocacy research so that we can take into account the experiences of BIPOC, women, LGBTQ+ individuals and groups, poverty-stricken communities, and global non-western perspectives.

Situating teaching and learning in the age of climate change as part of an epistemopolis that requires a transdisciplinary approach to problem solving is especially important because, as Mauser et al. (2013) point out, "no definitive blueprint exists yet" for creating "new forms of learning and problem-solving" between "different parts of society and academia that have not traditionally been in close contact" (p. 427). Current transdisciplinary discussions encourage us to see the climate crisis as part of the larger theoretical framework of how language constructs knowledge, limits knowledge, and, if we transcend the limitations of our terministic screens, pushes knowledge in new directions by redefining, blending, and expanding existing boundaries. Bernstein (2013) argues that as a "response to a host of concerns about the pitfalls of specialization and the compartmentalization of knowledge, a globalized economy, shifts in the center of gravity in knowledge production, the ethics of research, and environmental crisis," transdisciplinarity "has gained recognition as a mode of research applied to real world problems that need not only to be understood in new ways but also demand practical solutions" (p. 12). As he emphasizes, "for transdisciplinarians concerned with justice, sustainability, and ending poverty, war, genocide, hunger, or other such wicked problems, theoretical solutions do not suffice, even though they realize that wicked problems by definition may be impossible to solve" (p. 12). Similar to the discussions of other transdisciplinarians, Bernstein's (2013) comments remind us of the importance of spaces – knowledge cities and knowledge societies – that encourage stakeholders to participate in knowledge creation, knowledge revision, and knowledge distribution in order to address the difficult program of climate change.

## Postcolonial Ecocriticism and Critical Ecofeminism: Bringing Theory to Practice

In their discussion of environmental and natural resource management strategies, USAID warns that "climate change is a threat that sees no borders and can harm us all" (USAID, 2022). They argue that "addressing the climate crisis must be a collective effort" where global partners need to cooperate in order to avert the climate crisis and implement "ambitious emissions reduction measures, protect critical ecosystems, transition to renewable energy, build resilience against the impacts of climate change, and promote the flow of capital toward climate-positive investments" (USAID, 2022). USAID's discussion of climate change brings to the forefront the importance of a transdisciplinary approach to problem solving and knowledge creation offered by knowledge societies. A successful transdisciplinary approach also requires theoretical frameworks that address abstract as well as practical principles for solving complex problems connected to sustainability and the current climate crisis. One such framework is that of postcolonial and critical ecofeminism, a framework that, according to Greta Gaard (1993), "has evolved from various fields of feminist inquiry and activism: peace movements, labor movements, women's health care, and the anti-nuclear, environmental, and animal liberation movements" (p. 1).

Postcolonial and critical ecofeminism has emerged and is still emerging as part of an anti-colonial and ecosocial framework which provides a critique of Western capitalism as the conquest of society and nature (Banerjee, 2016; Carlassare, 2000; Gaard, 2017; Huggan & Tiffin, 2015; Mies & Shiva, 1993; Plumwood, 2004). As Plumwood (2004) points out, it also challenges "nature/culture and human/nature dualisms" and asks us "to rethink the concepts of both *woman and the human* in ecological terms that are respectful of non-human difference, sensitive to human continuity with non-human nature, and attentive to the embodiment of all life and the embedment of human culture in the more than human world" (p. 51). The focus on respect in postcolonial and critical ecofeminism is especially important in discussions of the many diverse experiences and needs of BIPOC, women, and LGBTQ+ individuals and groups. In addition, such a framework encourages us to pay attention to local, national, and global poverty-stricken communities where, for example, food security and natural resources are limited, or where environmental disasters have led to increased disease rates, hunger, and displacement because, as Elizabeth Ferris (2008) reports, natural disasters affect people in poverty and marginalized people more severely, with consequences including "unequal access to assistance; discrimination in aid provision; enforced relocation; sexual and gender-based violence; loss of documentation; recruitment of children into fighting forces; unsafe or involuntary return or resettlement; and issues of property restitution" (Ferris, 2008).

The critical exploration of essentialist concepts and eurocentric perspectives found in some of the early ecofeminist writings is especially relevant in the establishment of critical ecofeminism which includes a focus on race, gender, sexuality, socio-economic status, and global environmental concerns (Gaard, 2017; Harper, 2012; Huggan & Tiffin, 2015; Sturgeon, 2009, 2016; Wright, 2018). It shows, as Gaard (2017) postulates, the "scholarly activist engagements with environmental justice, interspecies justice, queer climate justice, posthumanisms (i.e. plant studies), and sustainability efforts" (p. xvi). Gaard sees critical ecofeminism as benefitting from "past lessons about gender and racial essentialism, as well as from the more contemporary critical dimensions of economic, posthumanist, and postcolonial analysis" (p. xxiii). Sturgeon (2009), to counter what she calls "mainstream environmentalisms" rooted in Western culture, calls for a feminist environmental justice approach that uses an "intersectional approach (seeing at all times an interactive relationship among inequalities of gender, race, sexuality, class, and nation) and revealing the connections between social inequalities and environmental problems to uncover the systems of power that continue to generate the complex problems that we face" (p. 6). Such increased awareness of the complexities of climate change advocacy, then, requires us to look at expanded communication frameworks that take into account the multiplicity of issues to be addressed and solutions to be found.

The transdisciplinary nature of postcolonial and critical ecofeminism is especially important considering the initial tentative relationship between ecocriticism, feminism, and postcolonial theories, all emerging as correctives of untenable situations, but neither, according to Banerjee (2016) drawing from the knowledges of the other. As Banerjee (2016) reminds us about ecocriticism and postcolonialism, "both fields emerged at the intersection between humanities concerns and political activism and have hence centrally been concerned with the mooring of the humanities in material and social realities" (p. 194). In addition, critical ecofeminism's concern with humanity and nature (Carlassare, 1994, 2000; Gaard, 1993, 2017; Plumwood, 2004), and its focus on "context dependency and diversity" (Carlassare, 2000, p. 102), provides an additional perspective on resisting "ecological destruction and the legacies of patriarchy, capitalism, and imperialism" (p. 102). The emergence of postcolonial ecocriticism and critical ecofeminism, where "an ecological dimension is inextricably intertwined with postcolonial concerns and neo-colonial developments" (p. 205), is a promising step in bringing together perspectives from different fields in order to find new solutions in the fight against the climate crisis.

Learning from different theoretical fields and perspectives such as postcolonial ecocriticism has encouraged critical ecofeminist scholars to embrace multiple perspectives in the fight against anthropomorphic climate change. This transdisciplinary framework for addressing the impact of race, culture, gender, sexuality, religion, socio-economic status, ability, and politics on the environment can provide an in-depth understanding, for example, of the interconnectedness of environmental degradation and human activities. Postcolonial and critical ecofeminist principles, as Gaard (2017) points out, provide an additional incentive to create a collaborative environment where researchers are encouraged to emphasize "listening to one's research subjects, to the oppressed, to one's activist and scholarly community" (p. xvii). Drawing on multiple disciplines and movements is a basic tenet of postcolonial and critical ecofeminism because, Gaard (1993) argues, "the ideology which authorizes oppressions such as those based on race, class, gender, sexuality, physical abilities, and species is the same ideology which sanctions the oppression of nature" (p. 1).

## ANTHROPOMORPHIC CLIMATE CRISIS: HARNESSING THE ENERGY

The United Nations (UN), in their report on the climate crisis, points out that "it is clear that business as usual is not enough" when "climate change is the defining crisis of our time" (UN, 2022). As they point out, "no corner of the globe is immune from the devastating consequences of climate change. Rising temperatures are fueling environmental degradation, natural disasters, weather extremes, food and water insecurity, economic disruption, conflict, and terrorism. Sea levels are rising, the Arctic is melting, coral reefs are dying, oceans are acidifying, and forests are burning" (UN, 2022). According to USAID (2022), "we have a narrow moment to pursue action in order to protect our environment and to seize the opportunity that tackling climate change presents" (USAID, 2022). USAID highlights the need to transition to renewable energy, improve conservation efforts, prepare for and combat climate disasters, provide resources to create climate-smart agriculture, manage water resources, and reduce greenhouse gas emissions (USAID, 2022). The very real threat of rising temperatures globally, more frequent climate disasters, and increasing food and water insecurities caused by soil degradation, the UN (2022) points out, is also a catalyst for conflict since climate change increases competition for resources and forces people to migrate to other regions and countries (UN, 2022).

In their discussion on "What We Know: The Reality, Risks, and Response to Climate Change", the American Association for the Advancement of Science (AAAS, 2022) reports that "about 97% of climate scientists have concluded that human-caused climate change is happening" (AAAS, 2022) even though "surveys show that many Americans think climate change is still a topic of significant scientific disagreement" (AAAS, 2022). Ignoring scientific evidence and suppressing an EPA report that affirmed that the climate crisis is human-caused (Guenot, 2021) encouraged the rollback of climate and environmental regulations during the Trump administration. According to Kann (2021), these came at a time "when the science has never been clearer on the urgent need for the planet's biggest polluters to make big cuts to the greenhouse gas emissions" (Kann, 2021). Because the U.S. also left the Kyoto Protocol under George W. Bush, and left the Paris Climate Agreement under Trump, slowing down and reversing any progress in slowing down, much less reversing, anthropomorphic climate change and responding to the climate crisis on multiple levels has become more difficult and also more urgent (Kann, 2021).

Even though continuing disasters show us that climate change is real, climate science skeptics and deniers show us that the arguments made by climate scientists have not reached a significant number of individuals nor have the data on anthropomorphic climate change impacted major players of the industry – especially the industry sectors focused on non-renewable energy (Besley & Peters, 2020; Chomsky & Pollen, 2020; Mathers, 2020; Parry & Poland, 2019; Tangney, 2021). As Besley and Peters (2020) point out, "major fossil fuel companies have worked to cast doubt on the reliability of the scientific research despite the overwhelming majority of scientists supporting [human-caused climate change]" (p. 1351). This has created a climate change "denial machine" and a "climate change counter-movement" that focused on "conservative politicians, media and think tanks" (p. 1351). To counter such denial, Besley and Peters (2020) point out that we need to provide ourselves with skills that are "practical, cognitive, social, ethical, and political" (p. 1355) so that we can participate successfully in discussions on the current climate crisis.

The ability to reach a diverse audience becomes especially important in the efforts of the Climate Science Alliance (2022) which sees as its mission to "safeguard natural and human communities in the face of a changing climate" (Climate Science Alliance, 2022). Their boundary-spanning projects have created "partnerships which increase awareness of climate change impacts, promote solutions, and facilitate action" (Climate Science Alliance, 2022). As they point out, "alliance partners focus their efforts on boundary-spanning projects, sharing their skills, expertise, and knowledge in order to bridge the gap between research and application within the community" (Climate Science Alliance, 2022).

Participating successfully in climate crisis action certainly requires critical skills based not only on theoretical frameworks but also put to the test in communities, businesses, political organizations, and educational settings locally, nationally, and across the globe. This means that it is not enough for individuals and groups to learn about and know about the short- and long-term impact of climate change. Although such knowledge is important, it does not always lead to positive action that can then result in positive change. Instead, individuals might de-emphasize or ignore the problem, or they might become paralyzed or angry about the current climate crisis and ecological problems, including ocean acidification, rainforest destruction, global warming, oil spills, flooding, wildfires, chemical and e-waste, food waste, textile waste, and global pandemics. It is certainly important to realize the dangers of continuing on a similar path and raise awareness of the many untenable practices that put our communities, countries, and nations in danger. However, it is most important to harness the energy of individuals and communities who not only know about climate change but who have the critical skills to participate in transformative climate action on a local, national, and global level.

The theoretical and action-oriented lens of postcolonial ecofeminism with its focus on transdisciplinary knowledge exchange provides an opportunity to encourage discussions among many different stakeholders. It allows us to transform and transcend established terministic screens (Burke, 1965, 1966) and to share knowledge among diverse individuals and groups. This epistemological framework – what Echeverría (2011) called an epistemopolis or knowledge city that exists within a knowledge society – encourages learning from each other, the transfer of knowledge, and the creation of new knowledge to address the need for working together on finding solutions for the growing climate crisis.

## BEING PART OF THE SOLUTION: BRIDGING THEORY AND PRACTICE IN A TRANSFORMATIVE EPISTEMOPOLIS

The urgency of the climate crisis, and the need for bringing together multiple stakeholders in an effort to move beyond terministic screens – which among other things allow climate crisis deniers to use politics and the media to undermine the immediacy of the crisis – was the initial impetus for creating an online graduate-level course that could participate in transforming and transcending current discussions on climate change. The course, "Environmental Rhetoric in Public Spaces," encouraged students to hone their rhetorical awareness in order to participate successfully in climate change discussion. Students were asked to refine their verbal, written, and multimodal communication skills – whether presenting ideas to a group of people, writing a letter, report, email, website material, or social media entries – in order to participate as positive agents of change. Communication, in other words, needed to be persuasive and needed to take into account purpose, audience, stakeholders, and context. In other words, the course emphasized that public writing focuses on the goals and situations that require the need to write, and it focuses on the expectations, goals, situations, and needs of the listener and reader. As a result, students were asked to pay close attention to research, design of the document, medium in which the document is presented, and media used to distribute information.

In particular, "Environmental Rhetoric in Public Spaces" focused on the theories and practices of environmental rhetoric in public spaces such as social media spaces, documentaries, and written texts produced for public audiences. As practicing members of professional communities, students were asked to explore various approaches to how specific professional communities use written communication, and they explored their roles and responsibilities for successful communication in these organizations. They analyzed professional cultures, social contexts, genres, new media, and audiences to determine how they shape the various purposes and forms of writing, especially climate change writing and environmental rhetoric.

Readings examined transdisciplinary practices, especially those used by ecofeminists, and discussions prompted students to look at the importance of participating in an epistemopolis and in knowledge societies in order to address the growing climate crisis and the complexities of sustainable practices. Students, many of whom were current middle, high school, and community college teachers, and others who were journalists or worked in various industries, were especially engaged in studying environmental rhetoric and written, visual, and multimodal communication on climate change. They quickly addressed how climate change impacts not only them but impacts their students or their co-workers, often to a paralyzing degree that made action impossible. Students provided frequent input that helped them understand the different perspectives each of them brought to the discussions. Because of students' diverse cultural, social, ethnic, socio-economic, religious, and regional backgrounds, they were encouraged to provide concrete and relevant evidence for their arguments in order to show that they did their research and that they considered multiple perspectives and multiple solutions for encouraging climate change action.

To encourage critical communication and active participation skills concerning climate change and sustainability practices, the course's scaffolding practices were based on postcolonial and critical ecofeminist practices where students focused on "listening to one's research subjects, to the oppressed, to one's activist and scholarly community" (Gaard, 2017, p. xvii) and emphasized transdisciplinary approaches to knowledge creation. They included several measures that provided students with opportunities to join discussions on the environment and sustainable measures to address the anthropomorphic impact on the climate crisis. Students engaged in course introductions which were based on their experiences and on what they expected to gain from participating in the course. Additionally, they were exposed to textual and multimodal readings focused on theory and practical applications so that they could then participate in discussions that connected the readings to their experiences and to the experiences of the communities in which they participated. After creating a strong foundation based on the readings and discussions, they then created publicly accessible multimodal blog entries geared towards applying their theoretical and practical knowledge about environmental concerns to climate change activism and climate advocacy. In other words, the course encouraged students to build on their personal experiences and apply ecofeminist practices and transdisciplinary approaches to participate successfully in transforming and transcending the current practices of climate change activism and advocacy by using communication strategies that took the diverse knowledges, skills, and needs of multiple stakeholders into consideration.

As several students pointed out in the initial course introductions, they wanted to be climate activists and advocates for the environment. However, because of how difficult it seemed to be fully engaged, they often remained at the sidelines without participating in the discussions when those discussions were getting contentious. Many chose to participate in the course because they realized that remaining at the periphery of climate action was no longer enough, and that participating more actively was important in order to create environments for initiating positive changes. Students discussed their experiences growing up in environments where family members refused to believe in anthropomorphic climate change, where climate change was not addressed, or where involvement was relatively passive and included dinner time discussions and comments on how individuals were powerless against the growing dangers of climate change. They also addressed their current positionalities at taking small steps to decrease their carbon footprint by being fully vegan, participating in vegan Mondays, buying second-hand clothing, separating trash from recyclables, participating in climate action marches, or using public transportation or bicycles for getting to school and/or work.

The different student voices, and the experiences they brought to the table, showed the student group that they were part of a community that was concerned about climate change and that wanted to become more involved in finding ways to actively participate as climate change activists and climate action advocates. They were excited about learning more about the different theoretical approaches, the current discussions on climate change communication, the opportunities for climate change activism, and how to make better evidence-based decisions on climate change action, advocacy, and communication practices by participating in a knowledge society where, according to Echeverría (2011) they could ""promote, facilitate, and marshal knowledge flow among very different communities" (p. 27).

Students' enthusiasm and curiosity about climate change communication remained strong throughout the course, and the readings became the basis for continued discussion on individual and group involvement in climate action and sustainability movements. The textual and multimodal, multimedia, and social media readings for the course were organized into four modules. First, the general framework exposed students to the rhetorical principles for climate change communication and environmental rhetoric in global and intercultural settings and to ecofeminism as a theoretical lens for addressing climate change communication. Readings introduced students to Smith's (2017) rhetorical dimensions of myth and narrative to highlight the importance of a coherent story when trying to influence an audience. As Smith (2014) points out, "storytelling helps to transform a set of facts, which might otherwise be unpersuasive, into a coherent narrative that advances a point of view" (p. 30). In connection with Gaard's (2017), Weiss andd Moskop's (2020) and Plumwood's (2004) discussion on critical ecofeminism; Armstrong, Krasny, and Schuldt's (2018) discussion on how to communicate climate change; Constantino and Weber's (2021) reflections on the psychological and political agency of narratives to create change; and McArdle's (2021) focus on intersectional climate urbanism, students were able to familiarize themselves with a wide variety of approaches to climate change discussions. Many were especially drawn to McArdle's (2021) call for action, letting her readers know that "there is an ethical responsibility on us to imagine and create better alternative futures" (p. 304). As she points out, "intersectional climate urbanism considers all factors that oppress and empower people and is one step towards a more inclusive climate-changed future" (p. 304).

After the initial exposure to ecofeminist theories, intersectionality, and the importance of creating successful narratives, students focused on learning about and participating in transdisciplinary approaches to climate change discussions during the second module. Reading Labosier and Fay's (2019) discussion of a co-taught science and rhetoric course provided a reminder that science teaching includes a "civic mission" to prepare "a nonscientific public to appropriately utilize science in carefully forming opinions on public matters and boost credibility in voicing public opinions in deliberative public settings" (p. 1903). As the authors point out, "students had opportunities to witness the collision of two scholarly paradigms – the scientific and the humanistic – in ways that demonstrated the benefits and limitations of each" (p. 1907). Additional readings (Gee, 2004; Porter, 1986; Bladow and Ladino, 2018; Halpern, 2021) reiterated the importance of intertextuality and transdisciplinarity in addressing climate change, bringing to the forefront the need for collaborative efforts in addressing and changing the ongoing climate crisis.

Discussions of transdisciplinarity were followed by the third module which emphasized the importance of subject matter and genre knowledge in climate change communication and environmental rhetoric, Slovic's (2016) work on "Narrative Scholarship as an American Contribution to Global Ecocriticism," and Rodríguez-Labajos and Ray's (2021) discussion on the importance of artworks in environmental activism, especially because "art is thriving as a pathway to knowledge-sharing and the creation of new ideas" (p. 102268), encouraged students to pay attention to how subject matter can be viewed through many different epistemological, axiological, and ontological frameworks. Similarly, discussions on food, health, global justice, and cultural reproduction (Rawlinson, 2015; Parascoli, 2014; Harper, 2010, 2012; Chuck, Fernandes, & Hyers, 2016) provided the impetus for students to look closely at how different genres can disseminate information most successfully.

The final module focused on participating in an epistemopolis and knowledge society by examining social media and global communication practices and their effects on climate change and environmental rhetoric. This module was specifically focused on opportunities for participating in climate change action and included TED talks as well as social media sites that encouraged readers to be part of positive change. Goodall (2020), for example, reminded her audience that we are part of the environment and live with it and not separately from it. UNESCO's (2019) focus on why we need to teach and learn about climate change was especially pertinent for the middle and high school teachers in the class, and

COPD26's (2021) 55 gitaton challenge encouraged students to contribute as change agents to slow and halt the environmental crisis. These texts, in conjunction with others that brought to the forefront the multiple perspectives and ways in which diverse individuals and groups participated in climate action and had become climate advocates, were especially powerful for addressing our positionalities and responsibilities within the natural as well as human-made environments.

To scaffold possible ways to participate as climate change advocates and activists, students posted their responses to the textual, multimedia, and social media texts, and they collaborated on idea exchanges throughout the semester. The collaborative engagement with their classmates, and the positive feedback on possible ways of participating as climate change advocates and activists, guided students to find ways to participate in the current exchange and to use their theoretical knowledge and their individual lenses to create multimedia pieces that would transcend and transform current knowledge, and that could become part of a knowledge society in search for innovative solutions to the climate crisis. Students' increased critical communication skills, awareness of what is already part of the discussion, and awareness of what is still needed promoted continual exchanges of ideas and concepts, revisions of initial schemes, and possible action plans for encouraging climate change advocacy. In other words, students' increased familiarity with the current discussions on climate change and environmental rhetoric, and their understanding of the importance of transdisciplinary practices, exemplified in this case by postcolonial and critical ecofeminism, created a supportive environment for becoming actively engaged as members of knowledge communities and knowledge societies that work together in order to make a difference to currently untenable situations. Such active engagement was especially important when students used their social media presence and created a blogging portfolio that brought together theory and practice as the basis for participating in transdisciplinary knowledge communities.

Students' engagement in discussions of sustainability, climate activism, and climate change advocacy provided the starting point for moving from critical learners to engaged citizens and active participants. They were able to use their voices to build on, transform, and transcend the terministic screens of current climate action discourse. In their blog portfolios, students advocated for ethical and responsible climate change action, especially in relation to traditionally minoritized groups and individuals such as BIPOC, women, LGBTQ+ individuals, and people living in poverty. They also promoted earth-forward women leadership and advocated for including ecofeminist principles when exploring sustainability solutions and climate action. Others addressed the need to bring food scarcity, life expectancy, and race inequities to the center of climate advocacy. The importance of conscious and conscientious climate change communication, climate action, climate advocacy, and of looking beyond currently held beliefs, became an important rallying point expressed in the blog portfolios.

The positive effects of learning about the theories and practices of climate change communication and sustainability efforts were not limited to the classroom. Students pointed out by the end of the course how much more involved they are in their communities, and how they use their knowledge to work with organizations and groups that are actively engaged in sustainability efforts and climate action. As one student pointed out, the readings, discussions, and the blog portfolio in "Environmental Rhetoric in Public Spaces" "has influenced much of the work I do in the environmental sector. It also inspired me to get involved in activist work in my community after class ended, which was something I always wanted to do but hadn't." Students used what they learned and experienced as members of a transdisciplinary class community and transformed their own actions, transcended stumbling blocks, and started to participate in knowledge communities and knowledge societies focused on climate advocacy.

## THEORY TO ACTION: FUTURE DIRECTIONS

The immediate success of "Environmental Rhetoric in Public Spaces" – increasing awareness of theoretical frameworks, participating in public discussions on climate change advocacy, and actively engaging as members of knowledge societies – shows how important it is to create safe spaces where students can explore, broaden, and practice their understanding of the interconnectedness of the natural world and humans. The short-term effects of greater engagement with climate change action and advocacy shows how important it is to continue work on best practices for not only raising awareness about the current crises related to climate change but for also increasing ethical participation in climate action. Future studies can address the long-term impact of working on the theories as well as the practices of climate change action and advocacy.

Certainly, courses such as "Environmental Rhetoric in Public Spaces" should not stand alone. For future transdisciplinary work that can become part of a knowledge society, it is important to consider how this course can participate in transdisciplinary knowledge exchange on sustainability, environmental justice, climate action, and climate advocacy. As a first step, "Environmental Rhetoric in Public Spaces" has become a part of a newly created graduate certificate in Environmental Narrative. Ideally, the integration of a course similar to "Environmental Rhetoric in Public Spaces" into a master's degree on global sustainability rhetoric, environmental humanities, environmental science communication for a global audience, climate action and advocacy communication would provide a more rounded experience on how to engage in transdisciplinary climate change communication and action.

## REASON FOR HOPE: CONCLUDING THOUGHTS

On July 6, 2022, *The Ocean Cleanup* announced on Facebook that "Interceptor 007 has arrived in LA County" (The Ocean Cleanup, 2022a). *The Ocean Cleanup*, a non-profit organization with headquarters in Rotterdam, Netherlands was founded by Boyan Slat in 2013 (*The Ocean Cleanup*, 2022b) after Slat's (2012) TED talk on cleaning the world's oceans of plastic pollution went viral. Ten years later, the organization includes engineers, researchers, scientists, computational modelers, and support staff with a mission of "developing and scaling technologies to rid the world's oceans of plastic" (*The Ocean Cleanup*, 2022b). Success stories are posted on *The Ocean Cleanup* website, on Facebook, Twitter, and Instagram. This multimodal social media approach encourages audiences from across the globe to learn about how one person envisioned and put into practice a transformative company that employs individuals from many different backgrounds and with many different experiences. Instead of waiting for a government organization to take action, Boyan Slat saw an opportunity for transcending imagined boundaries and moving beyond what was seen to be possible. He collaborated with multiple stakeholders and applied the principles of a knowledge society – "the plurality of communities of knowledge" (Echeverría, Alonso, and Oiarzabal, 2011, p. 9) – in his fight against oceanic plastic pollution.

On August 3, 2022, Re:wild – an organization that focuses on wildland and wildlife restoration and that partners with earth advocates around the globe – reported on the successful efforts to rewild California by planting over 100,000 trees and native plants in the Santa Monica Mountains. Over 2,000 volunteers have worked with the National Park Service to "rewild" an area that was "hard-hit by fires in recent years" (Putnam, 2022). Re:wild also participated in efforts to prevent the extinction of the saola, rare wild cattle that was found in Vietnam in 1992. In collaboration with the European Union, USAID, and

WWF-Viet Nam, Re:wild intends to secure the last saola "for a conservation breeding program to ensure the species survival" (Mayer & Murphy, 2022). According to Re:wild (2022), "radical change requires radical collaborations" which allows them to "scale impact through the replication and amplification of proven solutions, and to act quickly where need meets opportunity" (Our Work, 2022). Re:wild's focus on solutions – which include "creating and managing protected areas, protecting and restoring ecosystems, working with Indigenous people on their land rights, and preventing wildlife crime" – makes it essential to tailor their work to "local ecological, cultural, and socioeconomic contexts and implemented by our local partners" (Our Work, 2022).

On August 16, 2022, President Joe Biden signed into law an inflation reduction bill that provides approximately 370 billion dollars over the next decade to fight climate change. The bill includes allocations for clean energy technologies such as solar energy and electric vehicles, climate research grants, eco-friendly jet fuel, clean-energy investment credits, and global pollution clean-up efforts (Vaidyanathan, 2022). As Vaidyanathan (2022) reports, "the legislation would cut US greenhouse-gas emissions by about 30–40% below 2005 levels by 2030." This, she continues, will bring "the country closer to delivering on its pledge of a 50% reduction, which Biden made last year." In addition, "it signals to other nations that the United States, a major emitter that has historically pumped the largest share of greenhouse gases into Earth's atmosphere, is on board to address climate change" (Vaidyanathan, 2022).

The efforts of environmental groups, climate change activists and advocates, non-profits, and governments show hope for addressing best ways forward to fight anthropomorphic climate change. We can participate as members of knowledge societies where transdisciplinary climate change action and advocacy can be explored, discussed, revised, and applied, and where a postcolonial and critical ecofeminist lens can guide us to take into account the multiple perspectives of traditionally marginalized individuals and groups.

## REFERENCES

Alvargonzález, D. (2011). Multidisciplinarity, interdisciplinarity, transdisciplinarity, and the sciences. *International Studies in the Philosophy of Science*, *25*(4), 387–403. doi:10.1080/02698595.2011.623366

American Association for the Advancement of Science (AAAS). (2022). *What we know: The reality, risks, and response to climate change.* Retrieved from https://whatweknow.aaas.org/get-the-facts/

Angelstam, P., Andersson, K., Annerstedt, M., Axelsson, R., Elbakidze, M., Garrido, P., Grahn, P., Jönsson, K. I., Pedersen, S., Schlyter, P., Skärbäck, E., Smith, M., & Stjernquist, I. (2013). Solving problems in social–ecological systems: Definition, practice and barriers of transdisciplinary research. *Ambio*, *42*(2), 254–265. doi:10.100713280-012-0372-4 PMID:23475660

Armstrong, A. K., Krasny, M. E., & Schuldt, J. P. (2018). *Communicating climate change: A guide for educators.* Comstock Publishing Associates.

Bae, G., & Yeung, J. (2022, August 9). *Record rainfall kills at least 9 in Seoul as water floods buildings, submerges cars.* CNN. https://www.cnn.com/2022/08/09/asia/seoul-south-korea-rain-flooding-intl-hnk/index.html

Bagheri, A., & Hjorth, P. (2007). Planning for sustainable development: A paradigm shift towards a process-based approach. *Sustainable Development*, *15*(2), 83–96. doi:10.1002d.310

Bernstein, J. H. (2015). Transdisciplinarity: A review of its origins, development, and current issues. *Journal of Research Practice*, *11*(1), R1. https://jrp.icaap.org/index.php/jrp/article/view/510/41

Besley, T., & Peters, M. A. (2020). Life and death in the Anthropocene: Educating for survival amid climate and ecosystem changes and potential civilisation collapse. *Educational Philosophy and Theory*, *52*(13), 1347–1357. doi:10.1080/00131857.2019.1684804

Bladow, K., & Ladino, J. (Eds.). (2018). *Affective ecocriticism: Emotion, embodiment, environment*. University of Nebraska Press. doi:10.2307/j.ctv75d0g8

Burke, K. (1965). Terministic Screens. *Philosophy and the Arts*, *39*, 87–102.

Burke, K. (1966). *Language as symbolic action: Essays on life, literature and method*. U of California P. Print doi:10.1525/9780520340664

Burke, K. (1969). *A rhetoric of motives*. University of California Press.

Burns, T. R. (2012). The sustainability revolution: A societal paradigm shift. *Sustainability*, *4*(6), 1118–1134. doi:10.3390u4061118

Carlassare, E. (1994). Destabilizing the criticism of essentialism in ecofeminist discourse. *Capitalism, Nature, Socialism*, *5*(3), 50–66. doi:10.1080/10455759409358597

Carlassare, E. (2000). Socialist and cultural ecofeminism: Allies in resistance. *Ethics and the Environment*, *5*(1), 89–106. doi:10.1016/S1085-6633(99)00025-X

Chomsky, N., & Pollin, R. (2020). *Climate crisis and the global green new deal: The political economy of saving the planet*. Verso Books.

Chuck, C., Fernandes, S. A., & Hyers, L. L. (2016). Awakening to the politics of food: Politicized diet as social identity. *Appetite*, *107*, 425–436. doi:10.1016/j.appet.2016.08.106 PMID:27554183

Climate Science Alliance. (2022). *Who we are*. Climate Science Alliance. https://www.climatesciencealliance.org

Constantino, S. M., & Weber, E. U. (2021). Decision-making under the deep uncertainty of climate change: The psychological and political agency of narratives. *Current Opinion in Psychology*, *42*, 151–159. doi:10.1016/j.copsyc.2021.11.001 PMID:34861621

COPD26. (2021). *The 55 Gigaton Challenge*. Ted Talk. https://www.ted.com/talks/countdown_the_55_gigaton_challenge/

Darbellay, F. (2015). Rethinking inter-and transdisciplinarity: Undisciplined knowledge and the emergence of a new thought style. *Futures*, *65*, 163–174. doi:10.1016/j.futures.2014.10.009

Echeverría, J. (1999). *Los señores del aire: Telépolis y el tercer entorno*. Destino.

Echeverría, J. (2011). Epistemopolis: From knowledge communities to knowledge cities. In J. Echeverría, A. Alonso, & P. Oiarzabal (Eds.), *Knowledge communities*. Center for Basque Studies, University of Nevada.

Echeverría, J., Alonso, A., & Oiarzabal, P. (Eds.). (2011). Knowledge communities. Center for Basque Studies, University of Nevada, Reno.

Edwards, A. R. (2005). *The sustainability revolution: Portrait of a paradigm shift*. New Society Publishers.

Ferris, E. (2008). *Natural disasters, human rights, and the role of national human rights institutions*. Brookings. https://www.brookings.edu/on-the-record/natural-disasters-human-rights-and-the-role-of-national-human-rights-institutions/

Gaard, G. (1993). Living interconnections with animals and nature. In G. Gaard (Ed.), *Ecofeminism: Women, animals, nature* (pp. 1–12). Temple University Press.

Gaard, G. (2017). *Critical ecofeminism*. Lexington Books.

Gallastegui, M. C., & Galarraga, I. (2011). Climate change and knowledge communities. In J. Echeverría, A. Alonso, & P. Oiarzabal (Eds.), *Knowledge communities*. Center for Basque Studies, University of Nevada.

Gee, J. P. (2004). *An introduction to discourse analysis: Theory and method*. Routledge. doi:10.4324/9780203005675

Goodall, J. (2020). *Every day you live, you impact the planet*. Ted Talk. https://www.ted.com/talks/jane_goodall_every_day_you_live_you_impact_the_planet#t-3393

Guenot, M. (2021, May 13). *In a report suppressed under Trump, the EPA has said for the first time that humans caused the climate crisis*. Business Insider. https://www.businessinsider.com/epa-climate-crisis-man-made-report-suppressed-trump-2021-5?op=1

Hall, J. (2018, November 3). Rewriting disciplines, rewriting boundaries: Transdisciplinary and translingual challenges for WAC/WID. *Across the Disciplines*, 15(3), 1-10. http://wac.colostate.edu/atd/trans_wac/intro.pdf

Halpern, M. (2021). Scientific integrity and advocacy: keeping the government honest. In P. DellaSala (Ed.), *Conservation Science and Advocacy for a Planet in Peril* (pp. 149–175). Elsevier. doi:10.1016/B978-0-12-812988-3.00003-X

Harper, A. B. (2010). Social justice beliefs and addiction to uncompassionate consumption. In A. B. Harper (Ed.), *Sistah vegan: Black female vegans speak on food, identity, health and society* (pp. 20–41). Lantern Books.

Harper, A. B. (2012). Going beyond the normative white 'post-racial' gegan epistemology. In P. Williams-Forson & C. Counihan (Eds.), *Taking Food Public: Redefining Foodways in a Changing World* (pp. 155–174). Routledge.

Huggan, G., & Tiffin, H. (2015). *Postcolonial ecocriticism: Literature, animals, environment* (2nd ed.). Routledge. doi:10.4324/9781315768342

Kann, D. (2021, Jan. 18). "The lost years": Climate damage that occurred on Trump's watch will endure long after he is gone. *CNN*. Retrieved from https://www.cnn.com/2021/01/18/politics/trump-climate-legacy-bidens-challenge/index.html

Klein, J. T. (2004). Prospects for transdisciplinarity. *Futures*, *36*(4), 515–526. doi:10.1016/j.futures.2003.10.007

Kuhn, T. (1970). *The structure of scientific revolutions* (2nd ed.). University of Chicago Press.

Lave, J., & Wenger, E. (1991). *Situated learning: Legitimate peripheral participation*. Cambridge University Press.

Leemans, R., & Moore, H. (2013). Transdisciplinary global change research: The co-creation of knowledge for sustainability. *Current Opinion in Environmental Sustainability*, *5*(3-4), 420–431.

Mahan, J. L., Jr. (1970). *Toward transdisciplinary inquiry in the humane sciences* [Doctoral dissertation, United States International University]. UMI No. 702145. Retrieved from ProQuest Dissertations & Theses Global.

Mathers, R. (2020). An anthropology of climate change deniers. In D. Mathers (Ed.), *Depth Psychology and Climate Change* (pp. 29–48). Routledge.

Mauser, W., Klepper, G., Rice, M., Schmalzbauer, B. S., Hackmann, H., Leemans, R., & Moore, H. (2013). Transdisciplinary global change research: The co-creation of knowledge for sustainability. *Current Opinion in Environmental Sustainability*, *5*(3-4), 420–431. doi:10.1016/j.cosust.2013.07.001

Max-Neef, M. A. (2005). Foundations of transdisciplinarity. *Ecological Economics*, *53*, 5–16.

Mayer, L. R., & Murphy, D. (2022, August 10). *The European Union, Re:wild and WWF-Viet Nam mobilize emergency response to prevent imminent extinction of Asian "unicorn."* Re:wild. https://www.rewild.org/press/the-european-union-re-wild-and-wwf-viet-nam-mobilize-emergency-response-to

McArdle, R. (2021). Intersectional climate urbanism: Towards the inclusion of marginalised voices. *Geoforum*, *126*, 302–305. doi:10.1016/j.geoforum.2021.08.005

NASA. (2022, August 10). *Death valley flash flooding*. NASA Earth Observatory. https://earthobservatory.nasa.gov/images/150181/death-valley-flash-flooding

Nicolescu, B. (2010). Methodology of transdisciplinarity: Levels of reality, logic of the included middle, and complexity. *Transdisciplinary Journal of Engineering & Science, 1*(1), 19-38.

Nicolescu, B. (2012). Transdisciplinarity: The hidden third, between the subject and the object. *Human and Social Studies*, *1*(2), 13–28.

Parasecoli, F. (2014). Food, identity, and cultural reproduction in immigrant communities. *Social Research*, *81*(2), 415–439.

Parry, C., & Poland, M. (2019). "Going on" into climate crisis. *Green Letters*, *23*(4), 331–336.

Piaget, J. (1972). The epistemology of interdisciplinary relationships. In *Interdisciplinarity: Problems of teaching and research in universities* (pp. 127–139). Organisation for Economic Co- operation and Development.

Plumwood, V. (2004). Gender, eco-feminism and the environment. In R. White (Ed.), *Controversies in Environmental Sociology* (pp. 43–60). Cambridge University Press.

Pohl, C., Klein, J. T., Hoffmann, S., Mitchell, C., & Fam, D. (2021). Conceptualising transdisciplinary integration as a multidimensional interactive process. *Environmental Science & Policy, 118*, 18–26.

Porter, J. E. (1986). Intertextuality and the discourse community. *Rhetoric Review, 5*(1), 34–47.

Putnam, M. (2022, August 3). *Rewilding California: Project reaches halfway point in planting over 100,000 native plants in largest-ever restoration effort in the Santa Monica Mountains.* Re:wild. https://www.rewild.org/news/rewilding-california-project-reaches-halfway-point-in-planting-over-100-000

Rao, U., & Saul, A. (2021). From the green revolution to the green chemistry revolution: In pursuit of a paradigm shift in agricultural sustainability. In X. Savarimuthu, U. Rao, & M. F. Reynolds (Eds.), *Go Green for Environmental Sustainability* (pp. 47–66). CRC Press.

Rawlinson, M. C. (2015). Food, health, and global justice. *International Journal of Feminist Approaches to Bioethics, 8*(2), 1–9.

Re:wild (2022). *Our work.* Re:wild. https://www.rewild.org/our-work

Rodríguez-Labajos, B., & Ray, I. (2021). Six avenues for engendering creative environmentalism. *Global Environmental Change, 68*, 102269.

Schiefelbein, M. (2022, August 20). *Chinese farmers struggle as scorching drought wilts crops.* The Associated Press. https://apnews.com/article/china-asia-droughts-chongqing-ddd4b-c18741f4710e5fbd4db7070d3d8

Schmitz, R. (2022, August 17. *Germany's Rhine is at one of its lowest levels. That's trouble for the top EU economy.* All Things Considered. https://www.npr.org/2022/08/17/1117861780/germany-rhine-low-water-level-shipping

Senge, P. M., & Käufer, K. H. (2000). Communities of leaders or no leadership at all. In B. Kellerman & L. R. Matusak (Eds.), *Cutting Edge: Leadership.* James McGregor Burns Academy of Leadership Press.

Slat, B. (2012). *How the oceans can clean themselves.* TED Talk. Retrieved from https://www.youtube.com/watch?v=ROW9F-c0kIQ

Slovic, S. (2016). Narrative Scholarship as an American Contribution to Global Ecocriticism. In H. Zapf (Ed.), *Handbook of Ecocriticism and Cultural Ecology* (pp. 315–333). DeGruyter.

Smith, C. R. (2017). *Rhetoric and human consciousness: A history* (5th ed.). Waveland Press.

Sturgeon, N. (2016). *Ecofeminist natures: Race, gender, feminist theory, and political action.* Routledge.

Sturgeon, N. L. (2009). *Environmentalism in popular culture: Gender, race, sexuality, and the politics of the natural.* University of Arizona Press.

Tangney, P. (2021). Are "Climate Deniers" Rational Actors? Applying Weberian Rationalities to Advance Climate Policymaking. *Environmental Communication, 15*(8), 1077–1091.

Tennant, M. (2019). Psychology and Adult Learning: The Role of Theory in Informing Practice (4th ed.). Routledge., https://doi.org/10.4324/9780429023255.

The Associated Press. (2022, August 19). *Winds drive major wildfire in Spain; Portugal goes on alert.* The Associated Press. https://apnews.com/article/wildfires-fires-valencia-a219c8a7ff5542b0b3732afd-7fc19890

The Ocean Cleanup. (2022a). *The interceptor 007 has arrived in LA County.* Facebook. https://www.facebook.com/TheOceanCleanup/videos/731077404702075/

The Ocean Cleanup. (2022b). *About.* https://theoceancleanup.com/about/

UNESCO. (2019). *Why we urgently need to teach and learn about climate change.* UNESCO. https://en.unesco.org/news/why-we-urgently-need-teach-and-learn-about-climate-change

United Nations. (2022). *The climate crisis – A race we can win.* UN. https://www.un.org/en/un75/climate-crisis-race-we-can-win

USAID. (2022). *Climate change.* https://www.usaid.gov/climate

Vaidyanathan, G. (2022, August 17). Biden signs historic climate bill as scientists applaud. *Nature Magazine.* https://www.scientificamerican.com/article/biden-signs-historic-climate-bill-as-scientists-applaud/

Weiss, P., & Moskop, W. (2020, November). Ecofeminist manifestos: Resources for feminist perspectives on the environment. *Women's Studies International Forum, 83,* 102418.

Wenger, E. (1998). Communities of practice: Learning as a social system. *Systems Thinker.* http://www.co-i-l.com/coil/knowledge-garden/cop/lss.shtml

Wenger, E. (1999). *Communities of practice. Learning, meaning and identity.* Cambridge University Press.

Wright, L. (2018). Vegans in the interregnum: The cultural moment of an enmeshed theory. In Thinking Veganism in Literature and Culture: Towards a Vegan Theory. Springer.

## ADDITIONAL READING

Almassi, B. (2012). Climate change, epistemic trust, and expert trustworthiness. *Ethics and the Environment, 17*(2), 29–49. doi:10.2979/ethicsenviro.17.2.29

Biehl, J. (1991). *Rethinking ecofeminist politics.* South End Press.

Darbellay, F. (2015). Rethinking inter-and transdisciplinarity: Undisciplined knowledge and the emergence of a new thought style. *Futures, 65,* 163–174. doi:10.1016/j.futures.2014.10.009

DeLuca, K. M. (1999). *Image politics: The new rhetoric of environmental activism.* Guilford.

Engelbrecht, P. (2004). Transdisciplinary collaboration. *Keys to Educational Psychology,* 247-257.

Gaard, G. (2011). Ecofeminism revisited: Rejecting essentialism and re-placing species in a material feminist environmentalism. *Feminist Formations*, *23*(2), 26–53. doi:10.1353/ff.2011.0017

Mobjörk, M. (2010). Consulting versus participatory transdisciplinarity: A refined classification of transdisciplinary research. *Futures*, *42*(8), 866–873. doi:10.1016/j.futures.2010.03.003

## KEY TERMS AND DEFINITIONS

**Climate Change Activism:** Participation in transformative action to raise awareness and demand change in support of the environment.

**Ecofeminism:** Foregrounding gender to analyze the relationship between human beings and the natural world.

**Environmental Justice:** Supports equal access to a safe, healthy, and sustainable environment and fights against marginalization and oppression.

**Knowledge Societies:** Creates environments where knowledge can be shared by all members.

**Sustainable Solutions:** Balanced approaches to natural resources that ensure the long-term well-being of humans and the natural world.

**Trans-Disciplinarity:** Requires participation from multiple stakeholders to find solutions for specific issues.

# Chapter 14
# The Significance of Collective Self-Directed Learning Competencies for the Sustainability of Higher Education

**Jean Henry Blignaut**
https://orcid.org/0000-0001-7326-4136
*Research Unit Self-Directed Learning, Faculty of Education, North-West University, South Africa*

**Charlene du Toit-Brits**
*North-West University, South Africa*

## ABSTRACT

*Few scholarly studies have addressed SDL in HE. Competency improvement and curriculum change are important HE learning opportunities. Curricula should emphasize knowledge acquisition, future-oriented evaluation, and global accountability to meet HE's SDGs. Sustainable learning, living, and working must be explored alongside HE for sustainable development. New learning strategies and cultures are needed. It should be sustainable, open-minded, self-directed, and participatory. CSDL is essential for sustained capabilities and HE's growth. HE must promote SDL to engage pupils. This chapter claims that SDL skills are vital for HE's progress. Participatory learning builds these skills, which needs a university-wide approach. Using explicit, null, and hidden curricula creates meaningful learning experiences, linking theory and practice. Self-directed, sustained learning ought to be HE's focus. SDL should replace directed learning in HESD. Lastly, participatory learning might generate independently responsible and accountable thinkers who respect sustainable development.*

DOI: 10.4018/978-1-6684-6172-3.ch014

## INTRODUCTION

Globally, diversity is a necessary focal point in all spheres of life, but arguably most importantly, in education. In the words of former South African President Nelson Mandela, "education is the most powerful weapon you can use to change the world." In addition, education can also contribute to sustainable living spaces globally. Higher Education that is sustainable will not only be able to meet the needs of a diverse student population, as we have in the South African context, but it can sustain itself and survive into the future. Most Higher Education Institutions (HEI) have strategic goals focused on promoting diversity, equality, and inclusion, among other ideals. If achieved, these can promote lifelong learning beyond the walls of the HEI and lead to sustainable higher education.

The most important aspect to remember is that people from all walks of life are involved in HE: They are from different backgrounds, face different challenges and must deal with different problems. Therefore, HE should not exclude anyone and reflect the lives of the students who are enrolled for higher education degrees. As such, consultation between, and the participation of, various stakeholders such as academics, students, policy designers/developers, managers, curriculum specialists and researchers are an absolute necessity.

It seems likely that the sustainability of HE has looked to participatory learning as a means to readdress learning methods with strong links between the two (Sun, Hong & Dong, 2022). Developing sustainable competencies necessitates instructive strategies that emphasize learning processes and methods much more than the compilation of knowledge and facts. Developing sustainable competencies through instructive strategies helps to instruct individuals with capacities for participation, change, innovation, creativity, and resilience through SDL competencies, such as critical thinking, holistic thinking, problem-solving, and teamwork (Sun, Hong & Dong, 2022). HE that deals only with cognitive knowledge is insufficient. This approach to learning must be founded on contemporary living habits, where individuals in complicated circumstances can be inspired to discover innovative thoughts and strategies and partake in the learning processes, to progressively move their learning and social communities to sustainable development (Rieckmann, 2018). Such active student-centered learning methods can reinforce students' thinking, feelings, actions, and mindfulness, transforming how they perceive and exist in the world around them. These active teaching-learning processes increase knowledge recollection, fostering motivation and higher-order learning and SDL competencies (Sun, Hong & Dong, 2022).

## BACKGROUND

Since the 1970s, the idea of SDL has been evident in HE. To us, SDL has always been a HE catchphrase that commonly appears in academic writing. However, experience has shown us that, although SDL has been discussed in theoretical terms in conversations about education, it has seldom been put into full practice in HE. The construction of appropriate educational learning environments in HE is still a problem that must be overcome to enhance and promote student-centered learning capabilities and ensure higher education sustainability (Brockett & Hiemstra, 2019; Du Toit-Brits, 2020; Loeng, 2020; Olivier, 2021).

The current shortage in higher education is an apparent reason for the rising emphasis on SDL skills since it is critical to transforming educational practice from a traditional lecturer responsibility to a facilitator and mediator of SDL competencies (Du Toit-Brits, 2018b; Du Toit-Brits, 2020). Considering that SDL is based on social constructivism as a theory of learning (see Piaget, 1928; Vygotsky, 1978), it

## The Significance of Collective Self-Directed Learning Competencies

is widely recognized that it offers a solid platform for planning constructively engaged student learning (Brockett & Hiemstra, 2019; Sun, Hong & Dong, 2022). Although SDL is often provided as a type of individual learning, it should not be forgotten that learning environments must support CSDL capabilities for HE to remain sustainable (Gusmão Caiado et al., 2018; Martins et al., 2019).

The authors believe that describing the core elements of CSDL is essential for incorporating such skills into HEand ensuring that a lack of information does not constrain practice. Consequently, we review the academic production of CSDL competencies concerning pursuing HE's sustainable development. This chapter aims to explore CSDL competencies to contribute to sustainable HE and as a way to ensure the survival and quality of HE. The discussion follows the curriculum in HE as an essential vehicle for promoting sustainable development, supported by SDL and collaboration among many stakeholders associated with HEIs and those served by the HEI.

## CAPITALISING ON HIGHER EDUCATION CURRICULA FOR SUSTAINABLE DEVELOPMENT

In 2015, the sustainable development goals (SDGs) for the future were adopted by the United Nations and its member states (United Nations, 2022), which include more than 100 countries across the world (International Science Council, 2013). These SDGs are quality education and reduced inequalities (United Nations Development Programme, 2022). Education – as in formal schooling, whether in primary, secondary, or HE – can assist in reaching these goals. The roles of educators and educational institutions in transforming the communities and societies around them are of great importance. Educators and educational institutions form part of the various stakeholders that could aid in reaching the set SDGs as a collective by 2030. This chapter addresses how HE can be more sustainable in South Africa. That being said, stakeholder engagement with local communities as a whole and the ability of universities to have a good influence on quality education and reduced inequalities are critical. Universities should uphold this responsibility (Barnett, 2007; Goddard, 2009; Lo et al., 2017). Universities are primarily known for their contributions to advancing research and, most importantly, their roles in ensuring the further education of adults who pursue HE degrees after high school. The latter-mentioned function comprises the HE curricula that are offered to students.

Historically, curriculum components have been taught explicitly as part of any institution's purposeful teaching and learning objectives (the overt curriculum) (Wilson, 2022). However, other components are also thought to be part of an institution's everyday routines, such as sports activities (also known as the hidden curriculum) or knowledge that has not been taught explicitly, owing to its perceived insignificance (also known as the null curriculum) (Wilson, 2022). These null portions of the curriculum are thus excluded from everyday teaching considerations. Although the curriculum is a broad notion with many variations, it comprises everything from the content taught, the activities organized by educational institutions' staff to the experiences students gain from their education (cf. Olivia, 1997). Certain curriculum components become less significant as time passes, while others intentionally become more visible and obvious. Portions of clearly taught curricula occur continually, while other portions shift in and out of null and hidden curricula.

The authors consider contextuality necessary for creating a curriculum that honors the knowledge and histories of marginalized peoples. Context is the experiences and actions that mold pupils' values (de Sousa, 2021). Therefore, contextual education would be an education that recognizes and reflects the lives and histories of those participating in the learning process.

Considering the aforementioned line of argument, what would contribute to HE's sustainability? Based on the information presented above, the authors believe that curricula should allow for direct involvement and adapting what is learned to match everyone's frame of reference and educational background to their contexts. Students should perceive themselves in their education and become self-directed via curricular involvement. Such instruction may help an HEI continue its fundamental duties. These duties sometimes include teaching, research, and day-to-day administration according to the university's purpose, vision, and objectives (cf. McMillin & Dyball, 2009).

Some approaches are suggested to promote the sustainability of HE, some starting from the top and others starting from the bottom. Among these approaches are the "Whole-of-University Approach" by McMillan and Dyball (2009) or the four phases required to ensure the long-term viability of the university (Velazquiz et al., 2006). Both these approaches start at the top. Moreover, approaches starting from the bottom that is intended to promote sustainable HE (with a focus on Business, Science, and Engineering courses regarding the advancement of technology) include the work of Benn and Dunphy (2009), Reid and Petocz (2006), Sammalisto and Lindhqvis (2008), Sherren (2005); and Vaughter et al., (2013).

While most of the work of the mentioned scholars focuses on approaches meant to ensure sustainable HE, the collective focus is nevertheless narrow: cultural aspects, for example, or a change in how the university is seen within a larger community. However, universities have an enormous responsibility to the people living around them (Chankseliani & McCowan, 2021), among other things, to advance the lives of their surrounding communities and improve the livelihoods of many people – all with the crucial aim of ensuring sustainable development (cf. Blasco, Brusca & Labrador, 2020). Exploring how HE sustainability can be promoted is therefore crucial. That being said, the elements McMillin and Dyball (2009) focused on in their research are central to the South African context; hence the authors' line of argument is based on their essential work.

Being sustainable as an HEI, specifically a university, requires a "Whole-of-University Approach" regarding teaching and learning (McMillin & Dyball, 2009). Such an approach highlights the need for, and the importance of, working together as a collective and interaction between the operational side, the research conducted at the university and the curriculum of such a university (which includes teaching and learning). The research conducted at a university influences the curriculum as much as the curriculum influences the research, whereas research and operations have an equal influence on one another (*ibid.*). Nevertheless, the curriculum directly influences how a university functions (*ibid.*). However, the guiding policies of a university should be influenced by the curriculum and not the other way around. Furthermore, what is taught at universities should be reflected in their research outputs, putting forward a high regard for the scholarship of teaching and learning, community-based research, and communities of practice. With this notion in mind, the authors believe that top-down and bottom-up approaches are insufficient for the sustainable development of HEIs. Therefore, the authors' stance in this chapter is influenced by the bigger picture of a university's context rather than by any perspective that universities are isolated entities.

The authors believe that scholarship of teaching and learning, community-based research and communities of practice serve as platforms for the generation of valuable data that can be shared with a university's surrounding communities. In turn, the authors believe that a university's longevity is promoted by focusing on providing meaningful and sustainable education. Such education can benefit the community surrounding a university, making it sustainable and enabling it to survive by adapting to changing times while working towards transforming and improving people's lives.

Based on the work of Mcmillin and Dyball (2009), any focus on making a university sustainable comprises three components. Since the authors are not policy experts, it falls outside the authors' usual research to elaborate on a university's policies and determine the social effects or consequences of its core functions, such as research and teaching and learning. While the emphasis in this chapter is on teaching, learning, and research, the authors also recognize that policy documents should not hinder the quality of students created by and leaving a university. Many people beyond the university's walls participate in sustainable HE, which benefits their communities. The authors propose that participatory learning in HE is needed for sustainable development.

## Participatory Learning to Contribute to Higher Education for Sustainable Development

Since 2015, nations worldwide have worked towards achieving the goals for sustainable development by 2030. Doing so needs to become an integral element of education at all levels. Above and beyond the SDGs mentioned in the agenda, education is considered a critical intervention to achieve the agenda. Therefore, education on all levels can contribute to sustainable development. Apart from the requirement for individuals to be lifelong students, the authors argue that HE is indispensable to determining who would support sustainable development in their work and the communities in which they live. Higher education for sustainable development (HESD) is a comprehensive and progressive approach focusing on learning objectives, subject information, different pedagogical approaches, and educational contexts (Watson, Lozano, Noyes & Rodgers, 2013). Sustainable development education requires an action-oriented, transformational pedagogy that promotes SDL, collaborative problem-solving, interdisciplinarity, and transdisciplinarity and integrates formal and informal learning to create basic sustainability capacities (Kioupi & Voulvoulis, 2019; Sipos, Battisti & Grimm, 2008; Tilbury, 2011). As an educational task, promoting sustainable development has not been well defined, nor have precise results been indicated (Kioupi & Voulvoulis, 2019). Education supporting sustainable development should produce certain traits, abilities, and attitudes (ibid.). Developing these traits, abilities and attitudes involves effective information transfer and communal knowledge generation (ibid.). Therefore, interactive learning is crucial.

Based on the above information, the authors maintain that for a university to produce HESD, it must be sustainable. Thus, a university's sustainability is underpinned by the creation of participatory learning and by adopting instructional practices that encourage students to be present and actively contribute to their learning and the learning of others. Participatory learning can be seen as a form of learning that puts the student first, puts the *doing* back into their hands, and allows them to teach one another (Intra-agency Network for Education in Emergencies – INEE, 2022). Therefore, the *doing* is epitomized by an idea that learning which allows for participation, is based on core principles, i.e., giving those who have been silenced agency and voice.

These core principles include relying on contextual knowledge about the diverse people in an environment for subject content and allowing students to also be the lecturer – in an approach geared towards mutual teaching and learning between students and the lecturer (Institute of Development Studies, 2022). Moreover, education that is mindful of diversity and is geared towards promoting sustainable development is also framed around principles that include a mutual willingness to unlearn and relearn. This technique requires lecturers to recognize how their views affect instructional material (Blignaut, 2021). Students' unique education requires them to be self-directed, creative, motivated and engaged while working together, using information relevant to their homes, schools, and communities (Jenkins, 2012). Learning together (Dominguez, 2012) is tied to the social constructivist learning philosophy, in which students actively produce learning material rather than passively receive it (Piaget, 1928; Vygotsky, 1978). Instead of only providing students with information, participatory learning enables them to connect socially and actively (de Sousa, 2021) to establish a shared understanding and to ask and answer genuinely relevant issues (Fischer, 2013). Students might recover their lives via self-directed collaborative learning.

Finally, the authors maintain that by engaging students self-directedly and actively in the learning process and allowing them to engage actively with learning content, they can express themselves and have their voices heard. The implication is that their perspectives are valued and used to influence and shape the teaching of curricula and learning components. The above information shows that the specific survival skills that need to be developed for people to make a valuable contribution to their communities after they have left university are developed, but that when this objective is achieved, it only addresses the *what* and not the *how*. Performing a task requires skills, competence, knowledge and attitudes (McNeill, 2022). Using skills effectively requires an amalgamation of knowledge and attitudes to acquire the competencies needed to be thoughtful in every aspect of their lives. In other words, to reflect on every action and reaction that would apply to their functioning within a larger community. Competency development, therefore, becomes a key driver for sustainable development and HE sustainability.

## Competency Development: Using Higher Education Curricula for Sustainable Development

The authors argue that if competencies are the knowledge, attitudes and skills required to perform a task (cf. O'Brien, 2020), then what is taught to students at HE and how they react to what they are taught plays a significant role in their future job success. What they are taught should typically be aimed at developing competencies to survive within the 21st century and the fourth industrial revolution (4IR). Doing so should not move away from contextual education so that students will find meaning beyond the walls of their educational institutions.

Some of the currently trending workplace competencies that reflect the promotion of SDL (cf. Du Toit-Brits & Blignaut, 2019) include communication, working as part of a team, leadership, accountability, perception, abstract thinking, solving problems, attentiveness and flexibility to learn as you go (e.g., formal or informal lifelong learning), the ability to teach others and the use of technology (Venable, 2021). A balance between theory and practice (not only theory) that entails capitalizing on opportunities in which theory is utilized to address issues that emerge in practical situations is central to work-life competence and citizen competency. The disparity in HE between theory and practice is real and can mean that students are not adequately prepared for life beyond university, where they will deal with real-life problems that need to be solved.

The gaps between theory and practice that can contribute to competencies also promote ESD. The authors argue that the explicit, null and hidden curricula be integrated where teaching and learning promote praxis. In other words, transformational learning should occur. Such learning occurs through pedagogies that reflect praxis (Arnold & Mundy, 2020). The authors have adopted the view of Marcus Aurelius (120-180AD) regarding praxis: whatever someone does is for the good of the people around them. In HE, how education occurs comprises the use of various instructional practices. That being said, instructional practices that are based on praxis pedagogies will be, among other ideals, democratic,

## The Significance of Collective Self-Directed Learning Competencies

supportive of dialogue and reciprocal, where input from peers is valued, focusing on solving the most pertinent issues that arise contextually (cf. Arnold et al., 2014; Arnold, Edwards, Hooley, & Williams, 2013). Education and what is learned might be re-imagined in environments where students unlearn and re-learn, evolving continually and via interactions (Arnold & Mundy, 2020). The lecturer should advise and not control the education of students and what they do with it, which requires the elimination of power relations in education. Participatory learning changes power dynamics from the ruler–subject to lecturer–student partnerships, where they learn from multiple viewpoints/sources of information and empower one another. Arnold and Mundy (2020:14) term them "learning circles." Learning together in lecture rooms and elsewhere includes explicit, null, and hidden curriculums.

Learning circles allow students and community members to share unique frames of reference and personal experiences. At the same time, lecturers may reflect on their teaching approaches and the areas they might improve (cf. Arnold & Mundy, 2020). Students and lecturers can better understand one another, which may benefit the greater university community. In conversations, individuals communicate what they believe, know, and have learned to solve societal problems (ibid.). Finally, students acquire confidence, and a community is built (ibid.). These learning circles represent praxis and the social learning foundations of SDL, showing how self-directed students are created.

## SELF-DIRECTED LEARNING: THE FORGOTTEN INGREDIENT IN HIGHER EDUCATION

SDL "has been one of the fastest-growing and most-researched areas of education [...] and is an essential skill for the 21st century" (Guglielmino, 2013: 2). Knowing how to learn is crucial for self-directed students to function efficiently in an increasingly technological and knowledge-based community (Ginzburg, Santen & Schwartzstein, 2020; Loeng, 2020). SDL also needs to be seen as a multifaceted mixture of skills and different ways of thinking – this is necessary because of the complexities that people face within all facets of their lives (Kidane, Roebertsen & Van der Vleuten, 2020). Because of this multifaceted mixture of skills and these different ways of thinking, SDL must be a dominant approach in all learning environments (Du Toit-Brits, 2020). For the sake of this chapter, it must be acknowledged that the above explanation conveys the essence of SDL as a requirement in HE teaching and learning.

Currently, dialogue in HE focuses on a few preferred vital words like "blended", "hybrid", "synchronous", and "asynchronous." These words generally feature in debates about the issue of a lecturer's role in the learning environment and in discussions where hardly any authentic SDL conversation occurs (Robinson & Persky, 2020; Sun, Hong & Dong, 2022). Of course, some researchers contend that discussions about asynchronous teaching report on SDL by explaining that asynchronous teaching does suggest that students access learning materials in a self-directed manner. However, it is commonly believed that SDL requires students that they should take responsibility and ownership of their learning processes (Brockett & Hiemstra, 2019; Sun, Hong & Dong, 2022). Nevertheless, asynchronous teaching and learning conversations emphasize that teaching content can be accessed anytime and anywhere. Nevertheless, this is not the original purpose of SDL. In HE, SDL's purpose is expected mainly to focus on the following: i) setting up learning goals, ii) locating and implementing learning resources, iii) implementing learning activities and actions, iv) evaluating learning accomplishments, and v) re-evaluating teaching and learning strategies (Kidane, Roebertsen & Van der Vleuten, 2020; Robinson & Persky, 2020). This chapter suggests that SDL emphasizes individual autonomy, independence, responsibility, growth and progress, which are HE ideologies. HE should produce self-directed graduates who can take responsibility for their learning and academic success.

In 1991, Knapper and Cropley advocated that adult learning and lifelong learning should be acknowledged and implemented in HEI since students need lifelong learning abilities (Karatas & Arpaci, 2021; Sun, Hong & Dong, 2022). SDL may involve academics with diverse ideas on education to enhance educational processes. SDL highlights HE's focus on empowering students to take ownership of their learning. It mimics lifelong learning. These ideas and concepts are important because HE must create marketable skills in a rapidly changing, employment-scarce society. This view is supported by Karatas and Arpaci (2021) and Sun et al. (2022).

Furthermore, recent evidence suggests that educators favor SDL, especially those who envisage students to be vigorously involved in every aspect of the educational process and who criticize the view that students are customers of HE (Sun et al., 2022). Therefore, the authors argue that fostering SDL in students is vital and creating a HE learning environment based on SDL. In addition, the authors propose that the intention of HE must be to facilitate and improve student competency in learning. Thus, SDL in HE constitutes a scenario where students participate and contribute to various individual and collective learning endeavors with their peers in more extensive reading of learning materials and resources, to name only one (Loeng, 2020; Sun, Hong & Dong, 2022).

## Self-Directed Learning Competencies for the Sustainability of Higher Education

The responsibility of HE has been analyzed extensively (Barnett, 2007; Blasco, Brusca, & Labrador, 2020; Breed, 2016; Chankseliani, & McCowan, 2021). It has been acknowledged that HE must participate in and promote the establishment and construction of a sustainable world to cultivate the sustainability of HE. HE education should shift from providing students with information and skills to helping them determine and improve their learning needs (Sun et al., 2022). Hence, SDL skills are crucial. These SDL skills are part of sustainable learning since they require active student participation and emphasize the need to comprehend whatever is learned. These SDL skills can also be seen as being able to self-assess ones learning needs and progress, reflection, information management, critical thinking, critical evaluation, problem-solving, creative thinking, action competence, and systems thinking (Patterson, Crooks, & Lunyk-Child, 2002; Tekkol & Demirel, 2018). Given what has been said, it is likely that these abilities are interrelated so that students may guide and manage their learning. To progress personally and professionally, students must be self-directed and acquire knowledge, skills, and traits. Thus, students ought to have confidence, abilities, and knowledge in these areas.

Worldwide, students in HE must become confident in implementing SDL competencies, as they are expected to be self-directed learners who are experienced, motivated, enthusiastic, practically oriented, independent, autonomous, goal-oriented, responsible, proactive, and to be learners who know the worth of learning (Ginzburg, 2020; Mbagwu et al., 2020). CSDL competencies depend not only on the learning opportunity but also on the aptitude and skill needed to make informed choices between various learning options (Karatas & Arpaci, 2021). Having students develop these competencies requires a paradigmatic move of "unlearning" and "relearning" through SDL (Guglielmino & Long, 2011; Guglielmino, 2013; Hiemstra, 2013; Robinson & Persky, 2020).

As seen from the above point of view, HE principles like independence, prior knowledge, goal-orientation and autonomy are all incorporated into the aspects of SDL (Mbagwu et al., 2020). Despite these assets, SDL in HE is still confronted with the crucial issue of properly implementing SDL in its learning environments. Effective implementation of SDL competencies necessitates a shift from "behaviorist" instruction to "constructivist" teaching approaches (Van Deur, 2017). As indicated earlier in this section, SDL is a student-centered approach that can be implemented in HE to instill SDL competencies into students. In this chapter, the authors contend also that for SDL to be implemented effectively in HE, this paradigm shift is needed, as well as a recognition of the significance of the CSDL competencies that are required for the sustainability of HE (van Woezik, Koksma, Reuzel, Jaarsma & van der Wilt, 2021). Given all that has been mentioned so far, one may propose that SDL offers students various necessary competencies to flourish and succeed in a complex, changing and demanding community (Kidane et al., 2020; Mbagwu, Chukwuedo & Ogbuanya, 2020).

In contrast to the behaviorist approach to learning, the constructivist approach focuses on active learning (AL) and SDL that implements problem-based learning (PBL), collective learning, metacognition, grit, determination, self-esteem and self-confidence to acquire critical skills (Karatas & Arpaci, 2021; Mbagwu et al., 2020; van Woezik et al., 2021). HE should help students to focus their learning on fostering sustainable development beyond formal schooling. Students must have opportunities to apply responsibility and autonomy in their learning processes and to develop competencies that encourage and empower them to promote SDL in HE for sustainability (De Beer & Mentz, 2019). Furthermore, HE is expected to prepare students to take up their responsibilities in defining the communities in which they live (Du Toit-Brits, 2018a).

Through active student-centered learning, self-directed students may develop the traits and abilities necessary for effectively facilitating SDL skills for individuals and their communities. Various teaching and learning approaches may encourage meaningful learning. To help students develop self-direction and CSDL competencies, they should have opportunities to work collaboratively, enhancing their shared knowledge and understanding (van Woezik et al., 2021). Student contributions and explanations in group work projects may assist them in acquiring CSDL competencies while also enhancing their subject matter comprehension and self-confidence (Breed, 2016; Mbagwu et al., 2020). Collective learning may increase SDL: students work in small groups, and interactive online HE environments can provide CSDL tasks (De Beer & Mentz, 2019; van Woezik et al., 2021). HE should promote CSDL abilities to produce autonomously thinking people via communal interactions, and not identical products from conventional learning. CSDL is a significant aspect of competency-based training for both employers and employees.

## Collective Self-Directed Learning

Engaging in an SDL environment changes and shifts students' educational paths. HE prepares students for community dynamics and changes in the world of work (Shteynberg, Hirsh, Bentley & Garthoff, 2020; Sun et al., 2022). As described in the preceding section, students must have strong SDL skills to satisfy future job demands. HE must therefore employ student teaching and learning approaches based on self-directed, contextual, and constructive concepts (Momennejad, 2022).

In this regard, the authors recommended that for effective learning to occur, students must learn collectively, feel safe enough to communicate their learning struggles with real-life issues from everyday practice, and be empowered to meet their learning needs with collective responsibility and accountability. In essence, it is an essential element of CSDL to inspire students to foster a collective vision, take collective (joint) actions, and assess and reflect on their personal and collective learning processes and learning outcomes. This view is supported by Lodders and Meijers (2017); and Momennejad (2022). This chapter recommends that CSDL be regarded as a "work-related learning process" where students are partners of a collective who work together towards CSDL. CSDL must enable students to join learning communities and encourage knowledge-building and professional development (Momennejad, 2022). That being said, working with other students may encourage, develop, and improve self-direction (Kemp, Baxa & Cortes, 2022). Research demonstrates that students may benefit from studying in groups (Balasooriya, Olupeliyawa & Iqbal, 2016; Hill, Peters Salvaggio, Vinnedge & Darden, 2020).

A gap in the existing literature on SDL excludes an essential aspect of adult education philosophy, namely that of purposeful collectively. Students and lecturers can be seen working collectively in SDL (Kim & Yang, 2020). This aspect is essential when working collectively in study groups and gives students a sense of support and motivation. Students can gain better knowledge and understanding of learning materials from various viewpoints and further benefit from the responses of others through the joint support function (Balasooriya et al., 2016; Hill et al., 2020).

In the authors' opinion, SDL focuses on the individual student's learning requirements and objectives, but students also need to feel connected when engaging in autonomous learning and communal SDL (Breed, 2016; Kemp, Baxa & Cortes, 2022; Ottu, 2017). Therefore, CSDL needs students to mix SDL with working as a team. The authors believe that working together does not imply that students must have comparable learning objectives. Instead, students should collaborate to inspire, evaluate, exchange perspectives, and reflect on learning materials and the learning process. In addition, it is necessary to maintain collaboration, together with an effective teaching-learning technique for promoting SDL in HE (Kemp, Baxa & Cortes, 2022). Students have to be self-directed and independent with CSDL. They must be part of a team working together. Students who collaborate may have self-control and learning responsibility.

For this reason, although SDL focuses on the individual student (Merriam 2001), and although there is a notably individualistic approach to SDL, the authors argue that students do not learn or work independently (Breed, 2016, Ottu, 2017) and that a CSDL environment plays a vital role in the learning experiences of students. For us, learning is generally influenced by the social learning environment. Therefore, CSDL must be a habit of practice in HE learning environments, where lecturers must construct learning opportunities collectively grounded on SDL. Moore et al. (2007) designed the CSDL framework for "real-life" problem-solving (Kemp, Baxa & Cortes, 2022; Ottu, 2017) where students may study in groups to facilitate learning via shared discussion, analysis, and reflection (Ottu, 2017). These collective learning opportunities may increase i) deeper learning, ii) student accomplishment, iii) deep learning, iv) critical thinking, v) communication skills, vi) problem-solving abilities, vii) teamwork, and viii) self-management skills (Balasooriya et al., 2016; Hill et al., 2020). Hence, collective learning can be supportive of SDL.

CSDL is characterized by a student-centered teaching approach that enables students to guide themselves (individually or collectively) in the learning process, thus supporting their progress as self-directed students in their environment(s). HE curriculum must promote CSDL and push lecturers and students to solve real-world challenges. Such an HE curriculum might foster student ownership. A sustainability-focused curriculum will empower students to participate in deep learning, which changes their communities. This sustainability-driven curriculum should concentrate on a global learning environment to provide students with CSDL opportunities to enhance SDL competencies. CSDL, respects people's freedom and responsibility to use the HE curriculum for sustainable development and HE sustainability.

*The Significance of Collective Self-Directed Learning Competencies*

## COLLECTIVE SELF-DIRECTED LEARNING (CSDL) IN HIGHER EDUCATION FOR SUSTAINABLE DEVELOPMENT (HESD) FRAMEWORK

Using the above information in sections one, two and three, the authors present their framework for realizing and depicting HESD. 'IN' and 'FOR' are used as metaphors in the framework and as prepositions in the title of the framework. In addition, the metaphors represent the importance of inclusion and reality, and the need for contextual education is strengthened. Furthermore, 'IN' resembles inclusion as the norm and 'FOR' is focused on reality – perhaps where 'others' are put first and where the education is focused on reality. Putting 'others' first, those who are seen as 'other' can promote equality and aid in recognizing each other as fellow students and not as strangers. In the case of this chapter, and with the framework presented below in mind, the purpose of (higher) education is not *to replace an empty mind with an open mind,* as argued by Malcolm Forbes, but for HE to be offered from a space/place with an open mind, considering multiple understandings of phenomena where learning, un-learning and re-learning can occur.

Below is a framework that offers the authors' unique contribution to HESD. This framework represents the stakeholders involved in promoting HESD working together. In other words, there is a constant interaction between the stakeholders. Such a framework reflects an integrated reciprocal approach to promoting the sustainability of HE through CSDL. Although the framework below represents elements of a whole university approach (as in the work of McMillin & Dyball, 2009) as a departure point, it is not static, neither one-sided nor linear. The authors' framework is neither top-down nor bottom-up but rather integrated and reciprocal, which can help transform power relations from the HEI once perceived as the "know-it-all" to that of forming a larger body of knowledge comprised of people from the community of which the university is a part – as opposed to the university being a community unto itself or functioning as an entity outside of a community. That being said, the framework the authors propose highlights the stakeholders, processes, and engagements that would be necessary to promote HESD through CSDL. The letters A to H and X (as reflected in the CSDSD framework below) are explained below.

*Figure 1. Collective self-directed sustainable development framework*

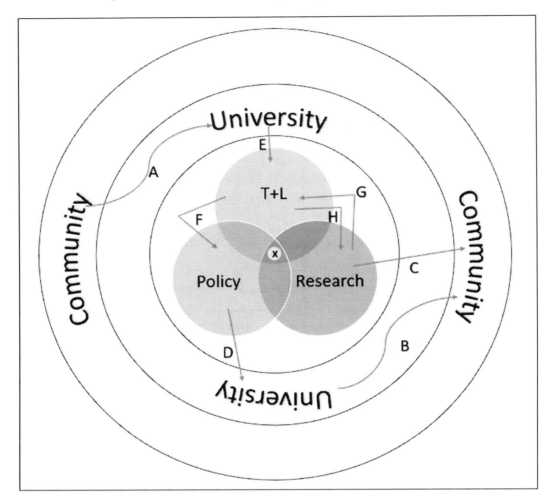

The arrow marked A connects the concept community to the concept university. It signifies how a community feeds into a university. Likewise, the arrow marked B connects the concept university to the concept community, signifying how a university feeds into a community. In other words, the figure highlights the importance of these aspects, to be seen and functioning as dependents rather than as total opposites and widely scattered from each other. Together, arrows A and B indicate that a community is nothing without a university and that a university is nothing without a community. Universities are there to transform communities. When this transformative interaction happens properly, universities play a valuable role in contributing to sustainable development within communities and ensuring their prevalence and the social justifications for their place and necessity in a community. The arrow connection marked C indicates how research should be participatory – involving the community surrounding the university- and that the research should feed into the community. By implication, any reporting on research and its practical community benefits should serve as a guide in this stage.

Arrow connections D, E and F all influence each other directly. Arrow connection D indicates the connection that exists between policy and the university. Policy ultimately guides the university in con-

## The Significance of Collective Self-Directed Learning Competencies

ducting its functions. Arrow connection E indicates the link between the university and teaching and learning. The university exists for the sake of teaching and learning, which includes CSDL. Supposing that teaching and learning did not occur at universities or that they did not promote sustainable development in communities through empowering students as change agents throughout the learning process, then the university would have no place in the community. Arrow connection F indicates the link between teaching and learning on the one hand and policy on the other. Collective SD teaching and learning should inform policy, not the other way around. Moving backward from F to E and E to D, it is evident that each of these avenues in the framework significantly affects the other. F signifies that teaching and learning should inform policy so that policy does not contradict one of the university's core functions: teaching and learning. E is the direct connection from the university to teaching and learning, which is influenced by arrow connection A.

By offering contextually reflective education based on the community, the university caters to the community. In doing so, each one feeds into the other – teaching and learning feed into research when scholarship of teaching and learning is reported as research findings. Those research findings again feed into the community. Moreover, influencing policy through teaching and learning feeds into the university. If policies allow for contextualized education based on the people around the university, the curricula are bound to be mindful of diversity and offer an education to which students can relate.

The arrow connections G and H indicate the links between research on the one hand and teaching and learning on the other. One should inform the other. Through scholarship of teaching and learning and communities of practice between academics and community members, these two core functions of the university can inform one another to transform the people the university serves in a community-based research capacity.

As indicated by the framework above, HEIs must construct a learning environment supporting CSDL. Therefore, it is clear from the framework that the focus of HE needs to be on better alignment with students and, by implication, on the community and better relevance to the community's specific needs. Additionally, the educational method should put the student at the center of teaching and learning while striving to inspire students to be responsible and accountable for their learning activities. The university learning environment should foster a climate conducive to CSDL. Universities can promote SDL skills and students' self-directedness by using suitable teaching methods. However, within the traditional teaching-learning idea of the teaching and learning environment of HEIs, students are passive agents. In this *operating idea* of HEIs, an HEI does not keep up with a community's needs, interests and expectations. As a result, the role of HE needs to focus on cultivating sustainable CSDL competencies in the learning process. In this learning process, the interaction between the university and the community only occurs when stakeholders play an essential role in guiding students towards self-directedness.

An HEI should educate students with collective self-directed learning skills to fulfill ever-changing skills shortages in a complex, fast-globalizing 21st-century context. The world's evolving requirements and transitions affect all aspects of life, including HE. HEIs and communities must collaborate to generate lifelong self-directed students. After graduating, students must find work to utilize their self-direction and SDL skills. Therefore, HEIs should teach them about CSDL and its actions. Students from a constructivist teaching-learning environment may continue to learn, un-learn, and re-learn throughout their lives, which encourages lifelong learning and may help students to recognize that learning is a lifelong process.

The proposed framework also indicates that constructivist teaching-learning conceptions and effective collective self-directed learning ideas should have a positive relationship. From the framework, the authors learn that HEIs must adapt their education and training systems to 21st-century expectations, emphasizing citizenship, social cohesion, and lifelong learning. In this context, HE and the community highlight the importance of CSDL skills. The authors believe HE should concentrate on establishing sustainable CSDL competencies in the learning process since existing HE students' CSDL skills and lifetime learning must evolve in this direction.

The X in the framework above indicates the center of the entire supply chain (including parts A to H) through which the authors believe HESD occurs through CSDL. Interaction with all the arrows is the goal – so that students are more self-directed and use their competencies in their communities, meaning that universities transform the communities that they serve. Therefore, sustainable development from the side of HE cannot be seen as an individualistic process. On the contrary, it is based on constant interactions between people who possess the knowledge and those who want to acquire knowledge and promotes new understandings that display different frames of reference.

## RECOMMENDATIONS

As stated at the beginning of this chapter, the chapter aims to explore CSDL competencies to contribute to sustainable HE as a way to ensure the survival and quality within HE. Based on the aim of this chapter, as recommendations, the authors propose changes within the HE sector for HESD to occur through CSDL. HE must adapt its curriculum to CSDL as crucial an initiative to transform teaching and learning. HEIs should concentrate on why and how to learn, not what to learn. This notion relates to competence development and shifting away from focusing on what to study to appropriately applying what was learned and comprehending how that knowledge may alter education and support sustainable growth to secure HE's existence. Understanding and information should be tied to students' lived experiences. Transforming teaching and learning requires that CSDL should guide it. Thus, lecturers should be facilitators who support students via curriculum content and structure. The authors further propose that CSDL should be strengthened through policy. The collective component of SDL is essential in encouraging and supporting sustainable lifelong learning. Therefore, policies and guidelines in HE need to be favorable to creating and sustaining CSDL environments and learning processes. This idea supports policy being informed by teaching and learning and not the other way around. The authors also propose promoting CSDL. Students must be driven to study and take responsibility actively. CSDL is a lifelong learning opportunity in higher education that students must pursue.

## FUTURE RESEARCH DIRECTIONS

Based on the solutions and recommendations provided in the preceding section, future research directions could include exploring the possible curriculum adaptations that could be made to promote CSDL in HE. Furthermore, future research could include developing a model or drawing up guidelines to shift learning in HE to why learning is important and how to apply the content learned to real-life situations rather than what is deemed important content and what is not. In addition, more community-based research is required to reflect those in the community where examples can be drawn from teaching and learning. Another possible avenue to pursue is research on policies used at HEIs as an initiative to adapt or re-write policies to be inclusive and reflective of the communities the HEI serves.

## CONCLUSION

This chapter explored CSDL competencies as a means of contributing to sustainable HE and ensuring the sustainability of HE. The relevance of this chapter is that with the framework adopted in HE it could promote the inclusion of community members' needs, related to the problems they experience that can be solved through the education offered. Furthermore, the authors emphasized the importance of curriculum in HE to foster sustainable development, supported by SDL and collaboration among various stakeholders within and outside the HEI. CDSL is vital not just for students in HE but also for the long-term growth and survival of HE. Promoting CSDL in higher education necessitates curriculum designers and developers (lecturers and curriculum specialists) to consider the context and community around the HE to promote student access and success, such as improving people's lives. Furthermore, CSDL fosters a collaborative SDL culture in HE by providing many SDL opportunities. "Learning cities" are leaner, more concentrated learning models that enable collaborative, action-oriented learning environments. A CSDL culture promotes learning "beyond the walls" and the development of CSDL ecosystems. HE must allow students to learn by unlearning and relearning together. Adopting the previously described framework may help, as it allows for a comprehensive and all-inclusive approach to executing the many duties of HEI and the results that follow from them.

Nonetheless, HEIs have the potential to become lifelong learning institutions focused on sustainable growth and the long-term viability of higher education. However, doing so implies that HEIs accept the duty of adapting to incorporate the society around them. Finally, this chapter demonstrates that HE requires a more unified, self-directed, and long-term CSDL strategy.

## REFERENCES

Arnold, J., Burridge, P., Cacciattolo, M., Cara, C., Edwards, T., Hooley, N., & Neal, G. (2014). *Researching the signature pedagogies of praxis teacher education*. AARE-NZARE.

Arnold, J., Edwards, A., Hooley, P., & Williams, J. (2013). Site-based teacher education for enhanced community knowledge and culture: Creating the conditions for 'philosophical project knowledge. *Australian Educational Researcher*, *40*(1), 61–75. doi:10.100713384-012-0070-z

Arnold, J., & Mundy, B. (2020). Praxis pedagogy in teacher education. *Smart Learning Environments*, *7*(8), 1–14.

Balasooriya, C., Olupeliyawa, A., & Iqbal, M. P. (2016). *Innovative assessment that combines collaborative and self-directed learning with integration and application of knowledge: teamwork group projects*. Association of American Medical Colleges. Retrieved February 12, 2022, from https://www.mededportal.org/doi/full/10.15766/mep_2374-8265.10452

Barnett, R. (2007). Recovering the civic university. In L. McIlrath & I. MacLabhrainn (Eds.), *Higher Education and Civic Engagement: International Perspectives* (pp. 25–36). Ashgate.

Benn, S., & Dunphy, D. (2009). Action research as an approach to integrating sustainability into MBA programs. *Journal of Management Education*, *33*(3), 276–295. doi:10.1177/1052562908323189

Blasco, N., Brusca, I., & Labrador, M. (2020). Drivers for universities' contribution to the sustainable development goals: An analysis of Spanish public universities. *Sustainability*, *13*(1), 89. doi:10.3390u13010089

Blignaut, J. H. (2021). *An exploration of gender and sexual diversity development and inclusion within the curriculum of a selected higher education institution: challenges and opportunities* (Unpublished doctoral thesis). North-West University, Potchefstroom.

Breed, B. (2016). Exploring a cooperative learning approach to improve self-directed learning in higher education. *Journal for New Generation Sciences*, *14*(3), 1–21.

Brien, O. E. (2020). Enhancing 21st century learning using digital learning objects and multiple intelligence theory: a conceptual model. In R. Z. Zheng (Ed.), Examining multiple intelligences and digital technologies for enhanced learning opportunities (pp. 19-40). Hershey, PA: IGI Global.

Brockett, R. G., & Hiemstra, R. (2019). *Self-direction in adult learning: perspectives on theory, research, and practice*. Routledge.

Chankseliani, M., & McCowan, T. (2021). Higher education and the sustainable development goals. *Higher Education*, *81*(1), 1–8. doi:10.100710734-020-00652-w PMID:33173242

De Beer, J., & Mentz, E. (2019). The use of Cultural-Historical Activity Theory in researching the affordances of indigenous knowledge for self-directed learning. In J. De Beer (Ed.), *The decolonisation of the curriculum project: The affordances of indigenous knowledge for self-directed learning* (pp. 87–116). AOSIS.

De Sousa, L. O. (2021). Learning experiences of a participatory approach to educating for sustainable development in a South African higher education institution yielding social learning indicators. *Sustainability*, *13*(6), 3210. doi:10.3390u13063210

Dominguez, R. G. (2012). Participatory Learning. In R. M. Seel (Ed.), *Encyclopedia of the Sciences of Learning*. Retrieved February 11, 2022, from https://link.springer.com/referenceworkentry/10.1007%2F978-1-4419-1428-6_1903

Du Toit-Brits, C. (2018a). Towards a transformative and holistic continuing self-directed learning theory. *South African Journal of Higher Education*, *32*(4), 51–65. doi:10.20853/32-4-2434

Du Toit-Brits, C. (2018b). Die onderwyser as beoefenaar en bemiddelaar van selfgerigte leer. *Tydskrif vir Geesteswetenskappe*, *58*(2), 376–386. doi:10.17159/2224-7912/2018/v58n2a11

Du Toit-Brits, C. (2020). Unleashing the power of self-directed learning: Criteria for structuring self-directed learning within the learning environments of higher education institutions. *Africa Education Review*, *17*(2), 20–32. doi:10.1080/18146627.2018.1494507

Du Toit-Brits, C., & Blignaut, H. (2019). Posisionering van voortgesette selfgerigte leervaardighede in een-en-twintigste-eeuse onderwys. *Tydskrif vir Geesteswetenskappe*, *59*(4), 512–529. doi:10.17159/2224-7912/2019/v59n4a4

Fischer, G. (2013). Learning, social creativity, and cultures of participation. In A. Samino & V. Ellis (Eds.), *Learning and collective creativity: Activity-theoretical and sociocultural studies* (pp. 210–227). Taylor & Francis/Routledge.

Ginzburg, S. B., Santen, S. A., & Schwartzstein, R. M. (2020). Self-directed learning: A new look at an old concept. *Medical Science Educator*, *31*(1), 229–331. doi:10.100740670-020-01121-w PMID:34457877

Goddard, J. (2009). *Reinventing the Civic University*. NESTA. Retrieved January 22, 2022, from https://www.nesta.org.uk/report/re-inventing-thecivic-university

Guglielmino, L. M. (2013). The case for promoting self-directed learning in formal educational institutions. SA-. *Education Journal*, *10*(2), 1–18.

Guglielmino, L. M., & Long, H. B. (2011). Perspectives: The international society for self-directed learning and the international self-directed learning symposium. *International Journal of Self-Directed Learning*, *8*(1), 1–6.

Gusmão Caiado, R. G., Leal Filho, W., Quelhas, O. L. G., Luiz de Mattos Nascimento, D., & Ávila, L. V. (2018). A literature-based review on potentials and constraints in the implementation of the sustainable development goals. *Journal of Cleaner Production*, *198*, 1276–1288. doi:10.1016/j.jclepro.2018.07.102

Hiemstra, R. (2013). Facilitating adult self-directed learning. In R. Hiemstra (Ed.), *A fest of learning: international perspectives on adult learning and change* (pp. 25–46). Information Age Publishing, INC.

Hill, l. M., Peters, M., Salvaggio, M., Vinnedge, J., & Darden, A. (2020). Implementation and evaluation of a self-directed learning activity for first-year medical students. *Medical Education Online*, *25*(1), 1717780.

Institute for Development Studies. (2022). *About participatory methods*. Retrieved February 11, 2022, from https://www.participatorymethods.org/page/about-participatory-methods

International Science Council. (2013). *UN announces list of countries for Working Group on Sustainable Development Goals*. Retrieved June 14, 2022, from https://council.science/current/news/un-announces-list-of-countries-for-working-group-on-sustainable-development-goals/

Intra-agency Network of Education in Emergencies (INEE). (2022). *Participatory learning*. Retrieved August 11, 2022, from https://inee.org/eie-glossary/participatory-learning

Jenkins, H. (2012). *Play (Participatory learning and YOU!)*. Retrieved February 11, 2022, from http://henryjenkins.org/blog/2012/12/play-participatory-learning-and-you.html

Karatas, K., & Arpaci, I. (2021). The role of self-directed learning, metacognition, and 21st century skills predicting the readiness for online learning. *Contemporary Educational Technology*, *13*(3), ep300. doi:10.30935/cedtech/10786

Kemp, K., Baxa, D., & Cortes, C. (2022). Exploration of a collaborative self-directed learning model in Medical Education. *Medical Science Educator*, *32*(1), 195–207. doi:10.100740670-021-01493-7 PMID:35003877

Kidane, H. H., Roebertsen, H., & Van der Vleuten, C. P. (2020). Students' perceptions towards self-directed learning in Ethiopian medical schools with new innovative curriculum: A mixed-method study. *BMC Medical Education*, *20*(1), 1–10. doi:10.118612909-019-1924-0 PMID:31914977

Kim, S., & Yang, E. B. (2020). Does group cohesion foster self-directed learning for medical students? A longitudinal study. *BMC Medical Education*, *20*(1), 1–5. doi:10.118612909-020-1962-7 PMID:32085775

Kioupi, V., & Voulvoulis, N. (2019). Education for sustainable development: A systemic framework for connecting the SDGs to educational outcomes. *Sustainability*, *11*(21), 6104. doi:10.3390u11216104

Lo, C. W. H., Pang, R. X., Egri, C. P., & Li, P. H. Y. (2017). University social responsibility: conceptualization and an assessment framework. In D. Shek & R. Holliuster (Eds.), *University Social Responsibility and Quality of Life* (pp. 37–59). Springer. doi:10.1007/978-981-10-3877-8_4

Lodders, N., & Meijers, F. (2017). Collective Learning, Transformational Leadership and New Forms of Careers Guidance in Universities. *British Journal of Guidance & Counselling*, *45*(5), 532–546. doi:10.1080/03069885.2016.1271864

Loeng, S. (2020). Self-Directed Learning: A Core Concept in Adult Education. *Education Research International*, *2020*, 1–12. doi:10.1155/2020/3816132

Martins, V. W. B., Rampasso, I. S., Anholon, R., Quelhas, O. L. G., & Leal Filho, W. (2019). Knowledge management in the context of sustainability: Literature review and opportunities for future research. *Journal of Cleaner Production*, *229*, 489–500. doi:10.1016/j.jclepro.2019.04.354

Mbagwu, F. O., Chukwuedo, S. O., & Ogbuanya, T. C. (2020). Promoting Lifelong Learning Propensity and Intentions for Vocational Training among Adult and Vocational Educational Undergraduates. *Vocations and Learning*, *13*(3), 419–437. doi:10.100712186-020-09245-1

McMillin, J., & Dyball, R. (2009). Developing a whole-of-university approach to educating for sustainability: Linking curriculum, research and sustainable campus operations. *Journal of Education for Sustainable Development*, *3*(1), 55–64. doi:10.1177/097340820900300113

McNeill, J. (2022). *Skills vs. Competencies – What's the difference, and why should you care?* Retrieved February 11, 2022, from https://qr.page/g/M9H26KjlIe

Merriam, S. B. (2001). Andragogy and self-directed learning: Pillars of adult learning theory. *New Directions for Adult and Continuing Education*, *2001*(89), 3–14. doi:10.1002/ace.3

Momennejad, I. (2022). Collective minds: social network topology shapes collective cognition. *Philosophical Transactions of The Royal Society B Biological Sciences*, *377*(1843), 20200315.

Moore, T., Houde, J., Hoggan, C., & Wagner, J. (2007). Re-viewing Adult Learning: A Collaborative Self-Directed Learning Model for Adult Educators. In *Proceedings of Adult Education Research Conference* (vol. 32, pp. 195–207). Retrieved February 22, 2022, from https://newprairiepress.org/aerc/2007/papers/72

Olivia, P. (1997). *The curriculum: Theoretical dimensions*. Longman.

Olivier, J. (2021). Online access and resources for open self-directed learning in Africa. In D. Burgos & J. Olivier (Eds.), *Radical Solutions for Education in Africa: Open education and self-directed learning in the continent* (pp. 1–16). Springer. doi:10.1007/978-981-16-4099-5_1

Ottu, I. F. (2017). Cooperative stakeholding: Optimising students' educational practice through need-centred self-determination, connectedness with learning environment and passion. *Journal of Education and Practice*, *8*(4), 1–33.

Patterson, C., Crooks, D., & Lunyk-Child, O. (2002). A New Perspective on Competencies for Self-Directed Learning. *The Journal of Nursing Education*, *41*(1), 25–31. doi:10.3928/0148-4834-20020101-06 PMID:11843104

Piaget, J. (1928). *Judgement and reasoning in the child*. Routledge & Kegan Paul.

Reid, A., & Petocz, P. (2006). University lecturers' understanding of sustainability. *Higher Education*, *51*(1), 105–123. doi:10.100710734-004-6379-4

Rieckmann, M. (2018). Learning to transform the world: Key competencies in Education for Sustainable Development. In A. Leicht, J. Heiss, & W. J. Byun (Eds.), *Issues and trends in education for sustainable development* (pp. 39–59). UNESCO.

Robinson, J. D., & Persky, A. M. (2020). Developing self-directed students. *American Journal of Pharmaceutical Education*, *84*(3), 292–296. doi:10.5688/ajpe847512 PMID:32313284

Sammalisto, K., & Lindhqvist, T. (2008). Integration of sustainability in higher education: A study with international perspectives. *Innovative Higher Education*, *32*(4), 221–233. doi:10.100710755-007-9052-x

Sherren, K. (2005). Balancing the disciplines: A multidisciplinary perspective on sustainability curriculum content. *Australian Journal of Environmental Education*, *21*, 97–106. doi:10.1017/S0814062600000987

Shteynberg, G., Hirsh, J. B., Bentley, R. A., & Garthoff, J. (2020). Shared worlds and shared minds: A theory of collective learning and a psychology of common knowledge. *Psychological Review*, *127*(5), 918–931. doi:10.1037/rev0000200 PMID:32309965

Sipos, Y., Battisti, B., & Grimm, K. (2008). Achieving transformative sustainability learning: Engaging head, hands and heart. *International Journal of Sustainability in Higher Education*, *9*(1), 68–86. doi:10.1108/14676370810842193

Sun, W., Hong, J. C., Dong, Y., Huang, Y., & Fu, Q. (2022). Self-directed Learning Predicts Online Learning Engagement in Higher Education Mediated by Perceived Value of Knowing Learning Goals. *The Asia-Pacific Education Researcher*, 1–10. doi:10.100740299-022-00653-6

Tekkol, İ. A., & Demirel, M. (2018). An Investigation of Self-Directed Learning Skills of Undergraduate Students. *Frontiers in Psychology*, *9*, 1–14. doi:10.3389/fpsyg.2018.02324 PMID:30532727

Tilbury, D. (2011). *Education for Sustainable Development: An Expert Review of Processes and Learning*. UNESCO. Retrieved, February 11, 2022, from https://unesdoc.unesco.org/ark:/48223/pf0000191442

United Nations. (2022). *Sustainable Development Agenda*. Retrieved June 14, 2022, from https://www.un.org/sustainabledevelopment/development-agenda/

United Nations Development Programme. (2022). *The Sustainable Development Goals in Action*. Retrieved June 14, 2022, from https://www.undp.org/sustainable-development-goals

Van Deur, P. (2017). *Managing self-directed learning in primary school education: emerging research and opportunities*. IGI Global.

Van Woezik, T. E. T., Koksma, J. J. J., Reuzel, R. P. B., Jaarsma, D. C., & van der Wilt, G. J. (2021). There is more than 'I' in self-directed learning: An exploration of self-directed learning in teams of undergraduate students. *Medical Teacher*, *43*(5), 590–598. doi:10.1080/0142159X.2021.1885637 PMID:33617387

Vaughter, P., Wright, T., McKenzie, M., & Lidstone, L. (2013). Greening the ivory tower: A review of educational research on sustainability in post-secondary education. *Sustainability*, *5*(5), 2252–2271. doi:10.3390u5052252

Velazquez, L., Munguia, N., Platt, A., & Taddei, J. (2006). Sustainable university: What can be the matter? *Journal of Cleaner Production*, *14*(9-11), 810–819. doi:10.1016/j.jclepro.2005.12.008

Venable, M. (2021). *10 Workplace competencies employers want*. Retrieved February 11, 2022, from https://www.bestcolleges.com/blog/workplace-competencies-employers-want/

Vygotsky, L. (1978). *Mind in society: The development of higher psychological processes*. Harvard University Press.

Watson, M. K., Lozano, R., Noyes, C., & Rodgers, M. (2013). Assessing curricula contribution to sustainability more holistically: Experiences from the integration of curricula assessment and students' perceptions at the Georgie Institute of Technology. *Journal of Cleaner Production*, *61*, 106–116. doi:10.1016/j.jclepro.2013.09.010

Wilson, L. O. (2022). *Types of curriculum*. Retrieved, February 11, 2022, from https://thesecondprinciple.com/instructional-design/types-of-curriculum/

## ADDITIONAL READING

Argento, D., Einarson, D., Mårtensson, L., Persson, C., Wendin, K., & Westergren, A. (2020). Integrating sustainability in higher education: A Swedish case. *International Journal of Sustainability in Higher Education*, *21*(6), 1131–1150. doi:10.1108/IJSHE-10-2019-0292

Leal-Filho, W., Frankenberger, F., Salvia, A. L., Azeiteiro, U., Alves, F., Castro, P., Will, M., Platje, J., Lovren, V. O., Brandli, L., Price, E., Doni, F., Mifsud, M., & Ávila, L. V. (2021). A framework for the implementation of the Sustainable Development Goals in university programmes. *Journal of Cleaner Production*, *299*, 1–12. doi:10.1016/j.jclepro.2021.126915

Leal-Filho, W., Raath, S., Lazzarini, B., Vargas, V. R., de Souza, L., Anholon, R., Quelhas, O. L. G., Haddad, R., Klavins, M., & Orlovic, V. L. (2018). The role of transformation in learning and education for sustainability. *Journal of Cleaner Production*, *199*, 286–295. doi:10.1016/j.jclepro.2018.07.017

Mahon, K., Edwards-Groves, C., Francisco, S., Kaukko, M., Kemmis, S., & Petrie, K. (Eds.). (2020). *Pedagogy, education, and praxis in critical times*. Springer. doi:10.1007/978-981-15-6926-5

Shephard, K. (2008). Higher Education for Sustainability: Seeking Affective Learning. *International Journal of Sustainability in Higher Education, 9*(1), 87–98. doi:10.1108/14676370810842201

UNESCO. (2009). *UNESCO World Conference on Sustainable Development: Bonn Declaration 2009.* https://unesdoc.unesco.org/images/0018/001887/188799e.pdf

UNESCO. (2010). *Teaching and Learning for a Sustainable Future.* http://www.unesco.org/education/tlsf/extras/desd.html

Zguir, M. F., Dubis, S., & Koç, M. (2021). Embedding Education for Sustainable Development (ESD) and SDGs values in curriculum: A comparative review on Qatar, Singapore and New Zealand. *Journal of Cleaner Production, 319,* 1–22.

## KEY TERMS AND DEFINITIONS

**Collective Learning:** Learning together in a group with individuals from various backgrounds.

**Contextual Learning:** Learning supported by knowledge that helps students make personal connections.

**Hidden Curriculum:** What students take away from university that is not explicitly taught but profoundly impacts whom they become and how they see the world.

**Null Curriculum:** Subject matter intentionally or inadvertently overlooked by an educator as they regard particular concepts as irrelevant.

**Overt Curriculum:** The explicit subject content students are exposed to intentionally throughout their chosen courses in HE.

**Social Constructivism:** A school of thought that maintains that individuals do not learn alone but as part of a larger group engaging with the subject matter.

# Chapter 15
# Voice and Photovoice of the Bangladeshi Migrant Workers in Malaysia:
## An Ethnography of the 3rd Space With Reciprocity

**Jahid Siraz Chowdhury**
https://orcid.org/0000-0002-1016-0441
*Department of Social Administration and Justice, Universiti Malaya, Malaysia*

## ABSTRACT

*This chapter has an inspirational event. During this pandemic, the authors have been volunteering among the Bangladeshi migrant workers in Malaysia, concomitantly finding that marginal people are unsecured for the severe food crisis. In doing this volunteering, a few questions were raised: What is the state's responsibility for the marginal people's food supply? Why does the state ignore its presence? Is there any philosophical reason? And how can these activities be theorized? Finally, how can these people survive? How can it be theorized? The authors endeavoured to answer these questions from the critical paradigm by adopting the philanthropic accountability model. In this empirical study, they argue by applying or testing the Ubuntu for politics and policy about a practical way forward in this new normal for a happier, sustainable, and healthier community.*

## INTRODUCTION

This chapter is, to an extent, a practice of the Ubuntu Model (Gade, 2012; Chowdhury et al., 2021) in the Malaysian context. If we feel the aim of social work, in effect, the social sciences, is to "make for individual and/or societal happiness (some refer to this as well-being or community well-being at the collective level) and planetary sustainability (Musikanski, Phillips, Bradbury, de Graaf & Bliss, 2020, p.2). This chapter is an academic and practical endeavor in the New Normal era. In the Pandemic, we

DOI: 10.4018/978-1-6684-6172-3.ch015

### Voice and Photovoice of the Bangladeshi Migrant Workers in Malaysia

realized even before the Pandemic (Phillips, 2012) that the major focus is life and/or the food--the question of survival (Long, 2020; Adams, 2020; Gupta & Pal, 2020; Ali, 2020; Smith & Judd, 2020)) regardless the geographical boundary, either if western (Mook, Murdock & Gundersen, 2020) or in the East. This study, along with the Ubuntu model, is creating a legacy of goodwill (Phillips, Seifer Antczak, 2013, p. 139) for a *'Sustainable communities'* in Malaysia. For sustainability, enhancing democracy is a basic goal of cooperatives [in Malaysia]. At the same time, democracy is a central core tenet of community development theory, and is "valued as a means, not as an end, serving the instrumental purpose of broadening the inputs available in the system (Cook, 1994, p. 11 in Phillips, 2012, p.192)." Large numbers of people in Malaysia are still at risk of food health as a consequence of the COVID-19 Pandemic. Understandably, unemployment or lack of savings is the justification. It is indeed, however, surfaced scenario. Rather, we do agree that policy strategies are reason to global food security (Glauber, Laborde, Martin, & Vos, 2020; Vos, Martin & Laborde, 2020; World Bank, 2020; Thomas, 2012; Caduff, 2020; Khan & Naushad, 2020).

From our volunteering experience in Malaysia, we realized that countries such as Malaysia, where thousands of foreign workers dwell and are already lost their jobs, struggle, and will intensify in the days ahead. Keeping aside the deadly numbers, the most attendant issues are for those who are living in the world's marginality (Congressional Research Service, 2020; Nuno, 2020). In this chapter, we are focusing on the food crisis. "Food is central to individual and community well-being and represents a nexus for exploring community development (Phillips, 2012, p. 198) as a referral point for furtherance. We agree, yet that, "[n]o one can accurately predict the final financial damage from COVID-19" (Khan & Naushad, 2020, p. 25) but we are in a New Normal stage, a new order, where the old is unfit. The old normal is dominated by profiteering ethics, justice, and a social system. Amongst all the dire needs in the New Normal, food is premiering as it is directly associated with life (WHO, 2020; Glauber et al., 2020; Galanakis, 2020). In developing nations, academics are diligently and critically examining the appalling issue of food security and, in turn, proposing the way forward for the New Normal (for example, in Sri Lanka, Ranasinghe, 2020; in China, Wang & Sue, 2020; in Amazonian nations, Kaplan et al., 2020; in Kenya, Odhiambo, Weke & Ngare, 2020). Narrowing down the issue, few scholars (Wenham, Smith & Morgan, 2020; Peterman, et al, 2020) are focusing on the gender issue as a marginal community. As we indicated the State's recently taken policies and implications are the major reason for food issues. However, both academia and policy are ignoring the Bangladeshi migrant workers in Malaysia, *one known study* appeared (Mia & Griffiths, 2020), though Mia and Griffith's chapter derived from secondary data, therefore, failed to give a compacted way forward except a conclusion call to be humanitarian for not returning to Bangladesh. Not only from an academic point of view but, we consider the community's standpoint, and from a humanitarian ground, perhaps, this study is pertinent and claims originality concerning both academia and community welfare. To us, it is impossible to condone food insecurity at this time. We will turn now to see the context, and how our academic position is connected with the community.

## WHAT WE HAVE DONE AND WHAT NEEDS TO DO? LITERATURE REVIEW

A fascinating, inspirational event has led to this researcht. During this Pandemic, I have volunteered among Bangladeshi migrant workers (BMWs) in Malaysia. I discovered that these BMWs have not only an absence of legal protection and food insecurity but are relatively quite unaware of Malaysian culture and charity organizations and are unconscious of their rights. Since then, I have surfed the academic works done over the last dedicated in this region and found that the situation is worse even the academic research demonstrated. Anecdotal evidence suggests that these figures are significantly underreported regarding unauthorized migrants. In Malaysia 70% of total construction labor comes from BMWs, and this is the 3rd in foreign workers.

A few labor surplus countries (especially Bangladesh) and Malaysia, Indonesia, and Brunei have implemented various control measures (such as airport inspections and, border surveillance, military patrols) to prevent undocumented immigration. However, these measures have proven ineffective against experienced traffickers and their human cargo. As a result, our policies should address, include, and adopt the study populations we hope to engage.

Given a large number of Bangladeshi migrant workers with their undeniable contribution to the economies of Malaysia (Anderson, 2022; Haque & Ghani, 2020, Ullah, 2022; Karim, 2014, 2017), it is vital to understand and learn about the adaptation of Bangladeshi migrant workers to Malaysian culture. Following that, a social policy can be designed to enable their cultural adaption and coping techniques to promote their health and wellbeing in Malaysia. It is critical to allow workers to accomplish their jobs optimally, particularly in the workplace. Bangladeshi migrant laborers are also highly renowned for their exemplary performance and excellent service in all growth sectors, as evidenced in numerous heavy-duty tasks. On the other side, the question of why the state ignores its presence arises. Is there a philosophical reason for this? And how can we theorize these activities? Finally, how will these folks survive? What is theorized? We attempted to answer these questions from a humanistic view using the IRP. This study centers around the ontological question of whether or not these BMWs are a part of the nation.

To rationalize the significance of this study, it is demonstrated that the survival, fitness, Quality of Life (QoL) and health-seeking behavior of migrant workers is significantly related to the socio-economic development and human resource requirements for a newly developed country as well as the livelihood of a poor economy. To compare Malaysia with Bangladesh in this perspective, it is well-documented that Bangladesh is presently an extremely impoverished country, ranking 133rd in the world's median HDI index (UNDP, 2022). The country's economic situation deteriorated further when it revealed a prolonged current account deficit and a persistent downward trend in the foreign exchange rate. Regarding population, Bangladesh has the highest population density in the world, with fast dwindling arable land, thus impoverishing vast numbers of unemployed farmers and forcing them to travel to towns and cities in quest of urgent employment. "It suffers significant unemployment rates in both the public and commercial sectors, as well as persistent poverty for at least one-third of the work force" (Karim, 2013b, p. 178). Because of the country's structural economic conditions, low levels of economic activity, and high incidence of poverty, many of the country's educated and less-educated young workforce have sought opportunities in many foreign countries, including Malaysia, to work temporarily as migrant workers as an alternative source of income.

On the other hand, Malaysia is a fast-industrializing country with significant economic development that necessitates an enormous need for foreign employees to carry out these tasks as a supplemental workforce. Workers are brought in from nearby Southeast Asian nations such as Thailand, the Philippines, and Indonesia to make up for the shortage. Simultaneously, labor was imported from South Asian countries, including India, Pakistan, Bangladesh, and Nepal. Bangladeshi migrants first arrived in Malaysia in 1986 as plantation workers, but a bilateral agreement struck between the two nations in 1992 permitted Bangladeshis to work in several development sectors (Karim, 2017).

From an academic, and organizational viewpoint, some leading universties and institutions, like in famous Asia Research Institute (ARI) of Singapore National University, Asian Studies of University Malaya, Institute of Malaysians and International Studies of University Kebngsan Malaysia are in zenith names in this issues. Professor Erich Thomson, C Y Koh, C. Goh, K, Wee of NSU, Ahasn Ullah of UBD, Brunei, Zehadul Karim of IIUM are a few among many. Along with ILO, we IOM came in 1951, the International Organization for Migration (IOM) is a Related Agency of the United Nations and the leading intergovernmental organization in the field of migration. What I claim here, these scholarly works are aimng two things, one justifies self-interest, and two, they are absent experts. For instance, what the people get benefitted from the ARI's series discussion 'Materializing Changes for Migrant workers.' The reasoning is in ontology, we need to seek an Autonomous Sociology that Hussein Alatas asserted over 50 yaers before (1972), and recently it has been revived by Farid Alatas (2006) maybe, with little amendment of this philosophical stand, we may look at the current phenomenon of BMWs. As a note,

*It is quite true that the younger Alatas' work is by far the "most important, detailed, and comprehensive theory of academic dependency to date" (Schöpf 2020, 8). According to the latter, An autonomous social science tradition is defined as one which independently raises problems, creates concepts and creatively applies methodologies without being intellectually dominated by another tradition. This does not mean that there are no influences from, and no learning involved from other traditions. Ideas are not to be rejected on the grounds of their national or cultural origins. (Alatas 2006, 112 in an unpublished paper in Thord World Quaterly)[1].*

Bangladeshi migrants have been working in Malaysia in large numbers since long. Bangladeshi migrants have historically worked in great numbers in Malaysia. This was possible because the governments of Malaysia and Bangladesh have also signed bilateral agreements. Because these three regions are geographically close, inhabited by BMWs, their cultures are similar. However, any systemic research was not conducted so far that includes these three locations of Malaysia with similar objectives by applying a field-based empirical inquiry.

It is well known that, due to significant fundamental national disparities, a large portion of Bangladesh's unemployed labor force temporarily migrates to Malaysia and working all law-ranked job sectors. We will argue in this empirical study that using or testing IRP for politics and policy is a feasible path forward in this New Normal for a happier, more sustainable, and healthier community in these three locations.

## Analysis for the Migration/Registration Theory of Change Is It LTR?

It is worth noting that since their first arrival in 1986, all are, in my view, virtually absent, or we term them 'Absent Experts.' Understandably, the methodological position does not allow them to be part of the studies people?. At large and significantly, most works follow and sit within the Durkheimian sociology of knowledge which says, consider social fact as things (Durkheim, 2014), hence, failed to provide a space for the BMWs and reach the policy arena. We place some of the leading works on BMWs issue in table 1.

*Table 1. The scholarly attention on BMWs*

| Epistemological Filed | Researchers | Major Focus |
|---|---|---|
| Anthropology | Karim, 2013, 2014, 2017; Karim et al., 2015 | Health and socio-economic condition |
| | Hilsdon (2007) | Female workers |
| | Rashid, 2011 | Theoretical study |
| | Ahlin and Li, 2019 | Methodological study |
| Social work | Anderson, 2021 | socio-cultural adjustment |
| | Reza and Subramaniam, 2019 | Social Wellbeing |
| | Jmail and Dutta, 2021 Raihan and Dutta, U. (2021 | Economic wellbeing |
| Sociology | Zaman & Hussain, 2019 Zaman et al, 2021 | Social Capital and social wellbeing |
| | Ullah, 2022 | |
| | Lee, 2010 | Identity and recognition (being-becoimg_ |
| Economics | Haque, M. W., & Ghani, N. A. (2020 Uddin, M., & Mohammed, A. A. (2021 | Economic aspect of BMWs |
| Education | Erling et al., 2015 | English is lack |
| | Chowdhury & Chakraborty, 2021 | |
| | Mobarak et al., 2020 | |

Table 1 is a nutshell of our claim that academicians were concerned about BMWs, yet, they caught fished without sweating their clothes; hence they were absent. We endeavored to present from anthropology, sociology, social work, economics and Education; unfortunately, and given justice, none has come out with any implementing model where people, academia and policymakers are in the same nexus. However, a detailed examination of these studies research leads us to conclude that people's voices have been emasculated and blended with academicians. These studies lack of being instructive and empirical in epistemology, and they fail to address liberation and sustainability, and therefore an actual development is left far behind. The same can be said of most stories published in newspapers and periodicals over the previous two decades, since migration came to the fore. There may be multiple answers, depending on the weight and strength. Still, when the people's perspective is key, the reality is that nothing is more significant than people's view, especially when marginalized and victims of structural violence. Except for a little, even marginal among the research crowd, some (Chowdhury et al., 2022, Chowdhury, 2022) are assertive and talk about volunteering and active participation. To begin, we may address the growing gap between academia and migrant workers, which has been caused by their methodological approach, as other scholars have already done. This reasoning would be relatively marginal because the tendency was observable when, to date, BMWs are still a living phenomenon. Many researchers, more or less, plausible reasons, combined or taken singly, are the difference in what sort of public was intended and (partially) the dissonance produced by citing positively these works, which are as 'absent experts' to the Migration discourse.

However, as social science practitioners, we should not rule out the possibility that, in general, the sustainable output could simply be ignored in exposing, highlighting, and emphasizing the dispossession of Bangladeshi migrant workers as human beings and citizens of Malaysia. Many of researchers have been and will be working with similar indignation, maybe academically rigorous, but in the question of Phrenetic, reciprocity, and contribution, these are not saying trash; however, they stand with justifying self-interest (Spivak, 2004) only instead of common interest. Of course, we can either condemn ourselves to silence (Alatas, 2021) or remove the 'other' through epistemic suppression (Foley, 2010; Chilisa, 2019; Smith, 2021). These cited researchers may eventually reduce the application of knowledge in practical domains, and readership goes very tiny club.

The applied trend of Education tagged with Brazilian educatinist philosopher Paolo Friere who started this practical implication of 'education' (not merely education faculty rather entire Education. I put a capital E to indicate the entirety of the knwolede discourse) move in the 1970s, eventually influencing many disciplines like anthropology, sociology, Education, etc. From the lens of Anthropology (Bejarano et al., 2019) and Educational Anthropology, in specific (Pelissier,1991; Foley, 2010; Schensul, 2011), if we locate this study, which allows me to "search for a cultural concept that addresses power relations, social inequality, and exploitation (Foley, 2010, p.81). Recently, there has a shift taken our notice that educational anthropology comes to the marginal and disadvantaged people and their welfare (Dar & Najar, 2018) and activity-based research (Dar, 2021; Gosine, 2021).

Naturally, a more thorough investigation of those writings (like an archaeological dig) may show an underlying presence of notions and interpretations workers in the coming days. These prior studies are, in turn, the gap, barriers, and opportunities for us.

## THE CONTEXT OF THIS STUDY AND CONNECTION TO THE COMMUNITY

Taking this ground, we revealed, as documented by Bangladesh Manpower Employment and Training-BMET, 8,80,584 Bangladeshi migrant laborers reached in Malaysian since 1976-2017, and 2017-2019, 1,76, 000 workers came.[2] Even recent studies (Reza & Subramaniam, 2019; Hossain, 2020; Ruji, 2019; Karim, et al, 2017; Noh, Wahab, Bakar Ah & Islam, 2016) came in fore about Bangladeshi migrant workers and their poor condition in leading healthy lives. These studies are, however, these are more evocative and conducted before the Pandemic. For instance, Noh, Wahab, Bakar Ah & Islam (2016) showed that these migrant workers have limited access to public health that leads to more severity during and after this Pandemic.

### A Brief Story…

Around 2 am March 17, 2020, the first author received a text message in WhatsApp, 17 Bangladeshi migrant workers are starving. Immediately, he shared this with other Bangladeshi peers of University Malaya. And the next day, evening, we were able to send some food for them. It was the starting, and by June 21, 2020, we provided food (Rice, potatoes, lentils, noodles, flour, sugar, cooking oil, onion, and mixed spice powder) to 410 people. This process is ongoing…

It is our connectivity with the community. Being academicians, we could not look the other way around but to be engaged in this appalling situation.

Due to Movement Control Order (MCO) by the Malaysian government, placed since 18th March 2020, thousands of workers have lost jobs, even now, the Recovery phase of MCO is in place, however, the migrant workers are yet jobless because of fewer customers in the restaurants, hotels are shut, construction sites are under the close monitor of Standard Operational Practice (SOP). Our observational fieldwork took places in three areas:

*Filed visit (FV) Cluster -1: Kota Damansara is a town located in the district of Petaling Jaya, Selangor, Malaysia. The total landscape stretched over 4,000 acres of land (16 Square k.m).*

*FV Cluster-2: Nilai is a town between district Sepang and district Seremban, Negeri Sembilan, Malaysia. It is a fast-rising town due to its proximity and connection to Kuala Lumpur, Putrajaya, and Kuala Lumpur International Airport.*

*FV Cluster -3: Ampang or Ampang Hill, in the eastern part of Kuala Lumpur (KL) in the Titiwangsa constituency, is a district and town area.*

Bangladeshi migrant workers are an existing entity in Malaysia as the 8th highest among foreign workers (Andaya & Andaya, 2016. p. 3). So, given this context, connectivity, and background, perhaps, we should inform the adopted methodology in this study.

## METHODOLOGY: CRITICAL PARADIGM AND UBUNTU

A theory is, for us and should be, a means of liberatory practice (hooks, 1991), a seed in our backyard (Harvey, 2000, p. 94) for a 'change agent' of the society' (Musikanski et al., 2020, p. 1) and tool governance so that this methodology can be accountable (Kraeger & Robichau, 2017) for political and policy for the marginal people. Relying on this theme, this study aligns with the Critical paradigm that maintains an ideological relation with Ubuntu. In further, this study adopts a 'cultural interface' (Nakata, 2007) that submits to analyze the gap between the state policies and the community.

This model is like a measuring tape, in this study, empirically we applied and found that there has a gaping hole in between the policy and marginal people like the Bangladeshi migrant workers. That is, in other words, a 'cultural interface,the gap between the policy planners and political decisions--have been widening. For national solidarity, a healthier community, and a sustained future, we would recommend reducing the gaps.

Besides, our theoretical understanding developed from other a few concepts such is, 'Historical ontology', 'Biopower' (Dreyfus & Rabinow, 2014), 'Metaphysics of presence' (Derrida, 1979), Disaster Capitalism (Klein, 2007) for comprehension and analysis.

*Along with this theoretical position, we feel, a solution is pertinent: volunteering is a means to be reciprocal with the people to whom we are working with. As we stated this Ubuntu and its position gives us a pathway, where academia, community, and the policies may string together, and as a whole, this is in other sense, reciprocity. These reciprocal links may broaden three demeanors, connectivity with the people, collaboration for the people with policy implications, and contribution to the welfare of the people. For collecting data, we used the interview (including telephonic), observational fieldwork, and a few sharing circles as it is widely practiced in Critical methodology (Chilisa, 2012, Smith, L., 2012). "My analysis of the historical development of the written discourses on ubuntu (Gade 2011) suggests that after the term 'ubuntu' appeared in writing in 1846, more than a century passed before the first authors began to define ubuntu more broadly than simply as a human quality. If I am correct, then it was not until the second half of the 1900s that ubuntu began to be defined as a philosophy, an ethic, African humanism, and as a worldview in written sources. Furthermore, my historical findings indicate that it was in the period from 1993 to 1995 that the Nguni proverb 'umuntu ngumuntu ngabantu' was used for the first time to describe what ubuntu is. In recent years some SAADs have used the proverb to explain what ubuntu is (e.g. Bhengu 1996: 6; Tshoose 2009: 14).*

*Furthermore, there are also members of the SAADs group who define ubuntu as a philosophy, an ethic, African humanism, or as a worldview. This can be illustrated with some quotes:*

*Ubuntu is a philosophy that could assist in rebuilding within and amongst different communities (Motsei 2007: 10).*

*It [ubuntu] is a social ethic, a unifying vision enshrined in the Zulu maxim 'umuntu ngumuntu ngabanye' ('one is a person through others') (Makgoba 1999: 153). That healthy atmosphere also emanated from the authentic African humanism (ubuntu) that pervaded the college (Buthelezi 2004: 129).*

*Ubuntu stresses the importance of community, solidarity, caring, and sharing. This worldview [ubuntu] advocates a profound sense of interdependence and emphasizes that our true human potential can only be realized in partnership with others (Ngcoya 2009: 1) (Gade, 2012, p. 492, emphasizing ours, original citation kept).*

In further we refere to (Chowdhury et al, 2022; Chowdhury et al., 2021). The Methodolohical stance, we may visualize in figure 1.

*Figure 1. Research design*

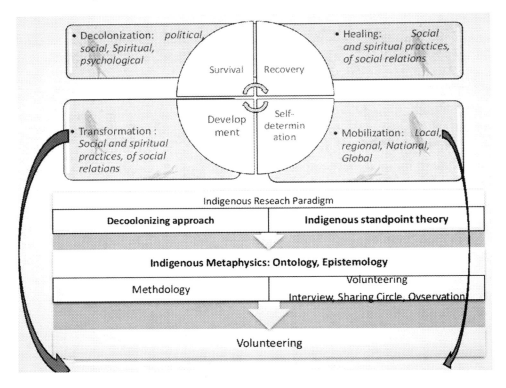

## FINDINGS AND ANALYSIS

The Malaysian Government took a few timely and practical steps for protecting the people during this Pandemic. If we locate the important elements from these packages, the information is as follows:

- *On March 27, 2020, the Malaysian government issued its second stimulus package to combat the economic impact of the COVID-19 Pandemic.*
- "One-off RM 800 financial assistance for unmarried individuals earning RM2,000 per month and below" has been announced by Prihatin Rakyat Economic Stimulus Package (Prihatin) (Ministry of Finance, 2020:4).
- *Selangor, a state of Malaysia, as an instance, also announced stimulus package, let us take the key point of this package, that includes* "incentives for licensed traders and hawkers (New Straits Times, 20 March 2020).

Keeping this information given above, let us brief the respondents' profiles may help to grasp the theme of the chapter.

*Table 2. Respondents' socio-economic profile (Malaysian workers).*

|  | Age | Education | Income (Till March 2020 | Profession |
|---|---|---|---|---|
| Malaysian Respondents | 27 | Higher secondary 70% | 2000 (70%) | Waiter (30%) |
|  |  | Secondary 20% | 1500-1999 (20%) | Construction worker (60%) |
|  |  | Below secondary 10% | <1500 (10%) | Cleaner (10%) |
| Regular Meal |  | 3 times with less meal: 10% | 2 times with less 70% | 1 time full meal: 20% |

Source: Fieldvisit

In Malaysia, we interviewed 90 males, and 3 families. The respondents are of average aged 27. Their monthly income was an average RM 2000 (70%) before COVID-10. However, the respondents from Malaysia are observed, interviewed, and discussed in a 'sharing circle' (Chilisa, 2011) instead of a Focus Group Discussion. Besides that, we observed more than 400 migrant workers in various locations. All the adults interviewed here, reported experiences of food insecurity since Malaysia went into official lockdown (March 18, 2020). It was supposed to be two weeks, however, due to the spread of the virus, the authority must extend till 9th June 2020 in different phases. The experience we faced is severe. For instance, one group of people from the Kota Damansara area said like this.

A Kota Damansara resident said,

*Brother, we wake up in mid-day so that we save the morning food for launch-(A respondent, a Bangladeshi worker, it was before that fasting month -Ramadan].*

*Can you brother provide us with some chicken, for a long time, we have not cooked any meat.*

*Ramadan [fasting for Muslims] is coming brother; how will we survive?*

Nilay respondents said that,

*Last 3 weeks potato paste(আলুভর্তা) and red lentil with rice is the only food we have been consuming.*

These statements when we compare with the findings of observations and FGD, perhaps, may point in the themes. The Bangladeshi migrant workers are

- consuming reduced meals than usual.
- by routinely bouncing food (like morning food).

- being starved however unable to eat
- not cooking every day, because they couldn't provide anything or even though they couldn't have the food. Everyone else addressing one or more of these questions was listed as insecure.

What we have been known from the people that they do not wake up in the morning skipping or reducing the size of their meals, experiencing hunger but not eating, and/or going a whole day without eating because they could not afford or access food. An additional 70% of adults reported feeling very worried or fairly worried about getting the food they need during the

COVID-19 outbreak, having two meals a day with less amount of normal quantity. Worthwhile to mention that those meals are mainly with potato paste, red lentils, or even sometimes they keep the leftover rice from dinner in water, and at morning eat it with onion and fried red dry or green chili (পান্তাভাত see figure 2).

*Figure 2. The Meal of a respondent*

On 27 May 2020, the first author received a text: 'Brother, I have no food for today, can you arrange some meat or fish, one onion and one garlic.' (see figure 4).

*Figure 3. A text message for food*

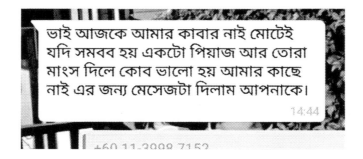

The author had arranged from his own house. This is a small group of people among the vast numbers of Bangladeshi workers in Malaysia, nonetheless, it represents the greater picture. In compliance with the national food security surveillance data from Malaysia, food insecurity-risk groups are currently in threat. These include unemployed adults, family-owned adult women, income-less adults, and these are, again, for those people who are citizens here.

Families with children are in the worst situation. We did not capture the malnutritional status of the respondents, however, it is explicit that by consuming potato paste, *panta vat*, red lentils, at best one can survive, but will not get proper and a balanced diet.

*Figure 4. Our Volunteering with the 3rd Space people*

In the case of Malaysia, the food crisis, again, we admit, for the locals is not an issue because of these stimulus packages, however, these excluded, the Bangladeshi migrant workers. We gave herein a few photos in figure 3 out of thousands form our volunteering, as we stated as a method of survival. It is not possible for a human being, at least for us, to construe the situation in a language format. Some statements, pictures, observation is indeed more than enough if one can feel it at all. And since now (June 10, 2020), Malaysia lifts MCO to the recovery phase, on the hand, starting the New Normal. Nothing has changed for the migrant workers and yet we have been doing volunteering for saving people's lives. The pictures are out of the explanation, when we see a pile of rice with onion and chili is the menu, language shows its limit to explain the condition. Yet, we are trying to decipher the deadly situation in text format, in academia, the discussion, and explanation.

## DISCUSSION

In this chapter, we are to scrutinize the state's perception (ontology) about the reality of marginal people. Nor the Malaysian government or the Bangladeshi High Commission of Malaysia, or the Government of Bangladesh has announced package, funds for these poor people in Malaysia. The only exception is, the Bangladesh High Commission donated a small amount of food[3] as a one-off. They have not provided any funds to pay room rent, buy food, and other everyday essentials for survival. It is one aspect of our argument. The Bangladeshi migrant workers are not an emblematical entity here, they are instead living as 'being' entity, but the reality is that they are not 'owning' or 'belonging'. We do feel that an "institutionalized understanding of ethnicity as about belonging, rather than 'being' (Rocha, 2019)" is vital for incorporating these people. About ten years before, Malaysian professor Raymond Lee concerned about marginality. "It is not my purpose here to construct such a model but only to provide the inklings of this model by alerting the reader to the yet unmapped relations between the nation-state and globalized liquidity and marginality. It is hoped that future cosmopolitanism research will take note of these relations (Lee, 2010: 184)." Yet, the marginality is such a concern in this Pandemic, we can not condone.

In addition to above, democracy is a central core tenet of community development theory, and is "valued as a means, not as an end, serving the instrumental purpose of broadening the inputs available in the system" (Cook, 1994, p. 11 in Phillips, 2012,p.192). So, taking the Ubuntu's message, we felt that lacking of a state's inclusionary policy is one reason for starving.

Volunteering' or philanthropic activities, if we take Ubuntu spirit which never allws to stay alone, live alone (Gade, 2012) and within itself is a method in social work (Chowdhury et al, 2022; Wilson & Son, 2018). But has to be in the state's policy inclusion within a democratic demeanor. We are not as radical as the philosopher Slavoj Zizek or Andrew Liu, who knows that the right preventive measure against coronavirus is the opportunity to willingly revoke from capitalism. This assertion is utopia. We instead prefer to take this journey forward with an ontological turn. Academicians must work for the people in air-cooled rooms with sun-burned streets. At the same time, state initiatives will represent the voice of the population.

Labor migration is perhaps an indelible byproduct of globalization—an unavoidable feature of the modern world. Relatively poor people, particularly in an overpopulated country like Bangladesh, seek a secure space in the globe. Well-known that Bangladeshi Migrant Workers (hereafter BMWs) have played a vital role in the Malaysian economy. The contribution of Bangladeshi migrant construction workers to Malaysia's infrastructural development is significant (Haque et al., 2020; Uddin & Mohammad, 2021). Malaysia, for example, is the most preferred destination country for Bangladeshis, where between 300,000 and 500,000 undocumented Bangladeshi migrants live (Shibli, 2020; Erling et al., 2015; Zaman et al., 2021; Raihan & Dutta, 2021). As the Immigration and Labour Departments limit services, many migrant workers in Malaysia have faced stigma, discrimination and xenophobia, especially concerning health, security, labor, and housing (Subramaniam, 2020). Mostly there are serving in 3D (dirty, demeaning and dangerous) type of work since most of them are unskilled and inexperienced for high profile jobs) (see Rahman et al, 2014, p 127; Haque & Ghani, 2020).

Similarly, in some Southeast Asian countries, such as Malaysia, one-fourth of the migrants are Bangladeshi (Jamil & Dutta, 2021, p 1385). The documented number is that "[u]nder the terms of a deal with Bangladesh, renegotiated in 2016, Malaysia sought to bring in up to 1.5 million Bangladeshi workers (Anderson, 2021, p. 93) and the current number is 2, 30,000 where unofficial number is higher (Haque & Ghani, 2020, Zaman et.al., 2021; Karim et al., 2015). Noticeably, the relationship between Bangladesh and Malaysia is quite historical, as the first mosque, according to Bierre (2006), was built in Penang in 1803. As observed, Indonesia accounted for 40% of the total, Nepal second with 22%, and Bangladesh third with 13% (Haque & Ghani, 2020).

In this Pandemic, the situation came with an accurate picture. I was working with them very closely as volunteering by my motivation (Chowdhury et al., 2022a, 2022b, 2020, 2021) with the BMWs and practically saw the food insecurity. There are many scholars like Jamil and Dutta's experience is direr.

Amid this Pandemic, "[c]onsequently, being capacitated to withstand such stress, young Bangladeshi workers exhibited desperation; a few of them tried to/committed suicide (2021, p. 1400) which aligns with the caveats and other studies (Karim, 2017, 2014). And it is seen that, 87% of Bangladeshi workers do not have access to health care in Malaysia (Rahman, 2022).

There have been numerous studies on Bangladeshi migrant workers over the last two decades, but two fundamental gaps remain. No studies with a combination of three adjust areas have appeared. Two, no single study has emerged with a methodology that aims to train and educate workers who come to a foreign soil, unfamiliar area, or even stranger work environment. Though Malaysia is the home of the second largest BMWs, we anticipate that by combining this country's three central locations, our study will focus on a large region and numbers. The rigor and novelty of this study are based not just on the regional coverage but also on the intention: sustained Community development for both workers and host countries.

The first primary focus of this study is the socio-economic status of BMWs in Malaysia, specifically Kuala Lumpur, Penang, and Johor Baru. This study then descends to the three regions to comprehend the BMWs' perspective on their lives and their vision of how to overcome obstacles, and closes with the development of a model. Following SDGs-11, and SDGs 8, which mentioned "Target 8.5: Full employment and decent work with equal pay and ILO Convention 169, this study intends to build a Training Module to familiarize workers with foreign life and foreign land to ensure a safe, secure, and sustainable community in Malaysia.

BMWs are in academic focus (Table 1), and we assume that 'absent experts have been working for them in Malaysian context by many local and Bangladeshi researchers, but now we propose as clarification that our proposal distinguishes what scholars have done. Again, as a continuous and living phenomenon, we must consider that concerns are evolving and coming under tension from a variety of other factors such as health, quality of life, a decent workplace, sustainability, and, most obviously, social justice and human rights. Many studies ended with such an assertion; for instance, Anderson said,

*Finally, this examination of the specific policy moves in Malaysia suggests there is a need for more research on the complexity of migration policymaking (2021. p.98).*

Or, Uddin and Mohammd (2021) said,

*The study suggested that adequate measures should be taken to provide pre-departure training on job and host county's culture to the expected migrant workers. The government of the native country should also monitor the activities of recruiting agencies.*

Scrutinizing these two statements, with all respect, can we find the scholars in these 'scientific' works? These abstract suggestions are often heard amid this Pandemic and come from people who usually do not know research and data analysis. These suggestions are very superficially, yet, informative, and to a specific point, are helpful in my endorsement that they are 'Absent experts.' However, these scientific works can not do anything unless their methodology permits engagement and activity. Despite—or perhaps because of—the availability of research works, it hlped me to find a space, hence I endeavor to work with a combination of international treaties, local acts, and BMWs standpoint in successfully achieving the SDGs.

In meeting the aims of this research, this study leans with the Indigenous Research paradigm (IRP). It is worth noting that, according to its terminology, IRP does not have to be for Indigenous people and their challenges; instead, this is the most suitable methodology for capturing the marginal point of view with emancipation, research, recovery, and development (Smith, 2021;, Nakata, 2009;). Epistemologically, we are with the spirit of humanism, and Educational Anthropology (Pelissier,1991; Foley, 2010; Schensul, 2011), which allows me to think about the social phenomenon from a practical aspect with power relations. This study informs Homi Bhabha's Third Space, Martin Nakata's Cultural Interface, George Murcus' Mutisited Ethnography, and BMW's Standpoint as theory. I aim for a Mixed-Method technique to collect data and achieve the goal, albeit an Ethnographic method is preferred. It follows a Mixed-Method approach to data collection and to reach the objective, though an Ethnographic method is a premier. This study informs intensive ethnographic fieldwork, field surveys, interviews with BMWs, government officials, employers, local policymakers, social researchers, sharing circles with employers and workers, and virtual gatherings with BMWs of three regions.

Moreover, on analytical tools, it adopted Foucauldian interpretative analytics, qualitative thematic analysis, critical and mediated discourse analysis of international treaties and local acts along with bilateral accords will facilitate the study's aimings. On axiology, this study takes the mandate to follow a Reciprocal approach in which the researchers are a part of the people. It must understandably follow the respective University norms and state law. In IRP, researchers are encouraged to make a practical contribution, to maintain a life-long relationship, and to do research in a phronetic manner (Aristotle's *Nichomachean Ethics*, books V, VI), that is, to employ knowledge for the welfare of the 'Polis' (Greek translation comes as a community).

If we see, in Malaysian contexts, the policy (democratic accountability to include all of the people within it), then performance and transparency would come in fore parallelly. This is an absolute ontological matter, at a time, a methodological gap—deeply rooted in the historical construction of the new liberal ideology. The state policies, per se, 'metaphysics of presence' Derrida (1979) for controlling the marginal people as biopolitics (Dreyfus & Rabinow, 2014), are reflecting the colonial legacy in Malaysia, and this is the base of historical ontology (Foucault, 1990). The old normal, in all means, dominated not only the social system with profiteering path and academia too. Therefore, we have not seen that these migrant people can be an agenda od research, or academicians stood with philanthropic activities.

In academia, some seminal works are our inspiration here for picking the Accountability model. Particularly, the botanical knowledge and social science, and its relation to imperialism, science has been at stake since 1494 (Crosby, 1972; Shiva; 2016; Harvey, 2000). Thus, we agreed, no research is value-free (bell hooks, David harvey). Even our analysis in this study is value-laden. The New Normal policy implications should aware of being "most imposing inheritance is the state apparatus (Lee)." We stated before, state policies caused the people's starve. American Indian scholar Vine Deloria, Australia aboriginal Martin Nakata are, since long, advocating, acting, and contributing for a localized critical stand. So theoretically, this chapter is a 'test-run' of Ubuntu. Concomitantly this chapter is parsing and reflecting people's transformation (Harvey), and liberty (bell hooks). We feel that the academicians do not act with the spirit of 'practical-critical' consciousness, probably it is time to refrain ourselves. In this study, we have been working as a volunteer for the people. Volunteering is a conduit between citizens and academicians who can medicate.

Seeing through Disaster capitalism, Biopolitics and in reverese, if we adopt Ubuntu approach, the migrant workers, particularly those were working in restaurants, and hotels—are not allowed to re-join. This gives us many outcomes:

1. In the scenario of Malaysia, Agamben's (2005) State of Exception' turns into the 'state of Normality' in the New Normal era.
2. By biopolitics marginal people have been controlled, managed.
3. By Disaster Capitalism, concurrently, the state vacates the old policies, and during the New Normal, new policies introduce that ultimately serve the neoliberals.
4. During this exceptional stage, the state has no measure for the Marginal people, only 'volunteering' survived them, though this volunteering, as tested in the Malaysian perspective lacks coordination of legal provision (state policies), performance accountability, and finally the democratic accountability.

For the New Normal:

5. So, we need the Standpoint, which gives people's voice to the policy planners in implementing the Ubuntu with full swing, connecting, collaborating with all social dimensions as demonstrated in the figure 1.
6. We need a reciprocal manner where nothing is imposed instead all stakeholders will be driven by an Ihsanic philosophy (Good deeds for the good deed, good actions for good action)
7. Agamben, and Foucault Thomas (2012) were aware that this special feature would become permanent. It's not about good or bad, but it is always risky, to fully commit to the concept of biopolitics if we instinctively endorse it without ever contemplating it.
8. The state of exception is going to the state of normal in the New Normal era. Despite the absence of enough evidence, either from Malaysia or the Bangladesh High Commisson in Malaysia, to make a final policy direction, yet some assumptions can make. This study perturbs with re-examining the future of studies. Based on present trajectories, yet we see a few theoretical observations.

The change to New Normal would be worthwhile if its values and morals were to become context-specific and to stand to gain its vulnerable groups.

## CONCLUSION FOR THE WAY FORWARD AND FURTHER RESEARCH

We hope, and we hope again, that more social research will appear soon. Our endeavors have been marked by both the continuity of the old normality and the discontinuity of the marginal life of the people. During this drastic situation, volunteering has been a practical instrument for lifesaving. However, volunteering or philanthropic would be more effective, if it had proper coordination with ALL social dimensions as we showed in figure -1.

Malaysia is planning for a soft-landing as the Malaysian prime minister indicated in the Eid greetings (24. 05. 2020, *The Malaysiakini*, 2020). And pressing for a plan to exit the MCO through the Community leaders. We propose that if the locals' community leaders are instructed by an inclusive policy, at least, we can see the minimal distance in the 'cultural interface' that will definitely bring social harmony, and well democratic environment, in effect, a happy society. Ubuntu is, to an extent, a sense of 'we' feelings. Gustavo Esteva's proposal of using the word 'we' as a verb--is a magnificent philosophical analogy of commonness, volunteering and philanthropic activities .

We think Harvey's *The New Imperialism* is very insightful here. Privatization schemes are not covering or protecting the marginal people unless it is 'Accountable'.

*I (the first author) am not a good scholar, I feel like my heart is rusted with loads of sins as I can't do much about the people we are working with, and we are 'intellectual.' But, every time I bring food to the poor, I feel that someone removes the rust of my heart and brings life back in it. I feel so relieved. We have thus become quite subjective, value-laden to our people, for whom we are graced in this world and perhaps in the New Normal.*

What good it would be if all the social dimensions are in accountable. To end, this chapter, "fundamentally, [our] research is [not only] the process of discovery and exploration, but a tool for exploitation and means of the marginal communities" (Phillips, Trevan & Kraeger, 2020, p1). Days will come, lets us finish with poetry lines:

*It is a time for us to cherish,*

*those who were lost, and those who served.*

*It is a time to bear witness to this silence, feeling it's poignant music.*

*The sound of our lives our loves*

*This Spring of two thousand and twenty. (In lockdown) (O'Malley, 2020).*

## REFERENCES

Adams, V. (2020). Disasters and Capitalism… and COVID-19. *Somatosphere Website, 26*.

Agamben, G. (2005). State of exception. *Nova Srpska Politička Misao, 12*(1-4), 135-145.

Ahlin, T., & Li, F. (2019). From field sites to field events. *Medicine Anthropology Theory, 6*(2). Advance online publication. doi:10.17157/mat.6.2.655

Ahsan Ullah, A. K. M. (2013). Theoretical rhetoric about migration networks: A case of a journey of Bangladeshi workers to Malaysia. *International Migration (Geneva, Switzerland), 51*(3), 151–168. doi:10.1111/j.1468-2435.2009.00579.x

Alatas, S. F. (2006). Editorial introduction: The idea of autonomous sociology: Reflections on the state of the discipline. *Current Sociology, 54*(1), 5–6. doi:10.1177/0011392106058830

Alatas, S. H. (2006). The autonomous, the universal and the future of sociology. *Current Sociology, 54*(1), 7–23. doi:10.1177/0011392106058831

Ali, I. (2020). The COVID-19 Pandemic: Making Sense of Rumor and Fear: Op-Ed. *Medical Anthropology, 39*(5), 1–4. doi:10.1080/01459740.2020.1745481 PMID:32212931

Anderson, J. T. (2021). Managing labour migration in Malaysia: Foreign workers and the challenges of 'control' beyond liberal democracies. *Third World Quarterly, 42*(1), 86–104. doi:10.1080/01436597.2020.1784003

Bejarano, C. A., Juárez, L. L., García, M. A. M., & Goldstein, D. M. (2019). *Decolonizing ethnography: Undocumented immigrants and new directions in social science.* Duke University Press.

Caduff, C. (2020). *What Went Wrong Corona and the World after the Full Stop.* https://www.academia.edu/download/63190746/What_Went_Wrong.pdf

Chilisa, B. (2019). *Indigenous research methodologies.* Sage Publications, Incorporated.

Chowdhury, J. S., Abd Wahab, H., Saad, M. R. M., Mathbor, G., & Hamidi, M. (2022). *Ubuntu Philosophy in the New Normalcy.* Springer Nature.

Chowdhury, J. S., Abd Wahab, H., Saad, M. R. M., Roy, P. K., Hamidi, M., & Ahmad, M. M. (2021). Ubuntu Philosophy: 'I Am Because We Are'–A Road to 'Individualism' to Global Solidarity. In Handbook of Research on the Impact of COVID-19 on Marginalized Populations and Support for the Future (pp. 361-381). IGI Global.

Chowdhury, J. S., Abd Wahab, H., Saad, R. M., & Roy, P. (2022b). "Ihsanic" Philosophy as an Alternative to Social Justice: A Concepirical (Conceptual+ Empirical) Reflection From the Bioprospecting Domain in Bangladesh. In Social Justice Research Methods for Doctoral Research (pp. 25-46). IGI Global.

Chowdhury, M. B., & Chakraborty, M. (2021). The impact of COVID-19 on the migrant workers and remittances flow to Bangladesh. *South Asian Survey, 28*(1), 38–56. doi:10.1177/0971523121995365

Córdova, T. (1998). Power and knowledge: Colonialism in the academy. *Living Chicana Theory*, 17-45.

Dar, W. A. (2021). Pedagogy for its own sake: Teacher's beliefs about activity-based learning in rural government schools of Kashmir. *Quality Assurance in Education, 29*(2/3), 311–327. doi:10.1108/QAE-01-2021-0013

Dar, W. A., & Najar, I. A. (2018). Educational anthropology, tribal education and responsible citizenship in India. *South Asia Research, 38*(3), 327–346. doi:10.1177/0262728018800759

De Bierre, J. (2006). Penang: Through Gilded Doors. Areca Books.

Deloria, V. (2001). American Indian metaphysics. *Winds of Change*, 49-67.

Dreyfus, H., & Rabinow, P. (2014). *Michel Foucault: Beyond structuralism and hermeneutics.* University of Chicago Press. doi:10.4324/9781315835259

Erling, E. J., Seargeant, P., Solly, M., Chowdhury, Q. H., & Rahman, S. (2015). *English for economic development: a case study of migrant workers from Bangladesh.* Academic Press.

Esteva, G. (2020). Alternative paths of transformation. *Globalizations, 17*(2), 225–231. doi:10.1080/14747731.2019.1670959

Ferrante, L., & Fearnside, P. M. (2020). Protect Indigenous peoples from COVID-19. *Science, 368*(6488), 251–251. doi:10.1126cience.abc0073 PMID:32299940

Foley, D. (2010). The rise of class culture theory in educational anthropology. *Anthropology & Education Quarterly, 41*(3), 215–227. doi:10.1111/j.1548-1492.2010.01084.x

Foucault, M. (1990). The history of sexuality: An introduction, volume I. Vintage.

Gade, C. B. (2012). What is ubuntu? Different interpretations among South Africans of African descent. *South African Journal of Philosophy, 31*(3), 484–503. doi:10.1080/02580136.2012.10751789

Galanakis, C. M. (2020). The Food Systems in the Era of the Coronavirus (COVID-19) Pandemic Crisis. *Foods, 9*(4), 523. doi:10.3390/foods9040523 PMID:32331259

Glauber, J., Laborde, D., Martin, W., & Vos, R. (2020). COVID-19: Trade restrictions are worst possible response to safeguard food security. International Food Policy Research Institute.

Gosine, K. (2021). Reconciling divergent realms in the lives of marginalized students. In *Visual and Cultural Identity Constructs of Global Youth and Young Adults* (pp. 78–95). Routledge. doi:10.4324/9781003055822-6

Gupta, R., & Pal, S. K. (2020). Trend Analysis and Forecasting of COVID-19 outbreak in India. medRxiv.

Haque, M. W., & Ghani, N. A. (2020). Economic aspects of quality of life of Bangladeshi construction workers in Malaysia. *Journal of Asian Development, 6*(1), 30–38. doi:10.5296/jad.v6i1.16725

Harvey, D. (2000). Reinventing geography. *New Left Review, 4*, 75.

Hilsdon, A. M. (2007). Introduction: Reconsidering Agency—Feminist Anthropologies in Asia. *The Australian Journal of Anthropology, 18*(2), 127–137. doi:10.1111/j.1835-9310.2007.tb00084.x

hooks, b. (1991). Theory as liberatory practice. *Yale JL & Feminism, 4*, 1

Hossain, M. I. (2020). Impacts of social remittances on economic activities: Labour migration from a village of Bangladesh to Malaysia. *Migration and Development*, 1–18.

Jamil, R., & Dutta, U. (2021). Centering the Margins: The precarity of Bangladeshi low-income migrant workers during the time of COVID-19. *The American Behavioral Scientist, 65*(10), 1384–1405. doi:10.1177/00027642211000397

Kaplan, H. S., Trumble, B. C., Stieglitz, J., Mamany, R. M., Cayuba, M. G., Moye, L. M., ... Thompson, R. C. (2020). Voluntary collective isolation as a best response to COVID-19 for indigenous populations? A case study and protocol from the Bolivian Amazon. *Lancet, 395*(10238), 1727–1734. doi:10.1016/S0140-6736(20)31104-1 PMID:32422124

Karim, & Rohaiza, & Basir. (2017). Roles and Social Adaptability of Bangladeshi Migrant Workers in Commercialized Farming of Cameron Highlands, Malaysia. *European Journal of Soil Science, 55*(3), 375–361.

Karim, A. H. M. (2015). Zehadul, and Nurazzura Mohamad Diah. "Health seeking behavior of the Bangladeshi migrant Workers in Malaysia: Some suggestive recommendations in Adjustive context. *Asian Social Science, 11*(10), 348.

Karim, A. Z., Diah, N. M., Mustari, S., & Sarker, M. S. I. (2015). Bangladeshi Migrant Workers in Malaysia: Their Socio-Cultural Background and Work-Adaptability. *South Asian Anthropologist*, *15*(1), 1–7.

KhanN.NaushadM. (2020). Effects of Corona Virus on the World Community. Available at SSRN 3532001. doi:10.2139/ssrn.3532001

KhanS. A.MahiM.ZainuddinM.IslamE. (2020). At what costs? A proposal for estimating migration costs in the Bangladesh-Malaysia corridor. Available at SSRN 3708959. doi:10.2139/ssrn.3708959

Khondaker, M. S. I. (2021). Tun Mahathir's administration of Malaysia's relationship with Bangladesh: A preliminary appraisal. *Religación: Revista de Ciencias Sociales y Humanidades*, *6*(30), 1. doi:10.46652/rgn.v6i30.868

Klein, N. (2007). *The shock doctrine: The rise of disaster capitalism*. Metroolitan Book.

Kraeger, P., & Robichau, R. (2017). Questioning stakeholder legitimacy: A philanthropic accountability model. *Journal of Health and Human Services Administration*, 470–519. PMID:29393613

Lee, R. L. (2010). On the margins of belonging: Confronting cosmopolitanism in the late modern age. *Journal of Sociology (Melbourne, Vic.)*, *46*(2), 169–186. doi:10.1177/1440783309355064

Long, M. A., Gonçalves, P., Paul, B. S., & Defeyter, M. (2020). Food Insecurity in Advanced Capitalist Nations: A Review. *Sustainability*, *12*(9), 3654. doi:10.3390u12093654

Mia, M. A., & Griffiths, M. D. (2020). The economic and mental health costs of COVID-19 to immigrants. *Journal of Psychiatric Research*, *128*, 23–24. doi:10.1016/j.jpsychires.2020.06.003 PMID:32512405

Ministry of Finance. (2020). *Prihatin Rakyat Economic Stimulus Package (Prihatin) (2020)*. Ministry of Finance.

Mobarak, A. M., Sharif, I., & Shrestha, M. (2020). Returns to low-skilled international migration: Evidence from the Bangladesh-Malaysia migration lottery program. *World Bank Policy Research Working Paper*, (9165).

Mook, L., Murdock, A., & Gundersen, C. (2020). Food Banking and Food Insecurity in High-Income Countries. *Voluntas*, *31*(5), 1–8. doi:10.100711266-020-00219-4

Musikanski, L., Phillips, R., Bradbury, J., de Graaf, J., & Bliss, C. L. (2020). *Happiness, Well-being and Sustainability: A Course in Systems Change*. Routledge. doi:10.4324/9781003043232

Nakata, M. (2007). *Disciplining the savages, savaging the disciplines*. Aboriginal Studies Press.

New Straits Times. (2020). *Covid-19: Rm127.78 Million Economic Stimulus Package For Selangor*. Author.

Noh, N. A., Wahab, H. A., Bakar Ah, S. H. A., & Islam, M. R. (2016). Public Health Services for Foreign Workers in Malaysia. *Social Work in Public Health*, *31*(5), 419–430. doi:10.1080/19371918.2015.1125321 PMID:27177326

NunoF. (2020). Economic effects of coronavirus outbreak (COVID-19) on the world economy. Available at SSRN 3557504.

O'Malley, K. D. (2020). A Covid Spring. *Irish Journal of Psychological Medicine*, 1–2. PMID:32406347

Odhiambo, J., Weke, P., & Ngare, P. (2020). Modeling Kenyan Economic Impact of Corona Virus in Kenya Using Discrete-Time Markov Chains. *Journal of Financial Economics*, *8*(2), 80–85.

Pelissier, C. (1991). The anthropology of teaching and learning. *Annual Review of Anthropology*, *20*(1), 75–95. doi:10.1146/annurev.an.20.100191.000451

Peterman, A., Potts, A., O'Donnell, M., Thompson, K., Shah, N., Oertelt-Prigione, S., & van Gelder, N. (2020). Pandemics and violence against women and children. *Center for Global Development Working Paper, 528*.

Phillips, R. (2012). Food cooperatives as community-level self-help and development. *International Journal of Self Help & Self Care*, *6*(2), 189–203. doi:10.2190/SH.6.2.f

Phillips, R., Seifer, B., & Antczak, E. (2013). *Sustainable communities: Creating a durable local economy*. Routledg. doi:10.4324/9780203381212

Phillips, R., Trevan, E., & Kraeger, P. (2020). Introduction to the Research Handbook on Community Development. In *Research Handbook on Community Development*. Edward Elgar Publishing. doi:10.4337/9781788118477.00005

Rahman, A. (2020). A Study on irregular migration from Bangladesh to Malaysia through the Bay of Bengal and the Andaman Sea. *Otoritas: Jurnal Ilmu Pemerintahan*, *10*(2), 120–131. doi:10.26618/ojip.v10i2.4640

Rahman, M., Uddin, M. S. J., & Albaity, M. (2014). Socio-economic conditions of Bangladeshi migrant workers in Malaysia. *Journal of Basic and Applied Scientific Research*, *4*, 246–252.

Rahman, M. M., Arif, M. T., Safii, R., Tambi, Z., Akoi, C., Jantan, Z., Halim, S. A., & Hafiz, A. (2019). Cultural adaptation by Bangladeshi migrant workers in Sarawak, Malaysia: An empirical study. *Indonesian Journal of Cultural and Community Development*, *4*, 10–21070. doi:10.21070/ijccd.v2i3.91

Raihan, J., & Dutta, U. (2021). Centering the margins: the precarity of Bangladeshi low-income migrant workers during the time of COVID-19. *The American Behavioral Scientist*, 1384–1405.

Ranasinghe R. (2020). Post-COVID19 (Novel Corona) Economic Recovery: Critical Review on Economic Immunity of Sri Lanka. Available at SSRN 3587179. doi:10.2139/ssrn.3587179

Rashid, S. (2011). Anthropology of migration: Concept, theories and Bangladesh perspective. *Green University Review*, *2*(1), 83–100.

Reza, M. M., & Subramaniam, T. (2019). Economic and social wellbeing of the Bangladeshi migrant workers in Malaysia. In *Social research methodology and new techniques in analysis, interpretation, and writing* (pp. 106–134). IGI Global. doi:10.4018/978-1-5225-7897-0.ch006

Reza, M. M., & Subramaniam, T. (2019). Economic and social wellbeing of the Bangladeshi migrant workers in Malaysia. In Social Research Methodology and New Techniques in Analysis, Interpretation, and Writing (pp. 106-134). IGI Global. doi:10.4018/978-1-5225-7897-0.ch006

Rocha, Z. L. (2019). Strict versus flexible categorizations of mixedness: Classifying mixed race in Singapore and New Zealand. *Social Identities*, *25*(3), 310–326. doi:10.1080/13504630.2018.1499221

Schensul, J. J. (2011). Building an applied educational anthropology beyond the academy. *A Companion to the Anthropology of Education*, 112-134.

Shibli, A. (2021) A case for improving labour conditions in Southeast Asia. *The Daily Star*. https://www.thedailystar.net/opinion/opendialogue/news/case-improving-labour-conditionssoutheast-asia-2031329

Smith, J. A., & Judd, J. (2020). COVID-19: Vulnerability and the power of privilege in a pandemic. *Health Promotion Journal of Australia*, *31*(2), 158–160. doi:10.1002/hpja.333 PMID:32197274

Smith, L. T. (2021). *Decolonizing Methodologies: Research and Indigenous Peoples*. Zed Books. doi:10.5040/9781350225282

Subramaniam, G. (2020). *The compounding impacts of COVID-19 on migrant workers across Asia* (Part 1). Academic Press.

Sunam, R. (2022). Infrastructures of migrant precarity: Unpacking precarity through the lived experiences of migrant workers in Malaysia. *Journal of Ethnic and Migration Studies*, 1–19. doi:10.1080/1369183X.2022.2077708

The Malaysiakini. (2020). *Raya Message*. Pm Indicates Exit Plan Led By Community Leaders. Malaysiakini.Com/News/527097

Thomas, T. D. (2012). Political Implications of Emergency Management. *Journal of Environmental Science & Engineering*, *1*(3), 397–402.

Uddin, M., & Mohammed, A. A. (2021). Adjustment Factors on the Work Performance of Bangladeshi Temporary Contract Workers in Malaysia. *The Indian Journal of Labour Economics*, *64*(2), 333–349. doi:10.100741027-021-00309-x

Ullah, A. A., Ferdous, J., & Chattoraj, D. (2022). Social, Political and Cultural Remittances: Implications for the Origin and Destination Countries. *Millennial Asia*.

Wang, Q., & Su, M. (2020). A preliminary assessment of the impact of COVID-19 on environment–A case study of China. *The Science of the Total Environment*, *728*, 138915. doi:10.1016/j.scitotenv.2020.138915 PMID:32348946

Wenham, C., Smith, J., & Morgan, R. (2020). COVID-19: The gendered impacts of the outbreak. *Lancet*, *395*(10227), 846–848. doi:10.1016/S0140-6736(20)30526-2 PMID:32151325

Wilson, J., & Son, J. (2018). The connection between neighboring and volunteering. *City & Community*, *17*(3), 720–736. doi:10.1111/cico.12324

World Bank. (2020). *Self-employed, total employment (modeled ILO estimate)* [Data file]. Washington, DC: World Bank. Retrieved April 13, 2020, from https://data.worldbank.org/indicator/sl.emp.self.zs

World Health Organization-WHO. (2020). *Coronavirus disease 2019 (COVID-19): Situation report, 72*. WHO.

Yusoff, N. N., Hamedani, S. S., Deli, M. M., Alia, M. H., & Rahman, M. R. C. A. (n.d.). *Migrant Food Handlers' Impacts on Food Quality and Safety in Malaysia Food Service Industry*. Academic Press.

Zaman, B., & Hussain, R. B. M. (2019). Usage of social capital among migrant workers for their livelihoods in Malaysia. In *Social research methodology and new techniques in analysis, interpretation, and writing* (pp. 160–189). IGI Global. doi:10.4018/978-1-5225-7897-0.ch008

Zaman, B., Islam, M. R., & Hussain, R. B. M. (2021). Fieldwork experience: challenges and managing risks as a female researcher. In *Field Guide for Research in Community Settings* (pp. 201–210). Edward Elgar Publishing. doi:10.4337/9781800376328.00023

## ADDITIONAL READING

Chowdhury, J. S., Abd Wahab, H., Saad, M. R. M., Roy, P. K., Hamidi, M., & Ahmad, M. M. (2021). Ubuntu Philosophy: 'I Am Because We Are'–A Road to 'Individualism' to Global Solidarity. In Handbook of Research on the Impact of COVID-19 on Marginalized Populations and Support for the Future (pp. 361-381). IGI Global.

Chowdhury, J. S., Wahab, H. A., Saad, R. M., Reza, H., & Ahmad, M. M. (Eds.). (2022). *Reciprocity and its practice in social research*. IGI Global. doi:10.4018/978-1-7998-9602-9

## KEY TERMS AND DEFINITIONS

**3D Jobs:** BMWs are mostky adopted, recruited and employed for 3D jobs. Mostly there are serving in 3D (dirty, demeaning and dangerous) type of work since most of them are unskilled and inexperienced for high profile jobs).

**Bangladeshi Migrant Workers (BMW):** The Bangladeshi men and women wo comes in Malaysia for non-skilled jobs.

**Pantavat:** Worthwhile to mention that those meals are mainly with potato paste, red lentils, or even sometimes they keep the leftover rice from dinner in water, and at morning eat it with onion and fried red dry or green chili (পান্তাভাত).

## ENDNOTES

[1] I adopted this appropriate statement, as an it has congruency with me. The Project of an Autonomous Social Science Tradition (ASST) and the Challenge of Scientometrics (in press).

[2] http://www.bmet.gov.bd/site/page/e3e5ce2a-7580-45e3-ab8f-ef7c55b8cc25/-

[3] A packet of 5-kilogram Rice, 7 potatoes, I liter cooking oil, a pack of salt per person.

# Chapter 16
# Ensuring Quality Education to Achieve the Sustainable Development Goals (SDGs) in Bangladesh

**Shamim Hosen**
https://orcid.org/0000-0002-6929-3062
*Bangladesh Public Administration Training Centre (BPATC), Bangladesh*

**Md. Shafiul Islam**
*University of Rajshahi, Bangladesh*

## ABSTRACT

*Bangladesh's development paradigm would change visibly once the Sustainable Development Goals (SDGs) are implemented by 2030. Quality tertiary education can act as a catalyst for the country's economic and social development, enabling it to realize its full potential. By 2030, the entire national system will have undergone gradual modification to accommodate the "Development Junction." Therefore, the main goal of this research is to identify the institutional and procedural barriers to ensuring quality tertiary education to fulfil the Sustainable Development Goals. Multiple primary data gathering techniques have been used in this study's mixed (qualitative and quantitative) approach. Again, in this study, both thematic and descriptive analyses were used. Finally, based on the findings, several recommendations have been put together for policy formation to ensure quality tertiary education in order to meet the Sustainable Development Goals.*

## INTRODUCTION

Inequality still exists despite outstanding economic growth and a significant decline in poverty over the past 20 years (World Bank, 2018). Quality education (UNESCO, 2004; Billah, 2017; Budiharso & Tarman, 2020) is regarded as one of the most powerful and successful methods, among others, for achiev-

DOI: 10.4018/978-1-6684-6172-3.ch016

ing sustainable development (Islam, Uddin, Nandy, & Hosen, 2019) to address myriad difficulties and reducing inequalities. It is generally accepted that the development of a country is more heavily influenced by highly educated individuals than by the mere number of educated individuals. The Sustainable Development Goals 4 (Owens, 2017) and quality education (Billah, 2017) go hand in hand, ensuring that all learners get the information and abilities necessary to advance sustainable development (UN, 2015). In order to produce trained people resources who will immediately contribute to improved and higher-quality output and ultimately Bangladesh's sustainable growth, it is crucial to guarantee quality higher education. However, the nation is behind in this area. This study has explored the issues against these depressing backdrops, concentrating on institutional deficiencies at the tertiary-level education sector.

Today, a nation like Bangladesh is thought to need both an education and a quality education to develop. As a result, from the elementary level to the higher level, quality in the education sector counts at every step. Furthermore, the development of the economy and society is significantly influenced by higher education (Islam, Uddin, Nandy, & Hosen, 2019). But the tertiary level of education has emerged as one of the key topics of discussion for its constantly declining quality (Hossain, 2017). Academics, researchers in education, and other interested parties all acknowledge that Bangladesh's higher education has become worse over the past 20 years (Aminuzzaman, 2011, Hossain, 2017), and the trend is still in place. As a result, one of the difficult problems that have emerged is how to meet the development crossroads (Karim & Fair, 2007) and achieve SDGs by 2030 (Bhattacharya, Rezbana, & Khatun, 2018).

Moreover, questions now arise about whether governance matters for quality education. Is Bangladesh's tertiary education of excellent quality hindered by any institutional issues? This study investigates the response to these queries. Even though there are numerous indicators for decreasing the standard of education (Ehsan, 2007; Nagoba & Mantri, 2015; Akter, 2017; Islam et al., 2017), little research has been done specifically on institutional gaps (Chowdhury, Hossain, & Rahman, 2013; J. Hossain, 2017; Cavallone, Manna, & Palumbo, 2020; Grudowski & Szczepańska, 2021). In order to improve the quality of tertiary education (Ullah, 2020) in the nation, it is essential and possible to conduct research to identify institutional shortcomings that have a negative impact.

Finding institutional deficiencies at the tertiary level in Bangladesh is the study's overarching goal. However, it addresses some particular goals such as, to identify institutional weaknesses in producing skilled human resources through high-quality education; to determine the extent to which tertiary-level educational institutions are struggling to meet the development agenda; and to suggest policy options for enhancing institutional capacity at tertiary level education in the nation. To achieve its goals, the study posed the following research questions.

1. Are there any institutional obstacles to providing Bangladeshi students with high-quality postsecondary education?
2. Are tertiary level educational institutions properly coordinated and cooperating?
3. In relation to SDG-4, what functions do financial and non-financial resources play in ensuring the quality of tertiary education?

The University Grants Commission (UGC) of Bangladesh has stated repeatedly in its numerous yearly reports about the decline in tertiary education quality (Ullah, 2020) and the importance of ensuring an excellent education for the growth of the country (UGC, 2016 & 2017). The Bangladesh Education Statistics 2021 also discusses the shortage of quality higher education in the nation (BANBEIS, 2022). Qualified tertiary education (Ullah, 2020) can immediately aid in achieving the development landmark by 2030 (Islam, Uddin, Nandy, & Hosen, 2019). Despite numerous studies and conclusions about the enhancement of educational quality, little has been discovered so far about institutional constraints. To provide quality tertiary education in the nation, which is also regarded as one of the most effective ways to achieve the SDGs, it was therefore significant to thoroughly investigate the institutional gaps.

## LITERATURE REVIEW

No matter a nation's caste, race, developed status, or level of development, quality education is crucial for its progress (UNESCO, 2005). The need for sustainable development globally cannot be satisfied by education alone. Academics, professionals, and development partners are now highlighting the importance of quality education at all levels, particularly at the postsecondary level, for sustainable development. It has been noted that graduates plan to enter the labor market (Hossain, 2021) shortly after completing their postsecondary education in a variety of roles, hoping to use their newfound knowledge to advance their particular fields. Additionally, it has been noticed that just a select few people can manage to get employment while the others struggle, and in many situations, companies claim they are not obtaining quality grades. Thus, quality of education is needed (Solaiman, 2018) not only for preparing skilled manpower for the job market, but it needs to contribute to boosting economic productivity, leading to achieving sustainable development goals (SDGs) which are related to SGD 4 (Owens, 2017; Islam, Uddin, Nandy, & Hosen, 2019). The management of the educational institutions would adhere to the Act, rules, and guidelines that the government would offer for quality education at all levels.

### Education

Education is the process of obtaining knowledge—specific knowledge or skills, preparing for adulthood, and empowering judgmental abilities. Education also facilitates the development of ethics, values, customs, beliefs, and actions. In addition, education develops in us a perspective on life and the outside world that motivates us to grow into something better. Thus, education lessens the challenges people face and creates opportunities for larger possibilities, such as prosperity, progress, and development, in both the public and private sectors (Encyclopedia of Britannica, 2020).

### Quality Education

The economic growth of a country largely depends on quality education rather than the number of people who obtained higher education. But quality education does not exist in a vacuum. Consideration of social, economic, political, cultural, historical, and geographical diversities within and between nations is a crucial determinant of quality in a given society (UNESCO, 2004).

According to UNICEF (2000), *"quality education is one that welcomes the learner and can adapt to meet learning needs"* (UNICEF, 2000, p.3). UNESCO states that *"a quality education understands the past, is relevant to the present, and has a view of the future. Quality education relates to knowledge-building and the skillful application of all forms of knowledge by unique individuals who function both independently and concerning others"* (UNESCO, 2003). Billah (2017) has said that "Quality education means teaching not just facts, but how to determine those facts. It involves critical thinking, learning to work with others, and work independently, a broad range of subjects" (Billah, 2017, p.1).

Importantly, quality is frequently described as a relative concept. The quality depends on who uses the term and the context in which it is used. To various people, it has varied meanings. The same person may adopt various conceptualizations at various times. This calls into question "whose quality?" Students, employers, teaching and non-teaching staff, the government and its financial agencies, accreditors, validators, auditors, and assessors, including professional organisations, are just a few examples of the various "stakeholders" in higher education (Hossain, 2017; Islam, Uddin, Nandy, & Hosen, 2019). Thus, indicators like the faculty recruitment system, student enrollment procedures, curriculum content, learning environments, logistical support, national education policy related to higher education, and others were discussed in this study because they are thought to be crucial for ensuring quality education from Bangladesh's perspective.

## Quality of an Education System

An education system's quality is determined by taking a summative look at the student's learning outcomes (Linn & Miller, 2005), the system's equity and inclusivity, and the system's relevance as determined by the employability of graduates. The foundations of a high-quality educational system could be summed up as follows, though it is difficult to fully express what this idea entails: i) the caliber and accessibility of teachers; (ii) the adequate and pertinent use of high-quality curricula, learning materials, and facilities; and (iii) systematic assessments, with analyses of these assessments feeding back into the policy (J. Hossain, 2014). The most significant factor in determining whether learning will be of a high caliber among these needs, according to research, is the effectiveness of the teachers (Schacter & Thum 2004; Glewwe & Kremer 2006). An efficient management and accountability mechanism is a crucial and key component in this regard. Contrarily, direct and indirect incentives produce the best outcomes for quality in a system of education.

## Indicators of Quality Education

It relies on a few things how the global phenomena (Hosen, 2020) are developing and how new needs for quality education are arising. The common indicators of quality education are included in considering a review of the research (UNESCO, 2003, 2004, 2014; World Bank, 2013, 2018; UNICEF, 2000; ADB, 2011).

*Figure 1. Indicators of quality education*

The aforementioned elements are generally thought to be crucial for quality education. The characteristics of these components should be good for getting qualitative changes in education, ranging from primary level to tertiary level if they are treated as quality indicators (Islam, Uddin, Nandy, & Hosen, 2019). Thus, depending on the need and makeup of a country, different countries may have different indications or variables of educational quality.

## Sustainable Development Goal-4

The fourth of the agenda 2030 is known as SDG 4 (Owens, 2017). It has 10 (ten) objectives that range from primary education to adult education. It covers education at all levels, from preschool to university. It means to offer free, equitable, and high-quality education to adolescents, adults, and those pursuing technical and vocational fields. However, the focus of this study is on SDG-4 objective 4.3, which emphasizes quality tertiary education (Ullah, 2020) from the perspective of Bangladesh.

## Development Junction

The present government has set objectives for Bangladesh, including becoming an upper-middle-income nation by 2031(GED, 2020). The country is also expected to reach a development crossroads by 2030 as a result of achieving the SDGs by that year and becoming a fully developed nation by 2041 as a result of putting "Vision 2041" into practice (GED, 2020). The Second Perspective Plan 2021–2041 (GED, 2020) has already been authorized by the government to meet the goals. As a result, it is claimed that by 2030, the country will have seen noticeable developmental changes. This time frame has been dubbed Development Junction (Islam, Uddin, Nandy, & Hosen, 2019). The phrase "Development Junction" refers to the stage at which the nation is anticipated to complete the government's key development objective by 2030. The current government used this phrase in their election manifesto before the 2018 national election (Bangladesh Awami League, 2018). In addition, it is anticipated that the SDGs also known as the Global Agenda, will be accomplished by 2030. This will pave the way for the nation to get moving and attain the long-anticipated objective of becoming a developed nation on the world map.

## Achieving SDG and Higher Education Scenario: Structure and Governance

The country will have seen noticeable developmental changes by 2030 (Rahman, 2021). This time frame has been dubbed Development Junction when the nation is anticipated to complete the government's key development objective by 2030 (Rahman, 2021). It is anticipated that the SDGs' main objectives will be met by 2030, paving the path for the nation to go forward and realize its long-anticipated goal of becoming a developed nation by 2041. Although, numerous challenges still exist to the implementation procedure of SDGs in Bangladesh (Hosen, Islam, & Alam, 2019; Rahman, 2021).

Moreover, need-based quality education is necessary worldwide, but especially in Bangladesh, to overcome all obstacles (Hossain, 2017) and assume a standard position in the world. As a result, successive governments have prioritized the education sector on the national agenda and taken some actions in this direction. In Bangladesh, there are three main categories of educational streams: general education, madrasah education, and technical-vocational education (Islam, Uddin, Nandy, & Hosen, 2019). Each of these streams has been divided into five levels: primary, junior, secondary, higher secondary, and tertiary. The levels are: i) primary level, ii) junior level, iii) secondary level, and iv) higher secondary level (J. Hossain, 2014). Figure 2 that follows illustrates it.

*Figure 2. Educational Governance System in Bangladesh*
Source: Islam, 2017; Islam, Uddin, Nandy, & Hosen, 2019

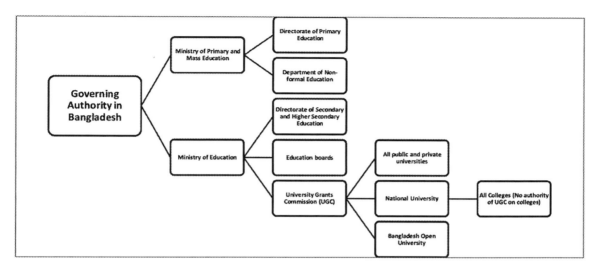

In addition, there are 105 private universities and 49 public universities in the nation, while the government funds public universities in the higher education sector through the University Grants Commission (UGC, 2018). Two types of institutions make up Bangladesh's tertiary education system: colleges associated with the National University and universities that provide degrees (Ehsan, 2021). The following figure 3 shows higher education along with the number of students enrolled in various public universities (including colleges) around the nation.

*Figure 3. Students' Ration in Different Tertiary level institutions in Bangladesh*
Source: UGC Annual Report 2018

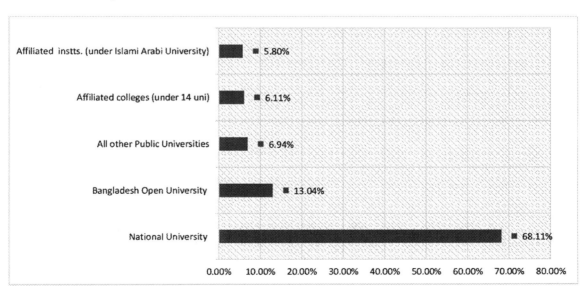

The University Grants Commission of Bangladesh serves as a driving force behind funding distribution to public universities and the administration of these universities' operations (Chowdhury, Hossain, & Rahman, 2013). The private universities must obtain UGC clearance to function and confer degrees, despite the fact that they do not receive any financing from the government. All colleges at the tertiary level are governed by National University (NU), but it lacks the power to hire teachers. Bangladesh Public Service Commission (BPSC) conducts a countrywide competitive public service examination as part of the selection process. The Ministry of Education (MoE) is in charge of hiring, assigning, moving, and promoting teachers (Islam, 2017). Although private universities have exploded in recent years, higher education in Bangladesh has always been dominated by the public sector. Again, it is up to the Ministry of Education (MoE) to create an overall policy framework and a budget for publicly funded educational institutions.

*Figure 4. Tertiary Level Education Streams in Bangladesh*
*Source: Prodhan, 2016; Islam, 2017*

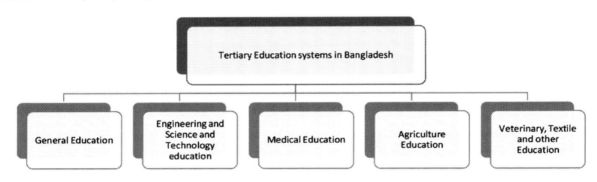

The 1973-founded UGC serves as a bridge between the government and universities to control university operations, and it is charged with regulating academic choices made at the tertiary level in the nation. The nation's higher education is divided into five streams. They are i) general education; (ii) science, technology, and engineering; (iii) medical; (iv) agriculture; and (v) veterinary, textile, and other education (Prodhan, 2016). These are counted as the tertiary higher education institutions in Bangladesh.

## Critical Discussion on Previous Studies

Studies found that university administrators will take steps to offer quality education through the use of best practices in pedagogy, a sound curriculum, modern instructional methods, recruiting skilled professors, and so forth. There are, however, several works of literature on quality education in the nation.

Akter (2017) outlines the elements that are viewed as markers for raising the standard of higher education in Bangladesh's private universities (Akter, 2017). There are nine elements of quality education; including peer quality, various direct and indirect facilities, administrative effectiveness, political phenomena, gender effects, teaching method quality, course/curriculum content quality, and expected satisfaction with tertiary education (Akter, 2017; Ullah, 2020)). He discovers, among many other things, that part-time and inexperienced teachers are among the reasons why the quality of education at many private colleges is below par (Nagoba & Mantri, 2015). He also makes clear that the research, laboratory, and library facilities in these universities are frequently subpar. In this study, a comparison of amenities between public and private universities is discussed.

In his study, Ehsan (2008) stated that the persistence, stability, and continuity of academic affairs—such as the holding of regular classes, the regular graduation of graduates, the absence of violence on campus, the absence of politics in the academic culture, etc.—are indicative of the quality of higher education overall. Therefore, the institutionalization of academic matters in higher education institutions is regarded as providing quality education. Once more, Ehsan examines the governance status in both private and public colleges around the nation. In contrast to public colleges, which have many governance issues, he finds that private institutions have a shortage of qualified full-time faculty members (Ehsan, 2008).

It is also found traditional features lack quality in tertiary-level education (J. Hossain, 2014). J. Hossain (2014) revealed that organizational structural lapses, governance problems, modern teaching approach gaps, syllabus and curriculum, infrastructural shortage, policies, and decision problems, lack of professionalism, and so on are impediments (J. Hossain, 2014) to ensuring quality control on the tertiary level education in Bangladesh.

Islam et al. (2017), however, focus on the existing quality, highlighting discrepancies between practices and quality as well as accreditation (G. Islam, Ali, I. Islam, & M. Islam, 2017). Another study points to various governance problems as the cause of Bangladesh's poor higher education quality. They talk about how laws and regulations aren't being followed (Rabbani & Chowdhury, 2014). Moreover, they discover a lack of professionalism. In Bangladesh, nepotism and politics are regarded as being much more significant hiring criteria than academic credentials. They also take into account how pupils would perceive the policy concerns. Monem and Banianmin talk about the state of higher education in Bangladesh, focusing on various problems and opportunities (Monem & Baniamin, 2010).

Indeed, it is evident that a country's economy is driven by the quality of its education, not the number of people who pursue higher education. Quality higher education may therefore be crucial in this regard. According to the World Bank, having access to high-quality education leads to improved socioeconomic results, such as lower infant mortality and income inequality (World Bank, 2013). However, higher education is getting more and more competitive, so Chowdhury, Hossain, and Rahman (2013) emphasized how top universities need to promote their schools both domestically and abroad. Higher education should focus on standards, welfare, and sustainable development. The authors placed special emphasis on how students saw and anticipated the current public and private university education systems, as well as the issues and difficulties that these institutions of higher learning were currently facing (Chowdhury, Hossain, & Rahman, 2013). The study found that institutional and personal factors are the two primary groups of factors that have an impact on students' decisions. Therefore, measuring the quality of their services is a crucial responsibility for those organizations that provide feedback on these aspects of quality (Chowdhury, Hossain, & Rahman, 2013). This study contributed to the existing literature alongside identifying new dimensions of institutional setbacks to ensure quality education.

## METHODS

This study was carried out using a mixed-method technique, which is thought to be reasonable for reaching the goals. Qualitative study methods are used to respond to queries about experiences, meaning, understanding, and perspective, most often from the viewpoint of participants (Hammarberg, Kirkman & Lacey, 2016) whereas quantitative research is the systematic empirical investigation of observable phenomena via statistical, mathematical, or computational techniques (Given, 2008). The purposive sampling (Robinson, 2014) method has been used. For data collection, both primary and secondary sources are used.

In this study, a total of 292 respondents were gathered from five higher education institutions: Dhaka University, Rajshahi University, Dhaka College, Rajshahi College, and Rajshahi Government City College. Survey questions, focus group discussions, and KII were employed as the primary data collection instruments. In this study, 274 participants from the chosen Higher Education Institutes (HEIs) were surveyed. Among them, 104 were academics, while the remaining 170 were students. In addition, 18 KIIs and 4 FGDs were completed for this study. Among the student respondents, 68% of them are male and 32% of them are female. Again, the respondent's representation is as followed figure.

*Figure 5. Respondent's University and College*

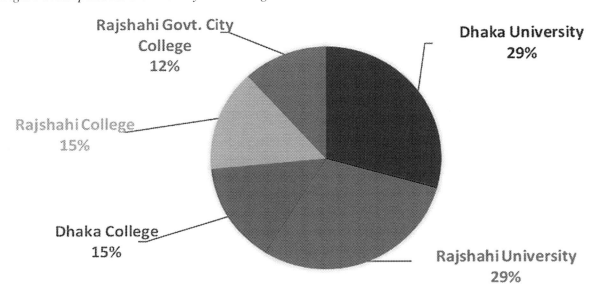

## Conceptual Framework

The conceptual framework for this study's research endeavour is as follows. The institutional deficiencies at tertiary-level academic institutions (Chowdhury, Hossain, & Rahman, 2013) are thought to be obstacles to quality education (Cavallone, Manna, & Palumbo, 2020). By proposing a few procedures, the assurance of quality education provided by the implementation of SDG 4 (Owens, 2017) will be highlighted. The knowledge-based economic society (Kefela, 2010) will also bring about a significant transformation to reach SDGs by 2030. Thus, the natural progression of the occurrence of this study (Camp, 2001) is as below.

*Figure 6. Conceptual Framework*

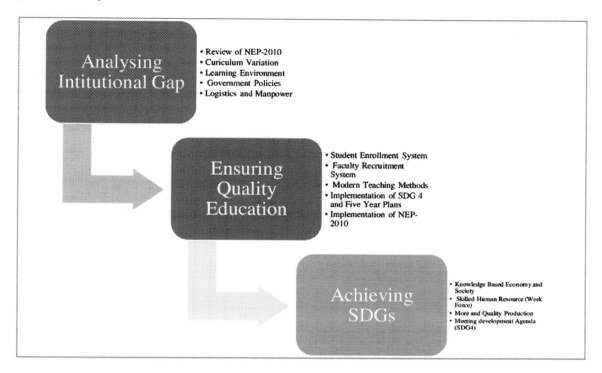

## DATA ANALYSIS AND DISCUSSION

Traditional higher education is insufficient for an independent nation like Bangladesh to meet its needs today. As a result, the system as a whole needs to be drastically restructured. The study has identified two categories of quality indicators: physical and non-physical. However, this paper focused on the main non-physical quality factors, with a particular emphasis on the curriculum, teacher preparation and education, salary, amenities, etc.

For tertiary-level educational institutions, curriculum creation is an important concern. It has a connection to SDG-4.7.1. The study reveals that each department of public institutions has a curriculum development committee (committee of courses), which proposes to add new courses and change or remove the existing course(s) from the syllabus at the start of each academic session. The suggestion made by the appropriate department is typically accepted by the universities' statutory bodies. At the meeting of the curriculum creation committee, all academic members of the relevant department and subject specialists approved and nominated by the university administration participated and offered their knowledge and skills. In the case of colleges, however, it has not occurred. College teachers have very little opportunity to exchange their knowledge and skills to create curricula. By the National University authority, it is handled centrally. The study has also discovered that no regional or international university's model curriculum is used while developing curricula. The study found that a sizable percentage of educational institutions, or roughly 67 per cent, do not adhere to any model for curriculum development, whereas 31 per cent of institutions of higher education use a partial model.

It has been discovered that national and international development objectives, such as the SDGs, five-year development plans, and national education strategies, are frequently ignored when establishing curricula. It is found that about 36% of the curriculum was created by the central authority, which only partially adhered to the national development objective, and that roughly 64% of the curriculum development authority did not. The National Education Policy of 2010 has not been followed or followed closely by a significant portion of curriculum creation, or around 62%, according to the report. According to the National Education Policy of 2010, 38% of curriculum development is governed by the federal government.

The study found that while the local job market is largely followed, essentially little consideration is given to the global job market when developing curricula. Only around 10% of the curriculum-building process is influenced by national and international labour markets, whereas roughly 50% and 25% of the national labour market, respectively, are not followed. According to the survey, the curriculum development authority has only tracked roughly 25% of the domestic employment market and less than 5% of the international job market.

According to this study, 62% of respondents believed that colleges and universities lacked fundamental strategies for teacher development and education, while 38% believed that college instructors' facilities were severely constrained and highly centralized. Additionally, it is found that the HEIs in the nation do not offer any professional development opportunities. At HEIs, rewards for good deeds are not used. ICT-based teaching-learning activities are underutilized at the tertiary level. The COVID-19 pandemic is extremely widely observed. The tertiary-level HEIs were shut down and unable to resume their academic, instructive, and educational operations. The study finds that it took place as a result of a lack of professional development training.

Nearly 40% of the faculties are found to be lacking in funding for research, conferences, seminars, workshops, and symposiums. Only a small portion or a lack of research, conference, seminar, workshop, and symposium grants are held by about 60% of the faculties. Data also demonstrate that conferences, seminars, and workshops are not encouraged to be attended. The motivation of the faculty members drives them to participate in such activities. It has been discovered that public university faculty members have very few amenities, while there are none for college professors.

One of the essential components of high-quality education is considered by educational institutions to be qualified professors. This problem was also emphasized in SDG-4. It is shown that 47% of respondents believe that the universities and tertiary-level colleges have enough qualified faculty members. On the other hand, roughly 42% of respondents think that there aren't enough qualified and skilled teachers working at their institutions. It affects both topic knowledge and how the course content is delivered. It should be noted that colleges are the primary setting where it is revealed. However, this question has received no responses from around 11% of the respondents. Once more, the survey shows that the learning atmosphere at the HEIs in the nation is not conducive as one may anticipate.

## Discussion

In Bangladesh, there are numerous national and international agendas and programs to guarantee quality education and sustainable development. These strategies and initiatives are discussed from the standpoint of Bangladesh's development and high standards of instruction. The five-year plans are regarded as the main strategies for the nation's growth. The government carried out five straight five-year plans from 1973 and the 2002 fiscal year, as well as a temporary two-year plan from 1979–1980. The current government again decided to return to the five-year plans after deviating from the process. The eighth five-year plan is currently in progress. The government has already adopted the second perspective plan for the years 2021–2041(GED, 2020), which aims to make the country a developed one by 2041 and a middle-income one by 2031(GED, 2020). The nation already possesses the designation of a developing country. A delta plan has already been approved by the government. The administration is adamantly devoted to carrying out the national-level strategic plans and to achieving the SDGs objectives (Sarker, 2019; Rahman, 2021). The following list summarizes the study's main decisions.

## National Education Policy (NEP) 2010

The 28 chapters of the NEP address the country's education system (Ministry of Education, 2010; Prodhan, 2016; Ehsan, 2021) from pre-primary to tertiary levels. But the purpose of this research is to examine the state of tertiary education. Particular attention is paid to understanding the practical reality when constructing the course curriculum under the NEP 2010 criteria (Ministry of Education, 2010). It has been discovered that the country's HEIs are not constructing their course curricula per the NEP 2010. There aren't any standards for establishing and creating university course curricula that would directly support the execution of the NEP-2010. Still, it is implemented inadvertently through many momentary endeavours.

According to FGD, whereas public universities offer research funds to faculty members, this is not the case at colleges. It has been discovered that while research papers, articles, and even research degrees like the MPhil and PhD are necessary and mandatory for the promotion of faculty members at public institutions, they are not necessary for the promotion of college professors. The discrepancy among teachers in universities and colleges is thus made clear, even though they all hold the same titles, such as professor, associate professor, assistant professor, and lecturer. Despite teaching in honors and masters programs at university colleges, college professors do not require a research degree or publications to be promoted. This is in contrast to teachers at public universities. In addition, it is made clear that no plans have yet been made for the training of newly hired professors at public universities.

## Curriculum Development

Tertiary education is a large field of study, and it is anticipated that there won't be a set number of textbooks for each subject; instead, there will be recommended reading, and students will be encouraged to read more literature for their education. Therefore, it is generally acknowledged that the tertiary-level curriculum would vary. Now, it is anticipated that each course would have a learning outcome. However, albeit moving slowly, initiatives to enhance public university curricula and syllabi have already started. In this aspect, the Institutional Quality Assurance Cell (IQAC) is attempting to assist. Although relatively little, it is offering training to become acquainted with this new system in the context of Bangladesh (Raqib, 2019). Additionally, it is giving faculty members instructions on how to create course outlines. Despite differences in curriculum, it is anticipated that if the rules are followed correctly, a favorable outcome will be seen. For this, faculty members would require additional training, workshops, or similar activities. Students from two Rajshahi University departments—the Department of Material Science and the Department of Human Resources and Population Development—have been seen protesting, even while on a hunger strike, to demand their subject code for various competitive job examinations, including the BCS exam. Additionally, it was noted that the students staged a protest to call for the renaming of a department.

## Professional Development

The learning process in education never ends. Following graduation and the beginning of a job, it won't stop. Career-minded people can develop their skills and conduct themselves more professionally at work by continuing their education. To ensure that teachers receive the best possible education for their students as well as to improve their effectiveness and sense of fulfilment in other areas of their work (Nagoba & Mantri, 2015), school administrators in the field of education management must support professional development for teachers (Raqib, 2019).

While public universities offer research funds to their academic members, colleges do not. Even though they have the same titles—professor, associate professor, assistant professor, and lecturer—teachers at universities and colleges are found to differ. When faced with the realities of poor pay and low social status, excessive workloads, huge classrooms, scarce opportunities for professional development, etc., it might be difficult to ensure that all schools have an adequate number of trained and competent teachers. Thus, quality education is partially depending on the professional development of the teachers.

## Teacher Education and Training

The importance of teachers, their education and training, and their viewpoints are only highlighted by the evolving global phenomena (Hosen, 2020) and the emerging demands for quality education (Nagoba & Mantri, 2015; Raqib, 2019). This is odd considering that there is a growing global concern about the lack of teachers in general, let alone those who have the necessary training (Raqib, 2019) to handle the challenges they are experiencing (UNESCO, 2003). However, the actual situation is hardly acceptable. There is a dearth of trained teachers in several fields in many nations.

With the realities of low pay and poor social standing, excessive workloads, huge classrooms, scarce opportunities for professional development, etc., it can be difficult to ensure that all schools have an adequate number of trained and competent teachers. Even while many nations have implemented policies to enhance teacher preparation and working circumstances, in some cases, teacher preparation is becoming worse (UNESCO, 2004). Teachers in private colleges do not receive training, despite NAEM offering it to those who teach in government colleges. The right to receive professional development training is likewise not available to professors at public universities. According to UGC (2018), National University's affiliated colleges are lacking in qualified instructors. The study explored that individual and institutional result changes due to the investment in training activities (Taylor et al., 2009; Tharenou et al., 2007). Indeed, adequate training has an elemental power to upsurge the knowledge, skills, and abilities, shortly KSA of the employees, which ultimately and positively changes the organization (Becker & Huselid, 1998).

## Teachers' Pay and Facilities

The anticipated monthly income for a lecturer in the Bangladesh region is BDT 83,000, with an average pay of BDT 33,000 (Glassdoor, 2022). These figures indicate the median, which is the middle value between the ranges from the unique Total Pay Estimate algorithm and based on wages gathered from registered users. But the actual scenario in the case of tertiary-level college teachers is not satisfactory. The survey reveals the realities of low pay and facilities, low social status, severe workloads, huge courses, and few opportunities for professional development. These result in poor student evaluations, little time spent on academic tasks, and little motivation.

## ICT-based Modern Teaching-Leaning Activities

A few schools affiliated with National University have the infrastructure and other logistical assistance necessary to give honors courses followed by master's degrees, according to professors at colleges who participated in focus groups and key informant interviews. Additionally, they acknowledged that there is no possibility for research in colleges. To advance their careers, they do not need to have a research degree or publish in the field.

It is discovered that neither colleges nor universities now use ICT-based modern teaching-learning activities (Rana & Rana, 2020). Whatever is put into practice depends on each faculty member. Additionally, it is seen in the COVID-19 pandemic. Public universities could not begin their academic operations until June 2020 due to a paucity of ICT-based teaching-learning activities. They are now making a tentative attempt. Thus, ICT-based modern teaching-learning activities are significantly important for establishing a knowledge-based innovative society for achieving SDGs.

## Learning Environment

Teaching and learning are the regular activities of an educational institution. A good teaching and learning environment (Rana & Rana, 2020) consists of a well-balanced combination of physical, psychological, and service delivery factors, including the standard of the school's facilities, class size, infrastructure, and other quality dimensions, as well as a climate that is free from discrimination, good teacher behavior, and effective school discipline policies (Hossain & Jahan, 2021; Hossain, 2017). The learning environment is a crucial element of quality education. For a high-quality education, the learning environment on campus and in the department are both crucial. However, the unrest in the nation frequently has an impact on the environment for learning in institutions of higher learning. Several kinds of harassment, including ragging, physical and mental abuse, sexual harassment, and theft of property like laptops and cell phones, are reportedly experienced by students. Students frequently experience insecurity. Additionally, it is made obvious that the learning environment in residence halls and on campuses is less inviting than one might assume for university education. It has already received a lot of attention because of recent events at BUET, Dhaka University, and other campuses all around the country.

## Higher Education Strategy

There should be a clear plan for higher education in the nation, and this strategy should be shared with academics at HEIs as a "full" document so that it may be taken into account when creating course curricula and contributing to national development. The government has a strategy, but university and college professors are unsure of what they think of it. The participants in the KII and FGDs conveyed their opinion that there are numerous documents on various development agendas available on various ministries' web portals. However, the UGC, the country's top authority on higher education institutions, does not have any of these records posted on its website. All policy documents about education should be accessible on the organization's website.

## Faculty Recruitment System

The faculty is one of a school's most valuable resources. One of the most crucial components of quality education is a skilled teacher. Each teacher has a unique educational background, degree, amount of work experience, and work ethic. These factors all affect how effectively they perform in the classroom. To fill instructor shortages and improve academic standards, educational institutions frequently use a teacher recruiting technique (Zulfikar, Wahana, Maylawati, Taufik, & Hodijah, 2018).

It is well known that the vice-chancellors selected by public universities have a significant impact on the recruitment process. Despite serving on numerous committees and bodies, vice chancellors of public institutions are regarded as "all in all". The final judgment rests with their "will". Additionally, it has been noted that the VCs' decisions on various matters of policy are influenced by "political phenomena". Research also exposed a vicious cycle of fraud or corruption in the entry-level hiring procedure in public universities (Transparency International Bangladesh, 2016). On the other hand, the National University authority lacks this authority when it comes to hiring teachers.

## SDGs Achieving Strategies Through Quality Education

The agenda-2030 is built around the 17 SDGs and their 169 linked targets (Khatun & Saadat, 2021). The Sustainable Development Goals (SDGs) are a set of aims and objectives that all countries should adhere to tackle the most pressing issues plaguing the world, such as ending hunger and poverty (United Nations, 2015). It has been identified that overall challenges for Bangladesh to meet the targets of SDGs are (i) management, coordination, and leadership, (ii) aligning SDG implementation with national planning and policy process, (iii) partnership and stakeholder participation including institutional arrangements, (iv) data-related issues and capacity of the national statistical agencies, and (v) financing and other means of implementation including systemic issues (Bhattacharya, Rezbana, & Khatun, 2018; Hosen, Islam, & Alam, 2019)). However, to overcome these challenges, quality education might be the best solution.

*Ensuring Quality Education to Achieve the Sustainable Development Goals (SDGs) in Bangladesh*

*Table 1. Sustainable Development Goals and Way to Achieve SDGs*

| Sustainable Development Goals | Role of Quality Education |
|---|---|
| Goal 1: End poverty in all its forms everywhere | If quality education has been insured, then profession and entrepreneurship will be established to end poverty |
| Goal 2: End hunger, achieve food security and improved nutrition and promote sustainable agriculture | Quality education will establish awareness regarding food security, nutrition, and sustainable agriculture. |
| Goal 3: Ensure healthy lives and promote well-being for all at all ages | Once again, quality education will assure a healthy lifestyle by promoting overall well-being. |
| Goal 4: Ensure inclusive and equitable quality education and promote lifelong learning opportunities for all | This is the focus of this study which will ultimately reach the development junction by 2030. |
| Goal 5: Achieve gender equality and empower all women and girls | Quality education at the tertiary level will increase the sense of gender equality and decrease the glass ceiling effect of society. |
| Goal 6: Ensure availability and sustainable management of water and sanitation for all | As healthy lives are the wealth of a nation, here quality education can play a vital role. |
| Goal 7: Ensure access to affordable, reliable, sustainable and modern energy for all | A sense of modernity is mandatory for the sustainable development of a nation where quality education opens the doors to awareness of modern energy. |
| Goal 8: Promote sustained, inclusive and sustainable economic growth, full and productive employment and decent work for all | Quality education can create employment opportunities through which sustainable growth can be achieved. |
| Goal 9: Build resilient infrastructure, promote inclusive and sustainable industrialization and foster innovation | Innovation and sustainable infrastructure and building can move the country in forwarding steps where quality education is a must. |
| Goal 10: Reduce inequality within and among countries | Equity and equality can be established by ensuring quality education which will decrease inequality in the country. |
| Goal 11: Make cities and human settlements inclusive, safe, resilient and sustainable | Innovative ideas with quality works can improve the cities' and human residents' beautiful and sustainable places. |
| Goal 12: Ensure sustainable consumption and production patterns | Quality education will create judicious eyes on sustainable consumption and manufacturing. |
| Goal 13: Take urgent action to combat climate change and its impacts | Only awareness of nature can preserve it and make an environment-friendly ecosystem. |
| Goal 14: Conserve and sustainably use the oceans, seas and marine resources for sustainable development | Quality education for a blue economy can sustainably utilize marine resources. |
| Goal 15: Protect, restore and promote sustainable use of terrestrial ecosystems, sustainably manage forests, combat desertification, and halt and reverse land degradation and halt biodiversity loss | The environment is essential for sustainable development and quality is important to grow up consciousness. |
| Goal 16: Promote peaceful and inclusive societies for sustainable development, provide access to justice for all and build effective, accountable and inclusive institutions at all levels | Employees with quality education and ethics can create services more sustainable and inclusive for the people. |
| Goal 17: Strengthen the means of implementation and revitalize the Global Partnership for Sustainable Development Finance | It has been recognized that without a sustainable partnership, obtaining SDGs will be a tough job. Therefore, quality education for diplomacies and foreign delegations is mandatory. |

Source: Goals are adopted from UN SDGs A/RES/70/1

In Bangladesh, there are numerous national and international agendas and programs to guarantee quality education and sustainable development. Bangladesh ratifies several plans and projects as a United Nations member. These goals and initiatives are, however, described from the standpoint of Bangladesh's development and high standards of education. Moreover, the five-year plans are regarded as the main strategies for the development of any country. The government carried out five straight five-year plans from 1973 and the 2002 fiscal year, as well as a temporary two-year plan from 1979–1980. After straying from the procedure, the present government opted to go back to the five-year plans. The 8th Five-Year Plan is currently being implemented. The second perspective plan, 2021-2041, has already been authorized by the government and aims to make the country middle-income by 2031 and developed by 2041. The nation has previously been designated as a developing nation. An existing delta plan has been approved by the government. The government is very devoted to achieving the SDGs' aims and firmly committed to implementing national-level strategic plans (Sarker, 2019; Rahman, 2021; Khatun & Saadat, 2021).

## CONCLUSION

In summary, tertiary-level quality education can operate as an engine that directly contributes to the economic and social growth of the nation to attain the dream development. Additionally, it would support the SDGs. It can be claimed that none of the institutional shortcomings that are thought to be necessary for quality education can be closed quickly. The problems in raising the standard of education are not linear nor one-dimensional. On multiple fronts, it necessitates concurrent policy actions. Based on the findings, it is stated that to measure the quality of tertiary education, a national framework for higher education quality should be developed, and indicators should be used. A two-year or one-year professional degree should be made mandatory along with other particular requirements for entry-level faculty recruitment at the tertiary level for qualified and skilled faculty members. This degree should be implemented for professional development. For this, professional development institutes for teaching and research should be created. Public universities should be organized into numerous categories based on the disciplines they teach. For instance, Bangladesh University of Engineering and Technology (BUET) should be present in abundance at engineering colleges, while agriculture universities should have agriculture specialities.

In addition, both science and technology Science and technology-focused subjects should be employed to establish universities, followed by disciplines connected to social science, the arts, and the humanities for general universities, and business-related disciplines for business universities. The performance of academic disciplines and universities should then be evaluated. It is important to take into account the context at the national, regional, and global levels. To reduce institutional gaps that would help the nation's growth crossroads, there should be central standards for creating or launching new departments, which should consider the market demands as well as the link to various institutional requirements. To ensure the country's sustained development, technical and vocational education needs to be strengthened rather than only general higher education, which is already thriving. The national university admits colleges, but the university administration has no control over college admissions or teacher promotion. Even yet, it lacks the power to transfer professors. Therefore, justifiable reform is required in this case. The NEP-2010's requirement to implement a separate pay scale for teachers is a very crucial problem.

However, this choice of sample size still might be the limitation of this study. It was not possible to include all universities, public and private, in the scope of this study project due to time and budget limitations. Only two colleges and three institutions have been chosen for this investigation. The study's inability to include all subjects from all faculties, notwithstanding the selection of a constrained number of higher education institutions, is another disadvantage. Due to time constraints, only the fields under the faculties of social science, arts, and business studies have been chosen. Even though it is true that some portions of the sample from the large population may not be regarded to be representative, it is thought that this would open up new possibilities for future research.

## CONFLICT OF INTEREST

There is no conflict of interest in publishing and sharing the study's findings. The authors agreed to publish the study findings.

## ETHICAL CONSIDERATION

The rules of research ethics were followed in the conduct of this investigation. There was no disclosure of the respondents' personal information, and nothing negative happened while data was being collected in the field.

## FUNDING

This study was financed by the National Academy for Educational Management (NAEM), Ministry of Education, the People's Republic of Bangladesh.

## ACKNOWLEDGMENT

The National Academy for Educational Management (NAEM), Ministry of Education, People's Republic of Bangladesh is greatly acknowledged by the authors for giving the funding required to carry out the study. The participants and responders in the survey, KII, and interview ought to know how much the authors appreciate their kind cooperation.

## REFERENCES

Akter, A. (2017). Factors to Improve the Quality of Higher Education in the Non Government Universities in Bangladesh. *International Journal of Education Culture and Society*, 2(4), 132–142. doi:10.11648/j.ijecs.20170204.15

Aminuzzaman, S. M. (2011). Quality Issues of Higher Education. *The Journal of General Education*, 1(1), 1–15.

BANBEIS. (2022). Bangladesh Education Statistics 2021. Dhaka: Bangladesh Bureau of Educational Information and Statistics (BANBEIS), Ministry of Education.

Bangladesh Awami League. (2018). *Bangladesh on the march towards Prosperity: Election Manifesto 2018*. Bangladesh Awami League.

Beattie, A. (2021, June 29). *The 3 pillars of corporate sustainability*. https://www.investopedia.com/articles/investing/100515/three-pillars-corporate-sustainability.asp

Becker, B. E., & Huselid, M. A. (1998). High performance work systems and firm performance: A synthesis of research and managerial implications. *Research in Personnel and Human Resources Management*, *16*, 53–101.

Bhattacharya, B., Rezbana, U. S., & Khatun, A. (2018). *Implementation Challenges of SDGs Country Study*. CPD.

Billah, M. (2017, June 19). What we mean by 'quality education'? *The Independent*.

Budiharso, T., & Tarman, B. (2020). Improving Quality Education through Better Working Conditions of Academic Institutes. *Journal of Ethnic and Cultural Studies*, *7*(1), 99–115. doi:10.29333/ejecs/306

Camp, W. G. (2001). Formulating and Evaluating Theoretical Frameworks for Career and Technical Education Research. *Journal of Vocational Educational Research*, *26*(1), 27–39. doi:10.5328/JVER26.1.4

Cavallone, M., Manna, R., & Palumbo, R. (2020). Filling in the gaps in higher education quality: An analysis of Italian students' value expectations and perceptions. *International Journal of Educational Management*, *34*(1), 203–216. doi:10.1108/IJEM-06-2019-0189

Chowdhury, S. A., Hossain, M. M., & Rahman, M. A. (2013). Extended GAPs Model to Assess the Quality of Education. *Journal of Business Studies*, *34*(1), 165–183.

Delors, J., Mufti, I. A., Amagi, I., Carneiro, R., Chung, F., Geremek, B., Gorham, W., Kornhauser, A., Manley, M., Quero, M. P., Savane, M., Singh, K., Stavenhagen, R., Suhr, M. W., & Nanzhao, Z. (1996). *Learning: The Treasure Within. Report to UNESCO of the International Commission on Education for the Twenty-First Century*. UNESCO Publishing.

Ehsan, M. (2008). *Higher Education Governance in Bangladesh: The Public-Private Dilemma*. https://www.britannica.com/

GED. (2020). Making Vision 2041 A Reality: Perspective Plan of Bangladesh 2021-2041. GED.

Given, L. M. (2008). *The SAGE Encyclopedia of Qualitative Research Methods*. SAGE Publications. doi:10.4135/9781412963909

Glassdoor. (2022, October 9). *How much does a Lecturer make in Bangladesh?* https://www.glassdoor.com/Salaries/bangladesh-lecturer-salary SRCH_IL.0,10_IN27_KO11,19.htm

Grudowski, P., & Szczepańska, K. (2021). Quality Gaps in Higher Education from the Perspective of Students. *Foundations of Management*, *13*(1), 35–48. doi:10.2478/fman-2021-0003

Hammarberg, K., Kirkman, M., & Lacey, S. (2016). Qualitative research methods: When to use them and how to judge them. *Human Reproduction (Oxford, England)*, *31*(3), 498–501. doi:10.1093/humrep/dev334 PMID:26759142

Haywood-Farmer, J. (1988). A conceptual model of service quality. *International Journal of Operations & Production Management*, *8*(6), 19–29. doi:10.1108/eb054839

Hosen, S. (2020). What is the Driving Force of Globalization? *International Journal of Publication and Social Studies*, *5*(2), 90–100. doi:10.18488/journal.135.2020.52.90.100

Hosen, S., Islam, M. S., & Alam, M. M. (2019). Challaenges of Implementation of the SDG 16 for Ensuring Better Oublic Service in Bangladesh. In P. D. Alam, D. M. Alam, & D. D. Begum (Ed.), *1st International Conference on Information and Knowledge Management* (p. 166). EWU and BPATC.

Hossain, J. (2014). Quality Control on Higher Education System in Bangladesh. *South American Journal of Academic Research, 1*(2), 156–162.

Hossain, M. B. (2017). Factors Affecting Higher Education Quality in Bangladesh: An Attempt to Improve Higher Education Quality in Bangladesh through HEQEP. *International Journal of Science and Business, 1*(1), 47–59.

Hossain, M. K., & Jahan, N. (2021). Teaching-learning environment of private educational institute:A case study on Ispahani Public School and College, Chittagong,Bangladesh. *Journal of Business. Management and Social Research, 11*(1), 585–594. doi:10.18801/ijbmsr.110121.62

Hossain, N. A. (2021, December 17). *The pandora's box in Bangladesh's labour market*. https://whiteboardmagazine.com/2700/the-pandoras-box-in-bangladeshs-labour-market/

Islam, M. G., Ali, M. N., Islam, I., & Islam, M. Z. (2017). Quality Assurance and Accreditation Mechanisms of Higher Education Institutions: Policy Issues and Challenges in Bangladesh. *European Journal of Education Studies, 3*(5), 278–304. doi:10.5281/zenodo.495792

Islam, S. (2017). Contribution of HEQEP in Ensuring Quality Education at Higher Level in Bangladesh: A Political Economy Perspective. In *International Integrative Research Conference on Education, Governance and Development*. OSDER Publications.

Islam, S., Uddin, T. M., Nandy, N., & Hosen, S. (2019). Quality Education at Tertiary Level in Bangladesh for Achieving Development Junction. *NAEM Journal, 14*(28), 9–21.

Karim, A. T., & Fair, C. C. (2007). Bangladesh at the crossroads: A more stable future in sight? *Strategic Comments, 7*(3), 1–2.

Kefela, G. T. (2010). Knowledge-based economy and society has become a vital commodity to countries. *International NGO Journal, 5*(7), 160–166.

Khatun, F., & Saadat, S. Y. (2021). *Implementation of the SDGs in Bangladesh: Domestic Challenges and Regional Considerations*. South and South-West Asia Office. https://www.unescap.org/sites/default/d8files/knowledge-products/SSWA%20DP%2021-02_SDG%20Implementation%20in%20Bangladesh.pdf

Linn, R. L., & Miller, M. D. (2005). Measurement and Assessment in Teaching (8th ed.). Pearson/Merrill Prentice Hall.

Ministry of Education. (2010). *Nationa Education Policy*. Dhaka: Ministry of Education, Government of the People's Republic of Bangladesh. https://reliefweb.int/report/bangladesh/national-education-policy-2010-enbn

Ministry of Education. (2010). *National Education Policy*. Ministry of Education, People's Republic of Bangladesh.

Mohajan, H. (2017, December 28). *Research Methodology, 83457.* https://mpra.ub.uni-muenchen.de/83457/1/MPRA_paper_83457.pdf

Monem, M., & Baniamin, H. M. (2010). Higher Education in Bangladesh: Status, Issues and Prospects. *Pakistan Journal of Social Science, 30*(2), 293–305.

Nagoba, S. B., & Mantri, B. S. (2015). Role of Teachers in Quality Enhancement in Higher Education. *Journal of Krishna Institute of Medical Sciences University, 4*(1), 177–182.

Owens, T. L. (2017). Higher education in the sustainable development goals framework. *European Journal of Education, 52*(4), 414–420. doi:10.1111/ejed.12237

Prodhan, M. (2016). The present situation of education system in Bangladesh and scope for improvement. *Journal of Education and Social Sciences, 4*(June), 122–132.

Rabbani, G., & Chowdhury, S. (2014). Quality of Higher Education in Bangladesh: Governance Framework and Quality Issues. *Beykent University Journal of Social Sciences, 7*(1), 78-91.

Rahman, M. M. (2021). Achieving SustainableDevelopment Goals of Agenda2030 in Bangladesh: The crossroadof the governance and performance. *Public Administration and Policy, 24*(2), 195–211. doi:10.1108/PAP-12-2020-0056

Rana, K., & Rana, K. (2020). ICT integration in teaching and learning activities in higher education: A case study of Nepal's teacher education. *Malaysian Online Journal of Educational Technology, 8*(1), 36–47. doi:10.17220/mojet.2020.01.003

Raqib, A. (2019). Innovations in Teachers Training at Higher Education in Bangladesh. *Social Science Review, 36*(1), 221–231.

Robinson, R. S. (2014). Purposive Sampling. In A. C. Michalos (Ed.), *Encyclopedia of Quality of Life and Well-Being Research.* Springer., doi:10.1007/978-94-007-0753-5_2337

Sarker, M. A. (2019). *Bangladesh Delta Plan (BDP) 2100.* General Economics Division, Bangladesh Planning Commission.

Solaiman, M. (2018, August 27). Teacher-student ratio not ideal at many public universities. *Daily Sun.*

Taylor, P. J., Russ-Eft, D. F., & Taylor, H. (2009). Transfer of management training from alternative perspectives. *The Journal of Applied Psychology, 94*(1), 104–121. doi:10.1037/a0013006 PMID:19186899

Tharenou, P., Saks, A. M., & Moore, C. (2007). A review and critique of research on training and organizational-level outcomes. *Human Resource Management Review, 17*(3), 251–273. doi:10.1016/j.hrmr.2007.07.004

TIB. (2016). *Recruitment of Lecturers in Public Universities: Governance Challenges and Ways Forward.* Transparency International Bangladesh.

UNESCO. (2003). *Promoting Quality Education: Education for Peace, Human Rights and Democracy; Education for Sustainable Development; Curricula, Educational Tools and Teacher Training.* United Nations Educational, Scientific and Cultural Organization.

UNESCO. (2004). Quality Education for All Young People. In *47th International Conference on Education of UNESCO* (pp. 56, 52, 49, 46, 115-116). Geneva: UNESCO.

UNESCO. (2005). *Guidelines for quality provision in cross-border higher education*. UNECO Publishing.

UNICEF. (2000). *Defining Quality in Education*. Programme Division Working Paper Series, UNICEF. https://www.unicef.org/programme/girlseducation/papers.htm

United Nations. (2015). *Transforming Our World: The 2030 Agenda for Sustainable Development*. United Nations.

University Grants Commission. (2014). *UGC Annual Report, 2014*. University Grants Commission, Ministry of Education.

University Grants Commission. (2016). *UGC Annual Report, 2016*. University Grants Commission, Ministry of Education.

University Grants Commission. (2017). *UGC Annual Report, 2017*. University Grants Commission, Ministry of Education.

World Bank. (2013). *Bangladesh Education Sector Review: Seeding Fertile Ground - Education that Works for Bangladesh*. Dhaka: World Bank. https://openknowledge.worldbank.org/handle/10986/17853

World Bank. (2018, November 15). *Bangladesh: Reducing Poverty and Sharing Prosperity*. https://www.worldbank.org/en/results/2018/11/15/bangladesh-reducing-poverty-and-sharing-prosperity

Zulfikar, W. B., Wahana, A., Maylawati, D. S., Taufik, I., & Hodijah, H. S. (2018). An approach for teacher recruitment system using simple additive weighting and TOPSIS. In *IOP Conference Series: Materials Science and Engineering. 434* (pp. 1–8). IOP Publishing Ltd. doi:10.1088/1757-899X/434/1/012059

## ADDITIONAL READING

Arcaro, J. (1995). *Quality in Education: An Implementation Handbook*. Routledge.

Ehsan, S. M. A. (2021). Revisiting Tertiary Education System in Bangladesh: In Quest for Unraveling Existing Issues and Challenges. *Journal of Contemporary Governance and Public Policy*, *2*(1), 45–66. doi:10.46507/jcgpp.v2i1.33

Hoque, N., Mowla, M. M., Chowdhury, H. A., & Uddin, S. M. (2013). Quality Education in Bangladesh: A survey on private business school. *Information and Knowledge Management*, *3*(5), 117–122.

Mukhopadhyay, M. (2020). Quality in education. In *Total quality management in education* (pp. 1–18). SAGE Publications Pvt Ltd. doi:10.4135/9789353885977.n1

Mukhopadhyay, M. (2021). *Total quality management in education*. SAGE Publications Pvt Ltd. doi:10.4135/9789353885977

Rinehart, G. (2016). *Quality Education: Why It Matters, and How to Structure the System to Sustain It*. Stormwatch.

Sarkar, H. S., Rana, S., & Zitu, A. R. (2013). Challenges of Quality Higher Education in Bangladesh: A study on Public University. *Journal of Education and Practice*, *4*(8), 151–159.

Tazuddi, S. M. (2020). A Review of Quality Education in Bangladesh. *International Journal of Innovative Science and Research Technology*, *5*(8), 317–320. doi:10.38124/IJISRT20AUG046

Uddin, N., & Uddin, M. N. (2018). Overview of the challenges to achieve sustainable development goals in Bangladesh. *The International Journal of Social Sciences and Humanities Invention*, *5*(2), 4453–4460. doi:10.18535/ijsshi/v5i2.10

Ullah, M. N. (2020). Ingredients of Quality Education at Tertiary Level: An Assessment of Higher Education in Bangladesh. *International Journal of Engineering Applied Sciences and Technology*, *4*(11), 546–556. doi:10.33564/IJEAST.2020.v04i11.097

Zajda, J. I., Bacchus, M. K., & Kach, N. (1995). *Excellence and Quality in Education: International studies in education, society, and social change*. James Nicholas Publishers.

## KEY TERMS AND DEFINITIONS

**Development Junction:** The 'Development Junction' means a point of the stage where the country is expected to achieve the major development agenda of the government by 2030. This term has been adopted by the current Awami League government in their election manifesto before the national election in 2018.

**Higher Education Institution (HEI):** Universities, colleges, and professional schools that offer courses in disciplines like law, theology, medicine, business, music, and art are all considered higher education institutions.

**Qualified Education:** Quality education involves critical thinking, learning to work with others, and working independently, in a broad range of subjects.

**Sustainable Development Goals (SDG):** The 2030 Agenda for Sustainable Development, which has 17 SDGs, was adopted by the General Assembly in September 2015 (United Nations, 2015). The new Agenda emphasizes a holistic approach to attaining sustainable development for all, building on the idea of "leaving no one behind". Environmental, economic, and social sustainability are the three pillars of the sustainable development concept (Beattie, 2021).

**Tertiary Education:** The degree of education that comes after secondary school is known as tertiary education (Ullah, 2020), sometimes known as third-level, third-stage, or post-secondary education. Tertiary education in Bangladesh comprises two categories of institutions: degree-awarding universities and colleges affiliated with the National University (Ehsan, 2021).

**Transparency International Bangladesh (TIB):** A civil society organization devoted to battling corruption, which has its headquarters in Berlin.

**University Grant Commission (UGC):** The University Grants Commission (UGC), established in 1973, acts as a catalyst between the government and universities to regulate university affairs and it has the mandate to oversee academic decisions at the tertiary level in the country.

# Compilation of References

Abramenka, V. (2015). *Students' motivations and barriers to online education.* Academic Press.

Acar-Çiftçi, Y., & Gürol, M. (2015). A conceptual framework regarding the multicultural education competencies of Teachers. *Hacettepe University Journal of Education, 30*(1), 1-14.

Achkovska-Leshkovska, E., & Davchev, V. (2013). Intercultural Education: Analysis of the primary school textbooks in the Republic of Macedonia. *International Journal of Cognitive Research in Science, Engineering and Education, 1*(2), 51–56.

Achuthan, K., & Murali, S. S. (2017). Virtual lab: An adequate multi-modality learning channel for enhancing students' perception in chemistry. In Computer Science On-line Conference. Springer. doi:10.1007/978-3-319-57264-2_42

Achuthan, K., Francis, S. P., & Diwakar, S. (2017). Augmented reflective learning and knowledge retention perceived among students in classrooms involving virtual laboratories. *Education and Information Technologies, 22*(6), 2825–2855. doi:10.100710639-017-9626-x

Adams, V. (2020). Disasters and Capitalism… and COVID-19. *Somatosphere Website, 26.*

Agamben, G. (2005). State of exception. *Nova Srpska Politička Misao, 12*(1-4), 135-145.

Ahlin, T., & Li, F. (2019). From field sites to field events. *Medicine Anthropology Theory, 6*(2). Advance online publication. doi:10.17157/mat.6.2.655

Ahmed, F., Zhao, F., Faraz, N. A., & Qin, Y. J. (2021). How inclusive leadership paves way for psychological well-being of employees during trauma and crisis: A three-wave longitudinal mediation study. *Journal of Advanced Nursing, 77*(2), 819–831. doi:10.1111/jan.14637 PMID:33231300

Ahsan Ullah, A. K. M. (2013). Theoretical rhetoric about migration networks: A case of a journey of Bangladeshi workers to Malaysia. *International Migration (Geneva, Switzerland), 51*(3), 151–168. doi:10.1111/j.1468-2435.2009.00579.x

Aissaoui, N. (2021). *The digital divide: A literature review and some directions for future research in light of COVID-19.* Global Knowledge, Memory and Communication. doi:10.1108/GKMC-06-2020-0075

Ajzen, I. (2002). Perceived behavioural control, self-efficacy, locus of control, and the theory of planned behaviour. *Journal of Applied Social Psychology, 32*(4), 665–683. doi:10.1111/j.1559-1816.2002.tb00236.x

Akrivou, K., & Bradbury-Huang, H. (2015). Educating integrated catalysts: Transforming business schools toward ethics and sustainability. *Academy of Management Learning & Education, 14*(2), 222–240. doi:10.5465/amle.2012.0343

Akter, A. (2017). Factors to Improve the Quality of Higher Education in the Non Government Universities in Bangladesh. *International Journal of Education Culture and Society, 2*(4), 132–142. doi:10.11648/j.ijecs.20170204.15

Al Balushi, H. (2020). The reasons of using L1 in ESL classrooms. *Language Teaching Research Quarterly*, *16*, 56–70. doi:10.32038/ltrq.2020.16.04

Al-Amir, B. (2017). Saudi female teachers' perspectives of the use of L1 in the EFL classrooms. *English Language Teaching*, *10*(6), 12–20. doi:10.5539/elt.v10n6p12

Alatas, S. F. (2006). Editorial introduction: The idea of autonomous sociology: Reflections on the state of the discipline. *Current Sociology*, *54*(1), 5–6. doi:10.1177/0011392106058830

Alatas, S. H. (1972). The Captive Mind In Development Studies. *International Social Science Journal*, *24*(1), 9–25.

Alatas, S. H. (2006). The autonomous, the universal and the future of sociology. *Current Sociology*, *54*(1), 7–23. doi:10.1177/0011392106058831

Aldrich, A. S., & Lotito, N. J. (2020). Pandemic performance: Women leaders in the Covid-19 crisis. *Politics & Gender*, *16*(4), 960–967. doi:10.1017/S1743923X20000549

Ali, A. (1998). *Santals of Bangladesh*. Institute of Social Research & Applied Anthropology.

Ali, I. (2020). The COVID-19 Pandemic: Making Sense of Rumor and Fear: Op-Ed. *Medical Anthropology*, *39*(5), 1–4. doi:10.1080/01459740.2020.1745481 PMID:32212931

Ali, M. (2002). *Dinajpurer Adivasi*. Adivasi Academy.

Ali, W. (2018). Influence of evolving technology in emerging online lives of the digital native university students. *Asia Pacific Journal of Contemporary Education and Communication Technology*, *4*(2), 141–155. doi:10.25275/apjcectv4i2edu15

Alomaim, T. (2018). *Language education policy and language practices in teaching English as a foreign language in a Saudi newly established university: An interpretive case study* [Unpublished thesis]. University of Birmingham.

Alrabah, S., Wu, S., Alotaibi, A., & Aldaihani, H. (2016). English teachers' use of learners' L1 (Arabic) in college classrooms in Kuwait. *English Language Teaching*, *9*(1), 1–11. doi:10.5539/elt.v9n1p1

Al-Shammari, H. T. (2021). The extent to which teachers of social curriculum at the intermediate stage possess e-learning skills. *Turkish Journal of Computer and Mathematics Education*, *12*(13), 3619–3626.

Alvargonzález, D. (2011). Multidisciplinarity, interdisciplinarity, transdisciplinarity, and the sciences. *International Studies in the Philosophy of Science*, *25*(4), 387–403. doi:10.1080/02698595.2011.623366

Alves, A. C., Mesquita, D., Moreira, F., & Fernandes, S. (2012). Teamwork in Project-Based Learning: engineering students' perceptions of strengths and weaknesses. *Third International Symposium on Project Approaches in Engineering Education (PAEE'2011): Aligning Engineering Education With Engineering Challenges*, 1-13.

Ameny-Dixon, G. M. (2004). Why multicultural education is more important in higher education now than ever: A global perspective. *International Journal of Scholarly Academic Intellectual Diversity*, *6*, 1–12.

American Association for the Advancement of Science (AAAS). (2022). *What we know: The reality, risks, and response to climate change*. Retrieved from https://whatweknow.aaas.org/get-the-facts/

Aminuzzaman, S. M. (2011). Quality Issues of Higher Education. *The Journal of General Education*, *1*(1), 1–15.

Amstelveen, R. (2019). Flipping a college mathematics classroom: An action research project. *Education and Information Technologies*, *24*(2), 1337–1350. doi:10.100710639-018-9834-z

Anderson, J. T. (2021). Managing labour migration in Malaysia: Foreign workers and the challenges of 'control'beyond liberal democracies. *Third World Quarterly*, *42*(1), 86–104. doi:10.1080/01436597.2020.1784003

## Compilation of References

Anderson, W. (2019). *All Connected Now: Life in the First Global Civilization.* Routledge. doi:10.4324/9780429037122

Andreas, S. (2018). Effects of the decline in social capital on college graduates' soft skills. *Industry and Higher Education, 32*(1), 47–56. doi:10.1177/0950422217749277

Angelstam, P., Andersson, K., Annerstedt, M., Axelsson, R., Elbakidze, M., Garrido, P., Grahn, P., Jönsson, K. I., Pedersen, S., Schlyter, P., Skärbäck, E., Smith, M., & Stjernquist, I. (2013). Solving problems in social–ecological systems: Definition, practice and barriers of transdisciplinary research. *Ambio, 42*(2), 254–265. doi:10.100713280-012-0372-4 PMID:23475660

Antonio, A. L., Chang, M. J., Hakuta, K., Kenny, D. A., Levin, S., & Milem, J. F. (2004). Effects of racial diversity on complex thinking in college students. *Psychological Science, 15*(8), 507–510. doi:10.1111/j.0956-7976.2004.00710.x PMID:15270993

Arif, M., Gan, C., & Nadeem, M. (2021). Regulating non-financial reporting: evidence from European firms' environmental, social and governance disclosures and earnings risk. *Meditari Accountancy Research, 30*(3). doi:10.1108/MEDAR-11-2020-1086

Armstrong, A. K., Krasny, M. E., & Schuldt, J. P. (2018). *Communicating climate change: A guide for educators.* Comstock Publishing Associates.

Arnold, J., Burridge, P., Cacciattolo, M., Cara, C., Edwards, T., Hooley, N., & Neal, G. (2014). *Researching the signature pedagogies of praxis teacher education.* AARE-NZARE.

Arnold, J., Edwards, A., Hooley, P., & Williams, J. (2013). Site-based teacher education for enhanced community knowledge and culture: Creating the conditions for 'philosophical project knowledge. *Australian Educational Researcher, 40*(1), 61–75. doi:10.100713384-012-0070-z

Arnold, J., & Mundy, B. (2020). Praxis pedagogy in teacher education. *Smart Learning Environments, 7*(8), 1–14.

Arnold, R. D., & Wade, J. P. (2015). A definition of systems thinking: A systems approach. *Procedia Computer Science, 44,* 669–678. doi:10.1016/j.procs.2015.03.050

Arquero, J. L., Byrne, M., Flood, B., & Gonzalez, J. M. (2009). Motives, expectations, preparedness, and academic performance: A study of students of accounting at a Spanish university. *Revista de Contabilidad-Spanish Accounting Review, 12*(2), 279–299. doi:10.1016/S1138-4891(09)70009-3

Arquero, J. L., & Fernández Polvillo, C. (2019). Estereotipos contables. Motivaciones y percepciones sobre la contabilidad de los estudiantes universitarios de Administración de Empresas y Finanzas y Contabilidad. *Revista de Contabilidad-Spanish Accounting Review, 22*(1), 88–99. doi:10.6018/rc-sar.22.1.354341

Artino, A. R., Jr., & Stephens, J. M. (2009). Academic motivation and self-regulation: A comparative analysis of undergraduate and graduate students learning online. *The Internet and Higher Education, 12*(3–4), 146–151.

Astin, A. W., & Astin, H. S. (2000). *Leadership reconsidered: Engaging higher education in social change.* The Kellogg Foundation.

Atkinson, D. (1993). *Teaching monolingual classes.* Longman.

Aydın, H., & Acar-Çiftçi, Y. (2014). A study on the necessity of multicultural education in Turkey. *SDU Journal of Social Sciences., 33*(1), 197–218.

Aydın, H., & Tonbuloğlu, B. (2014). Graduate students' perceptions on multicultural education: A qualitative case study. *Eurasian Journal of Educational Research, 0*(57), 29–50. doi:10.14689/ejer.2014.57.3

Azad, H. (2014). *Parbbatya Chattogram: Sobuj Paharer Vitor Diye Hingsar Jharna Dhara*. Agami Prakashani.

Bae, G., & Yeung, J. (2022, August 9). *Record rainfall kills at least 9 in Seoul as water floods buildings, submerges cars.* CNN. https://www.cnn.com/2022/08/09/asia/seoul-south-korea-rain-flooding-intl-hnk/index.html

Bagaji, A., & Okhidemeh, E. (2014). Perspectives on stress and its management for individual well-being and organisational productivity. *International Journal of Public Administration and Management Research*, *2*(2), 129–147.

Bagheri, A., & Hjorth, P. (2007). Planning for sustainable development: A paradigm shift towards a process-based approach. *Sustainable Development*, *15*(2), 83–96. doi:10.1002d.310

Baker, R. S., Clarke-Midura, J., & Ocumpaugh, J. (2016). Towards general models of effective science inquiry in virtual performance assessments. *Journal of Computer Assisted Learning*, *32*(3), 267–280. doi:10.1111/jcal.12128

Balasooriya, C., Olupeliyawa, A., & Iqbal, M. P. (2016). *Innovative assessment that combines collaborative and self-directed learning with integration and application of knowledge: teamwork group projects*. Association of American Medical Colleges. Retrieved February 12, 2022, from https://www.mededportal.org/doi/full/10.15766/mep_2374-8265.10452

Baldwin, M. (2001). Working together, learning together, co-operative inquiry in the development of complex practice by teams of social workers. In P. Reason & H. Bradbury (Eds.), *The Sage handbook of action research* (pp. 287–293). Sage.

BANBEIS. (2022). Bangladesh Education Statistics 2021. Dhaka: Bangladesh Bureau of Educational Information and Statistics (BANBEIS), Ministry of Education.

Bangladesh Awami League. (2018). *Bangladesh on the march towards Prosperity: Election Manifesto 2018*. Bangladesh Awami League.

Banks, J. A. (1995a). Multicultural Education and Curriculum Transformation. *The Journal of Negro Education*, *64*(4), 390–400. doi:10.2307/2967262

Banks, J. A. (1995b). Multicultural Education: Its effects on students' racial and gender role attitudes. In J. A. Banks & C. Banks (Eds.), *Handbook of research on multicultural education* (pp. 617–627). Macmillan.

Banks, J. A. (2009). *The Routledge International Companion to Multicultural Education*. Routledge. doi:10.4324/9780203881514

Barkat, A. (2016). *Political economy of unpeopling of indigenous peoples: The case of Bangladesh*. Mukto Buddhi Prokasana.

Barker, M. C., & Mak, A. S. (2013). From classroom to boardroom and ward: Developing generic intercultural skills in diverse disciplines. *Journal of Studies in International Education*, *17*(5), 573–589. doi:10.1177/1028315313490200

Barnett, R. (2007). Recovering the civic university. In L. McIlrath & I. MacLabhrainn (Eds.), *Higher Education and Civic Engagement: International Perspectives* (pp. 25–36). Ashgate.

Barnett, R. (2011). The coming of the ecological university. *Oxford Review of Education*, *37*(4), 439–455. doi:10.1080/03054985.2011.595550

Barnett, R. (2018). *The ecological university. A feasible utopia*. Routledge.

Barnett, R., & Jackson, N. (Eds.). (2020). *Ecologies for learning and practice: Emerging ideas, sightings, and possibilities*. Routledge.

Basilaia, G., & Kvavadze, D. (2020). Transition to online education in schools during a SARSCoV-2 coronavirus (COVID-19) pandemic in Georgia. *Pedagogical Research*, *5*(4). Advance online publication. doi:10.29333/pr/7937

## Compilation of References

Baumeister, R. F., & Leary, M. R. (1995). The need to belong: Desire for interpersonal attachments as a fundamental human motivation. *Psychological Bulletin*, *117*(3), 497–529. doi:10.1037/0033-2909.117.3.497 PMID:7777651

Bazier, C. C. (2015). *An analysis of instructor extraversion and student learning style* [Doctoral dissertation]. Walden University.

Beabout, B. (2012). Turbulence, Perturbance, and Educational Change. Complicity. *An International Journal of Complexity and Education.*, *9*(2). Advance online publication. doi:10.29173/cmplct17984

Beans, H., Maireva, C., & Muza, C. (2020). Zimbabwe higher education institutions' preparedness in responding to Covid-19 induced disruptions to education. *Journal of New Vision in Educational Research*, *1*(2), 267–282.

Beard, L. A., & Harper, C. (2002). Student perceptions of online versus on campus instruction. *Education*, *122*(4), 658–663.

Beattie, A. (2021, June 29). *The 3 pillars of corporate sustainability*. https://www.investopedia.com/articles/investing/100515/three-pillars-corporate-sustainability.asp

Becker, B. E., & Huselid, M. A. (1998). High performance work systems and firm performance: A synthesis of research and managerial implications. *Research in Personnel and Human Resources Management*, *16*, 53–101.

Beechler, S., & Javidan, M. (2007). Leading with a global mindset. In M. Javidan, R. M. Steers, & M. A. Hitt (Eds.), *The Global Mindset* (pp. 131–169). Elsevier. doi:10.1016/S1571-5027(07)19006-9

Bejarano, C. A., Juárez, L. L., García, M. A. M., & Goldstein, D. M. (2019). *Decolonizing ethnography: Undocumented immigrants and new directions in social science*. Duke University Press.

Belay, D. G. (2022). COVID-19 Pandemic, Distance Learning, and Educational Inequality in Rural Ethiopia. In Global Risk and Contingency Management Research in Times of Crisis (pp. 244-262). IGI Global.

Beltrão, K. L., & Barcante, L. C. (2016). Teaching principles and fundamentals of business excellence to undergraduate students through a game. *Total Quality Management & Business Excellence*, *27*(5), 681–698. doi:10.1080/14783363.2015.1043116

Bendell, T. (2016). *Building anti-fragile organisations: Risk, opportunity and governance in a turbulent world*. Routledge. doi:10.4324/9781315570426

Benjaminsen, T. A., & Svarstad, H. (2021). *Political ecology: A critical engagement with global environmental issues*. Springer Nature. doi:10.1007/978-3-030-56036-2

Benn, S., & Dunphy, D. (2009). Action research as an approach to integrating sustainability into MBA programs. *Journal of Management Education*, *33*(3), 276–295. doi:10.1177/1052562908323189

Ben-Zvi, T. (2010). The efficacy of business simulation games in creating decision support systems: An experimental investigation. *Decision Support Systems*, *49*(1), 61–69. doi:10.1016/j.dss.2010.01.002

Bergan, S., & Damian, R. (2010). Higher Education for Modern Societies – Competences and Values. Publishing Council of Europe Higher Education Series No. 15, Council of Europe Publishing.

Berkes, F. (2007). Understanding uncertainty and reducing vulnerability: Lessons from resilience thinking. *Natural Hazards*, *41*(2), 283–295. doi:10.100711069-006-9036-7

Bernstein, J. H. (2015). Transdisciplinarity: A review of its origins, development, and current issues. *Journal of Research Practice*, *11*(1), R1. https://jrp.icaap.org/index.php/jrp/article/view/510/41

Besley, T., & Peters, M. A. (2020). Life and death in the Anthropocene: Educating for survival amid climate and ecosystem changes and potential civilisation collapse. *Educational Philosophy and Theory*, *52*(13), 1347–1357. doi:10.1080/00131857.2019.1684804

Besra, L. (2014). *A Critical Review of Democracy and Governance Challenges in Bangladesh with special refences to a human rights-based approach for the Development of marginalized indigenous people* [PhD thesis]. Flinders of Institute of Public Policy Management.

Bhaduri, R. M. (2019). Leveraging culture and leadership in crisis management. *European Journal of Training and Development*, *43*(5/6), 554–556. doi:10.1108/EJTD-10-2018-0109

Bhattacharya, B., Rezbana, U. S., & Khatun, A. (2018). *Implementation Challenges of SDGs Country Study*. CPD.

Bhavani, G., Mehta, A., & Dubey, S. (2020). Literature review: Game-based pedagogy in accounting education. *International Journal of Financial Research*, *11*(6), 165–176. doi:10.5430/ijfr.v11n6p165

Billah, M. (2017, June 19). What we mean by 'quality education'? *The Independent*.

Bilsland, C., Carter, L., & Wood, L. N. (2019). Work integrated learning internships in transnational education: Alumni perspectives from Vietnam. *Education + Training*, *61*(3), 359–373. doi:10.1108/ET-07-2017-0094

Birnbaum, R. (1992). *How academic leadership works: Understanding success and failure in the college presidency*. Jossey-Bass.

Black, A. L. (2018). Responding to longings for slow scholarship: Writing ourselves into being. In A. Black & S. Garvis (Eds.), *Women activating agency in academia: Metaphors, manifestos and memoir* (pp. 23–34). Routledge. doi:10.4324/9781315147451-3

Black, A. L., Crimmins, G., & Jones, J. K. (2017). Reducing the drag: Creating v formations through slow scholarship and story. In S. Riddle, M. Harmes, & P. A. Danaher (Eds.), *Producing pleasure in the contemporary university*. Sense. doi:10.1007/978-94-6351-179-7_11

BlackChen, M. (2015). To lead or not to lead: Women achieving leadership status in higher education. *Advancing Women in Leadership Journal*, *35*, 153–159.

Bladow, K., & Ladino, J. (Eds.). (2018). *Affective ecocriticism: Emotion, embodiment, environment*. University of Nebraska Press. doi:10.2307/j.ctv75d0g8

Blasco, N., Brusca, I., & Labrador, M. (2020). Drivers for universities' contribution to the sustainable development goals: An analysis of Spanish public universities. *Sustainability*, *13*(1), 89. doi:10.3390u13010089

Blau, P. M. (1964). *Exchange and power in social life*. John Wiley.

Blay-Palmer, A., Landman, K., Knezevic, I., & Hayhurst, R. (2013). Constructing resilient transformative communities through sustainable food hubs. *Local Environment*, *18*(5), 521–528. doi:10.1080/13549839.2013.797156

Blignaut, J. H. (2021). *An exploration of gender and sexual diversity development and inclusion within the curriculum of a selected higher education institution: challenges and opportunities* (Unpublished doctoral thesis). North-West University, Potchefstroom.

Bloom, B. S. (1956). Taxonomy of educational objectives: the classification of educational goals. In M. D. Engelhart, E. J. Furst, W. H. Hill, & D. R. Krathwohl (Eds.), *Handbook 1: Cognitive Domain*. David McKay.

Boca, G. D., & Saraçlı, S. (2019). Environmental Education and Student's Perception, for Sustainability. *Sustainability*, *11*(6), 1553. doi:10.3390u11061553

*Compilation of References*

Boffo, V. (2019). Employability and higher education: A category for the future. *New Directions for Adult and Continuing Education*, *2019*(163), 11–23. doi:10.1002/ace.20338

Bolt, D. B., & Crawford, R. A. (2000). *Digital divide: Computers and our children's failure*. Bantam.

Bolton, A., Goosen, L., & Kritzinger, E. (2021). An Empirical Study into the Impact on Innovation and Productivity Towards the Post-COVID-19 Era: Digital Transformation of an Automotive Enterprise. In L. C. Carvalho, L. Reis, & C. Silveira (Eds.), *Handbook of Research on Entrepreneurship, Innovation, Sustainability, and ICTs in the Post-COVID-19 Era* (pp. 133–159). IGI Global. doi:10.4018/978-1-7998-6776-0.ch007

Bonnard, C. (2020). What is employability for higher education students? *Journal of Education and Work*, *33*(5-6), 425–445. doi:10.1080/13639080.2020.1842866

Booth, R., & Abdul, G. (2022, July 19). UK reaches hottest ever temperature as 40.2C recorded at Heathrow. *The Guardian*. https://www.theguardian.com/uk-news/2022/jul/19/uk-weather-record-hottest-day-ever-heatwave

Borodzicz, E., & Van Haperen, K. (2002). Individual and group learning in crisis simulations. *Journal of Contingencies and Crisis Management*, *10*(3), 139–147. doi:10.1111/1468-5973.00190

Bosch, C. (2016). *Promoting Self-Directed Learning through the Implementation of Cooperative Learning in a Higher Education Blended Learning Environment* [Doctoral dissertation]. North-West University.

Boswell, S. W. (2011, Nov 1). *Digital Divide Definition*. Retrieved from https://wiki.uiowa.edu/display/edtech/Digital+Divide+Definition

Bousquet, F., Botta, A., Alinovi, L., Barreteau, O., Bossio, D., Brown, K., Caron, P., Cury, P., D'Errico, M., DeClerck, F., Dessard, H., Enfors Kautsky, E., Fabricius, C., Folke, C., Fortmann, L., Hubert, B., Magda, D., Mathevet, R., Norgaard, R. B., ... Staver, C. (2016). Resilience and development: Mobilizing for transformation. *Ecology and Society*, *21*(3), 40. doi:10.5751/ES-08754-210340

Bowen, T. (2018). Becoming professional: Examining how WIL students learn to construct and perform their professional identities. *Studies in Higher Education*, *43*(7), 1148–1159. doi:10.1080/03075079.2016.1231803

Bowers, M. R., Hall, J. R., & Srinivasan, M. M. (2017). Organizational culture and leadership style: The missing combination for selecting the right leader for effective crisis management. *Business Horizons*, *60*(4), 551–563. doi:10.1016/j.bushor.2017.04.001

Bowman, B. T. (1994). Cultural diversity and academic achievement. Urban Education Program. Urban Monograph Series, 10-22.

Boyd, D. (2004). The characteristics of successful online students. *New Horizons in Adult Education and Human Resource Development*, *18*(2), 31–39. doi:10.1002/nha3.10184

Bradshaw, D. (1999). *Transforming lives, Transforming communities: A conceptual framework for further education*. Adult Education Resource and Information Service (ARIS), Language Australia.

Branson, C. M., Franken, M., & Penney, D. (2016). Middle leadership in higher education: A relational analysis. *Educational Management Administration & Leadership*, *44*(1), 128–145. doi:10.1177/1741143214558575

Bratton, J., Gold, J., Bratton, A., & Steele, L. (2021). *Human resource management*. Bloomsbury Publishing.

Brazhkin, V., & Zimmerman, H. (2019). Students' perceptions of learning in an online multiround business simulation game: What can we learn from them? *Decision Sciences*, *17*(4), 363–386.

Breed, B. (2016). Exploring a cooperative learning approach to improve self-directed learning in higher education. *Journal for New Generation Sciences, 14*(3), 1–21.

Brewer, M. B. (1991). The social self: On being the same and different at the same time. *Personality and Social Psychology Bulletin, 17*(5), 475–482. doi:10.1177/0146167291175001

Brien, O. E. (2020). Enhancing 21st century learning using digital learning objects and multiple intelligence theory: a conceptual model. In R. Z. Zheng (Ed.), Examining multiple intelligences and digital technologies for enhanced learning opportunities (pp. 19-40). Hershey, PA: IGI Global.

British Broadcasting Corporation (BBC). (2021, September 10). *More people trying to give up their lockdown dogs, says charity*. https://www.bbc.co.uk/news/uk-58518892

British Educational Research Association Guidelines. (2018). *BERA Ethical Guidelines for Educational Research*. Available at: https://www.bera.ac.uk/wp-content/uploads/2018/06/BERA-Ethical-Guidelines-for-EducationalResearch_4thEdn_2018.pdf?noredirect=1

Brocato, B. R., Bonanno, A., & Ulbig, S. (2015). Student perceptions and instructional evaluations: A multivariate analysis of online and face-to-face classroom settings. *Education and Information Technologies, 20*(1), 37–55. doi:10.100710639-013-9268-6

Brockett, R. G., & Hiemstra, R. (2019). *Self-direction in adult learning: perspectives on theory, research, and practice*. Routledge.

Brooman, S. (2011). Enhancing Student Engagement by Building upon the 'Tectonic Plates' of Legal Education. *The Liverpool Law Review, 32*(2), 109–112. doi:10.100710991-011-9097-x

Bruckmüller, S., Ryan, M. K., Rink, F., & Haslam, S. A. (2014). Beyond the glass ceiling: The glass cliff and its lessons for organizational policy. *Social Issues and Policy Review, 8*(1), 202–232. doi:10.1111ipr.12006

Bruner, E. M. (1997). Ethnography as narrative. In *Memory, identity, community: The idea of narrative in the human sciences* (pp. 264–280). State University of New York Press.

Budiharso, T., & Tarman, B. (2020). Improving Quality Education through Better Working Conditions of Academic Institutes. *Journal of Ethnic and Cultural Studies, 7*(1), 99–115. doi:10.29333/ejecs/306

Buhl, A., Schmidt-Keilich, M., Muster, V., Blazejewski, S., Schrader, U., Harrach, C., Schäfer, M., & Süßbauer, E. (2019). Design thinking for sustainability: Why and how design thinking can foster sustainability-oriented innovation development. *Journal of Cleaner Production, 231*, 1248–1257. doi:10.1016/j.jclepro.2019.05.259

Burchell, N., & Kolb, D. (2006). Stability and change for sustainability. *University of Auckland Business Review, 8*(2), 33–41.

Burd, B. A., & Buchanan, L. E. (2004). Teaching the teachers: Teaching and learning online. *RSR. Reference Services Review, 32*(4), 404–412. doi:10.1108/00907320410569761

Burke, C. (2014). Fleeting pockets of anarchy. Streetwork. The exploding school. *Paedagogica Historica, 50*(4), 433–442. doi:10.1080/00309230.2014.899376

Burke, K. (1965). Terministic Screens. *Philosophy and the Arts, 39*, 87–102.

Burke, K. (1966). *Language as symbolic action: Essays on life, literature and method*. U of California P. Print doi:10.1525/9780520340664

Burke, K. (1969). *A rhetoric of motives*. University of California Press.

## Compilation of References

Burnard, K., & Bhamra, R. (2011). Organisational resilience: Development of a conceptual framework for organisational responses. *International Journal of Production Research*, *49*(18), 5581–5599. doi:10.1080/00207543.2011.563827

Burns, T. R. (2012). The sustainability revolution: A societal paradigm shift. *Sustainability*, *4*(6), 1118–1134. doi:10.3390u4061118

Burrell, S. M., & Heiselt, A. K. (2012). Presidential perspectives of crisis preparedness at Christian higher education institutions. *Christian Higher Education*, *11*(4), 260–271. doi:10.1080/15363759.2010.544614

Burrows, A., & Borowczak, M. (2019). Computer science and engineering: Utilizing action research and lesson study. *Educational Action Research*, *27*(4), 631–646. doi:10.1080/09650792.2019.1566082

Bushman, R. M., Piotroski, J. D., & Smith, A. J. (2004). What Determines Corporate Transparency? *Journal of Accounting Research*, *42*(2), 207–252. doi:10.1111/j.1475-679X.2004.00136.x

Byram, M., Gribkova, B., & Starkey, H. (2002). *Developing the intercultural dimension in language teaching: A Practical introduction for teachers*. Council of Europe Publishing.

Byrne, M., & Flood, B. (2005). A study of accounting students' motives, expectations, and preparedness for higher education. *Journal of Further and Higher Education*, *29*(2), 111–124. doi:10.1080/03098770500103176

Byrne, M., Flood, B., Hassall, T., Joyce, J., Montano, J. L. A., Gonzalez, J. M. G., & Tourna-Germanou, E. (2012). Motivations, expectations, and preparedness for higher education: A study of accounting students in Ireland, the UK, Spain, and Greece. *Accounting Forum*, *36*(2), 134–144. doi:10.1016/j.accfor.2011.12.001

Caduff, C. (2020). *What Went Wrong Corona and the World after the Full Stop*. https://www.academia.edu/download/63190746/What_Went_Wrong.pdf

Camillus, J. C. (2008). Strategy as a wicked problem. *Harvard Business Review*, *86*(5), 98–101.

Campbell, J. (1988). *The power of myth*. Random House.

Camp, W. G. (2001). Formulating and Evaluating Theoretical Frameworks for Career and Technical Education Research. *Journal of Vocational Educational Research*, *26*(1), 27–39. doi:10.5328/JVER26.1.4

Canagarajah, S. (1999). *Resisting linguistic imperialism in English teaching*. Oxford University Press.

Cannon, J. R. (2002). Distance learning in science education. In J. W. Altschuld & D. D. Kumar (Eds.), *Evaluation of Science and Technology Education at the Dawn of a New Millennium* (pp. 243–265). Kluwer Academic/Plenum Publishers. doi:10.1007/0-306-47560-X_10

Capra, F., & Luisi, P. L. (2016). *A systems view of life: A unifying vision*. Cambridge University Press.

Carenys, J., Moya, S., & Perramon, J. (2017). Is it worth it to consider videogames in accounting education? A comparison of a simulation and a videogame in attributes, motivation and learning outcomes. *Revista de Contabilidad-Spanish Accounting Review*, *20*(2), 118–130. doi:10.1016/j.rcsar.2016.07.003

Carlassare, E. (1994). Destabilizing the criticism of essentialism in ecofeminist discourse. *Capitalism, Nature, Socialism*, *5*(3), 50–66. doi:10.1080/10455759409358597

Carlassare, E. (2000). Socialist and cultural ecofeminism: Allies in resistance. *Ethics and the Environment*, *5*(1), 89–106. doi:10.1016/S1085-6633(99)00025-X

Carmeli, A., Reiter-Palmon, R., & Ziv, E. (2010). Inclusive leadership and employee involvement in creative tasks in the workplace: The mediating role of psychological safety. *Creativity Research Journal*, *22*(3), 250–260. doi:10.1080/10400419.2010.504654

Carmo, C., & Ribeiro, C. (2022). Mandatory Non-Financial Information Disclosure under European Directive 95/2014/EU: Evidence from Portuguese Listed Companies. *Sustainability*, *14*(8), 4860. Advance online publication. doi:10.3390u14084860

Carnes, M., Morrissey, C., & Geller, S. (2008). Women's health and women's leadership in academic medicine: Hitting the same glass ceiling? *Journal of Women's Health*, *17*(9), 1453–1462. doi:10.1089/jwh.2007.0688 PMID:18954235

Carr, F., & Kemmis, S. (1986). *Becoming Critical: Education, Knowledge and Action Research*. Falmer Press.

Carvalho, H. C., & Mazzon, J. A. (2019). Embracing complex social problems. *Journal of Social Marketing*, *10*(1), 54–80. doi:10.1108/JSOCM-03-2019-0049

Cataylst. (2019). *Pyramid: Women in S&P 500 Companies*. https://www.catalyst.org/research/women-in-sp-500-companies/

Cavallone, M., Manna, R., & Palumbo, R. (2020). Filling in the gaps in higher education quality: An analysis of Italian students' value expectations and perceptions. *International Journal of Educational Management*, *34*(1), 203–216. doi:10.1108/IJEM-06-2019-0189

Cavinato, A. G., Hunter, R. A., Ott, L. S., & Robinson, J. K. (2021). Promoting student interaction, engagement, and success in an online environment. *Analytical and Bioanalytical Chemistry*, *413*(6), 1513–1520. doi:10.100700216-021-03178-x PMID:33479816

Cenar, I. (2020). Non-financial Reporting and Performance in Pre-university Education. *Ovidius University Annals, Economic Sciences Series*, *20*(2), 830-836. https://stec.univ-ovidius.ro/html/anale/RO/wp-content/uploads/2021/03/Section%205/5.pdf

Centers for Disease Control and Prevention. (2020). *COVID-19 hospitalization and death by race/ethnicity*. Available at: https://www.cdc.gov/coronavirus/2019-ncov/covid-data/investigations-discovery/hospitalization-death-by-race-ethnicity.html

Chakma and Maitrot. (2016). *Working paper on – How Ethnic Minorities became poor and stay poor in Bangladesh: A Qualitative enquiry*. EEP/ Shiree.

Chamorro-Premuzic, T., & Furnham, A. (2008). Personality, intelligence and approaches to learning as predictors of academic performance. *Personality and Individual Differences*, *44*(7), 1596–1603. doi:10.1016/j.paid.2008.01.003

Chankseliani, M., & McCowan, T. (2021). Higher education and the sustainable development goals. *Higher Education*, *81*(1), 1–8. doi:10.100710734-020-00652-w PMID:33173242

Chassagne, N. (2018). Sustaining the good life: Buen vivir as an alternative to sustainable development. *Community Development Journal: An International Forum*, *54*(3), 482–500. doi:10.1093/cdj/bsx062

Cha, Y. K., Gundara, J., Ham, S. H., & Lee, M. (2017). *Multicultural Education in Glocal Perspectives: Policy and Institutionalization*. Springer. doi:10.1007/978-981-10-2222-7

Checkland, P. (2000). Soft systems methodology: A thirty year retrospective. *Systems Research and Behavioral Science*, *17*(1), 11–58. doi:10.1002/1099-1743(200011)17:1+<::AID-SRES374>3.0.CO;2-O

Checkland, P., & Poulter, J. (2010). Soft systems methodology. In M. Reynolds & S. Holwell (Eds.), *Systems approaches to managing change: A practical guide* (pp. 191–242). Springer. doi:10.1007/978-1-84882-809-4_5

**Compilation of References**

Chellammal, T. (2021). A Study of Students Perspective on E-Learning. *International Journal of Advanced Research in Commerce Management and Finance*, *1*(1), 11–16.

Cheng, M., Adekola, O., Albia, J., & Cai, S. (2021). Employability in higher education: A review of key stakeholders' perspectives. *Higher Education Evaluation and Development*, *16*(1), 16–31. doi:10.1108/HEED-03-2021-0025

Cheng, Y. C. (2009). Hong Kong educational reforms in the last decade: Reform syndrome and new developments. *International Journal of Educational Management*, *23*(1), 65–86. doi:10.1108/09513540910926439

Chen, Y. C. (2020). Dialogic pathways to manage uncertainty for productive engagement in scientifc argumentation. *Science & Education*, *29*(2), 331–375. doi:10.100711191-020-00111-z

Chhinzer, N., & Russo, A. M. (2018). An exploration of employer perceptions of graduate student employability. *Education + Training*, *60*(1), 104–120. doi:10.1108/ET-06-2016-0111

Chilisa, B. (2017). Decolonising transdisciplinary research approaches: An African perspective for enhancing knowledge integration in sustainability science. *Sustainability Science*, *12*(5), 813–827. doi:10.100711625-017-0461-1

Chilisa, B. (2019). *Indigenous research methodologies*. Sage Publications, Incorporated.

Cho, C. H., & Patten, D. M. (2007). The role of environmental disclosures as tools of legitimacy: A research note. *Accounting, Organizations and Society*, *32*(7–8), 639–647. doi:10.1016/j.aos.2006.09.009

Choi, S. B., Tran, T. B. H., & Kang, S. W. (2016). Inclusive leadership and employee well-being: The mediating role of person-job fit. *Journal of Happiness Studies*, *18*(6), 1877–1901. doi:10.100710902-016-9801-6

Choi, S. B., Tran, T. B. H., & Park, B. I. (2015). Inclusive leadership and work engagement: Mediating roles of affective organizational commitment and creativity. *Social Behavior and Personality*, *43*(6), 931–943. doi:10.2224bp.2015.43.6.931

Chomsky, N., & Pollin, R. (2020). *Climate crisis and the global green new deal: The political economy of saving the planet*. Verso Books.

Chong, S. (2005). The logic of Hong Kong teachers: An exploratory study of their teaching culturally diverse students. *Teaching Education*, *16*(2), 117–129. doi:10.1080/10476210500122691

Chowdhury, J. S., Abd Wahab, H., Saad, M. R. M., Roy, P. K., Hamidi, M., & Ahmad, M. M. (2021). Ubuntu Philosophy: 'I Am Because We Are'–A Road to 'Individualism'to Global Solidarity. In Handbook of Research on the Impact of COVID-19 on Marginalized Populations and Support for the Future (pp. 361-381). IGI Global.

Chowdhury, J. S., Abd Wahab, H., Saad, R. M., & Roy, P. (2022b). "Ihsanic" Philosophy as an Alternative to Social Justice: A Concepirical (Conceptual+ Empirical) Reflection From the Bioprospecting Domain in Bangladesh. In Social Justice Research Methods for Doctoral Research (pp. 25-46). IGI Global.

Chowdhury, J. S., Abd Wahab, H., Saad, M. R. M., Mathbor, G., & Hamidi, M. (2022). *Ubuntu Philosophy in the New Normalcy*. Springer Nature.

Chowdhury, M. B., & Chakraborty, M. (2021). The impact of COVID-19 on the migrant workers and remittances flow to Bangladesh. *South Asian Survey*, *28*(1), 38–56. doi:10.1177/0971523121995365

Chowdhury, S. A., Hossain, M. M., & Rahman, M. A. (2013). Extended GAPs Model to Assess the Quality of Education. *Journal of Business Studies*, *34*(1), 165–183.

Christian, J., & Walley, L. (2016). Termite tales: Organisational change – A personal view of sustainable development in a university – As seen from the "tunnels.". In W. Leal Filho, L. Brandli, O. Kuznetsova, & A. Paco (Eds.), *Integrative approaches to sustainable development at university level* (pp. 525–538). Springer.

Chuck, C., Fernandes, S. A., & Hyers, L. L. (2016). Awakening to the politics of food: Politicized diet as social identity. *Appetite*, *107*, 425–436. doi:10.1016/j.appet.2016.08.106 PMID:27554183

Cifuentes, L. (2021). *A guide to administering distance learning*. Brill. doi:10.1163/9789004471382

Clarke, M. (2018). Rethinking graduate employability: The role of capital, individual attributes and context. *Studies in Higher Education*, *43*(11), 1923–1937. doi:10.1080/03075079.2017.1294152

Clark, R. E. (1983, Winter). Reconsidering research on learning from media. *Review of Educational Research*, *53*(4), 445–459. doi:10.3102/00346543053004445

Climate Science Alliance. (2022). *Who we are*. Climate Science Alliance. https://www.climatesciencealliance.org

Coaffee, J. (2019). *Futureproof: How to build resilience in an uncertain world*. Yale University Press.

Coban, A. E., Karaman, N. G., & Doğan, T. (2010). Investigation of preservice teachers' perspectives on cultural diversity in terms of various demographic variables. *Abant Izzet Baysal University Journal of Faculty of*, *10*(1), 125-131.

Cobb, P. (1994). Where is the mind? Constructivist and sociocultural perspectives on mathematical development. *Educational Researcher*, *23*(7), 13–19. doi:10.3102/0013189X023007013

Cohen, A. S., Morrison, S. C., & Callaway, D. A. (2013). Computerized facial analysis for understanding constricted/blunted affect: Initial feasibility, reliability, and validity data. *Schizophrenia Research*, *148*(1-3), 111–116. doi:10.1016/j.schres.2013.05.003 PMID:23726720

Cohen, E. G., & Lotan, R. A. (1995). Producing equal-status interactions in the heterogeneous classroom. *American Educational Research Journal*, *32*(1), 99–120. doi:10.3102/00028312032001099

Cohen, L., Manion, L., & Morrison, K. (2007). *Research Methods in Education* (6th ed.). Routledge Falmer. doi:10.4324/9780203029053

Cohen, L., Manion, L., & Morrison, K. (2011). *Research methods in education*. Rutledge Flamer.

Colares, A. C., & Amorim, N. B. (2020). Motivação dos discentes em ciências contábeis na ótica da teoria da autodeterminação. *International Journal of Accounting and Reporting*, *14*, 1–18. doi:10.34629/ric.v14i0.e-020008

Collins, P. H. (1990). *Black feminist thought: feminist theory and the construction of knowledge*. Routledge.

Conceição, S. (2002). The sociocultural implications of learning and teaching in cyberspace. *New Directions for Adult and Continuing Education*, *2002*(96), 37–46. doi:10.1002/ace.77

Constantino, S. M., & Weber, E. U. (2021). Decision-making under the deep uncertainty of climate change: The psychological and political agency of narratives. *Current Opinion in Psychology*, *42*, 151–159. doi:10.1016/j.copsyc.2021.11.001 PMID:34861621

Coombs, W. T. (2007). Protecting organization reputations during a crisis: The development and application of situational crisis communication theory. *Corporate Reputation Review*, *10*(3), 163–176. doi:10.1057/palgrave.crr.1550049

Cooper, C. D., Scandura, T. A., & Schriesheim, C. A. (2005). Looking forward but learning from our past: Potential challenges to developing authentic leadership theory and authentic leaders. *The Leadership Quarterly*, *16*(3), 475–493. doi:10.1016/j.leaqua.2005.03.008

Cooperrider, D., & Godwin, L. (2022). Strengths-based megacommunities and the appreciative inquiry's complete convention: Creating wholepower, willpower and waypower for our world's Earthshot moment. *AI Practitioner*, *24*(1), 94–106. doi:10.12781/978-1-907549-50-2-8

## Compilation of References

COPD26. (2021). *The 55 Gigaton Challenge*. Ted Talk. https://www.ted.com/talks/countdown_the_55_gigaton_challenge/

Córdova, T. (1998). Power and knowledge: Colonialism in the academy. *Living Chicana Theory*, 17-45.

Cork, S. (Ed.). (2010). *Resilience and transformation: Preparing Australia for uncertain futures*. CSIRO Publishing. doi:10.1071/9780643098138

Cormier, D., & Magnan, M. (2007). The revisited contribution of environmental reporting to investors' valuation of a firm's earnings: An international perspective. *Ecological Economics*, *62*(3–4), 613–626. doi:10.1016/j.ecolecon.2006.07.030

Corntassel, J. (2008). Toward sustainable self-determination: Rethinking the contemporary Indigenous-rights discourse. *Alternatives*, *33*(1), 105–132. doi:10.1177/030437540803300106

Correll, S. (2017). Reducing gender biases in modern workplaces: A small wins approach to organisational change. *Gender & Society*, *31*(6), 725–750. doi:10.1177/0891243217738518

Cundiñr, N. L., & Stockdale, M. S. (2013). Social psychological perspectives on discrimination against women leaders. Women and Management: Global Issues and Promising Solutions [2 volumes]: Global Issues and Promising Solutions, 155.

Curtis, D. D., & Lawson, M. J. (2001). Exploring collaborative online learning. *Journal of Asynchronous Learning Networks*, *5*(1), 21–34.

Dale, R., & Robertson, S. (2014). Global education policy. In N. Yeates (Ed.), *Global Social Policy*. Policy Press.

Darbellay, F. (2015). Rethinking inter-and transdisciplinarity: Undisciplined knowledge and the emergence of a new thought style. *Futures*, *65*, 163–174. doi:10.1016/j.futures.2014.10.009

Darling-Hammond, L., Flook, L., Cook-Harvey, C., Barron, B., & Osher, D. (2020). Implications for educational practice of the science of learning and development. *Applied Developmental Science*, *24*(2), 97–140. doi:10.1080/10888691.2018.1537791

Dar, W. A. (2021). Pedagogy for its own sake: Teacher's beliefs about activity-based learning in rural government schools of Kashmir. *Quality Assurance in Education*, *29*(2/3), 311–327. doi:10.1108/QAE-01-2021-0013

Dar, W. A., & Najar, I. A. (2018). Educational anthropology, tribal education and responsible citizenship in India. *South Asia Research*, *38*(3), 327–346. doi:10.1177/0262728018800759

Davidman, L., & Davidman, P. (1997). *Teaching with a multicultural perspective: A practical guide*. Longman.

Dawis, R. V., & Lofquist, L. H. (1984). *A psychological theory of work adjustment*. University of Minnesota Press.

De Beer, J., & Mentz, E. (2019). The use of Cultural-Historical Activity Theory in researching the affordances of indigenous knowledge for self-directed learning. In J. De Beer (Ed.), *The decolonisation of the curriculum project: The affordances of indigenous knowledge for self-directed learning* (pp. 87–116). AOSIS.

De Bierre, J. (2006). Penang: Through Gilded Doors. Areca Books.

De la Campa, J., & Nassaji, H. (2009). The amount, purpose, and reasons for using L1 in L2 classrooms. *Foreign Language Annals*, *42*(4), 742–759. doi:10.1111/j.1944-9720.2009.01052.x

de Moraes Sarmento Rego, I. (2015). Mobile Language Learning: How Gamification Improves the Experience. In Y. Zhang (Ed.), *Handbook of Mobile Teaching and Learning* (pp. 705–720). Springer., doi:10.1007/978-3-642-54146-9_76

De Sousa, L. O. (2021). Learning experiences of a participatory approach to educating for sustainable development in a South African higher education institution yielding social learning indicators. *Sustainability*, *13*(6), 3210. doi:10.3390u13063210

Debnath, M. K. (2010). *Living on the Edge: The predicament of a rural indigenous Santal community in Bangladesh* (Doctoral dissertation).

Debnath, M. K. (2012). The invisible agenda: Civilising mission or missionizing civilization. *International Journal of Human Rights*, *16*(3), 461–473. doi:10.1080/13642987.2011.572550

Debnath, M. K. (2020). A community under siege: Exclusionary education policies and indigenous Santals* in the Bangladeshi context. *Third World Quarterly*, *41*(3), 453–469. doi:10.1080/01436597.2019.1660634

Deci, E. L., & Ryan, R. M. (1985). Conceptualizations of Intrinsic Motivation and Self-Determination. In *Intrinsic Motivation and Self-Determination in Human Behavior. Perspectives in Social Psychology*. Springer. doi:10.1007/978-1-4899-2271-7_2

Deci, E. L., & Ryan, R. M. (2008). Self-determination theory: A macrotheory of human motivation, development, and health. *Canadian Psychology*, *49*(3), 182–185. https://psycnet.apa.org/doi/10.1037/a0012801. doi:10.1037/a0012801

Deffuant, G., & Gilbert, N. (Eds.). (2011). *Viability and resilience of complex systems: Concepts, methods and case studies from ecology and society*. Springer Science & Business Media. doi:10.1007/978-3-642-20423-4

Deloria, V. (2001). American Indian metaphysics. *Winds of Change*, 49-67.

Delors, J., Mufti, I. A., Amagi, I., Carneiro, R., Chung, F., Geremek, B., Gorham, W., Kornhauser, A., Manley, M., Quero, M. P., Savane, M., Singh, K., Stavenhagen, R., Suhr, M. W., & Nanzhao, Z. (1996). *Learning: The Treasure Within. Report to UNESCO of the International Commission on Education for the Twenty-First Century*. UNESCO Publishing.

D'Errico, F., Paciello, M., De Carolis, B., Vattanid, A., Palestra, G., & Anzivino, G. (2018). *Cognitive emotions in e-learning processes and their potential relationship with students' academic adjustment*. Academic Press.

Deudney, D. (2018). Turbo change: Accelerating technological disruption, planetary geopolitics, and architectonic metaphors. *International Studies Review*, *20*(2), 223–231. doi:10.1093/isr/viy033

Dewey, J. (1938). *Experience and education*. Macmillan Publishing Company.

Dietrich, N., Kentheswaran, K., Ahmadi, A., Teyché, J., Bessière, Y., Alfenore, S., Laborie, S., Bastoul, D., Loubière, K., Guigui, C., Sperandio, M., Barna, L., Paul, E., Cabassud, C., Liné, A., & Hébrard, G. (2020). Attempts, successes, and failures of distance learning in the time of COVID-19. *Journal of Chemical Education*, *97*(9), 2448–2457. doi:10.1021/acs.jchemed.0c00717

Dirani, K. M., Abadi, M., Alizadeh, A., Barhate, B., Garza, R. C., Gunasekara, N., Ibrahim, G., & Majzun, Z. (2020). Leadership competencies and the essential role of human resource development in times of crisis: A response to Covid-19 pandemic. *Human Resource Development International*, *23*(4), 380–394. doi:10.1080/13678868.2020.1780078

Dogs Trust. (2022, July 14). *Cost-of-living crisis starts to bite dog owners, shows new poll*. https://www.dogstrust.org.uk/latest/2022/dogs-trust-cost-of-living

Dolapçı, E. (2019, Spring). *The examination of the relationships among teachers' multicultural self-efficacy, school climate, and teachers' attitudes towards refugee students* [Master's thesis]. Kastamonu University.

Dominguez, R. G. (2012). Participatory Learning. In R. M. Seel (Ed.), *Encyclopedia of the Sciences of Learning*. Retrieved February 11, 2022, from https://link.springer.com/referenceworkentry/10.1007%2F978-1-4419-1428-6_1903

Dooley, K. J. (1997). A complex adaptive systems model of organization change. *Nonlinear Dynamics Psychology and Life Sciences*, *1*(1), 69–97. doi:10.1023/A:1022375910940

Dörner, D., & Funke, J. (2017). Complex problem solving: What it is and what it is not. *Frontiers in Psychology*, *8*, 1153.

Draijer, C., & Schenk, D. J. (2004). Best practices of business simulation with SAP R/3. *Journal of Information Systems Education*, *15*(3), 244–261.

Dreyfus, H., & Rabinow, P. (2014). *Michel Foucault: Beyond structuralism and hermeneutics*. University of Chicago Press. doi:10.4324/9781315835259

Du Pisani, J. A. (2006). Sustainable development–historical roots of the concept. *Environmental Sciences*, *3*(2), 83–96. doi:10.1080/15693430600688831

Du Toit, A. (2018). *Developing a framework for the effective structuring and implementation of entrepreneurship education in Consumer Studies* (Doctoral dissertation). University of South Africa. Retrieved from http://hdl.handle.net/10500/24948

Du Toit, A., & Kempen, E. L. (2018). Entrepreneurship education: Enhancing the value of Consumer Studies in South African secondary schools. In A scholarly compendium for teaching and learning (Vol. 1, pp. 185-212). Academic Press.

Du Toit, A. (2016). Foundations in the South African senior phase curriculum for entrepreneurship education in consumer studies. *Journal of Consumer Sciences*, *44*, 11–20. https://www.ajol.info/index.php/jfecs/article/download/143699/133413/0

Du Toit, A. (2021). Harnessing education through entrepreneurship in consumer studies to address youth unemployment in South Africa. *Journal of Consumer Sciences*, *49*, 1–14. https://www.ajol.info/index.php/jfecs/article/download/210186/198144

Du Toit-Brits, C. (2018a). Towards a transformative and holistic continuing self-directed learning theory. *South African Journal of Higher Education*, *32*(4), 51–65. doi:10.20853/32-4-2434

Du Toit-Brits, C. (2018b). Die onderwyser as beoefenaar en bemiddelaar van selfgerigte leer. *Tydskrif vir Geesteswetenskappe*, *58*(2), 376–386. doi:10.17159/2224-7912/2018/v58n2a11

Du Toit-Brits, C. (2020). Unleashing the power of self-directed learning: Criteria for structuring self-directed learning within the learning environments of higher education institutions. *Africa Education Review*, *17*(2), 20–32. doi:10.1080/18146627.2018.1494507

Du Toit-Brits, C., & Blignaut, H. (2019). Posisionering van voortgesette selfgerigte leervaardighede in een-en-twintigste-eeuse onderwys. *Tydskrif vir Geesteswetenskappe*, *59*(4), 512–529. doi:10.17159/2224-7912/2019/v59n4a4

DuBrin, A. J. (2013). *Handbook of research on crisis leadership in organizations*. Edward Elgar Publishing. doi:10.4337/9781781006405

Dumay, J. (2016). A critical reflection on the future of intellectual capital: From reporting to disclosure. *Journal of Intellectual Capital*, *17*(1), 168–184. doi:10.1108/JIC-08-2015-0072

Duncan, G. (2015). Innovations in appreciative inquiry: Critical appreciative inquiry with excluded Pakistani women. In P. Reason & H. Bradbury (Eds.), *The Sage handbook of action research* (pp. 107–123). Sage. doi:10.4135/9781473921290.n6

Duncan, H. E., Range, B., & Hvidston, D. (2013). Exploring student perceptions of rigor online: Toward a definition of rigorous learning. *Journal on Excellence in College Teaching*, *24*(4), 5–28.

Dunn, R., Beaudry, J., & Klavas, A. (1989). *Survey on Research on Learning Styles Educational Leadership*. Academic Press.

Dyer, B., & Song, X. M. (1998). Innovation strategy and sanctioned conflict: A new edge in innovation? *Journal of Product Innovation Management*, *15*(6), 505–519. doi:10.1111/1540-5885.1560505

Dymitrow, M., & Halfacree, K. (2018). Sustainability – differently. *Bulletin of Geography. Socio-Economic Series*, *40*(40), 7–16. doi:10.2478/bog-2018-0011

Earl, A., VanWynsberghe, R., Walter, P., & Straka, T. (2018). Adaptive education applied to higher education for sustainability. *International Journal of Sustainability in Higher Education*. e Cunha, M. P., Clegg, S. R., & Kamoche, K. (2012). Improvisation as "real time foresight". *Futures*, *44*(3), 265–272.

Echeverría, J., Alonso, A., & Oiarzabal, P. (Eds.). (2011). Knowledge communities. Center for Basque Studies, University of Nevada, Reno.

Echeverría, J. (1999). *Los señores del aire: Telépolis y el tercer entorno*. Destino.

Echeverría, J. (2011). Epistemopolis: From knowledge communities to knowledge cities. In J. Echeverría, A. Alonso, & P. Oiarzabal (Eds.), *Knowledge communities*. Center for Basque Studies, University of Nevada.

Cunha, M. P. E., & Putnam, L. L. (2019). Paradox theory and the paradox of success. *Strategic Organization*, *17*(1), 95–106.

Edwards, A. R. (2005). *The sustainability revolution: Portrait of a paradigm shift*. New Society Publishers.

EFRAG. (2021). *Conceptual Framework for Non-Financial Information Standard Setting*. Retrieved from https://www.efrag.org/Assets/Download?assetUrl=%2Fsites%2Fwebpublishing%2FSiteAssets%2FEFRAG%2520PTF-NFRS_A3_FINAL.pdf

Egan, T. M., & Akdere, M. (2004). *Distance learning roles and competencies*. Academy of Human Resource Development.

Ehsan, M. (2008). *Higher Education Governance in Bangladesh: The Public-Private Dilemma*. https://www.britannica.com/

Elliott, J. (1991). *Action Research for Educational Change*. Open University Press.

Elo, S., Kääriäinen, M., Kanste, O., Pölkki, T., Utriainen, K., & Kyngäs, H. (2014). Qualitative content analysis: A focus on trustworthiness. *SAGE Open*, *4*(1). doi:10.1177/2158244014522633

Elsass, P. M. (1993). The paradox of success: Too much of a good thing? *The Academy of Management Perspectives*, *7*(3), 84–85.

Elsenbroich, C., & Gilbert, N. (2014). *Modelling norms*. Springer.

Elsubbaugh, S., Fildes, R., & Rose, M. B. (2004). Preparation for crisis management: A proposed model and empirical evidence. *Journal of Contingencies and Crisis Management*, *12*(3), 112–127. doi:10.1111/j.0966-0879.2004.00441.x

Ely, R. J., & Thomas, D. A. (2001). Cultural diversity at work: The effects of diversity perspectives on work group processes and outcomes. *Administrative Science Quarterly*, *46*(2), 229–273. doi:10.2307/2667087

English, P., De Villiers Scheepers, M. J., Fleischman, D., Burgess, J., & Crimmins, G. (2021). Developing professional networks: The missing link to graduate employability. *Education + Training*, *63*(4), 647–661. doi:10.1108/ET-10-2020-0309

Erbas, Y. (2019). A qualitative case study of multicultural education in Turkey: Definitions of multiculturalism and multicultural education. *International Journal of Progressive Education*, *15*(1), 23–43. doi:10.29329/ijpe.2019.184.2

Erdal, Y., Kiziltepe, Z., Seggie, F. N., & Sekerler, S. A. (2014). The Learning styles and personalities traits of undergraduate: A case at a state university in Istanbul. *The Anthropologist*, *18*(2), 591–600. doi:10.1080/09720073.2014.11891577

Erkens, M., Paugam, L., & Stolowy, H. (2015). Non-financial information: State of the art and research perspectives based on a bibliometric study. Comptabilite Controle Audit, 21(3), 15-92. doi:10.3917/cca.213.0015

Erling, E. J., Seargeant, P., Solly, M., Chowdhury, Q. H., & Rahman, S. (2015). *English for economic development: a case study of migrant workers from Bangladesh*. Academic Press.

*Compilation of References*

Esser, I.-M., MacNeil, I., & Chalaczkiewicz-Ladna, K. (2020). Engaging stakeholders in corporate decision-making through strategic reporting: An empirical study of FTSE 100 companies (Part 2). *European Business Law Review, 31*(2), 209–242. http://eprints.gla.ac.uk/177301/

Estatutos da Aula do Comércio. (1759). Série Preta N° 2193/9. Instituto dos Arquivos Nacionais/Torre do Tombo.

Esteva, G. (2020). Alternative paths of transformation. *Globalizations, 17*(2), 225–231. doi:10.1080/14747731.2019.1670959

European Commission. (2014). *Directive of the European Parliament and of the Council of 22 October 2014 amending Directive 2013/34/EU as regards disclosure of non-financial and diversity information by certain large undertakings and groups.* https://eur-lex.europa.eu/legal-content/EN/TXT/PDF/?uri=CELEX:32014L0095&from=EN

European Commission. (2019). *Communication from the Commission Guidelines on non-financial reporting: Supplement on reporting climate-related information (2019/C 209/01).* https://eur-lex.europa.eu/legal-content/EN/TXT/PDF/?uri=CELEX:52019XC0620(01)&from=EN

European Commission. (2021). *Proposal for a Directive of the European Parliament and of the Council amending Directive 2013/34/EU, Directive 2004/109/EC, Directive 2006/43/EC, and Regulation (EU) N. 537/2014, as regards Corporate Sustainability Reporting.* https://eur-lex.europa.eu/legal-content/EN/TXT/PDF/?uri=CELEX:52021PC0189&from=EN

European Parliament (EP). (2015). *Report on women's careers in science and universities, and glass ceiling encountered.*

Evdokimova, M., & Kuzubov, S. (2021). Non-Financial Reporting And The Cost Of Capital In BRICS Countries. *Higher School of Economics Research Paper No. WP BRP, 83.* https://wp.hse.ru/data/2021/06/25/1430000555/83FE2021.pdf

Everitt, J., Neary, S., Delgardo Fuentes, M. A., & Clark, L. (2008, November). *Personal guidance: What works?* London: The Careers & Enterprise Company.

Faas, D., Hajisoteriou, C., & Angelides, P. (2014). Intercultural education in Europe: Policies, practices, and trends. *British Educational Research Journal, 40*(2), 300–318. doi:10.1002/berj.3080

Farjoun, M. (2010). Beyond dualism: Stability and change as a duality. *Academy of Management Review, 35*(2), 202–225.

Fawns, T., Mulherin, T., Hounsell, D., & Aitken, G. (2021). Seamful learning and professional education. *Studies in Continuing Education, 43*(3), 360–376. doi:10.1080/0158037X.2021.1920383

Ferguson, K. J., Wolter, E. M., Yarbrough, D. B., Carline, J. D., & Krupat, E. (2009). Defining and describing medical learning communities: Results of a national survey. *Academic Medicine, 84*(11), 1549–1556. doi:10.1097/ACM.0b013e3181bf5183 PMID:19858814

Ferns, S., Dawson, V., & Howitt, C. (2019). A collaborative framework for enhancing graduate employability. *International Journal of Work - Integrated Learning, 20*(2), 99-111.

Ferrante, L., & Fearnside, P. M. (2020). Protect Indigenous peoples from COVID-19. *Science, 368*(6488), 251–251. doi:10.1126cience.abc0073 PMID:32299940

Ferris, E. (2008). *Natural disasters, human rights, and the role of national human rights institutions.* Brookings. https://www.brookings.edu/on-the-record/natural-disasters-human-rights-and-the-role-of-national-human-rights-institutions/

Festinger, L. (1954). A theory of social comparison processes. *Human Relations, 1*(2), 117–140. doi:10.1177/001872675400700202

Fiksel, J. (2015). *Resilient by design: Creating businesses that adapt and flourish in a changing world.* Island Press.

Fischer, G. (2013). Learning, social creativity, and cultures of participation. In A. Samino & V. Ellis (Eds.), *Learning and collective creativity: Activity-theoretical and sociocultural studies* (pp. 210–227). Taylor & Francis/Routledge.

Foley, D. (2010). The rise of class culture theory in educational anthropology. *Anthropology & Education Quarterly*, *41*(3), 215–227. doi:10.1111/j.1548-1492.2010.01084.x

Folke, C., Carpenter, S., Elmqvist, T., Gunderson, L., Holling, C. S., & Walker, B. (2002). Resilience and sustainable development: Building adaptive capacity in a world of transformations. *Ambio*, *31*(5), 437–440.

Foucault, M. (1990). The history of sexuality: An introduction, volume I. Vintage.

Fraccascia, L., Sabato, A., & Yazan, D. M. (2021). An industrial symbiosis simulation game: Evidence from the circular sustainable business development class. *Journal of Industrial Ecology*, *25*(6), 1688–1706. doi:10.1111/jiec.13183

Francis, J., Nanda, D., & Olsson, P. (2008). Voluntary disclosure, earnings quality, and cost of capital. *Journal of Accounting Research*, *46*(1), 53–99. doi:10.1111/j.1475-679X.2008.00267.x

Fredericksen, E., Pickett, A., Shea, P., Pelz, W., & Swan, K. (2000). Student satisfaction and perceived learning with online courses: Principles and examples from the SUNY learning network. *Journal of Asynchronous Learning Networks*, *4*(2), 1–29.

Freeman, G., & Wash, P. (2013). You can lead students to the classroom, and you can make them think: Ten brain-based strategies for college teaching and learning success. *Journal on Excellence in College Teaching*, *24*(3), 99–120.

French, S., & Niculae, C. (2005). Believe in the model: Mishandle the emergency. *Journal of Homeland Security and Emergency Management*, *2*(1), 24–35. doi:10.2202/1547-7355.1108

Friend, M. (2018). Remarks of a philosopher of mathematics and science. In A. Riegler, K. Muller, & S. Umpleby (Eds.), *New horizons for second-order cybernetics* (Vol. 60, pp. 327–332). World Scientific.

Froman, L. (2010). Positive psychology in the workplace. *Journal of Adult Development*, *17*(2), 59–69.

Furnham, A., Jackson, C. J., & Miller, T. (1999). Personality, learning style and work performance. *Personality and Individual Differences*, *27*(6), 1113–1122. doi:10.1016/S0191-8869(99)00053-7

Furnham, A., Monsen, J., & Ahmetoglu, G. (2009). Typical intellectual engagement, Big Five personality traits, approaches to learning and cognitive ability predictors of academic performance. *The British Journal of Educational Psychology*, *79*(4), 769–782. doi:10.1348/978185409X412147 PMID:19245744

Gaard, G. (1993). Living interconnections with animals and nature. In G. Gaard (Ed.), *Ecofeminism: Women, animals, nature* (pp. 1–12). Temple University Press.

Gaard, G. (2017). *Critical ecofeminism*. Lexington Books.

Gade, C. B. (2012). What is ubuntu? Different interpretations among South Africans of African descent. *South African Journal of Philosophy*, *31*(3), 484–503. doi:10.1080/02580136.2012.10751789

Galanakis, C. M. (2020). The Food Systems in the Era of the Coronavirus (COVID-19) Pandemic Crisis. *Foods*, *9*(4), 523. doi:10.3390/foods9040523 PMID:32331259

Gallastegui, M. C., & Galarraga, I. (2011). Climate change and knowledge communities. In J. Echeverría, A. Alonso, & P. Oiarzabal (Eds.), *Knowledge communities*. Center for Basque Studies, University of Nevada.

Galusha, J. M. (2008). *Barriers to Learning in Distance Education*. Retrieved from http://www.infrastruction.com/barriers.htm

**Compilation of References**

García-Peñalvo, F. J., Corell, A., Abella-García, V., & Grande-de-Prado, M. (2021). Recommendations for Mandatory Online Assessment in Higher Education During the COVID-19 Pandemic. In *Radical Solutions for Education in a Crisis Context* (pp. 85–98). Springer. doi:10.1007/978-981-15-7869-4_6

Gardner, J. (1963). *Self-renewal: The individual and the Innovative society*. Harper and Row.

Garibay, J. C. (2015). *Creating a positive classroom climate for diversity*. UCLA Diversity & Faculty Development.

Garikipati, S., & Kambhampati, U. (2021). Leading the fight against the pandemic: Does gender really matter? *Feminist Economics*, *27*(1-2), 401–418. doi:10.1080/13545701.2021.1874614

Garrison, D. R., & Arbaugh, J. B. (2007). Researching the community of inquiry framework: Review, issues, and future directions. *The Internet and Higher Education*, *10*(3), 157–172. doi:10.1016/j.iheduc.2007.04.001

Garrison, R. (2000). Theoretical challenges for distance education in the 21st century: A shift from structural to transactional issues. *International Review of Research in Open and Distributed Learning*, *1*(1), 1–17. doi:10.19173/irrodl.v1i1.2

Gartzia, L., Ryan, M. K., Balluerka, N., & Aritzeta, A. (2012). Think crisis–think female: Further evidence. *European Journal of Work and Organizational Psychology*, *21*(4), 603–628. doi:10.1080/1359432X.2011.591572

Gasman, M., & Nguyen, T. H. (2015). Myths dispelled: A historical account of diversity and inclusion at HBCUs. *New Directions for Higher Education*, *2015*(170), 5–15. doi:10.1002/he.20128

Gay, G. (1990). Achieving educational equality through curriculum desegregation. *Phi Delta Kappan*, *72*, 56–62.

Gay, G. (2000). *Culturally responsive teaching*. Teachers College Press.

Gay, G. (2004). Beyond Brown: Promoting equality through multicultural education. *Journal of Curriculum and Supervision*, *19*(3), 193–216.

Gay, G., & Howard, T. C. (2000). Multicultural teacher education for the 21st century. *Teacher Educator*, *36*(1), 1–16. doi:10.1080/08878730009555246

GED. (2020). Making Vision 2041 A Reality: Perspective Plan of Bangladesh 2021-2041. GED.

Gee, J. P. (2004). *An introduction to discourse analysis: Theory and method*. Routledge. doi:10.4324/9780203005675

Gee, J. P. (2008). A sociocultural perspective on opportunity to learn. In P. A. Moss, D. C. Pullin, J. P. Gee, E. H. Haertel, & L. J. Young (Eds.), *Assessment, equity, and opportunity to learn* (pp. 76–108). Cambridge University Press. doi:10.1017/CBO9780511802157.006

Geiger, O. G., & Bostow, D. E. (1976). Contingency-managed college instruction: Effects of weekly quizzes on performance on examination. *Psychological Reports*, *39*(3), 707–710. doi:10.2466/pr0.1976.39.3.707

Gerstenhaber, J. A., & Har-El, Y. E. (2021). Virtual biomaterials lab during COVID-19 pandemic. *Biomedical Engineering Education*, *1*(2), 353-358.

Ghuman, U., & Olmstead, W. (2015). Utilizing flux and chaos: A case study of wicked problems in environmental management. *International Journal of Organization Theory and Behavior*, *18*(4), 379–404. https://doi.org/10.1108/IJOTB-18-04-2015-B001

Giannini, G. (1999). 'Drop-in' sessions: Information literacy responding to student needs. *Australian Academic and Research Libraries*, *30*(3), 212–218. doi:10.1080/00048623.1999.10755094

Giezen, M. (2012). Keeping it simple? A case study into the advantages and disadvantages of reducing complexity in mega project planning. *International Journal of Project Management*, *30*(7), 781–790.

Gigliotti, R. A. (2019). *Crisis leadership in higher education: Theory and practice*. Rutgers University Press.

Gill, S. S., Naeem, U., Fuller, S. Chen, Y., & Uhlig, S. (2022a). How Covid-19 Changed Computer Science Education. *ITNOW*, *64*(2), 60–61.

Gill, S. S., Fuller, S., Cabral, A., Chen, Y., & Uhlig, S. (2023a). An Operating System Session Plan Towards Social Justice and Intercultural Development in Microteaching for Higher Education. In E. Meletiadou (Ed.), *Handbook of Research on Fostering Social Justice Through Intercultural and Multilingual Communication* (pp. 1–15). IGI Global.

Gill, S. S., Fuller, S., Cabral, A., Chen, Y., & Uhlig, S. (2023b). Curriculum Redesign for Cloud Computing to Enhance Social Justice and Intercultural Development in Higher Education. In E. Meletiadou (Ed.), *Handbook of Research on Fostering Social Justice Through Intercultural and Multilingual Communication* (pp. 44–61). IGI Global.

Gill, S. S., Thibodeau, D., Kaur, R., Naeem, U., & Stockman, T. (2023c). Reflection on Teaching Observation for Computer Science and Engineering to Design Effective Teaching Resources in Transnational Higher Education. In G. R. Morris & L. Li (Eds.), *Handbook of Research on Developments and Future Trends in Transnational Higher Education* (pp. 62–80). IGI Global.

Gill, S. S., Xu, M., Ottaviani, C., Patros, P., Bahsoon, R., Shaghaghi, A., & Uhlig, S. (2022b). AI for next generation computing: Emerging trends and future directions. *Internet of Things*, *19*, 100514. doi:10.1016/j.iot.2022.100514

Ginzburg, S. B., Santen, S. A., & Schwartzstein, R. M. (2020). Self-directed learning: A new look at an old concept. *Medical Science Educator*, *31*(1), 229–331. doi:10.100740670-020-01121-w PMID:34457877

Given, L. M. (2008). *The SAGE Encyclopedia of Qualitative Research Methods*. SAGE Publications. doi:10.4135/9781412963909

Glass, C., & Cook, A. (2016). Leading at the top: Understanding women's challenges above the glass ceiling. *The Leadership Quarterly*, *27*(1), 51–63. doi:10.1016/j.leaqua.2015.09.003

Glassdoor. (2022, October 9). *How much does a Lecturer make in Bangladesh?* https://www.glassdoor.com/Salaries/bangladesh-lecturer-salary SRCH_IL.0,10_IN27_KO11,19.htm

Glassman, M. (2020). The internet as a context for participatory action research. *Education and Information Technologies*, *25*(3), 1891–191. doi:10.100710639-019-10033-1

Glauber, J., Laborde, D., Martin, W., & Vos, R. (2020). COVID-19: Trade restrictions are worst possible response to safeguard food security. International Food Policy Research Institute.

Goddard, J. (2009). *Reinventing the Civic University*. NESTA. Retrieved January 22, 2022, from https://www.nesta.org.uk/report/re-inventing-thecivic-university

Goi, C. L. (2019). The use of business simulation games in teaching and learning. *Journal of Education for Business*, *94*(5), 342–349. doi:10.1080/08832323.2018.1536028

Gokbulut, B. (2020). The effect of Mentimeter and Kahoot applications on university students'-learning. World Journal on Educational Technology. *Current Issues*, *12*(2), 107–116.

Gondwe, S. S. (2020). Archival education and training opportunities in Malawi: After 50 years, why have we not done well? In S. Keakopa & T. Mosweu (Eds.), *Cases on electronic record management in the ESARBICA region* (pp. 277–297). IGI Global. doi:10.4018/978-1-7998-2527-2.ch015

*Compilation of References*

González-Howard, M., & McNeill, K. L. (2016). Learning in a community of practice: Factors impacting English-learning students' engagement in scientific argumentation. *Journal of Research in Science Teaching*, *53*(4), 527–553. doi:10.1002/tea.21310

Goodall, J. (2020). *Every day you live, you impact the planet*. Ted Talk. https://www.ted.com/talks/jane_goodall_every_day_you_live_you_impact_the_planet#t-3393

Good, G. E., & Sherrod, N. (2001). The psychology of men and masculinity: Research status and future directions. In R. Unger (Ed.), *Handbook of the Psychology of Women and Gender* (pp. 201–214). Wiley.

Goosen, L. (2015). Educational Technologies for Growing Innovative e-Schools in the 21st Century: A Community Engagement Project. In D. Nwaozuzu, & S. Mnisi (Ed.), *Proceedings of the South Africa International Conference on Educational Technologies* (pp. 49 - 61). Pretoria: African Academic Research Forum.

Goosen, L. (2018a). Sustainable and Inclusive Quality Education Through Research Informed Practice on Information and Communication Technologies in Education. In L. Webb (Ed.), *Proceedings of the 26th Conference of the Southern African Association for Research in Mathematics, Science and Technology Education (SAARMSTE)* (pp. 215 - 228). Gabarone: University of Botswana.

Goosen, L., & Mukasa-Lwanga, T. (2017). Educational Technologies in Distance Education: Beyond the Horizon with Qualitative Perspectives. In U. I. Ogbonnaya, & S. Simelane-Mnisi (Ed.), *Proceedings of the South Africa International Conference on Educational Technologies* (pp. 41 - 54). Pretoria: African Academic Research Forum.

Goosen, L., & Van der Merwe, R. (2015). e-Learners, Teachers and Managers at e-Schools in South Africa. In C. Watson (Ed.), *Proceedings of the 10th International Conference on e-Learning (ICEL)* (pp. 127 - 134). Nassau: Academic Conferences and Publishing International.

Goosen, L. (2004). *Criteria and Guidelines for the Selection and Implementation of a First Programming Language in High Schools*. Potchefstroom Campus: North West University. Retrieved from http://hdl.handle.net/10394/226

Goosen, L. (2018b). Trans-Disciplinary Approaches to Action Research for e-Schools, Community Engagement, and ICT4D. In T. A. Mapotse (Ed.), *Cross-Disciplinary Approaches to Action Research and Action Learning* (pp. 97–110). IGI Global. doi:10.4018/978-1-5225-2642-1.ch006

Goosen, L. (2018c). Ethical Data Management and Research Integrity in the Context of e-Schools and Community Engagement. In C. Sibinga (Ed.), *Ensuring Research Integrity and the Ethical Management of Data* (pp. 14–45). IGI Global. doi:10.4018/978-1-5225-2730-5.ch002

Goosen, L. (2018d). Ethical Information and Communication Technologies for Development Solutions: Research Integrity for Massive Open Online Courses. In C. Sibinga (Ed.), *Ensuring Research Integrity and the Ethical Management of Data* (pp. 155–173). IGI Global. doi:10.4018/978-1-5225-2730-5.ch009

Gordy, L. L., & Pritchard, A. M. (1995). Redirecting our voyage through history: A content analysis of social studies textbooks. *Urban Education*, *30*(2), 195–218. doi:10.1177/0042085995030002005

Gorham, E. (2001). *Multicultural teaching competence as perceived by elementary school teachers* (Order No. 3106783). Available from ProQuest Dissertations & Theses Global. (304729078). Retrieved from https://www.proquest.com/dissertations-theses/multicultural-teaching-competence-as-perceived/docview/304729078/se-2

Gorski, P. C. (1999). *A brief history of multicultural education*. Available online also at: http://www.edchange.org/multicultural/papers/edchange_history.html

Gosine, K. (2021). Reconciling divergent realms in the lives of marginalized students. In *Visual and Cultural Identity Constructs of Global Youth and Young Adults* (pp. 78–95). Routledge. doi:10.4324/9781003055822-6

Gouldner, A. W. (1960). The norm of reciprocity: A preliminary statement. *American Sociological Review*, *25*(2), 161–178. doi:10.2307/2092623

Gouthro, P., Taber, N., & Brazil, A. (2018). Universities as inclusive learning organizations for women? *The Learning Organization*, *25*(1), 29–39. doi:10.1108/TLO-05-2017-0049

Grant, C. A., & Khurshid, A. (2009). Multicultural education in a global context: Addressing the varied perspectives and themes. In R. Cowen & A. M. Kazamias (Eds.), *Second international handbook of comparative education* (pp. 403–416). Springer. doi:10.1007/978-1-4020-6403-6_26

Grasha, A. (1996). *Teaching with style*. Alliance.

Grober, U. (2007). *Deep roots-A conceptual history of sustainable development*. Academic Press.

Grudowski, P., & Szczepańska, K. (2021). Quality Gaps in Higher Education from the Perspective of Students. *Foundations of Management*, *13*(1), 35–48. doi:10.2478/fman-2021-0003

Guenot, M. (2021, May 13). *In a report suppressed under Trump, the EPA has said for the first time that humans caused the climate crisis*. Business Insider. https://www.businessinsider.com/epa-climate-crisis-man-made-report-suppressed-trump-2021-5?op=1

Guglielmino, L. M. (2013). The case for promoting self-directed learning in formal educational institutions. *SA-. Education Journal*, *10*(2), 1–18.

Guglielmino, L. M., & Long, H. B. (2011). Perspectives: The international society for self-directed learning and the international self-directed learning symposium. *International Journal of Self-Directed Learning*, *8*(1), 1–6.

Guimon, J., & Narula, R. (2020, April 22) A happy exception: The pandemic is driving global scientific collaboration. *Issues in Science and Technology*. https://ingsa.org/covidtag/covid-19-commentary/guimon-collaboration/

Gunawan, G., Harjono, A., Sahidu, H., & Herayanti, L. (2017). Virtual laboratory to improve students' problem-solving skills on electricity concept. *Journal Pendidikan IPA Indonesia*, *6*(2), 257–264. doi:10.15294/jpii.v6i2.9481

Gundara, J. S. (2015). *The case of international education in a multicultural world*. Mosaic Press.

Gupta, R., & Pal, S. K. (2020). Trend Analysis and Forecasting of COVID-19 outbreak in India. medRxiv.

Gurin, P. (1999). *The compelling need for diversity in education*. Expert report. http://www.umich.edu/~urel/admissions/legal/expert/gurintoc.html

Gurin, P., Dey, E., Hurtado, S., & Gurin, G. (2002). Diversity and Higher Education: Theory and Impact on Educational Outcomes. *Harvard Educational Review*, *72*(3), 330–367. doi:10.17763/haer.72.3.01151786u134n051

Guri-Rosenblit, S., & Gros, B. (2011). E-learning: Confusing terminology, research gaps and inherent challenges. *International Journal of E-Learning & Distance Education/Revue internationale du e-learning et la formation à distance*, *25*(1). Retrieved from https://www.ijede.ca/index.php/jde/article/view/729

Gusmão Caiado, R. G., Leal Filho, W., Quelhas, O. L. G., Luiz de Mattos Nascimento, D., & Ávila, L. V. (2018). A literature-based review on potentials and constraints in the implementation of the sustainable development goals. *Journal of Cleaner Production*, *198*, 1276–1288. doi:10.1016/j.jclepro.2018.07.102

Gustafsson, J. (2017). *Single case studies vs. multiple case studies: A comparative study*. Academic Press.

## Compilation of References

Haddock-Fraser, J., Rands, P., & Scoffham, S. (2018). *Leadership for sustainability in higher education.* Bloomsbury Publishing.

Hager, P., Sleet, R., & Kaye, M. (1994). The relation between critical thinking abilities and student study strategies. *Higher Education Research & Development, 13*(2), 179–188. doi:10.1080/0729436940130208

Hall, J. (2018, November 3). Rewriting disciplines, rewriting boundaries: Transdisciplinary and translingual challenges for WAC/WID. *Across the Disciplines, 15*(3), 1-10. http://wac.colostate.edu/atd/trans_wac/intro.pdf

Halpern, M. (2021). Scientific integrity and advocacy: keeping the government honest. In P. DellaSala (Ed.), *Conservation Science and Advocacy for a Planet in Peril* (pp. 149–175). Elsevier. doi:10.1016/B978-0-12-812988-3.00003-X

Hammarberg, K., Kirkman, M., & Lacey, S. (2016). Qualitative research methods: When to use them and how to judge them. *Human Reproduction (Oxford, England), 31*(3), 498–501. doi:10.1093/humrep/dev334 PMID:26759142

Hamouche, S. (2021). Human resource management and the COVID-19 crisis: Implications, challenges, opportunities, and future organizational directions. *Journal of Management & Organization, 1*, 1–16. doi:10.1017/jmo.2021.15

Hanna, W. (2007). The new Bloom's taxonomy: Implications for music education. *Arts Education Policy Review, 108*(4), 7–16. doi:10.3200/AEPR.108.4.7-16

Haque, M. W., & Ghani, N. A. (2020). Economic aspects of quality of life of Bangladeshi construction workers in Malaysia. *Journal of Asian Development, 6*(1), 30–38. doi:10.5296/jad.v6i1.16725

Harney, B., & Collings, D. G. (2021). Navigating the shifting landscapes of HRM. *Human Resource Management Journal.* Advance online publication. doi:10.1111/1748-8583.12343

Harper, A. B. (2010). Social justice beliefs and addiction to uncompassionate consumption. In A. B. Harper (Ed.), *Sistah vegan: Black female vegans speak on food, identity, health and society* (pp. 20–41). Lantern Books.

Harper, A. B. (2012). Going beyond the normative white 'post-racial' gegan epistemology. In P. Williams-Forson & C. Counihan (Eds.), *Taking Food Public: Redefining Foodways in a Changing World* (pp. 155–174). Routledge.

Harring, R. D. (1992). Biracial children: An increasing concern for elementary and middle school counselors. *Elementary School Guidance & Counselling,* 123-130.

Harvey, D. (2000). Reinventing geography. *New Left Review, 4*, 75.

Hasan, M. M. (2020). *Mining Conflict, Indigenous Peoples and Environmental Justice: The Case of Phulbari Coal Project in Bangladesh* [PhD Thesis]. https://www.ilo.org/wcmsp5/groups/public/---ed_norm/ normes/documents/publication/wcms_205225.pdf https://www.un.org/development/desa/indigenouspeoples/declaration-on-the-rights-of-indigenous-peoples.html

Haski-Leventhal, D. (2020). *The purpose-driven university: Transforming lives and creating impact through academic social responsibility.* Emerald Group Publishing.

Hassan, S., & Jiang, Z. (2021). Facilitating learning to improve performance of law enforcement workgroups: The role of inclusive leadership behaviour. *International Public Management Journal, 24*(1), 106–130. doi:10.1080/10967494.2019.1680465

Hawick, L., Cleland, J., & Kitto, S. (2017). Getting off the carousel: Exploring the wicked problem of curriculum reform. *Perspectives on Medical Education, 6*(5), 337–343.

Hays, J. (2012). *Wicked problem: Educating for complexity and wisdom* [Paper presentation]. The Wise Management in Organisational Complexity Conference, Shanghai, China.

Hays, J. (2015b). *Privilege, proviso, and paradox: Leadership in—and for—a changing world*. Available at: https://www.researchgate.net/publication/323424440_Privilege_Proviso_and_Paradox_Leadership_in-and_for-a_Changing_World

Hays, J. M. (2010). Mapping wisdom as a complex adaptive system. *Management & Marketing, 5*(2).

Hays, J. M. (2010). The ecology of wisdom. *Management & Marketing, 5*(1).

Hays, J. (2008). Dynamics of organisational wisdom. *The Business Renaissance Quarterly, 2*(4), 77–122.

Hays, J. (2013a). The team learning pyramid. *Journal of Leadership, Management & Organization Studies, 3*(1), 1–19.

Hays, J. (2013b). Wicked problem: educating for complexity and wisdom. In M. Thompson & D. Bevan (Eds.), *Wise management in organisational complexity* (pp. 134–150). Palgrave Macmillan.

Hays, J. (2015a). *Chaos to capability: Educating professionals for the 21st century*. Unitec Press.

Hays, J. (2015c). *Citizenship, democracy, and professionalism for a sustainable future* [paper presentation]. *The Unitec Community Development Conference*, Auckland, New Zealand.

Hays, J. (2017). A wise course: educating for wisdom in the 21st century. In W. Küpers & O. Gunnlaugson (Eds.), *Wisdom learning: Perspectives on wising-up business and management education* (pp. 185–210). Routledge.

Hays, J., & Reinders, H. (2018). Critical learnership: A new perspective on learning. *International Journal of Learning. Teaching and Educational Research, 17*(1), 1–25.

Hays, J., & Reinders, H. (2020). Sustainable learning and education: A curriculum for the future. *International Review of Education, 66*(1), 29–52. doi:10.100711159-020-09820-7

Hays, J., & Reinders, H. (2021). Viability of the sustainable development ecosystem. In M. Khosrow-Pour (Ed.), *Encyclopedia of organizational knowledge, administration, and technologies* (pp. 812–830). IGI.

Haywood-Farmer, J. (1988). A conceptual model of service quality. *International Journal of Operations & Production Management, 8*(6), 19–29. doi:10.1108/eb054839

Hazy, J., & Silberstang, J. (2009). Leadership within emergent events in complex systems: Micro-enactments and the mechanisms of organisational learning and change. *International Journal of Learning and Change, 3*(3), 230–247.

HEA. (2015). *Framework for student engagement through partnership*. Available: https://www.heacademy.ac.uk/sites/default/files/downloads/studentenagagement-through-partnership-new.pdf

Healey, G. W. (1974). *Self-concept: a comparison of Negro-, Anglo-, and Spanish-American students across ethnic, sex, and socioeconomic variables*. R & E Research Associates.

Heatherton, T. F., & Wyland, C. L. (2003). Assessing self-esteem. In S. J. Lopez & C. R. Snyder (Eds.), *Positive psychological assessment: A handbook of models and measures* (pp. 219–233). American Psychological Association. doi:10.1037/10612-014

Heffes, E. M. (2008). FASB chairman advocates 'improving and adopting' IFRS for U.S. companies. *Financial Executive, 24*(7). https://link.gale.com/apps/doc/A185460066/AONE?u=anon~976de3b9&sid=googleScholar&xid=32f32333

Heinberg, R. (2015). *Afterburn: Society beyond fossil fuels*. New Society Publishers.

Hernández-Lara, A., & Serradell-López, E. (2018). Student interactions in online discussion forums: Their perception on learning with business simulation games. *Behaviour & Information Technology, 37*(4), 419–429. doi:10.1080/0144929X.2018.1441326

*Compilation of References*

Hiemstra, R. (2013). Facilitating adult self-directed learning. In R. Hiemstra (Ed.), *A fest of learning: international perspectives on adult learning and change* (pp. 25–46). Information Age Publishing, INC.

Higher Technical and Vocational Education in China. (2019, June 20). *Annual Conference of China Higher Vocational Education Quality Report in Beijing 2019*. https://www.tech.net.cn/news/show-66627.html

Hill, l. M., Peters, M., Salvaggio, M., Vinnedge, J., & Darden, A. (2020). Implementation and evaluation of a self-directed learning activity for first-year medical students. *Medical Education Online, 25*(1), 1717780.

Hilsdon, A. M. (2007). Introduction: Reconsidering Agency—Feminist Anthropologies in Asia. *The Australian Journal of Anthropology, 18*(2), 127–137. doi:10.1111/j.1835-9310.2007.tb00084.x

Hodge, E., Bossé, M. J., Faulconer, J., & Fewell, M. (2006). Mimicking proximity: The role of distance education in forming communities of learning. *International Journal of Instructional Technology and Distance Learning, 3*(12), 3–12.

Hoegl, M., & Parboteeah, K. P. (2007). Creativity in innovative projects: How teamwork matters. *Journal of Engineering and Technology Management, 24*(1-2), 148–166. doi:10.1016/j.jengtecman.2007.01.008

Hoepfl, M. C. (1997). Choosing qualitative research: A primer for technology education researchers. *Journal of Technology Education, 9*(1), 47–63. doi:10.21061/jte.v9i1.a.4

Holden, L. M. (2005). Complex adaptive systems: Concept analysis. *Journal of Advanced Nursing, 52*(6), 651–657.

Hollander, E. (2009). *Inclusive leadership: The essential leader-follower relationship*. Routledge.

Holtzman, D. M., & Kraft, E. M. (2011). A comparison of qualitative feedback from alumni and employers with a national study for assessment of business curricula. *American Institute of Higher Education 6th International Conference Proceedings, 4*, 173-179.

Ho, M. H., Fido, D., & Simonovic, B. (2021). An investigation of the Learning Motivation of Student Studying Accounting Courses in China. *International Journal of Learning and Teaching, 7*(3), 219–225. doi:10.18178/ijlt.7.3.219-225

Homanová, Z., & Havlásková, T. (2019). H5P interactive didactic tools in education. *11th International Conference on Education and New Learning Technologies*, 1-6.

Honey, P., & Mumford, A. (1992). *The manual of learning styles*. Academic Press.

hooks, b. (1991). Theory as liberatory practice. *Yale JL & Feminism, 4*, 1

Horm, D. M. (2003). Preparing early childhood educators to work in diverse urban settings. *Teachers College Record, 105*(2), 226–244. doi:10.1111/1467-9620.00237

Hosen, S. (2020). What is the Driving Force of Globalization? *International Journal of Publication and Social Studies, 5*(2), 90–100. doi:10.18488/journal.135.2020.52.90.100

Hosen, S., Islam, M. S., & Alam, M. M. (2019). Challaenges of Implementation of the SDG 16 for Ensuring Better Oublic Service in Bangladesh. In P. D. Alam, D. M. Alam, & D. D. Begum (Ed.), *1st International Conference on Information and Knowledge Management* (p. 166). EWU and BPATC.

Hossain, N. A. (2021, December 17). *The pandora's box in Bangladesh's labour market*. https://whiteboardmagazine.com/2700/the-pandoras-box-in-bangladeshs-labour-market/

Hossain, J. (2014). Quality Control on Higher Education System in Bangladesh. *South American Journal of Academic Research, 1*(2), 156–162.

Hossain, M. B. (2017). Factors Affecting Higher Education Quality in Bangladesh: An Attempt to Improve Higher Education Quality in Bangladesh through HEQEP. *International Journal of Science and Business*, *1*(1), 47–59.

Hossain, M. I. (2020). Impacts of social remittances on economic activities: Labour migration from a village of Bangladesh to Malaysia. *Migration and Development*, 1–18.

Hossain, M. K., & Jahan, N. (2021). Teaching-learning environment of private educational institute:A case study on Ispahani Public School and College, Chittagong,Bangladesh. *Journal of Business. Management and Social Research*, *11*(1), 585–594. doi:10.18801/ijbmsr.110121.62

Howard, J. L., Bureau, J., Guay, F., Chong, J., & Ryan, R. (2021). Student Motivation and Associated Outcomes: A meta-Analysis from Self-Determination Theory. *Perspectives on Psychological Science*, *16*(6), 1300–1323. doi:10.1177/1745691620966789 PMID:33593153

Huang, X., Cao, J., Zhao, G., Long, Z., Han, G., & Cai, X. (2022a). The employability and career development of finance and trade college graduates. *Frontiers in Psychology*, *12*, 719336. doi:10.3389/fpsyg.2021.719336 PMID:35082712

Huang, Y. M., Silitonga, L. M., & Wu, T. T. (2022b). Applying a business simulation game in a flipped classroom to enhance engagement, learning achievement, and higher-order thinking skills. *Computers & Education*, *183*, 104494. doi:10.1016/j.compedu.2022.104494

Hubbard, K. (2021). Using Data-Driven Approaches to Address Systematic Awarding Gaps. In *Doing Equity and Diversity for Success in Higher Education* (pp. 215–226). Palgrave Macmillan. doi:10.1007/978-3-030-65668-3_16

Hue, M. T. (2011). Developing resiliency in students with behavioral problems in Hong Kong secondary schools: Teachers' narratives from a school guidance perspective. *Pastoral Care in Education*, *29*(4), 261–272. doi:10.1080/02643944.2011.626067

Hue, M. T., & Kennedy, K. J. (2012). Creation of culturally responsive classrooms: Teachers' conceptualization of a new rationale for cultural responsiveness and management of diversity in Hong Kong secondary schools. *Intercultural Education*, *23*(2), 119–132. doi:10.1080/14675986.2012.686021

Huggan, G., & Tiffin, H. (2015). *Postcolonial ecocriticism: Literature, animals, environment* (2nd ed.). Routledge. doi:10.4324/9781315768342

Hughes, M., Salamonson, Y., & Metcalfe, L. (2020). Student engagement using multiple-attempt 'Weekly Participation Task' quizzes with undergraduate nursing students. *Nurse Education in Practice*, *46*, 22–36. doi:10.1016/j.nepr.2020.102803 PMID:32526682

Hutchins, H. M., & Wang, J. (2008). Organizational crisis management and human resource development: A review of the literature and implications to HRD research and practice. *Advances in Developing Human Resources*, *10*(3), 310–330. doi:10.1177/1523422308316183

IFRS Foundation. (2020). *Effects of climate-related matters on financial statements*. https://www.ifrs.org/content/dam/ifrs/supporting-implementation/documents/effects-of-climate-related-matters-on-financial-statements.pdf

IFRS Foundation. (2021, November 3). *Global sustainability disclosure standards for the financial markets*. https://www.ifrs.org/news-and-events/news/2021/11/global-sustainability-disclosure-standards-for-the-financial-markets/

Ilgaz, H., & Gulbahar, Y. (2017). *Why Do Learners Choose Online Learning: The Learners' Voices*. International Association for Development of the Information Society.

Inal, S., & Turhanli, I. (2019). Teachers' opinions on the use of L1 in EFL classes. *Journal of Language and Linguistic Studies*, *15*(3), 861–875. doi:10.17263/jlls.631526

*Compilation of References*

Inigo, E. A., & Albareda, L. (2016). Understanding sustainable innovation as a complex adaptive system: A systemic approach to the firm. *Journal of Cleaner Production*, *126*, 1–20.

Institute for Development Studies. (2022). *About participatory methods*. Retrieved February 11, 2022, from https://www.participatorymethods.org/page/about-participatory-methods

Institute of Student Employers (ISE). (2022). *ISE Development Survey*. https://ise.org.uk/page/ise-development-survey-22

International Science Council. (2013). *UN announces list of countries for Working Group on Sustainable Development Goals*. Retrieved June 14, 2022, from https://council.science/current/news/un-announces-list-of-countries-for-working-group-on-sustainable-development-goals/

Intra-agency Network of Education in Emergencies (INEE). (2022). *Participatory learning*. Retrieved August 11, 2022, from https://inee.org/eie-glossary/participatory-learning

Ippolito, K. (2007). Promoting intercultural learning in a multicultural university: Ideals and realities. *Teaching in Higher Education*, *12*(5–6), 749–763. doi:10.1080/13562510701596356

Irawan, A. W., Dwisona, D., & Lestari, M. (2020). Psychological Impacts of Students on Online Learning During the Pandemic COVID-19. *KONSELI: Jurnal Bimbingan dan Konseling (E-Journal)*, *7*(1), 53-60.

Isaias, P., & Issa, T. (2014). Promoting communication skills for information systems students in Australian and Portuguese higher education: Action research study. *Education and Information Technologies*, *19*(4), 841–861. doi:10.100710639-013-9257-9

Islam, M. G., Ali, M. N., Islam, I., & Islam, M. Z. (2017). Quality Assurance and Accreditation Mechanisms of Higher Education Institutions: Policy Issues and Challenges in Bangladesh. *European Journal of Education Studies*, *3*(5), 278–304. doi:10.5281/zenodo.495792

Islam, S. (2017). Contribution of HEQEP in Ensuring Quality Education at Higher Level in Bangladesh: A Political Economy Perspective. In *International Integrative Research Conference on Education, Governance and Development*. OSDER Publications.

Islam, S., Uddin, T. M., Nandy, N., & Hosen, S. (2019). Quality Education at Tertiary Level in Bangladesh for Achieving Development Junction. *NAEM Journal*, *14*(28), 9–21.

Jackson, D., & Tomlinson, M. (2020). Investigating the relationship between career planning, proactivity and employability perceptions among higher education students in uncertain labour market conditions. *Higher Education*, *80*(3), 435–455. doi:10.100710734-019-00490-5

Jackson, D., & Tomlinson, M. (2022). The relative importance of work experience, extra-curricular and university-based activities on student employability. *Higher Education Research & Development*, *41*(4), 1119–1135. doi:10.1080/07294360.2021.1901663

Jahan, F. (2020). *The issue of identity: state denial, local controversies and everyday resistance among the Santal in Bangladesh* [PhD Thesis]. Hale University.

Jamil, R., & Dutta, U. (2021). Centering the Margins: The precarity of Bangladeshi low-income migrant workers during the time of COVID-19. *The American Behavioral Scientist*, *65*(10), 1384–1405. doi:10.1177/00027642211000397

Jan, S. K., & Vlachopoulos, P. (2018). Infuence of learning design of the formation of online communities of learning. *International Review of Research in Open and Distributed Learning*. . doi:10.19173/irrodl.v19i4.3620

Janoff-Bulman, R. (2010). *Shattered assumptions*. Simon and Schuster.

Jeje, Y. (2006). *Southern Alberta Landscapes: Meeting the Challenges Ahead: Export Coefficients for Total Phosphorus, Total Nitrogen and Total Suspended Solids in the Southern Alberta Region: a Review of Literature.* Alberta Environment.

Jenkins, H. (2012). *Play (Participatory learning and YOU!).* Retrieved February 11, 2022, from http://henryjenkins.org/blog/2012/12/play-participatory-learning-and-you.html

Jiang, Z., Hu, X., Wang, Z., & Jiang, X. (2019). Knowledge hiding as a barrier to thriving: The mediating role of psychological safety and moderating role of organizational cynicism. *Journal of Organizational Behavior, 40*(7), 800–818. doi:10.1002/job.2358

Jia, S., Li, Y., & Fang, T. (2022). System dynamics analysis of COVID-19 prevention and control strategies. *Environmental Science and Pollution Research International, 29*(3), 3944–3957.

Jiménez-Aleixandre, M. P. (2014). Determinism and underdetermination in genetics: Implications for students' engagement in argumentation and epistemic practices. *Science & Education, 23*(2), 465–484. doi:10.100711191-012-9561-6

Jin, L., & Cortazzi, M. (2011). Re-evaluating traditional approaches to second language teaching and learning. In E. Hinkel (Ed.), *Handbook of research in second language teaching and learning* (Vol. 2, pp. 558–575). Routledge.

Junco, R. (2012). The relationship between frequency of Facebook use, participation in Facebook activities, and student engagement. *Computers & Education, 58*(1), 162–171. doi:10.1016/j.compedu.2011.08.004

Kann, D. (2021, Jan. 18). "The lost years": Climate damage that occurred on Trump's watch will endure long after he is gone. *CNN.* Retrieved from https://www.cnn.com/2021/01/18/politics/trump-climate-legacy-bidens-challenge/index.html

Kantur, D., & İşeri-Say, A. (2012). Organizational resilience: A conceptual integrative framework. *Journal of Management & Organization, 18*(6), 762–773.

Kapilan, N., Vidhya, P., & Gao, X. Z. (2021). Virtual laboratory: A boon to the mechanical engineering education during covid-19 pandemic. *Higher Education for the Future, 8*(1), 31–46. doi:10.1177/2347631120970757

Kaplan, H. S., Trumble, B. C., Stieglitz, J., Mamany, R. M., Cayuba, M. G., Moye, L. M., ... Thompson, R. C. (2020). Voluntary collective isolation as a best response to COVID-19 for indigenous populations? A case study and protocol from the Bolivian Amazon. *Lancet, 395*(10238), 1727–1734. doi:10.1016/S0140-6736(20)31104-1 PMID:32422124

Karakiewicz, J. (2016). Interventions in complex urban systems: how to Eenable modeling to account for disruptive innovation. In Understanding complex urban systems (pp. 113-127). Springer.

Karatas, K., & Arpaci, I. (2021). The role of self-directed learning, metacognition, and 21st century skills predicting the readiness for online learning. *Contemporary Educational Technology, 13*(3), ep300. doi:10.30935/cedtech/10786

Kareem, J. (2016). The influence of leadership in building a learning organization. *IUP Journal of Organizational Behaviour, 15*(1), 7–18.

Karim, A. H. M. (2015). Zehadul, and Nurazzura Mohamad Diah. "Health seeking behavior of the Bangladeshi migrant Workers in Malaysia: Some suggestive recommendations in Adjustive context. *Asian Social Science, 11*(10), 348.

Karim, A. T., & Fair, C. C. (2007). Bangladesh at the crossroads: A more stable future in sight? *Strategic Comments, 7*(3), 1–2.

Karim, A. Z., Diah, N. M., Mustari, S., & Sarker, M. S. I. (2015). Bangladeshi Migrant Workers in Malaysia: Their Socio-Cultural Background and Work-Adaptability. *South Asian Anthropologist, 15*(1), 1–7.

Karim, & Rohaiza, & Basir. (2017). Roles and Social Adaptability of Bangladeshi Migrant Workers in Commercialized Farming of Cameron Highlands, Malaysia. *European Journal of Soil Science, 55*(3), 375–361.

*Compilation of References*

Kashefi, H., Ismail, Z., & Yusof, Y. M. (2012). The impact of blended learning on communication skills and teamwork of engineering students in multivariable calculus. *Procedia: Social and Behavioral Sciences, 56*, 341–347. doi:10.1016/j.sbspro.2012.09.662

Kaufman, H. (2015). A review of predictive factors of student success in and satisfaction with online learning. *Research in Learning Technology, 23*. Advance online publication. doi:10.3402/rlt.v23.26507

Kaymakamoglu, S., & Yıltanlılar, A. (2019). Non-native English teachers' perceptions about using Turkish (L1) in EFL classrooms: A case study. *International Online Journal of Education & Teaching, 6*(2), 327–337. https://iojet.org/index.php/IOJET/article/view/614

Kayumova, S., & Tippins, D. J. (2021). The quest for sustainable futures: Designing transformative learning spaces with multilingual black, brown, and Latinx young people through critical response-ability. *Cultural Studies of Science Education, 16*(3), 821–839. doi:10.100711422-021-10030-2 PMID:34484464

Kazakov, R., Howick, S., & Morton, A. (2021). Managing complex adaptive systems: A resource/agent qualitative modelling perspective. *European Journal of Operational Research, 290*(1), 386–400.

Keengwe, J., & Kidd, T. T. (2010). Towards best practices in online learning and teaching in higher education. *Journal of Online Learning and Teaching, 6*(2), 533–541.

Kefela, G. T. (2010). Knowledge-based economy and society has become a vital commodity to countries. *International NGO Journal, 5*(7), 160–166.

Kelly, G. J. (2007). Discourse in science classrooms. In S. K. Abell & N. G. Lederman (Eds.), *Handbook of research on science education* (pp. 443–469). Lawrence Erlbaum.

Kemmis, S., & McTaggart, R. (1988). *The action research planner*. Deakin University.

Kemp, K., Baxa, D., & Cortes, C. (2022). Exploration of a collaborative self-directed learning model in Medical Education. *Medical Science Educator, 32*(1), 195–207. doi:10.100740670-021-01493-7 PMID:35003877

Kennedy, K. J., & Hue, M. T. (2011). Researching ethnic minority students in a Chinese context: Mixed methods design for cross cultural understandings. *Comparative Education, 47*(3), 343–354. doi:10.1080/03050068.2011.586766

Kerr, P. (2019). *The use of L1 in English language teachingPart of the Cambridge Papers in ELT series*. Cambridge University Press. Retrieved from cambridge.org/cambridge-papers-elt

Kettleborough, H. (2019). Gaia's graveyards: Bearing witness as first-person inquiry. *Action Research Journal, 17*(3), 292–322.

KhanN.NaushadM. (2020). Effects of Corona Virus on the World Community. Available at SSRN 3532001. doi:10.2139/ssrn.3532001

KhanS. A.MahiM.ZainuddinM.IslamE. (2020). At what costs? A proposal for estimating migration costs in the Bangladesh-Malaysia corridor. Available at SSRN 3708959. doi:10.2139/ssrn.3708959

Khatun, F., & Saadat, S. Y. (2021). *Implementation of the SDGs in Bangladesh: Domestic Challenges and Regional Considerations*. South and South-West Asia Office. https://www.unescap.org/sites/default/d8files/knowledge-products/SSWA%20DP%2021-02_SDG%20Implementation%20in%20Bangladesh.pdf

Khondaker, M. S. I. (2021). Tun Mahathir's administration of Malaysia's relationship with Bangladesh: A preliminary appraisal. *Religación: Revista de Ciencias Sociales y Humanidades, 6*(30), 1. doi:10.46652/rgn.v6i30.868

Khoo, E., & Forret, M. (2011). Evaluating an online learning community: Intellectual, social and emotional development and transformations. *Waikato Journal of Education, 16*(1).

Kidane, H. H., Roebertsen, H., & Van der Vleuten, C. P. (2020). Students' perceptions towards self-directed learning in Ethiopian medical schools with new innovative curriculum: A mixed-method study. *BMC Medical Education, 20*(1), 1–10. doi:10.118612909-019-1924-0 PMID:31914977

Kim, S., & Yang, E. B. (2020). Does group cohesion foster self-directed learning for medical students? A longitudinal study. *BMC Medical Education, 20*(1), 1–5. doi:10.118612909-020-1962-7 PMID:32085775

Kinash, S., & Crane, L. (2015). Enhancing graduate employability of the 21st century learner. *Proceedings of the International Mobile Learning Festival 2015: Mobile Learning, MOOCs and 21st Century Learning.*

Kinash, S. (2011). Next generation of what. *Education Technology Solutions, 44*, 52–54.

Kinash, S., Wood, K., & Knight, D. (2013). Digital immigrant teachers and digital native students: What happens to teaching? *Education Technology Solutions, 54*, 56–58.

King, N., & Brooks, J. (2018). Thematic analysis in organisational research. In C. Cassell, A. L. Cunliffe, & G. Grandy (Eds.), *The Sage handbook of qualitative business and management research methods* (pp. 219–236). Sage.

Kinzie, M. B., & Joseph, D. R. D. (2008). Gender differences in game preferences of middle school children: Implications for educational game design. *Educational Technology Research and Development, 56*(5-6), 643–663. doi:10.100711423-007-9076-z

Kioupi, V., & Voulvoulis, N. (2019). Education for sustainable development: A systemic framework for connecting the SDGs to educational outcomes. *Sustainability, 11*(21), 6104. doi:10.3390u11216104

Klein, J. T. (2004). Prospects for transdisciplinarity. *Futures, 36*(4), 515–526. doi:10.1016/j.futures.2003.10.007

Klein, N. (2007). *The shock doctrine: The rise of disaster capitalism.* Metroolitan Book.

Knights, D., & Richards, W. (2003). Sex discrimination in UK academia. *Gender, Work and Organization, 10*(2), 213–238.

Kolb, D. A. (1984). *Experiential Learning: Experience as the Source of Learning and Development.* Prentice-Hall, Inc.

Kolb, D. A. (2014). *Experiential learning: Experience as the source of learning and development.* Prentice Hall.

Kolb, D. M. (2000). More than just a footnote: Constructing a theoretical framework for teaching about gender in negotiation. *Negotiation Journal, 16*(4), 347–356. doi:10.1111/j.1571-9979.2000.tb00763.x

Komarraju, M., Karau, S. J., Schmeck, R. R., & Avdic, A. (2011). The Big Five personality traits, learning styles, and academic achievement. *Personality and Individual Differences, 51*(4), 472–477. doi:10.1016/j.paid.2011.04.019

König, L. S., & Ribarić, H. M. (2019). Is there a mismatch between employers' and university teachers' perceptions on graduate employability in Croatia? *Journal of Managerial Issues, 24*(1), 87–102.

Kopnina, H. (2015). Neoliberalism, pluralism and environmental education: The call for radical re-orientation. *Environmental Development, 15*, 120–130. doi:10.1016/j.envdev.2015.03.005

Kostoulas-Makrakis, N. (2012). *The earth charter's integrated ethical approach to learning to live together sustainably: An example of an international master course* [Paper presentation]. *16th UNESCO-APEID International Conference*, Bangkok, Thailand.

Kour, J., El-Den, J., & Sriratanaviriyakul, N. (2019). The role of positive psychology in improving employees' performance and organizational productivity: An experimental study. *Procedia Computer Science, 161*, 226–232.

*Compilation of References*

Kraeger, P., & Robichau, R. (2017). Questioning stakeholder legitimacy: A philanthropic accountability model. *Journal of Health and Human Services Administration*, 470–519. PMID:29393613

Krasodomska, J., Michalak, J., & Świetla, K. (2020). Directive 2014/95/EU: Accountants' understanding and attitude towards mandatory non-financial disclosures in corporate reporting Directive 2014 / 95 / EU disclosures incorporate reporting. *Meditari Accountancy Research*, *28*(5), 751–779. doi:10.1108/MEDAR-06-2019-0504

Krathwohl, D. (2002). A revision of bloom's taxonomy: An overview. *Theory into Practice*, *41*(4), 212–218. doi:10.120715430421tip4104_2

Kreitz, P. A. (2008). Best practices for managing organizational diversity. *Journal of Academic Librarianship*, *34*(2), 101–120.

Krishnamurthy, S. (2020). The future of business education: A commentary in the shadow of the Covid-19 pandemic. *Journal of Business Research*, *117*, 1–5. doi:10.1016/j.jbusres.2020.05.034 PMID:32501309

Kristofík, P., Lament, M., & Musa, H. (2016). The Reporting of Non-Financial Information and the rationale for its standardisation. *Business Administration and Management*, (2), 157–175. doi:10.1016/j.jaci.2012.05.050

Kritzinger, E., Loock, M., & Goosen, L. (2019). Cyber Safety Awareness – Through the Lens of 21st Century Learning Skills and Game-Based Learning. *Lecture Notes in Computer Science*, *11937*, 477–485. doi:10.1007/978-3-030-35343-8_51

Kruck, S. E., Sendall, P., Ceccucci, W., Peslak, A., & Hunsiger, S. (2014). Does personality play a role in computer information systems course performance? *Issues in Information Systems*, *15*(2), 383–392.

Kucuktas, S. (2016). *Examination of faculty members' multicultural teaching competencies at a four-year institution* [Ph.D. Thesis]. Auburn University.

Kuhn, T. (1970). *The structure of scientific revolutions* (2nd ed.). University of Chicago Press.

Kumaravadivelu, B. (2006). *Understanding language teaching from method to postmethod*. Lawrence Erlbaum Associates. doi:10.4324/9781410615725

Kurio, J., & Reason, P. (2021). Voicing rivers through ontopoetics: A co-operative inquiry. *River Research and Applications*, *38*(3), 376–384. doi:10.1002/rra.3817

La Torre, M., Sabelfeld, S., Blomkvist, M., Tarquinio, L., & Dumay, J. (2018). Harmonising non-financial reporting regulation in Europe: Practical forces and projections for future research. *Meditari Accountancy Research*, *26*(4), 598–621. doi:10.1108/MEDAR-02-2018-0290

Ladson-Billings, G. (1992). Culturally relevant teaching: The key to making multicultural education work. In C. A. Grant (Ed.), *Research and Multicultural Education* (pp. 106–121). The Falmer Press.

Lambirth, A., & Cabral, A. (2017). Issues of Agency, Discipline and Criticality: An Interplay of Challenges Involved in Teachers Engaging in Research in a Performative School Context. *Educational Action Research*, *25*(4), 650–666. doi:10.1080/09650792.2016.1218350

Lambirth, A., Cabral, A., & McDonald, R. (2019). Transformational professional development: (re)claiming agency and change (in the margins). *Teacher Development*, *23*(3), 387–405. doi:10.1080/13664530.2019.1605407

Landis, J. R., & Koch, G. G. (1977). An application of hierarchical kappa-type statistics in the assessment of majority agreement among multiple observers. *Biometrics*, *33*(2), 363–374. doi:10.2307/2529786 PMID:884196

LaPorta, P. J. (2020). *The Psychological Effects of Patriarchy and Courtship: Eighteenth Century Women's Mentalities in Pamela and Clarissa*. State University at New York.

Larrinaga, C., Carrasco, F., Correa, C., Llena, F., & Moneva, J. (2002). Accountability and accounting regulation: The case of the Spanish environmental disclosure standard. *European Accounting Review*, *11*(4), 723–740. doi:10.1080/0963818022000001000

Lasagabaster, D. (2013). The use of L1 in CLIL classes: The teachers' perspective. *Latin American Journal of Content and Language Integrated Learning*, *6*(2), 1–21. doi:10.5294/laclil.2013.6.2.1

Lautensach, A. (2018). Educating as if sustainability mattered. In Proceedings of the 11th Annual International Conference of Education. Research and Innovation. https://doi.org/10.21125/iceri.2018.0352.

Lau, Y. Y., & Ng, A. K. Y. (2015). The motivations and expectations of students pursuing maritime education. *WMU Journal of Maritime Affairs*, *14*(2), 313–331. doi:10.100713437-015-0075-3

Lau, Y. Y., Ng, A. K. Y., Tam, K. C., & Chan, E. K. K. (2018). An investigation on the professionalization of education in maritime logistics and supply chains. *Maritime Business Review*, *3*(4), 394–413. doi:10.1108/MABR-08-2018-0029

Lave, J., & Wenger, E. (1991). *Situated learning: Legitimate peripheral participation*. Cambridge University Press.

Lave, J., & Wenger, E. (1991). *Situated Learning: Legitimate Peripheral Participation*. Cambridge University Press. doi:10.1017/CBO9780511815355

Lawson, D., Stevenson, K. T., Peterson, M. M., Carrier, S. J., Strnad, R., & Seekampa, E. (2018). Intergenerational learning: Are children key in spurring climate action? *Global Environmental Change*, *53*, 204–208. doi:10.1016/j.gloenvcha.2018.10.002

Leach, J., & Scott, P. (2003). Individual and sociocultural views of learning in science education. *Science & education*, *12*(1), 91–113. doi:10.1023/A:1022665519862

Leal, E. A., Miranda, G. J., & Carmo, C. R. S. (2013). Teoria da autodeterminação: Uma análise da motivação dos estudantes do curso de ciências contábeis. *Revista Contabilidade & Finanças*, *24*(62), 162–173. doi:10.1590/S1519-70772013000200007

Lean In and McKinsey & Company. (2018). *Women are Doing Their Part. Now Companies Need to do Their Part, Too*. Available at: https://womenintheworkplace.com/2018#!

Leana, C. R., & Barry, B. (2000). Stability and change as simultaneous experiences in organizational life. *Academy of Management Review*, *25*(4), 753–759.

Leavy, P. (Ed.). (2014). *Oxford library of psychology. The Oxford handbook of qualitative research*. Oxford University Press. doi:10.1093/oxfordhb/9780199811755.001.0001

Lee, J., & Macaro, E. (2013). Investigating age in the use of L1 or English-only instruction: Vocabulary acquisition by Korean EFL learners. *Modern Language Journal*, *97*(4), 887–901. doi:10.1111/j.1540-4781.2013.12044.x

Leemans, R., & Moore, H. (2013). Transdisciplinary global change research: The co-creation of knowledge for sustainability. *Current Opinion in Environmental Sustainability*, *5*(3-4), 420–431.

Lee, R. L. (2010). On the margins of belonging: Confronting cosmopolitanism in the late modern age. *Journal of Sociology (Melbourne, Vic.)*, *46*(2), 169–186. doi:10.1177/1440783309355064

Lefrancois, G. R. (2019). *Theories of human learning*. Cambridge University Press.

Lehtonen, A., & Salonen, A. & Cantell, H. (2019). Climate change education: A new approach for a world of wicked problems. In C. Cook (Ed.), Sustainability, human well-being, and the future of education (pp. 339-374). Palgrave Macmillan.

*Compilation of References*

Letiche, H., Lissack, M., & Schultz, R. (2011). *Coherence in the midst of complexity: Advances in social complexity theory.* Springer.

Leung, C.-H., & Hue, M.-T. (2017). Understanding and enhancing multicultural teaching in preschool. *Early Child Development and Care, 187*(12), 2002–2014. doi:10.1080/03004430.2016.1203308

Levin, S., Xepapadeas, T., Crépin, A. S., Norberg, J., De Zeeuw, A., Folke, C., Hughes, T., Arrow, K., Barrett, S., Daily, G., Ehrlich, P., Kautsky, N., Mäler, K., Polasky, S., Troell, M., Vincent, J., & Walker, B. (2013). Social-ecological systems as complex adaptive systems: Modeling and policy implications. *Environment and Development Economics, 18*(2), 111–132.

Lewin, K. (1946). Action research and minority problems. *The Journal of Social Issues, 2*(4), 4–46. doi:10.1111/j.1540-4560.1946.tb02295.x

Lewis, N., & Shore, C. (2019). From unbundling to market making: Reimagining, reassembling and reinventing the public university. *Globalisation, Societies and Education, 17*(1), 11–27. doi:10.1080/14767724.2018.1524287

Lewis, T. G. (2014). *Book of extremes: Why the 21st century isn't like the 20th century.* Springer.

Libbrecht, P., & Goosen, L. (2015). Using ICTs to Facilitate Multilingual Mathematics Teaching and Learning. In R. Barwell, P. Clarkson, A. Halai, M. Kazima, J. Moschkovich, N. Planas, & M. Villavicencio Ubillús (Eds.), *Mathematics Education and Language Diversity* (pp. 217–235). Springer. doi:10.1007/978-3-319-14511-2_12

Light, J. (2001). Rethinking the digital divide. *Harvard Educational Review, 71*(4), 709–734. doi:10.17763/haer.71.4.342x36742j2w4q82

Linn, R. L., & Miller, M. D. (2005). Measurement and Assessment in Teaching (8th ed.). Pearson/Merrill Prentice Hall.

Littlewood, W., & Yu, B. (2011). First language and target language in the foreign language classroom. *Language Teaching, 44*(01), 64–77. doi:10.1017/S0261444809990310

Liu, G., Yin, X., Pengue, W., Benetto, E., Huisingh, D., Schnitzer, H., Wang, Y., & Casazza, M. (2018). Environmental accounting : In between raw data and information use for management practices. *Journal of Cleaner Production, 197*, 1056–1068. doi:10.1016/j.jclepro.2018.06.194

Lo, C. W. H., Pang, R. X., Egri, C. P., & Li, P. H. Y. (2017). University social responsibility: conceptualization and an assessment framework. In D. Shek & R. Holliuster (Eds.), *University Social Responsibility and Quality of Life* (pp. 37–59). Springer. doi:10.1007/978-981-10-3877-8_4

Lockwood, N. R. (2005). Crisis management in today's business environment. *SHRM Research Quarterly, 4*, 1–9.

Lodders, N., & Meijers, F. (2017). Collective Learning, Transformational Leadership and New Forms of Careers Guidance in Universities. *British Journal of Guidance & Counselling, 45*(5), 532–546. doi:10.1080/03069885.2016.1271864

Loeng, S. (2020). Self-Directed Learning: A Core Concept in Adult Education. *Education Research International, 2020*, 1–12. doi:10.1155/2020/3816132

Long, M. A., Gonçalves, P., Paul, B. S., & Defeyter, M. (2020). Food Insecurity in Advanced Capitalist Nations: A Review. *Sustainability, 12*(9), 3654. doi:10.3390u12093654

Longo, S., Clark, B., Shriver, T., & Clausen, R. (2016). Sustainability and environmental sociology: Putting the economy in its place and moving toward an integrative socio-ecology. *Journal of Sustainability, 8*(5), 437–454. doi:10.3390u8050437

Lotz-Sisitka, H., Wals, A. E., Kronlid, D., & McGarry, D. (2015). Transformative, transgressive social learning: Rethinking higher education pedagogy in times of systemic global dysfunction. *Current Opinion in Environmental Sustainability, 16*, 73–80.

Lovelock, J. (1995). *The ages of Gaia: A biography of our living earth*. Norton.

Lukashova, L. (2020). Evaluation of the synergetic effect from implementation of economic activity by small business entities. *Technology Audit and Production Reserves*, *1*(4), 51.

Luse, A., & Rursch, J. (2021). Using a virtual lab network testbed to facilitate real-world hands-on learning in a networking course. *British Journal of Educational Technology*, *52*(3), 1244–1261. doi:10.1111/bjet.13070

Lyons, O. (2004). *The ice is melting* [Paper presentation]. 24th Annual E. F. Schumacher lectures. https://centerforneweconomics.org/publications/the-ice-is-melting/

Madu, B. C. (2012). Organization culture as driver of competitive advantage. *Journal of Academic and Business Ethics*, *5*, 1.

Mahan, J. L., Jr. (1970). *Toward transdisciplinary inquiry in the humane sciences* [Doctoral dissertation, United States International University]. UMI No. 702145. Retrieved from ProQuest Dissertations & Theses Global.

Mahboob, A., & Lin, A. (2016). Using local languages in English language classroom. In W. Renandya & H. Widodo (Eds.), *English language teaching today:Linking theory to practice* (pp. 25–40). Springer Nature. doi:10.1007/978-3-319-38834-2_3

Mahwari, W. (2016). *Designing a model for pre-service EFL teacher education programs: An exploratory study in the Yemeni context*. Retrieved December 2016, from https://www.awej.org/index.php?option=com_content&view=article&id=1038

Malcolm, M. (2013). Transforming lives and 'the measure of their states'. *Journal of Pedagogic Development*, *3*(3).

Marcela, V. (2015). Learning strategy, personality traits and academic achievement of university students. *Procedia: Social and Behavioral Sciences*, *174*, 3473–3478. doi:10.1016/j.sbspro.2015.01.1021

Maria, D. (2011). Complex adaptive systems: A trans-cultural undercurrent obstructing change in higher education. *International Journal of Vocational and Technical Education*, *3*(2), 9–19.

Marina, B. L. H. (2004 February 16-20). *The multicultural competence among faculty and administrators in a predominantly white institution*. Paper presented at the 7th International Conference on The First-Year Experience, Maui, HI.

Martin, F., Ritzhaupt, A., Kumar, S., & Budhrani, K. (2019). Award-winning faculty online teaching practices: Course design, assessment and evaluation, and facilitation. *The Internet and Higher Education*, *42*, 34–43. doi:10.1016/j.iheduc.2019.04.001

Martins, V. W. B., Rampasso, I. S., Anholon, R., Quelhas, O. L. G., & Leal Filho, W. (2019). Knowledge management in the context of sustainability: Literature review and opportunities for future research. *Journal of Cleaner Production*, *229*, 489–500. doi:10.1016/j.jclepro.2019.04.354

Maslow, A. H. (1943). A theory of human motivation. *Psychological Review*, *50*(4), 370–396. doi:10.1037/h0054346

Mata, C., Fialho, A., & Eugénio, T. (2018). A decade of environmental accounting reporting: What we know? *Journal of Cleaner Production*, *198*, 1198–1209. doi:10.1016/j.jclepro.2018.07.087

Mathers, R. (2020). An anthropology of climate change deniers. In D. Mathers (Ed.), *Depth Psychology and Climate Change* (pp. 29–48). Routledge.

Maughan, E., & Reason, P. (2001). A co-operative inquiry into deep ecology. *ReVision*, *23*(4), 18–24.

Mawson, M., & Haworth, A. C. (2018). Supporting the employability agenda in university libraries. *Information and Learning Science*, *119*(1/2), 101–108. doi:10.1108/ILS-04-2017-0027

Max-Neef, M. A. (2005). Foundations of transdisciplinarity. *Ecological Economics*, *53*, 5–16.

*Compilation of References*

Maxwell, J. A. (1998). Designing a qualitative study. In L. Bickman & D. J. Rog (Eds.), *Handbook of Applied Social Research Methods* (pp. 69–100). Sage Publications, Inc.

Mayer, L. R., & Murphy, D. (2022, August 10). *The European Union, Re:wild and WWF-Viet Nam mobilize emergency response to prevent imminent extinction of Asian "unicorn."* Re:wild. https://www.rewild.org/press/the-european-union-re-wild-and-wwf-viet-nam-mobilize-emergency-response-to

Mazon, G., Pereira Ribeiro, J. M., Montenegro de Lima, C. R., Castro, B. C. G., & Guerra, J. B. (2020). The promotion of sustainable development in higher education institutions: Top-down bottom-up or neither? *International Journal of Sustainability in Higher Education*, *21*(7), 1429–1450. doi:10.1108/IJSHE-02-2020-0061

Mbagwu, F. O., Chukwuedo, S. O., & Ogbuanya, T. C. (2020). Promoting Lifelong Learning Propensity and Intentions for Vocational Training among Adult and Vocational Educational Undergraduates. *Vocations and Learning*, *13*(3), 419–437. doi:10.100712186-020-09245-1

McArdle, R. (2021). Intersectional climate urbanism: Towards the inclusion of marginalised voices. *Geoforum*, *126*, 302–305. doi:10.1016/j.geoforum.2021.08.005

McGann, M., Wells, T., & Blomkamp, E. (2021). Innovation labs and co-production in public problem solving. *Public Management Review*, *23*(2), 297–316.

McMillin, J., & Dyball, R. (2009). Developing a whole-of-university approach to educating for sustainability: Linking curriculum, research and sustainable campus operations. *Journal of Education for Sustainable Development*, *3*(1), 55–64. doi:10.1177/097340820900300113

McNeill, J. (2022). *Skills vs. Competencies – What's the difference, and why should you care?* Retrieved February 11, 2022, from https://qr.page/g/M9H26KjIIe

Meadows, D. H., Meadows, D. L., Randers, J., & Behrens, W. W. (2018). The limits to growth. In *Green planet blues* (pp. 25–29). Routledge. doi:10.4324/9780429493744-3

Mehra, V. (2007). Teachers' attitude towards computer use Implications for Emerging Technology Implementation in Educational Institutions. *Journal of Teacher Education and Research*, *2*(2), 1–13.

Meletiadou, E. (2011). *Peer assessment of writing in secondary education: its impact on learners' performance and attitudes* (Unpublished MA thesis). University of Cyprus.

Meletiadou, E. (2013). EFL learners' attitudes towards peer assessment, teacher assessment and the process writing. In Selected Papers in Memory of Dr Pavlos Pavlou: Language Testing and Assessment around the Globe—Achievement and Experiences (pp. 312-32). Frankfurt am Main: Peter Lang GmbH.

Meletiadou, E. (2021d, November). Adopting a multilingual approach towards comprehension in assessment in Higher Education Institutions in the UK amidst the Covid-19 pandemic. *The Association for Assessment (AEA)-Europe Conference*. Retrieved from https://www.aea-europe.net/conferences/22nd-annual-conference/

Meletiadou, E. (2022d). Nurturing Student Writing Knowledge, Self-Regulation, and Attitudes in Higher Education: The Use of Self-Assessment as an Inclusive Practice. In Handbook of Research on Policies and Practices for Assessing Inclusive Teaching and Learning (pp. 27-53). IGI Global.

Meletiadou, E. (2022e, January 26-27). Iron fists in velvet gloves: exploring female educational leaders' experiences in Higher Education in the UK. *Applied Research Conference* (pp. 85-88). Chartered Institute of Personnel and Development (CIPD).

Meletiadou, E. (2022g). The Lived Experiences of Female Educational Leaders in Higher Education in the UK: Academic Resilience and Gender. In Handbook of Research on Practices for Advancing Diversity and Inclusion in Higher Education (pp. 1-19). IGI Global.

Meletiadou, E. (2022h). Profiling the Writing Competency of BAME Undergraduate Students: Fostering Inclusion and Academic Success to Improve Retention in Tertiary Education. In Handbook of Research on Practices for Advancing Diversity and Inclusion in Higher Education (pp. 20-48). IGI Global.

Meletiadou, E. (2022i). *Inclusive assessment: fostering social justice in education*. Retrieved from European Association for Educational Assessment: https://www.aea-europe.net/inclusive-assessment-fostering-social-justice-in-education/

Meletiadou, E. I. (2017). *Peer assessment: a dynamic learning-oriented tool for the development of writing skills* (PhD dissertation). University of Cyprus. Retrieved from https://gnosis.library.ucy.ac.cy/bitstream/handle/7/38983/Eleni_I_Meletiadou_PhD.pdf?sequence=5&isAllowed=y

Meletiadou, E. (2021a, July). Opening Pandora's box: How does peer assessment affect EFL students' writing quality? *Languages*, *6*(3), 115. Advance online publication. doi:10.3390/languages6030115

Meletiadou, E. (2021b, September). Exploring the impact of peer assessment on EFL students' writing performance. *IAFOR Journal of Education*, *9*(3), 77–95. doi:10.22492/ije.9.3.05

Meletiadou, E. (2021c, October). Using Padlets as E-Portfolios to Enhance Undergraduate Students' Writing Skills and Motivation. *IAFOR Journal of Education*, *9*(5), 67–83. doi:10.22492/ije.9.5.04

Meletiadou, E. (2022a, January 1). Learners' Perceptions of Peer Assessment: Implications for Their Willingness to Write in an EFL Context. *International Journal of Teacher Education and Professional Development*, *5*(1), 1–14. doi:10.4018/IJTEPD.295539

Meletiadou, E. (2022c). The Use of Peer Assessment as an Inclusive Learning Strategy in Higher Education Institutions: Enhancing Student Writing Skills and Motivation. In *Handbook of Research on Policies and Practices for Assessing Inclusive Teaching and Learning* (pp. 1–26). IGI Global. doi:10.4018/978-1-7998-8579-5.ch001

Meletiadou, E. (Ed.). (2022b, January 14). *Handbook of Research on Policies and Practices for Assessing Inclusive Teaching and Learning*. IGI Global. doi:10.4018/978-1-7998-8579-5

Meletiadou, E. (Ed.). (2022f, June). *Handbook of research on practices for advancing diversity and inclusion in higher education*. IGI Global. doi:10.4018/978-1-7998-9628-9

Meletiadou, E., & Tsagari, D. (2012). Investigating the attitudes of adolescent EFL learners towards peer assessment of writing. *Research in English as a Foreign Language in Cyprus*, *2*, 225–245.

Meletiadou, E., & Tsagari, D. (2016). The washback effect of peer assessment on adolescent EFL learners in Cyprus. In *Classroom-based assessment in L2 contexts* (pp. 138–160). Cambridge Scholars Publishing.

Meletiadou, E., & Tsagari, D. (2022). Exploring EFL teachers' perceptions of the use of peer assessment in external exam-dominated writing classes. *Languages*, *7*(1), 16. Advance online publication. doi:10.3390/languages7010016

Melloni, G., Caglio, A., & Perego, P. (2017). Saying more with less? Disclosure conciseness, completeness and balance in Integrated Reports. *Journal of Accounting and Public Policy*, *36*(3), 220–238. doi:10.1016/j.jaccpubpol.2017.03.001

Mena, J. A., & Rogers, M. R. (2017). Factors associated with multicultural teaching competence: Social justice orientation and multicultural environment. *Training and Education in Professional Psychology*, *11*(2), 61–68. doi:10.1037/tep0000143

*Compilation of References*

Merriam, S. B. (2001). Andragogy and self-directed learning: Pillars of adult learning theory. *New Directions for Adult and Continuing Education, 2001*(89), 3–14. doi:10.1002/ace.3

Meyer, J. P., Becker, T. E., & Vandenberghe, C. (2004). Employee commitment and motivation: A conceptual analysis and integrative model. *The Journal of Applied Psychology, 89*(6), 991.

Mia, M. A., & Griffiths, M. D. (2020). The economic and mental health costs of COVID-19 to immigrants. *Journal of Psychiatric Research, 128*, 23–24. doi:10.1016/j.jpsychires.2020.06.003 PMID:32512405

Miceli, A., Hagen, B., Riccardi, M. P., Sotti, F., & Settembre-Blundo, D. (2021). Thriving, not just surviving in changing times: How sustainability, agility and digitalization intertwine with organizational resilience. *Sustainability, 13*(4), 2052.

Mikyoung, K., & Moon, J. (2019). Inclusive leadership and creative performance: The role of psychological safety, feedback-seeking behaviour, and power-distance. *Korean Journal of Human Resource Development, 22*(4), 181–205. doi:10.24991/KJHRD.2019.12.22.4.181

Milem, J. F. (1992). *The Impact of College on Students' Racial Attitudes and Levels of Racial Awareness* [PhD Thesis, UCLA]. Ann Arbor: University Microforms International (UMI), Order Number 9301968.

Milem, J. F. (1994). College, students, and racial understanding. *Thought & Action, 9*(2), 51–92.

Minghui, Y., & Yuanxu, L. (2014). Research on the mechanism of inclusive leadership on employees' innovative behaviour [J]. *Scientific Progress and Countermeasures, 31*(10), 6–9.

Ministry of Education. (2010). *Motiona Education Policy*. Dhaka: Ministry of Education, Government of the People's Republic of Bangladesh. https://reliefweb.int/report/bangladesh/national-education-policy-2010-enbn

Ministry of Education. (2010). *National Education Policy*. Ministry of Education, People's Republic of Bangladesh.

Ministry of Finance. (2020). *Prihatin Rakyat Economic Stimulus Package (Prihatin) (2020)*. Ministry of Finance.

Miranda, C. (2020). *Generation Z: Re-thinking Teaching and Learning Strategies*. Retrieved from: https://www.facultyfocus.com/articles/teaching-and-learning/generation-z-re-thinking-teaching-and-learning-strategies/

Miranda, A. H. (2002). Best practices in increasing cross-cultural competence. In A. Thomas & J. Grimes (Eds.), *Best Practices in School Psychology IV* (Vol. 1, pp. 353–362). National Association of School Psychologists.

Miser, K. M., & Cherrey, C. (2009). Responding to campus crisis. In G.S. McClellan, J. Stringer, & Associates (Eds.), The handbook of student affairs administration (3rd ed., pp. 602-622). Jossey-Bass.

Mitchell, R., Boyle, B., Parker, V., Giles, M., Chiang, V., & Joyce, P. (2015). Managing inclusiveness and diversity in teams: How leader inclusiveness affects performance through status and team identity. *Human Resource Management, 54*(2), 217–239. doi:10.1002/hrm.21658

Mobarak, A. M., Sharif, I., & Shrestha, M. (2020). Returns to low-skilled international migration: Evidence from the Bangladesh-Malaysia migration lottery program. *World Bank Policy Research Working Paper*, (9165).

Mohajan, H. (2017, December 28). *Research Methodology, 83457*. https://mpra.ub.uni-muenchen.de/83457/1/MPRA_paper_83457.pdf

Mohammed, S. D. (2018). Mandatory Social and Environmental Disclosure : A Performance Evaluation of Listed Nigerian Oil and Gas Companies Pre- and Post-Mandatory Disclosure Requirements. *Journal of Finance and Accounting, 6*(2), 56–68. doi:10.11648/j.jfa.20180602.12

Mohr, K. A., & Mohr, E. S. (2017). Understanding Generation Z students to promote a contemporary learning environment. *Journal on Empowering Teaching Excellence*, *1*(1), 9.

Mohsin, A. (2001). *The state of "minority" rights in Bangladesh*. International Centre for Ethnic Studies.

Mohsin, A. (2002). *The Politics of Nationalism: The Case of the Chittagong Hill Tracts Bangladesh* (2nd ed.). The University Press Limited.

Momennejad, I. (2022). Collective minds: social network topology shapes collective cognition. *Philosophical Transactions of The Royal Society B Biological Sciences*, *377*(1843), 20200315.

Monbiot, G. (2022, July 18). Heatwave extreme weather climate crisis. *The Guardian*. https://www.theguardian.com/commentisfree/2022/jul/18/heatwave-extreme-weather-uk-climate-crisis

Monem, M., & Baniamin, H. M. (2010). Higher Education in Bangladesh: Status, Issues and Prospects. *Pakistan Journal of Social Science*, *30*(2), 293–305.

Montiel, I. (2008). Corporate social responsibility and corporate sustainability: Separate pasts, common futures. *Organization & Environment*, *21*(3), 245–269.

Mook, L., Murdock, A., & Gundersen, C. (2020). Food Banking and Food Insecurity in High-Income Countries. *Voluntas*, *31*(5), 1–8. doi:10.100711266-020-00219-4

Moon, J. (2007). The contribution of corporate social responsibility to sustainable development. *Sustainable Development*, *15*(5), 296–306.

Moore, T., Houde, J., Hoggan, C., & Wagner, J. (2007). Re-viewing Adult Learning: A Collaborative Self-Directed Learning Model for Adult Educators. In *Proceedings of Adult Education Research Conference* (vol. 32, pp. 195–207). Retrieved February 22, 2022, from https://newprairiepress.org/aerc/2007/papers/72

Moore, L. (2015). A day at the beach: Rising sea levels, horseshoe crabs, and traffic jams. *Sociology*, *49*(5), 886–902. doi:10.1177/0038038515573474

Moore, M. G. (1989). Three types of interaction. *American Journal of Distance Education*, *3*(2), 1–6. doi:10.1080/08923648909526659

Moorman, D., & Clark, K. (2012). *Student learning style and personality types: Their implications for teaching*. SOTL-Commons conference paper 33. http://digitalcommons.georgiasouthern.edu

Moreno-Gómez, J., Lafuente, E., & Vaillant, Y. (2018). Gender diversity in the board, women's leadership and business performance. *Gender in Management*, *33*(2), 104–122. doi:10.1108/GM-05-2017-0058

Morgan, S., Yazdanparast, A., & Rawski, G. (2018). Creating a distinctive business career outcome programme. *Journal of Vocational Education and Training*, *70*(2), 251–277. doi:10.1080/13636820.2017.1394356

Morley, L. (2013). The rules of the game: Women and the leaderist turn in higher education. *Gender and Education*, *25*(1), 116–131. doi:10.1080/09540253.2012.740888

Mowbray, D. (2008). Building resilience–an organisational cultural approach to mental health and well-being at work: a primary prevention programme. In A. Kinder, R. Hughes, & C. Cooper (Eds.), *Employee well-being support: A workplace resource* (pp. 309–321). John Wiley & Sons.

Mukeredzi, T. G. (2013). Professional Development Through Teacher Roles: Conceptions of Professionally Unqualified Teachers in Rural South Africa and Zimbabwe. *Journal of Research in Rural Education, 28*(11). https://citeseerx.ist.psu.edu/viewdoc/download?doi=10.1.1.398.2997&rep=rep1&type=pdf

Mupinga, D. M. (2003). Communicating with online students. *Sketches of Innovators in Education*.

Mupinga, D. M. (2005). Distance education in high schools: Benefts, challenges, and suggestions. *The Clearing House: A Journal of Educational Strategies, Issues and Ideas*, 78(3), 105–109. doi:10.3200/TCHS.78.3.105-109

Mupinga, D. M., Nora, R. T., & Yaw, D. C. (2006). The learning styles, expectations, and needs of online students. *College Teaching*, 54(1), 185–189. doi:10.3200/CTCH.54.1.185-189

Murphy, R. (2012). Sustainability: A wicked problem. *Sociologica*, 2, 1–23.

Musikanski, L., Phillips, R., Bradbury, J., de Graaf, J., & Bliss, C. L. (2020). *Happiness, Well-being and Sustainability: A Course in Systems Change*. Routledge. doi:10.4324/9781003043232

Naeem, U., Bosman, L., & Gill, S. S. (2022, March). Teaching and Facilitating an Online Learning Environment for a Web Programming Module. In *2022 IEEE Global Engineering Education Conference (EDUCON)* (pp. 769-774). IEEE. 10.1109/EDUCON52537.2022.9766757

Nagoba, S. B., & Mantri, B. S. (2015). Role of Teachers in Quality Enhancement in Higher Education. *Journal of Krishna Institute of Medical Sciences University*, 4(1), 177–182.

Nakata, M. (2007). *Disciplining the savages, savaging the disciplines*. Aboriginal Studies Press.

NASA. (2022, August 10). *Death valley flash flooding*. NASA Earth Observatory. https://earthobservatory.nasa.gov/images/150181/death-valley-flash-flooding

Neely, K. (2015). Complex adaptive systems as a valid framework for understanding community level development. *Development in Practice*, 25(6), 785–797.

Nembhard, I. M., & Edmondson, A. C. (2006). Making it safe: The effects of leader inclusiveness and professional status on psychological safety and improvement efforts in health care teams. Journal of Organizational Behaviour: *The International Journal of Industrial, Occupational and Organizational Psychology and Behaviour*, 27(7), 941–966. doi:10.1002/job.413

Netherlands Organization for Scientific Research. (2013). *Researchers' report*. Country Profile.

Neuendorf, K. A. (2018). Content analysis and thematic analysis. In P. Brough (Ed.), Advanced research methods for applied psychology (pp. 211-223). Routledge. doi:10.4324/9781315517971-21

New Straits Times. (2020). *Covid-19: Rm127.78 Million Economic Stimulus Package For Selangor*. Author.

Newell, R. W. (1981). Skepticism and Cognitivism: A Study in the Foundations of Knowledge. *Mind*, 90(357), 137–139. doi:10.1093/mind/XC.357.137

Nghuulondo, P., Kanyimba, A. T., & Haipinge, E. (n.d.). *The use of smart phones and mobile devices to access learning support services for distance education students at University of Namibia*. Retrieved from https://www.academia.edu/download/62292616/Patrick_Nghuulondo_Article_201920200306-79049-j26pb.pdf

Ng, P. M., Chan, J. K., Wut, T. M., Lo, M. F., & Szeto, I. (2021). What makes better career opportunities for young graduates? Examining acquired employability skills in higher education institutions. *Education + Training*, 63(6), 852–871. doi:10.1108/ET-08-2020-0231

Ngugi, J. K., & Goosen, L. (2021). Innovation, Entrepreneurship, and Sustainability for ICT Students Towards the Post-COVID-19 Era. In L. C. Carvalho, L. Reis, & C. Silveira (Eds.), *Handbook of Research on Entrepreneurship, Innovation, Sustainability, and ICTs in the Post-COVID-19 Era* (pp. 110–131). IGI Global. doi:10.4018/978-1-7998-6776-0.ch006

Nicholas, A. J. (2020). *Preferred Learning Methods of Generation Z*. Academic Press.

Nicolescu, B. (2010). Methodology of transdisciplinarity: Levels of reality, logic of the included middle, and complexity. *Transdisciplinary Journal of Engineering & Science, 1*(1), 19-38.

Nicolescu, B. (2012). Transdisciplinarity: The hidden third, between the subject and the object. *Human and Social Studies, 1*(2), 13–28.

Nieto, S. (2015). *The light in their eyes: Creating multicultural learning communities*. Teachers College Press.

Nilsson, W. (2015). Positive institutional work: Exploring institutional work through the lens of positive organizational scholarship. *Academy of Management Review, 40*(3), 370–398. doi:10.5465/amr.2013.0188

Nishimura, N. (1995). Addressing the Needs of Biracial Children: An Issue for Counsellors in a Multicultural School Environment. *The School Counsellor, 43*(1), 52-57. Retrieved March 27, 2021, from http://www.jstor.org/stable/23901428

Noh, N. A., Wahab, H. A., Bakar Ah, S. H. A., & Islam, M. R. (2016). Public Health Services for Foreign Workers in Malaysia. *Social Work in Public Health, 31*(5), 419–430. doi:10.1080/19371918.2015.1125321 PMID:27177326

Northouse, P. G. (2016). *Leadership: theory and practice* (7th ed.). Sage.

Novakowski, J. T. (2019). *Analyzing Teacher-Student Relationships in the Life and Thought of William James to Inform Educators Today*. Ohio State University.

Nunan, D. (1992). *Research methods in language learning*. Cambridge University Press.

Nuno F. (2020). Economic effects of coronavirus outbreak (COVID-19) on the world economy. Available at SSRN 3557504.

O'Byrne, L., Gavin, B., & McNicholas, F. (2020). Medical students and COVID-19: The need for pandemic preparedness. *Journal of Medical Ethics, 46*(9), 623–626. doi:10.1136/medethics-2020-106353 PMID:32493713

O'Malley, K. D. (2020). A Covid Spring. *Irish Journal of Psychological Medicine*, 1–2. PMID:32406347

Odhiambo, J., Weke, P., & Ngare, P. (2020). Modeling Kenyan Economic Impact of Corona Virus in Kenya Using Discrete-Time Markov Chains. *Journal of Financial Economics, 8*(2), 80–85.

OECD. (2005). *E-learning in tertiary education*. Available at http://www.cumex.org.mx/archivos/ACERVO/Elearning-Policybriefenglish.pdf

Olivia, P. (1997). *The curriculum: Theoretical dimensions*. Longman.

Olivier, J. (2021). Online access and resources for open self-directed learning in Africa. In D. Burgos & J. Olivier (Eds.), *Radical Solutions for Education in Africa: Open education and self-directed learning in the continent* (pp. 1–16). Springer. doi:10.1007/978-981-16-4099-5_1

Orebech, P., Bosselman, F., Bjarup, J., Callies, D., Chanock, M., & Petersen, H. (2005). *The role of customary law in sustainable development*. Cambridge University Press.

Organisation for Economic Co-operation and Development. (2020). *The potential of online learning for adults: early lessons from the COVID-19 crisis*. OECD Publishing.

Osmani, M., Hindi, N. M., & Weerakkody, V. (2018). Developing employability skills in information system graduates: Traditional vs. innovative teaching methods. *International Journal of Information and Communication Technology Education, 14*(2), 17–29. doi:10.4018/IJICTE.2018040102

## Compilation of References

Ottu, I. F. (2017). Cooperative stakeholding: Optimising students' educational practice through need-centred self-determination, connectedness with learning environment and passion. *Journal of Education and Practice*, *8*(4), 1–33.

Owens, T. L. (2017). Higher education in the sustainable development goals framework. *European Journal of Education*, *52*(4), 414–420. doi:10.1111/ejed.12237

Pallof, R. M., & Pratt, K. (2007). *Building online learning communities: Effective strategies for the virtual classroom*. John Wiley & Sons.

Pando-Garcia, J., Perianez-Canadillas, I., & Charterina, J. (2016). Business simulation games with and without supervision: An analysis based on the TAM model. *Journal of Business Research*, *69*(5), 1731–1736. doi:10.1016/j.jbusres.2015.10.046

Pappas, E., Pierrakos, O., & Nagel, R. (2013). Using Bloom's Taxonomy to teach sustainability in multiple contexts. *Journal of Cleaner Production*, *48*, 54–64. doi:10.1016/j.jclepro.2012.09.039

Parasecoli, F. (2014). Food, identity, and cultural reproduction in immigrant communities. *Social Research*, *81*(2), 415–439.

Paraskevi, A., & Nikolaos, M. (2017). Students from Different Cultural Backgrounds, Their Difficulties upon Elementary School Entry in Greece and Teachers' Intercultural Educational Practices. *Brock Journal of Education*, *5*(4), 2053–5813.

Parker, C. M., & Swatman, P. M. C. (1999). An Internet-mediated electronic commerce business simulation: Experiences developing and using TRECS. *Simulation & Gaming: An Interdisciplinary Journal*, *30*(1), 51–69. doi:10.1177/104687819903000107

Parris, T. M., & Kates, R. W. (2003). Characterizing and measuring sustainable development. *Annual Review of Environment and Resources*, *28*(1), 559–586. doi:10.1146/annurev.energy.28.050302.105551

Parry, C., & Poland, M. (2019). "Going on" into climate crisis. *Green Letters*, *23*(4), 331–336.

Pascarella, E. T., Whitt, E. J., Nora, A., Edison, M., Hagedorn, L. S., & Terenzini, P. T. (1996). What Have We Learned from the First Year of the National Study of Student Learning? *Journal of College Student Development*, *37*(2), 182–192.

Patterson, C., Crooks, D., & Lunyk-Child, O. (2002). A New Perspective on Competencies for Self-Directed Learning. *The Journal of Nursing Education*, *41*(1), 25–31. doi:10.3928/0148-4834-20020101-06 PMID:11843104

Patterson, J. T. (2000). *Brown V. Board of Education: A civil rights milestone and its troubled legacy*. Oxford University Press.

Patton, M. Q. (1990). *Qualitative evaluation and research methods* (2nd ed.). Sage Publications, Inc.

Paul, B. D. (2008). A history of the concept of sustainable development: Literature review. The Annals of the University of Oradea. *Economic Sciences Series*, *17*(2), 576–580.

Pazos, P., Cima, F., Kidd, J., Ringleb, S., Ayala, O., Gutierrez, K., & Kaipa, K. (2020). Enhancing Teamwork Skills Through an Engineering Service-learning Collaboration. *2020 ASEE Virtual Annual Conference Content Access, Virtual Online*, 1-6. 10.18260/1-2--34577

Peeters, E., Nelissen, J., De Cuyper, N., Forrier, A., Verbruggen, M., & De Witte, H. (2019). Employability capital: A conceptual framework tested through expert analysis. *Journal of Career Development*, *46*(2), 79–93. doi:10.1177/0894845317731865

Pelissier, C. (1991). The anthropology of teaching and learning. *Annual Review of Anthropology*, *20*(1), 75–95. doi:10.1146/annurev.an.20.100191.000451

Peltier, J. W., Chennamaneni, P. R., & Barber, K. N. (2022). Student anxiety, preparation, and learning framework for responding to external crises: The moderating role of self-efficacy as a coping mechanism. *Journal of Marketing Education*, *44*(2), 149–165. doi:10.1177/02734753211036500

Perrin, D. (2012). Coming to grips with complexity: dynamic systems theory in the research of newswriting. In C. Bazerman, C. Dean, J. Early, K. Lunsford, S. Null, P. Rogers, & A. Stansell (Eds.), *International advances in writing research: Culture, places, measures* (pp. 539–558). Parlor Press.

Perryman, A., Fernando, G., & Tripathy, A. (2016). Do gender differences persist? An examination of gender diversity on firm performance, risk, executive compensation. *Journal of Business Research*, *69*(2), 579–586. doi:10.1016/j.jbusres.2015.05.013

Perusso, A., van der Sijde, P., Leal, R., & Blankesteijn, M. (2021). The effectiveness and impact of action learning on business graduates' professional practice. *Journal of Management Education*, *45*(2), 177–205. doi:10.1177/1052562920940374

Peschl, M. F. (2019). Design and innovation as co-creating and co-becoming with the Future. *Design Management Journal*, *14*(1), 4–14.

Peterman, A., Potts, A., O'Donnell, M., Thompson, K., Shah, N., Oertelt-Prigione, S., & van Gelder, N. (2020). Pandemics and violence against women and children. *Center for Global Development Working Paper, 528*.

Phillips, R. (2012). Food cooperatives as community-level self-help and development. *International Journal of Self Help & Self Care*, *6*(2), 189–203. doi:10.2190/SH.6.2.f

Phillips, R., Seifer, B., & Antczak, E. (2013). *Sustainable communities: Creating a durable local economy*. Routledg. doi:10.4324/9780203381212

Phillips, R., Trevan, E., & Kraeger, P. (2020). Introduction to the Research Handbook on Community Development. In *Research Handbook on Community Development*. Edward Elgar Publishing. doi:10.4337/9781788118477.00005

Piaget, J. (1928). *Judgement and reasoning in the child*. Routledge & Kegan Paul.

Piaget, J. (1972). The epistemology of interdisciplinary relationships. In *Interdisciplinarity: Problems of teaching and research in universities* (pp. 127–139). Organisation for Economic Co-operation and Development.

Pierson, A. E., Clark, D. B., & Kelly, G. J. (2019). Learning Progressions and science practices. *Science & Education*, *28*(8), 833–841. doi:10.100711191-019-00070-0

Pillay, N. (2009). Human rights in United Nations action: Norms, institutions, and leadership. *European Human Rights Law Review*, *1*, 1–7.

Pizzi, S., Caputo, A., Corvino, A., & Venturelli, A. (2020). Management research and the UN sustainable development goals (SDGs): A bibliometric investigation and systematic review. *Journal of Cleaner Production*, *276*, 124033. doi:10.1016/j.jclepro.2020.124033

Plumwood, V. (2004). Gender, eco-feminism and the environment. In R. White (Ed.), *Controversies in Environmental Sociology* (pp. 43–60). Cambridge University Press.

Pohl, C., Klein, J. T., Hoffmann, S., Mitchell, C., & Fam, D. (2021). Conceptualising transdisciplinary integration as a multidimensional interactive process. *Environmental Science & Policy*, *118*, 18–26.

Polat, İ., & Kılıç, E. (2013). Multicultural education in Turkey and teachers' competencies in multicultural education. *Van Yuzuncu Yil University Journal of Faculty of Education*, *10*(1), 352-372.

Polat, S. (2009). Determining the level of characteristics of pre-service teachers towards culturally responsive education. *International Online Journal of Educational Sciences, 1*(1), 154–164.

Polio, C., & Duff, P. (1994). Teacher's language use in university foreign language classrooms: A qualitative analysis of English and target language alternation. *Modern Language Journal, 78*(3), 313–326. doi:10.1111/j.1540-4781.1994.tb02045.x

Pope, R. L., Reynolds, A. L., & Mueller, J. A. (2019). *Multicultural competence in student affairs: Advancing social justice and inclusion*. John Wiley & Sons.

Porter, J. E. (1986). Intertextuality and the discourse community. *Rhetoric Review, 5*(1), 34–47.

Postolov, K., Magdinceva Sopova, M., & Janeska-Iliev, A. (2017). *E-learning in the hands of generation Y and Z*. Academic Press.

Poulisse, N. (1990). The use of compensatory strategies by Dutch learners of English. Foris.

Pratt-Johnson, Y. (2006). Communicating cross-culturally: What teachers should know. *The Internet TESL Journal, 12*(2).

Preiser, R., Biggs, R., De Vos, A., & Folke, C. (2018). Social-ecological systems as complex adaptive systems. *Ecology and Society, 23*(4), 46.

Prikshat, V., Kumar, S., & Nankervis, A. (2018). Work-readiness integrated competence model. *Education + Training, 61*(5), 568–589. doi:10.1108/ET-05-2018-0114

Primavesi, A. (2013). *Exploring earthiness*. Cascade Books.

Prodhan, M. (2016). The present situation of education system in Bangladesh and scope for improvement. *Journal of Education and Social Sciences, 4*(June), 122–132.

Punch, K. F. (2013). *Introduction to social research: Quantitative and qualitative approaches*. Sage.

Putnam, M. (2022, August 3). *Rewilding California: Project reaches halfway point in planting over 100,000 native plants in largest-ever restoration effort in the Santa Monica Mountains*. Re:wild. https://www.rewild.org/news/rewilding-california-project-reaches-halfway-point-in-planting-over-100-000

Qi, W. (2012). On the New Development of the Framework of Higher Education Qualifications in England, Wales and Northern Ireland (FHEQ) and Its Enlightenment. *China Higher Education Research, 3*, 1–20.

QMUL. (2009). *The Queen Mary Statement of Graduate Attributes*. Available at http://www.arcs.qmul.ac.uk/media/arcs/docs/quality-assurance/QMULGraduate-Attributes.pdf

Quainoo, M. A., & Pasawano, T. (2022, April 22). *A Study of Blended E-Learning Platforms for Continuing Education During the Covid-19 Pandemic in Ghana*. doi:10.21203/rs.3.rs-1566095/v1

Quality Assurance agency (QAA). (2018). *The UK quality code for higher education*, https://www.qaa.ac.uk/en/quality-code

Rabbani, G., & Chowdhury, S. (2014). Quality of Higher Education in Bangladesh: Governance Framework and Quality Issues. *Beykent University Journal of Social Sciences, 7*(1), 78-91.

Rahman, M. M. (2020). *Organizational gap analysis in achieving SDGs in Bangladesh*. Academic Press.

Rahman, A. (2020). A Study on irregular migration from Bangladesh to Malaysia through the Bay of Bengal and the Andaman Sea. *Otoritas: Jurnal Ilmu Pemerintahan, 10*(2), 120–131. doi:10.26618/ojip.v10i2.4640

Rahman, M. M. (2021). Achieving SustainableDevelopment Goals of Agenda2030 in Bangladesh: The crossroadof the governance and performance. *Public Administration and Policy*, *24*(2), 195–211. doi:10.1108/PAP-12-2020-0056

Rahman, M. M., Arif, M. T., Safii, R., Tambi, Z., Akoi, C., Jantan, Z., Halim, S. A., & Hafiz, A. (2019). Cultural adaptation by Bangladeshi migrant workers in Sarawak, Malaysia: An empirical study. *Indonesian Journal of Cultural and Community Development*, *4*, 10–21070. doi:10.21070/ijccd.v2i3.91

Rahman, M., Uddin, M. S. J., & Albaity, M. (2014). Socio-economic conditions of Bangladeshi migrant workers in Malaysia. *Journal of Basic and Applied Scientific Research*, *4*, 246–252.

Raihan, J., & Dutta, U. (2021). Centering the margins: the precarity of Bangladeshi low-income migrant workers during the time of COVID-19. *The American Behavioral Scientist*, 1384–1405.

Rana, K., & Rana, K. (2020). ICT integration in teaching and learning activities in higher education: A case study of Nepal's teacher education. *Malaysian Online Journal of Educational Technology*, *8*(1), 36–47. doi:10.17220/mojet.2020.01.003

RanasingheR. (2020). Post-COVID19 (Novel Corona) Economic Recovery: Critical Review on Economic Immunity of Sri Lanka. Available at SSRN 3587179. doi:10.2139/ssrn.3587179

Randel, A. E., Galvin, B. M., Shore, L. M., Ehrhart, K. H., Chung, B. G., Dean, M. A., & Kedharnath, U. (2018). Inclusive leadership: Realizing positive outcomes through belongingness and being valued for uniqueness. *Human Resource Management Review*, *28*(2), 190–203. doi:10.1016/j.hrmr.2017.07.002

Randles, S., Wadham, H., Skritsovali, K., Hart, C., Hoque, S., Kettleborough, H., Klapper, R., Marron, R., Taylor, T., & Walley, L. (forthcoming). Leveraging hope & experience: Towards an integrated model of transformative learning, community & leadership for sustainability action & change. In W. Purcell & J. Haddock-Fraser (Eds.), The Bloomsbury handbook of sustainability in higher education. London: Bloomsbury.

Ranga, M., & Etzkowitz, H. (2015). Triple Helix systems: an analytical framework for innovation policy and practice in the Knowledge Society. *Entrepreneurship and knowledge exchange*, 117-158.

Rani, N. (2021). *Impact of mobile technology on students' achievements in higher education*. Waikato Institute of Technology. Retrieved from http://researcharchive.wintec.ac.nz/7810/

Rao, U., & Saul, A. (2021). From the green revolution to the green chemistry revolution: In pursuit of a paradigm shift in agricultural sustainability. In X. Savarimuthu, U. Rao, & M. F. Reynolds (Eds.), *Go Green for Environmental Sustainability* (pp. 47–66). CRC Press.

Rappaport, J. (2020). *Cowards don't make history: Orlando Fals Borda and the origins of participatory action research*. Duke University Press.

Raqib, A. (2019). Innovations in Teachers Training at Higher Education in Bangladesh. *Social Science Review*, *36*(1), 221–231.

Rashid, S. (2011). Anthropology of migration: Concept, theories and Bangladesh perspective. *Green University Review*, *2*(1), 83–100.

Rastegar Kazerooni, A., Amini, M., Tabari, P., & Moosavi, M. (2020). Peer mentoring for medical students during COVID-19 pandemic via a social media platform. *Medical Education*, *54*(8), 762–763. doi:10.1111/medu.14206 PMID:32353893

Ravetz, J. (2020). *Deeper city: Collective intelligence and the pathways from smart to wise*. Routledge. doi:10.4324/9781315765860

## Compilation of References

Rawlinson, M. C. (2015). Food, health, and global justice. *International Journal of Feminist Approaches to Bioethics*, *8*(2), 1–9.

Re:wild (2022). *Our work*. Re:wild. https://www.rewild.org/our-work

Reason, P., & Bradbury, H. (Eds.). (2001). *The Sage handbook of action research*. Sage.

Reddy, P., & Shaw, R. (2019). Becoming a professional: A longitudinal qualitative study of the graduate transition in BSc Psychology. *Education + Training*, *61*(2), 272–288. doi:10.1108/ET-10-2018-0210

Redmond, P., Heffernan, A., Abawi, L., Brown, A., & Henderson, R. (2018). An online engagement framework for higher education. *Online Learning*, *22*(1), 183-204.

Reichelt, M. (2009). A critical evaluation of writing teaching programmes in different foreign language settings. In R. Manchon (Ed.), *Writing in foreign language contexts. Learning, teaching and research* (pp. 183–206). Multilingual Matters. doi:10.21832/9781847691859-011

Reid, A., & Petocz, P. (2006). University lecturers' understanding of sustainability. *Higher Education*, *51*(1), 105–123. doi:10.100710734-004-6379-4

Reilly, J. R., Gallagher-Lepak, S., & Killion, C. (2012). "Me and my computer": Emotional factors in online learning. *Nursing Education Perspectives*, *33*(2), 100–105. doi:10.5480/1536-5026-33.2.100 PMID:22616408

Reinders, H., & Hays, J. (2020). Creativity and criticality in presencing. In O. Gunnlaugson & W. Brendel (Eds.), *Advances in presencing vol II: Individual approaches in theory u* (pp. 393–420). Trifoss Business Press.

Rennert-Ariev, P. (2008). The hidden curriculum of performance-based teacher education. *Teachers College Record*, *110*(1), 105–138. doi:10.1177/016146810811000105

Republic of Turkey Ministry of Interior Presidency of Migration Management. (2017, June) *Residence permit data*. https://www.goc.gov.tr/kurumlar/goc.gov.tr/YillikGocRaporlari/2016_yiik_goc_raporu_haziran.pdf

Reza, M. M., & Subramaniam, T. (2019). Economic and social wellbeing of the Bangladeshi migrant workers in Malaysia. In *Social research methodology and new techniques in analysis, interpretation, and writing* (pp. 106–134). IGI Global. doi:10.4018/978-1-5225-7897-0.ch006

Ribeiro, M. F., Saraiva, V., Pereira, P., & Ribeiro, C. (2019). Escala de Motivação Académica: Validação no Ensino Superior Público Português. *Revista de Administração Contemporânea*, *23*(3), 288–310. doi:10.1590/1982-7849rac2019180190

Richards, D., & Tangney, B. (2008). An informal online learning community for student mental health at university: A preliminary investigation. *British Journal of Guidance & Counselling*, *36*(1), 81–97. doi:10.1080/03069880701715671

Richardson, J. C., Arbaugh, J. B., Cleveland-Innes, M., Ice, P., Swan, K. P., & Garrison, D. R. (2012). Using the community of inquiry framework to inform effective instructional design. In L. Moller & J. B. Heuett (Eds.), *The Next Generation of Distance Education* (pp. 97–125). Springer. doi:10.1007/978-1-4614-1785-9_7

Richmond, A. S., & Cummings, R. (2005). Implementing Kolb's learning styles into online distance education. *International Journal of Technology in Teaching and Learning*, *1*(1), 45–54.

Rieckmann, M. (2018). Learning to transform the world: Key competencies in Education for Sustainable Development. In A. Leicht, J. Heiss, & W. J. Byun (Eds.), *Issues and trends in education for sustainable development* (pp. 39–59). UNESCO.

Rist, G. (2014). *The history of development: from western origins to global faith*. Bloomsbury Publishing.

Rittel, H., & Webber, M. (1973). Dilemmas in a general theory of planning. *Policy Sciences*, *2*(2), 155–169. doi:10.1007/BF01405730

Roberts, J. (2006). Limits to communities of practice. *Journal of Management Studies*, *43*(3), 623–639. doi:10.1111/j.1467-6486.2006.00618.x

Robinson, J. D., & Persky, A. M. (2020). Developing self-directed students. *American Journal of Pharmaceutical Education*, *84*(3), 292–296. doi:10.5688/ajpe847512 PMID:32313284

Robinson, R. S. (2014). Purposive Sampling. In A. C. Michalos (Ed.), *Encyclopedia of Quality of Life and Well-Being Research*. Springer., doi:10.1007/978-94-007-0753-5_2337

Rocha, Z. L. (2019). Strict versus flexible categorizations of mixedness: Classifying mixed race in Singapore and New Zealand. *Social Identities*, *25*(3), 310–326. doi:10.1080/13504630.2018.1499221

Rodrigues, H., Almeida, F., Figueiredo, V., & Lopes, S. (2019). Tracking e-learning through published papers: A systematic review. *Computers & Education*, *136*, 87–98. doi:10.1016/j.compedu.2019.03.007

Rodríguez-Labajos, B., & Ray, I. (2021). Six avenues for engendering creative environmentalism. *Global Environmental Change*, *68*, 102269.

Roelofs, K., Hagenaars, M., & Stins, J. (2010). Facing freeze: Social threat induces bodily freeze in humans. *Psychological Science*, *21*(11), 1575–1581.

Römgens, I., Scoupe, R., & Beausaert, S. (2020). Unraveling the concept of employability, bringing together research on employability in higher education and the workplace. *Studies in Higher Education*, *45*(12), 2588–2603. doi:10.1080/03075079.2019.1623770

Rosenthal, U., Boin, A., & Comfort, L. K. (2001). *Managing crises: Threats, dilemmas, opportunities*. Charles C. Thomas.

Roser, C., Sato, M., & Nakano, M. (2021). Would you like some wine? Introducing variants to the beer game. *Production Planning and Control*, *32*(6), 454–462. doi:10.1080/09537287.2020.1742370

Roy, A. (2020, April 3). The pandemic is a portal. *Financial Times*. https://www.ft.com/content/10d8f5e8-74eb-11ea-95fe-fcd274e920ca

Roy, P., Chowdhury, J. S., Abd Wahab, H., & Saad, R. (2022). Social Justice Through BPATC in Bangladesh Under the Shadow of Colonialism: Prospects and Challenges. *Social Justice Research Methods for Doctoral Research*, 303-319.

Roy, P., Chowdhury, J. S., Abd Wahab, H., & Saad, R. B. M. (2022). Ethnic Tension of the Bangladeshi Santal: A CDA of the Constitutional Provision. In Handbook of Research on Ethnic, Racial, and Religious Conflicts and Their Impact on State and Social Security (pp. 208-226). IGI Global. doi:10.4018/978-1-7998-8911-3.ch013

Roy, P. K., Hamidi, M., & Roy, S. (2022). Internet as a Field: An Analysis of the Santal Online Communities. In *Practices, Challenges, and Prospects of Digital Ethnography as a Multidisciplinary Method* (pp. 124–137). IGI Global. doi:10.4018/978-1-6684-4190-9.ch009

Russell, T. L. (1999). *The "no significant difference phenomenon."* North Carolina State University. Retrieved September 30, 2004, from: http://nt.media.hku.hk/no_sig_diff/ phenom1.html

Ryan, M. K., Haslam, S. A., Morgenroth, T., Rink, F., Stoker, J., & Peters, K. (2016). Getting on top of the glass cliff: Reviewing a decade of evidence, explanations, and impact. *The Leadership Quarterly*, *27*(3), 446–455. doi:10.1016/j.leaqua.2015.10.008

Ryan, R. M., & Deci, E. L. (2000). Self-determination theory and the facilitation of intrinsic motivation, social development, and well-being. *The American Psychologist*, *55*(1), 68–78. doi:10.1037/0003-066X.55.1.68 PMID:11392867

Ryan, R. M., & Deci, E. L. (2020). Intrinsic and extrinsic motivation from a self-determination theory perspective: Definitions, theory, practices, and future directions. *Contemporary Educational Psychology*, *61*, 101860. doi:10.1016/j.cedpsych.2020.101860

Sadeghi, N., Kasim, Z. M., Tan, B. H., & Abdullah, F. S. (2012). Learning styles, personality types and reading comprehension performance. *English Language Teaching*, *5*(4), 116–123. doi:10.5539/elt.v5n4p116

Sadler, T. D. (2009). Situated learning in science education: Socio-scientifc issues as contexts for practice. *Studies in Science Education*, *45*(1), 1–42. doi:10.1080/03057260802681839

Şahin, D. R., Çubuk, D., & Uslu, T. (2014). The effect of organizational support, transformational leadership, personnel empowerment, work engagement, performance, and demographical variables on the factors of psychological capital. *EMAJ*, *3*(3), 1–18. doi:10.5195/EMAJ.2014.49

Salancik, G. R., & Pfeffer, J. (1978). A social information processing approach to job attitudes and task design. *Administrative Science Quarterly*, *23*(2), 224–253. doi:10.2307/2392563 PMID:10307892

Salehi, Z., Mokhtari Nouri, J., Khademolhoseyni, S. M., & Ebadi, A. (2014). Studying the effect of education and implementation of Evidence-Based Nursing Guidelines on parents' satisfaction in NICU. *Journal of Applied Environmental and Biological Sciences*, *4*(8), 176–182.

Salomon, G. (2000). *E-moderating the key to teaching and learning online*. Kogan Page.

Sammalisto, K., & Lindhqvist, T. (2008). Integration of sustainability in higher education: A study with international perspectives. *Innovative Higher Education*, *32*(4), 221–233. doi:10.100710755-007-9052-x

Sancho, P., Corral, R., Rivas, T., González, M. J., Chordi, A., & Tejedor, C. (2006). A blended learning experience for teaching microbiology. *American Journal of Pharmaceutical Education*, *70*(5), 1–16. doi:10.5688/aj7005120 PMID:17149449

Sandanayake, T. C., Madurapperuma, A. P., & Dias, D. (2011). Affective E learning model for Recognising learner emotions. *International Journal of Information and Education Technology (IJIET)*, *1*(4), 315–320. doi:10.7763/IJIET.2011.V1.51

Sandel, M. (2012). *What money can't buy: The moral limits of markets*. Allen Lane.

Santos, A. L., & Rodrigues, L. L. (2021). Banks and climate-related information: The case of Portugal. *Sustainability (Switzerland)*, *13*(21), 12215. Advance online publication. doi:10.3390u132112215

Sarker, M. A. (2019). *Bangladesh Delta Plan (BDP) 2100*. General Economics Division, Bangladesh Planning Commission.

Sarker, M. A. R., Khan, N. A., & Musarrat, K. M. (2016). Livelihood and vulnerability of the Santals community in Bangladesh. *The Malaysian Journal of Social Administration*, *12*(1), 38–55. doi:10.22452/mjsa.vol12no1.2

Savigny, H. (2014). Women, know your limits: Cultural sexism in academia. *Gender and Education*, *26*(7), 794–809. doi:10.1080/09540253.2014.970977

Sayer, A. (2011). *Why things matter to people: Social sciences, values and ethical life*. Cambridge University Press. doi:10.1017/CBO9780511734779

Schabracq, M. (2003). Everyday well-being and stress in work and organisations. In M. Schabracq, J. Winnubst, & C. Cooper (Eds.), *The Handbook of work and health psychology* (pp. 7–36). John Wiley & Sons.

Schensul, J. J. (2011). Building an applied educational anthropology beyond the academy. *A Companion to the Anthropology of Education*, 112-134.

Schiefelbein, M. (2022, August 20). *Chinese farmers struggle as scorching drought wilts crops*. The Associated Press. https://apnews.com/article/china-asia-droughts-chongqing-ddd4bc18741f4710e5fbd4db7070d3d8

Schmitz, R. (2022, August 17. *Germany's Rhine is at one of its lowest levels. That's trouble for the top EU economy*. All Things Considered. https://www.npr.org/2022/08/17/1117861780/germany-rhine-low-water-level-shipping

Schroeder, S. M., & Terras, K. L. (2015). Advising experiences and needs of online, cohort, and classroom adult graduate learners. *The Journal of the National Academic Advising Association*, *35*(1), 42–55. doi:10.12930/NACADA-13-044

Schuck, S., Aubusson, P., Burden, K., & Brindley, S. (2018). Future—always coming never comes: embracing imagination and learning from uncertainty. In S. Schuck, P. Aubusson, K. Burden, & S. Brindley (Eds.), *Uncertainty in teacher education futures* (pp. 253–264). Springer.

Sediri, S., Trommetter, M., Frascaria-Lacoste, N., & Fernandez-Manjarrés, J. (2020). Transformability as a wicked problem: A cautionary tale? *Sustainability*, *12*(15), 5895. doi:10.3390u12155895

Sen, A. (2009). *The Idea of Justice*. Allan Lane Penguin Books.

Senge, P. M. (1990). *The fifth discipline: The art and practice of the learning organization*. Doubleday.

Senge, P. M., & Käufer, K. H. (2000). Communities of leaders or no leadership at all. In B. Kellerman & L. R. Matusak (Eds.), *Cutting Edge: Leadership*. James McGregor Burns Academy of Leadership Press.

Senne, F. (2021, June). Beyond connectivity: Internet for all. *Internet Sectoral Overview*, *13*(2), 1–10.

Shafie, H., & Kilby, P. (2003). *Including the excluded: ethnic inequality and Development in Northwest Bangladesh*. Academic Press.

Shahmoradi, L., Changizi, V., Mehraeen, E., Bashiri, A., Jannat, B., & Hosseini, M. (2018, September). The challenges of E-learning system: Higher educational institutions perspective. *Journal of Education and Health Promotion*, *7*. Advance online publication. doi:10.4103/jehp.jehp_39_18 PMID:30271801

Sharma, G. (2017). Pros and cons of different sampling techniques. *International Journal of Applied Research*, *3*(7), 749–752.

Sherren, K. (2005). Balancing the disciplines: A multidisciplinary perspective on sustainability curriculum content. *Australian Journal of Environmental Education*, *21*, 97–106. doi:10.1017/S0814062600000987

Sherry, L. (1995). Issues in distance learning. *International Journal of Educational Telecommunications*, *1*(4), 337–365.

Shibli, A. (2021) A case for improving labour conditions in Southeast Asia. *The Daily Star*. https://www.thedailystar.net/opinion/opendialogue/news/case-improving-labour-conditionssoutheast-asia-2031329

Shields, C. (2020). Transformative leadership. *Oxford research encyclopedia of education*. https://oxfordre.com/education/view/10.1093/acrefore/9780190264093.001.0001/acrefore-9780190264093-e-632

Shields, C. M. (2011). Transformative leadership: An introduction. In C. M. Shields (Ed.), *Transformative leadership: A reader*. Peter Lang.

Shields, C. M. (2017). *Transformative leadership in education: Equitable and socially just change in an uncertain and complex world*. Routledge. doi:10.4324/9781315207148

*Compilation of References*

Shochet, R., Fleming, A., Wagner, J., Colbert-Getz, J., Bhutiani, M., Moynahan, K., & Keeley, M. (2019). Defining learning communities in undergraduate medical education: A national study. *Journal of Medical Education and Curricular Development, 6*, 2382120519827911. doi:10.1177/2382120519827911 PMID:30937385

Shore, L. M., Randel, A. E., Chung, B. G., Dean, M. A., Holcombe Ehrhart, K., & Singh, G. (2011). Inclusion and diversity in work groups: A review and model for future research. *Journal of Management, 37*(4), 1262–1289. doi:10.1177/0149206310385943

Shteynberg, G., Hirsh, J. B., Bentley, R. A., & Garthoff, J. (2020). Shared worlds and shared minds: A theory of collective learning and a psychology of common knowledge. *Psychological Review, 127*(5), 918–931. doi:10.1037/rev0000200 PMID:32309965

Shu, H., & Gu, X. (2018). Determining the diferences between online and face-to-face student–group interactions in a blended learning course. *The Internet and Higher Education, 39*, 13–21. doi:10.1016/j.iheduc.2018.05.003

Siddiquei, N. L., & Khalid, R. (2018). The relationship between personality traits, learning styles and academic performance of E-Learner. *Open Praxis, 10*(3), 1–20. doi:10.5944/openpraxis.10.3.870

Simon, E., Dormer, K., & Hartshorne, J. (1971). *Lowson's textbook of botany*. University Tutorial Press.

Singhal, R., Kumar, A., Singh, H., Fuller, S., & Gill, S. S. (2021). Digital device-based active learning approach using virtual community classroom during the COVID-19 pandemic. *Computer Applications in Engineering Education, 29*(5), 1007–1033. doi:10.1002/cae.22355

Sipos, Y., Battisti, B., & Grimm, K. (2008). Achieving transformative sustainability learning: Engaging head, hands and heart. *International Journal of Sustainability in Higher Education, 9*(1), 68–86. doi:10.1108/14676370810842193

Slat, B. (2012). *How the oceans can clean themselves*. TED Talk. Retrieved from https://www.youtube.com/watch?v=ROW9F-c0kIQ

Slovic, S. (2016). Narrative Scholarship as an American Contribution to Global Ecocriticism. In H. Zapf (Ed.), *Handbook of Ecocriticism and Cultural Ecology* (pp. 315–333). DeGruyter.

Small, L., Shacklock, K., & Marchant, T. (2018). Employability: A contemporary review for higher education stakeholders. *Journal of Vocational Education and Training, 70*(1), 148–166. doi:10.1080/13636820.2017.1394355

Smith, L. M. (2014). The benefits of sustainability and integrated reporting. *Journal of Legal, Ethical and Regulatory Issues, 17*(2), 93–113. https://www.proquest.com/openview/bcb70ca0b973d8fbea1cdcd76a9bdcff/1?pq-origsite=gscholar&cbl=38868

Smith, W., Erez, M., Jarvenpaa, S., Lewis, M. W., & Tracey, P. (2017). Adding complexity to theories of paradox, tensions, and dualities of innovation and change: Introduction to organization studies special issue on paradox, tensions, and dualities of innovation and change. *Organization Studies, 38*(3-4), 303–317.

Smith, C. R. (2017). *Rhetoric and human consciousness: A history* (5th ed.). Waveland Press.

Smith, J. A., & Judd, J. (2020). COVID-19: Vulnerability and the power of privilege in a pandemic. *Health Promotion Journal of Australia, 31*(2), 158–160. doi:10.1002/hpja.333 PMID:32197274

Smith, L. T. (2021). *Decolonizing methodologies: Research and indigenous peoples*. Bloomsbury Publishing. doi:10.5040/9781350225282

Sneddon, C., Howarth, R. B., & Norgaard, R. B. (2006). Sustainable development in a post-Brundtland world. *Ecological Economics, 57*(2), 253–268. doi:10.1016/j.ecolecon.2005.04.013

Soares, S. E., & Sidun, N. M. (2021). Women leaders during a global crisis: Challenges, characteristics, and strengths. *International Perspectives in Psychology: Research, Practice, Consultation*, *10*(3), 130–137. doi:10.1027/2157-3891/a000020

Soeftestad, L. T. (1994). *Workshop on participatory development*. Academic Press.

Soeftestad, L. T. (2004). Biodiversity conservation, communication and language–is English a solution, a problem or both? *Policy Matters*, *13*, 281–283.

Solaiman, M. (2018, August 27). Teacher-student ratio not ideal at many public universities. *Daily Sun*.

Sosniak, L. A. (1994). *Bloom's taxonomy* (L. W. Anderson, Ed.). Univ. Chicago Press.

Southern, N. (2007). Mentoring for transformative learning: The importance of relationship in creating learning communities of care. *Journal of Transformative Education*, *5*(4), 329–338. doi:10.1177/1541344607310576

Souza, D. T., Jacobi, P. R., & Wal, A. E. J. (2019). Learning based transformations towards sustainability: A relational approach based on Humberto Maturna and Paulo Freire. *Environmental Education Research*, *25*(11), 1605–1619. doi:10.1080/13504622.2019.1641183

Souza, Z. A., & Miranda, G. J. (2019). Motivação de alunos de graduação em Ciências Contábeis ao longo do curso. *Enfoque: Reflexão Contábil*, *38*(2), 49–65. doi:10.4025/enfoque.v38i2.41079

Srichanyachon, N. (2014). The barriers and needs of online learners. *Turkish Online Journal of Distance Education*, *15*(3), 50–59. doi:10.17718/tojde.08799

Stacey, R. (1992). *Managing the unknowable: Strategic boundaries between order and chaos in organizations*. John Wiley & Sons.

Stefani, L., & Blessinger, P. (Eds.). (2017). *Inclusive leadership in higher education: International perspectives and approaches*. Routledge. doi:10.4324/9781315466095

Steinmayr, R., Weidinger, A. F., Schwinger, M., & Spinath, B. (2019). The importance of students' motivation for their academic achievement–replicating and extending previous findings. *Frontiers in Psychology*, *10*, 1730. doi:10.3389/fpsyg.2019.01730 PMID:31417459

Stemler, S. (2001). *An overview of content analysis. Practical assessment, research, and evaluation*. http://pareonline.net/getvn.asp?v=7&n=17

Stengers, I. (2018). *Another science is possible: A manifesto for slow science*. Polity.

Stenhouse, L. (1975). *Introduction to curriculum research and development*. Heinemann Educational.

Sterling, S. (2021). Concern, conception, and consequence: Re-thinking the paradigm of higher education in dangerous times. *Frontiers in Sustainability*, *2*, 743806. doi:10.3389/frsus.2021.743806

Stoll, L., & Earl, L. (2003). Making it last: Building capacity for sustainability. In B. Davies & J. West-Burham (Eds.), *Handbook of Educational Leadership and Management*. Pearson/Longman.

Storch, N., & Aldosari, A. (2010). Learners' use of first language (Arabic) in pair work in EFL class. *Language Teaching Research*, *14*(4), 355–375. doi:10.1177/1362168810375362

Storey, M., Killian, S., & O'Regan, P. (2017). Responsible management education: Mapping the field in the context of the SDGs. *International Journal of Management Education*, *15*(2), 93–103. doi:10.1016/j.ijme.2017.02.009

Stoten, D. (2018). Employability: A contested concept in higher education. *Journal of Pedagogic Development*, *8*(1), 9–17.

## Compilation of References

Sturgeon, N. (2016). *Ecofeminist natures: Race, gender, feminist theory, and political action*. Routledge.

Sturgeon, N. L. (2009). *Environmentalism in popular culture: Gender, race, sexuality, and the politics of the natural*. University of Arizona Press.

Sturmberg, J. (2018). *Health System Redesign*. Springer. doi:10.1007/978-3-319-64605-3_3

Subhash, S., & Cudney, E. A. (2018). Gamified learning in higher education: A systematic review of the literature. *Computers in Human Behavior*, *87*, 192–206. doi:10.1016/j.chb.2018.05.028

Subramaniam, G. (2020). *The compounding impacts of COVID-19 on migrant workers across Asia* (Part 1). Academic Press.

Sue, D. W., Arredondo, P., & McDavis, R. J. (1992). Multicultural counselling competencies and standards: A call to the profession. *Journal of Counseling and Development*, *70*(4), 47. doi:10.1002/j.1556-6676.1992.tb01642.x

Sugahara, S., & Lau, D. (2019). The effect of game-based learning as the experiential learning tool for business and accounting training: A study of management game. *Journal of Education for Business*, *94*(5), 297–305. doi:10.1080/08832323.2018.1527751

Suleman, F., & Laranjeiro, A. M. (2018). The employability skills of graduates and employers' options in Portugal: An explorative study of anticipative and remedial strategies. *Education + Training*, *60*(9), 1097–1111. doi:10.1108/ET-10-2017-0158

Sullivan, R., & Gouldson, A. (2012). Does voluntary carbon reporting meet investors' needs? *Journal of Cleaner Production*, *36*(January), 60–67. doi:10.1016/j.jclepro.2012.02.020

Sunam, R. (2022). Infrastructures of migrant precarity: Unpacking precarity through the lived experiences of migrant workers in Malaysia. *Journal of Ethnic and Migration Studies*, 1–19. doi:10.1080/1369183X.2022.2077708

Sun, S. (2008). Organizational culture and its themes. *International Journal of Business and Management*, *3*(12), 137–141.

Sunstein, C. R. (2004, April 26). Did Brown Matter? On the fiftieth anniversary of the fabled desegregation case, not everyone is celebrating. *The New Yorker*. Retrieved from https://www.newyorker.com/magazine/2004/05/03/did-brown-matter

Sun, W., Hong, J. C., Dong, Y., Huang, Y., & Fu, Q. (2022). Self-directed Learning Predicts Online Learning Engagement in Higher Education Mediated by Perceived Value of Knowing Learning Goals. *The Asia-Pacific Education Researcher*, 1–10. doi:10.100740299-022-00653-6

Sutton, M. (2005). The globalization of multicultural education. *Indiana Journal of International Legal Studies*, *12*(1), 97–108.

Swan, K., & Shea, P. (2005). The development of virtual learning communities. In S. R. Hiltz & R. Goldman (Eds.), *Asynchronous Learning Networks: The Research Frontier* (pp. 239–260). Hampton Press.

Tangney, P. (2021). Are "Climate Deniers" Rational Actors? Applying Weberian Rationalities to Advance Climate Policymaking. *Environmental Communication*, *15*(8), 1077–1091.

Tang, Y. M., Chen, P. C., Law, K. M. Y., Wu, C. H., Lau, Y. Y., Guan, J., He, D., & Ho, G. T. S. (2021). Comparative studies for students readiness in live online learning during the coronavirus (COVID-19) outbreak in higher education sector. *Computers & Education*, *168*, 104211. doi:10.1016/j.compedu.2021.104211 PMID:33879955

Tan, L. M., Laswad, F., & Chua, F. (2022). Bridging the employability skills gap: Going beyond classroom walls. *Pacific Accounting Review*, *34*(2), 225–248. doi:10.1108/PAR-04-2021-0050

Tarone, E. (1983). Some thoughts on the notion of 'communication strategy'. In C. Faerch & G. Kasper (Eds.), Strategies in Interlanguage Communication (pp. 61-74). Academic Press.

Tarquinio, L., & Posadas, S. C. (2020). Exploring the term "non-financial information": An academics' view. *Meditari Accountancy Research*, *28*(5), 727–749. doi:10.1108/MEDAR-11-2019-0602

Taylor, C. (2020). Slow singularities for collective mattering: New material feminist praxis in the accelerated academy. *Irish Educational Studies*, *39*(2), 255–272. doi:10.1080/03323315.2020.1734045

Taylor, D. (2021). On damaged and regenerating life: Spinoza and mentalities of climate catastrophe. *Crisis and Critique*, *8*(1), 476–501.

Taylor, D. G., & Frechette, M. (2022). The impact of workload, productivity, and social support on burnout among marketing faculty during the COVID-19 pandemic. *Journal of Marketing Education*, *44*(2), 02734753221074284. doi:10.1177/02734753221074284

Taylor, E. W. (2008). Transformative learning theory. *New Directions for Adult and Continuing Education*, *2008*(119), 5–15. doi:10.1002/ace.301

Taylor, P. J., Russ-Eft, D. F., & Taylor, H. (2009). Transfer of management training from alternative perspectives. *The Journal of Applied Psychology*, *94*(1), 104–121. doi:10.1037/a0013006 PMID:19186899

TCFD. (2017). *Final Report: Recommendations of the Task Force on Climate-Related Financial Disclosures*. https://www.fsb-tcfd.org/wp-content/ uploads/2017/06/

Teixeira, C., Gomes, D., & Borges, J. (2015). Introductory accounting students' motives, expectations, and preparedness for higher education: Some Portuguese evidence. *Accounting Education*, *24*(2), 123–145. doi:10.1080/09639284.2015.1018284

Tekkol, İ. A., & Demirel, M. (2018). An Investigation of Self-Directed Learning Skills of Undergraduate Students. *Frontiers in Psychology*, *9*, 1–14. doi:10.3389/fpsyg.2018.02324 PMID:30532727

Tellakat, M., Boyd, R. L., & Pennebaker, J. W. (2019). How do online learners study? The psychometrics of students' clicking patterns in online courses. *PLoS One*, *14*(3), e0213863. doi:10.1371/journal.pone.0213863 PMID:30908503

Tennant, M. (2019). Psychology and Adult Learning: The Role of Theory in Informing Practice (4th ed.). Routledge., https://doi.org/10.4324/9780429023255.

Thakore, R., Kavantera, A., & Whitehall, G. (2022). Systems-thinking theory: Decision-making for sustainable workplace transformations. In V. Danivska & R. Appel-Meulenbroek (Eds.), *A handbook of management theories and models for office environments and services* (pp. 25–35). Routledge.

Tharenou, P., Saks, A. M., & Moore, C. (2007). A review and critique of research on training and organizational-level outcomes. *Human Resource Management Review*, *17*(3), 251–273. doi:10.1016/j.hrmr.2007.07.004

The Associated Press. (2022, August 19). *Winds drive major wildfire in Spain; Portugal goes on alert*. The Associated Press. https://apnews.com/article/wildfires-fires-valencia-a219c8a7ff5542b0b3732afd7fc19890

The Malaysiakini. (2020). *Raya Message*. Pm Indicates Exit Plan Led By Community Leaders. Malaysiakini.Com/News/527097

The Ocean Cleanup. (2022a). *The interceptor 007 has arrived in LA County*. Facebook. https://www.facebook.com/TheOceanCleanup/videos/731077404702075/

The Ocean Cleanup. (2022b). *About*. https://theoceancleanup.com/about/

## Compilation of References

The United Nations. (2016). Retrieved from https://www.un.org/en/universal-declaration-human-rights/index.html

Thevanes, N., & Arulrajah, A. A. (2017). The search for sustainable human resource management practices: A review and reflections. In *Proceedings of Fourteenth International Conference on Business Management (ICBM)* (pp. 606-634). Academic Press.

Thomas, T. D. (2012). Political Implications of Emergency Management. *Journal of Environmental Science & Engineering*, *1*(3), 397–402.

TIB. (2016). *Recruitment of Lecturers in Public Universities: Governance Challenges and Ways Forward*. Transparency International Bangladesh.

Tilbury, D. (2011). *Education for Sustainable Development: An Expert Review of Processes and Learning*. UNESCO. Retrieved, February 11, 2022, from https://unesdoc.unesco.org/ark:/48223/pf0000191442

Tjosvold, D. (2008). The conflict-positive organization: It depends upon us. *Journal of Organizational Behavior: The International Journal of Industrial. Occupational and Organizational Psychology and Behavior*, *29*(1), 19–28.

Top-BOSS. (2022). Retrieved from https://www.top-boss.com/mbs-macro-business-simulation/

Townsend, B. L. (2002). Leave no teacher behind: A bold proposal for teacher education. *International Journal of Qualitative Studies in Education: QSE*, *15*(6), 727–738. doi:10.1080/0951839022000014402

Tran, T. T. T., & Nguyen, H. V. (2020). Gender preference in higher education leadership: Insights from gender distribution and subordinate perceptions and expectations in Vietnam universities. *International Journal of Leadership in Education*, 1–22.

Tripura, J. (2016). Reflection of the Santal Rebellion and the Situations of the Indigenous Peoples of Bangladesh. *Unread Voice*.

Tripura, P. (2018). *Prantikotar Khaad Theke Mohaakashe*. Samhati Publication.

Tripura, P. (2020). *Colonial Shadow in Bangladesh (Bangla books)*. Sangbed.

Tsagari, D., & Giannikas, C. (2018). Re-evaluating the use of the L1 in the L2 classroom: students vs. teachers. *Applied Linguistics Review*, 1-31. doi:10.1515/applirev-2017-0104

Tsagari, D., & Meletiadou, E. (2015). Peer Assessment of Adolescent Learners' Writing Performance. *Writing & Pedagogy*, *7*(2/3), 305–328. doi:10.1558/wap.v7i2-3.26457

Tsing, A. (2017). A threat to holocene resurgence is a threat to liveability. In M. Brightman & J. Lewis (Eds.), *The anthropology of sustainability* (pp. 51–65). Palgrave. doi:10.1057/978-1-137-56636-2_3

Turner, J. C., Christensen, A., Kackar-Cam, H. Z., Fulmer, S. M., & Trucano, M. (2018). The development of professional learning communities and their teacher leaders: An activity systems analysis. *Journal of the Learning Sciences*, *27*(1), 49–88. doi:10.1080/10508406.2017.1381962

Turzo, T., Marzi, G., Favino, C., & Terzani, S. (2022). Non-financial reporting research and practice: Lessons from the last decade. *Journal of Cleaner Production*, *345*(February), 131154. doi:10.1016/j.jclepro.2022.131154

Tyran, K. L. (2017). Transforming students into global citizens : International service learning and PRME. *International Journal of Management Education*, *15*(2), 162–171. doi:10.1016/j.ijme.2017.03.007

Uddin, M., & Mohammed, A. A. (2021). Adjustment Factors on the Work Performance of Bangladeshi Temporary Contract Workers in Malaysia. *The Indian Journal of Labour Economics*, *64*(2), 333–349. doi:10.100741027-021-00309-x

UK GDPR. (2018). *The General Data Protection Regulation (GDPR) Guidance for members*. Available at: https://www.local.gov.uk/sites/default/files/documents/The%2BGeneral%2BProtection%2BData%2BRegulation%2B%28GDPR%29%2B-%2BGuidance%2Bfor%2BMembers.pdf

Ullah, A. A., Ferdous, J., & Chattoraj, D. (2022). Social, Political and Cultural Remittances: Implications for the Origin and Destination Countries. *Millennial Asia*.

Umar, I. (2014). Factors influencing students' career choice in accounting: The case of Yobe State University. *Research Journal of Finance and Accounting*, 5(17), 59-62. https://core.ac.uk/download/pdf/234630127.pdf

UNCTAD. (2020, October 29). *International Accounting and Reporting Issues: 2019 Review*. https://isar.unctad.org/annual-review/

UNESCO. (2003). *Promoting Quality Education: Education for Peace, Human Rights and Democracy; Education for Sustainable Development; Curricula, Educational Tools and Teacher Training*. United Nations Educational, Scientific and Cultural Organization.

UNESCO. (2004). Quality Education for All Young People. In *47th International Conference on Education of UNESCO* (pp. 56, 52, 49, 46, 115-116). Geneva: UNESCO.

UNESCO. (2005). *Guidelines for quality provision in cross-border higher education*. UNECO Publishing.

UNESCO. (2014). *Education for Sustainable Development*. doi:10.4324/9781315876573

UNESCO. (2019). *Why we urgently need to teach and learn about climate change*. UNESCO. https://en.unesco.org/news/why-we-urgently-need-teach-and-learn-about-climate-change

UNESCO. (2020). *Education: From disruption to recovery*. Retrieved November 1, 2021, from https://en.unesco.org/covid19/educationresponse

UNESCO. (2021). *Exploring the impact of COVID-19 in Learning in Africa*. Retrieved from https://en.unesco.org/news/exploring-impact-covid-19-learning-africa

UNICEF. (2000). *Defining Quality in Education*. Programme Division Working Paper Series, UNICEF. https://www.unicef.org/programme/girlseducation/papers.htm

United Nations (UN). (2021, July 15). *Deeply negative impact of COVID pandemic, reverses SDG progress*. https://news.un.org/en/story/2021/07/1095942

United Nations Development Programme. (2022). *The Sustainable Development Goals in Action*. Retrieved June 14, 2022, from https://www.undp.org/sustainable-development-goals

United Nations Educational, Scientific and Cultural Organization (UNESCO). (2014). *UNESCO roadmap for implementing the global action programme on education for sustainable development*. Retrieved from https://unesdoc.unesco.org/images/0023/002305/230514e.pdf

United Nations. (2015). *Transforming Our World: The 2030 Agenda for Sustainable Development*. United Nations.

United Nations. (2022). Retrieved from https://www.un.org/en/transforming-education-summit?gclid=EAIaIQobChMI6PDkzs-d-gIV6cIWBR0G_wsgEAAYAiAAEgKPFfD_BwE

United Nations. (2022). *Sustainable Development Agenda*. Retrieved June 14, 2022, from https://www.un.org/sustainabledevelopment/development-agenda/

## Compilation of References

United Nations. (2022). *The climate crisis – A race we can win.* UN. https://www.un.org/en/un75/climate-crisis-race-we-can-win

University Grants Commission. (2014). *UGC Annual Report, 2014.* University Grants Commission, Ministry of Education.

University Grants Commission. (2016). *UGC Annual Report, 2016.* University Grants Commission, Ministry of Education.

University Grants Commission. (2017). *UGC Annual Report, 2017.* University Grants Commission, Ministry of Education.

Ünlü, İ., & Örten, H. (2013). Investigation of the perception of teacher candidates about multiculturism and multicultural education. Dicle University Journal of Ziya Gokalp Education Faculty, 21.

Urval, R., Kamath, A., Ullal, S., Shenoy, A., Shenoy, N., & Udupa, L. (2014). Assessment of learning styles of undergraduate medical students using the VARK questionnaire and the influence of sex and academic performance. *Advances in Physiology Education, 38*(3), 216–220. Advance online publication. doi:10.1152/advan.00024.2014 PMID:25179610

USAID. (2022). *Climate change.* https://www.usaid.gov/climate

Ustunel, E. (2016). *EFL classroom code-switching.* Palgrave Macmillan. doi:10.1057/978-1-137-55844-2

Vaidyanathan, G. (2022, August 17). Biden signs historic climate bill as scientists applaud. *Nature Magazine.* https://www.scientificamerican.com/article/biden-signs-historic-climate-bill-as-scientists-applaud/

Van Deur, P. (2017). *Managing self-directed learning in primary school education: emerging research and opportunities.* IGI Global.

Van Heerden, D., & Goosen, L. (2021). Students' Perceptions of e-Assessment in the Context of Covid-19: The Case of UNISA. In M. Qhobela, M. M. Ntsohi, & L. G. Mohafa (Ed.), *Proceedings of the 29th Conference of the Southern African Association for Research in Mathematics, Science and Technology Education (SAARMSTE)* (pp. 291-305). SAARMSTE.

Van Woezik, T. E. T., Koksma, J. J. J., Reuzel, R. P. B., Jaarsma, D. C., & van der Wilt, G. J. (2021). There is more than 'I' in self-directed learning: An exploration of self-directed learning in teams of undergraduate students. *Medical Teacher, 43*(5), 590–598. doi:10.1080/0142159X.2021.1885637 PMID:33617387

Varney, S. (2013). *A complexity perspective on organisational change: making sense of emerging patterns in self-organising systems* [Unpublished doctoral dissertation]. University of Reading, UK.

Vasileiou, K., Barnett, J., Thorpe, S., & Young, T. (2018). Characterising and justifying sample size sufficiency in interview-based studies: Systematic analysis of qualitative health research over a 15-year period. *BMC Medical Research Methodology, 18*(1), 1–18. doi:10.118612874-018-0594-7 PMID:30463515

Vasileva-Stojanovska, T., Malinovski, T., Vasileva, M., Jovevski, D., & Trajkovik, V. (2015). Impact of satisfaction, personality and learning style on educational outcomes in a blended learning environment. *Learning and Individual Differences, 38,* 127–135. doi:10.1016/j.lindif.2015.01.018

Vaughter, P., Wright, T., McKenzie, M., & Lidstone, L. (2013). Greening the ivory tower: A review of educational research on sustainability in post-secondary education. *Sustainability, 5*(5), 2252–2271. doi:10.3390u5052252

Velazquez, L., Munguia, N., Platt, A., & Taddei, J. (2006). Sustainable university: What can be the matter? *Journal of Cleaner Production, 14*(9-11), 810–819. doi:10.1016/j.jclepro.2005.12.008

Venable, M. (2021). *10 Workplace competencies employers want.* Retrieved February 11, 2022, from https://www.bestcolleges.com/blog/workplace-competencies-employers-want/

Verma, P., Nankervis, A., Priyono, S., Mohd Salleh, N., Connell, J., & Burgess, J. (2018). Graduate work-readiness challenges in the Asia-Pacific region and the role of HRM. *Equality, Diversity and Inclusion*, *37*(2), 121–137. doi:10.1108/EDI-01-2017-0015

Vickers, D., & Fox, S. (2010). Towards practice-based studies of HRM: An actor-network and communities of practice informed approach. *International Journal of Human Resource Management*, *21*(6), 899–914. doi:10.1080/09585191003729366

Vij, S., & Sharma, R. (2018). Experiential learning through business simulation game in strategic management. *20th Annual Convention of Strategic Management Forum, "Strategy, Innovation and Entrepreneurship Curriculum in the Era of Disruption"*.

Villegas, A. M., & Lucas, T. (2002). Preparing culturally responsive teachers: Rethinking the curriculum. *Journal of Teacher Education*, *53*(1), 20–32. doi:10.1177/0022487102053001003

Vroom, V. H., & Jago, A. G. (2007). The role of the situation in leadership. *The American Psychologist*, *62*(1), 17–24. doi:10.1037/0003-066X.62.1.17 PMID:17209676

Vygotsky, L. (1978). *Mind in society: The development of higher psychological processes*. Harvard University Press.

Vygotsky, L. S. (1978). *Mind in Society: The development of higher mental processes* (M. Cole, V. John-Steiner, S. Scribner, & E. Souberman, Eds.). Harvard University Press.

Vygotsky, L. S. (1986). *Thought and language*. MIT Press.

Wadham, H. (2020). Horse matters: Re-examining sustainability through human-domestic animal relationships. *Sociologia Ruralis*, *60*(3), 530–550. doi:10.1111oru.12293

Wagner, E. D. (1994). In support of a functional defnition of interaction. *American Journal of Distance Education*, *8*(2), 6–29. doi:10.1080/08923649409526852

Wahl, D. C. (2017). *Regeneration: A webinar with Fritjof Capra, Simon Robinson and Daniel Christian Wahl*. https://www.youtube.com/watch?v=DU699CwJiv4&ab_channel=SimonRobins

Walker, G., Daniels, S., & Emborg, J. (2008). Tackling the tangle of environmental conflict: Complexity, controversy, and collaborative learning. *Emergence*, *10*(4), 17–27.

Walumbwa, F. O., Cropanzano, R., & Goldman, B. M. (2011). How leader-member exchange influences effective work behaviours: Social exchange and internal-external efficacy perspectives. *Personnel Psychology*, *64*(3), 739–770. doi:10.1111/j.1744-6570.2011.01224.x

Wang, L., Law, K. S., Zhang, M. J., Li, Y. N., & Liang, Y. (2019). It's mine! Psychological ownership of one's job explains positive and negative workplace outcomes of job engagement. *The Journal of Applied Psychology*, *104*(2), 229–246. doi:10.1037/apl0000337 PMID:30211569

Wang, Q., & Su, M. (2020). A preliminary assessment of the impact of COVID-19 on environment–A case study of China. *The Science of the Total Environment*, *728*, 138915. doi:10.1016/j.scitotenv.2020.138915 PMID:32348946

Ward, C. (1973). *Anarchy in action*. Freedom Press.

Ward, C. (2004). *Anarchism: A very short introduction*. Oxford University Press. doi:10.1093/actrade/9780192804778.001.0001

Ward, C., & Fyson, A. (1973). *Streetwork: The exploding school*. Routledge.

Washington, H. (2015). *Demystifying sustainability: Towards real solutions*. Routledge. doi:10.4324/9781315748641

Watanabe, Y. (2004). Methodology in washback studies. In Washback in Language Testing: Research Context and Methods (pp. 19-36). Laurence Erlbaum & Associates.

Waterman, R. (1987). *The renewal factor*. Bantam.

Watson, M. K., Lozano, R., Noyes, C., & Rodgers, M. (2013). Assessing curricula contribution to sustainability more holistically: Experiences from the integration of curricula assessment and students' perceptions at the Georgie Institute of Technology. *Journal of Cleaner Production, 61*, 106–116. doi:10.1016/j.jclepro.2013.09.010

Weber, Y., and Tarba, S. (2014). Strategic agility: A state of the art introduction to the special section on strategic agility. *California Management Review, 56*(30), 5-12.

Weber, R. P. (1990). *Sage University paper series on quantitative applications in social sciences, No. 07-049. In Basic Content Analysis* (2nd ed.). Sage Publications, Inc.

WEF. (2018). *The global gender gap report 2018*. https://www.weforum.org/reports/theglobal-gender-gap-report-2018/

Wegener, D. T., & Petty, R. E. (1994). Mood management across affective states: The hedonic contingency hypothesis. *Journal of Personality and Social Psychology, 66*(6), 1034–1048. doi:10.1037/0022-3514.66.6.1034 PMID:8046576

Wei, L., & Garcia, O. (2017). From researching translanguaging to translaguaging research. In Research methods in language and education (pp. 227-240). Gewerbestrasse: Springer International Publishing.

Weick, K. E., & Sutcliffe, K. M. (2011). *Managing the unexpected: Resilient performance in an age of uncertainty* (Vol. 8). John Wiley & Sons.

Weiss, P., & Moskop, W. (2020, November). Ecofeminist manifestos: Resources for feminist perspectives on the environment. *Women's Studies International Forum, 83*, 102418.

Wenger, E. (1998). Communities of practice: Learning as a social system. S*ystems Thinker*. http://www.co-i-l.com/coil/knowledge-garden/cop/lss.shtml

Wenger, E. (1999). *Communities of practice. Learning, meaning and identity*. Cambridge University Press.

Wenham, C., Smith, J., & Morgan, R. (2020). COVID-19: The gendered impacts of the outbreak. *Lancet, 395*(10227), 846–848. doi:10.1016/S0140-6736(20)30526-2 PMID:32151325

Whelan, A., Walker, R., & Moore, C. (2013). *Zombies in the academy: Living death in higher education*. Intellect Books.

Whetten, D. A., & Cameron, K. S. (1984). *Instructors Manual for Developing Management Skills*. Scott, Foresman.

Whitehead, A. N. (1938/1968). *Modes of thought*. Free Press.

Wilbert, C., & White, D. (2011). *Autonomy solidarity possibility: The Colin Ward reader*. AK Press.

Williams, S., Karypidou, A., Steele, C., & Dodd, L. (2019). A personal construct approach to employability: Comparing stakeholders' implicit theories. *Education + Training, 61*(4), 390–412. doi:10.1108/ET-08-2017-0112

Wilson, L. O. (2022). *Types of curriculum*. Retrieved, February 11, 2022, from https://thesecondprinciple.com/instructional-design/types-of-curriculum/

Wilson, J., & Son, J. (2018). The connection between neighboring and volunteering. *City & Community, 17*(3), 720–736. doi:10.1111/cico.12324

Winchester, H. P., & Browning, L. (2015). Gender equality in academia: A critical reflection. *Journal of Higher Education Policy and Management, 37*(3), 269–281. doi:10.1080/1360080X.2015.1034427

Winkle-Wagner, R., & McCoy, D. L. (2016). Entering the (postgraduate) field: Underrepresented students' acquisition of cultural and social capital in graduate school preparation programs. *The Journal of Higher Education*, *87*(2), 178–205.

Wintergerst, A. C., & McVeigh, J. (2011). *Tips for teaching culture: Practical approaches to intercultural communication*. Pearson Education.

Winterton, J., & Turner, J. J. (2019). Preparing graduates for work readiness: An overview and agenda. *Education + Training*, *61*(5), 536–551. doi:10.1108/ET-03-2019-0044

Wooten, L. P., & James, E. H. (2008). Linking crisis management and leadership competencies: The role of human resource development. *Advances in Developing Human Resources*, *10*(3), 352–379. doi:10.1177/1523422308316450

World Bank. (2013). *Bangladesh Education Sector Review: Seeding Fertile Ground - Education that Works for Bangladesh*. Dhaka: World Bank. https://openknowledge.worldbank.org/handle/10986/17853

World Bank. (2018, November 15). *Bangladesh: Reducing Poverty and Sharing Prosperity*. https://www.worldbank.org/en/results/2018/11/15/bangladesh-reducing-poverty-and-sharing-prosperity

World Bank. (2020). *Self-employed, total employment (modeled ILO estimate)* [Data file]. Washington, DC: World Bank. Retrieved April 13, 2020, from https://data.worldbank.org/indicator/sl.emp.self.zs

World Health Organization-WHO. (2020). *Coronavirus disease 2019 (COVID-19): Situation report, 72*. WHO.

Wright Mills, C. (1959/2000). *The sociological imagination*. Oxford University Press.

Wright, L. (2018). Vegans in the interregnum: The cultural moment of an enmeshed theory. In Thinking Veganism in Literature and Culture: Towards a Vegan Theory. Springer.

Wu, C. K., & Lai, H. S. (2010). Learning style and personality type profiles of hospitality undergraduate students of Taiwan and the United States. *Airity Library*, *6*, 111-139. http://ge.cyut.edu.tw

Wu, D., & Hiltz, S. R. (2004). Predicting learning from asynchronous online discussions. *Journal of Asynchronous Learning Networks*, *8*(2), 139–152.

Yang, Y., & Montgomery, D. (2011). Behind Cultural Competence: The Role of Causal Attribution in Multicultural Teacher Education. *The Australian Journal of Teacher Education*, *36*(9). Advance online publication. doi:10.14221/ajte.2011v36n9.1

Yanping, L., Yang, T., & Pan, Y. J. (2012). Building and implementing inclusive leadership based on the perspective of new generation employee management. *China Human Resources Development*, *3*, 31–35.

Yeo, G. K., & Tan, S. T. (1999). Toward a multilingual experiential environment for learning decision technology. *Simulation & Gaming: An Interdisciplinary Journal*, *30*(1), 70–83. doi:10.1177/104687819903000108

Yigzaw, A. (2012). Impact of L1 use in L2 English writing classes. *Ethiop J. Educ. & Sc.*, *8*(1), 11–27.

Yin, R. K. (2009). Case study research: Design and methods. *Sage (Atlanta, Ga.)*.

Yin, R. K. (2013). Validity and generalization in future case studyevaluations. *Evaluation*, *19*(3), 321–332. doi:10.1177/1356389013497081

Yorks, L., Arnold, A., James, L., Rees, A., Hoffman-Pinilla, H., & Ospina, S. (2008). *The tapestry of leadership: lessons from six co-operative inquiry groups of social justice leaders*.

*Compilation of References*

Yudi, M. M., Ibrahim, N. N., Kamaruzaman, S. A., Haron, N. Q. A., Hamid, N. S., & Hambali, S. S. (2020). Accounting Students' Motivation for Getting Professionally Qualified. *Environment-Behaviour Proceedings Journal*, *5*(15), 41–48. doi:10.21834/ebpj.v5i15.2454

Yukl, G. A., & Becker, W. S. (2006). Effective empowerment in organizations. *Organizational Management Journal*, *3*(3), 210–231. doi:10.1057/omj.2006.20

Yusoff, N. N., Hamedani, S. S., Deli, M. M., Alia, M. H., & Rahman, M. R. C. A. (n.d.). *Migrant Food Handlers' Impacts on Food Quality and Safety in Malaysia Food Service Industry*. Academic Press.

Yusuf, I., & Widyaningsih, S. W. (2020). Implementing E-Learning-Based Virtual Laboratory Media to Students' Metacognitive Skills. *International Journal of Emerging Technologies in Learning*, *15*(5), 1–12. doi:10.3991/ijet.v15i05.12029

Zaman, B., & Hussain, R. B. M. (2019). Usage of social capital among migrant workers for their livelihoods in Malaysia. In *Social research methodology and new techniques in analysis, interpretation, and writing* (pp. 160–189). IGI Global. doi:10.4018/978-1-5225-7897-0.ch008

Zaman, B., Islam, M. R., & Hussain, R. B. M. (2021). Fieldwork experience: challenges and managing risks as a female researcher. In *Field Guide for Research in Community Settings* (pp. 201–210). Edward Elgar Publishing. doi:10.4337/9781800376328.00023

Zdziarski, E. L. (2006). Crisis in the context of Higher Education. In K. S. Harper, B. G. Paterson, & E. L. Zdziarski (Eds.), *Crisis management: Responding from the heart* (pp. 3–24). NASPA.

Zenger, J., & Folkman, J. (2019). *Women score higher than men in most leadership skill*. Harvard Business Review.

Zeni, J. (1998). A guide to ethical issues and action research. *Educational Action Research*, *6*(1), 9–19. doi:10.1080/09650799800200053

Zuber-Skerritt, O. (Ed.). (2021). *Action research for change and development*. Routledge. doi:10.4324/9781003248491

Zulfikar, W. B., Wahana, A., Maylawati, D. S., Taufik, I., & Hodijah, H. S. (2018). An approach for teacher recruitment system using simple additive weighting and TOPSIS. In *IOP Conference Series: Materials Science and Engineering. 434* (pp. 1–8). IOP Publishing Ltd. doi:10.1088/1757-899X/434/1/012059

Zulfiqar, S. (2021). Understanding and predicting students' entrepreneurial intention through business simulation games: A perspective of COVID-19. *Sustainability (New Rochelle, N.Y.)*, *13*(4).

# About the Contributors

**Eleni Meletiadou** is a Programme Director and Senior Lecturer at London South Bank University Business School, UK. Her research interests include language assessment, writing, blended learning, diversity, inclusion, and multilingualism.

\* \* \*

**Fábio Albuquerque** has a Ph.D. in Financial Economics and Accounting, a master's degree in Auditing, and a bachelor's degree in Accounting. He is the Coordinator Professor and Director of the Master in Accounting at Lisbon Accounting and Business School (ISCAL) / Instituto Politécnico de Lisboa, Portugal, in the scientific area of Accounting and Auditing. Prof. Albuquerque worked for several entities in accounting, financial reporting, and statistics, in addition to providing business consulting and training on national and international accounting and financial reporting standards. His research has covered accounting and auditing, as well as other scientific areas such as education. Reviewer of several scientific journals in the accounting and reporting fields. Member of editorial boards of several scientific journals.

**Abdullah Alfalagg** is an assistant professor at Hadhramout University. He teaches graduate and undergraduate students at the College of Arts in the Department of English. He is the managing editor for the Journal of the College of Arts, at Hadhramout University and a member of the editorial board for the International Journal of Literacy, Culture, and Language Education. He has sixteen years of experience teaching English in ESL and EFL contexts, including the USA, India, and Yemen. Dr. Alfalagg holds a Ph.D. in English language education from the English and Foreign Language University in India. As a Fulbright Scholar, he did M.A. in TESOL at Murray State University, KY in the U.S. He has published in the Asian-Pacific Journal of Second and Foreign Language Education. His research interests include teaching in higher education, enhancing reading and writing skills in ESL/EFL contexts, offering feedback to ESL/EFL students, English-Arabic translation, and sociocultural theory.

**Hsiao Shih-Kuei Arthur** is a Founder of Top-BOSS International Corporation and an Adjunct Lecturer at the National Taipei University of Commerce. He obtained a Master of Business Administration from National ChenChi University (Taiwan). He is also Vice President of the Chinese Association of Retail Education and a member of the Japan Association of Simulation and Gaming. His research interests are decision making, psychology, learning theory, educational technologies, and international studies.

*About the Contributors*

**Hassan Saeed Awadh Ba-Udhan** has seventeen-year experience of teaching English at schools, colleges, and universities. He has experience in teaching English for specific purposes, e.g. English for computer science, English for business, etc. He obtained his MA and Ph.D. degrees in TESL and Applied Linguistics from English and Foreign Languages University Hyderabad, India. By profession, he works as an associate professor of TESL and Applied Linguistics at the College of Arts of Seiyun University. Previously he taught at Seiyun College of Education of Hadhramout University. He has been appointed as the head of the English department of the College of Education of Hadhramout University, then of Seiyun University for six years. He has supervised pre-service and in-service teachers of primary and secondary schools. He has worked in the development of several English language school textbooks. He has presented several papers at international conferences. He also organized and participated actively in some conferences, workshops, and seminars in the field of ELT and Applied Linguistics both nationally and internationally. He has published several papers in international refereed journals of TESL and Applied Linguistics. He has been a teacher at Master's programs and a supervisor of MA research students. He has examined several dissertations and reviewed several promotion and journal papers. He has been selected as a member of several academic committees, e.g. the committee of assembling, preparation, and follow-up of the Needs of Seiyun University; the committee of academic development and quality assurance of Hadhramout University, and the translation committee of Seiyun University. His areas of interest include teacher training, English language material development, listening comprehension, and issues related to ELT, TESL, and Applied linguistics.

**Jean Henry Blignaut** has been involved in research and teaching at private and public higher education institutions for the past nine years. He is currently a lecturer for undergraduate and postgraduate students within the Curriculum Studies subject group in the Faculty of Education of the North-West University (NWU), as well as the programme leader for the BEdHons degree. Previously, Henry held the following positions: Junior Researcher; Head of Department for Business and Humanities faculties; Programme Manager of Information Technology; Academic Advisor; and Curriculum Designer. He obtained his PhD in 2021. So far, Henry has presented five conference papers as co-author at national as well as international conferences. His research focuses on curriculum development, self-direction of individuals, and diversity in education. He also supervises postgraduate students.

**Ana Cabral** is Academic Practice and Student Engagment Manager and a member of the Education and Recognition team within the Queen Mary Academy which provides strategic, developmental, practical, project and consultancy support for the development and enhancement of learning and teaching across QMUL.

**Yue Chen** (Senior Member, IEEE) is a Professor of Telecommunications Engineering at the School of Electronic Engineering and Computer Science, Queen Mary University of London (QMUL), U.K.. Prof Chen received the bachelors and masters degree from Beijing University of Posts and Telecommunications (BUPT), Beijing, China, in 1997 and 2000, respectively. She received the Ph.D. degree from QMUL, London, U.K., in 2003. Her current research interests include intelligent radio resource management (RRM) for wireless networks; cognitive and cooperative wireless networking; mobile edge computing; HetNets; smart energy systems; and Internet of Things.

**Jahid Chowdhury** obtained PhD form the Universiti of Malaya, Now working as a as a consultant at Universiti Malaya. He voluntarily working as a consultant for Bioprospecting in Malaysia, Universiti Malaya, before that he served as a faculty of Anthropology Shahjalal University of Science and Technology, Bangladesh. Former Research Associate, Victoria University and the University of South Pacific. On Covid-19, he, along with senior scholars, completed a Trilogy published by Universiti Malaya Press, IGI Global and Springer Nature. He is now working to develop a Selfosophic Society with academic endorsement. His publications include, Ubuntu Philosophy for the New Normalcy (Springer Nature); Reciprocity and Its Practice in Social Research (IGI Global).

**Charlene du Toit-Brits** (associate professor) is an NRF-rated researcher (C2 rating) in Curriculum Studies, Philosophy and Research Methodology at the North-West University. For the past 17 years, she has been actively involved in the training of teachers at the NWU Faculty of Education in distance education as well as fulltime education programmes. She has specifically been involved in designing different academic programmes for in-service training of school principals, teachers and education students in various subject specialities: Curriculum Studies, Comparative Education, and Research Methodology. Her research focuses on various elements of distance education, self-directed learning (SDL) within teacher education, as well as fostering SDL among teachers and school learners. Her research aims to inform the 21stcentury workplace and learning environment to enhance lifelong SDL and to inform scholarship on SDL within the unique South African landscape. She has published several articles in various journals, and she has supervised several master's and PhD students in the above-mentioned subject specialities.

**Stephanie Fuller** is the Queen Mary Academy's Academic Practice Taught Programmes Manager. The co-programme lead is Dr Angela Gallagher-Brett. Steph leads the Academy's taught programmes Certificate in Learning and Teaching (CILT) and Postgraduate Certificate in Academic Practice (PGCAP), with responsibility for managing the programmes, leading modules, teaching and supporting colleagues. Steph joined QMUL in 2014 as an Education Adviser and worked to support colleagues on the taught programmes by teaching and leading modules. She also led on dissemination of good practice through organising teaching and learning events including the Teaching and Learning Conference, and managed education grants and funding. She received her PhD in film studies from the University of East Anglia in 2013 (funded by the Arts & Humanities Research Council) and had her thesis published as a monograph. She has research interests in internationalisation and interdisciplinarity in HE, online learning and cultural history. Her current research project focuses on the development of communities of practice in online learning. She was awarded Senior Fellowship of the Higher Education Academy in 2018.

**Sukhpal Singh Gill** is a Lecturer (Assistant Professor) in Cloud Computing at School of Electronic Engineering and Computer Science, Queen Mary University of London, UK. Prior to this, Dr. Gill has held positions as a Research Associate at the School of Computing and Communications, Lancaster University, UK and also as a Postdoctoral Research Fellow at CLOUDS Laboratory, The University of Melbourne, Australia. Dr. Gill is serving as an Associate Editor in Wiley ETT and IET Networks Journal. He has co-authored 70+ peer-reviewed papers published in prominent international journals and conferences such as IEEE TCC, IEEE TSC, IEEE TII, IEEE IoT Journal, Elsevier JSS and IEEE CCGRID. His one review paper has been nominated and selected for the ACM 21st annual Best of Computing Notable Books and Articles as one of the notable items published in computing – 2016. His research interests

**About the Contributors**

include Cloud Computing, Fog Computing, Software Engineering, Internet of Things and Healthcare. For further information, please visit http://www.ssgill.me.

**Leila Goosen** is a full professor in the Department of Science and Technology Education of the University of South Africa. Prof. Goosen was an Associate Professor in the School of Computing, and the module leader and head designer of the fully online signature module for the College for Science, Engineering and Technology, rolled out to over 92,000 registered students since the first semester of 2013. She also supervises ten Masters and Doctoral students, and has successfully completed supervision of 43 students at postgraduate level. Previously, she was a Deputy Director at the South African national Department of Education. In this capacity, she was required to develop ICT strategies for implementation. She also promoted, coordinated, managed, monitored and evaluated ICT policies and strategies, and drove the research agenda in this area. Before that, she had been a lecturer of Information Technology (IT) in the Department for Science, Mathematics and Technology Education in the Faculty of Education of the University of Pretoria. Her research interests have included cooperative work in IT, effective teaching and learning of programming and teacher professional development.

**Sibylle Gruber** is a professor of Rhetoric, Writing, and Digital Media Studies where she teaches graduate and undergraduate courses in literacy studies, rhetoric and cultures, rhetorics of travel writing, computers and writing, and feminist studies. She has served as the University Writing Program Director, the Writing Center Director, and the Director of the Rhetoric, Writing, and Digital Media Studies Program. She has also worked as a mentor to create opportunities for first-generation, economically disadvantaged, and minority middle-school students to provide opportunities for a college education. She received the Women and Gender Studies Certificate of Appreciation, the Commission on the Status of Women Award for Outstanding Service on the Diversity Project, and the Spirit of Excellence Award in Recognition of Contributions to Quality, Excellence, and Continuous Improvement in Arizona State Government for her commitment to gender equity and her commitment to diversity, and student success. She is the author of of several book-length projects and has published widely on feminist rhetorics, literacy and identity, transnational literacies, technological literacies, composition theories and practices, cultural studies and the social and cultural aspects of communicative practices.

**Akın Gürbüz** is currently working at the School of Foreign Languages, Muğla Sıtkı Koçman University, in Turkey. He holds a PhD degree in ELT and has teaching experience of more than 10 years in language teaching. His research specialty and interests include teaching language skills, blended, and flipped learning, self-directed learning, discourse analysis, multicultural education, and professional development.

**Mashitah Hamidi** is Senior lecturer in Department of Social Administration and Justice of Universiti Malaya, Malaysia. She Obtained PhD from the University of La Trobe, Australia. Her areas of research include Development studies, Social Services System, Migration, and stateless group of people (Refugee).

**Clare Hart** is a Student Experience Officer and Sustainability Tutor in the Department of Strategy, Enterprise and Sustainability at Manchester Metropolitan University, UK. She holds an MSc in Psychology. Clare encourages students to take their passion and enthusiasm out into the wider world, and helps to coordinate the support network to do this.

## About the Contributors

**Anita Hashmi** is a PhD researcher at Manchester Metropolitan University. She uses applied genetics to assess the impact of an integrated conservation approach in black and white rhinos, Grevy's zebra, giraffe, and mountain bongo. She is also working as a research assistant on the Business School's project on "Animal rescue and rehoming in a post-pandemic world."

**Shamim Hosen** has been working as an Assistant Director at the Bangladesh Public Administration Training Centre (BPATC), Dhaka, Bangladesh since 2015. He has completed a Bachelor's and a Master's degree in political science from the University of Dhaka, Bangladesh. Second Master's in International Relations from the University of Aberdeen, United Kingdom. Mr. Hosen has conducted numerous research projects as a team member in distinguish fields. He has several publications from home and abroad. He is currently working on the Forced Migration, Organizational Culture and Development, Training Transfer, and Citizen Charter.

**Ana Isabel Dias** has a Ph.D in Economía y Empresa by the University of Extremadura / Spain; Master in Management with specialization in Finances by the University of Évora; Degree in Audit by Lisbon Accounting and Business School (ISCAL). Profesor in ISCAL in the department of Accounting and Audit. Author of scientific papers published in journals or presented in conferences; and of technical books in the area of financial reporting.

**Md. Shafiul Islam** is a Professor, Department of Public Administration, Rajshahi University, Bangladesh.

**Helena Mary Kettleborough** is a Lecturer at Manchester Metropolitan University Business School. Her research interests centre on using first- and second-person action research, incorporating social justice. Researching currently on community/student/staff collaborations around sustainability and on creating wider Gaian and cosmological paradigms for hopeful futures: www.linkedin.com/in/helena.kettleborough.

**Yui-yip Lau** is a Senior Lecturer from the Division of Business and Hospitality Management, College of Professional and Continuing Education, The Hong Kong Polytechnic University. Dr. Lau graduated from The Hong Kong Polytechnic University (PolyU) and received a BSc (Hons) in International Shipping and Transport Logistics. He further pursued studies at the University of Bristol where he received his Doctor of Education. Until now, he has published more than 290 research papers in international journals and professional magazines, contributed 15 book chapters, 3 books, and presented numerous papers at international conferences. He has collaborated with scholars from more than 20 countries and regions spreading over five continents on research projects. He has also secured over HK$ 10 million in research grants. Recently, he has been awarded a Certificate of Appreciation by the Institute of Seatransport in recognition of his outstanding performance in research and the Best Paper Award in international leading conferences. In addition, he has been appointed an Associate, University of Manitoba, Transport Institute, Winnipeg, Manitoba, Canada, and Visiting Scholar, East China Normal University. His research interests are cruise, ferry, maritime transport, air transport, impacts of climate change, maritime education and training, transport history, sustainability issues, supply chain management, health logistics, human remains, and regional development.

*About the Contributors*

**Roz Marron** is a Senior Lecturer at Manchester Metropolitan University Business School, UK. She has been teaching in HE for over 17 years and has a PhD in English literature. She is interested in pedagogical approaches to teaching sustainability literacy. Current research focuses on transformative learning, identity, and communities.

**Chan Kwai Nam** is the founder of icetech Hong Kong Co. Ltd. since 2011 and the chairman of the international association of business management simulation in 2022. He was graduated from University of Technology Sydney with Master Degree in Engineering Management on 2000. He has over 35 years experiences in consumer electronic product industry with over hundreds of products has been developed with supplier in mainland China and SE Asia countries. He is the exclusive distributor of Top Boss International Co. Ltd. who is a professional AI based Business Management Simulation provider in Asia market, their platform has been widely applied in TW and China with over 500 Universities. Michael collaborated with different Universities in delivering the training program and organized number of business management simulation in Hong Kong Polytechnic University, IVE Kwun Tong and Hong Kong Metropolitan University respectively from 2019 to 2022. Over the years he is evolved to meet the needs of the transformation of education by innovation and creativity simulation platform in various business category, he sustains his role not only in serving the University with his business simulation product but also in the contribution of the whole society by organizing the global competition to our youth generation. He hopes to provide the students with a quality program to cultivate your critical thinking, effective communication, problem solving and how to being a social responsibility citizen. Students usually have to wait until their first job to get hands-on training, which is a costly way to practice and learn. He brings the business world straight to the students and provide them with the most realistic business simulations ever designed.

**Sally Randles** is Chair of Sustainability and Innovation at Manchester Metropolitan University's Faculty of Business and Law, UK and is Faculty Lead for Sustainability. Sally's research investigates how organisations enact de-facto responsible innovation. She is engaged in EU-funded projects bringing together circular economy, social value innovation, and local policy.

**Parimal Roy** is a PhD Candidate, Department of Social Administration and Justice under Universiti Malaya, Malaysia. He Studied in Anthropology, in later he obtained papers on MBA, Project management, and Criminology (paper is better than a certificate) to enhance his versatile knowledge domain. He is currently working in a State own institution in the filed of Research,Training & Development of Bangladesh. Decolonizing, Indigenous Community, Ethnography, Project management - all are staking arena in the academic realm. His written book is Extra-marital love in folk songs; and Co-author of Captive minded intellectual; Quantitative Ethnography in Indigenous Research Methodology; Digital Ethnography from IGI Global; and so forth.

**Konstantina Skritsovali** is a Senior Lecturer at Liverpool Business School, UK. Her research interests revolve around sustainable business models, collaborative approaches across sectors and responsible management education. She is one of the PRME coordinators for the Liverpool Business School.

**C. Therasa**, B.Tech., MBA., Ph.D, Assistant Professor Assistant Professor in School of Management, SASTRA, Deemed University. She has received her B.Tech from SASTRA, Thanjavur and her MBA from Gnanam School of Business. She has two years of corporate experience as a Junior Consultant in Object Frontier Software Private Ltd. She has a Ph.D in Human Resource Management. Her areas of teaching and research interests include Organizational Behavior, Human Resource Management, Behavioral Psychology and Consumer Behavior. She has published 21 quality articles in Scopus indexed journals and 4 case studies in Case Centre. She has also presented several articles in National level and International level Conferences.

**Megan Tucker** is a recent Masters in Business (MBus) graduate of Manchester Metropolitan University. She is also a Carbon Literacy trainer and worked with Greater Manchester Poverty Action to generate the 2022 Poverty Monitor. Advocating sustainability, social justice and seeking a sense of community is the foundation of Megan's core values with additional hobbies in cooking and outside exploration of which stems from a childhood within the Shropshire hills. https://www.linkedin.com/in/meganrtucker109/.

**Steve Uhlig** obtained a Ph.D. degree in Applied Sciences from the University of Louvain, Belgium, in 2004. From 2004 to 2006, he was a Postdoctoral Fellow of the Belgian National Fund for Scientific Research (F.N.R.S.). His thesis won the annual IBM Belgium/F.N.R.S. Computer Science Prize 2005. Between 2004 and 2006, he was a visiting scientist at Intel Research Cambridge, UK, and at the Applied Mathematics Department of University of Adelaide, Australia. Between 2006 and 2008, he was with Delft University of Technology, the Netherlands. Prior to joining Queen Mary, he was a Senior Research Scientist with Technische Universität Berlin/Deutsche Telekom Laboratories, Berlin, Germany. Starting in January 2012, he is the Professor of Networks and Head of the Networks Research group at Queen Mary, University of London. Between 2012 and 2016, he was a guest professor at the Institute of Computing Technology, Chinese Academy of Sciences, Beijing, China. He's currently the Head of School of Electronic Engineering and Computer Science, QMUL.

**Helen Wadham** is a Senior Lecturer at Manchester Metropolitan University, UK. Her research explores sustainability via collaborative approaches across sectors and species. Current projects include off-grid living and how domestic animals influence the understanding and practice of sustainability in rural areas and organisations. She is a fellow of the Royal Anthropological Institute. https://orcid.org/0000-0002-9980-4409.

**Haris Abd Wahab** (PhD) is Professor in the Department of Social Administration and Justice, Faculty of Arts and Social Sciences, Universiti Malaya, Malaysia. He graduated in the field of human development and community development. He has conducted studies on community work, community development, volunteerism, and disability. He has extensive experience working as a medical social worker at the Ministry of Health.

**Macy Wong** is the Head of the CPCE Employability Services Office (CESO) and a Senior Lecturer in the Division of Business and Hospitality Management, College of Professional and Continuing Education, The Hong Kong Polytechnic University. After working in the business consultancy and commercial fields for several years, Dr Wong pursued her career in academia. Her academic training in Business Administration from Monash University and University of Newcastle leads her to interdisciplinary fields of research and teaching. Her research and teaching interests are in the fields of Strategic Management, International Business, Entrepreneurship, Human Resource Management and Higher Education. Her

**About the Contributors**

researches have been published in reputable peer-reviewed international journals. She has also presented her papers in international academic conferences. As the Head of CESO, Dr Wong is committed to leading CESO in infusing all-round employability services and employment related activities that are beneficial to students' career development. Dr Wong will oversee the strategic planning of CESO in enhancing students' employability and strengthening the school's industry connections through various employability and entrepreneurship services, activities and events including the Career Fair, Annual Employability Forum, various Placement & Scholarship Programmes, and Start-up Starter Programme and the like to support the story telling.

**Zhuang Yang** was a graduate of the Macao Institute for Tourism Studies (IFTM) and he was awarded the Bachelor Degree of Science in Hotel Management in 2022. Meanwhile, he won another Diploma in Hotel Management from the Swiss Hotel Management School (S.H.M.S.). In June 2022, he attended the Tourism Education Student Summit, an academic conference, where he presented his thesis to professionals from the hospitality and tourism industry. John worked at Wynn Resorts based in Macao and L.E.K. Consulting (Shanghai) and accumulated plenty of industry experience. During the undergraduate period, John participated in a series of research projects, and then worked as a research assistant under the supervision of professors at IFTM, helping to do the data collection and junior analysis. Besides, he worked as an interviewer for IFTM Tourism Research Centre (ITRC) for one year, through which job he was required to make an interview or deliver questionnaires to the citizens randomly on the street. From 2021 to 2022, he was involved in the publication of a book and was listed as the third author. John is currently studying for his master's program majoring in International Wine Management at the School of Hotel and Tourism Management of Hong Kong Polytechnic University (PolyU). John's research interests include tourism management, health tourism and logistics management. Before admission to PolyU, John passed the Wine & Spirit Education Trust (WSET) Level 2 in wines with a distinction grade. And he also won another wine-related certification from Bordeaux Wine School and tourism-related certifications from the American Hotel & Lodging Educational Institute (AH & LEI) and City & Guilds.

**Rana Yildirim** is a professor at the ELT Department of Çukurova University. She has an MSc and a PhD TESOL from Aston University, UK. She teaches on the undergraduate and graduate programme and supervises MA and PhD students. Her research interests include teaching English to young learners, gifted language learners and language teacher development at pre- and in-service levels.

# Index

3D Jobs 336

## A

Accessing Online Learning 167
Accounting Course 71, 81, 90, 96
Achieving SDGs 112, 337, 351
Action Research 43, 45-49, 52, 54-55, 57-65, 69, 170, 179, 202, 210, 224-227, 229, 307
Amotivation 71-72, 77-80, 88, 96
Arabic Language 251, 253, 257, 269
Assessment Analysis 43, 60
Awarding Gap 24-25, 28, 34

## B

Bangladesh 97-101, 106-114, 315-317, 319, 325-326, 329, 331-334, 337-338, 340-345, 347-350, 352-360
Bangladeshi Migrant Workers (BMW) 336
Biopolitics 314, 328-329

## C

Challenges 2, 12-14, 18-19, 21, 24-25, 28, 30, 32, 34-35, 37-39, 43, 45-46, 55, 61, 63, 70, 76, 78, 90, 108, 110-113, 115-116, 158, 164, 168, 172, 174-176, 178-179, 182-183, 202-205, 207-209, 211, 214, 216, 218-219, 224, 229-230, 232, 236-244, 252, 255, 278, 288, 294, 302, 308, 328, 331, 336, 339, 342, 350, 352, 356-360
Climate Change Activism 282, 292
Climate Change Advocacy 272, 279, 284-285
Cloud Computing 43-51, 53-54, 56-60, 62, 65, 67
Collaborative Approaches 202, 229
Collective Learning 293, 300-302, 310-311, 313
Community 24-28, 36-38, 64, 97-101, 106-114, 123, 138, 140, 160, 165, 169-174, 176-179, 182, 186, 189, 194-196, 199, 202, 204, 206, 208-220, 222, 225-226, 232, 274, 279-282, 284, 290, 297-299, 301, 303-307, 314-315, 317, 319-321, 326-329, 333-336
Contextual Learning 313
COVID-19 1-2, 4-9, 11, 13-16, 18, 24-26, 28-32, 34-41, 44, 62-64, 113, 139, 160, 164-165, 167-170, 172-177, 180, 182, 185, 198-200, 203, 314-315, 322, 324, 330-336, 348, 351
COVID-19 Crisis 1, 4-6, 8, 11, 13, 16, 24-25, 30-32, 34, 38, 165, 200
COVID-19 Pandemic 2, 5, 9, 13-16, 18, 24-26, 28-29, 34-37, 39-41, 44, 62-64, 160, 167, 169-170, 172-177, 180, 182, 185, 203, 315, 322, 330, 348, 351
Crisis Management 1-2, 4, 13, 17-20, 22-23, 169, 174
Critical Learnership 115-118, 120-121, 123-124, 126-132, 134, 138, 142
Cultural Diversity 18, 230-232, 237-238, 240, 242-245, 249
Culturally Responsive Teaching 246, 249
Culture 4-6, 12-15, 17, 20-21, 26, 36, 51, 55, 79, 81, 86-87, 99, 105, 120, 131-132, 135-136, 140, 170, 174, 206, 209, 220, 230-231, 234-235, 237, 241-242, 249, 278-279, 290-291, 307, 315-316, 327, 332, 345, 355
Customary Law 97, 104, 111, 114

## D

Development 1-2, 5, 16-20, 22, 24-28, 32-33, 36-37, 40-42, 46, 51, 54, 59-60, 62-65, 71, 73, 75-78, 80, 89, 91, 94-95, 97-118, 120-121, 123, 126-127, 129-136, 138-140, 142, 145-153, 159-164, 167-176, 178-187, 193-195, 198-201, 203-204, 208, 224-226, 229, 233-235, 245, 247-248, 250, 257, 266-267, 272-273, 275, 287, 290, 293-298, 301-313, 315-316, 318, 320, 326-328, 331-332, 334, 337-339, 341-342, 345, 347-354, 357-360
Development Junction 337, 342, 357, 360
Dimension of Attitude 249

*Index*

Dimension of Awareness 249
Dimension of Knowledge 250
Dimension of Skills 250
Disaster Capitalism 314, 320, 328-329, 333
Discontinuity 115-118, 120-121, 124-125, 127-128, 130-132, 134-135, 142-143, 329
Disruption 6, 118, 123, 125-127, 129-132, 134-135, 137, 142, 164, 168, 182, 214, 279
Diverse Students 232, 234, 238-243, 245, 250
Diversity 1-4, 14, 16, 18, 20-21, 36, 38, 49, 55-56, 58-59, 75, 92, 119, 164, 168, 171, 174-175, 179, 181, 206, 209, 229, 231-233, 235, 237-240, 242-246, 249-250, 279, 294, 297, 305, 308

## E

Ecofeminism 272-273, 278-279, 281, 283-284, 287-288, 292
Ecological University 202, 207, 224, 228-229
Education for Sustainable Development (ESD) 168, 202, 204, 229, 313
Engagement 3, 18, 21-22, 26-27, 35, 37-40, 43-44, 47, 49-51, 53-54, 56, 58, 60-63, 67, 69, 74, 78, 96, 110, 123-124, 147, 150, 160, 162, 170, 174, 179, 183-184, 189-190, 195, 197, 199, 201, 206, 210, 219, 256, 274, 284-285, 295, 307, 311, 327
Environmental Justice 111, 278, 285, 292
Experiential Learning 151, 163-164, 184, 186-187, 199
Extrinsic 71-74, 77-80, 83-84, 87-89, 94, 96
Extrinsic Motivation 77-80, 83, 87-89, 94, 96

## F

Formative Assessment 51, 56, 65, 171

## G

Gender Diversity 1-3, 20-21

## H

Hidden Curriculum 182, 295, 313
Higher Education 1, 17, 19-24, 29, 32, 37-42, 44-46, 53, 59, 62-64, 71-74, 79, 88, 91, 94-96, 98, 137, 140, 145-151, 160-164, 167-178, 180-184, 198, 201, 204, 222, 224-229, 231-232, 244-247, 251-253, 255-257, 259-269, 293-295, 297-300, 303, 306-308, 311-313, 338-340, 342-347, 351, 354-360
Higher Education Institution (HEI) 360

## I

Impediments 120, 337, 345
Inclusive Leadership 1-3, 12, 16-22
Individual and Collective Learning Competencies 293
Innovation 35, 40, 48, 108, 115, 117-123, 125-127, 129-132, 134-137, 139-142, 150, 152, 164, 170, 174-175, 177, 181, 294
Innovative Educational Tool 144, 151, 165
Interactive Learning 144, 151-152, 165, 189, 297
Intercultural Awareness 25, 35, 42
Intrinsic 71-72, 74, 77-80, 83-85, 87-89, 91, 94-96, 146, 187, 274
Intrinsic Motivation 71-72, 77-80, 83-85, 87-89, 91, 94-96

## K

Knowledge Societies 272, 274-278, 281, 284-286, 292
KOLBs Framework 183

## L

Language Teaching 200, 245, 252-253, 256, 258, 269-271
Leadership 1-6, 8, 12-23, 34, 36, 40, 44-45, 121, 126, 130-131, 138-139, 148, 150, 169-170, 175, 198, 205-207, 210, 217-218, 221-229, 284, 290, 298, 310, 352
Learner 26, 47, 65, 69, 99, 151, 162, 173, 183-184, 186, 189-190, 195-197, 200-201, 238, 241, 339
Learner Engagement 47, 183-184, 201
Learnership 115-118, 120-121, 123-124, 126-132, 134, 138, 142
Learning Communities 24, 26-27, 29, 38-42, 206, 227, 302
Learning Strategies 72, 183, 199, 293, 299
Learning Style 183-186, 188-190, 197-199, 201
Learning Styles 183-190, 197-201, 235
Linguistic Diversity 230, 232, 238

## M

Macro Business Simulation Game 144, 165
Malaysia 97, 184, 188, 314-317, 319-320, 322-323, 325-336
Motivation 3, 12, 17, 20, 23, 28, 37, 42, 44, 71-74, 76-80, 83-96, 98, 122-123, 129, 140, 161, 171, 174, 176, 180, 185, 191, 238, 240, 243, 252, 267, 294, 302, 326, 348, 351
Multicultural Education 230, 232-235, 240, 244-250

Multicultural Teaching Competency 230, 232, 250

## N

New Normal 216, 315, 317, 325, 328-330
Non-Financial Information 71-72, 74, 83, 86, 88, 90-96
Null Curriculum 295, 313

## O

Online Learning 25, 27-28, 39-40, 48-49, 54, 59-60, 64, 66, 145, 151, 160, 164-165, 167-168, 170, 172-174, 176-177, 182-185, 188-190, 192, 195-200, 309, 311
Online Teaching 28, 43, 51, 172, 180, 184
Overt Curriculum 295, 313

## P

Pantavat 336
Participatory Research 229
Philosophy 8, 84, 97, 109, 132-133, 135, 268, 286-287, 298, 302, 321, 329, 331-332, 336
Portuguese Students 71
Postcolonial Ecofeminism 272, 281
Professionalization 144, 163, 166
Project-Based Learning 61

## Q

QMPLUS 48, 51, 53, 56-57, 66, 69
Qualified Education 360
Quality Education 151, 168, 179, 185, 295, 337-342, 344-346, 348, 350-354, 356-360

## R

Reporting 71-76, 80-81, 83, 86-88, 90-96, 176, 304

## S

Santal 97-102, 106-114
Self-Determination Theory 71-72, 74, 76, 91, 93-94, 96
Self-Directed Learning 187, 198, 293, 299-301, 303, 305, 307-312
Skills 2, 6, 8, 13-15, 23, 25-29, 32-35, 37, 42, 44-46, 49-51, 53, 55-56, 58-59, 63-64, 67, 69, 71, 73-74, 77, 89-90, 96, 115, 118, 127, 131-135, 142, 146-151, 156, 159-160, 162-164, 170-171, 173, 176-177, 179-181, 183-184, 187, 189, 191, 194-195, 197, 201, 208, 214-215, 230-235, 240, 242-243, 249-250, 253, 267, 269, 272-273, 280-282, 284, 293-295, 298-302, 305-306, 309-311, 339, 347, 350
Slow Science 227, 229
Social Constructivism 294, 313
Spoon-Feeding Education 144-145, 160, 166
Students 13, 16, 23-51, 53-67, 69, 72-74, 76, 78-80, 82-91, 94-96, 102, 144-152, 154-178, 180-182, 184-186, 188-190, 194-204, 206-224, 231-235, 237-247, 249-269, 271-273, 281-285, 294-303, 305-307, 309-313, 332, 338, 340, 343, 345-346, 349-351, 356
Students' Attitudes 24-25, 30-32, 79, 171
Sustainability 1, 13, 23, 40, 48, 64, 72-76, 79, 86-96, 98, 102-105, 107-108, 111, 114-121, 123-132, 134-137, 139-140, 142-143, 146, 149, 158, 165, 168-170, 174-175, 177, 181, 183-184, 194, 202-207, 209-216, 219-229, 272, 274-275, 277-278, 282-285, 287-290, 293-294, 296-298, 300-303, 307-308, 310-315, 318, 327, 333, 355, 360
Sustainable 1, 24, 28, 33-34, 38, 41-46, 48-51, 53-54, 56, 59-60, 66, 69, 71, 73, 76, 80, 86, 94-95, 97-100, 102-114, 117-120, 122-123, 126, 130-132, 134-135, 138-142, 145-147, 160, 162, 165, 167-170, 172, 174-176, 179, 182-184, 187, 194, 201-204, 207, 213, 220, 224-226, 229, 273-274, 276-277, 281-282, 287, 292-298, 300-315, 317-318, 327, 334, 338-339, 341, 345, 348, 352-353, 358-360
Sustainable Development 1, 71, 73, 76, 80, 94-95, 97-100, 102-113, 120, 123, 126, 130, 134, 138-140, 142, 145-147, 160, 167-170, 172, 174-176, 182-184, 187, 194, 201-204, 225-226, 229, 272-273, 287, 293-298, 301-313, 337-339, 341, 345, 348, 352-353, 358-360
Sustainable Development Goals (SDG) 76, 360
Sustainable Learning 24, 28, 33-34, 38, 42-46, 48-51, 53, 56, 59-60, 66, 119, 123, 139, 142, 170, 293, 300
Sustainable Solutions 118, 122, 272-273, 276, 292
Systemic Change 229

## T

Teacher 22, 41-42, 55, 59, 64, 141, 151, 159-160, 166, 168-169, 171, 173, 176, 180-182, 186, 191, 195-197, 220, 232, 234-235, 237-240, 243-244, 246, 248-249, 251-253, 255-258, 265, 268-271, 307, 312, 331, 347-348, 350-352, 354, 358-359
Teachers' Perceptions 163, 171, 181, 251-252, 258, 260-261, 265, 268, 270
Teamwork 6, 43-45, 47, 49-51, 53, 56, 58-59, 61, 63-64, 69, 142, 148, 150, 153, 159, 294, 302, 307
Tertiary Education 40, 133, 174, 181, 231-232, 337-

*Index*

339, 341, 343-344, 349, 354, 359-360
Tertiary level 243, 337-338, 341, 343-345, 348, 354, 357, 360
Think-Pair-Share 48, 66
Traditional Classroom 28, 144-145, 160, 166, 173
Transdisciplinarity 272-273, 276-277, 283, 286-287, 289, 291-292, 297
Transformative Learning 204, 206-207, 210, 221-222, 225-229
Transparency International Bangladesh (TIB) 360

## U

Ubuntu 314-315, 320-321, 326, 328-329, 331-332, 336
University Grant Commission (UGC) 360
Upper Echelon 1

Using Mobile Technologies 167, 170, 172, 176
Using Students' L1 251-252, 255-257, 266-267, 269

## V

VARK 183, 185-186, 188, 201
Virtual Professional Learning Communities 24, 29
Volunteering 314-315, 318, 320, 325-326, 328-329, 335

## Y

Yemen 251-253, 255, 257, 259, 266-268

# Recommended Reference Books

IGI Global's reference books are available in three unique pricing formats:
Print Only, E-Book Only, or Print + E-Book.

Shipping fees may apply.

**www.igi-global.com**

ISBN: 9781522589648
EISBN: 9781522589655
© 2021; 156 pp.
List Price: US$ 155

ISBN: 9781799840756
EISBN: 9781799840763
© 2021; 282 pp.
List Price: US$ 185

ISBN: 9781799855989
EISBN: 9781799856009
© 2021; 382 pp.
List Price: US$ 195

ISBN: 9781799864745
EISBN: 9781799864752
© 2021; 271 pp.
List Price: US$ 195

ISBN: 9781799875710
EISBN: 9781799875734
© 2021; 252 pp.
List Price: US$ 195

ISBN: 9781799857709
EISBN: 9781799857716
© 2021; 378 pp.
List Price: US$ 195

**Do you want to stay current on the latest research trends, product announcements, news, and special offers?**
Join IGI Global's mailing list to receive customized recommendations, exclusive discounts, and more.
Sign up at: **www.igi-global.com/newsletters.**

Publisher of Timely, Peer-Reviewed Inclusive Research Since 1988

www.igi-global.com   Sign up at www.igi-global.com/newsletters   facebook.com/igiglobal   twitter.com/igiglobal   linkedin.com/igiglobal

# Ensure Quality Research is Introduced to the Academic Community

# Become an Evaluator for IGI Global Authored Book Projects

 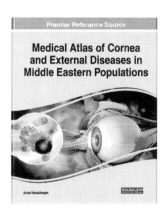 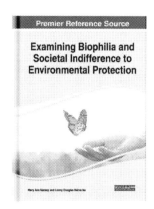 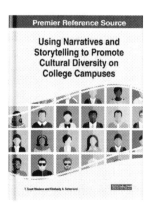

**The overall success of an authored book project is dependent on quality and timely manuscript evaluations.**

## Applications and Inquiries may be sent to:
### development@igi-global.com

Applicants must have a doctorate (or equivalent degree) as well as publishing, research, and reviewing experience. Authored Book Evaluators are appointed for one-year terms and are expected to complete at least three evaluations per term. Upon successful completion of this term, evaluators can be considered for an additional term.

If you have a colleague that may be interested in this opportunity, we encourage you to share this information with them.

Easily Identify, Acquire, and Utilize Published
Peer-Reviewed Findings in Support of Your Current Research

# IGI Global OnDemand

Purchase Individual IGI Global OnDemand Book Chapters and Journal Articles

**For More Information:**
www.igi-global.com/e-resources/ondemand/

## Browse through 150,000+ Articles and Chapters!

Find specific research related to your current studies and projects that have been contributed by international researchers from prestigious institutions, including:

- Accurate and Advanced Search
- Affordably Acquire Research
- Instantly Access Your Content
- Benefit from the InfoSci Platform Features

*It really provides an excellent entry into the research literature of the field. It presents a manageable number of highly relevant sources on topics of interest to a wide range of researchers. The sources are scholarly, but also accessible to 'practitioners'.*

- Ms. Lisa Stimatz, MLS, University of North Carolina at Chapel Hill, USA

## Interested in Additional Savings?

Subscribe to
**IGI Global OnDemand** *Plus*

Learn More

*Acquire content from over 128,000+ research-focused book chapters and 33,000+ scholarly journal articles for as low as US$ 5 per article/chapter (original retail price for an article/chapter: US$ 37.50)*

# 6,600+ E-BOOKS. ADVANCED RESEARCH. INCLUSIVE & ACCESSIBLE.

## IGI Global e-Book Collection

- **Flexible Purchasing Options** (Perpetual, Subscription, EBA, etc.)
- Multi-Year Agreements with **No Price Increases** Guaranteed
- **No Additional Charge** for Multi-User Licensing
- No Maintenance, Hosting, or Archiving Fees
- Transformative **Open Access Options** Available

*Request More Information, or Recommend the IGI Global e-Book Collection to Your Institution's Librarian*

## Among Titles Included in the IGI Global e-Book Collection

**Research Anthology on Racial Equity, Identity, and Privilege (3 Vols.)**
EISBN: 9781668445082
Price: US$ 895

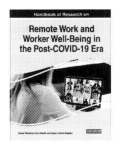

**Handbook of Research on Remote Work and Worker Well-Being in the Post-COVID-19 Era**
EISBN: 9781799867562
Price: US$ 265

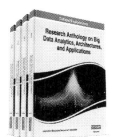

**Research Anthology on Big Data Analytics, Architectures, and Applications (4 Vols.)**
EISBN: 9781668436639
Price: US$ 1,950

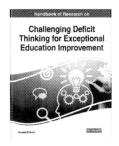

**Handbook of Research on Challenging Deficit Thinking for Exceptional Education Improvement**
EISBN: 9781799888628
Price: US$ 265

### Acquire & Open

When your library acquires an IGI Global e-Book and/or e-Journal Collection, your faculty's published work will be considered for immediate conversion to Open Access *(CC BY License)*, at no additional cost to the library or its faculty *(cost only applies to the e-Collection content being acquired)*, through our popular **Transformative Open Access (Read & Publish) Initiative**.

**For More Information or to Request a Free Trial, Contact IGI Global's e-Collections Team:** eresources@igi-global.com | 1-866-342-6657 ext. 100 | 717-533-8845 ext. 100

Printed in the United States
by Baker & Taylor Publisher Services